Atlas of
WORLD
HISTORY

William J. Fuecker
Summer Lake
Tigard, Oregon
December 1997

Atlas of
WORLD
HISTORY

John Haywood, Ph. D.

Honarary Teaching Fellow, University of Lancaster, UK

with

Brian Catchpole, M.A. • **Simon Hall,** M.A.
Edward Barratt, M.A.

BARNES
&NOBLE
BOOKS
NEW YORK

Project director Peter Furtado

Cartographic manager Richard Watts

Advisory editors Jeremy Black
Professor of History, University of Exeter, UK

K.M. Chaudhuri
Vasco da Gama Professor of European Exploration, European University Institute, Florence, Italy

Barry Cunliffe
Professor of European Archaeology, University of Oxford, UK

Brian M. Fagan
Professor of Anthropology, University of California, Santa Barbara, USA

J.E. Spence
Associate Fellow, Royal Institute of International Affairs, UK

Academic advisors J.I. Catto
Oriel College, University of Oxford, UK

Professor Robin Cohen
University of Warwick, UK

Professor J.H. Elliott
Regius Professor of Modern History, University of Oxford, UK

Professor Harold James
Princeton University, New Jersey, USA

Professor Maldwyn A. Jones
University of London, UK

Dr Stewart Lone
Australian Defence Force Academy

Dr Oswyn Murray
Balliol College, University of Oxford, UK

Professor A.J.S. Reid
The Australian National University

Professor Francis Robinson
Royal Holloway, University of London, UK

Dr Kate Spence
Christ's College, University of Cambridge, UK

Professor John K. Thornton
Millersville University, Pennsylvania, USA

This page:
Ottoman janissaries, c.AD 1820

Opposite above:
Chinese bronze horse, c.AD 200

Opposite below:
Mughal Indian rug design, c.1550

Following page:
Above: French revolutionary caricature, c.1789
Below: Russian revolutionary poster, c.1920

Art director Ayala Kingsley
Art editor Martin Anderson
Cartographic editor Tim Williams

Editors Susan Kennedy
            Peter Lewis
Cartographer Nathalie Johns
Picture research Claire Turner
Production Clive Sparling
Editorial assistance Marian Dreier
Typesetter Brian Blackmore
Illustrations Charles Raymond
Proof reader Lynne Elson
Index Ann Barrett

AN ANDROMEDA BOOK

Produced and prepared by
Andromeda Oxford Ltd
11–15 The Vineyard
Abingdon
Oxfordshire OX14 3PX

© Andromeda Oxford Ltd 1997

This edition published by
Barnes & Noble, Inc., by arrangement
with Andromeda Oxford Ltd

1997 Barnes & Noble Books

ISBN 0–7607–0687–5

Contents

USING THIS ATLAS

This book has a consistent organization and, wherever possible, a standard presentation, to help the reader understand the information shown on each map, and to trace a particular story from region to region, or from period to period. The book is arranged in six chronological parts, each with a brief introduction by a leading historian or archeologist.

WORLD MAPS AND REGIONAL MAPS

The detailed regional maps are arranged in an approximate chronological order, interspersed with unique world maps, each of which shows the world at a key moment in history.

World map spreads show the level of political or social complexity in standard categories from earliest times to the present. States and empires are shown in capital letters, dependencies or territories in upper-and-lower case. Societies or peoples which have not yet developed into states are shown in bold upper-and-lower-case type; the colors indicate their level of social organization.

World map spreads carry timecharts which are organized region by region. The text on these spreads includes many crossreferences to relevant spreads elsewhere in the Atlas.

Regional map spreads provide a survey of a part of the world between the dates shown in the map title.

Maps are shown in true cartographic projections, each one chosen for the best presentation of the information on the map. North is generally at the top of the page. Some degree of distortion may be found in the case of some maps, such as those of the whole of Asia, which cover a very large section of the world. Where necessary location maps have been included.

Regional map spreads include standard features. The maps use the typographical conventions of the world maps; thick gray lines indicate major borders, thin lines internal borders.

TYPOGRAPHICAL CONVENTIONS

World maps

FRANCE	state or empire
Belgian Congo	dependency or territory
Mongols	tribe, chiefdom or people
Anasazi culture	cultural group

Regional maps

HUNGARY	state or empire
Bohemia	dependency or territory
Slavs	tribe, chiefdom or people
ANATOLIA	geographical region
✗	battle
•	site or town

Campaigns or journeys are indicated by lines with arrowheads; thicker gray arrows are used for migrations or movements of large numbers of people. Trade routes are thinner lines, with arrowheads when the trade is specifically one-way.

Each item shown in the map key is referred to in the text at some point on the spread. The main text on each spread explains and amplifies the information drawn on the map.

The spread also carries a timeline, arranged in geographical or thematic sections. Extended events such as wars or dynasties are shown with colored bands; historical periods (such as "Bronze Age") are indicated with gray bands. Every regional map also carries between five and nine numbered "pointers". These refer to the captions elsewhere on the page, which offer additional historical detail about the places indicated.

Cross-references are provided in the panel on the bottom right; these list the numbers of other maps with related information, together with a suggestion of the relevant themes.

The volume index provides detailed references to the people, places, events and concepts covered in the text, timelines, numbered captions and map keys. For reasons of space it has not been possible to index every town or city shown on the maps, but the states and provinces on the maps are indexed, as are battles, sieges, peoples and journeys, exploration routes and so on.

Part 1

THE ANCIENT

Four million years of biological and cultural evolution are covered in this story of the development of humankind from its origins on the African savanna to the appearance of the literate civilizations and classical empires. The story is the product of research in many disciplines, but the central thread comes from thousands of archeological excavations, of inconspicuous scatters of stone tools and animal bones, hunting camps and farming villages as well as towns and spectacular cities.

Archeologists study and explain changes in societies, indeed in humanity itself, over immensely long periods of time. Why, for example, did some societies acquire farming skills? And how and why did humans cross from Siberia into Alaska and colonize the Americas? The archeologist tries to account for such developments in terms of social organization as well as technology and environmental change.

The key intellectual framework for our most distant past derives from the evolutionary theories of Charles Darwin, formulated in 1859. The theory of evolution by natural selection made it possible to imagine a vast antiquity, a blank timescape for human evolution to unfold over hundreds of thousands, if not millions, of years. Darwin and his contemporaries could only guess at the evolution of humanity. Today, study of the DNA in our body cells tells us that the hominid line – of which *Homo sapiens sapiens* is the culmination – separated from the other apes between four and five million years ago. Today, archeology tells us that human ancestors appeared in Africa and moved out to populate the rest of the world almost two million years ago, and that modern humanity may also have originated in Africa. With its help, we can not only wonder at the art of 30,000 years

THE AFRICAN RIFT VALLEY was the birthplace of humankind.

WORLD

ago, but also build up chronologies based on scientific analysis as well as on techniques of stylistic comparison. From archeology we know that literate civilizations developed in many places independently throughout the world. Historians using written sources, and archeologists using material remains, can then collaborate in piecing together a narrative of these civilizations.

Modern scholars think of evolution like the branches of a tree, with new species emerging as the endlessly proliferating limbs and twigs, which derive from a trunk of remote common ancestors. Human societies have evolved in many ways; but there are similarities, especially in social and political organization and in the ways in which people make their livings. A flexible classification of human societies into "prestate societies" and "state-organized societies" was made by the American anthropologist Elman Service.

The simplest prestate societies were small family bands, egalitarian groups with communal leadership based on experience. Usually hunters and gatherers of plant foods, band societies prevailed for an immensely long time, until the beginnings of farming. Some survived to modern times.

Early farmers lived in permanent villages, and needed new social institutions to settle quarrels and establish land ownership. Many village societies were "tribes", egalitarian groups with kin-based organization to regulate land ownership and undertake communal tasks. "Chiefdoms" were a development of tribes; power lay in the hands of a few people who controlled trade and accumulated wealth. "State-organized societies" or civilizations operated on a larger scale than chiefdoms. They involved cities and saw the development of a writing system. Early civilizations were centralized, with power concentrated in the hands of a supreme ruler at the pinnacle of a socially stratified society.

Four major themes dominate the long early chapter of our history: the origins of humanity, the evolution and spread of humans, the beginnings of agriculture, and the emergence of civilizations. All of these are bound up with the ways in which food has been secured. For 99 percent of all human history, people lived by hunting and gathering. Our earliest ancestors probably used fleetness of foot and opportunism to scavenge their meat from lion and leopard kills. Hunting may have begun at the same time as modern humans appeared. Stone-tipped spears, then barbed antler projectiles and spearthrowers allowed hunters to shoot game from a safe distance. When the bow-and-arrow came into use some 10,000 years ago, humans could hunt animals of every size and birds on the wing. And as the ice sheets retreated, people intensified the quest for food and permanent settlements began to emerge at some favored sites.

Hunting is often seen as the glamorous part of foraging, but edible plant foods formed the essential diet of humanity for four million years. Our ancestors knew which plants to eat as staples, and which to fall back on in lean times. It was only when populations rose at the en
d of the Ice Age that people began to plant wild grasses and tubers deliberately to extend the range of wild forms that had been gathered for millennia. And, in a remarkably short time – perhaps three thousand years – the growing of crops and the domestication of animals spread very widely.

Farming accelerated the pace of cultural change. At first, civilizations like those of the Egyptians, the Shang and the Sumerians were independent entities. Gradually, though, states became reliant on each other. By 500 BC, empires, much larger entities, played a leading role. But the first four million years had created human biological and cultural diversity and laid the foundations of our own world ■

H uman evolution began as the Earth's climate started to cool during the Miocene epoch (25–5 million years ago), and culminated about one million years ago in the Pleistocene Ice Age. During the early Miocene the global climate was warmer than today. Widespread tropical forests in Africa and Eurasia supported diverse populations of early hominoid apes, including a common ancestor of gorillas, chimpanzees and humans.

By the end of the Miocene ice caps had formed at the Poles, and drier conditions in Africa caused tropical forests to shrink. In east Africa, probably the birthplace of the hominids, this was exacerbated by geological movements that led to the uplift of the East African plateau and the formation of the Rift Valley. The ancestral hominids were confined to shrinking "islands" of forest surrounded by open woodland and savanna. As a result they learned to walk on two legs, allowing them to cover long distances on the ground.

The oldest known hominid, 4.4-million-year-old *Ardepithecus ramidus*, was probably bipedal, and the slightly later species *Australopithecus afarensis* certainly was, although (like later australopithecines) it retained a good tree-climbing ability. By 3 million years ago the australopithecines had evolved into two types, known as robusts and graciles. The robusts (named for their massive jaws and teeth) were not human ancestors. The gracile *Australopithecus africanus* had smaller teeth and jaws, and lived on plant foods and meat scavenged from the carcasses of the savanna's herd animals. The first hominid to be considered human, *Homo habilis*, appeared about 2.4 million years ago. This lived in a similar way to the gracile australopithecines, but had a larger brain – almost half the size of a modern human's, compared with a third, for australopithecines and chimpanzees. Whereas the australopithecines used simple tools such as stones and sticks, *Homo habilis* made sharp flakes and chipped pebble tools for butchering large animals. This simple toolmaking culture is known as the Oldowan, for the early hominid fossil site of Olduvai Gorge in the Rift Valley.

About 1.9 million years ago *Homo habilis* was replaced by *Homo erectus*, with a brain size about two-thirds that of modern humans. Over the next million years this proportion grew to three-quarters, the brain evolving rapidly as the climate fluctuated from dry glacial periods to moister, warmer inter-glacial periods. There was little time to adapt physically to new conditions, and intelligent animals that could cope by modifying their

| | | | 0 | | 600 km |
| 0 | | 400 mi | | | |

Hadar
Aa
Bodo
He
Middle Awash
Ar
Melka Kunture
Gadeb
Omo
Ra, other
Ileret
Ra
Ra, Hh, He
West Turkana
He
Koobi Fora
Ra, Hh, He
Chesowanja
Ra
Olorgasailie
Peninj
Ra
Olduvai Gorge
Ndutu
Ra, Hh, He.
other
Laetoli
Aa, other
Kalambo Falls
Kabwe
other

1,600,000 Earliest evidence of the use of fire, at Chesowanja, Kenya and Swartkrans (South Africa)

1,800,000 Populations of *Homo erectus* reach south and southeast Asia

c.3,500,000 "Lucy", the most complete *Australopithecus afarensis* found, lives at Hadar, Ethiopia

c.2,000,000 Stone choppers, from Olduvai Gorge, Tanzania, initiate the Oldowan culture

1,000,000 Beginning of the modern (Pleistocene) Ice Age

c.3,600,000 Hominid bipedal footsteps from this date have been found at Laetoli, Tanzania

c.2,400,000 Date of the oldest known stone tools, from Hadar, Ethiopia and the start of the African Lower Paleolithic

1,000,000 *Homo erectus* reaches Europe and Asia

| 4,000,000 years ago (ya) | 3,000,000 ya | 2,000,000 ya | 1,500,000 ya | 1,000,000 |

Homo habilis

Homo erectus

Ardepithecus ramidus

Australopithecus afarensis

Australopithecus africanus

Robust Australopithecines

Oldowan culture

LOWER PALEOLITHIC

PLIOCENE EPOCH

TERTIARY PERIOD

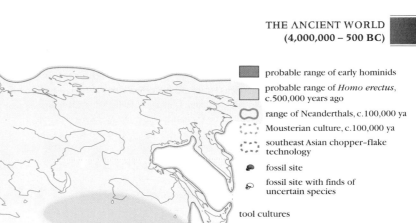

Greenland

Swanscombe
IIe
Pontnewydd
He
Boxgrove
He
Le Moustier
Hsn
La Chapelle-aux-Saints
Hsn
Neander Valley
Hsn
Steinheim
other
La Ferrassie
Hsn
Schöningen
Atapuerca
He
Gibraltar
Hsn
Krapina
Hsn
Vértesszöllös
He
Circeo
Hsn
Petralona
other
Torralba-Ambrona
Mt Carmel
Hsn
Ternifine
He
Tbilisi
He
Yerevàn
He
Teshik Tash
Hsn
Dederiyeh
Shanidar
Hsn
Salé
He
Qafzeh
Hsn, other
Kebibat
other
Yayo
He
Narmada
He
Zhoukoudien
He
Lantian
He
Bailongdong
He
Langtandong
He
Yunxián
He
Yuanmou
He
Tham Khuyen
He
Ban Mae
Tha
Trinil
He
Solo
He
Sangiran
He
Madagascar

EAST AFRICAN RIFT VALLEY
see inset

Makapansgat
Aaf
Sterkfontein
Ra
Kromdraai
Ra
Taung
Aaf
Swartkrans
Ra, Hh
Elandsfontein
other

omas
rries
He

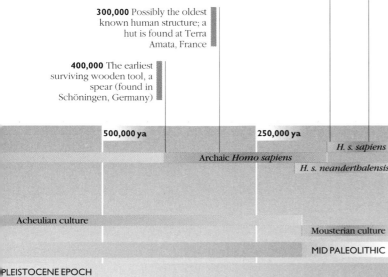

100,000 Modern humans begin their migration out of Africa

135,000 Date of the earliest anatomically modern human fossils, from Omo, Ethiopia

300,000 Possibly the oldest known human structure; a hut is found at Terra Amata, France

400,000 The earliest surviving wooden tool, a spear (found in Schöningen, Germany)

500,000 ya   250,000 ya

H. s. sapiens

Archaic *Homo sapiens*

H. s. neanderthalensis

Acheulian culture

Mousterian culture

MID PALEOLITHIC

PLEISTOCENE EPOCH

QUATERNARY PERIOD

behavior had evolutionary advantages. *Homo erectus* mastered the use of fire, and was a more able toolmaker than *Homo habilis*, using the symmetrical hand-ax (a butchery tool) of the Acheulian culture.

Homo erectus was the first hominid to live outside Africa. Perhaps as early as 1.8 million years ago it had spread through tropical south and southeast Asia and colonized temperate areas of Europe and northern China before one million years ago. *Homo erectus*, however, did not reach Australia or the Americas. It could survive in temperate climates but not in Arctic and sub-Arctic ones, usually prefering to live in savanna, steppe and open woodlands: the same hand-ax technology was widespread. However in southeast Asia it adapted to tropical forest life, using flake and chopper tools and bamboo. The isolated *Homo erectus* populations began to evolve in different ways after 500,000 years ago. In Africa and Europe a variety of large-brained forms showed a mixture of archaic and modern human characteristics. In Europe between 230,000 and 150,000 years ago, archaic *Homo sapiens* evolved into *Homo sapiens neanderthalensis*, its physique adapted to life on the cold steppes and tundras of Ice Age Eurasia. These Neanderthals developed the Mousterian toolmaking technique, which was also widely used by hunter–gatherer groups in North Africa and the Middle East (often called the Near East by archeologists). In Africa archaic humans evolved until anatomically modern humans, *Homo sapiens sapiens*, appeared by 135,000 years ago ∎

T he earliest known anatomically modern *Homo sapiens sapiens* had appeared in Africa by 135,000 years ago (ya). By 90,000 years ago anatomically modern humans existed in the Middle East; by 75,000 years ago they were in east Asia and by 40,000 in Europe and Australia. By the end of the Ice Age 10,000 years ago, only some oceanic islands, Antarctica and some parts of the high Arctic remained completely uninhabited.

Two rival explanations have been offered for these facts. One argues that the modern human races developed directly from the regional *Homo erectus* populations: modern Africans evolved from *Homo erectus* via African archaic *Homo sapiens*; modern Europeans from *Homo erectus* via European archaic *Homo sapiens* and Neanderthals and so on. Critics point out that parallel evolution of this sort over such a wide area is implausible and that there is no supporting fossil evidence. The second explanation, known as the single-origins or "out of Africa" model, is supported by genetic evidence suggesting that all modern humans derive from African ancestors who lived between about 285,000 and 150,000 years ago, and that all modern non-African humans are descendants of a single group of this ancestral population that migrated out of Africa around 100,000 years ago. According to this model, the descendants of this group spread across Eurasia. The anatomically modern humans had better developed speech abilities than the archaic natives, who could not compete with the newcomers and gradually became extinct.

This model is more compatible with the fossil and archeological evidence than the first. Between 120,000 and 90,000 years ago the African climate was more moist than it is today and bands of hunters and gatherers could have crossed the Sahara. The earliest known fossils of modern humans outside Africa date to about 90,000 years ago and were found in Israel – just the place and date predicted by the single-origins theory. Only in Africa have forms intermediate between archaic and modern humans been found. In Europe, the Neanderthals and early modern humans formed distinct populations that coexisted for over 10,000 years: the Neanderthals did not evolve into modern humans. In east and southeast Asia, the *Homo erectus* populations were replaced by modern humans with no trace of intermediate forms.

When the first modern humans reached the Middle East, the global climate was beginning to enter one of the most severe glacial periods of the Ice Age. Human technology was probably inadequate for survival in the arctic climates of Europe and central Asia, and these areas were left to the hardier Neanderthals. Instead the moderns moved east, reaching China and southeast Asia around 75,000 years ago. Here they developed boat- or raft-building skills and

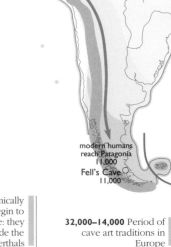

BERINGIA

Bluefish Cave
15–12,000

modern humans reach
Alaska around 15,000

ice free corridor
opens c.12–14,000

Cordilleran
Ice Sheet

Laurentide
Ice Sheet

Marmes
10,500

Folsom

Clovis

Clovis sites
occupied around
11,500–11,000

Little Salt Spring

Tepexpan
11–10,000

Pedra Pintada
14–13,000

Guitarrero Cave
c.10,000

modern humans
reach Patagonia
11,000

Fell's Cave
11,000

TIMELINE

	115,000 Onset of the last glaciation of the (Pleistocene) Ice Age	**90,000** Anatomically modern humans living at Qafzeh, Israel		**40,000** Anatomically modern humans begin to colonize Europe: they live alongside the indigenous Neanderthals	**32,000–14,000** Period of cave art traditions in Europe

The Americas

Europe

Middle East

Africa

East and South Asia

100,000 years ago   80,000 ya   60,000 ya   40,000 ya   30,000 ya.

c.120,000 Middle Stone Age flake-tool technology is well established in tropical Africa

120,000–90,000 Periods of higher rainfall make the Sahara habitable by humans

c.75,000 Glaciation causes Africa to become arid: the Sahara becomes impassable by humans

75,000 Anatomically modern humans inhabit China and southeast Asia

45,000 Date of the oldest known musical instrument, a flute, found in north Africa

35,000 Anatomically modern humans hunt large game in Eurasia

35,000 Australian aboriginal hunter–gatherer traditions emerge

28,000 The Solomon Islands are settled

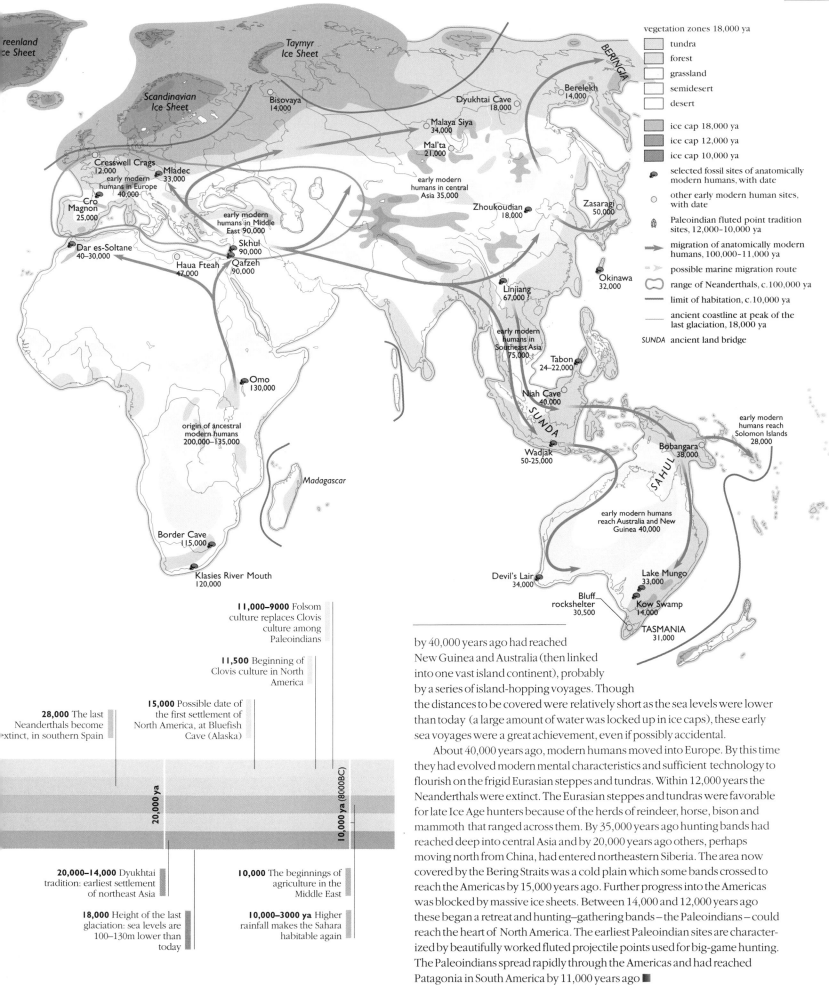

vegetation zones 18,000 ya

- tundra
- forest
- grassland
- semidesert
- desert

- ice cap 18,000 ya
- ice cap 12,000 ya
- ice cap 10,000 ya

- selected fossil sites of anatomically modern humans, with date
- other early modern human sites, with date
- Paleoindian fluted point tradition sites, 12,000–10,000 ya
- migration of anatomically modern humans, 100,000–11,000 ya
- possible marine migration route
- range of Neanderthals, c.100,000 ya
- limit of habitation, c.10,000 ya
- ancient coastline at peak of the last glaciation, 18,000 ya

SUNDA ancient land bridge

Greenland Ice Sheet

Scandinavian Ice Sheet

Taymyr Ice Sheet

BERINGIA

Bisovaya 14,000

Cresswell Crags 12,000
early modern humans in Europe 40,000
Mladec 33,000

Cro Magnon 25,000

Dar es-Soltane 40–30,000

early modern humans in Middle East 90,000

Haua Fteah 47,000
Qafzeh 90,000
Skhul 90,000

Malaya Siya 34,000
Mal'ta 21,000

Dyukhtai Cave 18,000

Berelekh 14,000

early modern humans in central Asia 35,000

Zhoukoudian 18,000

Zasaragi 50,000

Linjiang 67,000

Okinawa 32,000

Omo 130,000

early modern humans in Southeast Asia 75,000

Tabon 24–22,000

Niah Cave 40,000

SUNDA

Madagascar

Wadjak 50–25,000

Bobangara 38,000

early modern humans reach Solomon Islands 28,000

SAHUL

early modern humans reach Australia and New Guinea 40,000

Border Cave 115,000

Klasies River Mouth 120,000

origin of ancestral modern humans 200,000–135,000

Devil's Lair 34,000

Bluff rockshelter 30,500

Lake Mungo 33,000

Kow Swamp 14,000

TASMANIA 31,000

Timeline

11,000–9000 Folsom culture replaces Clovis culture among Paleoindians

11,500 Beginning of Clovis culture in North America

15,000 Possible date of the first settlement of North America, at Bluefish Cave (Alaska)

28,000 The last Neanderthals become extinct, in southern Spain

20,000 ya

10,000 ya (8000BC)

20,000–14,000 Dyukhtai tradition: earliest settlement of northeast Asia

18,000 Height of the last glaciation: sea levels are 100–130m lower than today

10,000 The beginnings of agriculture in the Middle East

10,000–3000 ya Higher rainfall makes the Sahara habitable again

by 40,000 years ago had reached New Guinea and Australia (then linked into one vast island continent), probably by a series of island-hopping voyages. Though the distances to be covered were relatively short as the sea levels were lower than today (a large amount of water was locked up in ice caps), these early sea voyages were a great achievement, even if possibly accidental.

About 40,000 years ago, modern humans moved into Europe. By this time they had evolved modern mental characteristics and sufficient technology to flourish on the frigid Eurasian steppes and tundras. Within 12,000 years the Neanderthals were extinct. The Eurasian steppes and tundras were favorable for late Ice Age hunters because of the herds of reindeer, horse, bison and mammoth that ranged across them. By 35,000 years ago hunting bands had reached deep into central Asia and by 20,000 years ago others, perhaps moving north from China, had entered northeastern Siberia. The area now covered by the Bering Straits was a cold plain which some bands crossed to reach the Americas by 15,000 years ago. Further progress into the Americas was blocked by massive ice sheets. Between 14,000 and 12,000 years ago these began a retreat and hunting–gathering bands – the Paleoindians – could reach the heart of North America. The earliest Paleoindian sites are characterized by beautifully worked fluted projectile points used for big-game hunting. The Paleoindians spread rapidly through the Americas and had reached Patagonia in South America by 11,000 years ago ∎

Anatomically modern humans from Africa reached what is now the Middle East some 90,000 years ago, but it was not until the beginning of the Upper Paleolithic period, about 40,000 years ago, that they were able to move into Europe. Unlike the indigenous Neanderthals, who were physically adapted to the harsh Ice Age climate, the early anatomically modern humans were poorly equipped to survive in Europe until, some 50,000–40,000 years ago, they also acquired a fully modern human mental capacity. This enabled them to adapt to the cold climate through technological and social innovation, and compete on more than equal terms with the Neanderthals. The Neanderthals became extinct about 28,000 years ago. Whether it was as a result of a war of extermination or because superior modern human hunting techniques drove them into marginal environments is a subject of debate: current archeological opinion favors the latter.

Two parallel toolmaking traditions, the Châtelperronian and the Aurignacian, are found in Europe during the 10–12,000 years that modern humans and Neanderthals shared the continent. The Châtelperronian is apparently a development of the Mousterian tool culture and is thought to have been used by the Neanderthals. The Aurignacian has similarities with contemporary tool cultures in the Middle East and is therefore thought to have been introduced to Europe by anatomically modern humans. The Aurignacian and the succeeding Gravettian tool cultures both are fairly uniform over wide areas but later Upper Paleolithic tool cultures show greater variety between different regions. These variations are often in style rather than function and probably served as a way of expressing emerging ethnic identities. Typical Upper Paleolithic stone tools include scrapers, sharpened blades, burins – engraving tools used for antler harpoons – and bone points and needles were also used. The Solutrean culture introduced a sophisticated technique of pressure flaking which produced beautiful leaf shaped spear heads.

The most impressive characteristics of the Upper Paleolithic cultures are their art traditions, both decorated artifacts and cave-wall painting. The earliest Upper Paleolithic art dates from around 31,000 years ago but the traditions reached their peak in the Magdalenian (17,000–11,000 years ago), in the cave paintings of sites such as Lascaux and Altamira. The greatest concentration of Upper Paleolithic cave art is to be found in southwest France and northern Spain, an area with a particularly dense population at the time. The function of cave art is unknown but it is thought to have played a religious role. The most distinctive decorated artifacts are female "Venus" figurines made around 25,000 years ago. These have been found across Europe – evidence, perhaps, of a widespread religious cult.

Despite the cold, the tundras and steppes of Ice Age Europe were a very favorable environment for hunters, being filled with easily tracked herds of large grazing mammals. Upper Paleolithic hunters used a combination of semi-permanent base-camps – often sited at bottlenecks on animal migration routes, such as river crossings – and seasonal camps where particular game species were intensively exploited. Caves and south-facing rock shelters were favored camp sites, but in more exposed areas tents and huts were built.

The end of the last glaciation, around 10,000 years ago (8000 BC) marks the end of the Upper Paleolithic and the beginning of the Mesolithic

Upper Paleolithic, 40,000–10,000 years ago

- ▮ Levantine Aurignacian culture
- ▮ Aurignacian culture
- ◆ cave site
- ✋ cave site with painting
- ● open site
- ▲ open site with structure
- ⚱ "Venus" figurine find

Mesolithic, 10,000–6000 ya (8000–4000 BC)

- 🐚 major site
- 🐚 site with shell midden
- ▮ maximum extent of ice sheet during last glaciation, c.18,000 ya
- ▮ extent of ice sheet, 7000 BC
- ⋯⋯ northern limit of deciduous woodland, c.18,000 ya
- ▬▬ northern limit of deciduous woodland, 7000 BC
- ➤ migration of anatomically modern humans from Middle East, c.40,000 ya
- - - - ancient course of Thames/Rhine, 7000 BC
- —— modern coastline and drainage where altered

0   800 km
0   600 mi

"VENUS" figurines with exaggerated sexual characteristics were a feature of the Gravettian culture and probably symbolized fertility. This example is from Willendorf in Austria.

ATLANTIC OCEAN

Oronsay   Oban
Mount Sandel
Star Carr
Creswell Cra,
Paviland
Pincevent
Loire
PYRENEES
Douro
Tagus
Cabeço da Arruda

8

1

7

TIMELINE

	40,000 years ago (ya)	30,000	20,000	10,000 ya (8000 BC)
	Mousterian Châtelperronian			
	Aurignacian	Gravettian	Solutrean Magdalenian	
Cultural	c.41,000 Blade tool technology introduced to Europe	c.30,000 The earliest cave paintings in southwest France and northern Spain	c.20,000 The pressure-flaking technique of tool manufacture is adopted	14,000 Production of cave paintings at Altamira, Spain
		25,000–22,000 "Venus" figurines are found widely from Spain to Russia	17,000 The cave paintings at Lascaux, France, are made	8000 (6000 BC) Beginning of the transition to a farming way of life in southeast Europe
			16,000 Microlithic tools are developed	
Physical	c.40,000 The first anatomically modern humans enter Europe	c.28,000 The last remaining Neanderthals become extinct in Spain	18,000–15,000 The Ice Age is in its coldest phase	10,000 End of the last glaciation
	MID PALEOLITHIC	UPPER PALEOLITHIC		MESOLITHIC

period. As the climate became warmer, sea levels rose and dense forests advanced over most of Europe, bringing the big-game hunting way of life to an end. Large mammals were now fewer and more elusive, but a far greater diversity of plant foods, shellfish, fish, birds and small mammals was available. Mesolithic hunter–gatherers introduced many new devices to exploit these new food sources. The most important technological change was a reliance on microliths – small stone blades or flakes – used in combination to make composite tools such as knives, harpoons, fish spears and lightweight arrow heads. Nets, fish traps, shellfish scoops and dug-out canoes also came into widespread use for the first time in the Mesolithic.

Many areas of northern Europe which had previously been uninhabitable because of extreme cold or ice sheets received their first modern human inhabitants during the Mesolithic, while some which had been relatively densely populated, such as southwest France and the southwest steppes, became comparatively depopulated. The densest population moved to areas such as the Atlantic coast and southern Scandinavia. Hunter–gatherers here were able to adopt an increasingly sedentary way of life, making fewer and shorter migrations between camps. In southern Scandinavia and eastern Europe there were even permanent settlements occupied all year round. Task groups set out from these settlements to spend short periods at temporary seasonal camps to exploit locally abundant food resources.

The Mesolithic period came to an end with the adoption of the Neolithic farming way of life, a process which began about 6000 BC in southeast Europe and about two thousand years later in the British Isles and Scandinavia. In extreme northerly areas, an essentially Mesolithic way of life continued until the domestication of the reindeer early in the Christian era.

1 In the Upper Paleolithic, southwest France had light woodland for fuel, sheltered valleys with many caves, and lay across major animal migration routes; it was therefore Europe's most densely populated area.

2 Upper Paleolithic hunters used temporary camps to exploit particular game species. Solutré was a base for horse hunters, Predmosti for mammoth.

3 Cave paintings of woolly rhinoceros, horses and buffalo found at Vallon Pont d'Arc in 1994 are, at 30,000 years old, the oldest yet found.

4 On the treeless steppes, mammoth bones were used to build huts; a well-known example, c.18,000 years old, was found at Mezhirich.

5 The well-preserved Mesolithic settlement of Lepenski Vir includes many fish-head sculptures, perhaps indicating worship of a fish-deity.

6 Denmark, with marine, freshwater and terrestrial food sources in close proximity, was densely populated in the Mesolithic.

7 The first cemeteries, such as those at Cabeço da Arruda and Oleneostravski (about 170 burials each) date from the late Mesolithic (c.4250 BC).

8 Late Mesolithic hunter-gatherers (c.4000-3400 BC) visited Oronsay island several times a year for fish and shellfish.

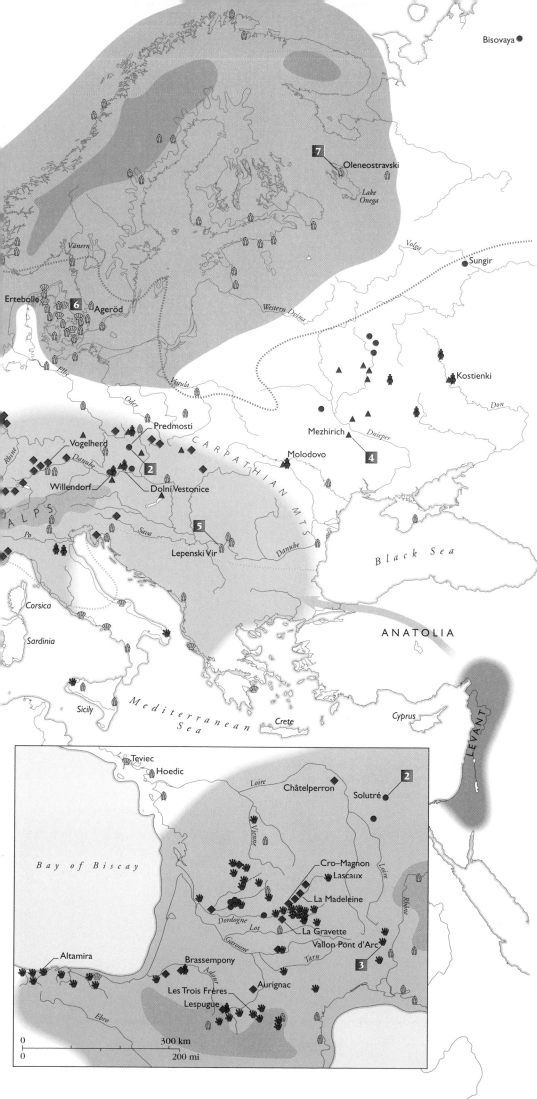

See also 2 (peopling the earth);
7 (Neolithic Europe)

F arming communities arose independently in many parts of the world between 10,000 and 5000 BC as a response to the environmental changes that followed the end of the Ice Age. The warmer climate was a mixed blessing: sea levels rose as the ice sheets melted, flooding huge areas of lowland hunting grounds. The savannas, steppes and tundras, all abundant in big game, shrank as the forests advanced.

In many areas, hunter–gatherers began to exploit small game birds, fish and plants to a greater extent than before. It was among these communities that agriculture first arose. Probably the first stage was planting the seeds of favored wild plant foods to guarantee their continuing availability. Next was the domestication of food plants by breeding strains with desirable characteristics. Because their seeds had a high carbohydrate content and were easy to store, the most important domesticated plant foods were strains of the cereals – wheat, barley, oats, rice, millet and maize – that still form the staple food crops today. Relatively few animal species have been domesticated; most of those have been herd animals, whose tendency to "follow the leader" makes them easier to manage. Animal domestication began with the management and selective culling of wild herds. Penning the animals followed, then selective breeding for desirable qualities. Most early centers of agriculture were rich in wild plants and animals suitable for domestication. Elsewhere agriculture relied on the introduction of crops and livestock from established farming areas.

Some communities of hunter–gatherers moved from casual cultivation of wild plants (incipient agriculture) to a full farming economy far more quickly than others. Farmers have to work harder than hunter–gatherers, and few made the transition willingly. Rising populations probably forced many to adopt cultivation to supplement wild food supplies. In the Fertile Crescent of the Middle East, where farming first developed, the transition from incipient agriculture to dependence on domesticated cereals took only three centuries, 8000–7700 BC, and domesticated animals replaced hunted wild animals a millennium later. In Mesoamerica a full farming way of life developed within a few centuries of the domestication of maize (▷ 17). In eastern North America hunting and gathering remained the main source of food for some three millennia after the first cultivation of domesticated food around 2500 BC. Even farmers who grew most of their food still exploited wild food sources.

Agriculture led to far-reaching technological developments. Most hunter–gatherers had to carry everything from camp to camp: farmers were sedentary, so weight became less critical. New tools, such as polished stone

EASTERN N AMERICA
goosefoot
gourds
marsh elder
sumpweed
sunflowers
c.1000

Hawaiian Islands

Bahamas

Cuba   Hispaniola
Puerto Rico
Jamaica

c.2300

c.1000

MESOAMERICA
avocados
beans
cotton
gourds
maize
peppers
pumpkins
squashes
tomatoes
turkeys

c.3500

c.4000

LOWLAND S AMERICA
manioc
peanuts
pineapples

c.3000

c.2000

ANDES
alpacas
beans
chili peppers
gourds
guinea pigs
llamas
potatoes

c.1000

c.500

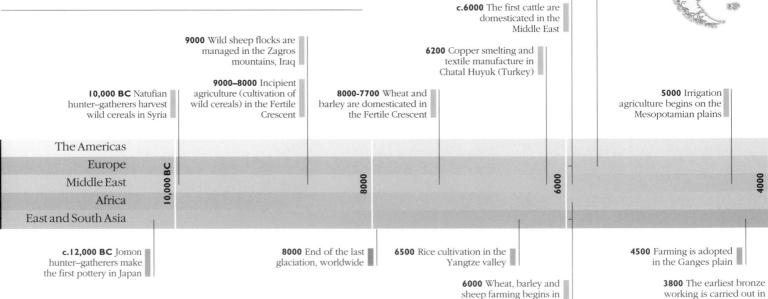

5400–4500 Bandkeramik culture: first farmers of central Europe

6000 Farming spreads across southern Europe

c.6000 The first cattle are domesticated in the Middle East

6200 Copper smelting and textile manufacture in Chatal Huyuk (Turkey)

9000 Wild sheep flocks are managed in the Zagros mountains, Iraq

9000–8000 Incipient agriculture (cultivation of wild cereals) in the Fertile Crescent

10,000 BC Natufian hunter–gatherers harvest wild cereals in Syria

8000-7700 Wheat and barley are domesticated in the Fertile Crescent

5000 Irrigation agriculture begins on the Mesopotamian plains

TIMELINE

The Americas
Europe
Middle East
Africa
East and South Asia

10,000 BC   8000   6000   4000

c.12,000 BC Jomon hunter–gatherers make the first pottery in Japan

8000 End of the last glaciation, worldwide

6500 Rice cultivation in the Yangtze valley

4500 Farming is adopted in the Ganges plain

6000 Wheat, barley and sheep farming begins in Egypt

3800 The earliest bronze working is carried out in the Middle East

6000 Earliest evidence for farming in the Indian subcontinent

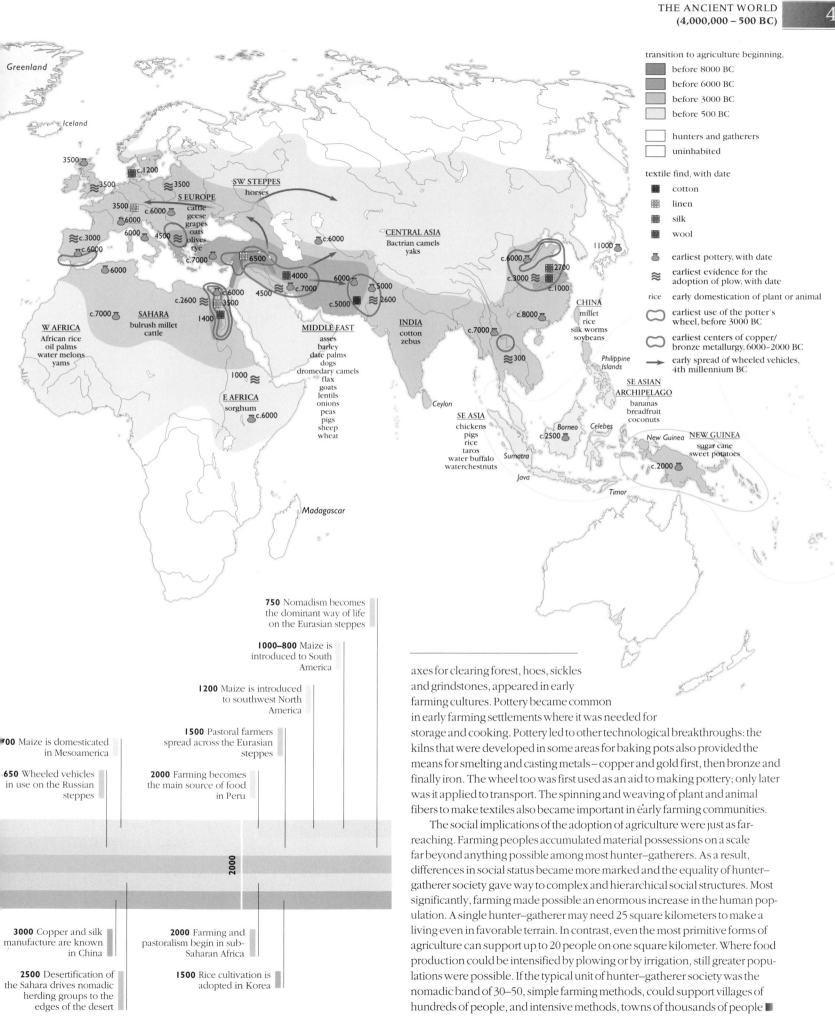

Greenland

Iceland

3500

3500

3500

c.1200

SW STEPPES
horses

3500

S EUROPE
cattle
geese
grapes
oats
olives
rye

c.6000

6000

6000

4500

c.3000

c.6000

6000

c.7000

6500

CENTRAL ASIA
Bactrian camels
yaks

c.6000

11000

c.6000

2700

c.3000

c.1000

4000

c.7000

6000

5000

4500

c.6000

3500

2600

c.8000

CHINA
millet
rice
silk worms
soybeans

1400

SAHARA
bulrush millet
cattle

c.2600

5000

W AFRICA
African rice
oil palms
water melons
yams

MIDDLE EAST
asses
barley
date palms
dogs
dromedary camels
flax
goats
lentils
onions
peas
pigs
sheep
wheat

INDIA
cotton
zebus

c.7000

Ceylon

300

Philippine
Islands

1000

E AFRICA
sorghum

c.6000

SE ASIA
chickens
pigs
rice
taros
water buffalo
waterchestnuts

SE ASIAN
ARCHIPELAGO
bananas
breadfruit
coconuts

Borneo

Celebes

c.2500

New Guinea

NEW GUINEA
sugar cane
sweet potatoes

Sumatra

Madagascar

Java

c.2000

Timor

transition to agriculture beginning,

before 8000 BC

before 6000 BC

before 3000 BC

before 500 BC

hunters and gatherers

uninhabited

textile find, with date

cotton

linen

silk

wool

earliest pottery, with date

earliest evidence for the
adoption of plow, with date

rice   early domestication of plant or animal

earliest use of the potter's
wheel, before 3000 BC

earliest centers of copper/
bronze metallurgy, 6000–2000 BC

early spread of wheeled vehicles,
4th millennium BC

750 Nomadism becomes
the dominant way of life
on the Eurasian steppes

1000–800 Maize is
introduced to South
America

1200 Maize is introduced
to southwest North
America

?00 Maize is domesticated
in Mesoamerica

1500 Pastoral farmers
spread across the Eurasian
steppes

650 Wheeled vehicles
in use on the Russian
steppes

2000 Farming becomes
the main source of food
in Peru

2000

3000 Copper and silk
manufacture are known
in China

2000 Farming and
pastoralism begin in sub-
Saharan Africa

2500 Desertification of
the Sahara drives nomadic
herding groups to the
edges of the desert

1500 Rice cultivation is
adopted in Korea

axes for clearing forest, hoes, sickles
and grindstones, appeared in early
farming cultures. Pottery became common
in early farming settlements where it was needed for
storage and cooking. Pottery led to other technological breakthroughs: the
kilns that were developed in some areas for baking pots also provided the
means for smelting and casting metals – copper and gold first, then bronze and
finally iron. The wheel too was first used as an aid to making pottery; only later
was it applied to transport. The spinning and weaving of plant and animal
fibers to make textiles also became important in early farming communities.

The social implications of the adoption of agriculture were just as far-
reaching. Farming peoples accumulated material possessions on a scale
far beyond anything possible among most hunter–gatherers. As a result,
differences in social status became more marked and the equality of hunter–
gatherer society gave way to complex and hierarchical social structures. Most
significantly, farming made possible an enormous increase in the human population. A single hunter–gatherer may need 25 square kilometers to make a
living even in favorable terrain. In contrast, even the most primitive forms of
agriculture can support up to 20 people on one square kilometer. Where food
production could be intensified by plowing or by irrigation, still greater populations were possible. If the typical unit of hunter–gatherer society was the
nomadic band of 30–50, simple farming methods, could support villages of
hundreds of people, and intensive methods, towns of thousands of people ■

The world's first cities and states emerged in the region of Sumeria in southern Mesopotamia in the Uruk period (4300–3100), named for the oldest and largest Sumerian city. States, with their social classes, centralized government and well-organized trade, became important mechanisms for coordinating flood control (important in this region) and other public works. Early Sumerian cities were dominated by temple complexes, and the priesthood probably took the lead in this organization. The Tigris and Euphrates rivers are subject to violent floods and unpredictable changes of course, events which must have seemed like the acts of capricious gods (the biblical story of the flood is of Sumerian origin). The priests claimed to be able to propitiate the gods, and this may have given them the authority to be accepted as rulers of their cities.

Most Sumerian cities of the Uruk period had a population between two and eight thousand people, although Uruk itself, the largest, had over 10,000; by 2700 BC this had risen to about 50,000. Most of these were farmers who traveled out each day to the surrounding fields. However, the food surpluses they produced were great and Sumerian society became the first to have the resources to support large numbers of people in specialist occupations: sculptors, potters, bronze-casters, stonemasons, bakers, brewers and weavers.

The temples became centers of redistribution where the surplus food of the countryside and craft products were gathered to be given out as rations, or traded abroad for raw materials that could not be found locally. These trade links ranged from India and Afghanistan to Egypt, and played an important part in spreading the influence of Sumerian civilization throughout the Middle East. It was a complex task to manage the redistribution of produce. Keeping track of all the transactions was beyond the ability of unaided memory and by around 3400 a system of pictographic writing, probably derived

			area of strongest Sumerian cultural influence
			kingdom of Lugalzagesi, c.2350
			city named in the Sumerian King List (compiled c.2100)
			other city
Mari			site of major temple
<u>Kish</u>			site of palace

origins of writing

▶   hollow clay spheres and impressed tablets (token system)

▶   inscribed clay tablets (Sumerian pictographic script), 3400–2900

▷   inscribed clay tablets (proto-Elamite script), 3100–2900

—   trade route

copper   imports to Mesopotamia

grain   exports from Mesopotamia

☐   area of alluvial soils

- - -   modern coastline and drainage where altered

| 0 | | | 300 km |
| 0 | | | 200 mi |

from an earlier token system, had been developed.

Sumerian civilization entered a new and troubled phase in the Early Dynastic period (2900–2334 BC). Massive defensive walls were built around the cities, bronze weapons were produced in increasing quantities and war begins to feature prominently as a subject of official art with rulers often being shown trampling on their enemies. This period also saw writing applied to purposes other than administration, as rulers began to record their glorious deeds to ensure their posthumous reputations. The gap between rich and poor widened and slavery appears in the records for the first time. Secular leaders now appear alongside the priest-kings. Some had the title *sangu* (accountant), suggesting that bureaucrats had achieved equal status with the priests. Others were called *lugal* (literally "big man"): these may have been war leaders, elected in times of emergency in the past, who had succeeded in making their power permanent. To show that their rule had divine approval these secular rulers built palaces next to the temple precincts, where they lived in opulence. In death they were given rich burials, such as those excavated at the Royal Cemetery at Ur, accompanied by the luxuries of their everyday lives and even their sacrificed retainers. Lacking the spiritual authority of the priesthood, the new secular rulers established their authority through law codes,

TIMELINE

	4000	3500	3000	2500
		Uruk period		Early Dynastic period

Political change

- **3500** The first cities develop in southern Mesopotamia
- **3400** Priests emerge as the rulers of the new Mesopotamian cities

Jemdet Nasr

- **2900** Defensive walls are built around many cities
- **2750** Secular rulers achieve increasing importance
- **2600–2500** Rich burials with human sacrifices take place in the "Royal Cemetery" at Ur
- **2350** Urukagina, king of Lagash, promulgates the first surviving law code
- **2350** Lugalzagesi, king of Umma and Uruk unites Sumeria and Akkad
- **2334** Sargon of Agade conquers Mesopotamia

Technological change

- **3800** The earliest arsenical bronze is produced at Tepe Yahya (Iran)
- **3600** The lost-wax process of casting copper and bronze is developed
- **3400** Writing comes into use in Sumeria
- **2900** Development of cuneiform script
- **2900** Tin bronze comes into use for the first time
- **2400** Four-wheeled war-wagons are used in Mesopotamia

NEOLITHIC   EARLY BRONZE AGE

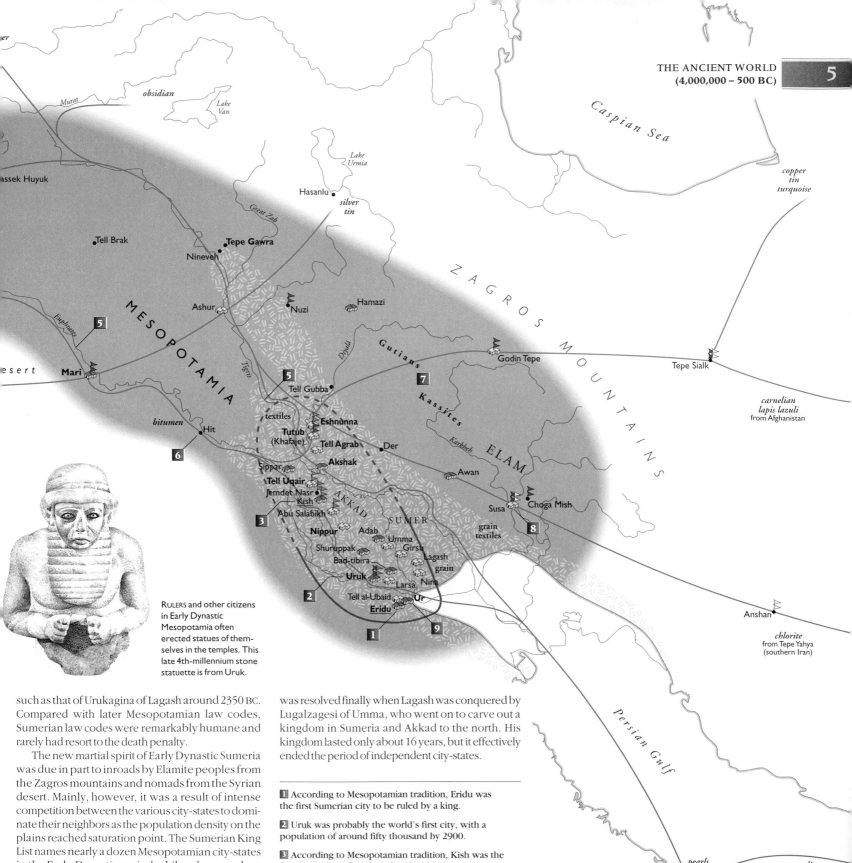

Caspian Sea

obsidian

Lake Van

*copper
tin
turquoise*

Murat

ⴰssek Huyuk

Great Zab

Lake Urmia

•Tell Brak

•**Tepe Gawra**

Hasanlu•

*silver
tin*

Nineveh•

M E S O P O T A M I A

Ashur•

5

Nuzi

Hamazi

Z A G R O S   M O U N T A I N S

Euphrates

Tigris

Mari

Tigris

Diyala

G u t i a n s

7

Godin Tepe•

Tepe Sialk

*carnelian
lapis lazuli
from Afghanistan*

K a s s i t e s

Karkheh

E L A M

bitumen

•Hit

5

•Tell Gubba

Eshnunna

textiles

Tutub
(Khafaje)

6

Tell Agrab

Der•

Akshak

Awan

Sippar•

A K K A D

Susa• Choga Mish

*grain
textiles*

8

Tell Uqair

Jemdet Nasr•

Kish

Abu Salabikh•

S U M E R

3

Nippur

Adab

Umma

Anshan•

Shuruppak

Girsu

Bad-tibira

Lagash
grain

*chlorite
from Tepe Yahya
(southern Iran)*

Uruk

Larsa

Nina

2

Tell al-Ubaid•

Ur

Eridu

9

1

RULERS and other citizens
in Early Dynastic
Mesopotamia often
erected statues of them-
selves in the temples. This
late 4th-millennium stone
statuette is from Uruk.

P e r s i a n   G u l f

*pearls
shells*

Dilmun•

*carnelian
ivory
steatite
timber*
from Meluhha
(Indus valley)

such as that of Urukagina of Lagash around 2350 BC.
Compared with later Mesopotamian law codes,
Sumerian law codes were remarkably humane and
rarely had resort to the death penalty.

The new martial spirit of Early Dynastic Sumeria
was due in part to inroads by Elamite peoples from
the Zagros mountains and nomads from the Syrian
desert. Mainly, however, it was a result of intense
competition between the various city-states to dominate their neighbors as the population density on the
plains reached saturation point. The Sumerian King
List names nearly a dozen Mesopotamian city-states
in the Early Dynastic period while others, such as
Lagash and Umma, are known from other sources.
Other cities had already lost their former independence: Girsu and Nina, for instance, were ruled by
Lagash by this date.

The early Early Dynastic was dominated by
rivalry between Kish, Uruk and Ur. This was ended
when Sumeria was conquered first by the Elamites
and then, after a brief revival by Kish, by Hamazi.
Hamazi was itself overthrown by Uruk after which
the city of Adab rose to a dominant position. By 2500
Mesilim of Kish seems to have been the nominal
overlord of Sumeria. The dominance of Kish was
ended around 2400 by Eannatum of Lagash, who
fought successfully against Kish, Akshak, Mari and
the Elamites. A dispute between Lagash and Umma

was resolved finally when Lagash was conquered by
Lugalzagesi of Umma, who went on to carve out a
kingdom in Sumeria and Akkad to the north. His
kingdom lasted only about 16 years, but it effectively
ended the period of independent city-states.

1 According to Mesopotamian tradition, Eridu was
the first Sumerian city to be ruled by a king.

2 Uruk was probably the world's first city, with a
population of around fifty thousand by 2900.

3 According to Mesopotamian tradition, Kish was the
first city to be refounded after the Flood.

4 Habuba Kabira was a Sumerian merchant colony
established around 3400, highlighting the growing
importance of long-distance trade.

5 The Tigris and Euphrates were the main transport
routes of Mesopotamia.

6 Hit was the main source of bitumen in
Mesopotamia, used for bonding courses of bricks.

7 The Gutians and Kassites were hill tribes who often
raided the Sumerian heartlands.

8 Susa was capital of Elam. Sumerians and Elamites
were frequently at war.

9 The "Royal Cemetery" at Ur revealed the existence
of a wealthy and powerful dynasty 2600–2500 BC.

See also 4 (agricultural
revolution); 6 (Egypt)

Ancient Egypt was totally dependent on the Nile. Below the First Cataract, the Nile flows through a narrow valley and, except where it broadens out into the Delta, its flood plain is nowhere more than a few kilometers wide, often less. The flood plain was probably the most favorable area for agriculture anywhere in the ancient world. The Nile flooded annually in the late summer, falling in the autumn and leaving the fields moist and fertilized with fresh silt ready for sowing. The crops grew through the warm Egyptian winter and were harvested in the spring before the next cycle of flooding. Egypt had little need of the complex irrigation systems and flood defenses of Mesopotamia, where the rivers flooded in spring, after the start of the growing season. Canals, however, were used to spread the floodwaters and increase the cultivable area. High yields were possible year after year: the farmers' surpluses were taken to state storehouses for distribution to administrators, craftsmen and priests, for trade or to build up reserves against the famine that would follow if the Nile flood failed. The Nile was also Egypt's main highway. The prevailing winds in Egypt blow north to south, enabling boats to travel upstream under sail and return downstream with the flow. Few settlements were far from the river, making it relatively easy to transport heavy loads of grain or stone over long distances. On either side of the narrow 800-kilometer (500-mile) fertile strip was the desert which isolated Egypt from the influence of other civilizations and protected it from invaders: Egyptian civilization was over 1,300 years old before it suffered its first major invasion.

Farming began in the Nile valley before 6000 BC and by 4000 BC it was populated by subsistence farmers. Chiefdoms and towns appeared by 3300. In the narrow confines of the valley competition was probably intense. Eventually, the southern chiefdoms amalgamated into an Upper Egyptian kingdom, which gained control over Lower Egypt. The first king known to have ruled all Egypt was Narmer, king of Upper Egypt who may have conquered Lower Egypt about 3000. This unification was consolidated by the foundation of Memphis as a new capital.

By the same date the hieroglyphic system of writing had appeared. The system worked on similar

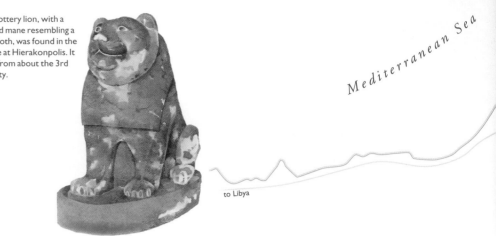

THIS pottery lion, with a stylized mane resembling a headcloth, was found in the temple at Hierakonpolis. It dates from about the 3rd Dynasty.

Mediterranean Sea

to Libya

principles to the Sumerian pictographic script; hieroglyphs were developed for use in record keeping and as labels in the late Predynastic period. Early hieroglyphs appear on a slate palette which Narmer had carved to commemorate his victories. This palette shows that the principle of theocratic kingship that would be the basis of the ancient Egyptian state was already well established. During the ensuing Early Dynastic period (2920–2575) the kings developed an efficient administration which made possible a dramatic increase in royal power at the beginning of the Old Kingdom (2575–2134), named for the kingdom ruled from Memphis by a succession of four dynasties.

The annual Nile flood was seen as a gift from the gods. The king claimed to be able to control the flood, but if the flood failed, his authority could be called into question. He was believed to be of divine descent and was held to be immortal. At his death immense effort was put into preserving his body and to providing it with a suitably regal tomb furnished with the luxuries of everyday life. Early royal tombs were built on platforms known as *mastabas*, but these were superseded by pyramids in the reign of King Djoser (r.2630–2611). Pyramid building climaxed in about 2550 with the 146-meter-high Great Pyramid, built for Khufu, and the slightly smaller pyramid of his son Khephren. These enormous

buildings are impressive evidence of the power the kings exercised over their subjects. However the large pyramids strained the resources of the kingdom: later ones were more modest and no more royal pyramids were built after the 17th century BC, by which time ideas of the afterlife had changed.

Egypt was governed by an efficient central and local bureaucracy. The kingdom was treated as the personal property of the king and the central bureaucracy was an extension of the royal household. The highest official was the vizier, who supervised the administration of justice and taxation. Below the vizier were chancellors, controllers of stores and other officials, supported by a staff of scribes trained in mathematics and writing. For the purposes of local government, Egypt was divided into provinces, or *nomes*, under governors selected from the royal or noble families.

During the 5th Dynasty (2465–2323) the monarchy was weakened by granting out lands as rewards and favors to the nobility. The provincial governorships became hereditary and drifted out of the control of the king. A period of low Nile floods then began around 2150, bringing famine and starvation, and the remaining royal authority crumbled. The Old Kingdom state collapsed and Egypt was divided between rival dynasties in Upper and Lower Egypt in what is known as the First Intermediate period.

TIMELINE

		3000	2500	2000
		Predynastic period	Early Dynastic Period	Old Kingdom	Middle Kingdom
Dynasties		**c.3000** Upper and Lower Egypt are united; Memphis is founded by Narmer	**2575** Snofru founds the 4th Dynasty and establishes the powerful Old Kingdom, based at Memphis	**2134** End of the Old Kingdom, as Egypt divides into two rival kingdoms
		2920 Traditional Egyptian date for the foundation of the 1st Dynasty	**2400** Royal power goes into decline	
Cultural		**6000** Farming begins in the Nile valley	**c.2630** The Step Pyramid is built at Saqqara	**2150** A succession of low floods brings famine and unrest
		c.4000 Copper is in use in Egypt	**c.2550** The Great Pyramid is built for Khufu at Giza	
		c.3300 The Naqada II period sees the growth of towns in the Nile valley		
		c.3300–3000 The hieroglyphic script is developed		
		3000	2500	2000

1 The First Cataract was the traditional southern frontier of Egypt through most of its history.

2 Hierakonpolis and Naqada were the first towns to develop in Egypt, c.3300.

3 Saqqara is the site of the oldest pyramid, the Step Pyramid, c.2630.

4 Giza is the site of the largest pyramids, including the Great Pyramid of Khufu.

5 The mountains of the Eastern Desert were the chief source of minerals.

6 Graffiti show that the Egyptians were exploiting Sinai's mineral wealth as early as the 3rd Dynasty (2649-2575).

7 The Egyptians maintained a trading post at Buhen in Nubia during the Old Kingdom.

8 Memphis was capital of Egypt for most of the Early Dynastic period and Old Kingdom.

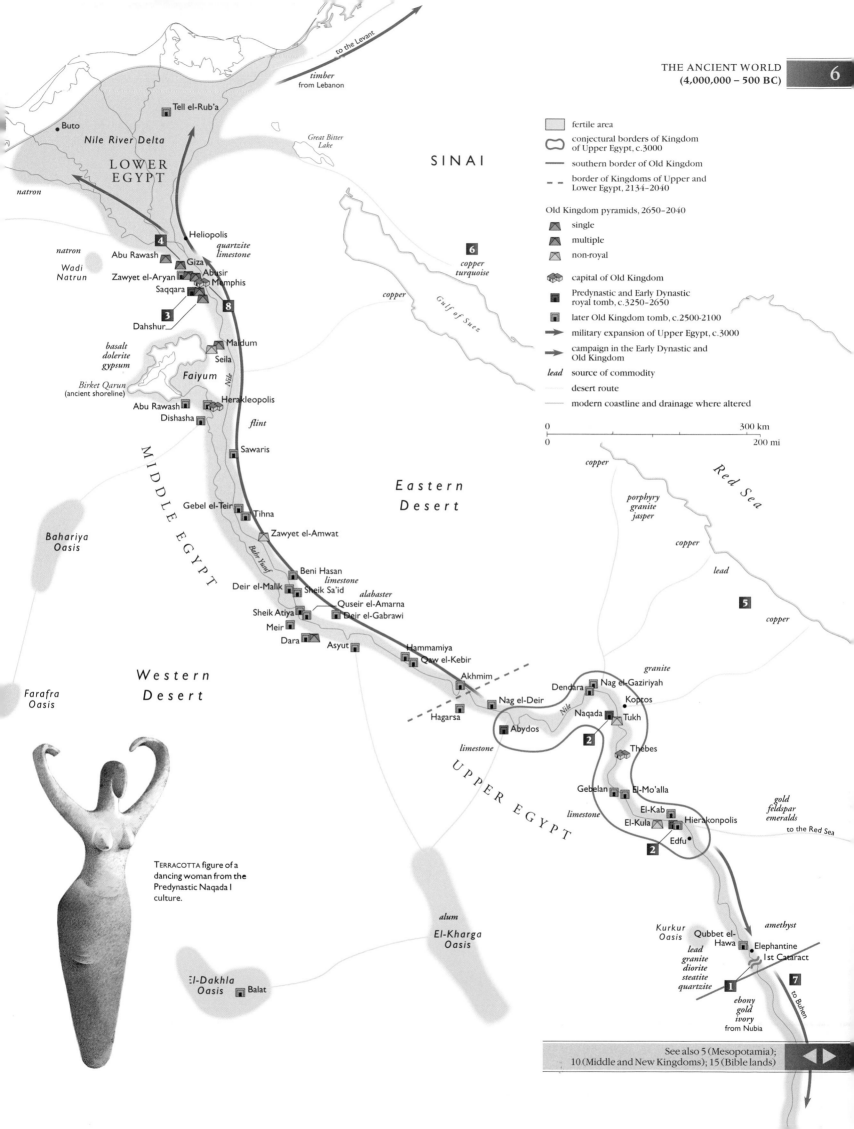

to the Levant

timber
from Lebanon

Tell el-Rub'a

Buto

Nile River Delta

LOWER
EGYPT

natron

SINAI

Great Bitter
Lake

Legend

fertile area

conjectural borders of Kingdom
of Upper Egypt, c.3000

southern border of Old Kingdom

border of Kingdoms of Upper and
Lower Egypt, 2134–2040

Old Kingdom pyramids, 2650–2040

single

multiple

non-royal

capital of Old Kingdom

Predynastic and Early Dynastic
royal tomb, c.3250–2650

later Old Kingdom tomb, c.2500-2100

military expansion of Upper Egypt, c.3000

campaign in the Early Dynastic and
Old Kingdom

lead   source of commodity

desert route

modern coastline and drainage where altered

0 — 300 km
0 — 200 mi

natron

Wadi
Natrun

Heliopolis

*quartzite
limestone*

4

Abu Rawash

Giza

Zawyet el-Aryan

Abusir

Memphis

Saqqara

3

8

Dahshur

*basalt
dolerite
gypsum*

Maidum

Seila

Birket Qarun
(ancient shoreline)

Faiyum

Abu Rawash

Herakleopolis

Dishasha

flint

Sawaris

MIDDLE EGYPT

Bahr Yusuf

Nile

*copper
turquoise*

6

copper

Gulf of Suez

Eastern
Desert

copper

*porphyry
granite
jasper*

Red Sea

Bahariya
Oasis

Gebel el-Teir

Tihna

Zawyet el-Amwat

copper

lead

Beni Hasan
limestone

Deir el-Malik

Sheik Sa'id

alabaster

Quseir el-Amarna

Deir el-Gabrawi

Sheik Atiya

Meir

Dara

Asyut

Hammamiya

Qaw el-Kebir

5

copper

Western
Desert

Farafra
Oasis

Akhmim

Nag el-Deir

Hagarsa

granite

Dendara

Nag el-Gaziriyah

Koptos

Naqada

Tukh

Abydos

limestone

Nile

2

Thebes

UPPER EGYPT

Gebelan

El-Mo'alla

limestone

El-Kab

El-Kula

Hierakonpolis

Edfu

2

*gold
feldspar
emeralds*

to the Red Sea

TERRACOTTA figure of a
dancing woman from the
Predynastic Naqada I
culture.

alum

El-Kharga
Oasis

Kurkur
Oasis

Qubbet el-
Hawa

amethyst

Elephantine

1st Cataract

*lead
granite
diorite
steatite
quartzite*

1

7

to Buhen

El-Dakhla
Oasis

Balat

*ebony
gold
ivory*
from Nubia

See also 5 (Mesopotamia);
10 (Middle and New Kingdoms); 15 (Bible lands)

The spread of agriculture through Europe was a complex process of small-scale migrations by farming peoples and the adoption of farming techniques by Mesolithic hunter–gatherers. It took time to develop crop strains suited to the colder and wetter climates of central, western and northern Europe. Hunter–gatherers readily adopted some aspects of the material culture of neighboring farmers, such as pottery and polished stone axes, but only adopted food production when natural food sources were in short supply. In many areas, Mesolithic hunter–gatherers were already semi-sedentary, so the transition to a settled farming way of life was probably easily made when it became necessary.

Farming, based on cereals, legumes, sheep, goats and cattle, first began in Europe in Greece and the Balkans around 6500 BC. This pattern of farming spread from the Balkans around the Mediterranean coasts to southern France and Spain by 5000. Whether the adoption of farming in Europe was an indigenous development or was influenced by the farming societies of the Middle East is doubtful. Southeastern Europe was within the range of wild einkorn wheat, cattle, pigs and sheep and farming may have developed as a result of experimentation with cultivation and animal husbandry by indigenous hunter–gatherers. Cattle may have been domesticated independently in southeast Europe but some crops, such as emmer wheat and barley, were certainly introduced from the Middle East.

The earliest farming culture of central Europe is the Bandkeramik or Linear Pottery culture. This originated in the northern Balkans around 5400 BC and over a few centuries spread north and west across the band of fertile and easily worked loess soils that extends across Europe from Romania to the Rhineland. When the population of a village became too large, a daughter settlement was simply founded a few kilometers away. The indigenous Mesolithic hunter–gatherer bands were not displaced by the Bandkeramik people, who settled on vacant lands between them, usually along rivers. However, the steady encroachment by the farmers placed pressure on the hunter–gatherers' resources and they were gradually forced to adopt farming too: gradually the two populations became assimilated. After a delay of several centuries, the farming way of life spread

from central Europe into western Europe, then Britain and Scandinavia and the southwest steppes.

Farming in central and northern Europe was very different from that in the south. The cold winters led to spring sowing of crops (autumn sowing prevailed in southern Europe, the Middle East and north Africa) and there was greater emphasis on cattle and pigs, which were better suited to grazing in woodland than sheep and goats.

Neolithic settlements were generally small, with populations of only forty to sixty. The most common type of building was the wooden longhouse that accommodated both people and livestock. Except in treeless areas such as the Orkney Islands, where stone houses were built, settlements have left few traces; burials and ritual structures provide most evidence of the nature of Neolithic societies. In most of Europe the dead were buried in individual graves in cemeteries with offerings of stone tools, pottery and ornaments. There is little variation in the quantity and quality of grave goods, indicating that these communities were not divded between rich and poor. In many areas the dead were buried communally in megalithic tombs which remained in use for many generations. The tombs were usually covered with mounds of earth, and may have served as territorial markers as well as burial places, the presence of the community's ancestors legitimizing the ownership of the present generation. The Atlantic coast of western Europe, where the earliest megalithic tombs were built, was already relatively densely populated in Mesolithic times. Population pressure may have been felt after the introduction of agriculture, leading to a new concern with territoriality.

In the later Neolithic and the early Bronze Age, northwest Europe saw the construction of megalithic stone circles and circular earth structures known as henges. Some circles have astronomical alignments or form part of a complex ritual landscape but their exact functions are unknown. Some monuments are so large that they must have been built by chiefdoms able to command the resources

	6000	5000	4000	3000	2000
South, east & central Europe	**c.6500** Farming starts to appear in the Balkans **c.6500** Cattle are domesticated in the Balkans **c.6000** Farming spreads to Italy	**c.5400** The Bandkeramik farming culture of central Europe begins **c.5000** Hierarchical societies emerge in southeast Europe **c.4500** Copper smelting begins in the Balkans **c.4500** The plow is in use in southeast Europe	**c.4000** The horse is domesticated on the southwestern steppes	**c.3300** Copper smelting begins in central Europe **c.3200** Wheeled vehicles are in use in the Balkans and the southwestern steppes	**c.2500** Bronze is made in central Europe **c.2300** Bronze is in use in southeast Europe **c.2000** The Minoan palace civilization emerges in Crete
West and north Europe			**c.4500** Farming begins in western Europe **c.4300** The first megalithic tombs are built, in Brittany **c.4000** Farming is introduced into Britain and Scandinavia	**c.2900** Cord Impressed Pottery cultures appear in northern Europe	**c.2000** The main stage of Stonehenge is completed in southern Britain **c.2500** Bell Beaker cultures appear in western Europe **c.2400** Copper is first in use in western Europe

NEOLITHIC   BRONZE AGE

earliest farming cultures

early Aegean and Anatolian Painted Ware cultures, 7000-6000

Balkan Painted and Impressed Pottery cultures, 6500-4000

Impressed Pottery cultures, 6000-4000

Bandkeramik or Linear Pottery culture, 5400-4500

Bowl cultures, 4500-3300

Tripolye-Cucuteni cultures, 4200-3800

Funnel-necked Beaker cultures, 4200-2800

megalithic monument building, 4300-2000

stone circle or alignment

megalithic tomb

excavation of early farming village

other site

spread of copper working by 4500

spread of copper working by 3000

general direction of the spread of farming, 6000-3000

0   600 km
0   400 mi

BELL-BEAKER drinking cups with incised decoration have been found in graves all over western Europe. Pollen grains found in the bottom of some indicate that they had contained a mead-like drink.

and populations of wide areas. The emergence of more hierarchical societies in the later Neolithic is also reflected in burial practices. In cultures such as the Cord Impressed Ware culture of eastern Europe and the Bell Beaker cultures in western Europe, variations in the quality and quantity of grave goods in burials indicate differences of wealth and status in farming societies. In many areas these changes are associated with the introduction of copper and gold metallurgy.

Metallurgy developed separately in the northern Balkans around 4800 BC and in southern Spain about fifteen centuries later. Both copper and gold were used to make small tools and ornaments. At first only native metals were used, cold-hammered into shape, but by 4500 copper ores were being mined in the Balkans for smelting. Copper was smelted in Spain, Italy and probably Britain by 2400. Copper tools had few advantages over stone ones, but the elites valued metal for display objects. Only in the Bronze Age did metal tools begin to replace stone tools in everyday use.

1 Starcevo was one of the earliest farming settlements in the Balkans, 6000-4000 BC. Hunting and gathering, cereals and cattle were all important.

2 Horses were domesticated in the Tripolye-Cucuteni cultures in the 4th millennium BC.

3 Incised clay tablets from Tartaria show that a simple system of notation had developed in the Balkans by 5000.

4 Copper ores were being mined at Rudna Glava in 4500 BC, the earliest known in the world.

5 A major stone temple complex was built at Tarxien c.3500-2400 BC.

6 Some three thousand standing stones aligned in multiple rows make Carnac one of the largest megalithic sites. Its purpose is unknown.

7 The stone circle at Stonehenge was built in several phases spanning the Neolithic and Bronze Age (c.3000-1500 BC).

8 An "ice man", whose body was found in 1991, froze to death in the Otztaler Alps c.3350-3120 BC.

See also 3 (Mesolithic Europe); 4 (spread of agriculture); 12 Bronze Age Europe

The first civilization of east Asia developed in the Yellow river valley in the 18th century BC from indigenous Neolithic cultures. Farming began as early as 5800 BC on the broad band of loess soils that stretches across the Yellow river basin. By 5000 millet farming villages of the Yangshao culture were spread across much of the region. At the same time rice farming communities were spreading among the wetlands of the Yangtze valley. Rice farming spread to the Yellow river valley in the late 4th millennium and the Longshan cultures emerged. In favorable areas, the Longshan cultures practiced intensive rice cultivation using irrigation. The population rose, copper came into use, regional trading networks developed and a warrior class emerged. There is evidence of warfare, such as rammed earth fortifications and massacres of prisoners. A system of divination based on the use of "oracle bones" was developed.

According to Chinese traditions, civilization was founded by the emperor Huang Di around 2698 BC while the first dynasty, the Xia, was founded by Yu the Great in about 2205. However, there is no evidence for states in China in the 3rd millennium BC.

The first historically and archeologically attested Chinese dynasty is the Shang. This was founded about 1766 BC by King Tang, around the time of the appearance of the Erlitou culture. Cities with monumental buildings began to develop craft specialization and advanced bronze-casting techniques were adopted. The appearance of rich burials points to the emergence of a powerful ruling elite. A pictographic script came into use: the modern Chinese script is its direct descendant. Shang cultural influence extended across most of northern China and as far south as the Yangtze river. Like many early states, the Shang kingdom combined directly run provinces and vassal states.

Around 1122 the Shang king Di-xin was defeated and overthrown by his vassal king Wu of Zhou. The dynasty established by Wu became the longest lived of Chinese history and the early centuries of its rule were looked back on as a golden age. To legitimize their rule after their usurpation of the Shang, the Zhou rulers introduced the theory of the "Mandate

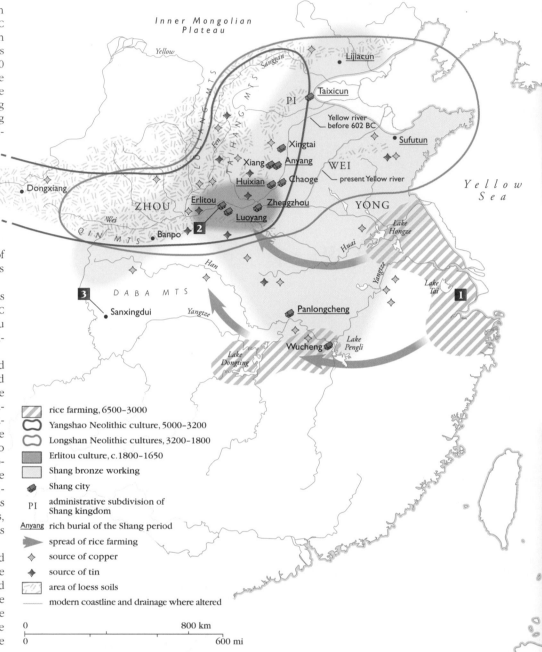

rice farming, 6500–3000
Yangshao Neolithic culture, 5000–3200
Longshan Neolithic cultures, 3200–1800
Erlitou culture, c.1800–1650
Shang bronze working
Shang city
PI   administrative subdivision of Shang kingdom
Anyang   rich burial of the Shang period
spread of rice farming
source of copper
source of tin
area of loess soils
modern coastline and drainage where altered

0   800 km
0   600 mi

	3000	2000	1000	500
	Longshan cultures	Shang dynasty	Western Zhou	Eastern Zhou (to 256 BC)
				Springs and Autumns	Warring states (to 221 BC)
Political change	c.3200 The first ranked societies in China are found in the Longshan culture	c.2205–1766 Traditional dates of the probably legendary Xia dynasty	c.1400–1122 The Shang capital is at Anyang	
	c.3000 Towns and complex fortifications are built		c.1122 King Wu of Zhou overthrows the Shang	481–480 End of the Springs and Autumns period, and start of the Warring States period
		c.1766 Foundation of the Shang dynasty by king Tang	770 The Zhou capital is moved from Hao to Luoyang; royal authority declines	
		c.1557 The Shang capital is moved to Zhengzhou		
Cultural change	6500 Rice farming begins in the Yangtze valley	c.1900 The earliest Chinese bronzes are made, at Erlitou	c.1350 The war chariot is introduced into China	551–479 Life of Confucius, philosopher and sage
	c.5800 Beginning of millet farming in northern China	c.1600 Origins of pictographic writing in China	c.800 Rapid increase in the number of towns in China	
	c.3000 Introduction of the potter's wheel in China		c.1400–1122 Royal burials at Anyang include human sacrifices	c.600 Earliest use of iron in China
	3000	2000	1000	500

TIMELINE

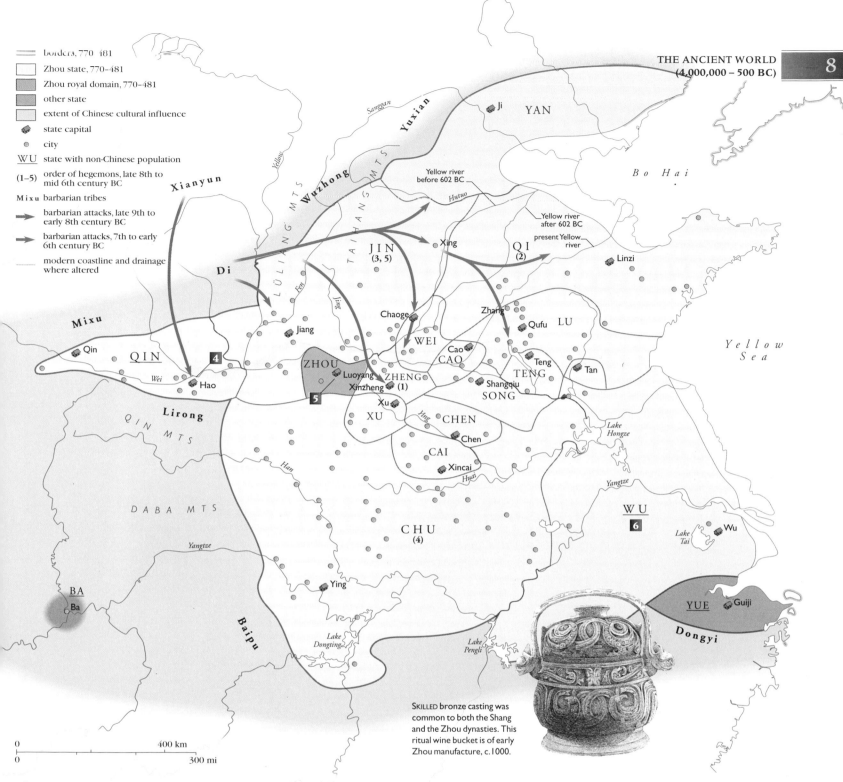

borders, 770–481

Zhou state, 770–481

Zhou royal domain, 770–481

other state

extent of Chinese cultural influence

state capital

city

WU state with non-Chinese population

(1–5) order of hegemons, late 8th to mid 6th century BC

Mixu barbarian tribes

barbarian attacks, late 9th to early 8th century BC

barbarian attacks, 7th to early 6th century BC

modern coastline and drainage where altered

SKILLED bronze casting was common to both the Shang and the Zhou dynasties. This ritual wine bucket is of early Zhou manufacture, c.1000.

of Heaven". The ruler was the "Son of Heaven" and "All under Heaven" was his lawful domain so long as he was just and moral. Should a ruler become unjust, Heaven would send him a warning and if he failed to reform, the Mandate would be given to another. Di-xin had been a sadist so Heaven had transferred the right to rule to the Zhou. This theory, which could be used both to condemn disobedience to the ruler and to justify successful usurpation, remained central to Chinese imperial ideology.

The Zhou kingdom was a decentralized feudal state, divided into fiefs governed by dukes chosen from among the king's relatives and trusted supporters. Only the royal domain was directly ruled by the king. In 770 barbarian attacks on Hao forced the Zhou to move their capital to Luoyang. This event was a turning-point in the history of the dynasty and marks the beginning of the period of disorder and fragmentation known as the Springs and Autumns period (after the title of the annals of the state of Lu).

Luoyang was more centrally situated than Hao

but it removed the dynasty from its traditional heartland in the west; its authority began to decline. By this time the king controlled less land than most of his dukes who now became, in effect, the rulers of independent states, making almost constant war on one another. However, the dukes continued to recognize the sovereignty of the king and also recognized the duke of the leading state of the time as hegemon (with general primacy over all other states). The Springs and Autumns period turned into the Warring States period (480–221), which saw the decline of feudal relationships and the rise of a professional bureaucracy.

The Springs and Autumns period was a brutal age but it saw great creativity in literature and religious and philosophical thought. The end of the period saw Confucius found the ethical system, which remains fundamental to Chinese thought. Iron working was adopted around 600, probably in Wu, though iron tools and weapons did not replace bronze in everyday use until the 2nd century BC.

1 More than a hundred wet-rice farming villages (using flooded fields) were established in this region 6500–4000 BC.

2 Erlitou was the site of the first Chinese bronzes c.1900 BC; it was probably also the first Shang capital.

3 The city and ritual offering pits at Sanxingdui, discovered in the 1990s, are evidence of a bronze-using civilization contemporary with the Shang.

4 Hao, in the original Zhou heartland, was abandoned as the capital in 770 after barbarian attacks. The move initiated a decline in Zhou authority.

5 The Zhou royal domain was limited to a small area around Luoyang by the 7th century.

6 Wu, the dominant state in southern China in the late 6th century, was destroyed by Yue in 473 BC.

See also 4 (agriculture), 26 (Warring states and after)

B y 2000 BC the revolutionary impact of agriculture had become clear. Farming was practiced on every continent and would overtake hunting and gathering as the way of life of most people well before the Christian era.

Not all early farming societies developed the same level of complexity. Poor soil, climate, endemic diseases of humans or livestock or a lack of suitable crops limited development in many areas. The greater the resources possessed by a society, the more complex it could become; in a few favorable environments (such as the northwest of North America), hunter-gatherer societies too achieved greater levels of social complexity.

Most early farming societies were kinship-based tribes of hundreds or a few thousand people living in villages or dispersed homesteads. Although they recognized ties of kinship, religion or language with others, each tribe was essentially independent. Differences of rank and status existed but leaders could rarely exercise coercive power over other tribes' people. Archeologically, such societies (known to anthropologists as "segmentary societies") can be recognized by communal burial practices, the remains of permanent homesteads and villages and communal works such as the megalithic tombs of prehistoric western Europe. In 2000 BC segmentary farming societies were dominant in south and southeast Asia, New Guinea, north Africa, northern Europe and parts of Mesoamerica and South America.

Where intensive agricultural techniques could be used, largescale hierarchical communities of up to 20,000 people, known as "chiefdoms", could develop. Rank and status were linked to lineage: the senior person of the senior lineage was the chief, who was thereby the ruler of the whole community. Chieftains could exercise coercive power, often through a warrior class, and support specialist craftsmen. Archeologically, chiefdoms show major construction projects requiring large resources of labor and wealth, such as Stonehenge in southern Britain (▷ 7). In chiefdoms the quantity and quality of grave goods placed with burials indicate the rank and status of the individual and a few burials are lavishly furnished. Chiefdoms commonly had a dominant central site such as a stronghold or ceremonial center, and smaller satellite settlements. In 2000 BC chiefdoms were established in the Middle East and southwest central Europe, in China and the Andes. In western Europe segmentary farming societies were giving way to chiefdoms at this time.

Arctic marine mammal hunters

Aleuts

Archaic Amerindian hunter–gatherers

Hawaiian Islands

Bahamas

Cuba
Hispaniola
Jamaica
Puerto Rico

maize farming replacing hunting and gathering

Valdivia tradition

Aspero tradition

Archaic Amerindian hunter–gatherers

Chinchoros tradition

3400 Earliest writing appears in Uruk (Iraq). City-states emerge in Sumeria (southern Mesopotamia)

c.4300 The first megalithic tombs are built in western Europe

3800 Bronze casting techniques employed for the first time in the Middle East

3500 Permanent fishing village settlements are inhabited in Peru

5000–2000 Hunting cultures spread across Arctic North America to Greenland

4000 Pottery first comes into use in the Americas (Guyana)

3500 Farming is established throughout Europe

c.3000 Foundation of the Egyptian state

The Americas			
Europe	4500 BC	4000	3500	3000
Middle East				
Africa				
East and South Asia				

4300–3100 Uruk period in Mesopotamia. The first cities are built.

3200–1800 Chinese Longshan advanced farming cultures; first towns are built in China

3000 Ancestral Austronesians migrate from Taiwan to the Philippines

3000–1700 Pastoral farming is established on the central Asian steppes (Afanasevo culture)

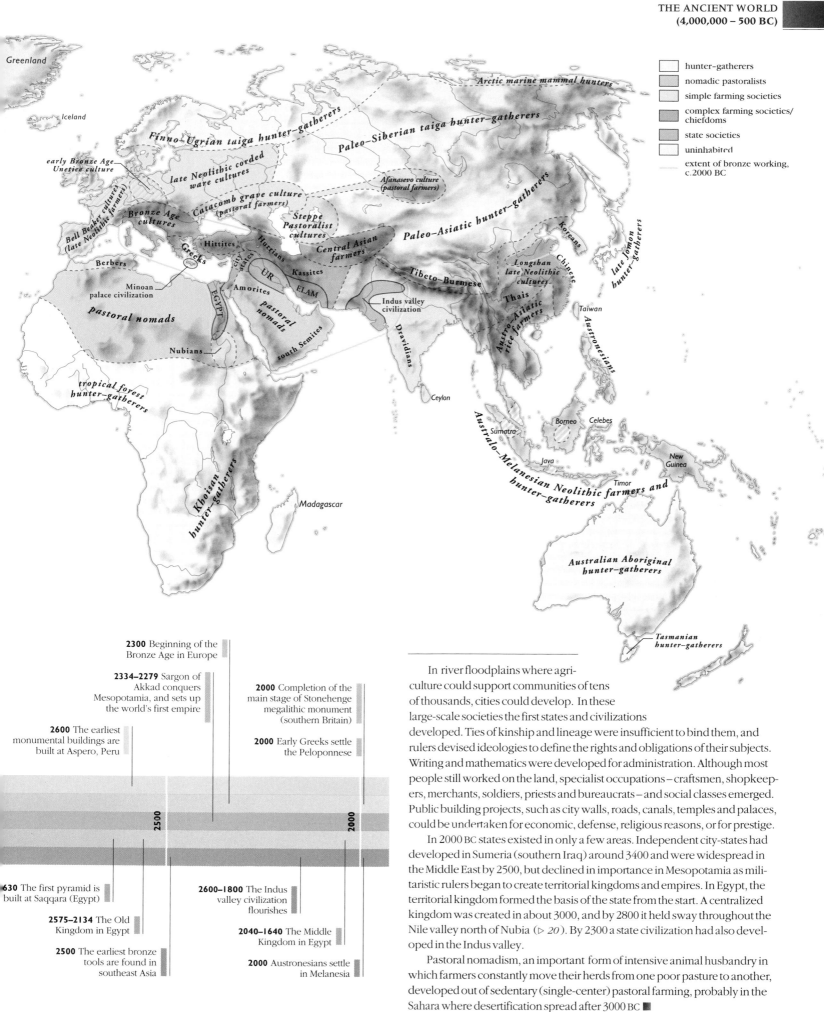

Legend:
- hunter-gatherers
- nomadic pastoralists
- simple farming societies
- complex farming societies/chiefdoms
- state societies
- uninhabited
- extent of bronze working, c.2000 BC

Timeline:

2300 Beginning of the Bronze Age in Europe

2334–2279 Sargon of Akkad conquers Mesopotamia, and sets up the world's first empire

2000 Completion of the main stage of Stonehenge megalithic monument (southern Britain)

2600 The earliest monumental buildings are built at Aspero, Peru

2000 Early Greeks settle the Peloponnese

2500

2000

2630 The first pyramid is built at Saqqara (Egypt)

2600–1800 The Indus valley civilization flourishes

2575–2134 The Old Kingdom in Egypt

2040–1640 The Middle Kingdom in Egypt

2500 The earliest bronze tools are found in southeast Asia

2000 Austronesians settle in Melanesia

In river floodplains where agriculture could support communities of tens of thousands, cities could develop. In these large-scale societies the first states and civilizations developed. Ties of kinship and lineage were insufficient to bind them, and rulers devised ideologies to define the rights and obligations of their subjects. Writing and mathematics were developed for administration. Although most people still worked on the land, specialist occupations – craftsmen, shopkeepers, merchants, soldiers, priests and bureaucrats – and social classes emerged. Public building projects, such as city walls, roads, canals, temples and palaces, could be undertaken for economic, defense, religious reasons, or for prestige.

In 2000 BC states existed in only a few areas. Independent city-states had developed in Sumeria (southern Iraq) around 3400 and were widespread in the Middle East by 2500, but declined in importance in Mesopotamia as militaristic rulers began to create territorial kingdoms and empires. In Egypt, the territorial kingdom formed the basis of the state from the start. A centralized kingdom was created in about 3000, and by 2800 it held sway throughout the Nile valley north of Nubia (▷ 20). By 2300 a state civilization had also developed in the Indus valley.

Pastoral nomadism, an important form of intensive animal husbandry in which farmers constantly move their herds from one poor pasture to another, developed out of sedentary (single-center) pastoral farming, probably in the Sahara where desertification spread after 3000 BC ■

The reunification of Egypt in 2040 BC by Mentuhotpe II (r.2061–2010), of the Theban dynasty of Upper Egypt, marks the start of the Middle Kingdom. A few decades later royal authority and political stability had been restored and the power of the provincial governors reduced. To rebuild a loyal administration, the Middle Kingdom rulers promoted propagandist literature, while statuary presented the king as the care-worn "good shepherd" of his people. Pyramid building was revived, though more modestly than in the Old Kingdom.

Egypt's neighbors were now becoming organized into chiefdoms and petty kingdoms, and the Middle Kingdom rulers had to pursue a more aggressive foreign policy than their predecessors. Under Amenemhet I (r.1991–1962), Lower Nubia was conquered; the frontier at the Second Cataract was garrisoned and heavily fortified by his successors. Egyptian influence was extended over the Levant during the reign of Senwosret III (r.1878–1841) and local rulers were forced to become vassals of Egypt. During the 18th century the bureaucracy began to grow out of control and for much of the time the effective rulers of Egypt were the viziers. In the 17th century there was considerable immigration from the Levant into the Delta. Most immigrants were absorbed into the lower classes of Egyptian society but one, Khendjer, became king around 1745 BC.

From around 1640 much of Egypt was ruled by the Hyksos, a Semitic people from the Levant, who gradually took over Lower Egypt, which they ruled from their capital at Avaris. Upper Egypt remained independent under a Theban dynasty but control over Lower Nubia was lost to the nascent kingdom of Kush. Hyksos rule, in what is known as the Second Intermediate period, made Egypt more open to foreign influences. Bronze came into widespread use, war chariots were introduced, as were weapons such as the composite bow and scale armor. New fashions in dress, musical instruments, domestic animals and crops were adopted through Hyksos influence. Otherwise, the Hyksos accepted Egyptian traditions and historical continuity was unbroken.

Under the Theban king Seqenenre II (died c.1555) the Egyptians began a long struggle to expel the Hyksos which was finally completed by Ahmose in 1532. This victory marks the beginning of the New Kingdom, under which the power and influence of ancient Egypt reached its peak. The Hyksos invasion had shown the Egyptians that their borders were no longer secure, and the New Kingdom was overtly militaristic and expansionist, reaching its greatest extent around 1500 under the warrior king Tuthmosis I. Tuthmosis conquered the entire Levant and established a frontier on the Euphrates. Lower Nubia was reconquered and Kush was overrun to beyond the Fourth Cataract. The primary motive of expansion into the Levant was to establish a buffer zone between Egypt and the aggressive powers of the Middle East; in Nubia, which had rich gold deposits, the motive was economic. In the Levant, local rulers were kept under the supervision of Egyptian officials and key cities were garrisoned. Nubia was subjected to full colonial government under a viceroy directly responsible to the king. Nubia was a great source of wealth to the New Kingdom, but the Egyptians faced a constant struggle to control the Levant, against local rebellions and expansionist powers such as the Hittite empire.

The power of Egypt declined after the reign of Amenophis IV (r.1353–1335). Amenophis, who changed his name to Akhenaten, was a radical religious reformer who attempted to replace Egypt's traditional polytheism with the monotheistic cult of the Aten, or sun disk. Akhenaten founded a new capital and promoted radically new art styles to symbolize the break with the past, but there was little popular enthusiasm for the new religion, which was abandoned after his death. In the ensuing period of political instability, Egypt lost control of the Levant to the Hittites. Campaigns by the kings (or pharaohs as they were now known) Sethos I (r.1306–1290) and Ramesses II "the Great" (r.1290–1224) to restore the Egyptian position were only partially successful and Ramesses eventually made peace with the Hittites.

Around 1200 the entire region was disrupted by

Map legend

Middle Kingdom (12th Dynasty, 1991–1783)

- zone of direct control
- zone of dominance

Second Intermediate period

- Hyksos Kingdom (15th Dynasty, 1640–1532)
- Theban (17th Dynasty, 1646–1550)
- Kingdom of Kush
- maximum extent of New Kingdom under Tuthmosis I, 1504–1492

- royal capital, with dynasty
- ■ city

royal tomb
- Middle Kingdom
- New Kingdom

fort or garrison
- ◆ Middle Kingdom
- ◇ New Kingdom

- sacked c.1200, probably by Sea Peoples
- Giza temple
- desert route used for communication between the Hyksos and Kushite allies
- gold deposit
- major migration
- modern coastline and drainage where altered

Libyan

0   300 km
0   200 mi

TIMELINE

	2000	1500	1000	500
	Middle Kingdom	New Kingdom	3rd Intermediate period	Late period

Political

2040 Egypt is reunified under the 11th Dynasty, based at Thebes

c.1960 Amenemhet I conquers Nubia, and the Egyptian frontier is established at the 2nd Cataract

1878–1841 Senwosret III reorganizes Egyptian local government

1640 A Semitic Hyksos dynasty (15th) rules Lower Egypt, initiating the 2nd Intermediate period

1550 Ahmose (18th Dynasty) begins to reunite Egypt

1532 The Hyksos are expelled from Egypt, beginning the New Kingdom

1504–1492 The Egyptian empire reaches its greatest extent under Tuthmosis I

1285 The Egyptian advance under Ramesses II into the Levant is halted by the Hittites at Qadesh

1180 An invasion of the Delta region by the "Sea Peoples" is driven off

1070 Fall of 21st Dynasty initiates 3rd Intermediate period

924 Shoshenq I ravages Israel and Judah

c.828–712 Egypt is split into five separate kingdoms

712-671 The Nubian 25th Dynasty reunites Egypt

671–651 The Assyrians occupy Egypt

525 The Persians conquer Egypt

332 Alexander the Great conquers Egypt

Cultural

2000–1640 Classical period of Egyptian literature

1800 Bronze working is introduced into Egypt

1600 The chariot is introduced into Egypt

c.1470 Queen Hatshepsut sends a trading expedition to east Africa

1353-1335 Akhenaten creates a short-lived monotheistic cult of the Aten at el-Amarna

c.750 Iron working is introduced into Egypt

	2000	1500	1000	500

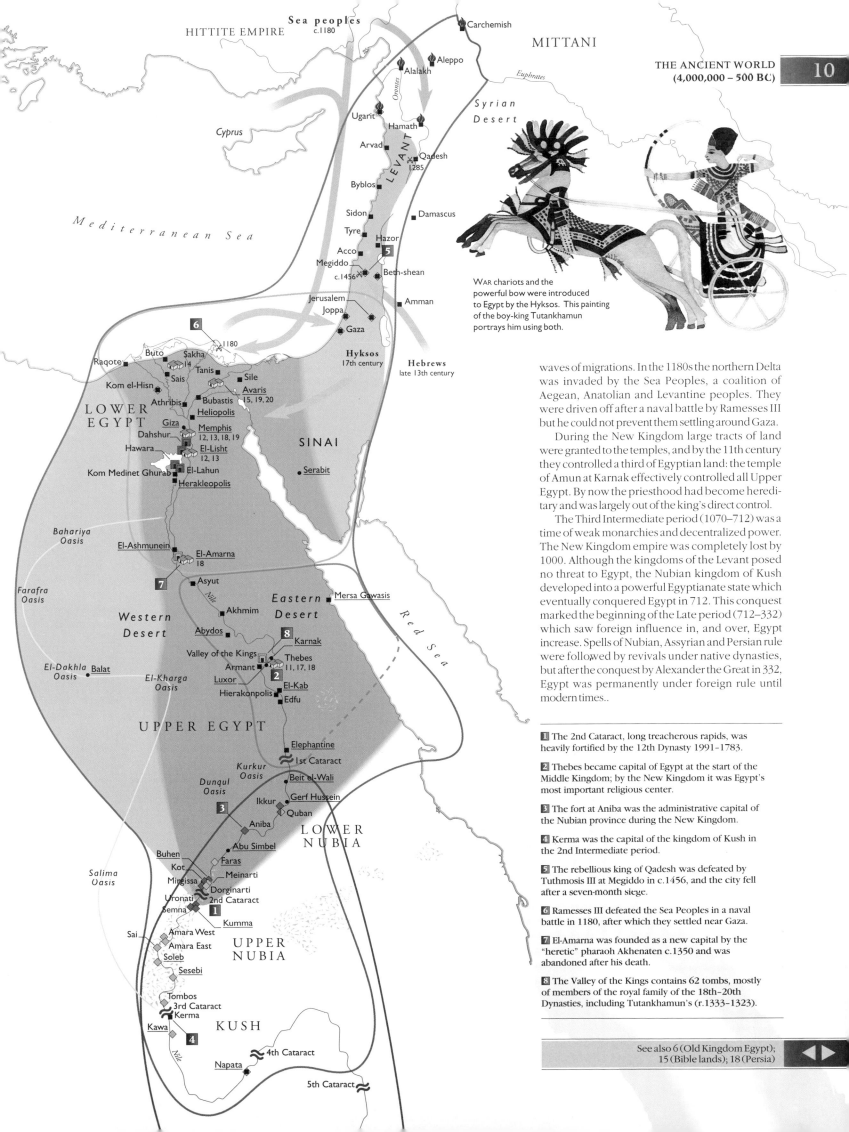

Sea peoples
c.1180

HITTITE EMPIRE

MITTANI

Carchemish

Aleppo
Alalakh

Ugarit
Hamath

Euphrates

*Syrian
Desert*

Arvad
Qadesh
1285

Cyprus

Byblos

Levant

M e d i t e r r a n e a n   S e a

Sidon
Damascus
Tyre
Hazor
Acco **5**
Megiddo
c.1456
Beth-shean

Jerusalem
Joppa
Amman
Gaza

WAR chariots and the
powerful bow were introduced
to Egypt by the Hyksos. This painting
of the boy-king Tutankhamun
portrays him using both.

6
1180
Buto
Sakha
Raqote
14
Tanis
Kom el-Hisn
Sais
Sile
Athribis
Avaris
15, 19, 20
Bubastis
Heliopolis
LOWER
EGYPT
Giza
Memphis
Dahshur
12, 13, 18, 19
Hawara
El-Lisht
12, 13
Kom Medinet Ghurab
El-Lahun
Herakleopolis

Hyksos
17th century

Hebrews
late 13th century

SINAI

Serabit

*Bahariya
Oasis*

El-Ashmunein
El-Amarna
18
7

*Farafra
Oasis*

Asyut

*Eastern
Desert*

Mersa Gawasis

*Western
Desert*

Akhmim

Abydos

Red Sea

El-Dakhla
Oasis
Balat
El-Kharga
Oasis

8
Karnak
Valley of the Kings
Thebes
11, 17, 18
Armant
2
Luxor
El-Kab
Hierakonpolis
Edfu

UPPER EGYPT

Elephantine
1st Cataract

*Kurkur
Oasis*

Beit el-Wali
*Dunqul
Oasis*
Gerf Hussein
Ikkur
Quban
3
Aniba

LOWER
NUBIA

*Salima
Oasis*

Abu Simbel
Buhen
Faras
Kor
Meinarti
Mirgissa
Dorginarti
Uronati
2nd Cataract
Semna
1
Kumma
Sai
Amara West
Amara East
UPPER
NUBIA
Soleb
Sesebi
Tombos
3rd Cataract
Kerma
Kawa
4
KUSH
Napata
4th Cataract
Nile
5th Cataract

waves of migrations. In the 1180s the northern Delta
was invaded by the Sea Peoples, a coalition of
Aegean, Anatolian and Levantine peoples. They
were driven off after a naval battle by Ramesses III
but he could not prevent them settling around Gaza.

During the New Kingdom large tracts of land
were granted to the temples, and by the 11th century
they controlled a third of Egyptian land: the temple
of Amun at Karnak effectively controlled all Upper
Egypt. By now the priesthood had become hereditary and was largely out of the king's direct control.

The Third Intermediate period (1070–712) was a
time of weak monarchies and decentralized power.
The New Kingdom empire was completely lost by
1000. Although the kingdoms of the Levant posed
no threat to Egypt, the Nubian kingdom of Kush
developed into a powerful Egyptianate state which
eventually conquered Egypt in 712. This conquest
marked the beginning of the Late period (712–332)
which saw foreign influence in, and over, Egypt
increase. Spells of Nubian, Assyrian and Persian rule
were followed by revivals under native dynasties,
but after the conquest by Alexander the Great in 332,
Egypt was permanently under foreign rule until
modern times..

1 The 2nd Cataract, long treacherous rapids, was
heavily fortified by the 12th Dynasty 1991-1783.

2 Thebes became capital of Egypt at the start of the
Middle Kingdom; by the New Kingdom it was Egypt's
most important religious center.

3 The fort at Aniba was the administrative capital of
the Nubian province during the New Kingdom.

4 Kerma was the capital of the kingdom of Kush in
the 2nd Intermediate period.

5 The rebellious king of Qadesh was defeated by
Tuthmosis III at Megiddo in c.1456, and the city fell
after a seven-month siege.

6 Ramesses III defeated the Sea Peoples in a naval
battle in 1180, after which they settled near Gaza.

7 El-Amarna was founded as a new capital by the
"heretic" pharaoh Akhenaten c.1350 and was
abandoned after his death.

8 The Valley of the Kings contains 62 tombs, mostly
of members of the royal family of the 18th–20th
Dynasties, including Tutankhamun's (r.1333-1323).

See also 6 (Old Kingdom Egypt);
15 (Bible lands); 18 (Persia)

Europe's first cities and states developed on the Aegean island of Crete around 2000 BC, where the Minoans developed a system of intensive agriculture based on wheat, olives and vines. Olives and vines grew well on rough hillsides and produced valuable commodities for long-distance trade, allowing good plowland to be kept for wheat production. Sheep were kept on Crete's mountain pastures and their wool supplied a textile industry that exported cloth to Egypt. Minoan pottery and metalwork was in demand throughout the eastern Mediterranean.

By 2000 BC Minoan society was controlled from palaces at Knossos, Phaistos, Mallia and Khania, probably the capitals of small kingdoms. A number of smaller palaces were probably subordinate centers. The palaces, which incorporated vast storehouses for grain, oil and other products, were centers for redistributing produce collected as taxes or tribute for rations to support administrators, craftsmen or traders. The Minoans had a hieroglyphic script by 2000, but this was superseded by a syllabic script three centuries later. Neither script has been deciphered so the ethnic identity of the Minoans is unknown, but they did not speak an Indo-European language and were therefore not Greeks.

Around 1700 most of the Minoan palaces were destroyed by fire, probably as a result of warfare between the palace states; they were subsequently rebuilt, but only Knossos regained its former splendor, taking control of the whole island and reducing the other palaces to tributary status. In 1626 the palaces were damaged by ash falls and earthquakes resulting from a volcanic eruption on the nearby island of Thera. The palaces were rebuilt and the Minoan civilization endured until it collapsed in about 1450 after conquest by the Mycenaeans.

The Mycenaeans, or Achaeans as they probably called themselves, were a Greek-speaking people who had moved to the Greek peninsula from the Balkans around 2000 BC. By around 1600 small kingdoms based on fortified towns were beginning to develop and a system of writing, based on the Cretan syllabic script, had been adopted. The earliest

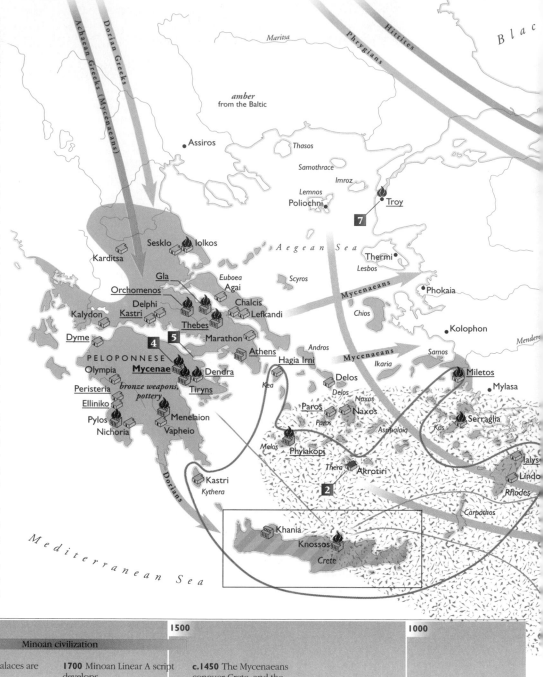

TIMELINE

		2000	1500	1000
Crete	c.6000 The first settlement of Crete		Minoan civilization	
	3000 Stone tombs are built on Crete, and trade develops with the Levant	2000 The first palaces are built on Crete	1700 Minoan Linear A script develops	c.1450 The Mycenaeans conquer Crete, and the palaces are destroyed
		2000 The Minoan hieroglyphic script develops	1700 Knossos is rebuilt as the main palace on Crete	
		2000 A Minoan colony is established at Kastri on Kythera	1626 Eruption of the volcano at Thera disrupts Cretan life	
Greece and the Aegean		c.2300 Bronze enters use in the Aegean region	Mycenaean civilization	Greek dark ages
		2000 The Achaeans (Mycenaeans) move south into Greece	1650 Emergence of Mycenaean urban life	c.1200 Invasions of the Sea Peoples
			c.1600 Rich shaft grave burials at Mycenae	c.1200 Fall of Mycenaean civilization and decline of urban life in Greece
			c.1450 The earliest Mycenaean palaces are built	c.1100 The Dorian peoples occupy Greece
			c.1450 The Mycenaean Linear B script is developed	1000 Iron is in widespread use in Greece
			1400 Walls are built around the Mycenaean cities	
		2000	1500	1000

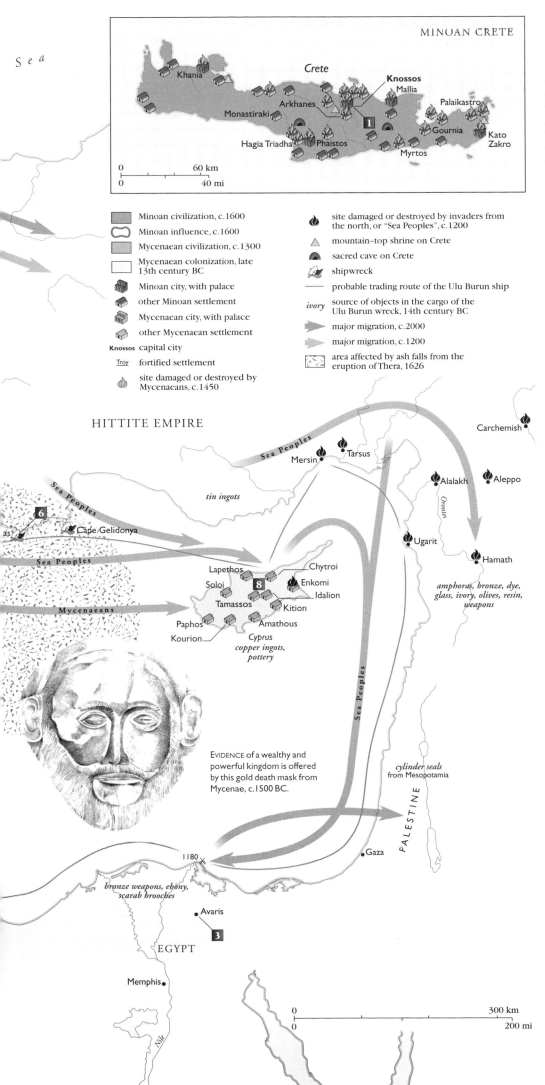

MINOAN CRETE

Sea

Crete

Khania
Arkhanes
Monastiraki
Knossos
Mallia
Palaikastro
Gournia
Kato Zakro
Hagia Triadha
Phaistos
Myrtos

0 ___ 60 km
0 ___ 40 mi

Legend

- Minoan civilization, c.1600
- Minoan influence, c.1600
- Mycenaean civilization, c.1300
- Mycenaean colonization, late 13th century BC
- Minoan city, with palace
- other Minoan settlement
- Mycenaean city, with palace
- other Mycenaean settlement
- **Knossos** capital city
- Troy fortified settlement
- site damaged or destroyed by Mycenaeans, c.1450
- site damaged or destroyed by invaders from the north, or "Sea Peoples", c.1200
- mountain-top shrine on Crete
- sacred cave on Crete
- shipwreck
- probable trading route of the Ulu Burun ship
- *ivory* source of objects in the cargo of the Ulu Burun wreck, 14th century BC
- major migration, c.2000
- major migration, c.1200
- area affected by ash falls from the eruption of Thera, 1626

HITTITE EMPIRE

Carchemish

Sea Peoples

Mersin
Tarsus

tin ingots

Sea Peoples

Cape Gelidonya

Sea Peoples

Mycenaeans

Alalakh
Aleppo

Orontes

Ugarit

Hamath

amphoras, bronze, dye, glass, ivory, olives, resin, weapons

Lapethos
Chytroi
Soloi
Enkomi
Idalion
Tamassos
Kition
Paphos
Amathous
Kourion
Cyprus copper ingots, pottery

EVIDENCE of a wealthy and powerful kingdom is offered by this gold death mask from Mycenae, c.1500 BC.

cylinder seals from Mesopotamia

PALESTINE

Gaza

1180 ✕

bronze weapons, ebony, scarab brooches

Avaris

EGYPT

Memphis

Nile

0 ___ 300 km
0 ___ 200 mi

---

evidence of Mycenaean civilization is a series of richly furnished shaft graves at Mycenae, dating to between 1650 and 1550. The grave goods reveal a wealthy warrior society and include hoards of bronze weapons, gold, silver and electrum tableware, jewelry and gold deathmasks. Mycenaean warriors rode to battle in horse-drawn chariots, but fought on foot with spear, sword and dagger. The towns were well defended, especially after the 14th century, by strong walls, built with massive blocks of stone and bastioned gateways. From the 15th century, Mycenaean rulers were buried in vaulted *tholos* (beehive shaped) tombs in which rituals related to a cult of kingship could be performed.

Each Mycenaean stronghold was ruled over by a king with a warrior aristocracy. The kings controlled many craftsmen – the king of Pylos employed about four hundred bronzesmiths – and hundreds of mainly female slaves. The royal palaces were smaller than those on Crete. According to a survey preserved in Homer's *Iliad*, known as the Catalog of Ships, there were some twenty kingdoms theoretically acknowledging the leadership of Mycenae.

Around 1450 the Mycenaeans expanded in the Aegean, conquering Crete and founding Miletos on the Anatolian coast: they may also have raided Egypt and the Hittite empire and, perhaps, they sacked Troy. They traded throughout the eastern Mediterranean and as far west as Malta, Sicily and Italy.

The Mycenaean civilization came to a violent end around 1200. Most of the major centers were sacked, town life came to an end and writing fell out of use. The whole Aegean entered a dark age which lasted about four centuries. The attackers were probably the Sea Peoples who also brought chaos to Egypt and the Levant. Some Mycenaeans sought refuge on Cyprus and on the coast of Anatolia; others may have joined with the Sea Peoples – Mycenaean influence is evident in Palestine where some of them settled. A power vacuum developed in Greece into which another Greek-speaking people, the Dorians, migrated around 1100, overrunning the Peloponnese, Crete and Rhodes: of the old Mycenaean centers only Athens retained its independence.

1 Knossos, the greatest of the Cretan palaces, was first built around 2000 and was rebuilt several times after earthquake damage or war.

2 The Minoan city of Akrotiri was preserved by ashfalls after the volcanic eruption on Thera in 1626.

3 Avaris was an Egyptian city which contained a Minoan colony founded in about 1550.

4 Mycenae had rich tombs and massive defenses built between 1600 and 1200. According to Homer, its king Agamemnon led the Greeks in the Trojan War.

5 A defensive wall was built across the Isthmus of Corinth in the late 13th century to protect the Peloponnese from invasion from the north.

6 A 14th-century shipwreck found at Ulu Burun near Kas had a cargo from around the east Mediterranean.

7 Troy was sacked twice in the 13th century, and again in 1100.

8 Mycenaeans reached Cyprus in the 15th century but the main settlement was 300 years later.

See also 10 (Egypt); 12 (Bronze Age Europe); 16 (Greek city-states)

The Bronze Age saw chiefdoms and warrior elites established across most of Europe. Beyond the Aegean, states were not formed until the Iron Age was well advanced and in northern and eastern Europe not until the early Middle Ages. The chiefdoms were competitive communities: fortifications were built in great numbers and new weapons such as swords and halberds were invented. Superb crafted display objects – ornaments, weapons, "parade-ground" armor, tableware, cult objects – made of bronze and precious metals, express the competitiveness of the period. Long-distance trade, particularly in tin and amber, arose to satisfy the demand for metals and other precious objects in areas where such resources were lacking. The increase in trade aided the spread of ideas and fashions and led to a high degree of cultural uniformity.

The earliest known use of bronze in Europe, in the Unetice culture in central Europe about 2500 BC, was probably an independent development and not the result of influence from the Middle East. Bronze came into use in southeast Europe, the Aegean and Italy two hundred years later, followed by Spain and, finally, the British Isles in about 1800. Scandinavia, with no workable deposits of copper or tin, continued in the Stone Age until the middle of the 2nd millennium BC. By this time bronze had entered Scandinavia, brought by traders in exchange for amber and, probably, furs.

Bronze technology led to a rapid increase in the use of metals. Bronze weapons and tools kept an edge better than stone or copper, could easily be resharpened and when broken could be melted down and recast. It was expensive, however, and its use was largely confined to the social elites in the early Bronze Age. Stone tools, sometimes copying the style of prestigious bronze tools, continued in everyday use. Large quantities of bronze artifacts, often of the highest quality, were buried or sunk in bogs as offerings to the gods.

The social distinctions of Bronze Age society are apparent in burial practices: a minority of burials being richly furnished with grave goods and the majority with few offerings. In the earlier Bronze

early Bronze Age cultures, c.2300–1800

- late megalithic cultures
- Bell Beaker cultures
- Nordic late Neolithic cultures
- Cord Impressed Pottery cultures
- Catacomb Grave cultures
- Unetice culture
- Danubian–Carpathian Bronze Age cultures
- Balkan Bronze Age cultures
- early Aegean Bronze Age cultures
- North Italian Bronze Age cultures
- South Italian Bronze Age cultures

spread of Urnfield cultures in late Bronze Age

- by 14th century
- by 12th century
- by 9th century

- early Bronze Age barrow burial
- fortified site
- late Bronze Age urnfield
- metal hoard
- shipwreck
- settlement
- other site
- source of tin
- source of copper
- source of gold
- source of amber
- Mycenaean trade route
- main amber trade route

```
0                          600 km
0                  400 mi
```

Age three distinct burial practices are found. In southeast Europe the normal practice was burial of rich and poor alike in flat grave cemeteries. In most of eastern, northern and western Europe, the poor were buried in flat graves but the rich were buried under earth mounds known as barrows. Barrows required a communal effort to build and are evidence of the power of the elites. In some parts of western Europe Neolithic-style communal burials in megalithic tombs continued until about 1200 BC.

In southern and central Europe, large villages, often fortified, developed but in northern and western Europe the settlement pattern was one of dispersed homesteads. Population rose across Europe and agricultural settlers moved into many marginal upland areas. These were abandoned late in the Bronze Age, perhaps because of climatic deterioration or because the poor soils had been exhausted. As agricultural land rose in value, clear boundaries were laid out between communities in

sub-Neolithic forest
hunters and gatherers

Rickeby
Hallunda
Tromøy
Vänern
Vättern
Kvarnby
Bulbjerg
Lake
Peipus
Rezne
Western Dvina
Trundholm
Brudevaelte
Egtved
Voldtofte
Kivik

VOTIVE offerings, thrown
into the bogs, include this
bronze and gold "chariot of
the sun" from Trundholm
(Denmark).

4
Drenthe
Barger-Oosterveld
Perleberg
Pustinka
Biskupin
Jankowo
Kamieniec
3
Nieder-Neundorf
Schweinert
Miejsce
oterfout
Court St Etienne
Leubingen
Helmsdorf
Grossenheim
Iwanowice
Ivanja
Moska
Dnieper
Donec group
Bad Nauheim
Flörsheim
Postoloprty
Oder
Vistula
Spissky Stvrtok
Gedinne
Heidesheim
Unetice
Barca
Rostov
Havré
Mannheim
5
Blucina
Veterov
Velatice
Usatove
Hagenam
Danube
Kelheim
Unter-Radl
Malé Kosihy
Mohi
Wasserburg
Ettins
Nitriansky Hrádok
Füzesabony
Suciu du Sus
Tudoromo
Kamenka
xheim
Baldegg
Volders
Caka
Vál
1
Wittnauer Horn
Hölting
Ptuj
Kisapostag
Tószeg
Periam
Monteoru
Cortaillod
Crestaulta
Ledro
Bled
Angarano
Dobova
Sava
Czorvas
Gomalova
Vattina
Danube
A
P
S
Polada
Canegrate
Fontanella
Girla Mare
Ezerovo
Cirna
Tarnava
Black Sea
Bismantora
Ezero
Luni
Corsica
Filitosa
Allumiere
Narce
Danja Slatina
ANATOLIA
Nuraghe
Albucci
Phlegraean
Fields
Scoglio del
Tonno
Hittites
Barumini
Sardinia
6
Troy
Lipara
Millazzo
Mycenae
Sicily
Cyprus
Borg in-Nadur
Malta
Mediterranean Sea
Crete
Knossos
Minoan
civilization

many areas, especially northwest Europe, and farmland was enclosed into small fields that could be managed more intensively. Farmers benefited from the introduction of heavier plows, wheeled vehicles and horses. European wild oats were domesticated at this time, probably as horse fodder.

Around 1350 the Urnfield culture, named for its distinctive burial practices, appeared in Hungary. Bodies were cremated and the ashes buried in funerary urns in flat grave cemeteries of hundreds, even thousands, of graves. As with earlier Bronze Age burial customs, a minority of graves included rich offerings, weapons and armor. Some of these graves were covered with barrows, demonstrating a degree of continuity with the past, but this was by no means universal: the powers enjoyed by chieftains in the early Bronze Age may have been undermined to an extent by the emergence of a warrior class. By the 9th century Urnfield customs had spread over most of continental Europe. Except in the west where it

was probably taken by migrating Celtic peoples, the Urnfield culture spread mainly as a result of the wide-ranging contacts on trade links. The later Bronze Age saw increased militarization, with extensive fortress building in western Europe and the introduction of the bronze slashing sword. Bronze armor was introduced, but probably for display only: it offers less protection than leather.

Small numbers of iron artifacts appeared in many areas about 1200. However, iron tools first became common only around 1000 in Greece and two hundred and fifty years later in northern Europe.

___

1 Bronze Age settlements along the northern fringes of the Alps were often built on islands in lakes for defense.

2 One of the last megalithic tombs to be used was at Island, in Ireland; it was still in use about 1200 BC about a millennium later than most megalithic tombs.

3 At Leubingen, an early Bronze Age barrow contains the remains of an elderly man accompanied by a girl, pottery, stone and bronze tools and weapons, and gold jewelry.

4 A late Bronze Age dismantled wooden "temple" was deliberately sunk into a peat bog at Barger-Oosterveld.

5 The Urnfield cemetery at Kelheim of 900–800 BC had more than 10,000 burials.

6 Defensive towers called *nuraghe* were built about 1800 BC in Sardinia; similar structures are found in Corsica and the Balearic islands.

7 A shipwreck from 800 BC off the southwest coast of Spain included more than 200 bronze weapons made in the Loire region.

___

See also 7 (Neolithic Europe); 11 (Minoans and Mycenaeans); 25 (Celts)

The fragility of the first civilizations was evident during the second millennium BC. Sumeria had vanished as a political entity shortly before 2000 BC, though its achievements were built upon by the Babylonian and Assyrian states which arose in the early second millennium. The rivalry between these two states was to endure until the middle of the first millennium. The other major power of the Middle East was the Hittite kingdom of Anatolia. One of the secrets of Hittite success is thought to have been their early mastery of iron working, in about 1500 BC. Meanwhile, Egypt expanded far south into Nubia and north into the Levant (▷ 6). In the eastern Mediterranean, the Minoans of Crete were replaced by the Mycenaean civilization that emerged on the Greek mainland around 1600. Around 1400 the Mycenaeans conquered Crete and introduced the Greek language; they also settled on Cyprus and in Anatolia (▷ 11).

This civilized world was thrown into chaos about 1200 by a wave of invasions. Mycenae was destroyed by invaders from the north, plunging Greece into a 400-year-long "dark age". Thracians, Phrygians and Anatolian Luvians overthrew the Hittite empire and nomadic Aramaeans occupied much of Mesopotamia. Egypt was invaded by mysterious Sea Peoples. Their fleets were driven from the Nile, but they settled in the Levant where they were known as the Philistines.

By 1000 stability was returning. The Hittites survived though as a shadow of their former selves. The Aramaeans had settled and were assimilating with the urbanized peoples of the conquered territories: their language became the common tongue of the Middle East for the next millennium. Assyria and Babylon were beginning to recover. The Levant was a mosaic of tiny states: of these, the Phoenician city-states and Israel acquired a historical importance out of all proportion to their size (▷ 15). Egyptian power was in decline and the Nubians, after a millennium of Egyptian domination, set up the kingdom of Kush. In sub-Saharan Africa, the transition to a farming way of life was beginning.

In Asia, the Indus valley civilization had collapsed around 1700; about 200 years later the Aryans, an Indo-European pastoralist people, migrated into India. In northern China the Neolithic Longshan cultures developed into the urbanized Shang state around 1766, marking the start of Chinese civilization. Around 1122 the Shang dynasty was ousted by the ruler of the Zhou sub-kingdom (▷ 8).

The Austronesian farming peoples continued to colonize the southeast Asian archipelagoes; by 2000 they had bypassed New Guinea and settled the western Pacific Bismarck archipelago around 1500 BC. The Lapita culture,

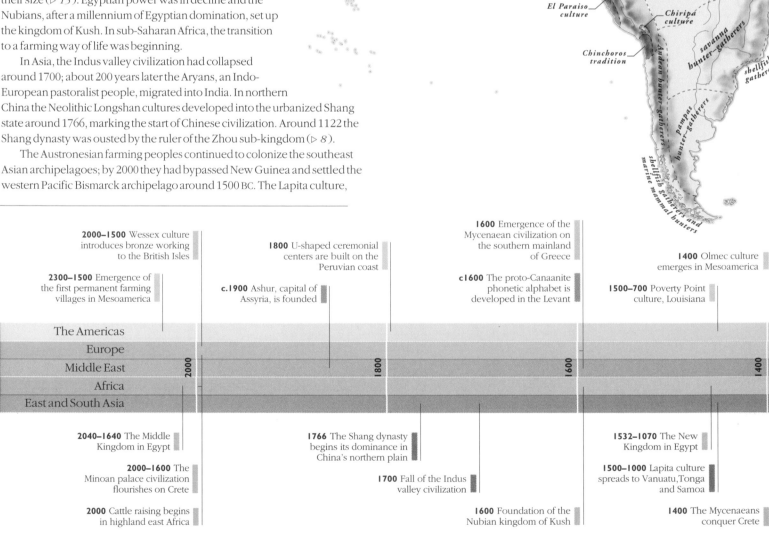

Timeline

2000–1500 Wessex culture introduces bronze working to the British Isles

2300–1500 Emergence of the first permanent farming villages in Mesoamerica

1800 U-shaped ceremonial centers are built on the Peruvian coast

c.1900 Ashur, capital of Assyria, is founded

1600 Emergence of the Mycenaean civilization on the southern mainland of Greece

c1600 The proto-Canaanite phonetic alphabet is developed in the Levant

1400 Olmec culture emerges in Mesoamerica

1500–700 Poverty Point culture, Louisiana

TIMELINE				
The Americas				
Europe				
Middle East	2000	1800	1600	1400
Africa				
East and South Asia				

2040–1640 The Middle Kingdom in Egypt

2000–1600 The Minoan palace civilization flourishes on Crete

2000 Cattle raising begins in highland east Africa

1766 The Shang dynasty begins its dominance in China's northern plain

1700 Fall of the Indus valley civilization

1600 Foundation of the Nubian kingdom of Kush

1532–1070 The New Kingdom in Egypt

1500–1000 Lapita culture spreads to Vanuatu, Tonga and Samoa

1400 The Mycenaeans conquer Crete

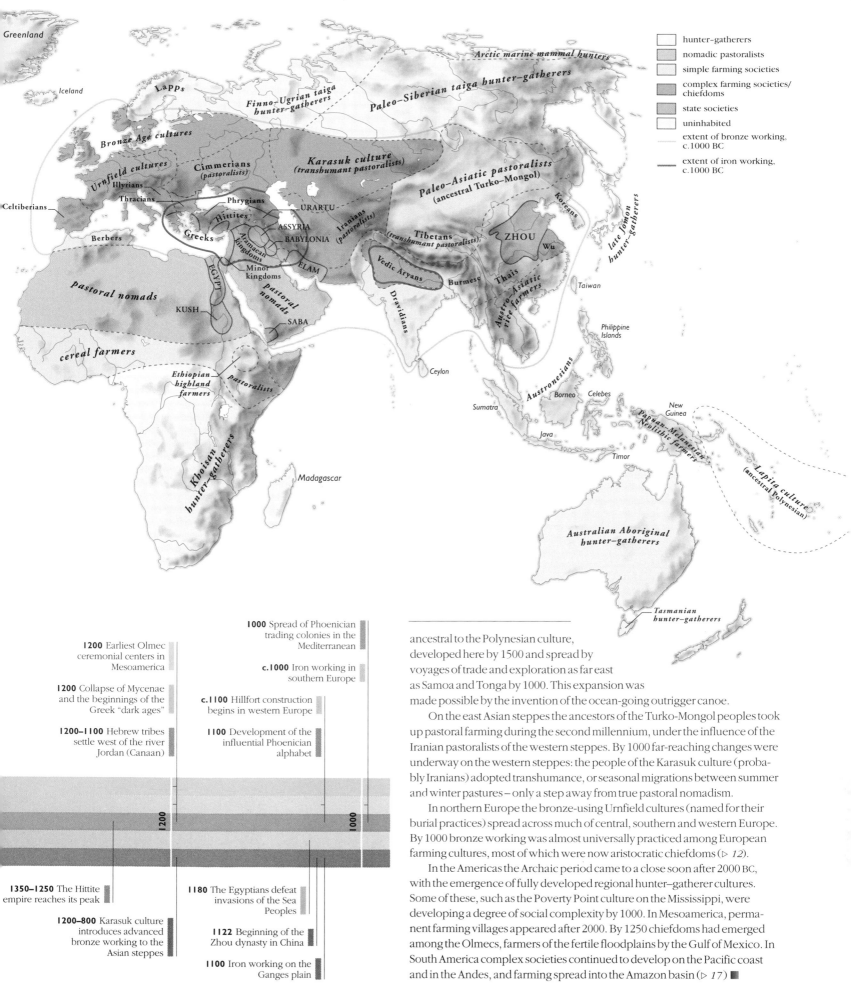

Map labels:

Greenland · Iceland · Lapps · Arctic marine mammal hunters · Finno-Ugrian taiga hunter-gatherers · Paleo-Siberian taiga hunter-gatherers · Bronze Age cultures · Urnfield cultures · Cimmerians (pastoralists) · Karasuk culture (transhumant pastoralists) · Paleo-Asiatic pastoralists (ancestral Turko-Mongol) · Koreans · late Jōmon hunter-gatherers · Illyrians · Thracians · Phrygians · URARTU · Hittites · ASSYRIA · Iranians (pastoralists) · Tibetans (transhumant pastoralists) · ZHOU · Wu · Celtiberians · Greeks · Aramaean kingdoms · BABYLONIA · Vedic Aryans · Burmese · Thais · Berbers · Minor kingdoms · ELAM · Austro-Asiatic rice farmers · Taiwan · EGYPT · pastoral nomads · Dravidians · Philippine Islands · Pastoral nomads · KUSH · SABA · Ceylon · Austronesians · cereal farmers · Ethiopian highland farmers · pastoralists · Borneo · Celebes · New Guinea · Sumatra · Papuan-Melanesian Neolithic farmers · Lapita culture (ancestral Polynesian) · Java · Timor · Khoisan hunter-gatherers · Madagascar · Australian Aboriginal hunter-gatherers · Tasmanian hunter-gatherers

Legend:
- hunter-gatherers
- nomadic pastoralists
- simple farming societies
- complex farming societies/chiefdoms
- state societies
- uninhabited
- extent of bronze working, c.1000 BC
- extent of iron working, c.1000 BC

Timeline:

1200 Earliest Olmec ceremonial centers in Mesoamerica

1200 Collapse of Mycenae and the beginnings of the Greek "dark ages"

1200–1100 Hebrew tribes settle west of the river Jordan (Canaan)

1000 Spread of Phoenician trading colonies in the Mediterranean

c.1000 Iron working in southern Europe

c.1100 Hillfort construction begins in western Europe

1100 Development of the influential Phoenician alphabet

1350–1250 The Hittite empire reaches its peak

1200–800 Karasuk culture introduces advanced bronze working to the Asian steppes

1180 The Egyptians defeat invasions of the Sea Peoples

1122 Beginning of the Zhou dynasty in China

1100 Iron working on the Ganges plain

ancestral to the Polynesian culture, developed here by 1500 and spread by voyages of trade and exploration as far east as Samoa and Tonga by 1000. This expansion was made possible by the invention of the ocean-going outrigger canoe.

On the east Asian steppes the ancestors of the Turko-Mongol peoples took up pastoral farming during the second millennium, under the influence of the Iranian pastoralists of the western steppes. By 1000 far-reaching changes were underway on the western steppes: the people of the Karasuk culture (probably Iranians) adopted transhumance, or seasonal migrations between summer and winter pastures – only a step away from true pastoral nomadism.

In northern Europe the bronze-using Urnfield cultures (named for their burial practices) spread across much of central, southern and western Europe. By 1000 bronze working was almost universally practiced among European farming cultures, most of which were now aristocratic chiefdoms (▷ 12).

In the Americas the Archaic period came to a close soon after 2000 BC, with the emergence of fully developed regional hunter–gatherer cultures. Some of these, such as the Poverty Point culture on the Mississippi, were developing a degree of social complexity by 1000. In Mesoamerica, permanent farming villages appeared after 2000. By 1250 chiefdoms had emerged among the Olmecs, farmers of the fertile floodplains by the Gulf of Mexico. In South America complex societies continued to develop on the Pacific coast and in the Andes, and farming spread into the Amazon basin (▷ 17) ■

By the 10th century the Aramaeans had begun to abandon their nomadic lifestyle and to settle in city-states across a wide area of the Levant and northern Mesopotamia. Simultaneously the Chaldeans were undergoing the same process in southern Mesopotamia. By settling down, the Aramaeans and Chaldeans lost most of the advantages that their loose nomadic organization had given them over the old military powers, and these now began to revive.

Like the Amorites a millennium earlier, the Aramaeans and Chaldeans adopted Mesopotamian culture but the Aramaeans, at least, kept their identity; their language and alphabet was the common tongue of the region by 500 BC. Mesopotamia experienced no further immigrations in this period but Anatolia and Iran saw the arrival of several waves of Iranian peoples, including the Medes and the Persians, who had both formed powerful kingdoms by the 6th century.

Of the Hittites, Assyria and Babylon, the three powers who had dominated the region before 1200, the Hittites made the least impressive recovery. With their heartland lost to the Phrygians, the Neo-Hittites (as they are now called) formed a number of small states in southern Anatolia, of which the most successful were Carchemish, Kummukhu (Commagene) and Khilakku (Cilicia). The Neo-Hittites were conquered by Assyria in the 8th century after which their identity became lost.

The Assyrian heartland around Ashur and Nineveh had survived the Aramaean invasions relatively unscathed and formed a strong base for recovery. The old pattern, established during the Middle Assyrian period, of expansion under able warrior kings followed by contraction under weak kings was continued in the new Assyrian empire.

Expansion began again in the reign of Adad-nirari II (r.911–891) and by the reign of Ashurnasirpal II (r.883–859) the empire dominated northern Mesopotamia and received tribute from the Levant as far south as Tyre. During Ashurnasirpal's reign Ashur, Assyria's ancient capital, declined in importance and was superseded by a new purpose-built capital at Kalhu.

In 854 a coalition of Levantine states tried to halt the expansion of Assyrian power in the region. The coalition met Shalmaneser III (r.858–824) in battle at Qarqar on the Orontes and, though Shalmaneser claimed complete victory, Assyrian power in the Levant did suffer a setback. Relations between Assyria and Babylon had been good since about 911 when the two states became allies. Shalmaneser gave military support to the Babylonians against the Chaldeans and also gave them assistance against internal enemies.

After Shalmaneser's reign Assyria was crippled by internal problems and went into decline for sixty years. Recovery and expansion began again in the reign of Tiglath-pileser III (r.744–727), who assumed overlordship over Babylon, reconquered the Levant and exacted tribute from Israel and Judah. Tiglath-pileser was responsible for a complete overhaul of the administration of the empire to assert central power. Hereditary provincial governors in the Assyrian heartlands were replaced by a hierarchy of officials under direct royal control. Traveling inspectors were sent out to examine the performance of local officials. A post system was introduced and officials were required to send regular reports to the capital. Representatives were appointed to the courts of vassal states to safeguard the interests of Assyria. Large numbers of subject peoples were resettled to prevent local opposition. Finally, in

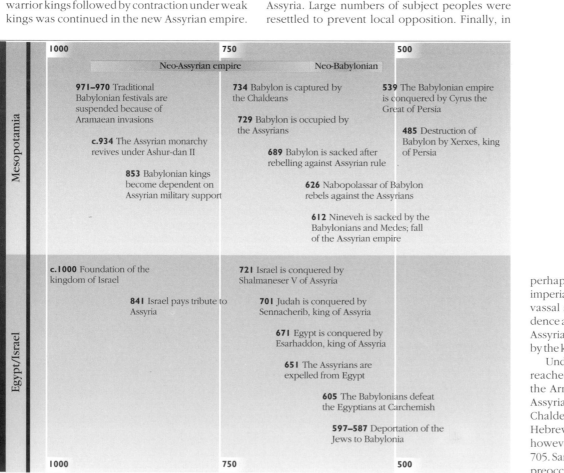

perhaps the greatest break with the imperial traditions of the past, rebellious vassal states lost their nominal independence and were reorganized as provinces of Assyria, directly ruled by officials appointed by the king.

Under Sargon II (r.721–705) Assyrian power reached its zenith. Sargon broke the power of the Armenian kingdom of Urartu and expanded Assyrian dominions with campaigns against the Chaldeans (who had seized Babylon), Elamites and Hebrews. Sargon's last campaign ended in defeat, however, and he was killed in battle in Anatolia in 705. Sargon's successor Sennacherib (r.704–681) was preoccupied with rebellions in Judah, with Babylon

Map legend:

growth of Neo-Assyrian empire
- under Ashur-dan II, 934–912
- under Ashurnasirpal II, 883–859
- maximum extent c.680–627

Neo-Babylonian empire under Nebuchadnezzar II, 604–562

area of Jewish resettlement by Nebuchadnezzar II, 597–581

■ Assyrian capital

major Assyrian campaign
- Ashurnasirpal, 883–859
- Tiglath-pileser III, 744–727
- Sargon II, 721–705
- Esarhaddon, 680–669
- Ashurbanipal, 668–c.627

Babylonian campaign against Assyria and Egypt, 616–600

migration of Indo-Iranian peoples, 9th–7th centuries

— modern coastline and drainage where altered

0   300 km
0   200 mi

TIMELINE

	1000	750	500
		Neo-Assyrian empire	Neo-Babylonian
Mesopotamia	**971–970** Traditional Babylonian festivals are suspended because of Aramaean invasions	**734** Babylon is captured by the Chaldeans	**539** The Babylonian empire is conquered by Cyrus the Great of Persia
		729 Babylon is occupied by the Assyrians	**485** Destruction of Babylon by Xerxes, king of Persia
	c.934 The Assyrian monarchy revives under Ashur-dan II	**689** Babylon is sacked after rebelling against Assyrian rule	
	853 Babylonian kings become dependent on Assyrian military support	**626** Nabopolassar of Babylon rebels against the Assyrians	
		612 Nineveh is sacked by the Babylonians and Medes; fall of the Assyrian empire	
Egypt/Israel	**c.1000** Foundation of the kingdom of Israel	**721** Israel is conquered by Shalmaneser V of Assyria	
	841 Israel pays tribute to Assyria	**701** Judah is conquered by Sennacherib, king of Assyria	
		671 Egypt is conquered by Esarhaddon, king of Assyria	
		651 The Assyrians are expelled from Egypt	
		605 The Babylonians defeat the Egyptians at Carchemish	
		597–587 Deportation of the Jews to Babylonia	
	1000	750	500

Map labels:

Phrygians
ANATOLIA
Cimmerians, c.705–c.695
Scythians, late 7th century
Caspian Sea
Murat
Lake Van
Tushpa
714
Lake Urmia
URARTU **4**
MANNEA
Medes, 9th century
il' Irmak
KUMMUKHU (COMMAGENE)
Tigris
Great Zab
Medes, 614–612
Neo-Hittites
CARCHEMISH
Nisibis
Dur-Sharrukin **1**
ZAGROS MOUNTAINS
8
Harran 608
605
Carchemish 605
Nineveh
Kalhu
Arbil
Hamadan (Ecbatana)
Ceyhan
7
Aramaeans
ASSYRIA
Aleppo
Orontes
Ashur
Arrapha
710–707
Ugarit
Qarqar 854
601
605
MESOPOTAMIA
Diyala
Arvad
Euphrates
615–612
729
LEVANT
Aramaeans
Syrian Desert
SYRIA
Tadmor (Palmyra)
Mari
653, 648–647
Karkheh
Byblos
ARAM
605
Phoenicians
Riblah
Der
Persians 8th century
Sidon
Damascus
600
Susa
Tyre
Dur-Kurigalzu
ELAM
3
Sippar
Babylon
BABYLONIA
Karkheh
PHILISTIA
ISRAEL
601
Borsippa **2**
Nippur
Jerusalem
MOAB
Lachish
Uruk
JUDAH
Ur
Chaldeans
EDOM
Arabs
Taima
Red Sea
Persian Gulf

LION hunting was symbolic to the Assyrians of royal power and only kings (Ashurbanipal in this bas-relief) were shown killing the animals.

and with Chaldean and Elamite attacks in the south. Assyrian expansion was renewed under Esarhaddon (r.680–669), who began the conquest of Egypt, and Ashurbanipal (r.668–c.627), who completed it and took great stores of booty back to Nineveh. This last conquest, however, succeeded only in over-extending the empire while Ashurbanipal's increasingly tyrannical rule spread discontent everywhere. Egypt regained its independence by 651 and, despite his subsequent conquest of Elam in 648, Ashurbanipal's reign ended in chaos. The Babylonian king Nabopolassar (626–605) rebelled against Assyrian rule and after ten years of fighting drove the Assyrians from Babylon.

In 615 Nabopolassar took the offensive and,

supported by the Medes, took Nineveh in 612. A rump kingdom held out at Harran until 609, but after that Assyrian resistance ended. The pharaoh Necho II (r.610–595) seized the opportunity offered by the collapse of Assyrian power to reoccupy the Levant but was defeated by the Babylonian crown prince Nebuchadnezzar at Carchemish in 605. The Babylonians followed up their victory by occupying virtually all of the territory previously held by Assyria. Nebuchadnezzar came to the throne in the following year and spent his reign (r.604–562) consolidating his empire, rebuilding the city of Babylon in imperial splendor and ruling very much within the Assyrian tradition.

Nebuchadnezzar's dynasty lasted only until 556 when it was overthrown in a palace coup. An official, Nabonidus (r.555–539), was chosen as king but his religious unorthodoxy soon made him unpopular in the Babylonian heartland. When the Persian king Cyrus the Great invaded in 539, Babylon surrendered without a fight, bringing to a quiet end an imperial tradition that was almost two thousand years old. Mesopotamian civilization survived for some centuries but gradually declined under the influence of Persian, and subsequently Hellenistic, culture, and had died out by the beginning of the Christian era.

1 The Assyrian capital moved: Ashur (c.1363–c.878); Kalhu (c.878–707); Dur-Sharrukin (707–705); Nineveh (705–612, when it was sacked by the Babylonians and Medes).

2 Though overshadowed militarily by Assyria before 626, Babylon was the dominant religious and cultural center of Mesopotamia.

3 Tyre was the leading Phoenician city; in the 9th century the Phoenicians established trade routes to the western Mediterranean.

4 Urartu developed as a rival to Assyria in the 8th century; its power was broken by Sargon II in 714.

5 Gordion was the capital of the Phrygians; its last king Mitas (Midas) killed himself after being conquered by the Cimmerians around 695.

6 Thebes, the most southerly point reached by the Assyrians, was sacked by Ashurbanipal in 663.

7 Pharaoh Necho II's attempt to seize the Levant was ended by the Babylonians at Carchemish.

8 Hamadan became the capital of a powerful Median empire after the fall of Assyria.

See also 15 (Bible lands); 10 (Egypt); 18 (Persians)

The Hebrew kingdoms of the Bible lands were dwarfed in scale and longevity by the great empires of the Middle East, yet their significance in world history is at least as great. The period of the independent monarchy, from the time of David to the Babylonian conquest in 587, was a formative time for Judaism and gave Jews a sense of historical destiny, driving them to preserve their religion and identity through centuries of foreign rule, exile and worldwide dispersal. Christianity and Islam both owe so much to Judaism that neither religion would have its present form had Judaism not survived.

The Hebrews migrated into Canaan in the early 12th century BC, a time when the great powers of the region were neutralized by troubles of various kinds. In their initial attacks under Joshua, the Hebrews occupied most of Canaan, which they settled in tribal units under chieftains (the "judges" of the biblical Book of Judges). However, many Canaanite enclaves remained and Hebrew expansion to the southwest was blocked by the Philistines who had settled in the area after being repulsed from Egypt in 1180. Most of the Canaanite enclaves were mopped up in the 11th century, but the Hebrews began to lose ground in the southwest to the Philistines.

The need for effective defense against the Philistines led the Hebrew tribes to unite under a monarchy. According to the Bible, the first king of the Hebrews was Saul (r.c.1020–c.1006), but it was his successor David who was responsible for consolidating the monarchy and creating the first Hebrew state. David conquered the Philistines, Ammonites, Moabites and Edomites and forced several of the Aramaean tribes of the Levant to accept his overlordship. These were great achievements, but he was aided by the temporary impotence of the powers who might otherwise have intervened. It was also to his advantage that the Aramaeans of the Levant (who had moved into the area after the fall of the Hittite empire) had settled in urban communities by 1000, and so were more vulnerable to attack than the still-nomadic Mesopotamian Aramaeans. Perhaps the most important event of David's reign was his capture of Jerusalem from the Canaanite Jebusites. By making Jerusalem his capital David ensured its lasting importance as a religious center.

David was succeeded by his son Solomon. Solomon's reign was largely peaceful, but maintaining his splendid court life and ambitious building projects, including the temple at Jerusalem, proved burdensome to his people. Some Hebrews were used as forced labor and territory was ceded to Tyre in return for supplying craftsmen and materials. He was criticized for tolerating the pagan religious practices of the many non-Hebrew wives he had acquired from diplomatic marriages. When his successor Rehoboam (r.928–911) dealt tactlessly with the economic complaints of the northern tribes, the kingdom split in two halves, Israel and Judah, and most of the non-Hebrew provinces fell away.

Map legend

probable border of the kingdom of Saul, c.1006

kingdom of David and Solomon
— border, 1006–928
— under direct rule
— vassal states and tributaries
→ campaigns of David, c.1006–965
Canaanite enclaves conquered by David
area ceded to Tyre by Solomon
fortress built by Solomon
other major building project by Solomon

0 — 200 km
0 — 150mi

TIMELINE

Political change

c.1220–1100 Initial settlement of the Hebrews in Canaan

c.1150–1050 Period of the "judges" (tribal leaders)

c.1020 Origins of the monarchy under Saul

c.1000 David (r.c.1006–965) captures Jerusalem

965–928 Solomon is king of Israel

c.928 Rebellion against Rehoboam; division of the Hebrew kingdom into Israel and Judah

924 Shoshenq I of Egypt invades Judah and Israel

854 The Assyrians defeat the Levantine states at Qarqar

841 Israel pays tribute to Assyria

721 Israel is conquered by Shalmaneser V, and the population of Samaria deported to Assyria

712–671 A Nubian dynasty rules all of Egypt

701 The Assyrians invade and conquer Judah

612 Fall of the Assyrian empire

609–605 Judah is under Egyptian control

597 The Babylonian king Nebuchadnezzar captures Jerusalem

587 Nebuchadnezzar sacks Jerusalem and deports the Jews to Babylon

539 Fall of Babylon and return of the exiled Jews

General

c.950 Solomon builds the temple of Jerusalem

c.850 The prophets Elijah and Elisha defend the Jewish faith against Levantine beliefs

c.735 The prophet Isaiah warns against Assyrian rule

587–539 Exilic period: Key books of the Old Testament approach their present form

Map labels:

Aleppo

Orontes

Euphrates

6

Qarqar
854

Ugarit

Hamath

Syrian   Desert

ARAM

Arvad

Tadmor

Riblah

Byblos

Cyprus

Sidon

Damascus

Tyre

Dan

Mediterranean
Sea

Acco

Hazor

Sea of Chinnereth
(Sea of Galilee)

Megiddo

Beth-shean

8

7

Samaria

Shechem

Joppa

5

KINGDOM OF ISRAEL

AMMON

Rabbah

Eltekeh
701

Gezer

9

Ashkelon

Jerusalem

Bethlehem

Gaza

Lachish

MOAB
independent of
Israel, 843 BC

Arad

Salt Sea
(Dead Sea)

PHILISTIA

KINGDOM
OF JUDAH

EGYPT

EDOM
independent of
Judah, 843 BC

Ezion-geber

LEVANT

PHOENICIA

ARAM-ZOBAH

ARAM-DAMASCUS

Jordan

Legend:

— border of former kingdom of Solomon
▨ greatest extent of kingdom of Israel
▧ greatest extent of kingdom of Judah
— border of state gaining independence
from kingdoms of Israel or Judah
▨ kingdom of Egypt, 924
▨ Assyrian empire, 722
⬭ Babylonian empire, 597

campaigns in Israel and Judah
➤ pharaoh Shoshenq I, 924
➤ Sennacherib, 701

0   150 km
0   100 mi

Disunity was a luxury the Hebrews could ill afford, as the power of both Egypt and Assyria was reviving. In 924 the pharaoh Shoshenq I (r.945–924) led a campaign through Philistia, Judah and Israel, sacking many cities and imposing tribute, although both kingdoms survived. In the 9th century relations between Israel and Judah was usually hostile and Israel often suffered attacks from Aram–Damascus, which was frequently allied to Judah. Under Omri and Ahab Israel became the most powerful kingdom in the region and played a leading role in attempts by the Levantine states to check the growing power of Assyria under Shalmaneser III. However, under Ahab's successor Jehu, Israel was forced to pay tribute to Assyria. In the early 8th century the kingdoms enjoyed relative peace and prosperity with Assyria in a period of decline, until Tiglath-pileser III (r.744–727) overran the Levant and forced vassal status on Israel and Judah. When Hoshea, king of Israel, rebelled against Assyria in 724 his capital Samaria was taken after a three-year siege and its population deported to Assyria. Despite receiving Egyptian support, a rebellion by Hezekiah, the king of Judah, was also put down by the Assyrians. As Assyrian power entered terminal decline in the 630s, Judah briefly regained independence under Josiah (r.640–609) who extended his authority over the old kingdom of Israel until he was killed in battle with the Egyptians at Megiddo. The Egyptians occupied the Levant but were defeated by the Babylonians at Carchemish in 605, after which Judah became a vassal state of Babylon.

In 597 Judah rebelled against Babylonian rule and was crushed by Nebuchadnezzar. Jerusalem was captured, the temple plundered and many of its citizens were deported to Babylonia. Ten years later Judah rebelled again but Jerusalem was taken after an eighteen-month siege. This was the end for independent Judah. Its last king Zedekiah was blinded and imprisoned with most of his nobles and more Hebrews were deported. Many others fled into exile in Egypt. Though a disaster in political terms, the Babylonian captivity was a creative period in Jewish history. Exile caused a great deal of religious reflection and it was the period when much of the Old Testament was written up in something close to its present form. Nor perhaps were the conditions of the exile extremely harsh. When Cyrus of Persia destroyed the Babylonian empire in 539 and gave the Jews leave to return home, thousands chose to remain where they were. Many others remained in Egypt. It was the beginning of the Diaspora.

HEBREW captives march into exile after the fall of Lachish in 701. Sennacherib commissioned this relief to record his triumph.

1 Saul was killed in battle against the Philistines at Gilboa c.1006.

2 Hebron was David's capital before his capture of Jerusalem from the Jebusite Canaanites c.1000.

3 The Aramaeans of Hamath submitted after David defeated the Aramaeans of Zobah and Damascus.

4 Solomon built a fleet at Ezion-geber to trade on the Red Sea with east Africa and Arabia.

5 Northern tribes rebelled against Rehoboam and formed the breakaway kingdom of Israel.

6 A coalition of Levantine states including Israel briefly checked Assyrian expansion at Qarqar, 854 BC.

7 Aram-Damascus emerged as a major rival to Israel in the 850s, but was conquered by Assyria in 732.

8 Samaria, the capital of Israel, was taken by the Assyrians in 721 after a three-year siege.

9 Jerusalem, capital of Judah, was sacked after the rebellion of 587, and its population deported to Babylon; they stayed until 539 when the victorious Achemenid Persians allowed them to return.

See also 10 (Egyptian empire);
14 (Assyrians and Babylonians)

During the dark ages (1200–800 BC), the Greeks lived in tribal communities under chiefs or kings who combined the roles of warleader and chief priest but who had to consult a council of elders and the warrior aristocracy. Their subjects sometimes paid tribute to the kings, but there was no regular system of taxation. There were no palaces, and kings lived in houses distinguished from those of their subjects only by their greater size. Town life almost ceased and such long-distance trade as survived was controlled by the Phoenicians. War, hunting and lavish displays of hospitality were the hallmarks of dark-age Greek culture. One of the most important developments of the period was that iron replaced bronze.

By the 9th century power began to pass to the hereditary aristocracy, and by the end of the 7th century only Sparta, Argos and Thera still had monarchies. Little is known about the institutions of aristocratic government but it was under their rule that trade and city life revived in Greece and that Greek colonization overseas began. The *polis* (city-state) became the dominant form of political organization. The cities dominated the countryside and became the main centers of political power, commerce and cultural life. The revival of trade made it necessary to re-invent writing in the 8th century, as the Mycenaean script had been entirely forgotten. The Greeks adopted the Phoenician consonantal alphabet and by adding separate signs for vowels turned it into a far more flexible and simple writing system. As a result writing became a common accomplishment in Greece. This was to be a major factor in the brilliant flowering of Greek civilization in the 6th and 5th century.

In the 7th century aristocratic government became unpopular. New military tactics, involving large numbers of heavily armed infantry, deprived them of their status as a warrior elite. There was discontent also among the newly rich who, not having aristocratic birth, were excluded from political power. In many Greek city-states these discontents led, between 660 and 485, to revolutions under popular leaders known as "tyrants" (a term describing rulers who had gained power through their own efforts, rather than by virtue of birth). Most tyrannies endured only a few decades before they were overthrown and replaced with "oligarchies", in which the aristocracy was influential but had no monopoly on power. Other Greek city-states reformed their constitutions without revolutions and by the 6th century most were ruled by oligarchies: the remaining strongholds of aristocratic power were in the north of Greece, where there were few cities, and in Sicily.

The most far-reaching political upheavals took place in Athens. Faced with mounting internal problems, the Athenians sought to avoid revolution by

- area of Greek settlement, 6th century BC
- Greek territory under royal or aristocratic rulers, c.600
- Spartan territory, 505
- allies of Sparta, 505
- major city-state, 6th century BC
- Athens — tyranny at some time between 660–485
- Persian conquests by 513
- ▲ site of pan-Hellenic festival
- ▪ Amphictonic shrine, with associated god named
- □ other major temple or shrine, with associated god named

0 — 200 km
0 — 150 mi

TIMELINE

		800	700	600	500
Political change		c.900 Foundation of Sparta	700–650 The "phalanx" infantry formation is developed	560–510 Rule of the tyrants in Athens	
		900–800 The first city-states are established in Ionia and Aeolia.	683 End of the monarchy in Athens	c.560 Sparta is the leading military power in Greece	
		c.800 Foundation of Corinth	657–580 Corinth, the leading power in Greece, is ruled by a tyranny	546–540 The Persians conquer Ionia	
		c.800 Beginning of the main period of Greek expansion overseas		509–507 A democratic constitution is implemented in Athens	
			c.640 The kingdom of Macedon is founded		
		800–750 Sparta conquers Laconia			
			594 Solon reforms the Athenian constitution	480 The Greeks defeat the Persians at Salamis	
Cultural change		800–700 The population begins to rise in Greece	c.650 Written law codes are created in Greece	550–500 Egyptian influences are felt on Greek art and architecture	
		776 The earliest known Olympic Games are held	c.650 A strong eastern influence is felt on Greek art		
		c.750 Homer composes the *Iliad* and the *Odyssey*	c.600 Coinage is adopted in the Greek mainland		
		c.750 The Greek alphabet is developed	c.580 A distinctive school of philosophy emerges in Ionia		
		800	700	600	500

1 A century of far-reaching political reforms transformed Athens from a backwater in 600 into a leading state in 500.

2 Regarded by the Greeks as a barbarian kingdom, Macedon had a mixed population of Illyrians, Thracians and Dorian Greeks.

3 Olympia was the wealthiest religious center in Greece; pan-Hellenic games were held in honor of Zeus every four years from 776 BC to AD 393.

4 The oracle of Apollo at Delphi was widely consulted by the Greek states on important political matters; it was famous for its ambiguous answers.

5 Corinth benefited from its strategic position on the isthmus between the Gulf of Corinth and the Aegean Sea to become a major trading power.

6 The Ionians were the most culturally sophisticated Greeks in the 7th and 6th centuries, taking advantage of close links with the Middle Eastern civilizations.

7 Argos was a bitter rival of Sparta for control of the Peloponnese from the 7th to the 5th century.

8 Coinage was introduced by Lydian kings in about 700; its use had spread to Greece by about 600.

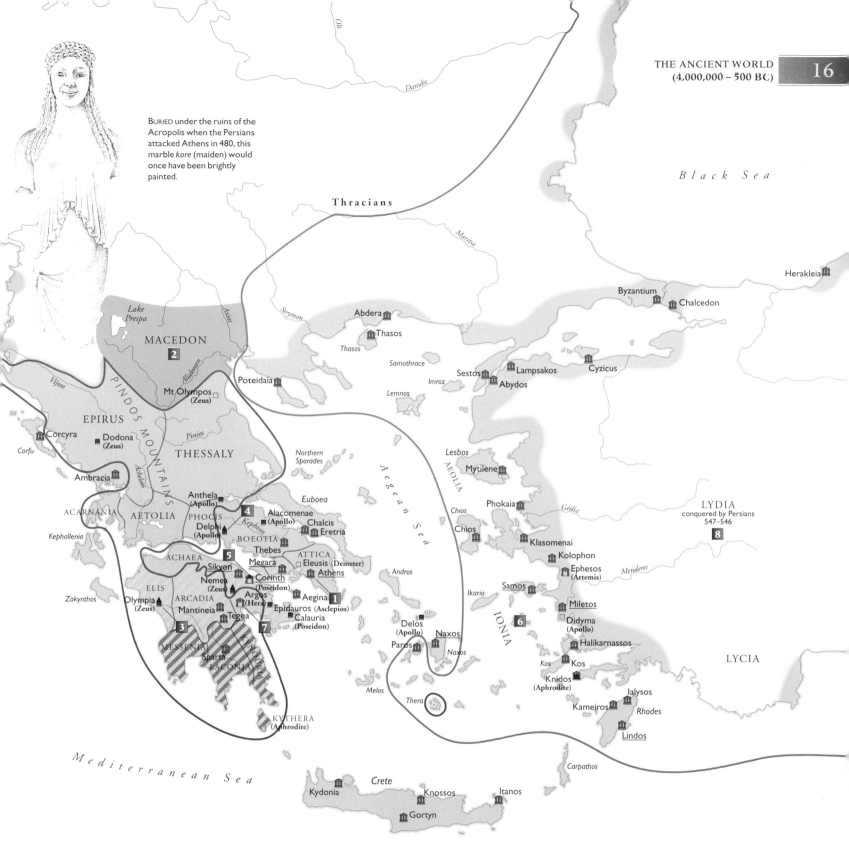

BURIED under the ruins of the Acropolis when the Persians attacked Athens in 480, this marble *kore* (maiden) would once have been brightly painted.

Black Sea

Thracians

Heracleia

Byzantium
Chalcedon

Abdera
Thasos
Thasos

Samothrace
Sestos
Lampsakos
Cyzicus
Imroz
Abydos

Lemnos

MACEDON
2

Poteidaia

Mt Olympos
(Zeus)

Lesbos
AEOLIA
Mytilene

LYDIA
conquered by Persians
547–546
8

EPIRUS

Corcyra
Dodona
(Zeus)

Corfu

Pinios

THESSALY

Northern Sporades

Aegean Sea

Chios
Phokaia

Chios

Ambracia

Anthela
(Apollo)

Euboea

Klasomenai
Kolophon
Ephesos
(Artemis)

Menderes

ACARNANIA
AETOLIA
Alacomenae
(Apollo)
Chalcis
Eretria

Kephallenia

PHOCIS
Delphi
(Apollo)

BOEOTIA
Thebes

ATTICA
Eleusis (Demeter)
Athens

Andros

Samos

IONIA
6

Miletos
Didyma
(Apollo)

ACHAEA
Sikyon
Nemea
(Zeus)
Corinth
(Poseidon)
Megara

Ikaria

Zakynthos

ELIS
Olympia
(Zeus)
ARCADIA
Mantineia
Tegea
Argos
(Hera)
Aegina
1
Epidauros (Asclepios)
Calauria
(Poseidon)

Halikarnassos

LYCIA

3
MESSENIA
Sparta
LACONIA
7

Delos
(Apollo)
Paros
Naxos

Naxos

Melos

Kos
Kos
Knidos
(Aphrodite)

Ialysos
Kameiros
Rhodes

Thera

KYTHERA
(Aphrodite)

Lindos

Mediterranean Sea

Carpathos

Kydonia
Crete
Knossos
Itanos

Gortyn

appointing Solon to reform the constitution in 594. The result was a compromise that satisfied nobody and in 546 the tyrant Peisistratus seized power. Peisistratus was an effective and popular ruler who broke the aristocratic hold on power and did much to address the problems of the peasantry. Peisistratos was succeeded by his less able son Hippias who was overthrown by an aristocratic faction in 510. After three years of internal strife the aristocratic party was defeated. The reformer Kleisthenes "took the people into partnership" and introduced a democratic constitution which gave all 45,000 male citizens the right to attend the assembly and vote on all major decisions and appointments.

By actively involving its citizens in government, Athens had become a self-confident and assertive

state by 500, but for most of the 6th century the most powerful state was Sparta, which had taken the lead in developing new infantry tactics in which armored spearmen fought in a close-packed phalanx, presenting an impenetrable hedge of spears to the enemy. Sparta formed a league of similar cities based on a hoplite franchise, through which it dominated the Peloponnese.

The first Greeks to fall under Persian power were the Ionians on the Anatolian coast. Since about 600 the Ionians had paid tribute to the kings of Lydia but relations were good: the Greeks adopted coinage as a result of Lydian influences and the Lydians themselves became increasingly Hellenized. Persian rule was not particularly oppressive but it was more unpopular than the loose control of the Lydians.

Despite their rivalries, Greeks had a strong sense of common identity by the 8th century, expressed through the name they gave themselves – Hellenes – and by religion. All Greeks worshiped the same gods and celebrated pan-Hellenic festivals, such as the Olympic Games, during which hostilities had to cease. The neutrality of shrines of pan-Hellenic importance was protected and supported by leagues (*amphictonies*) of neighboring states, such as the Amphictony of Delphi. A cultural heritage had also emerged, epitomized by the epic poems of Homer, which were composed in the 8th century.

See also 11 (Minoans and Mycenaeans);
12 (Bronze Age Europe); 18 (Persia)

The domestication of maize around 2700 made possible the development of permanent farming villages in Mesoamerica by 2300. Most early farmers practiced slash-and-burn agriculture, which cannot support dense populations. However, on fertile river flood-plains in the tropical forests of southeastern Mexico, reliable rainfall and year-round warmth made it possible to raise four crops of maize a year, which provided the economic base for the Olmec civilization.

By 1250 BC the Olmec lived in chiefdoms or small states ruled by a powerful hereditary elite. The most important sites were ceremonial centers with earth pyramid mounds and monumental stone sculptures of gods and chiefs. Associated with the ceremonial centers were settlements of two to three thousand people. The ritual centers were periodically destroyed and sculptures defaced or buried. Though possibly due to warfare between chiefdoms or states, it is more likely that this served a ritual purpose, marking the end of calendrical cycles, the death of a ruler or the accession of a new dynasty. Trade and gift exchange played an important part in the Olmec way of life. The Olmec lands have few natural resources and the raw materials for everyday tools, stone sculpture and status enhancing display objects had to be imported over long distances. Gift exchange played an important part in the diffusion of Olmec culture as the emerging elites of neighboring communities took up Olmec beliefs and artifacts to enhance their prestige. Late in their history, the Olmec developed a rudimentary hieroglyphic script which was used mainly for astronomical inscriptions. They used – and may have originated – both the Mesoamerican 260-day sacred year and the 52-year "long-count" calendar.

The Maya originated about 1200 BC in the Guatemalan highlands, developing from earlier Archaic cultures, and began to spread out into the lowlands of the Yucatán peninsula around 1000. By draining and canalizing swamps the Maya were able to

CARVED in rare blue jade, this tiny bust of a woman has the distinctive monumental quality which characterizes all Olmec sculpture.

Map legend:

Olmec, c.1250–400
Maya, c.1000
Maya, c.800
Zapotec, c.1400–400
◆ Olmec ceremonial center
● site with Olmec or Olmec influenced art
— Olmec trade route
◆ source of basalt
◆ source of hematite
◆ source of jade
◆ source of obsidian
◇ source of serpentine
— northern limit of farming cultures, c.500 BC

0 — 600 km
0 — 400 mi

Map labels: Pavón, Capacha, El Opeño, Tlatilco, Valley of Mexico, Cuicuilco, Tlapacoya, El Trapiche, Gualupita, Los Bocas, El Viejón, Chalcatzinco, Balsas, Tres Zapotes, Oxtotlitlan, Tehuacán Valley, Laguna de los Cerros, Juxtiahuaca, Monte Negro, San José Mogote, Las Limas, La Venta, Balancán, Oaxaca Valley, Dainzú, San Lorenzo, Monte Albán, Gulf of Mexico, Komchen, Dzibilchaltun, Yucatán Peninsula, Nakbe, Cuello, Lamanai, Uaxactún, Tikal, Padre Piedra, Pijijiapan, Xoc, Altar de Sacrificios, Salinas la Blanca, Izapa, Abaj Takalik, Copán, Kaminaljuyú, Chalchuapa, PACIFIC OCEAN

TIMELINE

Mesoamerica

3000 | 2000 | 1000 | 500

Olmec civilization

2700 Domestication of maize well under way

2300 Permanent farming villages develop in southern Mexico

2300 Pottery is first used in Mesoamerica

c.1400 The Olmec begin farming maize

1200 The earliest Olmec ceremonial center is built, at Tres Zapotes

1000–800 The Maya settle the Yucatán peninsula

c.800 Origins of the Zapotec hieroglyphic script

600 The earliest Maya temple-pyramids are built, such as at Nakbe

500–400 State formation begins in the Oaxaca valley

ARCHAIC PERIOD | EARLY PRECLASSIC | MIDDLE PRECLASSIC | LATE PRECLASSIC

Andes

c.3500 The earliest pottery-using cultures develop in Ecuador

c.3500 Permanent fishing villages on the coast of Peru

3000–2500 Domestication of alpacas and llamas, root crops and quinua in the highlands

2600 Monumental ceremonial centers of the Aspero tradition develop on the Pacific coast

1800–1500 Building of U-shaped ceremonial centers

1800–1500 Intensive agriculture and irrigation begin on the Pacific coast.

c.1750 Pottery comes into use in Peru

c.1440 The earliest known Andean metal work, at Waywaka

1000–800 Maize is introduced into the region

c.850 Chavín de Huántar is founded

c.600 Origins of the Lake Titicaca architectural styles

c.400 Spread of Chavín art styles

PRECERAMIC PERIOD | INITIAL PERIOD | EARLY HORIZON

produce sufficient food to support a complex society and by 600 towns, such as Nakbe and Komchen, with monumental temple pyramids, were developing. Complex societies also developed among the Zapotec people of the Oaxaca valley by the 1st millennium BC. Here food production was increased by simple irrigation techniques and terracing. By 400 BC there were at least seven small states in the valley, the most important of which was centered on Monte Albán, and a system of hieroglyphic writing had been developed. In the Valley of Mexico highly productive agriculture using *chinampas* – raised fields built on reclaimed swamps – led to the development of trading networks, a market economy, craft specialization and large villages by around 200 BC.

The earliest complex societies in South America developed on the desert coast of Peru in settled fishing communities during the Preceramic period (3750–1800 BC). The marine resources of this area are unusually rich and these communities were able to free labor for the construction of temples and ceremonial centers under the direction of village leaders. One of the earliest such centers was built at Aspero around 2600: it consisted of six mounds nine meters high, topped with masonry ceremonial structures. Cotton, squash and gourds (used as floats for fishing nets) were cultivated but farming did not make a significant contribution to the diet. In the highlands, herding alpacas or llamas and cultivation of root crops such as potatoes, ullucu and oca or quinua, a cereal, gradually replaced hunting and gathering during the Preceramic; permanent villages with small ceremonial buildings also developed.

During the Initial Period (1800–800 BC) the area of cultivable land in the coastal lowlands was greatly extended through irrigation works, diverting water from the rivers which flowed from the Andes through the desert to the coast. Pottery was adopted. Huge U-shaped ceremonial centers, requiring the control of considerable resources of labor, food supplies and raw materials, were constructed: one at Garagay is estimated to have required 3.2 million work-days to complete. These sites were probably focal points for local chiefdoms but burial practices show few distinctions of wealth or rank. Interaction between the fishing communities on the coast and the farming communities in the desert river valleys and the mountains was considerable, with salt, seaweed and dried fish from the coast being exchanged for carbohydrate foods such as root crops and grain from the highlands and river valleys.

The Early Horizon (about 800–200 BC) saw the development of sophisticated architecture and complex sculptural styles at the highland ceremonial center of Chavín de Huántar. The Chavín style was the culmination of styles which had originated as early as 1200 in other Andean and coastal sites and by 400 its influence had spread over a wide area of coastal and highland Peru. Chavín had a population of two to three thousand at its peak in the 4th century but thereafter it declined, without developing into a full urban civilization. Complex societies, united by common beliefs, also developed in the Lake Titicaca basin during the Early Horizon. Particularly important is the ceremonial center at Chiripa, built 600–400 BC, in which can be seen the origins of the architectural styles of the 5th-century AD Tiahuanaco state. Maize became an important crop in the Andes during this period.

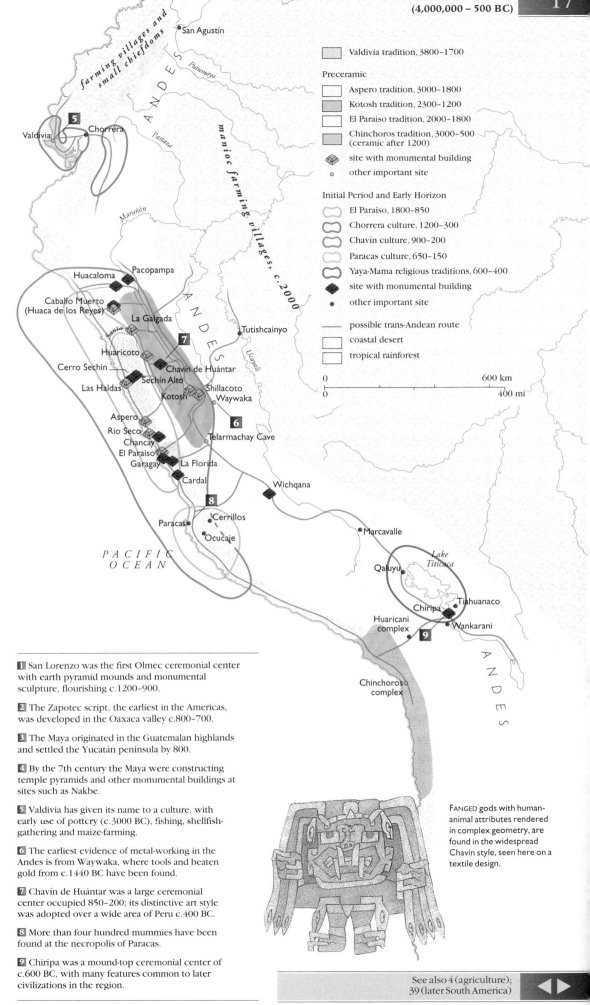

Key

Valdivia tradition, 3800–1700

Preceramic

Aspero tradition, 3000–1800

Kotosh tradition, 2300–1200

El Paraiso tradition, 2000–1800

Chinchoros tradition, 3000–500 (ceramic after 1200)

site with monumental building

other important site

Initial Period and Early Horizon

El Paraiso, 1800–850

Chorrera culture, 1200–300

Chavín culture, 900–200

Paracas culture, 650–150

Yaya-Mama religious traditions, 600–400

site with monumental building

other important site

possible trans-Andean route

coastal desert

tropical rainforest

0   600 km
0   400 mi

1 San Lorenzo was the first Olmec ceremonial center with earth pyramid mounds and monumental sculpture, flourishing c.1200–900.

2 The Zapotec script, the earliest in the Americas, was developed in the Oaxaca valley c.800–700.

3 The Maya originated in the Guatemalan highlands and settled the Yucatán peninsula by 800.

4 By the 7th century the Maya were constructing temple pyramids and other monumental buildings at sites such as Nakbe.

5 Valdivia has given its name to a culture, with early use of pottery (c.3000 BC), fishing, shellfish-gathering and maize-farming.

6 The earliest evidence of metal-working in the Andes is from Waywaka, where tools and beaten gold from c.1440 BC have been found.

7 Chavín de Huántar was a large ceremonial center occupied 850–200; its distinctive art style was adopted over a wide area of Peru c.400 BC.

8 More than four hundred mummies have been found at the necropolis of Paracas.

9 Chiripa was a mound-top ceremonial center of c.600 BC, with many features common to later civilizations in the region.

FANGED gods with human-animal attributes rendered in complex geometry, are found in the widespread Chavín style, seen here on a textile design.

See also 4 (agriculture);
39 (later South America)

The Persians who took Babylon in 539 were comparative newcomers to the region. An Indo-Iranian people, the Persians had followed their close relations the Medes from central Asia to Iran in the 8th century. The founder of the Persian monarchy was Achemenes, who gave his name to the dynasty, but it is uncertain when he ruled. In 648, when Ashurbanipal destroyed the Elamite kingdom and occupied western Elam, the Persians seized the opportunity to take its eastern territories. Despite this Persia was overshadowed by, and often subject to, the powerful Median kingdom. It was in the reign of Cyrus the Great that Persia rose to empire.

Cyrus' career as a great conqueror started when his nominal overlord, the Median king Astyages, invaded Persia around 550 following a rebellion. Astyages was deserted by his army and captured when he met Cyrus in battle at Pasargadae. Cyrus followed up this easy victory by taking the Median capital at Hamadan (Ecbatana). Cyrus was now the most powerful ruler in the region. In 547 he repulsed an invasion of Media by King Croesus of Lydia, who withdrew to his capital Sardis and disbanded his army for the winter. Cyrus, however, had nothing against winter campaigns and, when he arrived unexpectedly, Sardis fell after a siege of only fourteen days. Leaving his generals to complete the conquest of Lydia and the Ionian Greeks, Cyrus marched east to push deep into central Asia. In 539 he crowned his career by conquering Babylonia. Discontent over the religious unorthodoxy of its king Nabonidus was rife and, by posing as a servant of the god Marduk and restorer of orthodoxy, he was even welcomed in Babylon.

In little more than a decade Cyrus had built the largest empire the world had yet seen, with remarkably little hard campaigning. Clearly the close relationship between the Medes and Persians aided in what was more of a dynastic takeover than a conquest, and in Mesopotamia the experience of incorporation in the Assyrian and Babylonian empires had long-since mixed cultures, weakened local identities and accustomed people to imperial rule. As a result there was little spirit of resistance to what amounted, in practice, to no more than the advent of

a new imperial dynasty. Cyrus was diplomat as well as soldier and the consolidation of his empire owed much to his moderation. Demands for tribute were modest, he did not interfere with local customs, upheld the rights of the local priesthood and left local institutions of government intact.

Cyrus was killed in 530 on campaign against the Sakas in central Asia and was succeeded by his son Cambyses. Cambyses added Egypt and Libya to the empire before dying in mysterious circumstances,

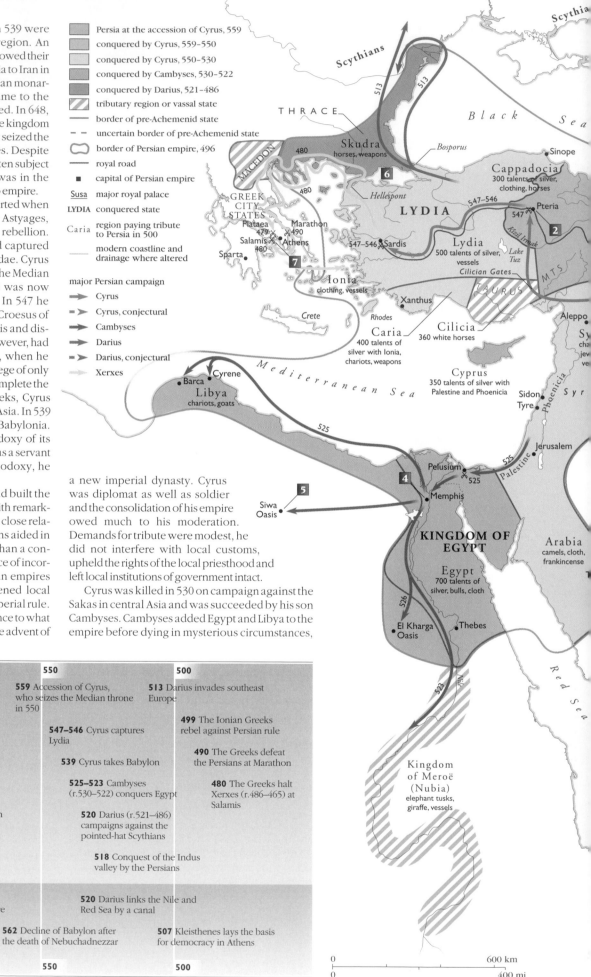

Persia at the accession of Cyrus, 559
conquered by Cyrus, 559–550
conquered by Cyrus, 550–530
conquered by Cambyses, 530–522
conquered by Darius, 521–486
tributary region or vassal state
border of pre-Achemenid state
uncertain border of pre-Achemenid state
border of Persian empire, 496
royal road
capital of Persian empire
Susa major royal palace
LYDIA conquered state
Caria region paying tribute to Persia in 500
modern coastline and drainage where altered

major Persian campaign
Cyrus
Cyrus, conjectural
Cambyses
Darius
Darius, conjectural
Xerxes

	600	550	500
Persian empire	**c.850** The Medes migrate into Iran from central Asia.	**559** Accession of Cyrus, who seizes the Median throne in 550	**513** Darius invades southeast Europe
	c.750 The Persians migrate into southern Iran from central Asia	**547–546** Cyrus captures Lydia	**499** The Ionian Greeks rebel against Persian rule
	c.640 Persia becomes a vassal state of Media	**539** Cyrus takes Babylon	**490** The Greeks defeat the Persians at Marathon
	c.630–553 Life of Zoroaster, the prophet of Iran and founder of the Parsee religion	**525–523** Cambyses (r.530–522) conquers Egypt	**480** The Greeks halt Xerxes (r.486–465) at Salamis
		520 Darius (r.521–486) campaigns against the pointed-hat Scythians	
		518 Conquest of the Indus valley by the Persians	
General	**612** Fall of Nineveh and collapse of Assyria's empire	**520** Darius links the Nile and Red Sea by a canal	
		562 Decline of Babylon after the death of Nebuchadnezzar	**507** Kleisthenes lays the basis for democracy in Athens

| 600 | 550 | 500 |

GOLD bracelets like this were shown as part of the Lydians' tribute, depicted on reliefs at Persepolis

Aral Sea

Sakas

Sogdiana
horses, jewelry, weapons

3 • Kyreskhata

Marakanda (Samarkand)

Pointed-hat Scythians
250 talents of silver, clothing, jewelry, horses

Pointed-hat Scythians

Bactria
360 talents of silver, camels, vessels

• Bactra

HINDU KUSH

Indus

Capisa •

Peshawar (Caspatyrus?)

C A U C A S U S M T S

Colchis
25 boys, 25 girls

Caspian Sea

Turan Lowland

Amu Dar'ya

546–539

Aria
camels, lionskin cloaks, vessels

Kabul •

• Taxila

Armenia
400 talents of silver, clothing, horses, vessels

Murat

Lake Van • Van

Araks

Lake Urmia

M E D I A N

Media
450 talents of silver, animal hides, clothing, jewelry, vessels, weapons

Chorasmia
300 talents of silver with Parthia and Aria, horses, jewelry, weapons

Parthia
camels, vessels

520

• Herat

Gandhara
170 talents of silver, bulls, weapons

Helmand

Chenab

547

Z A G R O S

E M P I R E

Assyria
animal hides, cloth, eunuchs, metals, rams, vessels

• Nineveh
• Arbil

Diyala

Hamadan

550

D a s h t - e L u t

Drangiana
camels, lionskin cloaks, vessels

• Kandahar

Sind
360 talents of gold dust, axes, weapons

BABYLONIAN EMPIRE

539

Elam
300 talents of silver, lioness & cubs, weapons

M O U N T A I N S

550

HINDU KINGDOMS

esert

Euphrates

539 × Opis

Sippar •

Babylon

• Nippur

Susa

1

550 × • Pasargadae
• Persepolis

Arachosia
animal hides, camels, vessels

c.518

Sutlej

Babylonia
1000 talents of silver with Assyria, bulls, cloth, eunuchs, vessels

Sagartia
600 talents of silver, cloth, horses

Indus

Tigris

PERSIA

Persian Gulf

Maka

Gulf of Oman

Arabian Sea

---

possibly murdered by his brother Smerdis. Smerdis was quickly overthrown and killed by Darius (r.521–486), a member of a junior Achemenid house. Darius faced rebellions from one end of the empire to the other but suppressed them all within a year. By 520 he was secure enough to campaign against the Caspian Scythians. In 518 he extended Persian control as far as, and possibly a little beyond, the Indus and in 513 he crossed into Europe; though he conquered Thrace, the expedition failed in its main objective of subduing the Black Sea Scythians. This failure encouraged a rebellion by the Ionian Greeks in 499. This was put down in 494 and Darius dispatched an expedition to punish the mainland Greeks for supporting the rebels. When this force was defeated by the Athenians at Marathon in 490, Darius began to plan for the conquest of Greece. The expedition was finally launched by his son Xerxes, but the decisive defeat of his fleet at Salamis in 480 and of his army at Plataea the following year brought the expansion of the empire to a halt.

Darius reorganized the empire into about twenty provinces under governors, or satraps, often relatives or close friends of the king. The system of taxation was regularized and fixed tributes, based on the wealth of each province, were introduced. Only Persia, which was not a conquered province, was exempt. The Assyrian imperial post system was expanded and the roads improved. Local garrison commanders remained directly responsible to the king. The official capital of the empire under Cyrus had been Pasargadae, but Hamadan was effectively the administrative capital. Darius moved the administrative capital to Susa and founded a new official capital at Persepolis. Under Darius the imperial administration used various local languages transcribed into cuneiform and written on clay tablets for documents, but his successors abandoned this system in favor of writing on parchment using the widespread Aramaic language and alphabet.

The Persian empire was a thoroughly cosmopolitan state which united elements of all the major civilizations of its time except the Chinese. By throwing together peoples from so many backgrounds, the empire promoted the diffusion and mixing of cultures and ended the isolation of the old civilizations.

1 Astyages, king of Media, was defeated by Cyrus at Pasargadae; Cyrus then took Hamadan and seized the Median throne.

2 Cyrus repulsed a Lydian invasion at Pteria, then captured the Lydian capital Sardis and King Croesus.

3 Kyreskhata was the strongest of a chain of forts built by Cyrus to protect the northern frontier.

4 After a hard-fought battle at Pelusium Cambyses captured Memphis (525) and took pharaoh Psammeticus III to Susa in chains.

5 A Persian force sent by Cambyses to capture Siwa vanished in the desert.

6 Darius built a bridge of boats over the Bosporus (513) to invade Europe; Xerxes did the same over the Hellespont in 480.

7 Persian expansion to the west was decisively halted by the Greeks at the naval battle of Salamis.

See also 15 (Babylon); 16 (Greece); 20 (invasion of Greece); 21 (Alexander)

◀ ▶

The number and size of organized states in the Middle East, India and the Mediterranean rose sharply between 1000 and 500 BC. A succession of empires dominated the Middle East. The first was the Assyrian empire which stretched from the Zagros mountains to Egypt by the 7th century. Assyrian rule was harsh and in 625 the Babylonians rebelled and seized most of the empire for themselves (▷ 14). Then the Iranian Medes pushed west, conquering the Caucasus and eastern Anatolia. In 550 Cyrus II "the Great", an Iranian king, seized the Median kingdom and founded the Persian empire. He then took western Anatolia and the Babylonian empire. By 500 the Persian empire extended from Egypt to the Indus (▷ 18).

State-organized societies had also spread throughout the Mediterranean world. By 700 Greece was a patchwork of independent city-states: by 500 these cities, and Athens in particular, entered a period of intellectual creativity unparalleled in world history (▷ 16). The Greeks and Phoenicians also founded trading colonies throughout the Mediterranean. Although the Phoenicians lost their independence by 500, Carthage, their colony in north Africa, was the leading power of the western Mediterranean. The Greek cities of Sicily and southern Italy had a powerful influence, notably on the Etruscans who dominated northern Italy by 500. North of the Alps the Urnfield cultures of central Europe were replaced by the aristocratic iron-using Celtic Hallstatt culture c.600.

States reappeared in the Indian subcontinent in the 9th century. The focus this time was the Ganges plain where Vedic Aryan chiefdoms began to coalesce into kingdoms and republics. By 500 the largest was the kingdom of Magadha. At the same time the Aryans extended southward, conquering the Dravidians and imposing Hindu religion on them. The Chinese Zhou kingdom expanded to the southeast after 1000, but what it gained in area it lost in internal cohesion. The Zhou kingdom was a decentralized feudal state and by the 8th century the powerful warlords had so undermined the power of the monarchy that it was powerless to prevent the kingdom from breaking up (▷ 8). Meanwhile the first chiefdoms emerged around 500 in Korea and in Van Lang in southeast Asia.

One far-reaching development of the early first millennium was the change in lifestyle of the Iranian peoples (Scythians, Sarmatians, Sakas and Yue Qi) of the Eurasian steppes from transhumant (seasonal) pastoralism to nomadic pastoralism. The steppe peoples had been pioneers in the use of horses: they had domesticated them for their meat around 4000 BC, they had harnessed them to wagons (4th millennium) and war chariots (2nd millennium) and by 1000 BC they had mastered

Timeline

700–100 Adena culture burial mound builders in the eastern woodlands of North America

800 Zapotecs develop hieroglyphic script in Mesoamerica

700 City-states flourish in Greece and the Aegean

800–500 Greek colonization of the Mediterranean and Black Sea

c.750 Emergence of the Celtic Hallstatt Iron Age culture north of the Alps

900–700 Nomadism becomes the dominant way of life on the Eurasian steppes

800 Emergence of the Etruscan civilization in Italy

750–705 Assyrian power reaches its peak

1000 Emergence of the kingdom of Israel

612 The collapse of the Assyrian empire

TIMELINE

The Americas
Europe
Middle East
Africa
East and South Asia

1000 · 900 · 800 · 700 · 600

1000–500 Formative period of Hinduism

900 The first states emerge on the Ganges plain

814 Foundation of the Phoenician colony of Carthage

712–671 Egypt is ruled by a Kushite dynasty from Nubia

600 Iron and bronze working develop in west Africa

800 The Aryans expand into southern India

600 Introduction of iron working into China

770–481 The "Springs and Autumns" period in China: the Zhou kingdom breaks up into minor states

c.590 The Nubian capital established at Meroë

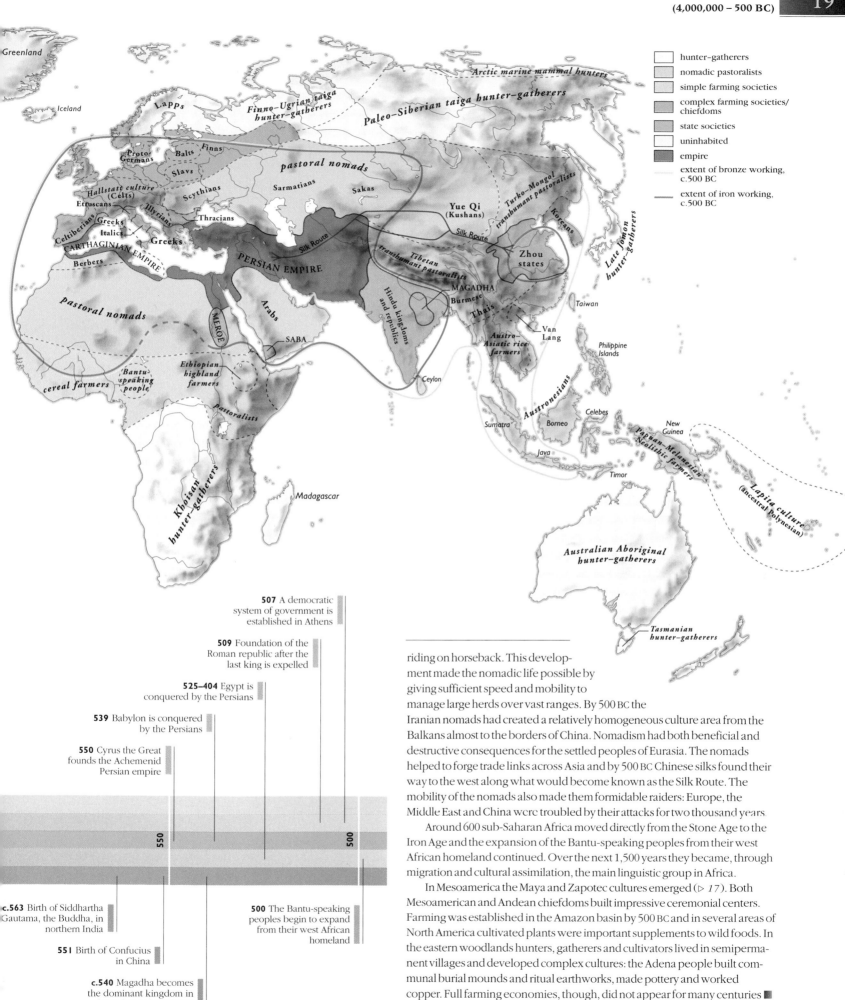

hunter-gatherers
nomadic pastoralists
simple farming societies
complex farming societies/
chiefdoms
state societies
uninhabited
empire
extent of bronze working,
c.500 BC
extent of iron working,
c.500 BC

Greenland

Iceland

Lapps

Finno–Ugrian taiga
hunter-gatherers

Arctic marine mammal hunters

Paleo-Siberian taiga hunter-gatherers

Proto-
Germans   Balts   Finns

Slavs

Hallstatt culture
(Celts)

Etruscans   Illyrians

Celtiberians   Greeks

Italics

CARTHAGINIAN EMPIRE   Greeks

Berbers

Scythians

Thracians

Sarmatians

pastoral nomads

Sakas

Yue Qi
(Kushans)

Turko-Mongol
transhumant pastoralists

Koreans

Zhou
states

Silk Route

PERSIAN EMPIRE

Silk Route

Tibetan
transhumant pastoralists

MAGADHA

Burmese

Late Jomon
hunter-gatherers

Pastoral nomads

MEROE

Arabs

SABA

Hindu kingdoms
and republics

Thais

Taiwan

Van
Lang

Austro-
Asiatic
farmers

cereal farmers

'Bantu-
speaking
people'

Ethiopian
highland
farmers

Pastoralists

Ceylon

Philippine
Islands

Austronesians

Madagascar

Khoisan
hunter-gatherers

Sumatra

Java

Borneo

Celebes

Timor

New
Guinea

Papuan-Melanesian
Neolithic farmers

Lapita culture
(ancestral Polynesian)

Australian Aboriginal
hunter-gatherers

Tasmanian
hunter-gatherers

507 A democratic
system of government is
established in Athens

509 Foundation of the
Roman republic after the
last king is expelled

525–404 Egypt is
conquered by the Persians

539 Babylon is conquered
by the Persians

550 Cyrus the Great
founds the Achemenid
Persian empire

550

500

c.563 Birth of Siddhartha
Gautama, the Buddha, in
northern India

500 The Bantu-speaking
peoples begin to expand
from their west African
homeland

551 Birth of Confucius
in China

c.540 Magadha becomes
the dominant kingdom in
the Indian subcontinent

riding on horseback. This development made the nomadic life possible by
giving sufficient speed and mobility to
manage large herds over vast ranges. By 500 BC the
Iranian nomads had created a relatively homogeneous culture area from the
Balkans almost to the borders of China. Nomadism had both beneficial and
destructive consequences for the settled peoples of Eurasia. The nomads
helped to forge trade links across Asia and by 500 BC Chinese silks found their
way to the west along what would become known as the Silk Route. The
mobility of the nomads also made them formidable raiders: Europe, the
Middle East and China were troubled by their attacks for two thousand years.

Around 600 sub-Saharan Africa moved directly from the Stone Age to the
Iron Age and the expansion of the Bantu-speaking peoples from their west
African homeland continued. Over the next 1,500 years they became, through
migration and cultural assimilation, the main linguistic group in Africa.

In Mesoamerica the Maya and Zapotec cultures emerged (▷ 17). Both
Mesoamerican and Andean chiefdoms built impressive ceremonial centers.
Farming was established in the Amazon basin by 500 BC and in several areas of
North America cultivated plants were important supplements to wild foods. In
the eastern woodlands hunters, gatherers and cultivators lived in semiperma-
nent villages and developed complex cultures: the Adena people built communal burial mounds and ritual earthworks, made pottery and worked
copper. Full farming economies, though, did not appear for many centuries ■

Part 2

THE CLASSICAL

I n the thirty generations between 500 BC and AD 600, populations increased across the globe; states with complex systems of social and economic control emerged; food production intensified, allowing artists, architects, poets and thinkers to develop their skills. All the major religions, with the exception of Islam, took root.

Amidst the vivid mass of detail, certain themes recur. In certain areas, favored by their access to natural resources and their position astride trade routes, centers of social or economic innovation sprang up. Powerful chiefs often commanded discrete territories. They copied and competed with one another, often acquiring prestige goods for display, in life and on death, for others to wonder at. Conspicuous consumption and ritual destruction of luxuries by burying them with chieftains meant that ever more prestige goods were needed. This gave momentum to trade and, sometimes, to warfare.

In some areas chiefdoms were transformed into states through a complex phase of warfare and social reordering. Thus the Mycenaean chiefdoms of the late second millennium BC became the young city-states of Greece two centuries later. On the other side of the world in about 500 BC, in the Oaxaca valley of Mesoamerica, three competing chiefdoms came together to found a new political capital on the mountain-top of Monte Albán; it remained preeminent for more than a thousand years. The unification of rival polities under a single authority was seen throughout the world. In 408 BC, a century after the foundation of Monte Albán, three rival Greek cities on the island of Rhodes agreed to found the city of Rhodes.

A dynamic relationship arose between these innovating centers and the peripheries around them. A complex state needed raw materials and human power to maintain it. A

THE AEGEAN SEA, scene of the ancient Greek experiments in civilization.

WORLD

regular supply of rare metals, exotic stones and woods, furs and fabrics was essential to support the structure of the social hierarchy, while human power, in the form of slaves or a supply of food for a free workforce, was needed to support the state's bureaucrats, soldiers, priests or scholars. The demands of centralizing powers thus encouraged trade with the surrounding peripheries. African and Indian communities were drawn into the economic sphere of the Roman empire, despite knowing little of the state that gave them pottery, coins and trinkets in return for raw materials and slaves. Communities closer to the centers were in a better position to learn from their neighbors and imitate them.

There was a continual drift of creative energy from the center to the periphery, as the seeds of innovation took root in the fertile periphery while the core decayed. The early core of Europe developed in the Greek cities around the Aegean; later, the focus for innovation was on the Greek mainland. Power then shifted to the central Mediterranean where Rome emerged preeminent. Six centuries later power moved to the peripheral Black Sea region, with the rise of Constantinople and the Byzantine empire. In Mesoamerica the same pattern can be seen, in the move of power from the Oaxaca valley to the Valley of Mexico and then the Maya area of the Yucatán.

The cycle of growth and decay and the inexorable shift of centers of power were accelerated by warfare and invasion. The Celtic tribes who attacked the Greco-Roman world in the fourth and third centuries BC confronted energetic states well able to defend themselves; but the Germanic peoples who attacked around AD 400 found the Roman empire in a state of decay. They rapidly overran Rome and set up a number of new kingdoms within the carcass of the old empire.

The collapse of empires – a common theme in this period – is a subject of great fascination. Each case is different and the reasons are always complex: natural catastrophy, population decline, economic over-extension, invasion, disease. In the prehistoric context of Mesoamerica, archeologists speculate about "ecological overshoot" and the destructive role of parasitic elites; whereas in China, detailed written records reveal the processes leading to the collapse of the Han empire – foreign wars, internal power struggles and peasant rebellions as the empire disintegrated into rival factions of local warlords.

Yet it is possible to turn the notions of center and periphery inside out and to see the states and empires of Europe, India and China not as centers but as developments on the periphery of the huge, central landmass of Asia – an unending steppe land, home of horse-riding nomads who for century after century moved out to strike terror into the hearts of their sedentary, civilized neighbors. In Europe the first recorded invaders were the Cimmerians, around 700 BC. Then followed the Scythians, the Sarmatians, the Alans and the Huns, the last contributing to the chaos at the end of the Roman era. Other groups moved into India, while the northern boundaries of China were constantly at risk – a threat which the Great Wall was eventually designed to avert. The history of Old World civilization was intimately bound up with the population pressures of the deepest Eurasian steppes.

During the millennium 500 BC–AD 600, many foundations of the modern world were created. Bronze and iron became widely available and steel was developed in Han China. The powers of wind and water were harnessed; horse-riding was transformed by the development of the stirrup; and science, astronomy and mathematics made enormous strides in the Hellenistic world, India, China and Mesoamerica. By AD 600 a plateau had been reached. There was to be little further advance until the fifteenth century when the arts of navigation and seamanship opened up the world ∎

After Cyrus, founder of the Persian empire, conquered Lydia in 546 BC, his generals mopped up the relatively insignificant Greek cities of Ionia, but in 499 they rebelled again under the leadership of Aristagoras of Miletos and introduced democratic rule. The rebels received aid from Athens and this provoked the Persian king Darius (r.521–486) to plan a punitive invasion of Greece after the revolt had been crushed in 494.

Darius' first invasion, in 492, was defeated by the weather when the fleet supporting his army was destroyed in a storm rounding Mount Athos. After a second expedition was humiliatingly defeated by the Athenians at Marathon in 490, Darius decided that the conquest of the whole of Greece was needed to secure the Persian position in Ionia. He died before his preparations were complete and it was left to his son Xerxes to carry out his plans. Meanwhile the Greeks prepared for an invasion, with Themistocles persuading Athens – by far the largest and wealthiest *polis* or city-state – to invest in an urgent naval building program.

The history of this invasion was memorably recorded by the Ionian-born Herodotos, the first major Greek prose writer and historian, later in the 5th century. Xerxes' army, said to have been 200,000 strong, was one of the largest forces ever assembled in antiquity and was supported by a fleet of perhaps a thousand ships. Faced with this vast force, most of the northern Greek states opted for neutrality or (in a few cases) alliance with Persia. The southern Greek states, however, united under the leadership of Athens and Sparta and prepared to resist the Persians. The resulting struggle was less uneven than expected. The very size of the Persian army proved a serious handicap; it was difficult to supply and impossible to control effectively on a battlefield; the quality of its troops varied enormously and only around 10,000 were elite troops. In contrast the Greeks, though greatly outnumbered, were heavily armed, experienced, disciplined and highly motivated: they were citizens defending their states, homes and families.

Persian wars, 499–448

- Greek states allied against Persia
- Greek states remaining neutral
- Greek vassals and allies of Persia
- Persian empire on accession of Xerxes, 486
- Persian empire after peace of Kallias, 448
- → Persian campaign under Darius, 492
- → Persian fleet (Marathon campaign), 490
- → Persian campaign under Xerxes, 480
- — border, 448

Athenian empire, 477–431

- Athens and the Delian league
- Athenian allies and conquests
- Spartan league
- *Skyros* Athenian military colony
- ☆ rebellion against Athens, with date

0 ————————— 200 km
0 ————————— 150 mi

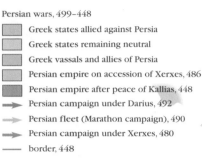

Italics

ATHENS had a strong coinage based on its local silver mines; the owl was the universally known symbol of the city.

The Greeks, led by Sparta, attempted to halt the Persian invasion at Thermopylae but were defeated after heroic resistance. The Persians went on to occupy Athens, although its population had been evacuated to Salamis. The Persian fleet, which was needed to outflank Spartan defenses on the Isthmus of Corinth, was now ambushed and destroyed by the Athenian navy at Salamis. Since it was clear that Greece could not now be conquered in a single campaign, Xerxes returned to Asia with half of the army: the remainder wintered in Greece only to be defeated decisively by a Spartan-led army at Plataea in the following year. The threat to Greece ended, the old rivalries of the Greek world resurfaced and Sparta and most of the other states withdrew from the war against Persia. Athens and its allies continued hostilities, destroying the last Persian garrisons in Europe, re-opening the Bosporus to Greek shipping by 475, and freeing the Ionian Greeks from

Persian rule in 468. The Athenians also intervened unsuccessfully against the Persians in Egypt in 454 and captured Cyprus in 450. Hostilities came to a formal end in 448 when the Persians recognized Ionian independence.

To pursue its war aims, Athens created the anti-Persian Delian league of Aegean cities, with a common treasury on the island of Delos to which all members contributed. As its richest member and greatest naval power, Athens dominated the league and came increasingly to regard it as its empire. Some states, such as Aegina, were forcibly enrolled, and if a dissatisfied member tried to withhold contributions, the Athenian fleet was sent to enforce obedience. When the Athenians moved the treasury to Athens in 454 its domination became even more apparent. Despite this, many members remained loyal, being grateful to Athens for its role in the Persian wars and for introducing democracy. After the end of the war with Persia the league became as much a commercial as a military organization, although still serving Athenian interests. Athenian coinage, weights and measures were introduced throughout the league.

Under the leadership of the highly nationalistic Pericles, Athens also extended its power on the mainland and by 460 had achieved a dominant position in central Greece. Sparta – unusual in still having a monarchical constitution – had the strongest army in Greece and was unwilling to surrender its primacy to the increasingly arrogant Athenians. Throughout the 460s the Spartans were preoccupied with a *helot* (serf) revolt, but moves to increase the influence of Athens within the Peloponnese led to the outbreak of war between the two rivals in 457.

Athens was unable to sustain a war against Persia and Sparta at the same time, but the peace treaty with Persia in 448 in some ways weakened the Athenian position. Without the fear of a return to Persian rule, many members of the Delian league felt less closely bound to Athens. Sparta, which had no navy, concentrated its attack on the Athenian position on the mainland of central Greece while attempting to foment rebellion in the league. The Athenians successfully put down rebellions in

TIMELINE

Political change

500

509–507 Kleisthenes introduces a democratic constitution in Athens

499–494 The Ionian cities rebel against Persian rule

492 Darius of Persia launches an expedition against Greece; it is defeated by the Athenians at Marathon in 490

480 Xerxes' invasion of Greece is stopped on sea at Salamis, and on land at Plataea (479)

475

478 Sparta withdraws from the alliance against Persia

478 The Delian league is set up, with Athens at its head

462–458 Democratic institutions are completed in Athens, with Pericles as the dominant political figure

457–445 The first Peloponnesian war between Athens and Sparta

450

447 Athens begins to establish military settlements in the Aegean

448 The peace of Kallias secures Ionian independence from Persia

Cultural change

c.500 The black-figure style of vase painting flourishes in Athens

484 The playwright Aeschylos wins the Athenian tragedy prize for the first time

c.460 The temple of Zeus at Olympia is built

449 Pericles begins to rebuild Athens, and starts work on the Parthenon (447–432)

500   **475**   **450**

Illyrians

Thracians

Apollonia

Black Sea

Epidamnos

Lake Ohrid

Lake Prespa

Marita

Bosporus
Byzantium
440

Apollonia

MACEDON
Persian vassal, 492

Pella

Amphipolis
Eion

7

Akanthos

Methone
Poteidaia
432

Abdera

465 *Thasos*
9

2

Mt Athos

Chersonesos **3**
Abydos

Hellespont

Cyzicus

Imbros

Troy

Lemnos

LYDIA

Aegean Sea

Northern Sporades

Larissa
Kosthanaia

THESSALY

Corcyra

EPIRUS

PINDOS MOUNTAINS

Pinios

Ambracia

Anaktorion

ACARNANIA

Thermopylae
480

4

Artemisium
480

Oreos

Euboea

Skyros

Mytilene

Lesbos

IONIA

Phokaia

Erythraia

Sardis

Delphi

PHOCIS

LOKRIS

BOEOTIA
Plataea
479

Thebes

ATTICA

EUBOEA 447
Chalcis
Eretria

Marathon
490

Chios

Kephallenia

ACHAEA

Megara

5

Athens

Andros

Elis

Corinth

Laurion

Ephesos
6

Buyuk Menderes

Zakynthos

ELIS

PELOPONNESE

ARCADIA

Argos

Tegea

Salamis
480

Troizen

Aegina

8

Ikaria

Delos

Samos *Samos*
440

Mycale
479

1

Miletos

Halikarnassos

Kos

Sparta

SPARTA

469
Naxos

Rhodes

Mediterranean Sea

Carpathos

Crete

Euboea and Thasos, but by 445 they had lost control in central Greece and agreed to peace terms which recognized Spartan dominance in the Peloponnese.

Despite being almost constantly at war, Athens flourished economically in the 5th century as a result of its dominance of eastern Mediterranean and Black Sea trade and its own rich silver mines – worked by more than 20,000 slaves – at Laurion in Attica. Athenian democratic institutions continued to be developed and by 458 all citizens (excluding slaves, women and foreigners) were eligible to vote for and (except for the poorest) to serve in the highest offices of the government and the judiciary. The triumph in the war with Persia led to an exceptional outburst of cultural confidence in Greece as a whole, and especially in Athens, where vase-painting, sculpture and drama all reached new heights. The

city, and notably its Acropolis, were rebuilt and the "classical" style of art and architecture matured. No other Greek city-state saw such a program of public building at this time.

1 The Greek cities of Ionia, led by Miletos, rebelled against Persian rule in 499 and sacked Sardis.

2 A Persian fleet was destroyed rounding Mt Athos in 492. To avoid the same thing happening in 480, the Persians dug a canal across the peninsula neck.

3 A bridge of boats was built across the Hellespont for Xerxes' expedition in 480.

4 At Thermopylae, the Greeks under Leonidas of Sparta were outflanked; most withdrew, but the Spartans' heroic stand inspired later Greek defense.

5 At the comprehensive Greek victory of Plataea, the Persian general Mardonios was killed and the leading Theban allies of the Persians were executed.

6 The last of the Persian fleet was destroyed at Mycale in 479.

7 Eion, the last important Persian stronghold in Europe, was captured by the Athenians in 475.

8 The common treasury of the Delian league was kept on Delos, but was removed to Athens in 454.

9 Delian league member Thasos rebelled in 465, but the Athenians invaded and tore down the city walls.

See also 16 (archaic Greece);
18 (Achemenid Persia)

In only eight years of tireless campaigning, Alexander of Macedon (r. 336–323) conquered the Persian empire and the Indus valley. Although his empire broke up on his death, Alexander's conquests determined that Hellenism would be the dominant cultural influence in the Middle East well into the Christian era.

Alexander was eighteen years old when his father, Philip II, was assassinated. He was bold, imaginative, well educated – Aristotle had been his tutor – and a promising soldier. In the first two years of his reign Alexander proved his abilities by securing Macedon's northern borders and subduing the rebellious Greeks. In 334, his home base now stable, Alexander launched his father's planned invasion of Persia, routing the army sent to stop him at the river Granicus. He then marched down the Anatolian coast, liberating and restoring the Greek cities of Ionia. Only Miletos and Halikarnassos, where the garrisons had been supplied by the Persian fleet, offered serious resistance. To prevent further naval interference, Alexander proceeded to conquer Phoenicia and Egypt, after first crushing a large Persian army, commanded personally by Darius III, at the river Issus in 333. With Persian naval power eliminated, Alexander marched into the heart of the Persian empire in 331, and at Gaugamela inflicted another humiliating defeat on Darius. Persian resistance crumbled, and Babylon and the Persian treasury at Susa were captured.

The following year, at the Persian Gates pass, Alexander destroyed the last sizeable Persian army and swept on to loot and burn the Persian capital, Persepolis. It took Alexander three more years of tough campaigning in Bactria and Sogdiana to complete his conquest of the Persian empire, before invading the Indus valley in 327. There, in 326, Alexander won his last major battle, over King Porus at the river Hydaspes. Alexander wanted to press on and invade the Ganges plain, but his soldiers, after marching 25,000 kilometers (15,000 miles), had had enough and they refused. Instead Alexander marched down the Indus to the sea and turned west, reaching Babylon in 324, where, the following year, aged only 32, he died, an overweight alcoholic.

Shortly before his death his adoption of the styles of oriental kingship had lost him the loyalty of some of his original Macedonian followers.

The most important factor in Alexander's success was his military genius, but he was also aided by the centuries-long tradition of imperial rule in the Middle East, which had weakened local identities and loyalties. The provincial populations of the Persian empire were used to foreign rule and, as Alexander respected local customs and did not make unreasonable demands for tribute, a change from Persian to Macedonian rule was a matter of indifference to them. Alexander's empire broke

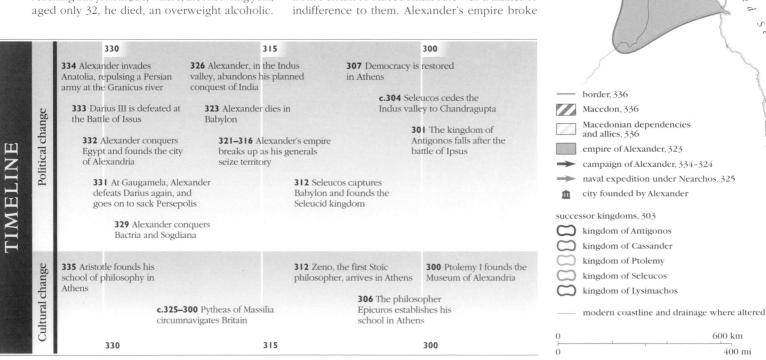

TIMELINE

Political change

330	315	300
334 Alexander invades Anatolia, repulsing a Persian army at the Granicus river	**326** Alexander, in the Indus valley, abandons his planned conquest of India	**307** Democracy is restored in Athens
333 Darius III is defeated at the Battle of Issus	**323** Alexander dies in Babylon	**c.304** Seleucos cedes the Indus valley to Chandragupta
332 Alexander conquers Egypt and founds the city of Alexandria	**321–316** Alexander's empire breaks up as his generals seize territory	**301** The kingdom of Antigonos falls after the battle of Ipsus
331 At Gaugamela, Alexander defeats Darius again, and goes on to sack Persepolis	**312** Seleucos captures Babylon and founds the Seleucid kingdom	
329 Alexander conquers Bactria and Sogdiana		

Cultural change

330	315	300
335 Aristotle founds his school of philosophy in Athens	**312** Zeno, the first Stoic philosopher, arrives in Athens	**300** Ptolemy I founds the Museum of Alexandria
		306 The philosopher Epicuros establishes his school in Athens
c.325–300 Pytheas of Massilia circumnavigates Britain		

Legend:
- — border, 336
- ▨ Macedon, 336
- ▢ Macedonian dependencies and allies, 336
- ▦ empire of Alexander, 323
- → campaign of Alexander, 334–324
- → naval expedition under Nearchos, 325
- 🏛 city founded by Alexander

successor kingdoms, 303
- kingdom of Antigonos
- kingdom of Cassander
- kingdom of Ptolemy
- kingdom of Seleucos
- kingdom of Lysimachos

---- modern coastline and drainage where altered

0	600 km
0	400 mi

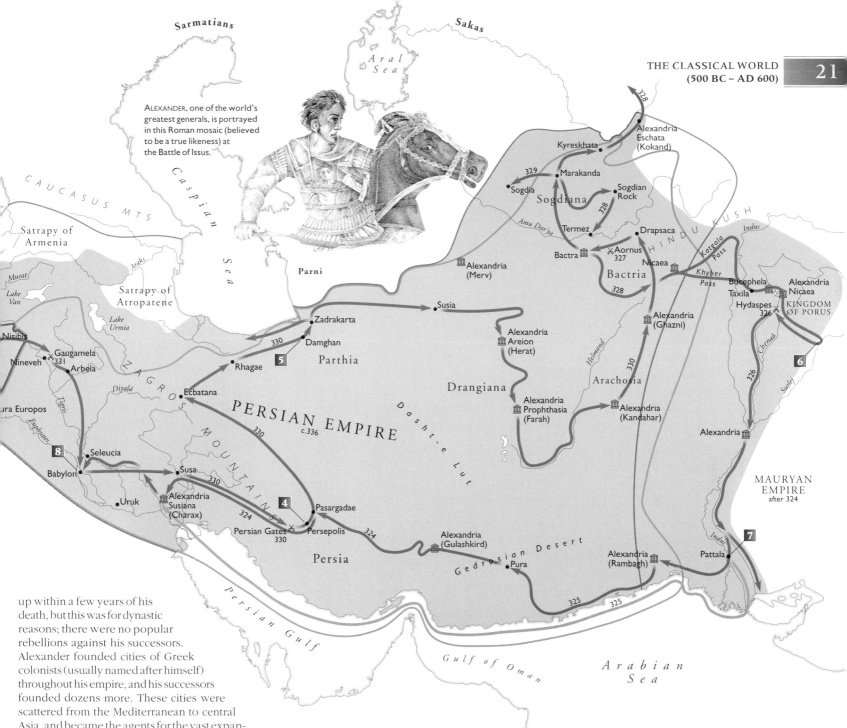

ALEXANDER, one of the world's greatest generals, is portrayed in this Roman mosaic (believed to be a true likeness) at the Battle of Issus.

Sarmatians

Sakas

Aral Sea

CAUCASUS MTS

Caspian Sea

Satrapy of Armenia

Parni

Satrapy of Atropatene

Murat

Lake Van

Lake Urmia

Nisibis

Gaugamela ✕ 331

Nineveh

Arbela

Diyala

Dura Europos

Tigris

Euphrates

ZAGROS MOUNTAINS

Ecbatana

Rhagae

Damghan

Zadrakarta

5

Parthia

Susia

Alexandria (Merv)

Sogdia

Marakanda

Kyreskhata

Alexandria Eschata (Kokand)

328

329

Sogdiana

Sogdian Rock

328

Termez

Amu Dar'ya

Drapsaca

HINDU KUSH

Indus

Bactra

Nicaea

✕ Aornus 327

Bactria

Katgala Pass

Khyber Pass

Taxila

Bucephela

Alexandria Nicaea

328

Hydaspes 326 ✕

KINGDOM OF PORUS

6

Chenab

326

Alexandria Areion (Herat)

Alexandria (Ghazni)

330

Arachosia

Helmand

Drangiana

Dasht-e Lut

Alexandria Prophthasia (Farah)

Alexandria (Kandahar)

Alexandria

PERSIAN EMPIRE
c.336

330

Seleucia

8

Babylon

Susa

330

Uruk

Alexandria Susiana (Charax)

324

4

Pasargadae

Persian Gates ✕ 330

Persepolis

324

Persia

Alexandria (Gulashkird)

Gedrosian Desert

Pura

325

325

MAURYAN EMPIRE
after 324

Alexandria (Rambagh)

Pattala

Indus

7

Sadej

Persian Gulf

Gulf of Oman

Arabian Sea

up within a few years of his death, but this was for dynastic reasons; there were no popular rebellions against his successors. Alexander founded cities of Greek colonists (usually named after himself) throughout his empire, and his successors founded dozens more. These cities were scattered from the Mediterranean to central Asia, and became the agents for the vast expansion of Greek cultural influence over west Asia that was perhaps the most important consequence of Alexander's conquests.

Alexander left as his heirs a posthumous son and a mentally ill brother, neither of whom was capable of ruling in his own right. The regent Perdiccas maintained the central administration until his murder in 321, but under his successor, Antipater (d.319), the governor of Macedon, power in the provinces was seized by the generals and the empire fragmented in a series of conflicts known as the Wars of the Diadochi ("successors"). By 304 five successor kingdoms had arisen. Cassander, Antipater's son, ruled in Macedon; Lysimachos in Thrace; Antigonos had seized power in Anatolia; Seleucos in Mesopotamia and the east; and Ptolemy in Egypt. Of the five, only Antigonos aspired to recreate Alexander's empire, but this simply united the other Diadochi against him. When Antigonos was killed in battle against the combined armies of Seleucos, Lysimachos and Cassander at Ipsus in 301, his kingdom was divided up among the victors: Lysimachos taking Anatolia, Seleucus Syria and Cilicia, and Ptolemy, who had been campaigning separately, Palestine and Cyprus. Although the battle

of Ipsus did not bring an end to the struggles of the Diadochi, it did set the seal on the break-up of Alexander's empire.

During the chaos that followed his death, Alexander's empire had also begun to fray at the edges. His conquests had been rapid and the rulers of the northern satrapies of Bithynia, Paphlagonia, Cappadocia, Armenia and Atropatene had been allowed to retain their provinces after making only token submission. Alexander's early death prevented these provinces being brought into full submission, and during the Diadochan wars they became fully independent kingdoms. The Indus valley was also lost by the Greeks after Alexander's death. Preoccupied with the war against Antigonos, Seleucos ceded the Indian provinces to the Mauryan empire in 304 in return for a herd of war elephants (which he used to good effect at Ipsus). In Greece, now only a small part of the Hellenistic world, the cities of the Corinthian league rebelled unsuccessfully against Macedonian control in 323 and then defected to Antigonos in 307. However, after the defeat of Antigonos at Ipsus, Macedonian control was restored.

1 Alexander won control of Anatolia after defeating an army sent to intercept him at the river Granicus.

2 Founded in 332, Alexandria was to become the largest and richest Greek city in the 3rd century.

3 The oracle of Amun at Siwa claimed Alexander to be son of the god and heir to the Egyptian throne.

4 The burning of the palace of Xerxes at Persepolis in 330 marked the end of the Panhellenic war of revenge but not of Alexander's personal desire for conquest.

5 Darius III was murdered at Damghan by his courtiers as he fled, seeking refuge in Bactria.

6 Only when Alexander's exhausted and homesick army refused to follow him into the Ganges valley did he at last relent and turn back.

7 Nearchos built a fleet of more than 100 ships at Pattala to explore and control the Gulf coast.

8 Alexander died in Babylon in 323, having caught a fever after several days of heavy drinking.

See also 18 (Achemenid Persia);
20 (Persian wars and Greece)

In 500 BC the world's most impressive state was the Achemenid empire of Persia, extending from Libya to the Indus. The empire's first setback occurred when Xerxes I invaded Greece (▷20). The quarrelsome Greek city-states united in the face of the common enemy and defeated the Persians at sea at Salamis and on land at Plataea. The Greeks went back to their quarrels and did little to follow up their victory: Persia lost its foothold in Europe but continued to dominate the Middle East for eighty years. Then, in 404, Egypt rebelled and Persian control was not restored until 343. In 380 Persia's Indian provinces were lost.

Late 5th-century Greece was dominated by rivalry between Sparta and Athens, culminating in the Peloponnesian war which engulfed most of the Greek world but settled nothing. Further indecisive wars between shifting alliances ensued. Meanwhile, the Balkan kingdom of Macedon rose unopposed under Philip II and in 338 all the Greek city-states were forcibly enrolled in the Macedonian-dominated Hellenic league. Philip planned to invade Persia but his assassination in 336 left it to his son Alexander to carry out his plans. In only six years he conquered almost all the Persian empire, opening the whole Middle East to Greek influence (▷21).

By the 4th century the old south Arabian kingdom of Saba had been joined by the new states of Qataban and Hadramaut, driven by a demand from the Mediterranean for the precious gums, frankincense and myrrh, which were produced in the region. By the same period Sabean influence was seen in Damot on the African Red Sea coast.

Through most of the 5th and 4th centuries the main power in the western Mediterranean was Carthage. Carthage was more interested in commerce than conquest and its empire grew little between 500 and 323. Most of central and western Europe was now dominated by Celtic peoples. Around 400, Celts crossed the Alps and invaded Italy, breaking the power of the Etruscans and settling the Po valley. Though still insignificant on the map, by 323 Rome was a major power in Italy, having conquered its Latin and Etruscan neighbors earlier in the century (▷23).

The strongest state in India in 500 was Magadha in the lower Ganges plain. From 364 it brought most of northern India under its control. Southern India was a mosaic of minor states and chiefdoms with little urban development. The Zhou kingdom of China, which had broken up into a dozen competing states in the 8th century, was still disunited, although many of the smaller states had been absorbed by the bigger players (▷26). The continual warfare stimulated

▷20 ▷21 ▷23 ▷26

c.450 Beginning of the La Tène phase of Celtic Iron Age culture

500–400 Mesoamerican state formation occurs in the Oaxaca valley (Monte Albán and Zapotec civilization)

450–400 Domestication of the reindeer in the Sayan Mountains of central Asia

c.400 Olmec civilization in steep decline

431–404 The Peloponnesian war takes place, between Athens and Sparta

509–507 Foundation of democracy in Athens

480–479 The Greeks defeat the Persian invasion

c.400 The Celts settle northern Italy; decline of Etruscan civilization

TIMELINE

The Americas
Europe
Middle East
Africa
East and South Asia

500
450
400

525 Egypt comes under Achemenid Persian control

483 Death of Siddhartha Gautama, the Buddha, in India

400–300 Iron working is practiced in east Africa

c.515 The Achemenid Persian empire is at its height

480–221 China breaks into competing kingdoms in the "Warring States" period

399 Death of Socrates, Greek philosopher, in Athens

479 Death of Confucius, Chinese philosopher

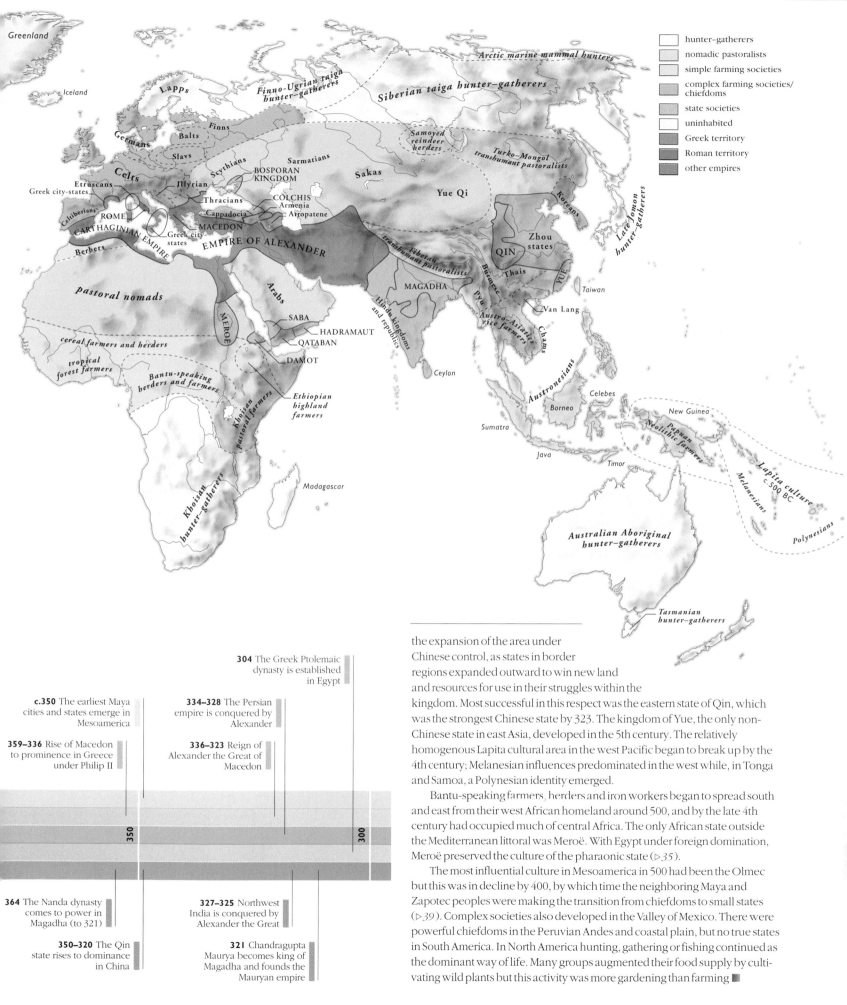

hunter-gatherers
nomadic pastoralists
simple farming societies
complex farming societies/
chiefdoms
state societies
uninhabited
Greek territory
Roman territory
other empires

Greenland

Iceland

Lapps

Finno-Ugrian taiga hunter-gatherers

Siberian taiga hunter-gatherers

Arctic marine mammal hunters

Germans

Balts

Finns

Slavs

Samoyed reindeer herders

Turko-Mongol transhumant pastoralists

Celts

Etruscans

Greek city-states

Illyrian

Scythians

Thracians

BOSPORAN KINGDOM

Sarmatians

Sakas

Yue Qi

Koreans

Late Jomon hunter-gatherers

Celtiberians

ROME

CARTHAGINIAN EMPIRE

Greek city-states

MACEDON

Cappadocia

COLCHIS

Armenia

Atropatene

EMPIRE OF ALEXANDER

Tibetan transhumant pastoralists

Zhou states

QIN

YUE

Van Lang

Berbers

Pastoral nomads

Arabs

MEROË

SABA

HADRAMAUT

QATABAN

DAMOT

MAGADHA

Hindu kingdoms and republics

Burmese

Pyu

Thais

Chams

Austro-Asiatic rice farmers

Taiwan

cereal farmers and herders

tropical forest farmers

Bantu-speaking herders and farmers

Khoisan pastoral farmers

Ethiopian highland farmers

Ceylon

Austronesians

Celebes

Sumatra

Borneo

Java

Timor

New Guinea

Papuan Neolithic farmers

Melanesians

Lapita culture c. 500 BC

Madagascar

Khoisan hunter-gatherers

Australian Aboriginal hunter-gatherers

Polynesians

Tasmanian hunter-gatherers

the expansion of the area under Chinese control, as states in border regions expanded outward to win new land and resources for use in their struggles within the kingdom. Most successful in this respect was the eastern state of Qin, which was the strongest Chinese state by 323. The kingdom of Yue, the only non-Chinese state in east Asia, developed in the 5th century. The relatively homogenous Lapita cultural area in the west Pacific began to break up by the 4th century; Melanesian influences predominated in the west while, in Tonga and Samoa, a Polynesian identity emerged.

Bantu-speaking farmers, herders and iron workers began to spread south and east from their west African homeland around 500, and by the late 4th century had occupied much of central Africa. The only African state outside the Mediterranean littoral was Meroë. With Egypt under foreign domination, Meroë preserved the culture of the pharaonic state (▷35).

The most influential culture in Mesoamerica in 500 had been the Olmec but this was in decline by 400, by which time the neighboring Maya and Zapotec peoples were making the transition from chiefdoms to small states (▷39). Complex societies also developed in the Valley of Mexico. There were powerful chiefdoms in the Peruvian Andes and coastal plain, but no true states in South America. In North America hunting, gathering or fishing continued as the dominant way of life. Many groups augmented their food supply by cultivating wild plants but this activity was more gardening than farming ◼

Founded probably around 800 BC, Rome had by about 600 BC fallen under the control of an Etruscan dynasty. Rome benefited from its strategic position on the lowest crossing point of the Tiber but remained a minor city. In 509 the monarchy was overthrown by an aristocratic coup and a republic was founded. The first century of its history was dominated by a struggle between the lower classes (the plebeians) and the leading families (the patricians). By the end of the 5th century the senate had codified the law and granted the plebeians their own representatives: the tribunes. In the 4th century the plebeians also won the right to run for the major offices of state – though voting in the popular assembly was structured to favor the richer classes. The extension of rights to the plebeians helped build a community of interest between the classes that sustained the republic through many crises.

Roman expansion began as a series of minor wars against its immediate neighbors. There was no imperial masterplan at this stage: these wars were intended primarily to make Rome more secure from attack. Around 400 BC, Gauls crossed the Alps and made extensive settlements in the Po valley, which became known as Cisalpine Gaul (Gaul "this side of the Alps") to distinguish it from the Gaulish homeland to the north. The Gauls raided widely, even sacking Rome in 390, but mainly they weakened the Etruscans. In 354 the Romans allied against the Gauls with the Samnites, a powerful tribal confederation, but the alliance did not last. The Romans and Samnites had competing interests in central Italy, which led to the inconclusive First Samnite War (343–341). Rome conquered the Latins (340–338), before renewing its conflict with the Samnites in the Second (327–304) and Third (298–290) Samnite wars. A Roman victory at Sentinum in 295 was followed by the collapse of Samnite power and by 290 Rome dominated central Italy. The Romans planted colonies of Roman citizens in subdued territories

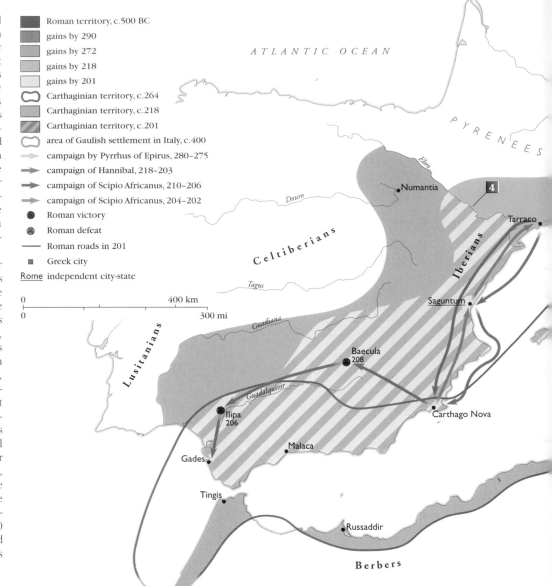

Roman territory, c.500 BC
gains by 290
gains by 272
gains by 218
gains by 201
Carthaginian territory, c.264
Carthaginian territory, c.218
Carthaginian territory, c.201
area of Gaulish settlement in Italy, c.400
campaign by Pyrrhus of Epirus, 280–275
campaign of Hannibal, 218–203
campaign of Scipio Africanus, 210–206
campaign of Scipio Africanus, 204–202
Roman victory
Roman defeat
Roman roads in 201
Greek city
Rome independent city-state

0   400 km
0   300 mi

and awarded their allies half-citizenship rights which could, if loyalty was proved, eventually be increased to full Roman citizenship.

The Romans began to bring the Greek cities of southern Italy under their sway. The Greeks appealed for protection to King Pyrrhus of Epirus. In 280 Pyrrhus invaded Italy after a hard-fought battle at Heraclea. The king's losses were so great that he remarked after the battle that a few more victories like this and he would lose the war. This is what in fact happened: the Romans resisted doggedly and in 275 Pyrrhus withdrew. Three years later the Romans took Tarentum, completing their conquest of peninsular Italy. Rome was now a Mediterranean power.

In 264 Rome went to war with Carthage, the major naval power of the western Mediterranean, over a dispute about spheres of influence in Sicily. The Romans called the Carthaginians "Poeni" (Phoenicians) – and the wars with Carthage came to be known as the Punic wars. Rome had no tradition of naval warfare but learned quickly, and in 260 its newly built fleet won its first victory over the Carthaginians at Mylae. In 255 the Romans tried to bring the war to a quick conclusion by invading north Africa but were repulsed. The war dragged on until 241, when the Carthaginians were vanquished at sea off Lilybaeum. Sicily became a Roman province; and in 238 the Romans also occupied Corsica

TIMELINE

Rome and Italy

509 The foundation of the Roman republic

c.450 The Laws of the Twelve Tables, the basis of Roman law, are laid down

c.400 Gauls settle Po valley and Etruscan power declines

396 Roman expansion begins with the capture of Veii

390 A wandering tribe of Gauls sacks Rome

c.380 City walls are built around Rome

343–290 The Samnite wars leave the Romans as the dominant power in Italy

280–275 Pyrrhus invades Italy but eventually withdraws

272 The Romans take Tarentum, completing the unification of peninsular Italy

c.222 The Romans conquer Cisalpine Gaul

216 At Cannae, Rome suffers its worst ever defeat, at the hands of Hannibal

201 End of the Second Punic War

Carthage

264–241 The First Punic War between Rome and Carthage

237–218 Carthaginian expansion occurs in Spain

218 Hannibal launches the Second Punic War

202 Rome defeats Carthage at the Battle of Zama

Gauls
(Celts)

ALPS

GAUL

Arausio

Narbo

Massilia

Emporiae
(Ampurias)

Mediolanum

Ticinus River
218

CISALPINE GAUL

Ligurians

Genua

Pisa

Po

Venetians

Aquileia

Trebia River
218

Ariminum

Ancona

Metaurus
River
207

Sentinum
295

Lake Trasimenus
217

Saturnia

Cosa

Umbrians

Castrum Novum

Etruscans

Veii

Rome

Latins

Ostia

Sabines

Corfinium

Samnites

Cannae
216

Beneventum

Caudine Forks
321

Capua

Neapolis

Paestum

Lucanians

Tarentum

Messapians

Heraclea
280

Bruttians

Croton

MAGNA GRAECIA

Aleria
Corsica

Sardinia

Carales

Balearic
Islands

Mediterranean Sea

Drepanum
249

Lilybaeum
241

Panormus

Messana

Sicily

Catana

Rhegium

Mylae
260

Agrigentum
262

Syracusae

Ecnomus
256

Malta

Hippo Regius

Utica

Carthage

Bagradas
255

Cirta
203

Zama
202

Hadrumetum

NUMIDIA

Kingdom of
Syphax

Kingdom of
Massinissa

Leptis Magna

Sava

Danube

Illyrians

Adriatic Sea

Epidamnus

MACEDON

Apollonia

Brundisium

EPIRUS

Ambracia

ELEPHANTS carried soldiers to
battle, but were used to scare
the enemy rather than as
cavalry. This Roman plate
shows one carrying a fort.

and Sardinia. In the 230s Carthage began to recoup its losses by expansion in Spain; and in the 220s Rome conquered Cisalpine Gaul. In 226 Rome and Carthage agreed on respective spheres of influence, but when Hannibal, Carthage's foremost general, attacked Saguntum, a city within Carthage's sphere but friendly to Rome, the Second Punic War broke out. Roman naval power compelled Hannibal to invade Italy by marching overland and crossing the Alps. In Italy Hannibal found ready allies in the newly conquered Gauls in the north and the Greek cities in the south – and also in the kingdom of Macedon, which viewed with concern the expansion of Roman power into Greece in the 220s. Hannibal was a brilliant general but lacked the strength to take Rome itself and so win the war. The Romans, after a catastrophic defeat at Cannae, did their best to avoid facing Hannibal in open battle, trying simply to contain him in southern Italy. The main Roman counterattack was aimed at Carthage's Spanish possessions. The decisive campaign began in 210 under Scipio Africanus, and by 206 the Carthaginians had been driven out of Spain. Then in 204 Scipio launched an invasion of north Africa and persuaded the Numidian king Massinissa to side with Rome. Hannibal was recalled from Italy to face Scipio, and in 202 the two generals met in battle at Zama. The result was a crushing defeat for Hannibal and

Carthage surrendered on harsh terms. Rome annexed Spain and the Balearic Islands, and the Numidians were given most of Carthage's north African territory. Carthage itself was reduced to a heartland in modern Tunisia: it had to disband its fleet and agree not to go to war without Rome's permission. Although in Spain the Romans faced rebellions – which for seventy years frustrated their attempts to gain control of their new possessions – Rome now dominated the western Mediterranean.

1 The capture of nearby Veii, an Etruscan city, in 396, was the first step in the Roman conquest of Italy.

2 Rome disputed control of Italy with the Samnites, a confederation of the Caraceni, Caudini, Hirpini and Pentri tribes, in a series of wars, from 343 to 290.

3 In the growing rivalry between Rome and Carthage, Sicily was the flashpoint that led in 264 to the outbreak of the First Punic War.

4 In 226 the Ebro was the agreed border between Roman and Carthaginian spheres of influence.

5 A Roman campaign against Illyria was mounted in 229–228 to suppress pirates infesting the Adriatic Sea.

6 Hannibal's crossing of the Alps took 15 days: only a handful of his original 38 elephants survived.

7 Hannibal's base for operations in southern Italy was at Tarentum until the Romans retook the city in 209.

8 Numidia's Berber kingdoms, longtime suppliers of cavalry to Carthage, sided with Rome at Zama in 202.

See also 12 (Bronze Age Europe);
29 (growth of the Roman empire)

Alexander's empire did not survive his death in 323 – the immediate cause of its breakup being his failure to provide an heir – and within a few years his generals had become the rulers of independent kingdoms). Seleucos built a state which incorporated most of Anatolia, Mesopotamia, and Iran and extended into central Asia; despite successful rebellions by the Bactrian Greeks in 239 and the Parthians in 238, the Seleucid kingdom was still the largest of the successor states in 200. Ptolemy seized Egypt and founded a dynasty which was to last until 31 BC, ending only with Cleopatra's suicide after the battle of Actium. Macedon itself fell to Antipater, who reasserted Macedonian supremacy in Greece in the face of an Athenian-led rebellion. Macedon was still the leading power in Greece in 200.

The leading power in the western Mediterranean by 200 was Rome. The Romans had completed the conquest of peninsular Italy in 272, and in 264 were drawn into a war with Carthage over Sicily. This, the First Punic War, dragged on for over twenty years until the Romans had wrested control of Sicily, Sardinia and Corsica. Carthaginian expansion in Spain, arousing Roman hostility once again, led in 218 to the outbreak of the Second Punic War. The Carthaginian general Hannibal surprised the Romans by attacking Italy from the north, but counterattacks in Spain and north Africa brought Rome crushing victory, and Carthage was shorn of its empire (▷23).

Several centuries of stability on the Eurasian steppes came to an end in the 3rd century as the Sarmatians began to push westward against the Scythians. On the far eastern steppes the Turko-Mongol pastoralists made the transition to a horse-mounted fully nomadic way of life around 300, and by 200 they were united in the powerful Xiong-nu confederation. Their use of the composite bow gave the Xiongnu a decided military advantage over their nomadic Iranian neighbors to the west and made them a formidable adversary for the newly united Chinese.

In 321 Chandragupta Maurya (321–c. 293) seized the throne of the kingdom of Magadha, overthrowing the Nanda dynasty. Chandragupta spent most of his reign building a strong central administration, but he defeated a Seleucid invasion, adding all of northwest India to his domains. His son Bindusara also conquered much of southern India. Under Ashoka the Mauryan empire reached its greatest extent. Appalled by his bloody conquest of the east coast kingdom of Kalinga in 261, Ashoka abjured further warfare and, becoming a Buddhist, tried to impose Buddhist standards of behavior on his people. Little is known about

323–280 Wars of the Diadochi: Alexander's generals split up his empire

323 Alexander the Great dies without naming a successor

264 Roman–Carthaginian rivalry in Sicily sets off the First Punic War

272 Rome completes its conquest of peninsular Italy

239 The Bactrian Greeks break away from the Seleucid kingdom

241 A Roman naval victory off Lilybaeum ends the First Punic war

TIMELINE

The Americas
Europe
Middle East   325
Africa
East and South Asia

300

275

250

321 Chandragupta Maurya, founder of the Mauryan empire, becomes king of Magadha

c.300 The Turko-Mongol tribes of the eastern steppes adopt a fully nomadic way of life

c.300 Beginning of rice farming in Japan

268–233 Reign of Ashoka: Buddhism spreads through the Mauryan empire

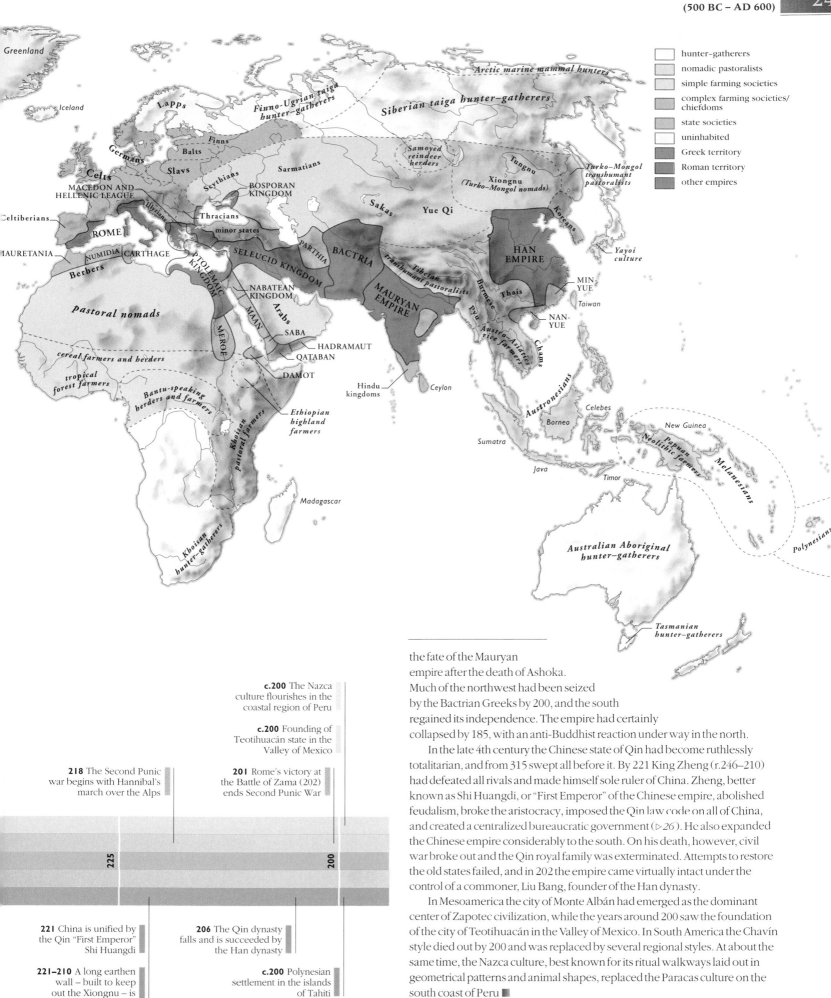

Map legend:

- hunter-gatherers
- nomadic pastoralists
- simple farming societies
- complex farming societies/chiefdoms
- state societies
- uninhabited
- Greek territory
- Roman territory
- other empires

Map labels:

Greenland · Iceland · Lapps · Finno-Ugrian taiga hunter-gatherers · Siberian taiga hunter-gatherers · Arctic marine mammal hunters · Finns · Germans · Balts · Slavs · Samoyed reindeer herders · Tungnu · Celts · Scythians · Sarmatians · Xiongnu (Turko~Mongol nomads) · Turko-Mongol transhumant pastoralists · Macedon and Hellenic League · Bosporan Kingdom · Sakas · Yue Qi · Koreans · Celtiberians · Illyrians · Thracians · minor states · Parthia · Bactria · Han Empire · Rome · Mauretania · Numidia · Carthage · Berbers · Ptolemaic Kingdom · Seleucid Kingdom · Tibetan transhumant pastoralists · Min-Yue · Yayoi culture · Nabatean Kingdom · Arabs · Mauryan Empire · Burmese · Thais · Taiwan · pastoral nomads · Maan · Saba · Hadramaut · Qataban · Damot · Meroe · Hindu kingdoms · Ceylon · Nan-Yue · Pyu · Austro-Asiatic rice farmers · Chams · cereal farmers and herders · tropical forest farmers · Bantu-speaking herders and farmers · Khoisan pastoral farmers · Ethiopian highland farmers · Austronesians · Celebes · Borneo · New Guinea · Papuan Neolithic farmers · Melanesians · Sumatra · Java · Timor · Madagascar · Khoisan hunter-gatherers · Australian Aboriginal hunter-gatherers · Polynesians · Tasmanian hunter-gatherers

Timeline:

218 The Second Punic war begins with Hannibal's march over the Alps

221 China is unified by the Qin "First Emperor" Shi Huangdi

221–210 A long earthen wall – built to keep out the Xiongnu – is completed in China

225

c.200 The Nazca culture flourishes in the coastal region of Peru

c.200 Founding of Teotihuacán state in the Valley of Mexico

201 Rome's victory at the Battle of Zama (202) ends Second Punic War

206 The Qin dynasty falls and is succeeded by the Han dynasty

c.200 Polynesian settlement in the islands of Tahiti

200

the fate of the Mauryan empire after the death of Ashoka. Much of the northwest had been seized by the Bactrian Greeks by 200, and the south regained its independence. The empire had certainly collapsed by 185, with an anti-Buddhist reaction under way in the north.

In the late 4th century the Chinese state of Qin had become ruthlessly totalitarian, and from 315 swept all before it. By 221 King Zheng (r.246–210) had defeated all rivals and made himself sole ruler of China. Zheng, better known as Shi Huangdi, or "First Emperor" of the Chinese empire, abolished feudalism, broke the aristocracy, imposed the Qin law code on all of China, and created a centralized bureaucratic government (▷26). He also expanded the Chinese empire considerably to the south. On his death, however, civil war broke out and the Qin royal family was exterminated. Attempts to restore the old states failed, and in 202 the empire came virtually intact under the control of a commoner, Liu Bang, founder of the Han dynasty.

In Mesoamerica the city of Monte Albán had emerged as the dominant center of Zapotec civilization, while the years around 200 saw the foundation of the city of Teotihuacán in the Valley of Mexico. In South America the Chavín style died out by 200 and was replaced by several regional styles. At about the same time, the Nazca culture, best known for its ritual walkways laid out in geometrical patterns and animal shapes, replaced the Paracas culture on the south coast of Peru ∎

The name Celts was used by Greek writers from the 5th century BC onward to describe a group of peoples of central and western Europe. Roman writers called the same peoples Gauls. The origins of the Celts are uncertain but are probably to be found in the northern Alps in the Bronze Age Urnfield (from mid-2nd millennium BC) and the late Bronze–early Iron Age Hallstatt cultures (1200–450 BC). There were at least two waves of Celtic migration out of central Europe. The first, from around 1000, took the Urnfield culture across western Europe into northern Spain by the 7th century; and a second, beginning in the 8th century, had by 500 BC spread the Hallstatt culture across France, Spain, Portugal, Germany, the Low Countries, and southern Britain.

A new phase of Celtic history began around 450 BC with the development in Germany and France of the La Tène culture. This was distinguished by a vigorous art style based on geometrical patterns and stylized animal images. It developed from Hallstatt art but also showed the influence of Etruscan and Scythian styles. The La Tène culture spread quickly across central and western Europe and reached the British Isles by about 400 BC, passed on partly by trade contacts and partly by smallscale migrations of continental Celts, such as the Parisii, who settled in Yorkshire. The La Tène culture did not spread to Spain, where the earlier Celtic settlers and the native population had become assimilated, forming a distinctive Celtiberian culture.

Around 400 BC there were major migrations of Celtic peoples into Italy and the lower Danube region. In Italy the Celts raided widely, sacked Rome, permanently weakened the Etruscans, and settled densely in the Po valley. The Celts on the lower Danube began to migrate into the Balkans in the 3rd century BC. A major raid on Delphi was repulsed, but the Hellenistic kingdom of Thrace was destroyed by their attacks. Three tribes crossed the Dardanelles and settled in central Anatolia, from where they raided the surrounding kingdoms.

The early 3rd century marked the high tide of Celtic expansion. The Romans began the conquest of the Celts of the Po valley at the battle of Telamon in 225 and captured the last center of resistance in Italy at Bononia (modern Bologna) in 192. The Thracians restored their kingdom around 220; and the Anatolian Celts were pacified by Pergamon in 230. In the 230s the Carthaginians began the conquest of the Celtiberians, and this was continued by the Romans after they had expelled the Carthaginians from Spain in 206. The Roman victory at Numantia in 133 brought them control of most of Spain, but Celtiberian resistance continued in the northwest until 19 BC. By the first century AD the continental Celts were caught firmly in a vise between the northward expansion of the Roman empire and the southward and westward expansion of the Germanic tribes and the Dacians. Between 58

- //// formative area of Hallstatt culture, 1200–750 BC
- ⌒ extent of Hallstatt culture, early 5th century BC
- ▢ Celts, c.500 BC
- ▢ Celtiberians, c.500 BC
- ▢ maximum extent of Celtic related peoples, 100 BC
- //// formative area of La Tène culture, 450 BC
- ⌒ La Tène culture, 2nd century BC
- ▢ area of Celtic state formation, 100 BC
- ⋯ surviving Celtic languages, c.AD 600
- ▶ migration of Celtic peoples, with date
- *Boii* Celtic peoples
- *Slavs* non-Celtic peoples
- ⊗ Celtic *oppidum*
- ⊗ other important Celtic site
- ⊗ La Tène vehicle burial
- — northern limit of Roman empire, 60 BC
- — northern limit of Roman empire, AD 79
- ▶ expansion of non-Celtic peoples, with date

0 ————— 600 km
0 ————— 400 mi

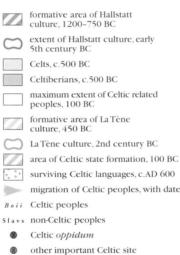

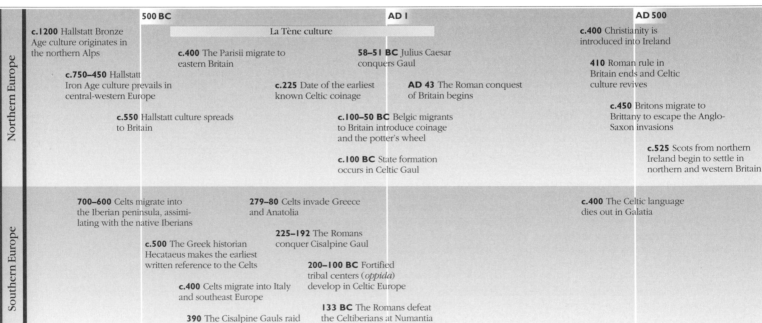

Northern Europe

| 500 BC | AD 1 | AD 500 |

La Tène culture

c.1200 Hallstatt Bronze Age culture originates in the northern Alps

c.400 The Parisii migrate to eastern Britain

58–51 BC Julius Caesar conquers Gaul

c.400 Christianity is introduced into Ireland

c.750–450 Hallstatt Iron Age culture prevails in central-western Europe

c.225 Date of the earliest known Celtic coinage

AD 43 The Roman conquest of Britain begins

410 Roman rule in Britain ends and Celtic culture revives

c.550 Hallstatt culture spreads to Britain

c.100–50 BC Belgic migrants to Britain introduce coinage and the potter's wheel

c.450 Britons migrate to Brittany to escape the Anglo-Saxon invasions

c.100 BC State formation occurs in Celtic Gaul

c.525 Scots from northern Ireland begin to settle in northern and western Britain

Southern Europe

700–600 Celts migrate into the Iberian peninsula, assimilating with the native Iberians

279–80 Celts invade Greece and Anatolia

c.400 The Celtic language dies out in Galatia

c.500 The Greek historian Hecataeus makes the earliest written reference to the Celts

225–192 The Romans conquer Cisalpine Gaul

c.400 Celts migrate into Italy and southeast Europe

200–100 BC Fortified tribal centers (*oppida*) develop in Celtic Europe

390 The Cisalpine Gauls raid and sack Rome

133 BC The Romans defeat the Celtiberians at Numantia

| 500 BC | AD 1 | AD 500 |

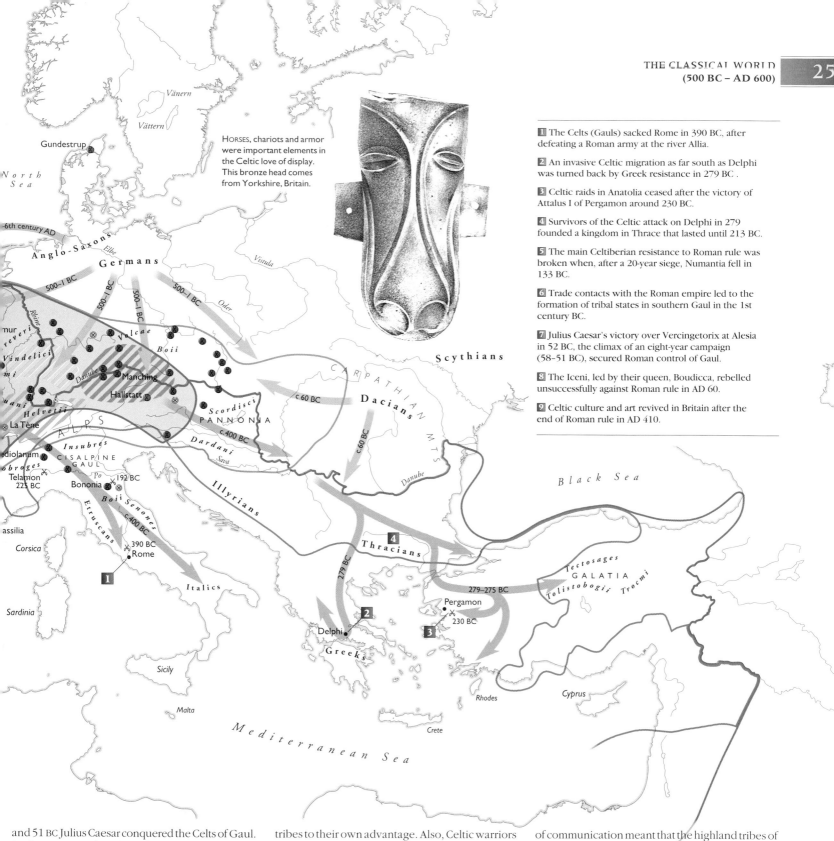

HORSES, chariots and armor were important elements in the Celtic love of display. This bronze head comes from Yorkshire, Britain.

North Sea

Gundestrup

Vänern

Vättern

6th century AD

Anglo-Saxons

Elbe

Germans

Vistula

Oder

500–1 BC

500–1 BC

500–1 BC

Rhine

reveri

Vulcae

Boii

mur

Vindelici

Danube

Manching

Hallstatt

Helvetii

La Tène

ALPS

Insubres

diolanum

CISALPINE GAUL

obroges

Telamon

Bononia

225 BC

×192 BC

Po

Boii

Senones

c.400 BC

Errusca

Scythians

CARPATHIAN

c.60 BC

Scordisci

PANNONIA

c.400 BC

Dardani

Sava

Illyrians

Dacians

MTS

c.60 BC

Danube

Black Sea

4

Thracians

279 BC

Tectosages

GALATIA

Tolistobogii *Trocmi*

279–275 BC

Pergamon

2

× 230 BC

3

assilia

Delphi

Corsica

Greeks

×390 BC

Rome

1

Italics

Sicily

Sardinia

Rhodes

Cyprus

Malta

Crete

Mediterranean Sea

1 The Celts (Gauls) sacked Rome in 390 BC, after defeating a Roman army at the river Allia.

2 An invasive Celtic migration as far south as Delphi was turned back by Greek resistance in 279 BC .

3 Celtic raids in Anatolia ceased after the victory of Attalus I of Pergamon around 230 BC.

4 Survivors of the Celtic attack on Delphi in 279 founded a kingdom in Thrace that lasted until 213 BC.

5 The main Celtiberian resistance to Roman rule was broken when, after a 20-year siege, Numantia fell in 133 BC.

6 Trade contacts with the Roman empire led to the formation of tribal states in southern Gaul in the 1st century BC.

7 Julius Caesar's victory over Vercingetorix at Alesia in 52 BC, the climax of an eight-year campaign (58–51 BC), secured Roman control of Gaul.

8 The Iceni, led by their queen, Boudicca, rebelled unsuccessfully against Roman rule in AD 60.

9 Celtic culture and art revived in Britain after the end of Roman rule in AD 410.

and 51 BC Julius Caesar conquered the Celts of Gaul. Under Augustus the tribes of the Alps and Pannonia were brought under Roman rule. By AD 1 the only independent Celts on mainland Europe were enclaves in German territory north of the Danube.

Celtic society was hierarchical and competitive and by the 2nd century BC was in the early stages of state formation. Fortified centers, or *oppida*, spread across Europe: some, such as Manching on the Danube, were large towns by the 1st century BC. Coinage and, in some areas, writing came into use. In southern Gaul small tribal states in direct contact with the Roman empire had developed by 60 BC. The Roman conquest prevented the Celts from developing a full urban civilization of their own.

The Celtic resistance to Rome failed for two main reasons. The Celts were politically disunited and the Romans easily exploited rivalries between states or

tribes to their own advantage. Also, Celtic warriors saw war as an opportunity to seek personal glory and this put them at a disadvantage to the drilled and disciplined legions. After the Roman conquest the La Tène culture died out on the continent and Celtic language was gradually replaced by Latin; but Celtic religion continued to be practiced. *Oppida* were superseded by planned Romanized towns.

Apart from two punitive raids by Caesar in 55–54 BC, it was AD 43 before the Romans began to subjugate the Celts in Britain. By this time contacts with the Romans across the Channel had already led to considerable Romanization of the southern British tribes and to the development of *oppida* and small tribal states. The Romans could never conquer all of Britain: the closest they came was in AD 83 when they defeated the Caledonians at "Mons Graupius". Harsh weather, mountainous terrain and long lines

of communication meant that the highland tribes of Scotland stayed independent, as did the Celts in Ireland, where pagan Celtic culture survived into the early Middle Ages. La Tène art died out in southern Britain in the 2nd century AD, but Celtic art traditions continued in the far north and Ireland, while Celtic languages survived throughout the British Isles. After the end of Roman rule in Britain in 410, Celtic art revived but was strongly influenced by late Roman and Anglo-Saxon art. The introduction of Christianity to Ireland in the 5th century inspired the development of a Celtic monastic civilization which, through missionary activity, had begun to exert a strong influence in Britain and the continent by 600.

See also 29 (growth of the Roman empire);
38 (Dark Ages)

Zhou China (1122–256 BC) was a decentralized feudal state: the king exercised direct authority only over his own domain, while the provinces were held as fiefs by dukes who ruled in his name. Gradually the dukes became, in effect, the rulers of independent states; the Zhou king reigned from his capital at Luoyang but did not rule. The Warring States period (480–221 BC) saw the stronger states eliminate the weaker and absorb their territory: by 300 eleven states were left, and by 256, when the last Zhou king was deposed, there were seven. By 221 one state – Qin – was supreme.

Qin's rise to dominance began under Xiao (r.361–338). Shang Yang, Xiao's prime minister, ended the power of the feudal aristocracy and enacted a series of reforms that turned Qin into a centralized state based on a settled and productive peasantry and a strong army. Qin's frontier position gave it opportunities for expansion at the expense of the tribal peoples to the west, while its mountainous borders protected it from the aggression of other states. By 315 it was the strongest of the surviving states. The Qin dukes had already abandoned the pretence of subservience to the Zhou by adopting the title of king. In the 3rd century Qin waged almost constant warfare against the other Chinese states, which failed to combine against it and were picked off one at a time. The unification of China was completed in a series of lightning campaigns by Zheng (r.246–210) between 230 and 221, after which he adopted the title Shi Huangdi, the "First Emperor".

Shi Huangdi is regarded as the founder of the Chinese empire and the pattern of centralized totalitarian government he established has endured to the present day. Qin laws and institutions were extended to the whole of China. The aristocracies of the defeated states were deported, the remnants of feudalism were abolished and a non-hereditary central and local bureaucracy was created. The empire was divided into 36 districts or commanderies, governed by civilian and military officials responsible directly to the autocratic emperor. Coinage, weights and measures, scripts and even the axle sizes of wagons were standardized. In an attempt to ensure that Chinese history began with him, Shi Huangdi ordered the destruction of all works of history, along with all "subversive" works of literature: scholars who protested were executed. Military campaigns extended the empire in the south while armies of conscripted laborers linked the frontier walls, which had been built by the Warring States against nomad invasions, into a continuous defensive system.

The cost of Shi Huangdi's reforms ruined the economy and his despotic rule caused such discontent that, after his death in 210, a civil war broke out. In 206 rebels massacred the entire Qin royal family. However, there was no restoration of the old states and the empire passed intact under the rule of Liu Bang, a commoner who had become a Qin official, and who became the first ruler of the Han dynasty. Gaozu (to use his more common posthumous title) ameliorated the severe Qin laws, reduced taxes and introduced reforms to restore prosperity. He rewarded some generals and bureaucrats with small fiefs but these were strictly controlled and the centralized state of Shi Huangdi was preserved.

The Former Han period (206 BC–AD 9) saw major territorial gains in central Asia and the south but northern China suffered severely from raids by the Xiongnu nomads until they were pacified in a long series of Han campaigns between 128 and 36 BC.

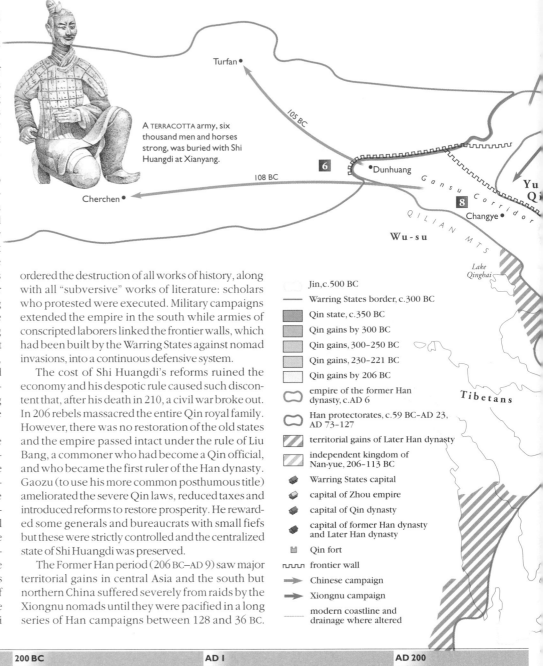

A TERRACOTTA army, six thousand men and horses strong, was buried with Shi Huangdi at Xianyang.

	Jin, c.500 BC
	Warring States border, c.300 BC
	Qin state, c.350 BC
	Qin gains by 300 BC
	Qin gains, 300–250 BC
	Qin gains, 230–221 BC
	Qin gains by 206 BC
	empire of the former Han dynasty, c.AD 6
	Han protectorates, c.59 BC–AD 23, AD 73–127
	territorial gains of Later Han dynasty
	independent kingdom of Nan-yue, 206–113 BC
	Warring States capital
	capital of Zhou empire
	capital of Qin dynasty
	capital of former Han dynasty and Later Han dynasty
	Qin fort
	frontier wall
	Chinese campaign
	Xiongnu campaign
	modern coastline and drainage where altered

TIMELINE

	400 BC	200 BC	AD 1	AD 200
	Warring States period	Former Han	Later Han	Three kingdoms period
Political change	**c.500** Jin becomes the leading Chinese state	**230–221** King Zheng of Qin unifies China	**117–115 BC** Han conquer Gansu corridor	**126** Peasant revolts against landowners
	c.400 Breakup of the Jin state	**221–210** Zheng unites China under the Qin dynasty and takes the title Shi Huangdi	**57 BC** Traditional date for foundation of the first Korean state, Silla	**189** Provincial warlords seize the Han capital, Luoyang
	361–338 Shang Yang turns Qin into a militaristic state	**209–202** Civil war: the Qin dynasty is overthrown and Han dynasty established	**AD 9** Courtier Wang Mang overthrows Han dynasty	**190** General Tung Cho installs a puppet emperor on Han throne
	c. 350–315 Qin becomes the leading state in China		**AD 23** Restoration of Han dynasty	
	256 Qin deposes the last Zhou king	**128–36 BC** The Han launch a series of campaigns to pacify the Xiongnu		**220** Deposition of last Han emperor: China splits into three kingdoms
Cultural change	**c. 500** Sun Tzu writes *The Art of War*	**175–150** Iron weapons and tools come into widespread use in China		**c.100** Introduction of Buddhism to China
	371–289 Mencius (Mengzi), Confucian philosopher			
	c.350 Crossbow invented	**c. 100** Sima Qian writes the history of China from the beginning to his own times		
	400 BC	200 BC	AD 1	AD 200

Places on map: Turfan, Cherchen, Dunhuang, Changye, Wu-su, Lake Qinghai, Tibetans, Gansu Corridor, Qilian Mts, 105 BC, 108 BC, 6, 8

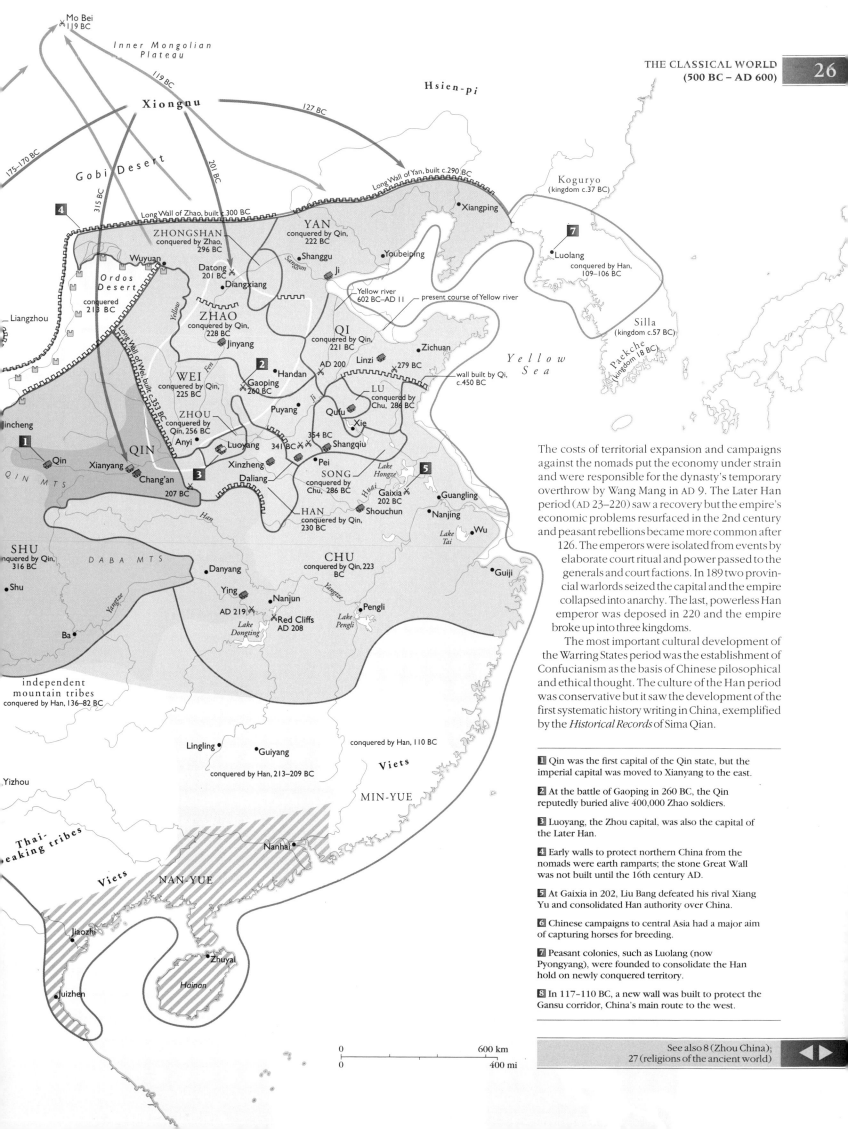

Mo Bei
✕ 119 BC

Inner Mongolian
Plateau

Hsien-pi

119 BC

127 BC

Xiongnu

Koguryo
(kingdom c.37 BC)

201 BC

Gobi Desert

175–170 BC

315 BC

Long Wall of Yan, built c.290 BC

Xiangping

7

Luolang
conquered by Han,
109–106 BC

4

Long Wall of Zhao, built c.300 BC

• Wuyuan

ZHONGSHAN
conquered by Zhao,
296 BC

Datong
✕ 201 BC

• Shanggu

YAN
conquered by Qin,
222 BC

Silla
(kingdom c.57 BC)

Ordos
Desert

Diangxiang

• Ji

Sanggan

Yellow river
602 BC–AD 11

present course of Yellow river

Liangzhou

conquered
213 BC

Yellow

ZHAO
conquered by Qin,
228 BC

• Jinyang

QI
conquered by Qin,
221 BC

Paekche
(kingdom 18 BC)

Long Wall of Wei, built c.353 BC

• Youbeiping

• Zichuan

Yellow
Sea

Fen

2

AD 200

Linzi

✕ 279 BC

wall built by Qi,
c.450 BC

Jincheng

WEI
conquered by Qin,
225 BC

• Handan

Gaoping
✕ 260 BC

• Puyang

Ji

LU
conquered by
Chu, 286 BC

1

Qin

ZHOU
conquered by
Qin, 256 BC

Qufu •

• Xie

QIN MTS

Xianyang

• Anyi

Luoyang

354 BC
341 BC ✕

• Shangqiu

5

Chang'an

QIN

3

Xinzheng

• Pei

207 BC

Daliang

Lake
Hongze

Gaixia
✕ 202 BC

• Guangling

Han

HAN
conquered by Qin,
230 BC

SONG
conquered by
Chu, 286 BC

Huai

Shouchun •

• Nanjing

• Wu

SHU
conquered by Qin,
316 BC

DABA MTS

• Danyang

Yangtze

CHU
conquered by Qin, 223
BC

Lake
Tai

• Guiji

• Shu

Ying
✕ AD 219

• Nanjun

✕ Red Cliffs
AD 208

Lake
Dongting

Lake
Pengli

• Pengli

• Ba

Yangtze

independent
mountain tribes
conquered by Han, 136–82 BC

• Lingling

• Guiyang

conquered by Han, 110 BC

Viets

Yizhou

MIN-YUE

conquered by Han, 213–209 BC

Thai-
speaking tribes

• Nanhai

Viets

NAN-YUE

• Jiaozhi

• Zhuyai

Hainan

• Juizhen

0   600 km

0   400 mi

The costs of territorial expansion and campaigns
against the nomads put the economy under strain
and were responsible for the dynasty's temporary
overthrow by Wang Mang in AD 9. The Later Han
period (AD 23–220) saw a recovery but the empire's
economic problems resurfaced in the 2nd century
and peasant rebellions became more common after
126. The emperors were isolated from events by
elaborate court ritual and power passed to the
generals and court factions. In 189 two provincial warlords seized the capital and the empire
collapsed into anarchy. The last, powerless Han
emperor was deposed in 220 and the empire
broke up into three kingdoms.
    The most important cultural development of
the Warring States period was the establishment of
Confucianism as the basis of Chinese pilosophical
and ethical thought. The culture of the Han period
was conservative but it saw the development of the
first systematic history writing in China, exemplified
by the Historical Records of Sima Qian.

1 Qin was the first capital of the Qin state, but the
imperial capital was moved to Xianyang to the east.

2 At the battle of Gaoping in 260 BC, the Qin
reputedly buried alive 400,000 Zhao soldiers.

3 Luoyang, the Zhou capital, was also the capital of
the Later Han.

4 Early walls to protect northern China from the
nomads were earth ramparts; the stone Great Wall
was not built until the 16th century AD.

5 At Gaixia in 202, Liu Bang defeated his rival Xiang
Yu and consolidated Han authority over China.

6 Chinese campaigns to central Asia had a major aim
of capturing horses for breeding.

7 Peasant colonies, such as Luolang (now
Pyongyang), were founded to consolidate the Han
hold on newly conquered territory.

8 In 117–110 BC, a new wall was built to protect the
Gansu corridor, China's main route to the west.

See also 8 (Zhou China);
27 (religions of the ancient world)

The years 1000 BC–AD 600 saw the emergence of every major world religion except Islam (a world religion is one that has endured and influenced diverse civilizations). Hinduism and Judaism had earlier roots but assumed their present form at this time; Christianity, Buddhism, Zoroastrianism, Daoism and Confucianism all arose 600 BC–AD 600.

Early Hinduism was based on the Vedas, hymns of the Aryans who invaded India around 1500 BC, but was also influenced by indigenous Dravidian traditions. Vedic Hinduism looked forward to a future existence in heaven; it was not until the 6th century BC that the belief in *karma* and rebirth, central to modern Hinduism, developed. The complex rituals of early Hinduism gave rise to a distinctive feature of Indian civilization, the caste system – the priestly Brahmins forming the highest caste. By 500 BC Hinduism dominated the Indian subcontinent, but discontent with Brahminical traditions grew on the Gangetic plain, where urbanization created a more materialistic society. New sects developed there, the most successful of them being Buddhism.

The founder of Buddhism was Siddhartha Gautama, known as the Buddha, or "Enlightened One." Many legends have become associated with the Buddha and little is known for certain of his life: even his original teachings are a matter of debate as the canon of Buddhist scripture was not written down until four centuries after his death. Buddhism remained a minor sect until the Mauryan emperor Ashoka converted in 260 BC. Under his patronage Buddhist missionaries spread the religion throughout India and to Ceylon and the Iranian nomads in central Asia. In northern India Buddhism supplanted Hinduism as the majority religion. It then spread from central Asia along the Silk Route, reaching China in the 1st century AD; Indian seafarers took it to southeast Asia in the 4th century. By the 3rd century AD Buddhism had divided into two schools: Theravada (Doctrine of the Elders), which adhered strictly to the established Buddhist canon, and Mahayana (Great Vehicle), a more liberal, eclectic

THE MENORAH symbolizes the survival of the Jewish people through the vicissitudes of history, including the Diaspora of the 1st century AD.

tradition. Hinduism responded to the rise of Buddhism by becoming more flexible and tolerant, and by AD 400 it was beginning to recover in India. In the 5th century Hinduism spread to southeast Asia.

The central influence on Chinese thought was the ethical teaching of Confucius. Its emphasis on respect for legitimate authority and moral education made this the official orthodoxy under the Han dynasty (206 BC–AD 220). In the disorder following the fall of the Han, Confucianism declined and Buddhism became a stronger influence in China. Buddhism was itself influenced by Chinese philosophies, particularly Daoism, a system inspired by the teachings of Lao Zi, a philosopher of the 6th century BC. The traditional Chinese practice of ancestor worship remained strong throughout these changes.

Although it was the religion of a minor and relatively unimportant people, the Hebrews, Judaism was the most influential religion of the Middle East. It was the first major monotheistic religion and its

TIMELINE

Middle East and Europe

600 BC	AD 1	AD 600
c.630–553 The life of Zoroaster, founder of Zoroastrianism	**c.6 BC–AD 30** The life of Jesus of Nazareth	**313** The Roman empire under Constantine officially tolerates Christianity
587 The Jews are deported to Babylonia by Nebuchadnezzar. This marks the beginning of the Diaspora	**AD 1–100** Mithraism spreads to the Roman empire	**c. 405** St Jerome completes the Vulgate Latin translation of the Bible
	AD 42–62 St Paul undertakes his missionary journeys throughout Asia Minor, Greece and to Rome	**c. 570** The birth of the prophet Muhammad
	AD 70–100 The Christian Gospels are written	**596** The English conversion to Christianity begins
		220–40 Zoroastrianism is the Persian state religion

South and east Asia

600 BC	AD 1	AD 600
800–400 The *Upanishads* of Hinduism are composed	**260** The Mauryan emperor Ashoka becomes a Buddhist and sends Buddhist missions to Ceylon and central Asia	**253–333** The life of Ko Hung, founder of religious Daoism
6th century The life of Lao Zi, the inspirer of Daoism	**c.240 BC** The *Dao De Jing*, the basic text of Daoism, is composed	**259** Chinese Buddhists begin pilgrimages to India
c.563–483 Life of Siddhartha Gautama, the Buddha		**300–500** The Hindu epics the *Ramayana* and the *Mahabharata* are written down in their final form
551–479 The life of the Chinese sage Confucius	**AD 1–100** Mahayana Buddhism develops	
600 BC	AD 1	AD 600

1 Although Hinduism is an ancient religion, few physical traces survive before the medieval period.

2 Ellora is the site of rock-cut temples of Buddhist, Hindu and Jain origin, dating from the 6th-8th centuries AD.

3 Southern Britain became Christian by the 4th century but reverted to paganism following the settlements of the Anglo-Saxons in the 5th century.

4 Christian monasticism originated on the edges of the Sahara desert, which developed from communities of hermits in the early 4th century.

5 Mithraism was popular in the Roman army: several Mithraic sites have been discovered on the strongly garrisoned Rhine frontier.

6 Armenia became the first state to adopt Christianity as its official religion, in about 300.

7 A major early Buddhist center developed around *stupas* (mounds) built by Ashoka to house relics of the Buddha and his followers.

8 Sacred Fire, believed to be a manifestation of Ahura Mazda, was the focus of ritual in Zoroastrian temples.

9 The influence of Daoism led Chinese Buddhists to found monasteries on mountains such as at Lingjiu (Vulture Peak).

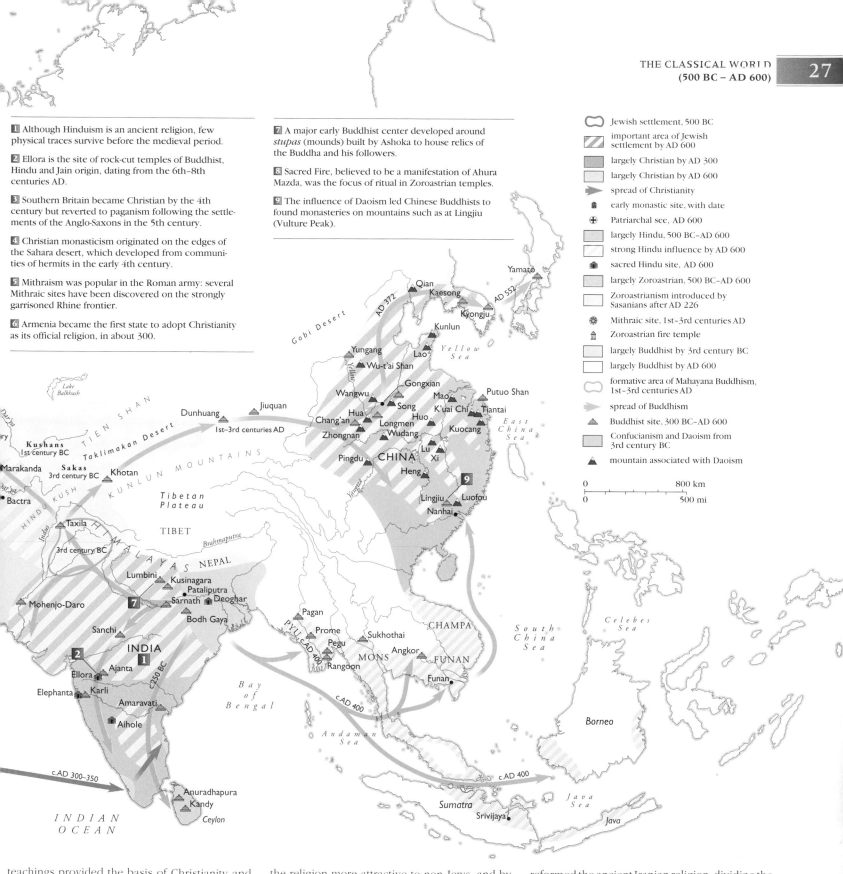

Legend:
- Jewish settlement, 500 BC
- important area of Jewish settlement by AD 600
- largely Christian by AD 300
- largely Christian by AD 600
- spread of Christianity
- early monastic site, with date
- Patriarchal see, AD 600
- largely Hindu, 500 BC-AD 600
- strong Hindu influence by AD 600
- sacred Hindu site, AD 600
- largely Zoroastrian, 500 BC-AD 600
- Zoroastrianism introduced by Sasanians after AD 226
- Mithraic site, 1st-3rd centuries AD
- Zoroastrian fire temple
- largely Buddhist by 3rd century BC
- largely Buddhist by AD 600
- formative area of Mahayana Buddhism, 1st-3rd centuries AD
- spread of Buddhism
- Buddhist site, 300 BC-AD 600
- Confucianism and Daoism from 3rd century BC
- mountain associated with Daoism

0 — 800 km
0 — 500 mi

teachings provided the basis of Christianity and Islam. Judaism was a national religion and did not actively seek converts among non-Jews; yet the Hebrews' turbulent history meant that it became very widespread in the Mediterranean and Middle East by AD 600. The Diaspora, or dispersal of the Jews, began in the 6th century BC when communities of exiles from Palestine were established in Egypt and Mesopotamia. The greatest dispersal of Jews occurred in the 1st and 2nd centuries AD, following rebellions in Palestine against Roman rule.

Christianity originated in the teachings of a Jew, Jesus of Nazareth, who rejected the current practice of Judaism. Christianity developed initially as a Jewish sect, but the influence of St Paul and others made

the religion more attractive to non-Jews, and by AD 70 its separation from Judaism was complete. Because of their refusal to pay formal homage to the state gods, Christians often faced persecution by the Roman emperors. Despite this Christianity was well established, especially in the eastern empire, by 312 when the emperor Constantine converted, introducing formal toleration the following year. Christianity made rapid progress after this, and in 391 it became the Roman empire's official religion. Christians came to believe that God had created the Roman empire specifically for the purpose of spreading Christianity.

An early rival to Christianity in the Roman empire was Mithraism, a derivative of the Persian Zoroastrian religion. Zoroaster, the religion's founder,

reformed the ancient Iranian religion, dividing the pantheon into good and evil deities. It developed into a dualist religion which taught that the chief god Ahura Mazda, aided by Mithra, was locked in combat to protect the world from his evil rival Ahriman. Zoroastrianism became the religion of the Achemenid rulers of Persia and flourished under the Parthians and Sasanians. Although in its pure form it won few converts outside Persia, its teaching on the nature of good and evil had an important influence on Hellenistic, Jewish, Christian and Islamic thought.

See also 30 (the Christian empire); 31 (early India); 44 (medieval world religions)

A decisive Roman victory at the battle of Cynoscephalae in 197 BC had broken the power of Macedon, who had supported Carthage in the Second Punic War. This victory opened the way for Roman domination of Greece. In 146 Rome brought the whole of Greece under direct control; and in the same year ruthlessly destroyed Carthage, though it had long ceased to be a threat (▷23). The Hellenistic kingdoms of the east were also powerless to prevent Roman expansion. By 64 BC most of Anatolia and the Levant were under Roman rule and Egypt had been made a protectorate. Direct rule was imposed on Egypt in 30 BC (▷29).

Rome's successes put its republican system of government – designed for a city-state, not a world empire – under increasing strain: and a succession of civil wars between 50 and 31 BC brought about the collapse of the Roman republic. The eventual victor, Octavian, created a new form of government – in effect, an absolute monarchy. King in all but name, he took the titles *princeps* (first citizen) and Augustus. His successors used the title *imperator* (commander or emperor).

In northern Europe, the Celts found themselves caught between the Romans, who were expanding northward, and the Germans, who were pushing south: by 1 BC the only remaining independent Celts were in the British Isles (▷25).

In Africa, the Sabean colonies had developed into the kingdom of Axum around 100 BC. At about the same time the dromedary camel was introduced to the northern Sahara, transforming the lives of the desert nomads much as horse riding had earlier changed the steppe pastoralist way of life, enabling them to range widely and raid settled peoples almost at will. By 1 BC pastoralism had spread among the Khoisan-speaking peoples as far south as the Transvaal region and Bantu-speaking peoples had begun to settle on the east African plateau (▷35).

Following his victory in the civil war in China (202), Liu Bang restored prosperity by introducing a series of agricultural and administrative reforms but, despite heroic efforts, failed to stop damaging raids by the nomadic Xiongnu who continued to be a serious threat to China until 38 BC. The Han period saw Chinese expansion in the south (▷26), where the non-Chinese kingdoms of Min-yue and Nan-yue were conquered, and in Korea. Small kingdoms had begun to develop in parts of Korea not under Chinese occupation by 50 BC.

The rise of the Xiongnu had a destabilizing effect on the Iranian nomads to the west. In 170 the Xiongnu inflicted a crushing defeat on the Yue Qi, who fled westward, unsettling the Sakas, before overrunning the Bactrian kingdom around 135. The Sakas headed south, first invading the Parthian empire and,

c.135 The westward-driven Yue Qi overrun the Bactrian kingdom

170–141 The Parthians conquer the Seleucid kingdom

146 Roman control is extended throughout Greece

c.100 Foundation of the Moche state in the region of Peru

The Americas			
Europe			
Middle East	200	150	100
Africa			
East and South Asia			

c.185 Fall of the Mauryan dynasty after Bactrians invade the Punjab

149–146 The Third Punic War: Rome levels the city of Carthage to the ground

101 China under the Han dynasty conquers Van Lang

170 The Hsiung-nu defeat the Yue Qi and dominate the eastern steppes

c.141 The Sakas invade the Parthian empire and northern India

c.100 The beginning of camel nomadism in the Sahara desert

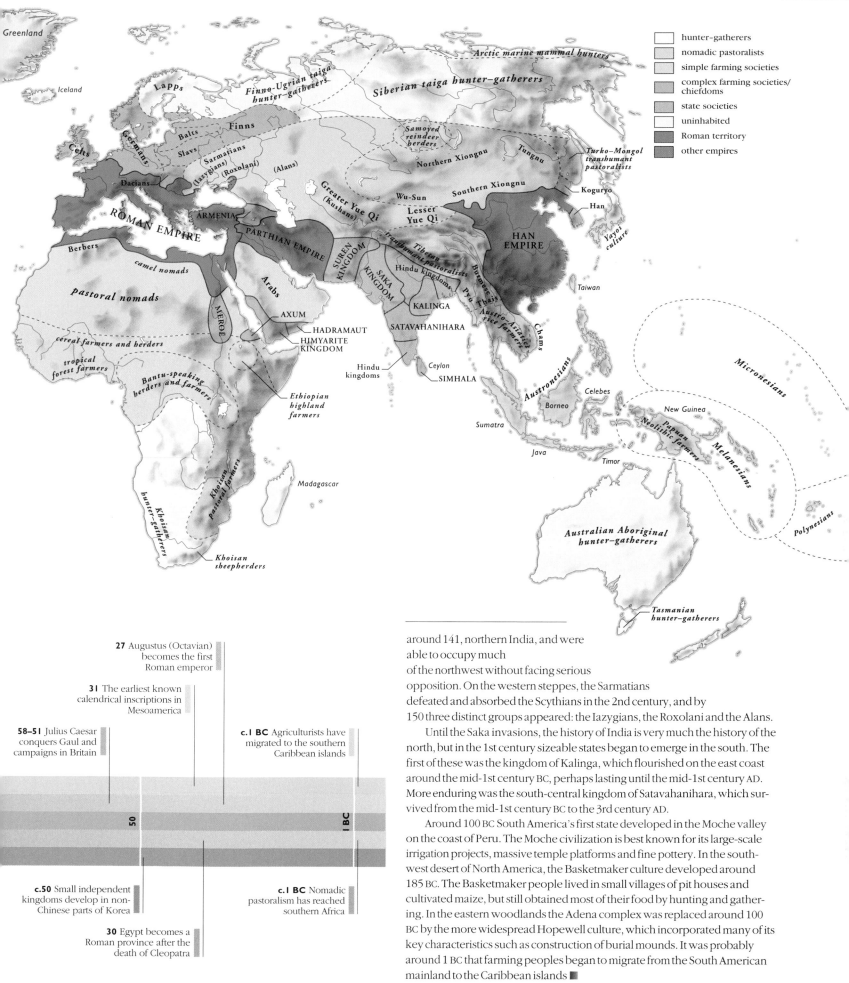

	hunter-gatherers
	nomadic pastoralists
	simple farming societies
	complex farming societies/chiefdoms
	state societies
	uninhabited
	Roman territory
	other empires

Greenland

Iceland

Lapps

Finno-Ugrian taiga hunter-gatherers

Siberian taiga hunter-gatherers

Arctic marine mammal hunters

Finns

Balts

Germans

Slavs

Celts

Sarmatians

(Iazygians)

(Roxolani)

(Alans)

Dacians

ROMAN EMPIRE

ARMENIA

PARTHIAN EMPIRE

Samoyed reindeer herders

Northern Xiongnu

Tungnu

Turko-Mongol transhumant pastoralists

Wu-Sun

Greater Yue Qi (Kushans)

Lesser Yue Qi

Southern Xiongnu

Koguryo

Han

HAN EMPIRE

Berbers

camel nomads

Pastoral nomads

Arabs

SUREN KINGDOM

SAKA KINGDOM

Tibetan transhumant pastoralists

Hindu kingdoms

Burmese

Pyu

Thais

Austro-Asiatic rice farmers

Yayoi culture

Taiwan

MEROE

AXUM

HADRAMAUT

HIMYARITE KINGDOM

KALINGA

SATAVAHANIHARA

Chams

cereal farmers and herders

tropical forest farmers

Bantu-speaking herders and farmers

Ethiopian highland farmers

Hindu kingdoms

Ceylon

SIMHALA

Austronesians

Micronesians

Sumatra

Borneo

Celebes

New Guinea

Papuan Neolithic farmers

Melanesians

Khoisan pastoral farmers

Madagascar

Java

Timor

Khoisan hunter-gatherers

Australian Aboriginal hunter-gatherers

Polynesians

Khoisan sheepherders

Tasmanian hunter-gatherers

27 Augustus (Octavian) becomes the first Roman emperor

31 The earliest known calendrical inscriptions in Mesoamerica

58–51 Julius Caesar conquers Gaul and campaigns in Britain

c.1 BC Agriculturists have migrated to the southern Caribbean islands

50

1 BC

c.50 Small independent kingdoms develop in non-Chinese parts of Korea

c.1 BC Nomadic pastoralism has reached southern Africa

30 Egypt becomes a Roman province after the death of Cleopatra

around 141, northern India, and were able to occupy much of the northwest without facing serious opposition. On the western steppes, the Sarmatians defeated and absorbed the Scythians in the 2nd century, and by 150 three distinct groups appeared: the Iazygians, the Roxolani and the Alans.

Until the Saka invasions, the history of India is very much the history of the north, but in the 1st century sizeable states began to emerge in the south. The first of these was the kingdom of Kalinga, which flourished on the east coast around the mid-1st century BC, perhaps lasting until the mid-1st century AD. More enduring was the south-central kingdom of Satavanihara, which survived from the mid-1st century BC to the 3rd century AD.

Around 100 BC South America's first state developed in the Moche valley on the coast of Peru. The Moche civilization is best known for its large-scale irrigation projects, massive temple platforms and fine pottery. In the southwest desert of North America, the Basketmaker culture developed around 185 BC. The Basketmaker people lived in small villages of pit houses and cultivated maize, but still obtained most of their food by hunting and gathering. In the eastern woodlands the Adena complex was replaced around 100 BC by the more widespread Hopewell culture, which incorporated many of its key characteristics such as construction of burial mounds. It was probably around 1 BC that farming peoples began to migrate from the South American mainland to the Caribbean islands ∎

Soon after the Second Punic War, Rome was drawn into further wars to protect its position in Italy, Spain and Greece. Cisalpine Gaul was reconquered by 191. The need to protect the new Spanish provinces from native attack drew Rome into a piecemeal conquest of the whole peninsula. Rome also launched a punitive campaign in 200 against Macedon, which had allied itself with Carthage in the Second Punic War. In 197, after the battle of Cynoscephalae, Macedon was forced to liberate the Greek city-states. At this time Rome took no territory for itself. However, the weight of constant disputes among the Greek cities and the Hellenistic kingdoms had become so onerous by 146 that the Romans imposed direct rule on Greece: opposition was ruthlessly suppressed. Also in 146 a Roman army, which had been besieging Carthage for three years, finally razed the city to the ground, its territory becoming the Roman province of Africa. Expansion into the Middle East began in 133, when the last king of Pergamon bequeathed his kingdom to Rome, and Pergamon became the province of Asia. Southern Gaul was conquered and became the province of Gallia Narbonensis in 121.

As the empire grew, the booty of successful campaigns – treasure and slaves – flooded back to Rome. The largest class of the early republic had been peasant freeholders, but they could not compete with the new slave-run estates of the rich and were forced off the land to swell the ranks of the urban poor. Demands for constitutional reform led to bitter class conflict in Rome, as defenders of aristocratic privilege resorted to acts of violence, such as the murder of the reformist tribune Tiberius Gracchus in 133. Gaius Marius then reformed the Roman army, opening recruitment for the first time to landless citizens. These soldiers looked to their commanders to reward their service with grants of land to settle on when discharged. This had a dramatic effect on Roman politics as successful generals could usually count on their armies to support their political ambitions. Success in war was now the surest route to political power: it was the main motive for Pompey's

campaigns in Anatolia and Syria (67–64 BC), Julius Caesar's conquest of Gaul (58–51 BC) and Crassus's ill-fated attack on Parthia, which ended in his death at Carrhae, in 53 BC. The generals' need to reward their veterans led to the foundation of colonies throughout the empire in the late republic: these became important agents of Romanization.

The competition for power between generals led to civil war in 49 BC and ultimately to the fall of the republic. The victor was Caesar, who defeated his opponent Pompey at Ilerda in Spain (49 BC) and Pharsalus in Greece (48 BC). By 44 BC Caesar had crushed all military opposition, but a month after he declared himself dictator for life he was murdered by republican conspirators. Instability and civil war continued until Caesar's nephew Octavian, later known as Augustus, defeated Mark Antony and Cleopatra at Actium in 31 BC. In 27 BC Augustus introduced a new constitutional settlement, which he claimed "restored the republic" but in reality

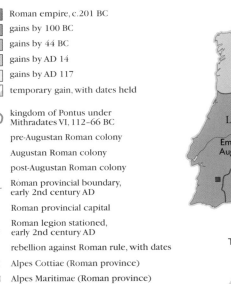

- Roman empire, c.201 BC
- gains by 100 BC
- gains by 44 BC
- gains by AD 14
- gains by AD 117
- temporary gain, with dates held
- kingdom of Pontus under Mithradates VI, 112–66 BC
- pre-Augustan Roman colony
- Augustan Roman colony
- post-Augustan Roman colony
- Roman provincial boundary, early 2nd century AD
- Roman provincial capital
- Roman legion stationed, early 2nd century AD
- rebellion against Roman rule, with dates
- AC Alpes Cottiae (Roman province)
- AM Alpes Maritimae (Roman province)
- AP Alpes Poeninae (Roman province)

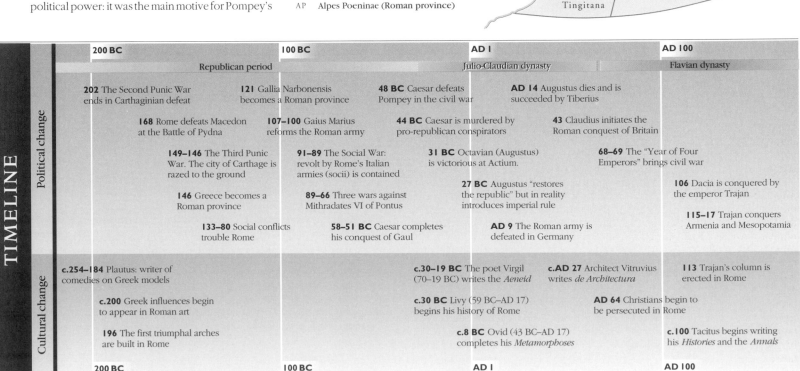

	200 BC	100 BC	AD 1	AD 100
	Republican period		Julio-Claudian dynasty	Flavian dynasty
Political change	**202** The Second Punic War ends in Carthaginian defeat	**121** Gallia Narbonensis becomes a Roman province	**48 BC** Caesar defeats Pompey in the civil war	**AD 14** Augustus dies and is succeeded by Tiberius
	168 Rome defeats Macedon at the Battle of Pydna	**107–100** Gaius Marius reforms the Roman army	**44 BC** Caesar is murdered by pro-republican conspirators	**43** Claudius initiates the Roman conquest of Britain
	149–146 The Third Punic War. The city of Carthage is razed to the ground	**91–89** The Social War: revolt by Rome's Italian armies (socii) is contained	**31 BC** Octavian (Augustus) is victorious at Actium.	**68–69** The "Year of Four Emperors" brings civil war
	146 Greece becomes a Roman province	**89–66** Three wars against Mithradates VI of Pontus	**27 BC** Augustus "restores the republic" but in reality introduces imperial rule	**106** Dacia is conquered by the emperor Trajan
	133–80 Social conflicts trouble Rome	**58–51 BC** Caesar completes his conquest of Gaul	**AD 9** The Roman army is defeated in Germany	**115–17** Trajan conquers Armenia and Mesopotamia
Cultural change	**c.254–184** Plautus: writer of comedies on Greek models		**c.30–19 BC** The poet Virgil (70–19 BC) writes the *Aeneid*	**c.AD 27** Architect Vitruvius writes *de Architectura*	**113** Trajan's column is erected in Rome
	c.200 Greek influences begin to appear in Roman art		**c.30 BC** Livy (59 BC–AD 17) begins his history of Rome	**AD 64** Christians begin to be persecuted in Rome
	196 The first triumphal arches are built in Rome		**c.8 BC** Ovid (43 BC–AD 17) completes his *Metamorphoses*	**c.100** Tacitus begins writing his *Histories* and the *Annals*
	200 BC	100 BC	AD 1	AD 100

TIMELINE

GAULS were respected opponents of the Romans in the west and in Anatolia; this statue of a dying Gaul was made in Pergamon, 2nd century BC.

introduced a monarchical type of government. He took the title *princeps* (first citizen), leaving it to his successors to call themselves *imperator* (emperor).

Expansion continued under the emperors. In Augustus' reign Egypt and Galatia were annexed, the last native resistance was extinguished in Spain, the Alpine tribes were conquered, and the empire's northern frontier was pushed to the Danube. Augustus also tried to conquer Germany but gave up the attempt after a humiliating defeat at the battle of the Teutoburgerwald in AD 9. This defeat convinced Augustus that the empire had reached its natural limits and he advised his successors not to seek any more territories. Despite this advice, the empire continued to expand for another century after the death of Augustus. Much of the expansion was simply a tidying-up operation. The annexation of Lycia (AD 43) and the client kingdom of Mauretania (AD 44)

gave Rome control of the entire Mediterranean coastline. In AD 43, Claudius, a weak emperor who needed a triumph to strengthen his position, began the conquest of Britain but only the southern two-thirds of the island were actually brought under Roman rule. The last emperor to pursue an all-out expansionist policy was Trajan. Between 101 and 106 Trajan conquered the Dacian kingdom, which posed a threat to the security of the Danube frontier. His ambition was to conquer the Parthian empire, and he brought Armenia and Mesopotamia under Roman rule. However, his successor Hadrian (r.117–38), judging these eastern conquests to be undefendable, withdrew from all of them except Edessa. Later in the 2nd century the border was pushed northward in Britain, and northern Mesopotamia was wrested from the Parthians, but from this time on the empire was mainly on the defensive.

1 Willed to the empire by the king of Pergamon, Asia became Rome's first Anatolian province in 133 BC.

2 Rebellions – the "Social War" – forced Rome to concede equal political rights to non-Roman Italians.

3 Mithradates VI of Pontus fought Rome in three wars from 89 until his final defeat in 66 BC.

4 Augustus' victory at Actium in 31 BC ended the civil war and brought Egypt under Roman rule.

5 Carthage, refounded as a Roman colony, became the center of Roman administration in Africa in 29 BC.

6 The Roman conquest of Britain began in AD 43, nearly a century after Caesar's raids in 55 and 54 BC.

See also 27 (religion);
30 (later Roman empire)

After Hadrian withdrew from Trajan's eastern conquests in 117, the borders of the Roman empire remained stable for almost 150 years. The only significant change was in the east, where successful campaigning by Septimius Severus between 195 and 198 wrested northern Mesopotamia from the Parthians. The 2nd century was a time of unrivaled peace and prosperity for the empire but this was not to last. The wealth of the empire was attractive to the Germanic tribes along the Rhine and Danube frontiers, and these began to unite in powerful confederations and raid Roman territory. In 167 Marcomannic raiders crossed into Italy, and though the emperor, Marcus Aurelius, successfully secured the borders, pressure on the northern frontier was thereafter continuous. Another problem was the imperial succession: there was no accepted way of deposing an incompetent or tyrannical emperor, nor of selecting a new emperor if a dynasty died out or was overthrown. When the incompetent, tyrannical Nero was overthrown in AD 68 the frontier armies promoted their own candidates for the succession, who then fought it out in a civil war. The same happened after the murder of the mad Commodus.

Pressure on the northern frontiers became critical in the 3rd century, and a new threat appeared in 226 when the Parthians were overthrown by the aggressive Persian Sasanian dynasty. In these conditions, the emperor had to be above all a good soldier. While rival candidates for power, promoted by different legions, fought each other for control of the empire, the borders were left undefended and open to invasion. For example, when Valerian (r. 253–60) withdrew troops from the Rhine to fight a usurper, the Franks immediately invaded Gaul. The efforts of emperors to buy the loyalty of their troops led them to debase the coinage to raise money, but this added runaway inflation to the empire's woes. Urban life now declined, especially in the west, where many towns shrank to a fortified administrative core. Civil war and invasion were incessant between 235 and 284: of the twenty-six emperors who ruled in this period all but one died by violence.

Not all the usurpers aimed at control of the whole empire. After Valerian was captured by the Persians at Edessa in 260, defense of the east devolved on Odenathus, ruler of the desert city of Palmyra. He defeated the Persians but then built an independent kingdom for himself. Under his wife and successor Queen Zenobia, it came to include Egypt, Syria and much of Anatolia. In the west the usurper Postumus founded an independent Gallic empire, winning over the people of Gaul, Britain and Spain; he promised to concentrate on defending the frontiers and not to march on Rome.

The Roman empire began to revive in the reign of Aurelian, with the reconquest of Palmyra (272) and the Gallic empire (274), though Dacia was permanently abandoned to the Germans. Political and economic stability were restored by Diocletian (r. 284–305), who reformed the whole structure of the empire. Diocletian greatly expanded the army and reformed the tax system to pay for it. Price regulation was introduced to curb inflation, though it drove goods off the markets. To restore respect to the imperial office, elaborate court ritual was introduced and the idea of the emperor as "first citizen" was abandoned: he was now "lord and god." Civilian and military

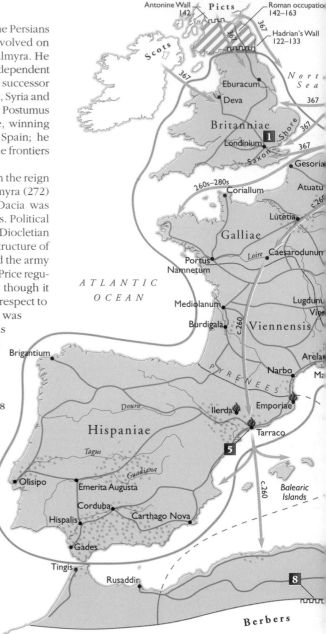

▢	Roman empire, c.235
▨	Roman territory lost permanently, 163–378
⬭	kingdom of Palmyra, 260–72
⬭	Gallic empire, 260–74
⬚	strong Christian communities by 300
Goths	major Germanic peoples, 3rd century
Picts	other barbarians, 3rd century
→	attacks on Roman empire, with dates
🜂	city sacked
✹	Roman victory
✹	Roman defeat
✹	battle between Roman forces
⌇⌇⌇	frontier wall or rampart
——	main road
Italia	Diocletianic diocese
— —	borders of Diocletianic dioceses

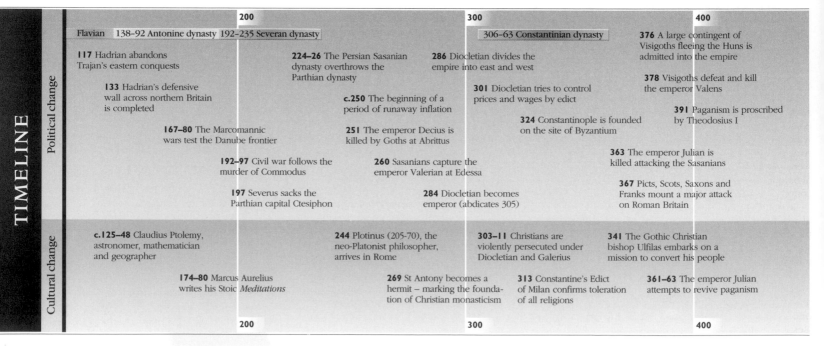

Political change

Flavian | 138–92 Antonine dynasty | 192–235 Severan dynasty | | 306–63 Constantinian dynasty

117 Hadrian abandons Trajan's eastern conquests

133 Hadrian's defensive wall across northern Britain is completed

167–80 The Marcomannic wars test the Danube frontier

192–97 Civil war follows the murder of Commodus

197 Severus sacks the Parthian capital Ctesiphon

224–26 The Persian Sasanian dynasty overthrows the Parthian dynasty

c.250 The beginning of a period of runaway inflation

251 The emperor Decius is killed by Goths at Abrittus

260 Sasanians capture the emperor Valerian at Edessa

284 Diocletian becomes emperor (abdicates 305)

286 Diocletian divides the empire into east and west

301 Diocletian tries to control prices and wages by edict

324 Constantinople is founded on the site of Byzantium

376 A large contingent of Visigoths fleeing the Huns is admitted into the empire

378 Visigoths defeat and kill the emperor Valens

391 Paganism is proscribed by Theodosius I

363 The emperor Julian is killed attacking the Sasanians

367 Picts, Scots, Saxons and Franks mount a major attack on Roman Britain

Cultural change

c.125–48 Claudius Ptolemy, astronomer, mathematician and geographer

174–80 Marcus Aurelius writes his Stoic *Meditations*

244 Plotinus (205–70), the neo-Platonist philosopher, arrives in Rome

269 St Antony becomes a hermit – marking the foundation of Christian monasticism

303–11 Christians are violently persecuted under Diocletian and Galerius

313 Constantine's Edict of Milan confirms toleration of all religions

341 The Gothic Christian bishop Ulfilas embarks on a mission to convert his people

361–63 The emperor Julian attempts to revive paganism

200 · 300 · 400

1 In the late 2nd century a chain of forts built on the east and south coasts of Britain was organized into an anti-piracy command, later known as the Saxon Shore.

2 After the Marcomanni attacked Aquileia in 167, the northern frontier was constantly threatened.

3 The importance of Rome declined in the 3rd and 4th centuries as it was abandoned by the emperor in favor of bases closer to the troubled frontiers.

4 Dacia could not be defended, and in 272 Aurelian abandoned it to the Goths and the Gepids.

5 Frankish invaders seized ships at Tarraco in 260 to launch pirate raids on north Africa.

6 Constantine the Great chose the small town of Byzantium as the site of a new capital for the empire.

7 After the emperor Julian was killed at Phrygia in 363 his army bought its freedom by ceding eastern Mesopotamia.

8 A network of ramparts, ditches, military roads and forts was built in the 3rd century to defend Rome's African frontier.

CHRISTIANITY spread widely before toleration was introduced in 313. This 2nd-century carving shows the *khi-rho* symbol for Christ.

authority were separated: provinces were subdivided and organized in dioceses under "vicars" who were directly responsible to the emperor. Diocletian realized that the problems of defending the empire were too great for one ruler and in 286 he appointed Maximian as co-emperor to rule the west while he concentrated on the east.

In the 4th century the empire underwent a cultural transformation as traditional paganism was supplanted by Christianity. The pagan Roman empire was a tolerant state and was prepared to accept any religion that did not involve human sacrifice, so long as its devotees were prepared to pay lip-service to the state gods. Christians were not prepared to do this and had faced frequent persecutions as a result, one of the worst being ordered by Diocletian. Despite this, Christianity had spread steadily through the urban lower and middle classes, and by 300 it was well established throughout the empire. In 312 the emperor Constantine (r. 306–37) became convinced that the Christian God had helped him win a victory over a rival at the Milvian Bridge, and in 313 he granted Christian toleration. Constantine subsequently presided over church councils, founded churches and was baptized on his deathbed. There is no reason to doubt the sincerity of his conversion, but he may also have seen Christianity as a unifying force for the embattled empire. Constantine's successors continued to promote Christianity, and the new religion began to exert a strong influence on all aspects of Roman life, from personal morality to art and literature. Christianity finally became the empire's official religion in 391, when Theodosius I abolished pagan worship.

See also 27 (world religions); 29 (earlier Roman empire); 33 (fall of the empire)

Around AD 50 the Kushans made northwest India part of an empire stretching from the Ganges to the Aral Sea. They were a clan of the Yue Qi nomads who had overrun the Greek kingdom of Bactria around 135 BC. The Kushan state was set up in Bactria around AD 25 by Kujala Kadphises, who invaded India and conquered Gandhara and the Northern Sakas around AD 50. Kujala's successor, Vima Kadphises (r.c.75–100), conquered the Indus valley and much of the Gangetic plain. The empire reached its peak under Kanishka (r.c.100–130). He was a devout Buddhist and a patron of the arts, supporting both the Indo-Hellenistic school of Gandhara and the Hindu school of Mathura. Under Kanishka's successors, the Kushan empire maintained its borders until the 3rd century, when most of the empire's western provinces were conquered by the Sasanian King Shapur I. Although the Kushans briefly regained their independence in the 4th century, the united Kushan empire was not restored.

The Kushan empire was never highly centralized and the king ruled through a host of dependent sub-kings or *yaghbus*. Kushan rulers used an eclectic range of titles, including *maharaja* (great king), *rajatiraja* (king of kings), the Greek title *basileus* (king) and *kaisara* (from the Latin *caesar*). They also instituted a cult of ruler worship and used the title *devaputra* (son of God). Kushan culture was equally eclectic, mixing Hellenistic, Indian and central Asian styles. Kushan rulers were tolerant in matters of religion. Most of the early rulers were Buddhists and the later ones Hindus, but all showed respect for a wide range of Persian, Greek and even Roman deities. The empire was always wealthy, prospering by its control of all the major trans-Asian overland trade routes. High-quality gold coinage was made by melting down gold Roman coins flooding into the empire to pay for luxury goods such as Chinese silk.

The Kushans did not have a monopoly on east–west trade. By the 1st century AD, Mediterranean seafarers had discovered how to exploit the monsoon winds to sail across the Indian Ocean, bringing increased trade between the Roman empire and southern India. The region's most valuable exports were spices, which the Romans paid for in gold. South Indian rulers did not issue their own coinage and Roman coins circulated freely. The most powerful south Indian state at this period was Satavahanihara; but the influx of wealth led to the formation of several small tribal kingdoms and cities in the region.

The decline of Kushan power made possible the rise of the Gupta kingdom in the 4th century. Minor princes in the Varanasi area in the later 3rd century, the Guptas may have been feudatories of Magadha. The dynasty began with the reign of Chandragupta I (r.320–35), who made an advantageous marriage alliance with the Licchavis. This brought him control of Magadha, the fertile and densely populated heartland of the former Mauryan empire. Chandragupta was succeeded by his son Samudragupta (r.335–80), whose long reign saw the kingdom expand across northern India, reducing the Kushans to tributary status. Samudragupta also fought a major campaign in the southeast, reducing many rulers to tributaries. He formed strong alliances with the Sakas and the Vakatakas (in power in Satavahanihara), but his son and successor, Chandragupta II (r.380–414), turned on the Western Sakas, conquered their kingdom and imposed direct rule. The empire ruled by Chandragupta II was almost as large as the Mauryan empire, but was very loose-knit. Gupta inscriptions approximately cover the area in which the dynasty exercised direct rule – the rest of the empire was ruled by tributary kings and barely-subdued tribes.

The Guptas were patrons of the arts and sciences and the period was one of great creativity. They were devout Hindus and some of the main features of Hinduism, such as image-worship, appeared under their rule. The Hindu epics of the *Ramayana* and the *Mahabharata* reached their final form at this time. Sanskrit poetry and drama flourished, causing the Gupta period to be regarded as the classical age of Indian literature. Advances were made in astronomy and mathematics, including the invention of the decimal system of numerals, later adopted by the Arabs and, through them, by the Europeans.

After the death of Chandragupta II, the empire ceased expanding but remained powerful, and under Skandagupta (r.c.455–67) defeated a major Hunnish invasion. However, a war of succession followed Skandagupta's death and the empire went into decline as tributary kings and nominally conquered tribes reasserted their independence. The final blow came from an invasion of the Hunas (Ephthalite Huns) in 505–11, who founded a kingdom in northwest India, destroying the last remnants of the Kushans. In 528 a coalition of Indian princes defeated the Hunas, but the Guptas played only a minor role in this campaign. Gupta rulers continued in Magadha until around 720, but only as mere princes. Except for a brief period under Harsha (r.606–47) of Kanauj, who united the states on the Gangetic plain, no supraregional state reappeared in India until the 13th century.

◖◗	core area of Kushan state, c.AD 25
◖◗	Kushan empire, mid 2nd century AD
◖◗	Satavahanihara, mid 2nd century
◖◗	Gupta kingdom of Chandragupta I, c.AD 320
▨	Gupta empire of Samudragupta, c.AD 370
▨	additions to Gupta empire by Chandragupta II, c.AD 410
VANGA	minor kingdom
Comari	important seaport for Roman trade
⬭	hoard of Roman coins
▮	Gupta inscription
——	trade route
➝	southern campaign of Samudragupta, c.AD 360
➤	migration of Kushans/Yue Qi
➤	migration of Ephthalites (Hunas)
- - -	ancient river course
——	modern coastline where altered

```
0                              400 km
0                         300 mi
```

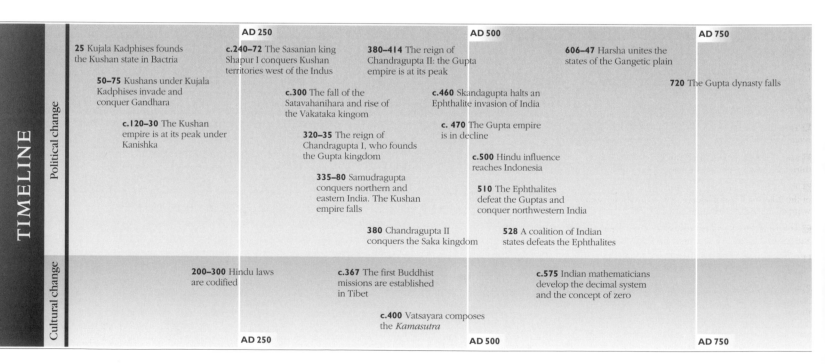

TIMELINE

Political change

AD 250

AD 500

AD 750

25 Kujala Kadphises founds the Kushan state in Bactria

50–75 Kushans under Kujala Kadphises invade and conquer Gandhara

c.120–30 The Kushan empire is at its peak under Kanishka

c.240–72 The Sasanian king Shapur I conquers Kushan territories west of the Indus

c.300 The fall of the Satavahanihara and rise of the Vakataka kingom

320–35 The reign of Chandragupta I, who founds the Gupta kingdom

335–80 Samudragupta conquers northern and eastern India. The Kushan empire falls

380 Chandragupta II conquers the Saka kingdom

380–414 The reign of Chandragupta II: the Gupta empire is at its peak

c.460 Skandagupta halts an Ephthalite invasion of India

c. 470 The Gupta empire is in decline

c.500 Hindu influence reaches Indonesia

510 The Ephthalites defeat the Guptas and conquer northwestern India

528 A coalition of Indian states defeats the Ephthalites

606–47 Harsha unites the states of the Gangetic plain

720 The Gupta dynasty falls

Cultural change

200–300 Hindu laws are codified

c.367 The first Buddhist missions are established in Tibet

c.400 Vatsayara composes the *Kamasutra*

c.575 Indian mathematicians develop the decimal system and the concept of zero

AD 250

AD 500

AD 750

Tashkent

Marakanda

c.135 BC

Kashgar

to China

to China

Merv

D 484

BACTRIA

Bactra

Surkh Kotal

HINDU

KUSH

2

AD 90

Khotan

KUNLUN

MTS

Kabul

c.AD 25

c.AD 50

GANDHARA

Khalatse

Peshawar

Taxila

Srinagar

AD 505

c.AD 460

8

AD 510

Sialkot

HIMALAYAS

Indus

c.AD 25

Northern Sakas

AD 510

Tibetans

Kandahar

Chenab

c.AD 75–100

Sutlej

SULAIMAN RANGE

KIRTHAR RANGE

PANCHALA

Ganges

Ahichhattra

CARVED wooden figures of
musicians exemplify the
congenial atmosphere for
Hindu learning and the arts
provided by the Gupta court.

Bairat

Mathura

Sravasti

KOSALA

Kusinagara

NEPALA

PUNDRA

Thar Desert

Kanauj

Ayodhya

Guptas

Licchavis

Yamuna

Prayaga

4

Pataliputra

9

Nalanda

Rajgir

Campa

Varanasi

Bodh Gaya

MAGADHA

Kausambi

VANGA

Pattala

7

AD 511

Pusyamitras

Tamralipti

Barbaricum

Vidisha

AD 510

Eran

Narmada

UTKALA

Ujjain

Western Sakas

Mahanadi

Bay of
Bengal

Valabhi

Barygaza

Tapti

Tosali

Junagadh

Girnar

DECCAN

KALINGA

Palura

3

Arabian Sea

Bhogavardhana

Vakatakas

Pratisthana

Godavari

6

Suppara

Simhapura

Kalliana

Pistapura

WESTERN GHATS

Tagara

Amaravati

EASTERN GHATS

Byzantium?

Krishna

Machilipatnam

Banavasi

5

Kaveri

Pallavas

1

southern border uncertain

Arikamedu

Ceras

Cholas

Kaveripatnam

Muziris

Madurai

Pandyas

Ceylon

Korkai

Anuradhapura

SIMHALA

Sigiriya

Comari

1 Arikamedu was a trading port in the 1st century
AD: many Roman artifacts have been excavated there.

2 A Chinese army defeated the Kushans in AD 90 at
Khotan, halting Kushan expansion in central Asia.

3 Junagadh is the site of the earliest known Sanskrit
inscription, erected c.150 by the Saka king Rudraman.

4 The main source of information on Samudragupta's
reign (c.335–75) is a pillar inscription at Prayaga.

5 Samudragupta's southern campaign (c 360) saw
thirteen kings and princes brought under Gupta rule.

6 The Vakatakas dominated central India after the fall
of the Satavahanihara kingdom in the 3rd century and
were close allies of the Guptas.

7 At Eran in 510 the Hunas defeated a Gupta army
and secured control of northwestern India.

8 Sialkot was the capital of the short-lived Huna
kingdom (c.505–30).

9 By c.600 a great Buddhist monastic university at
Nalanda, patronized by Gupta kings, housed thirty
thousand students.

See also 21 (Alexander's conquests);
27 (religions)

The area of the – now Christian – Roman empire in AD 400, though slightly greater than in 1 BC, disguises Rome's true position. Although the emperor Diocletian (r.284–305) had given the empire a new lease of life by dividing it into eastern and western halves and completely reforming the administration and army, Rome was a state under siege. Pressure on the empire's borders was constant and the cost of maintaining defenses ruinous, especially in the poorer west. When the Huns, a Turkic-dominated nomad confederation from somewhere in central Asia, arrived in eastern Europe around 372, destabilizing the Germanic tribes, the empire was plunged back into crisis (▷30). To the east, the Sasanians, who had overthrown the Parthian empire in 226, were also posing a threat.

From around AD 50 the Kushan clan, which had become dominant among the Yue Qi, established an empire extending from the Aral Sea to the Indian Ocean and into northwest India. The empire had fallen by the late 4th century. Northern India continued to be divided into small states, until around 350, when Samudragupta (d.c.380) founded the Gupta empire (▷31), which by 410 had reached its greatest extent under Chandragupta II (r.380–414).

Farther east, the authority of the Han dynasty, which had reached the summit of its power in the 1st century, began to decline. In 189 the empire collapsed in chaos as army and court factions struggled to control an isolated and powerless emperor. The dynasty was overthrown in 220, when the empire split into three kingdoms. In 280 unity was briefly restored, but civil war again broke out, giving the Xiongnu the opportunity to conquer the north of the country. A second wave of nomads – the Turkic Toba tribes – arrived in 386 and won control of the north. The Toba Wei state itself was threatened by the Juan-juan, a Mongol-dominated nomad confederation which arose in the late 4th century and controlled the eastern steppes by 400.

Small states sprang up in southern Japan in the 2nd or 3rd centuries, though most of these had been incorporated into the Yamato kingdom of Honshu by 400. The first southeast Asian states – the trading kingdom of Funan and the Cham kingdom of Champa – had developed by the 2nd century. Madagascar had been discovered and settled by Austronesian peoples from Indonesia in the 1st century AD, a voyaging feat to be matched by the Polynesians, who by 400 had colonized Hawaii and Easter Island.

In Africa the kingdom of Meroë collapsed around 350 as a result of nomad

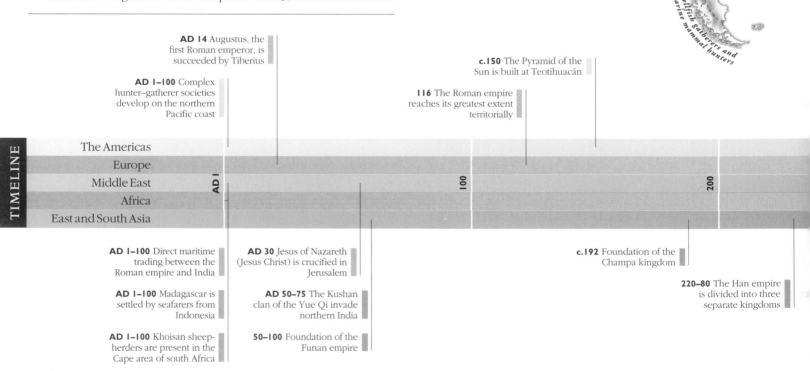

TIMELINE

AD 14 Augustus, the first Roman emperor, is succeeded by Tiberius

AD 1–100 Complex hunter–gatherer societies develop on the northern Pacific coast

c.150 The Pyramid of the Sun is built at Teotihuacán

116 The Roman empire reaches its greatest extent territorially

The Americas
Europe
Middle East
Africa
East and South Asia

AD 1–100 Direct maritime trading between the Roman empire and India

AD 30 Jesus of Nazareth (Jesus Christ) is crucified in Jerusalem

c.192 Foundation of the Champa kingdom

AD 1–100 Madagascar is settled by seafarers from Indonesia

AD 50–75 The Kushan clan of the Yue Qi invade northern India

220–80 The Han empire is divided into three separate kingdoms

AD 1–100 Khoisan sheep-herders are present in the Cape area of south Africa

50–100 Foundation of the Funan empire

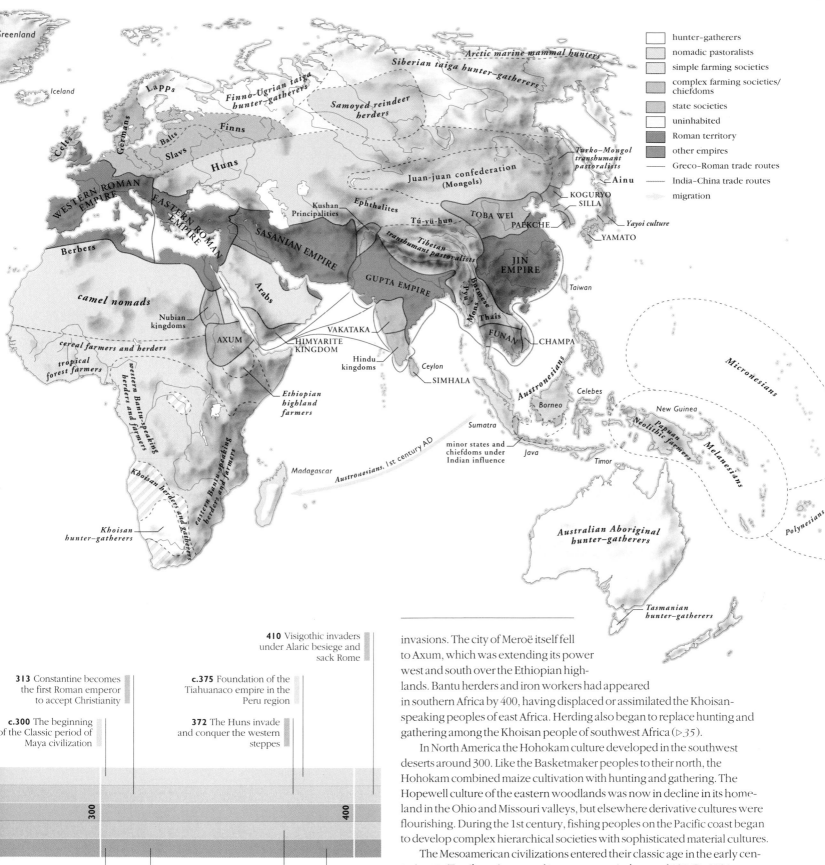

hunter-gatherers
nomadic pastoralists
simple farming societies
complex farming societies/ chiefdoms
state societies
uninhabited
Roman territory
other empires
Greco-Roman trade routes
India-China trade routes
migration

Greenland

Iceland

Lapps

Finno-Ugrian taiga hunter-gatherers

Arctic marine mammal hunters

Siberian taiga hunter-gatherers

Samoyed reindeer herders

Celts

Germans

Bals

Finns

Slavs

Huns

Turko-Mongol transhumant pastoralists

WESTERN ROMAN EMPIRE

EASTERN ROMAN EMPIRE

Juan-juan confederation (Mongols)

Ainu

KOGURYO
SILLA

Kushan Principalities

Ephthalites

Tú-yü-hun

TOBA WEI

PAEKCHE

Yayoi culture

YAMATO

Berbers

SASANIAN EMPIRE

Tibetan transhumant pastoralists

JIN EMPIRE

camel nomads

Arabs

GUPTA EMPIRE

Taiwan

Nubian kingdoms

AXUM

VAKATAKA

HIMYARITE KINGDOM

Burmese

Mon

Pyu

Thais

FUNAN

CHAMPA

cereal farmers and herders

tropical forest farmers

Hindu kingdoms

Ceylon

SIMHALA

Ethiopian highland farmers

Micronesians

western Bantu-speaking herders and farmers

Austronesians

Celebes

Borneo

New Guinea

Papuan Neolithic farmers

Melanesians

Sumatra

minor states and chiefdoms under Indian influence

Java

Timor

eastern Bantu-speaking herders and farmers

Madagascar

Austronesians, 1st century AD

Khoisan herders and farmers

Khoisan hunter-gatherers

Australian Aboriginal hunter-gatherers

Polynesians

Tasmanian hunter-gatherers

410 Visigothic invaders under Alaric besiege and sack Rome

313 Constantine becomes the first Roman emperor to accept Christianity

c.375 Foundation of the Tiahuanaco empire in the Peru region

c.300 The beginning of the Classic period of Maya civilization

372 The Huns invade and conquer the western steppes

300

400

300–400 Buddhism is introduced into south-east Asia

c.350 Axum overthrows the weakened kingdom of Meroë

00 The first states have appeared in Japan

386–397 The nomadic Toba tribe conquer the Wei state in north China

320 Foundation of the Gupta kingdom in northern India

invasions. The city of Meroë itself fell to Axum, which was extending its power west and south over the Ethiopian highlands. Bantu herders and iron workers had appeared in southern Africa by 400, having displaced or assimilated the Khoisan-speaking peoples of east Africa. Herding also began to replace hunting and gathering among the Khoisan people of southwest Africa (▷35).

In North America the Hohokam culture developed in the southwest deserts around 300. Like the Basketmaker peoples to their north, the Hohokam combined maize cultivation with hunting and gathering. The Hopewell culture of the eastern woodlands was now in decline in its homeland in the Ohio and Missouri valleys, but elsewhere derivative cultures were flourishing. During the 1st century, fishing peoples on the Pacific coast began to develop complex hierarchical societies with sophisticated material cultures.

The Mesoamerican civilizations entered their classic age in the early centuries AD. Teotihuacán entered its greatest period around 100. By 300 it was probably the world's fifth largest city, with a population of about 200,000. City-states with warlike ruling dynasties had developed across most of the Maya territories as the Classic period of Maya civilization began around 300. About 200 the Zapotec capital Monte Albán had a population of around 30,000. In South America, the coastal Moche state was at its peak from 200 to 400, and the Tiahuanaco state, in the Lake Titicaca highlands, was beginning a period of imperial expansion (▷39) ∎

The fragile stability of the 4th-century empire was maintained at great cost to its citizens. Taxation was kept at a high level to pay for the large armies needed to defend the frontiers against increasingly well organized Germanic barbarians; yet the economy, particularly in the west, was in decline. The rich used their political influence to avoid paying taxes, so the tax burden fell heavily upon the poorer classes. Even in Egypt's fertile Nile valley, peasant farmers could not afford to pay their taxes and abandoned their fields. The empire's population contracted and manpower shortages began to affect the armies. The western army relied increasingly on barbarian mercenaries to fill its ranks.

In the 370s pressures on the empire's northern frontier increased dramatically. The Huns, a Turkic nomad people, migrated to the eastern European steppes from central Asia and, around 372, crushed the Ostrogoths. The defeat of this the most powerful Germanic tribe caused panic among the rest. In 376 the Visigoths, seeking sanctuary from the Huns, requested permission to settle in the Roman empire. The eastern emperor, Valens, who saw the Visigoths as a valuable source of recruits for the army, settled them on vacant lands in Thrace. There, however, they were treated badly by the corrupt officials in charge of their settlement; and in 378 they rebelled, defeating and killing Valens in battle at Adrianople. Under a new agreement in 382 the emperor Theodosius gave the Visigoths the status of federates (allies); but they rebelled again in 395 under their ambitious new leader, Alaric. He had previously commanded Gothic troops in the Roman army, but now ravaged Greece and Dalmatia before invading Italy in 401. Stilicho, a Roman general of Germanic origin, drove the Visigoths back into Dalmatia; but the situation deteriorated in 406 when a coalition of Vandals, Suevi and Alans invaded Gaul before crossing the Pyrenees into Spain in 409. They were followed into Gaul by Franks, Burgundians and Alemanni. In 410 Alaric rebelled yet again, and when his demands were refused the Visigoths sacked Rome. Though no longer the administrative capital of the empire, Rome remained a potent symbol of its history and power, and the attack was deeply shocking. Alaric died soon afterward, and his successors were more inclined to cooperate with the Romans. In 425 the Visigoths, as allies of the Romans, attacked the Suevi, Alans and Vandals in Spain, before being settled on rich lands in Aquitaine as federates under nominal Roman suzerainty.

Although the Huns were indirectly responsible for the empire's woes, they initially maintained good

- border of Roman empire, 378
- - division between eastern and western Roman empires, 395
- northern limit of Germanic peoples, c.376
- eastern Roman empire, 480
- kingdom of Odoacer, 480
- kingdom of Syagrius, 480
- Burgundian kingdom (Germanic), 480
- Franks (Germanic), 480
- Ostrogoths (Germanic), 480
- Vandal kingdom (Germanic), 480
- Visigothic kingdom (Germanic), 480
- other Germanic peoples, 480
- temporary settlement of Vandals, with date
- federate settlement of Visigoths, with date
- Hun migration
- Alan, Suevi and Vandal migration
- Visigoth migration
- other migration

Goths major Germanic people, 4th century

Huns other barbarian peoples

- ■ capital city

Western Empire

400

402 Ravenna becomes the capital of the western empire

406 Vandals, Suevi and Alans invade Gaul

410 Visigoths under Alaric sack Rome

418 Visigoths are settled as federates in Aquitaine

429 The Vandals cross from Spain to north Africa

450

c.450 Beginning of Anglo-Saxon settlements in Britain

451 Aetius defeats Attila at the Catalaunian Plain

455 Vandals sack Rome

462–78 Visigothic expansion occurs in Gaul and Spain

476 Odoacer is proclaimed king of Italy

480 Death of Julius Nepos, the last legitimate western emperor

500

Eastern Empire

c.372 The Huns conquer the Ostrogoths

378 The Visigoths rebel; and the eastern emperor Valens is killed in battle at Adrianople

395 Death of Theodosius I. The division of the empire is made permanent

396–98 The Visigoths ravage Greece

413 The Theodosian walls are built in Constantinople

421–22 War with Sasanians

441 The Huns defeat the Romans at Naissus

453 Constantinople wins ecclesiastical supremacy over Alexandria at the Council of Chalcedon

400   **450**   **500**

---

1 The arrival of the Huns in eastern Europe around 370 completely destabilized the Germanic tribes, causing many to seek refuge in the Roman empire.

2 In 402 the capital of the western empire was moved from Rome to Ravenna, allowing more rapid communication with the northern frontier and Constantinople.

3 Most of Britain's garrison was withdrawn in 407 by the usurper Constantine to fight in a civil war. In 410 Honorius told the Britons to see to their own defenses.

4 Rome was sacked twice in the 5th century: in 410 by the Visigoths; and in 455 by the Vandals.

5 Saxons, Angles and Jutes from north Germany and Denmark began to settle in eastern Britain c.450.

6 The position and strong fortifications of Constantinople saved Anatolia from barbarian invaders in the 5th century.

7 In the 460s Visigoths, settled by the Romans in Aquitaine in 418, expanded into Gaul and Spain.

8 In 476 Italy came under the rule of Odoacer, a barbarian general, who deposed the "last" western emperor: the puppet usurper Romulus Augustulus, who was still a boy.

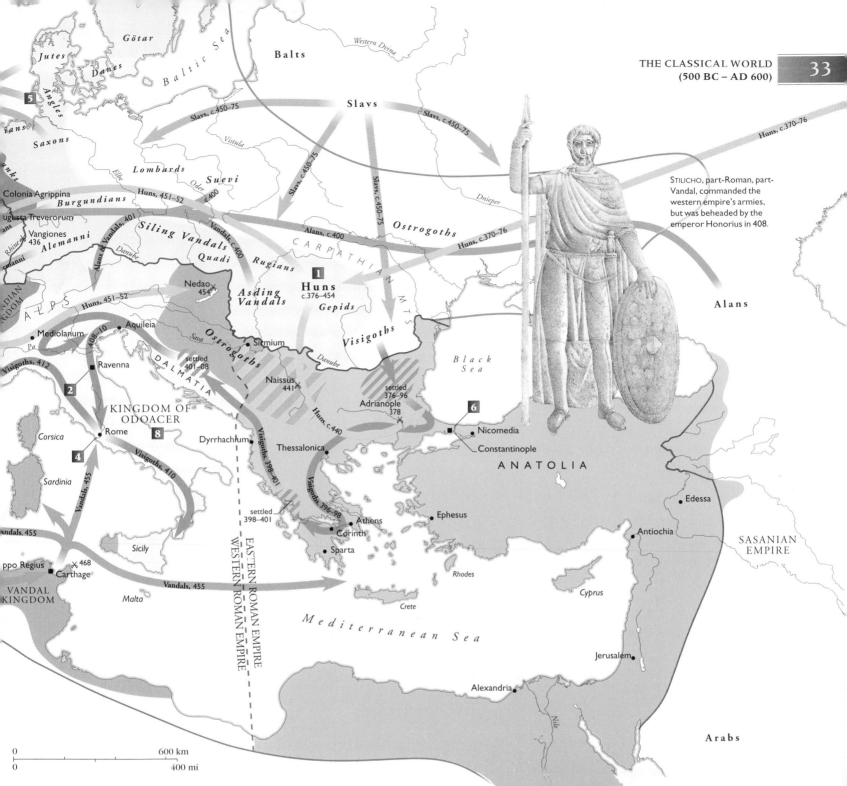

STILICHO, part-Roman, part-Vandal, commanded the western empire's armies, but was beheaded by the emperor Honorius in 408.

relations with Rome. The Roman general Aetius used Hun mercenaries widely in the 430s to impose federate status on the Burgundians and other barbarian settlers in Gaul, but in 441 Attila turned on the empire, ravaging the Balkans and pushing his western border to the Rhine. In 451 Attila invaded Gaul but was defeated by a coalition of Romans, Visigoths, Burgundians and Franks under Aetius at the Catalaunian Plain. After Attila's death in 453 the Huns' German subjects rebelled, breaking their power at the battle of Nedao in 454. The collapse of the Huns in fact worked against Rome: fear of them had kept Rome's Germanic allies reasonably loyal, now they had less cause to be cooperative.

In 429 the Vandals had crossed from Spain to Africa and in 439 captured Carthage and set up a completely independent kingdom. This was the most serious blow the barbarians had so far struck against the empire, as north Africa was Italy's main source of grain. The Vandals turned to piracy, and in 455 went on to sack Rome itself. The assassination in

this year of Aetius, the west's most able general, and of Valentinian III, last of the Theodosian dynasty, were further blows. The western empire now began to crumble and by the 470s was reduced to little more than Italy. The last legitimate western emperor, Julius Nepos, was driven out of Italy in 475 by a palace coup which placed a boy usurper, Romulus Augustulus, on the throne. The following year Odoacer, a barbarian general, deposed Augustulus and was proclaimed king by his soldiers. Odoacer recognized the suzerainty of the eastern emperor Zeno and offered to rule Italy as imperial viceroy. The deposing of Augustulus in 476 is widely accepted as marking the end of the western Roman empire, but Julius Nepos continued to rule a rump empire in Dalmatia from 475 until his death in 480. Dalmatia then became part of Odoacer's kingdom.

The main cause of the fall of the western Roman empire was its exposure to barbarian attack – far greater than in the east, which had only a short northern frontier. This problem was exacerbated by

the division of the empire in the 4th century, which deprived the poorer, less populated and more vulnerable west of the resources of the richer east. Eastern emperors did assist their western colleagues, but their main priority was ensuring that the east did not go the same way as the west. The west was also politically less stable than the east. From the time of Honorius onward western emperors were dominated by overbearing generals. After the death of Valentinian III in 455, the western emperors became the puppets of barbarian generals: when they outlived their usefulness or tried to act independently, they were murdered. The high cost of defending the empire undermined positive loyalty to it. There was little popular resistance to the barbarians and, as they were inefficient tax collectors, most people probably felt themselves better off without the empire.

See also 30 (the later Roman Empire);
34 (rise of Byzantium)

For twelve years after Odoacer's takeover of Italy, Zeno, the eastern emperor, did nothing. Then in 488 he commissioned Theodoric, king of the Ostrogoths, to overthrow Odoacer and rule Italy until he, the emperor, was able to claim sovereignty in person. By 493 Odoacer was dead and Theodoric was master of Italy. Under Theodoric, who wished to preserve Roman civilization, Italy enjoyed peace and prosperity, but there was no assimilation between Roman and Goth. The main barrier was religion. The Goths had converted to Christianity in the 4th century but were followers of the teachings of Arius, who denied the divinity of Christ – which their Roman subjects regarded as heretical. The Burgundians, Visigoths and Vandals were also Arians and assimilation was equally limited in those kingdoms. Arianism also prevented good relations between the barbarian kingdoms and the eastern emperor, who regarded himself as the guardian of orthodox Christianity. The only barbarians to escape the taint of heresy were the Franks, who converted directly from paganism to orthodox Christianity around 500. This earned them the friendship and support of the eastern emperors and the loyalty and cooperation of their Gallo-Roman subjects. Because of this the Frankish kingdom became the strongest power in western Europe by 600.

Although it was frequently at war with Sasanian Persia, the eastern empire prospered after the fall of the west. The emperor Anastasius (r. 491–518) even managed to cut taxes and still leave his successor, Justin (r. 518–27), with a full treasury. Justin was succeeded by his nephew Justinian (r. 527–65), the last great Roman emperor. Justinian had a very clear idea of the responsibilities of a Roman emperor, chief of which was maintaining the territorial integrity of the empire. To Justinian it was a disgrace that the western provinces of the empire were occupied by barbarians and he launched a concerted effort to recover them. In 533 he sent a force under Belisarius which, against expectations, destroyed the Vandal kingdom in north Africa. The Vandal campaign had been made possible by the cooperation of the pro-Roman Ostrogothic queen Amalasuntha,

who allowed the invasion fleet to use Sicily as a base. Amalasuntha's murder in 534 was used as a pretext for the invasion of Italy in 535. By 540 the Ostrogoth capital at Ravenna had fallen, but resistance was revived by Totila (r. 541–52). War with Persia diverted Roman forces to the east and the resulting stalemate in Italy was only broken in 552 when a new Roman army under Narses arrived from Constantinople. By 554 all of Italy south of the Po was in Roman hands, but north of the river Ostrogothic resistance continued until 562. The last of Justinian's conquests was southern Spain, seized opportunistically during a Visigothic civil war in 554.

Justinian's reconquests restored Roman control of the Mediterranean but put the empire under serious economic strain. The concentration of forces in the west left the Balkans exposed to Slavic raiding and settlement, and the Persians made serious

incursions in the east. Italy was devastated by years of war and much of the province was soon lost again following an invasion by the Lombards in 572. However, north Africa and Sicily proved to be valuable additions to the empire's resources.

In about 560 a new wave of nomads, the Avars, arrived in eastern Europe. The Romans paid them to wipe out the remnants of the Huns, but in 580 a dispute over possession of Singidunum (modern

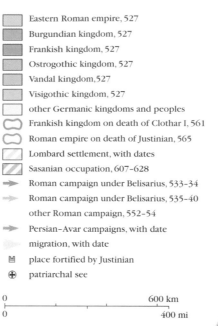

	Eastern Roman empire, 527
	Burgundian kingdom, 527
	Frankish kingdom, 527
	Ostrogothic kingdom, 527
	Vandal kingdom, 527
	Visigothic kingdom, 527
	other Germanic kingdoms and peoples
	Frankish kingdom on death of Clothar I, 561
	Roman empire on death of Justinian, 565
	Lombard settlement, with dates
	Sasanian occupation, 607-628
➡	Roman campaign under Belisarius, 533–34
➡	Roman campaign under Belisarius, 535–40
➡	other Roman campaign, 552–54
➡	Persian-Avar campaigns, with date
➡	migration, with date
	place fortified by Justinian
⊕	patriarchal see

0   600 km
0   400 mi

TIMELINE

Political change

500	550		600
486 Clovis, founder of the Frankish kingdom, defeats Syagrius, the last Roman ruler in Gaul, at Soissons	**526** Theodoric dies	**554** Justinian reconquers southern Spain	**592–602** The emperor Maurice campaigns against the Avars
489–93 Theodoric, king of the Ostrogoths, defeats Odoacer and wins Italy	**532** Justinian quells an anti-reform uprising in Constantinople	**561** The Frankish kingdom is divided between the sons of Clothar I	**607–27** War against Sasanian Persia ends with defeat of the Persians
c.503 Clovis becomes a convert to Christianity	**533–34** Justinian's general Belisarius conquers the Vandal kingdom in Africa	**568–82** The Lombards invade northern Italy	**610–22** Heraclius restructures the eastern Roman empire, creating what we now call the Byzantine empire
507 Clovis defeats the Visigoths at Vouillé, driving the Visigoths into the Iberian peninsula	**536–62** Belisarius and Narses conquer the Ostrogothic kingdom in Italy	**571** The Visigoths recapture Cordoba	**638** Arabs capture Jerusalem
	540 The Sasanian Persians sack Antiochia		

Cultural change

500	550		600
	529 Justinian closes the Academy at Athens	**565** Procopius (c.499-566) publishes the last of his histories of Justinian's reign	**591** Gregory of Tours (c.538-94), completes his *History [of the Franks]*
	529–34 Justinian codifies Roman law		**596–97** Pope Gregory the Great dispatches a mission to convert the Anglo-Saxons
	c.535–40 St Benedict (c.480-c.550) writes his monastic rule		

Danes

Balts

Baltic Sea

Saxons

Thuringians

Vistula

Elbe

Oder

Slavs

Don

Avars, 533–62 [4]

Huns

Lombards [6]

CARPATHIAN MTS

Bulgars

540s–80s

Alans

OSTROGOTHIC KINGDOM

568–72

Danube

Savi

Gepids

Singidunum

626

Cherson

Rhine

Danube

ALPS

Po

• Mediolanum

[3]

• Ravenna

572–82

Busta
Gallorum
✕ 552

• Salonae

Naissus

[7]

Narses

Black Sea

Trapezus

[1]

Corsica

Rome ⊕

Narses

Adrianople

Nicomedia [8]

Constantinople ⊕

• Nicaea

626

Neapolis •

Mons
✕ Lactacius
552

Thessalonica •

ANATOLIA

Sardinia

**EASTERN
ROMAN EMPIRE**

Ephesus •

Antiochia ✕

Euphrates

540

Tigris

Nineveh
✕ 627

Sicily

Catana •

[2]

• Syracusae

Athens •

Persians

Tricameron
533

• Carthage
✕ ad Decimum
533

Rhodes

Palmyra

Ctesiphon •

VANDAL
KINGDOM

Malta

Liberius

Cyprus

Damascus •

**SASANIAN
EMPIRE**

Crete

*Mediterranean
Sea*

Jerusalem ⊕

Leptis Magna

Cyrene •

Alexandria ⊕

Nile

Arabs

JUSTINIAN was portrayed in this mosaic at Ravenna, supported by religious and military forces.

prompted the governor of Africa to equip his son Heraclius with an army in 610 and send him to Constantinople to overthrow Phocas.

The reign of Heraclius was a turning point. The structure of the empire of Diocletian, Constantine and Justinian could not be revived. Heraclius spent the first years of his reign rebuilding the administrative and military structure of the empire. Greek, which had always been the majority language in the eastern empire, replaced Latin in official documents. Heraclius worked closely with the patriarch of Constantinople, who willingly used the wealth and authority of the church to support the state. While Heraclius was reforming the empire, the war with Persia continued to go badly and by 616 Syria, Palestine and Egypt had been lost. In 622 Heraclius launched a bold campaign directly into the heart of the Sasanian empire and five years later destroyed the Persian army at Nineveh, bringing the war to an end. Heraclius had saved the empire, but his reforms are considered to mark the end of the eastern Roman empire and the beginning of the medieval Greek Byzantine empire (named for the old Greek name for Constantinople).

Belgrade) led to war. For ten years the Avars raided the Balkans until the emperor, Maurice, launched a series of effective counterattacks in 592. Maurice was close to breaking Avar power, when his army mutinied in 602: he was deposed and murdered by his successor, Phocas, an incompetent despot. The administrative structure of the empire now began to fall apart. Slavs and Avars overran the Balkans and the Persians took the fortresses of Roman Mesopotamia one by one. The chaotic state of the empire

[1] Rome regained importance in the 6th century as the chief center of Christianity in western Europe.

[2] The Ostrogothic queen Amalasuntha allowed Justinian's general Belisarius to use Sicily as a base for his attack on the Vandals in 533.

[3] Ravenna, the Ostrogothic capital, was taken by Belisarius in 540; resistance continued for many years.

[4] The Avars, a Mongol people, migrated to Europe after being defeated by the Turks in central Asia (552).

[5] Civil war in the Visigothic kingdom gave Justinian the opportunity to reconquer southern Spain in 554.

[6] Originally Roman allies against the Ostrogoths, the Lombards invaded and settled Italy 568–82.

[7] Justinian's concentration on the west left the Balkans exposed to frequent Slav raids and settlement.

[8] A joint Persian–Avar attack on Constantinople in 626 failed when the Byzantine fleet prevented the two attacking armies from uniting.

See also 33 (fall of the western empire);
37 (Arab conquests)

The earliest African state formed in Egypt's Nile valley, where a centralized kingdom had emerged by 3000 BC. By this time desertification had turned the Sahara into a major barrier to travel and the only easy land route between Egypt and tropical Africa lay along the narrow valley of the middle Nile through Nubia. By 2500 several chiefdoms had emerged in Nubia. These were consolidated by 1700 into a large state, known to the Egyptians as Kush, whose capital was at Kerma. Nubia was rich in natural resources, especially gold, and was subjected to Egyptian plundering expeditions. It may, therefore, have been the impetus to organize an effective defense against the Egyptians that provided the impetus for state formation in this area. Kush was conquered by the Egyptians about 1500 at the start of Egypt's imperialistic New Kingdom period. When Egyptian power declined at the end of the New Kingdom (1070 BC), Kush regained its independence. In 770 the kings of Kush conquered southern Egypt and in 712 Shabaka (r.712–698) brought the whole kingdom under Nubian rule. Assyrian attacks on Egypt drove the Nubians from northern Egypt, and by 657 they had lost control of the whole country. The Egyptians expelled the Assyrians in 653 and launched campaigns into Nubia, forcing the Nubians to move their capital south to Meroë around 590. The kingdom of Meroë, as Kush is subsequently known, remained a major power that was taken seriously by the Persians, Greco-Macedonians and Romans who in turn ruled Egypt after 525 BC. In the 4th century Meroë suffered attacks from desert nomads; it collapsed about 350, after the capital was taken by the Axumites. Three small states, Nobatia, Makkura and Alwa, arose as successors to Meroë but Makkura conquered Nobatia in the 8th century.

Nubia was strongly influenced by Egyptian religion, kingship and culture. Until about 200 BC, when an indigenous Meroitic script was developed, Egyptian scripts and language were used for inscriptions, and the use of pyramids for royal burials continued into the Christian era, long after the practice had ceased in Egypt. Christianity was introduced to Nubia in the 6th century and remained strong until the region was put under pressure by the Arabs in the 13th century.

The second state to develop in tropical Africa, Axum emerged in northern Ethiopia in the 1st century AD. Urban development had begun at sites such as Yeha in the 5th century BC and the cultural development of the area was strongly influenced by the Sabeans of Arabia, whose alphabet, architecture and religion were adopted. In the 1st century AD the port of Adulis was exporting ivory, rhinoceros horn, tortoise-shell, obsidian and aromatic resins to the Roman empire via Red Sea trade routes. The city of Axum itself included complexes of monumental buildings and palaces. Among the most remarkable monuments at Axum are monoliths carved to resemble multistory buildings: the tallest still standing is 69 feet (21 meters) high. The kingdom of Axum reached a peak in the reign of King Ezana around 350. About this time also, Ezana converted to Christianity, the first African ruler to do so. In 522 the Axumites invaded and conquered the Yemen and held it until driven out by the Sasanians in 574. In the 8th century, attacks by the Arabs accelerated the decline of Axum, and by the 10th century power had shifted to the Ethiopian highlands.

Another area of Africa in which state formation occurred was the Maghrib, where the Berber kingdoms of Numantia and Mauretania emerged around 200 BC in the power vacuum left by the defeat of Carthage in the Second Punic War (226–201 BC). However, these states were soon swallowed up by the expanding empire of Rome. The most significant development in north Africa was the introduction of the camel to the Sahara around 100 BC. Camels were ideal for desert warfare, and settled communities on the fringes of the desert soon suffered badly from nomad raids. Camels also had the endurance for long desert crossings – horses, mules and bullocks had previously been the main beasts of burden in the Sahara. Now cross-desert trade began to expand, and by AD 500 camel caravans forged strong trade links between the Mediterranean and west Africa

(maritime links were never established, because of adverse winds south of Cape Bojador).

The earliest Iron Age culture of west Africa, the Nok culture of Nigeria (c. 500 BC– AD 400), is noted for its sophisticated terracotta sculptures, which are often seen as being ancestral to the art styles of the medieval Ibo and Yoruba peoples. By AD 600 many areas of west Africa had dense farming populations, and one city, Jenne-jeno, had developed as a regional trading center. Many large burial mounds in this region point to the emergence of powerful elites and the beginnings of state formation.

The major development in Africa south of the Equator was the expansion of the Bantu-speaking peoples, mixed farming and, later, iron working. The Bantu languages belong to the Niger-Kordofanian group, confined to tropical west Africa in the second millennium BC. The original homeland of the Bantu was in southern Nigeria and Cameroon, but around 2000 BC Bantu-speakers began to spread into central and east Africa, and by AD 500 they had reached southern Africa. Bantu languages were spread partly by migrations of iron-using farmers, but also by the assimilation to Bantu culture of the Khoisan-speaking Stone Age herders and hunter–gatherers of eastern and southern Africa.

Map legend

Nok early Iron Age culture, 6th century BC–5th century AD

maximum extent of Nubian power, 712–671 BC

kingdom of Meroë, 590 BC–AD 350

kingdom of Axum under Ezana, c.AD 350

Axumite occupation, AD 522–74

kingdom of Numidia, 2nd century BC

kingdom of Mauretania, 2nd century BC

origin of Bantu-speaking peoples, 2000 BC

northwestern Bantu by AD 500

eastern Bantu by AD 500

western Bantu by AD 500

spread of Bantu, with date

Niger-Kordofanian languages, 2nd millennium BC

border of Roman empire, AD 1

sub-Sahara African early Iron Age site

with evidence of iron production

other site

trading post, 1st–3rd century AD

early Christian church, 4th–6th century AD

probable trans-Saharan route

sea route

desert

tropical rainforest

0   1000 km

0   800 mi

Cape Bojador

1

Akjo

Senegal

Gambia

TIMELINE

Northern Africa

600 BC	AD 1	AD 600
712–671 Egypt is under Nubian rule	**c.200** Berber kingdoms emerge in north Africa	**c.350** Fall of the kingdom of Meroë
590 Meroë becomes the capital of Nubia	**146** The Romans destroy the city of Carthage	**c.350** King Ezana of Axum converts to Christianity
525–523 Egypt is conquered by Persia	**c.100 BC** The camel is introduced into the Sahara	**522–74** The kingdom of Axum rules in the Yemen
c.500 Sabeans settle in Ethiopia, later contributing to rise of the kingdom of Axum	**AD 1–100** The kingdom of Axum emerges	**c.540** The Nubians are converted to Christianity

Southern Africa

600 BC	AD 1	AD 600
700–600 Iron working is first known in the central Sahara region	**c.200** Date of the earliest occupation at Jenne-jeno	**c.400** City walls are built at Jenne-jeno
c.480 Taruga, Nigeria, flourishes as an iron working center	**c.AD 1** Khoisans in southern Africa are herding sheep	**400–500** Iron working reaches southern Africa
400–300 Iron working is established in the east African highlands	**AD 1–100** Madagascar is settled by Austronesians from southeast Asia	**500–600** Cattle and iron working are widespread in southern Africa
	100–300 Greco-Roman merchants sail to east Africa for ivory	

600 BC   AD 1   AD 600

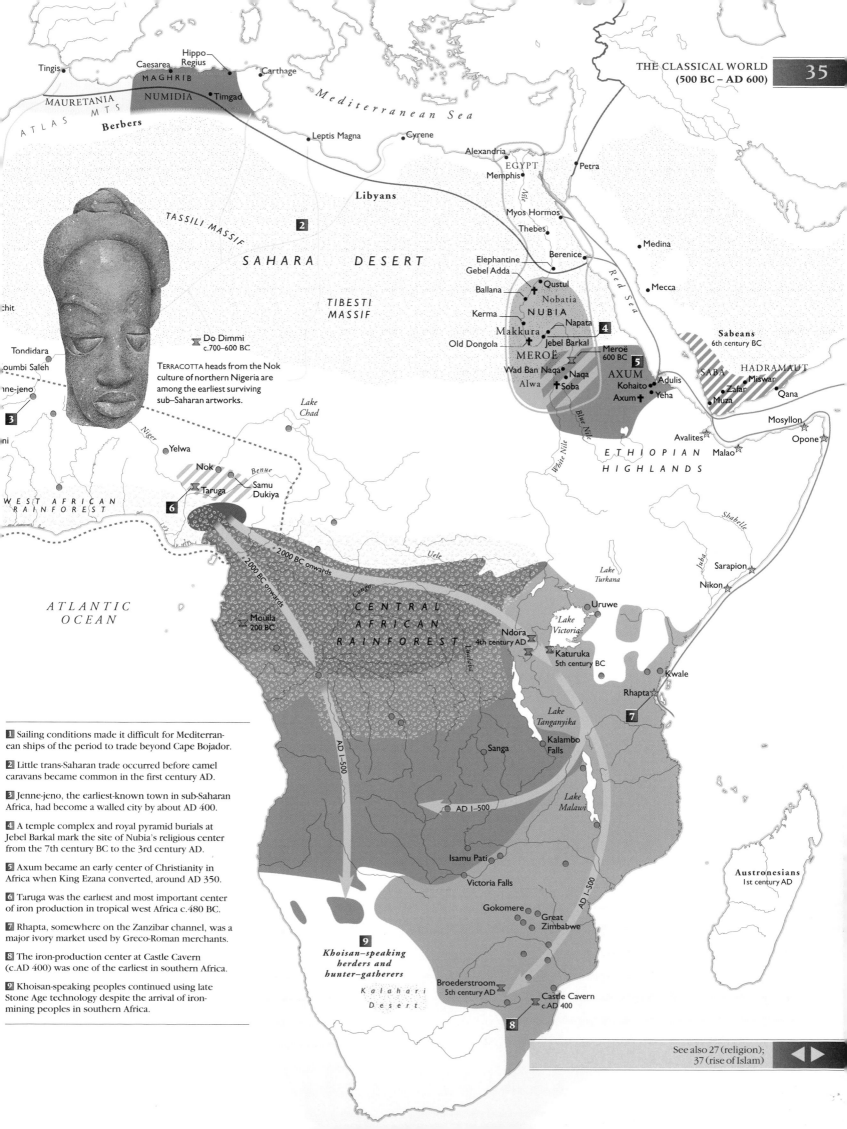

Tingis

Caesarea
Hippo
Regius
Carthage

MAGHRIB

MAURETANIA
NUMIDIA
Timgad

ATLAS MTS

Berbers

Mediterranean Sea

Leptis Magna
Cyrene

Alexandria
EGYPT
Memphis
Petra

SAHARA DESERT

TASSILI MASSIF

Libyans

Myos Hormos
Thebes

Medina

Berenice

TIBESTI
MASSIF

Elephantine
Gebel Adda
Ballana
Qustul
Nobatia
NUBIA
Kerma
Napata
Makkura

Mecca

Red Sea

Medina

Do Dimmi
c.700–600 BC

TERRACOTTA heads from the Nok
culture of northern Nigeria are
among the earliest surviving
sub–Saharan artworks.

Tondidara

oumbi Saleh

nne-jeno

3

chit

Lake
Chad

Niger

Yelwa

Old Dongola
Jebel Barkal

MEROË

Wad Ban Naqa
Alwa
Naqa
Soba

Meroë
600 BC

AXUM
Kohaito
Axum
Yeha

Adulis

Sabeans
6th century BC

SABA
HADRAMAUT
Miswar
Zafar
Muza
Qana

Mosyllon

Opone

Nok
Taruga
Samu
Dukiya

Benue

6

WEST AFRICAN
RAINFOREST

Avalites
Malao

ETHIOPIAN
HIGHLANDS

Blue Nile

White Nile

Uele

Shabelle

ni

ATLANTIC
OCEAN

2000 BC onwards

2000 BC onwards

Congo

CENTRAL
AFRICAN
RAINFOREST

Lake
Turkana

Sarapion

Nikon

Uruwe

Lake
Victoria

Ndora
4th century AD

Kwale

Mouila
200 BC

Lualaba

AD 1–500

Katuruka
5th century BC

Rhapta

7

AD 1–500

Sanga

Kalambo
Falls

Lake
Tanganyika

Lake
Malawi

AD 1–500

1 Sailing conditions made it difficult for Mediterranean ships of the period to trade beyond Cape Bojador.

2 Little trans-Saharan trade occurred before camel
caravans became common in the first century AD.

3 Jenne-jeno, the earliest-known town in sub-Saharan
Africa, had become a walled city by about AD 400.

4 A temple complex and royal pyramid burials at
Jebel Barkal mark the site of Nubia's religious center
from the 7th century BC to the 3rd century AD.

5 Axum became an early center of Christianity in
Africa when King Ezana converted, around AD 350.

6 Taruga was the earliest and most important center
of iron production in tropical west Africa c.480 BC.

7 Rhapta, somewhere on the Zanzibar channel, was a
major ivory market used by Greco-Roman merchants.

8 The iron-production center at Castle Cavern
(c.AD 400) was one of the earliest in southern Africa.

9 Khoisan-speaking peoples continued using late
Stone Age technology despite the arrival of iron-
mining peoples in southern Africa.

Isamu Pati

Victoria Falls

Gokomere

Great
Zimbabwe

Austronesians
1st century AD

9

*Khoisan-speaking
herders and
hunter-gatherers*

*Kalahari
Desert*

Broederstroom
5th century AD

Castle Cavern
c.AD 400

8

See also 27 (religion);
37 (rise of Islam)

The western half of the Roman empire, altogether poorer and less populated than the east, was also more exposed to Germanic barbarian attack. In 406 German tribes – Goths, Franks, Vandals and others – overran the Rhine frontier and by 476 the western Roman empire was almost entirely under their control. The wealthy eastern half of the Roman empire survived more or less unscathed and its emperor Justinian counter-attacked against the barbarians in the 530s, restoring Roman rule in Italy, north Africa and southern Spain (▷34). However, the empire was put back on the defensive after Justinian's death; much of Italy fell to the Lombards and most of southern Spain to the Visigoths by 600. The most successful of the Germanic invaders were the Franks, who had settled northern Gaul in the early 5th century. From 486 they were united by Clovis, who extended his kingdom into southern Gaul and east into Germany. By 600 the Frankish kingdom stretched from the Pyrenees almost to the Elbe. The end of Roman rule in Britain saw a revival of Celtic culture but in about 450 Angles and Saxons from north Germany began to settle the fertile east of Britain, driving the Celts to the hillier west.

Fear of the Huns drove the Germanic peoples to invade the Roman empire. The Huns extended their control as far west as the Rhine – further west than any steppe nomads in history – and raided both halves of the Roman empire under Attila (r. 433–453). However, after his death the Hun confederation broke up and returned to the steppes. Between 460 and 515 the Ephthalite (or "White") Huns destroyed the last Kushan principalities of central Asia, raided the Sasanian empire and conquered northwest India, only to be driven out in 528. On the eastern steppes, the Mongol-dominated Juan-juan confederacy was broken by a rebellion of the Turks in 552. By 600 the Turks had destroyed the Ephthalites and dominated the steppes as far west as the Aral Sea. The Khazars, another Turkic people, were established on the Caspian steppes. A part of the Juan-juan, the Avars, fled from the Turks and arrived on the European steppes in about 562 where they mopped up the remnants of the Huns and raided the Balkans. North of the Caucasus the Alans – the sole remnant of the Iranian peoples who had once dominated the steppes – re-emerged from Hunnic dominance in the 450s.

In Africa, Christianity had spread to Nubia and Axum by the 6th century, strengthening cultural and political links with the eastern Roman empire (▷35). With Roman encouragement, the Axumites conquered southwest Arabia in 528 but were expelled by the Sasanians in 574, ending Christian influence in Arabia just four years after the birth of Muhammad at Mecca. In west Africa intensive dry-rice farming led to a rising population on the upper Niger and the foundation of large villages in the 3rd and 4th centuries. One of these, Jenne-jeno, became the center of a wideranging network of west

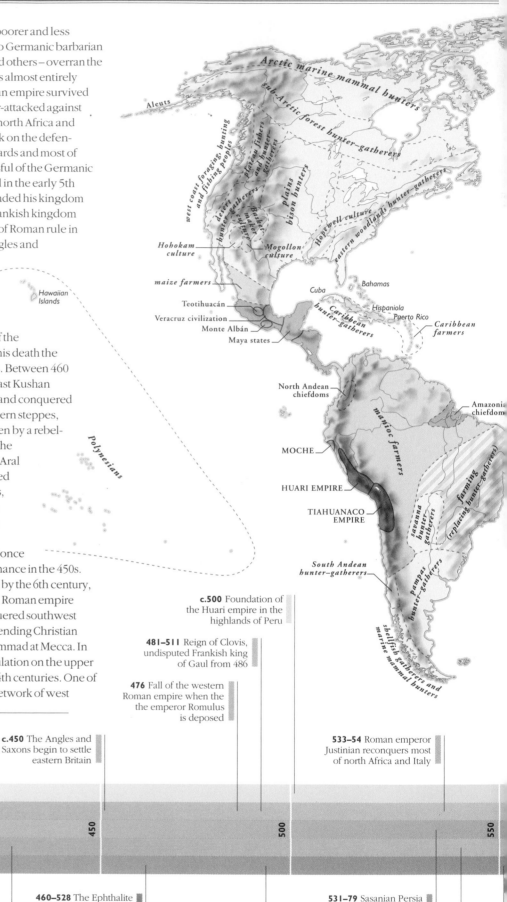

c.500 Foundation of the Huari empire in the highlands of Peru

481–511 Reign of Clovis, undisputed Frankish king of Gaul from 486

476 Fall of the western Roman empire when the the emperor Romulus is deposed

c.450 The Angles and Saxons begin to settle eastern Britain

410 The Visigoths, led by Alaric, sack Rome

533–54 Roman emperor Justinian reconquers most of north Africa and Italy

TIMELINE

	400	450	500	550
The Americas				
Europe				
Middle East				
Africa				
East and South Asia				

c.400 Iron working reaches southern Africa

c.400 Jenne-jeno flourishes as the first town in west Africa

429 A wealthy Vandal kingdom is set up in north Africa

460–528 The Ephthalite Huns ("Hunas") invade northwest India

c.470 Decline of the Gupta empire in northern India

531–79 Sasanian Persia achieves its maximum extent under Chosroes I

c.540 Christianity is introduced into Nubia

c.550 The Turkish khanates are dominant throughout central Asia

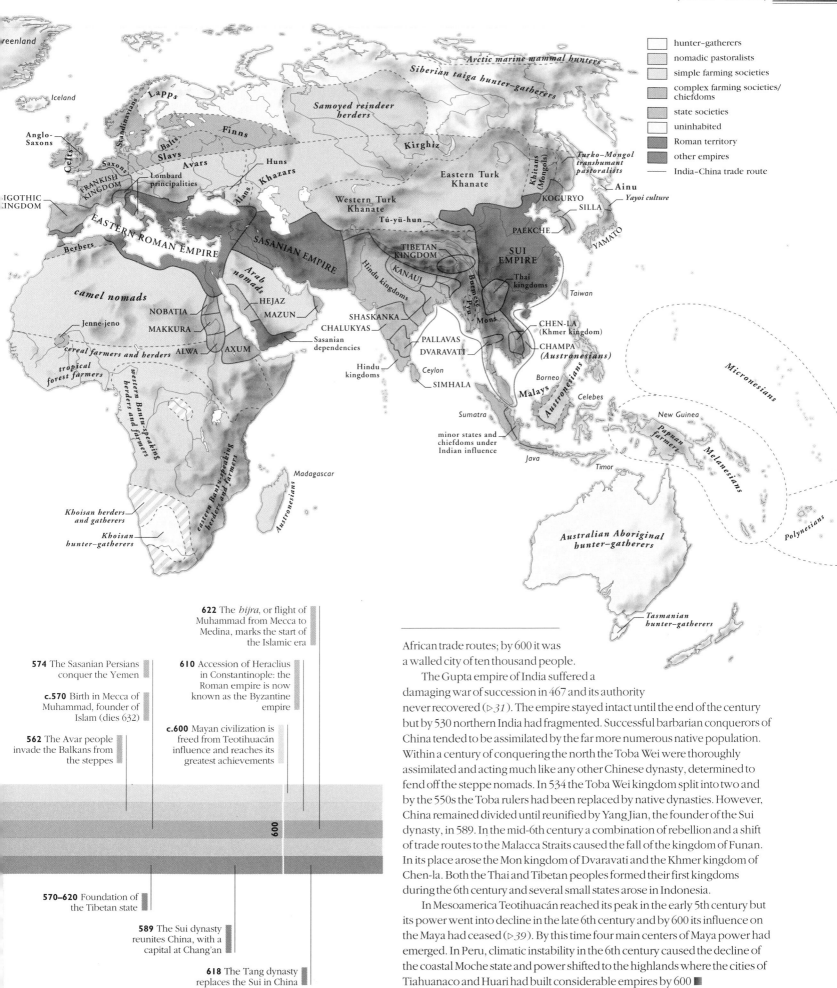

hunter-gatherers
nomadic pastoralists
simple farming societies
complex farming societies/chiefdoms
state societies
uninhabited
Roman territory
other empires
India-China trade route

Greenland

Iceland

Lapps

Anglo-Saxons

Scandinavians

Celts

Balts

Saxons

Slavs

Finns

Avars

Huns

Khazars

Kirghiz

Samoyed reindeer herders

Siberian taiga hunter-gatherers

Arctic marine mammal hunters

FRANKISH KINGDOM

Lombard principalities

Alans

Khitans (Mongols)

Turko-Mongol transhumant pastoralists

VISIGOTHIC KINGDOM

EASTERN ROMAN EMPIRE

Western Turk Khanate

Eastern Turk Khanate

Ainu

Yayoi culture

Berbers

SASANIAN EMPIRE

Tú-yü-hun

KOGURYO

SILLA

camel nomads

Arab nomads

TIBETAN KINGDOM

KANAUJ

SUI EMPIRE

PAEKCHE

YAMATO

NOBATIA

HEJAZ

MAZUN

Hindu kingdoms

Thai kingdoms

Taiwan

Jenne-jeno

MAKKURA

cereal farmers and herders

ALWA

AXUM

Sasanian dependencies

SHASKANKA

CHALUKYAS

PALLAVAS

DVARAVATI

Borneo

Pyu

Mons

CHEN-LA (Khmer kingdom)

CHAMPA (Austronesians)

Micronesians

tropical forest farmers

western Bantu-speaking herders and farmers

Hindu kingdoms

Ceylon

SIMHALA

Malays

Austronesians

Borneo

Celebes

New Guinea

Papuan farmers

Melanesians

eastern Bantu-speaking herders and farmers

Madagascar

Sumatra

minor states and chiefdoms under Indian influence

Java

Timor

Khoisan herders and gatherers

Khoisan hunter-gatherers

Austronesians

Polynesians

Australian Aboriginal hunter-gatherers

Tasmanian hunter-gatherers

622 The *hijra*, or flight of Muhammad from Mecca to Medina, marks the start of the Islamic era

574 The Sasanian Persians conquer the Yemen

610 Accession of Heraclius in Constantinople: the Roman empire is now known as the Byzantine empire

c.570 Birth in Mecca of Muhammad, founder of Islam (dies 632)

562 The Avar people invade the Balkans from the steppes

c.600 Mayan civilization is freed from Teotihuacán influence and reaches its greatest achievements

600

570–620 Foundation of the Tibetan state

589 The Sui dynasty reunites China, with a capital at Chang'an

618 The Tang dynasty replaces the Sui in China

African trade routes; by 600 it was a walled city of ten thousand people.

The Gupta empire of India suffered a damaging war of succession in 467 and its authority never recovered (▷31). The empire stayed intact until the end of the century but by 530 northern India had fragmented. Successful barbarian conquerors of China tended to be assimilated by the far more numerous native population. Within a century of conquering the north the Toba Wei were thoroughly assimilated and acting much like any other Chinese dynasty, determined to fend off the steppe nomads. In 534 the Toba Wei kingdom split into two and by the 550s the Toba rulers had been replaced by native dynasties. However, China remained divided until reunified by Yang Jian, the founder of the Sui dynasty, in 589. In the mid-6th century a combination of rebellion and a shift of trade routes to the Malacca Straits caused the fall of the kingdom of Funan. In its place arose the Mon kingdom of Dvaravati and the Khmer kingdom of Chen-la. Both the Thai and Tibetan peoples formed their first kingdoms during the 6th century and several small states arose in Indonesia.

In Mesoamerica Teotihuacán reached its peak in the early 5th century but its power went into decline in the late 6th century and by 600 its influence on the Maya had ceased (▷39). By this time four main centers of Maya power had emerged. In Peru, climatic instability in the 6th century caused the decline of the coastal Moche state and power shifted to the highlands where the cities of Tiahuanaco and Huari had built considerable empires by 600 ∎

Part 3

THE MEDIEVAL

S hortly after AD 600, the Islamic community was founded in Medina under the leadership of prophet Muhammad. For many centuries Islam and other civilizations farther east were the world's most dynamic cultures. The year 1492, however, saw Columbus reach the Antilles, the prelude to the conquest and settlement of the New World by Europeans; six years later Vasco da Gama sailed around Africa to India. The foundation of western hegemony was thus laid by the end of the fifteenth century.

Just as the "barbarian" invasions of the fifth century AD led to the eclipse of the classical civilization of Europe, so the Muslim Arab expansion ended the domination of old Persian empires in the Middle East and the surviving Roman empire in the eastern Mediterranean. The intensity of the success of Islam is still unexplained, but there is no doubt about its significance. The unification of large parts of the Mediterranean, the Middle East, and the Indian Ocean by the Umayyad and Abbasid caliphates was a cultural, technological, and economic as well as a political achievement. The use of the Arabic language played an important role: the Bedouins of the Arabian peninsula, the Berber converts of north Africa, Arab conquerors in Andalusia, the Copts of Egypt, the Nabateans of Mesopotamia, and the converted Iranians all shared the Koranic prayers recited in Arabic and a common body of family and civil law.

Islam revitalized old cities and founded new ones. Both Medina and Mecca attracted a huge number of pilgrims each year, while Damascus became the first Islamic capital under the Umayyads, greatly enlarged by successive caliphs. Under the Abbasids, the capital shifted to Baghdad, the first planned capital city to be built by Muslims. This in turn was followed

THE CAMEL CARAVAN drew east and west together in trade and culture.

WORLD

by Samarra. The Islamic world's great cities included Basra, Alexandria, Fustat, Cairo, Tunis, and Córdoba.

The urban gravitation of Islamic expansion required an economic surplus and food resources. This was achieved by bringing new land under cultivation and reviving existing regions of agricultural production. Arab engineers and farmers proved skilful in constructing irrigation projects. New plants such as hard wheat, sugar cane, citrus fruits, vegetables, and legumes were imported from India and southeast Asia and disseminated throughout the oasis agriculture of north Africa and into the arid areas of southern Spain.

Similar developments took place in China and southeast Asia. The Chinese perfected ways of containing the rivers of northern China to develop the rice-growing areas of Szechuan and the Yangtze valley. Population expansion, combined with the instability of climate, created a problem of feeding the world's most advanced empire. The Song emperors knew this problem to be a product of previous agricultural success, which had created crowded cities and rural areas. Relief in times of scarcity was provided by the state, which encouraged the cultivation of a strain of rice that ripened in two months, as against the three to six taken by traditional varieties.

Chinese civilization and administration was a matter of wonder to the rest of the world. China developed a class of professional bureaucratic administrators who were given formal instructions in writing and who had to report to the imperial court through written memoranda. Science, mathematics, and engineering flourished, and papermaking, the moving-type printing press and gunpowder were invented.

China's capacity for industrial production was evident in the quality of its porcelain and silk textiles. The Indian subcontinent had a similar lead in the production of cotton textiles. These products sustained a trade from the South China Sea to the eastern Mediterranean. Luxury goods were not the only articles of international trade. A network of trading cities grew up in response to the needs of this trade. Chinese ports such as Hangzhou were linked to Malacca in the tip of Malay peninsula, in turn connected to the seaports of India, the Gulf and the Red Sea. The city-states in east Africa completed the commercial rectangle.

The Mongol conquests dealt a severe blow to the ancient civilizations of the Indian Ocean and prepared the way for a resurgent Europe, where Arab intellectual knowledge had slowly penetrated through the intermediary of Jewish scholars and scientists living and working in Spain.

Europe's main contribution to world history to this point was its fighting technique. The adoption of the stirrup made it possible gradually to increase the armament of the mounted warrior using a heavy lance. A new breed of powerful horses appeared and the mounted knights were successful against the Turks during the Crusades. European success in the New World and the Indian Ocean later owed a great deal also to the invention of square-rigged ships armed with artillery capable of bombarding towns and cities. The reinforced hull made it possible to pierce gunports and add a gun-deck without encroaching on the vessel's cargo capacity. The result was a floating fortress that was also a floating warehouse.

European expansion was embedded in a larger process of scientific and intellectual advance. The new navigational methods – the use of compass, marine charts, mapmaking and astronomical navigation – were linked to the development of fighting ships. As a result, when, in the 15th century, Europeans sought routes to the east that would avoid the hostile Ottoman lands, the technology was at hand to enable them to dominate these new waters. The consequences were soon to be dramatically evident ■

T he great empires of the Mediterranean and the Middle East had for centuries been accustomed to raids by Arab border tribes. Though troublesome, these raids were prevented from becoming a serious threat by the political disunity of the Arabs. However, this situation changed dramatically in the early 7th century as a result of the rise of Islam.

The faith of Islam (meaning "submission to the will of God") was founded by Muhammad (c.570–632), a member of the Meccan Quraysh tribe. From about 610, Muhammad began to experience the revelations that formed the basis of the *Koran*. Muhammad's espousal of monotheism met with opposition from the Quraysh, so to escape persecution the prophet and his followers fled in 622 to Medina, a commercial rival of Mecca. This event, the *hijra* (flight), marks the beginning of the Muslim era and is the first year of the Islamic calendar. Muhammad used Medina as a base to fight the Quraysh and in 630 he returned to Mecca in triumph. However, Muhammad continued to live at Medina, which became the capital of a theocratic Islamic state. In the last two years of his life, Muhammad used diplomacy and force to spread Islam to other Arab tribes.

Muhammad was succeeded by his father-in-law Abu Bakr, the first *caliph* (successor). After putting down an anti-Islamic rebellion, Abu Bakr completed the political and religious unification of the Arabs. Under the next two caliphs, Umar and Uthman, the Arabs began an explosive expansion which saw the Byzantine empire lose the rich and populous provinces of Syria, Palestine, Egypt and Libya, and the complete destruction of the Persian Sasanian empire. On Uthman's death civil war broke out between supporters of the caliph Ali, Muhammad's son-in-law, and Muawiya, a member of Uthman's Umayyad family. After Ali's murder in 661, Muawiya became caliph, founding the Umayyad dynasty. Ali's son Husain tried to win the caliphate on Muawiya's

death but was killed in battle with the Umayyads at Karbala in 680. Consequently, Islam split into its two main branches: the Sunnites (from *sunna*, "tradition of Muhammad"), who formed a majority, and the Shiites (from *shi'atu Ali*, "party of Ali").

Arab expansion continued under the early Umayyads and by 715 the Islamic caliphate, extending from the Indus and central Asia to the Pyrenees, was the largest state the world had yet seen. Yet their attempts to complete the conquest of the Byzantine

empire and the west failed, with two unsuccessful sieges of Constantinople in 677 and 717 and defeat by the Franks at Poitiers in 732.

The caliphs were both religious and political leaders. Whereas the early caliphs had been elected, the Umayyads introduced hereditary succession, claiming divine appointment and demanding total obedience. By adapting Byzantine bureaucracy, they created an administrative system capable of ruling a world empire. As this empire could not be ruled effectively from the remote Arabian city of Medina, Muawiya moved the capital to Damascus in 661. The Umayyad period saw the beginning of the successful Arabization of the conquered populations through conversion to Islam, the adoption of Arabic as a common language, and by intermarriage. The Arabs in turn were influenced by the Persian and Byzantine civilizations that they had conquered. One of the most important cultural developments of

TIMELINE

Arab unification

625	675	725
610 Muhammad experiences his first vision	**656–61** Caliphate of Ali; civil war with Muawiya	
622 The *hijra*; Muhammad flees to Medina	**656** Standardization of the text of the *Koran* completed	
630 Mecca surrenders to Muhammad	**661–80** Muawiya caliph; founder of Umayyad dynasty	
632–34 Abu Bakr caliph after Muhammad's death		
634–44 Umar succeeds Abu Bakr as caliph		
644–56 Uthman's rule as caliph		

Conquests

625	675	725
607–27 The Sasanian empire is defeated by the Byzantines	**670–77** First Arab siege of Constantinople is defeated	**732** The Franks defeat the Arabs at Poitiers
636–38 Arabs overrun Syria and Palestine following victory at the Yarmuk River	**698** Carthage, the last Byzantine possession in Africa, falls to the Arabs	**740–43** The Berbers rebel against Arab rule
637 Arabs take Mesopotamia after victory at Qadisiya	**702** Berbers submit to the Arabs and accept Islam	**750** Overthrow of the Umayyad dynasty by the Abbasids
642 Fall of Alexandria to Arab forces	**711** The Arabs and Berbers invade Spain	
642 Sasanians defeated by Arabs at battle of Nehavend	**716–17** Second Arab siege of Constantinople is defeated	

1 Mecca was an important trading city and the main cult center for the pre-Islamic Arabs' pagan religion.

2 Arab military settlements, such as Al-Fustat (Cairo), were sited close to the edge of the desert, where the Arabs could take refuge in the event of rebellions.

3 The Taurus mountains proved an effective barrier against further Arab conquests in Anatolia.

4 The last Sasanian king, Yezdegird III, was murdered near Merv in 652, so ending Persian resistance.

5 Karbala became a major pilgrimage site for Shiite Muslims after Husain, Muhammad's grandson, was killed there by the Umayyads.

6 With the transfer of the Arab capital to Damascus in 661, Arabia gradually declined in significance.

7 The two attempts by the Arabs to take the heavily fortified city of Constantinople were costly failures.

8 Berber resistance to the Arabs was fierce; they were only subdued and converted to Islam in 702.

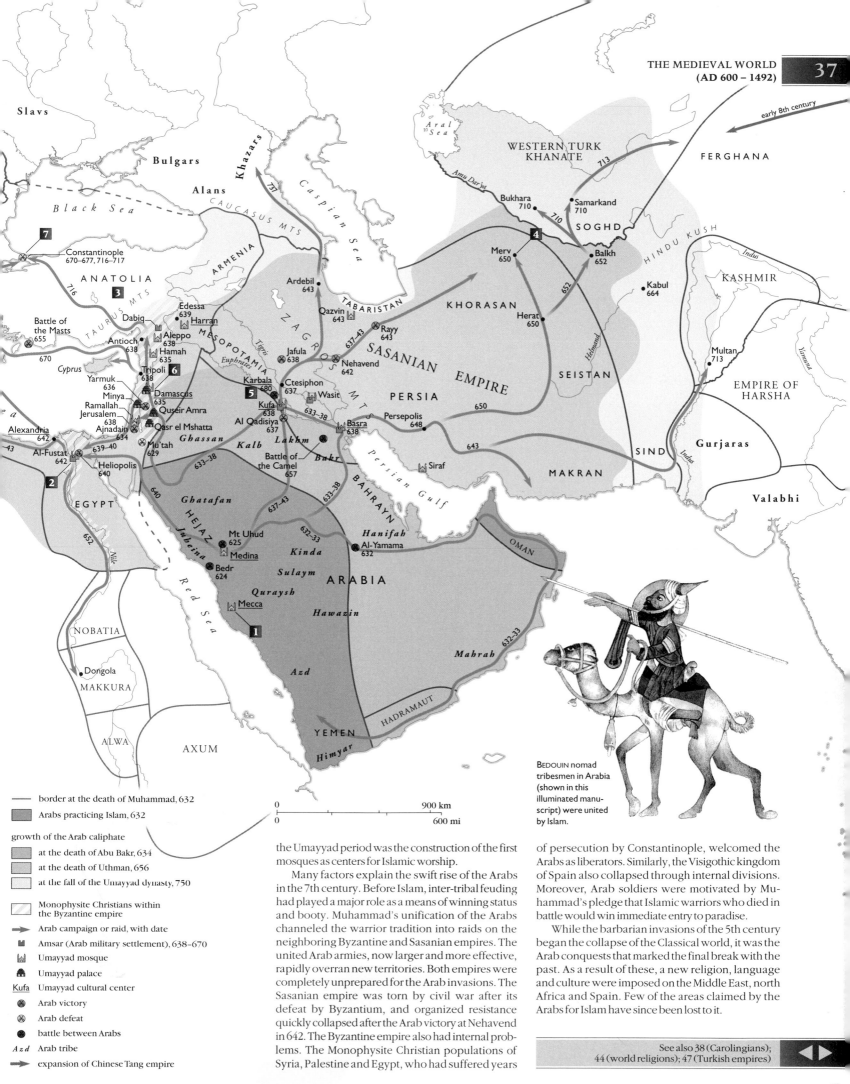

Slavs

Bulgars

Khazars

Alans

Black Sea

CAUCASUS MTS

Aral Sea

WESTERN TURK
KHANATE

713

FERGHANA

early 8th century

Caspian Sea

ARMENIA

Bukhara
710

Samarkand
710

SOGHD

Balkh
652

HINDU KUSH

Indus

KASHMIR

Constantinople
670–677, 716–717

ANATOLIA

737

Ardebil
643

TABARISTAN

Merv
650

Herat
650

652

Kabul
664

Yamuna

ZAGROS

KHORASAN

TAURUS MTS

716

Battle of
the Masts
655

670

Dabiq

Edessa
639

Harran

Aleppo
638

Hamah
635

MESOPOTAMIA

Qazvin
643

Rayy
643

637–43

Nehavend
642

SASANIAN
EMPIRE

SEISTAN

Helmand

Multan
713

EMPIRE OF
HARSHA

Antioch
638

Cyprus

Tripoli
638

6

Euphrates

Jafula
638

Tigris

Ctesiphon
637

PERSIA

650

EMPIRE OF
HARSHA

Yarmuk
636

Minya

Damascus
635

Quseir Amra

Karbala
680

Wasit

Persepolis
648

Ramallah

Jerusalem
638

Qasr el Mshatta

Kufa
638

Al Qadisiya
637

633–38

Basra
638

650

Gurjaras

Alexandria
642

43

Ajnadain
634

Ghassan

Kalb

Lakhm

Bakr

Battle of
the Camel
657

643

Siraf

SIND

Al-Fustat
642

Mu'tah
629

639–40

Heliopolis
640

2

EGYPT

Ghatafan

640

HEJAZ

Juheina

633–38

637–43

633–38

BAHRAYN

Persian Gulf

MAKRAN

Valabhi

Mt Uhud
625

Medina

Kinda

Sulaym

632–33

Hanifah

Al-Yamama
632

OMAN

Red Sea

Bedr
624

Quraysh

Mecca

1

ARABIA

Hawazin

632–33

NOBATIA

Dongola

MAKKURA

Azd

Mahrah

ALWA

AXUM

YEMEN

HADRAMAUT

Himyar

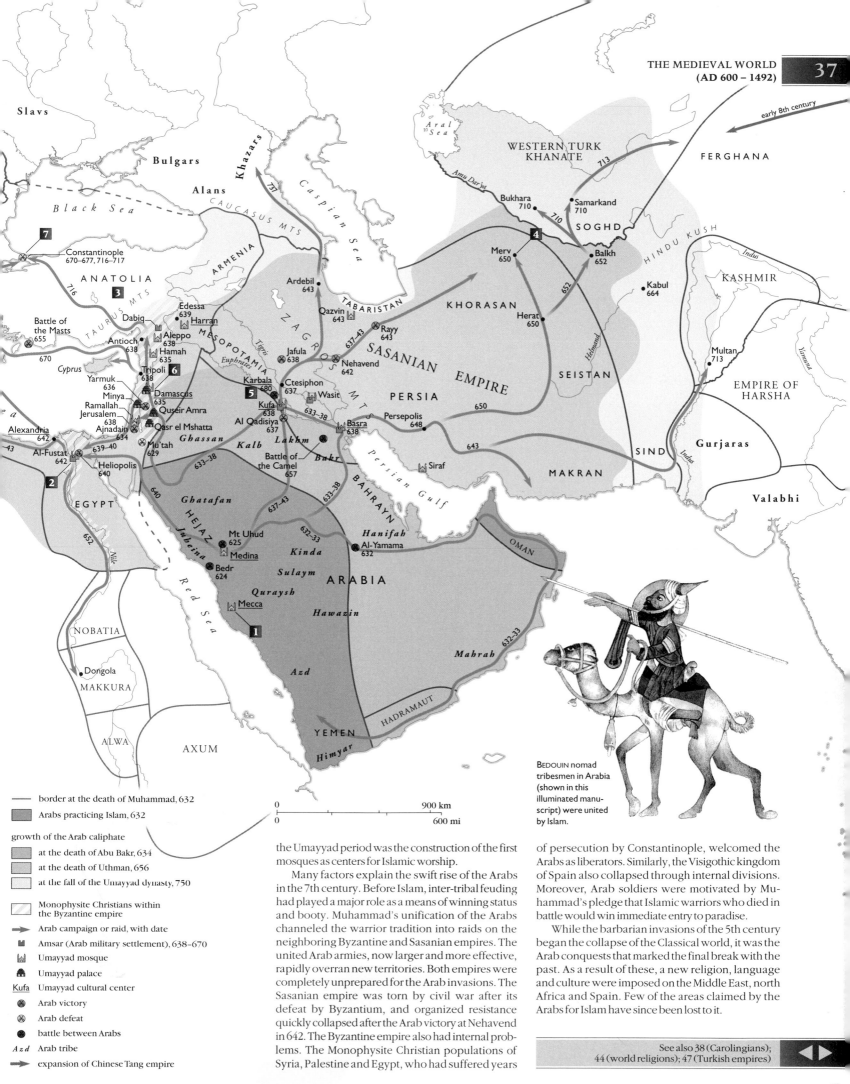

BEDOUIN nomad
tribesmen in Arabia
(shown in this
illuminated manu-
script) were united
by Islam.

— border at the death of Muhammad, 632

▨ Arabs practicing Islam, 632

growth of the Arab caliphate

▨ at the death of Abu Bakr, 634

▨ at the death of Uthman, 656

▨ at the fall of the Umayyad dynasty, 750

▢ Monophysite Christians within
the Byzantine empire

➤ Arab campaign or raid, with date

⛩ Amsar (Arab military settlement), 638–670

🕌 Umayyad mosque

🏛 Umayyad palace

<u>Kufa</u> Umayyad cultural center

⊗ Arab victory

⊗ Arab defeat

● battle between Arabs

Azd Arab tribe

➤ expansion of Chinese Tang empire

0 ———— 900 km
0 ———— 600 mi

the Umayyad period was the construction of the first mosques as centers for Islamic worship.

Many factors explain the swift rise of the Arabs in the 7th century. Before Islam, inter-tribal feuding had played a major role as a means of winning status and booty. Muhammad's unification of the Arabs channeled the warrior tradition into raids on the neighboring Byzantine and Sasanian empires. The united Arab armies, now larger and more effective, rapidly overran new territories. Both empires were completely unprepared for the Arab invasions. The Sasanian empire was torn by civil war after its defeat by Byzantium, and organized resistance quickly collapsed after the Arab victory at Nehavend in 642. The Byzantine empire also had internal problems. The Monophysite Christian populations of Syria, Palestine and Egypt, who had suffered years

of persecution by Constantinople, welcomed the Arabs as liberators. Similarly, the Visigothic kingdom of Spain also collapsed through internal divisions. Moreover, Arab soldiers were motivated by Muhammad's pledge that Islamic warriors who died in battle would win immediate entry to paradise.

While the barbarian invasions of the 5th century began the collapse of the Classical world, it was the Arab conquests that marked the final break with the past. As a result of these, a new religion, language and culture were imposed on the Middle East, north Africa and Spain. Few of the areas claimed by the Arabs for Islam have since been lost to it.

See also 38 (Carolingians);
44 (world religions); 47 (Turkish empires)

Of the Germanic kingdoms set up within the territory of the western Roman empire in the 5th century, only the Frankish and the Visigothic still survived in 600. The Visigothic kings preserved the late Roman administrative structure but, in contrast to the Franks, who were able to win the cooperation and loyalty of their subjects, they remained distant from their Hispano-Roman subjects. This was a fatal weakness. Faced with an invasion of Muslim Arabs and Berbers from North Africa in 711, the Visigoths received no support and the kingdom abruptly collapsed. The invaders took only two years to overrun most of the Iberian peninsula, bringing it within the Umayyad caliphate. Only in the mountains of the far north was there substantial resistance. Here the small Christian kingdom of Asturias developed, based at Oviedo. By 800 it had won back a sizable part of the northwest peninsula from the Arabs.

Since the mid 5th century the Merovingian dynasty had ruled the Frankish kingdom. They followed the Germanic custom of dividing the kingdom between all male heirs, leading to a complex sequence of subdivisions as generation succeeded generation. The succession was rarely a simple matter, and civil wars and assassinations were frequent. In the mid 7th century real authority passed into the hands of court officials known as the mayors of the palace. Frankish power declined and some peripheral areas of the kingdom were lost. Most were recovered early in the 8th century but Aquitaine, which broke away in 670, was not taken back until 768. The most successful of the mayors was Pepin II of Herstal (mayor 679–714), who was effective ruler of the entire kingdom by 687. Founder of the Carolingian dynasty, he began an expansion of Frankish power which continued under his son Charles Martel (mayor 714–41). In 732 he turned back an Arab invasion at Poitiers, ending Muslim expansion in the west.

Charles' successor Pepin III (r.741–68) formed an alliance with the papacy in 751. The year before, the Lombards (rulers of most of Italy since 568) had conquered the Byzantine exarchate of Ravenna and were threatening Rome itself. In return for military aid, the pope authorized Pepin to depose the last Merovingian king and assume the kingship of the Franks himself. Pepin died in 768, and the kingdom was divided between his two sons, Charlemagne and Carloman. On the latter's death in 771 Charlemagne was sole ruler; he doubled the size of the Frankish realm in thirty years of campaigning. He

Legend

- Visigothic kingdom before 711
- — border, c.732
- Byzantine empire, 732
- Umayyad caliphate, 732
- Frankish kingdom, 732
- Frankish gains, 732–768
- Frankish gains under Charlemagne, 768–814
- Frankish empire, 814
- kingdom of Asturias, 814
- Patrimony of St. Peter granted by Charlemagne
- Avar khanate, c.680–791
- Anglo-Saxon kingdoms
- Celtic kingdoms
- Bulgar peoples
- Slavic peoples
- ⊕ patriarchate
- ⊕ archbishopric
- ⌘ monastery
- ⌘ other ecclesiastical center
- ▦ palace
- ♨ early Viking raid
- ☆ trade center or port
- ᴫᴫᴫ defensive earthwork
- ▶ migration of peoples

```
0                                    600 km
0                                    400 mi
```

was also an energetic legislator and administrator and was devoutly religious, even intervening in matters of doctrine. He promoted missionary activity among the pagan Saxons in the northeast and, anxious to improve the quality of the clergy, encouraged the revival of classical learning known as the Carolingian renaissance. Charlemagne made considerable donations of land to the papacy and, influenced by Byzantine ideas of rulership, had himself crowned emperor by the pope on Christmas Day 800, an act he probably saw as restoring the Roman empire in the west. In line with Frankish custom, Charlemagne made provisions for his empire to be divided between his three sons after his death but was survived by only one, Louis the Pious.

In the British Isles, the Anglo-Saxons had overrun most of the fertile lowland zone by 600 and were

TIMELINE

The Franks

639 With the death of King Dagobert, a succession of short-lived kings sees power pass from the Merovingians to the mayors of the palace

689 Mayor Pepin II begins the conquest of the Frisians

732 Charles Martel defeats Arab invasion at Poitiers

751 Pope Zacharias authorizes the deposition of the last Merovingian king by Pepin III (d. 768)

771 Charlemagne becomes sole ruler of the Frankish kingdom

774 Charlemagne conquers Lombard kingdom of Italy

800 Charlemagne is crowned Roman emperor by Pope Leo III in Rome

814 Death of Charlemagne, succession of Louis the Pious

Western Christendom

c.600–635 Life of Isidore of Seville, theologian, historian and encyclopedist

616 The Visigoths expel the Byzantines from southern Spain

664 British churches adopt Roman Christianity at the Synod of Whitby: decline of Celtic Christianity

c.672–735 Life of Bede: monk, scholar, theologian and historian of early England

711–13 Arabs and Berbers conquer the Visigothic kingdom of Spain

718 The Danes fortify their southern border against Saxon attack

726 Iconoclast controversy causes a breach between the Byzantine and Roman churches

750 Lombards capture Ravenna, ending Byzantine power in central Italy

790 A dispute between King Offa of Mercia and Charlemagne disrupts cross-channel trade

793 The monastery of Lindisfarne is sacked by Viking raiders

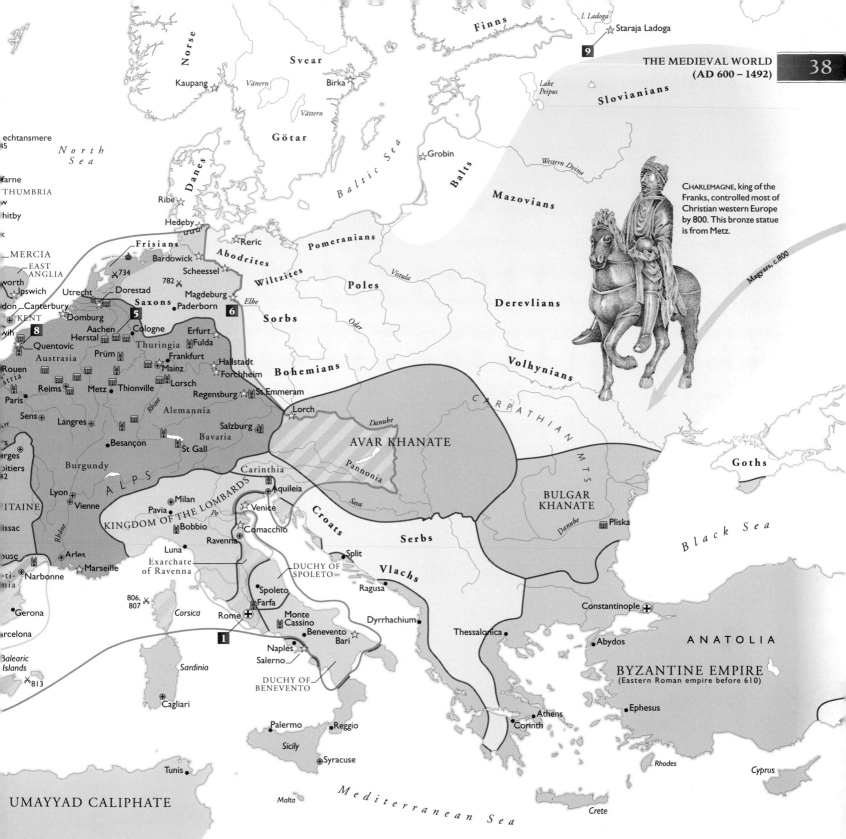

CHARLEMAGNE, king of the Franks, controlled most of Christian western Europe by 800. This bronze statue is from Metz.

Map labels:

Finns
L Ladoga
☆ Staraja Ladoga
9
Norse
Svear
Kaupang
Vänern
Birka
Slovianians
Lake Peipus
echtansmere
North Sea
Danes
Götar
Vättern
Western Dvina
Mazovians
farne
THUMBRIA
☆ Grobin
Baltic Sea
Balts
w
hitby
Ribe
Hedeby
Reric
Pomeranians
Poles
Magyars, c.800
MERCIA
EAST ANGLIA
Frisians
Abodrites
Bardowick
Scheessel
Wiltzites
Vistula
Derevlians
worth
Ipswich
734
782
Utrecht
Dorestad
Magdeburg
Saxons
Paderborn
Sorbs
6
Elbe
don
Canterbury
Domburg
Cologne
Oder
Volhynians
KENT
8
Aachen
Erfurt
Bohemians
wih
Quentovic
Herstal
Thuringia
Fulda
Frankfurt
CARPATHIAN MTS
Austrasia
Prüm
Mainz
Hallstadt
Rouen
Reims
Metz
Thionville
Lorsch
Forchheim
stria
Paris
Regensburg
St Emmeram
Goths
Sens
Langres
Alemannia
Lorch
Danube
rges
Salzburg
AVAR KHANATE
oitiers
Lyon
Besançon
Bavaria
Pannonia
BULGAR KHANATE
2
Vienne
St Gall
Burgundy
ALPS
Carinthia
Sava
Pliska
issac
ITAINE
Milan
KINGDOM OF THE LOMBARDS
Aquileia
Venice
Croats
Rhône
Pavia
Po
Serbs
Danube
Black Sea
Bobbio
Comacchio
Arles
Luna
Ravenna
Vlachs
Marseille
Exarchate of Ravenna
Split
Gerona
Narbonne
DUCHY OF SPOLETO
Ragusa
Constantinople
806, 807
Corsica
Spoleto
Farfa
Dyrrhachium
rcelona
Rome
1
Thessalonica
ANATOLIA
Balearic Islands
Monte Cassino
Benevento
Bari
Abydos
813
Naples
Salerno
BYZANTINE EMPIRE
(Eastern Roman empire before 610)
ti-nia
Sardinia
DUCHY OF BENEVENTO
Ephesus
Cagliari
Palermo
Reggio
Athens
Corinth
Sicily
Rhodes
Cyprus
Tunis
Syracuse
Mediterranean Sea
Malta
Crete

UMAYYAD CALIPHATE

beginning to form regional kingdoms, the most powerful being Northumbria. The Anglo-Saxon migrations into southern Britain had cut off British Christianity from contact with the Roman church. The Celtic church developed a distinctive identity and in Ireland fostered the creation of a monastic civilization that was to have significant influence on cultural and religious life in Europe. Irish and Roman missionaries both won converts among the Anglo-Saxons in the 7th century, and it was only with difficulty that the Celtic church was persuaded to rejoin the Roman church in 664. Northumbrian power declined after defeat by the Picts in 685, and in the 8th century the Mercian kingdom rose to dominance under Aethelbald (r.716–57) and Offa (r.757–96).

Frankish overrule brought a modest revival of trade and towns to western Europe, most marked around the southern North Sea and the Baltic, where ports and seasonal trading places developed by 800. Though threatened by the Viking raids that broke out in the 790s, it was the start of the process that shifted the focus of economic life from the Mediterranean to the North Sea and Atlantic coasts.

1 Rome found a new role as the seat of the papacy and the spiritual capital of western Christendom.

2 The Asturian victory at Covadonga is regarded as the beginning of the Christian reconquest of Spain.

3 King Offa of Mercia built a 240km (185 mile) earth and timber rampart on his frontier with the Welsh.

4 The Bretons fiercely resisted Frankish expansion: subdued by Charlemagne in 799, they revolted in 812.

5 Charlemagne built an impressive palace, administrative and ecclesiastical complex at Aachen in the 790s.

6 Charlemagne set up a chain of customs posts to regulate trade with the Slavs in 806.

7 Córdoba, the capital of Muslim Spain, was the largest city in western Europe by the 9th century.

8 Trading centers such as Hamwih and Quentovic were evidence of the growing commercial importance of northern Europe.

9 Scandinavian merchants were established at the Finnic settlement of Staraja Ladoga by 750.

See also 33 (fall of Roman empire); 37 (Arab conquests); 41 (Viking age)

The most sophisticated of the pre-Columbian civilizations of the Americas was the Maya of Guatemala, Petén and Yucatán. By draining and canalizing the swamplands, agricultural production rose in the Middle Preclassic period (700–300 BC), making it possible to support large populations. Chiefdoms and small states appeared and the first towns and monumental structures were built. During the Late Preclassic (300 BC–AD 300) powerful city-states emerged, writing came into use, advanced mathematical and astronomical studies were pursued, and a calendrical system was adopted. The new states were competitive and warlike and many cities were fortified. Underlying these developments may have been such factors as population pressure, agricultural intensification, long-distance trade and increased warfare. The main influences on the development of Mayan civilization were the Olmecs and the Zapotecs, from whom the Maya received, among other things, the 52-year "long count" calendar, writing and the sacred ball game.

The most important Maya center of the Late Preclassic period was the city of El Mirador, occupied 150 BC–AD 150. It had large temple pyramids, a fortified palace area, marketplaces and a population approaching 80,000. Causeways known as *sacbes* linked El Mirador with its subordinate villages. Although there is some evidence of writing at El Mirador, the best evidence for its use by the Pre-classic Maya comes from the southern highland area, where many *stelae* (stone monuments) were erected at sites like Kaminaljuyú, in the 1st and 2nd centuries AD, to commemorate royal ancestors. The earliest known inscription, found at El Baul, carries a "long-count" date equivalent to AD 36. The Maya did not invent writing themselves, but their hieroglyphic script was the only pre-Columbian script that could fully express the spoken language. The Mayan script included both ideographic and phonetic elements. About 800 glyphs are known. The southern Maya declined in the 3rd century AD and the tradition of erecting commemorative *stelae* died out. The cause was probably a volcanic eruption that blew apart

Mount Ilopango, covering thousands of square kilometers with ash and ruining agriculture for years.

Commemorative *stelae* with hieroglyphic inscriptions began to be erected by the Maya in the central lowland rainforest area around AD 300, a development that marks the beginning of the Classic period (AD 300–800). The earliest show clear stylistic links with the highland Maya. Until about AD 400 *stelae* were only erected at Tikal, Uaxactún and a few nearby centers, but thereafter the practice spread throughout the central area. Palenque, Yaxchilán, Copán and Calakmul all developed into major regional powers, but the dominant city-state for much of the Classic period was Tikal, with a population of 75,000–100,000. At its peak under King Stormy Sky (r.411–57), Tikal dominated most of the central area and maintained cultural and trade links

with Teotihuacán, the greatest power in Meso-america. Tikal went into decline after its defeat by Caracol in 562; and although it recovered under Ah Cacau (r.682–723) it did not regain its preeminence.

Warfare was common among the Classic Maya city-states, although the aim was more often to exact tribute and take prisoners than to annex territory permanently. The normal fate of prisoners was ritual torture and mutilation, after which they were sacrificed to the gods. Human sacrifices were needed to dedicate new temples, to accompany the dead and to mark important events such as the completion of calendrical cycles. Mayan rulers were expected to take part in painful bloodletting rites as a means of communicating with ancestral spirits. Marriage alliances were the usual means of forging friendly relations between states.

late Preclassic site with monumental sculpture, 300 BC–AD 300

other late Preclassic site, 300 BC–AD 300

area of Classic Maya civilization, AD 300–800

Puuc style

Chenes style

Rio Bec style

Cotzumalhuapan style

major Classic site

minor Classic site

pre-eminent regional center

influence of Tikal, 5th century AD

Tikal dynastic histories deciphered

city-state border, AD 790

trade route

cacao source of traded commodity

area with intensive agriculture

raised fields

stone-faced terraces

0   200 km
0   150 mi

MOSAIC jade mask found at Palenque, possibly a representation of Pacal, ruler of Palenque in the 7th century.

1 El Mirador was the largest Maya center in the Late Preclassic period, before being abandoned c.AD 150.

2 Lake Ilopango now fills the crater left by the catastrophic eruption of Mount Ilopango c.AD 200-250, which caused the decline of the southern Maya .

3 Tikal was the largest Maya city. It reached its peak under King Stormy Sky (r.AD 411-57) and dominated the central Maya until conquered by Caracol in 562.

4 Classic Maya ceremonial centers were often aligned on astronomical events. The earliest such center, at Uaxactún, was aligned on the midwinter, equinoctial and midsummer sunrises.

5 Copán, a major Maya center during the Classic period, was supplanted by Quirigua in 738.

6 The raised causeway, or *sacbe*, linking Cobá with Yaxuná runs for some 100 kilometers (62 miles).

7 Murals at Bonampak celebrating a victory of King Chan Muan c.790 provide vivid evidence of the warlike character of Maya civilization.

8 Power and population moved to the north in the Early Postclassic period (AD 900–1200), when Chichén Itzá became the dominant Maya center.

TIMELINE

	400 BC	AD I	AD 400	AD 800
Political change	500–100 BC Mayan forms of kingship develop		c.200–250 The eruption of Mount Ilopango devastates the southern Maya	695 King Jaguar Paw of Calakmul is captured and sacrificed by Ah Cacau of Tikal
	c.350–300 BC The earliest Maya city-states appear			
		c.150 BC–AD 150 El Mirador is the largest center of Mayan civilization	300–600 Teotihuacán is an influence on the Maya	800s The central Maya states are in decline
			411–57 Tikal is the dominant Maya center during the reign of King Stormy Sky	c.900 Chichén Itzá becomes the dominant Maya center
			562 Tikal is defeated by the state of Caracol	
		LATE PRECLASSIC PERIOD	CLASSIC PERIOD	POSTCLASSIC PERIOD
Cultural change	200–100 BC The earliest known Mayan writing dates from this time		c.300 Corbeled arches and vaults first appear in Mayan architecture	799 The last monuments are erected at Palenque
		AD 36 The earliest Mayan calendrical inscriptions, at El Baul, date from this year	800 The "long count" calendar falls into disuse	
			292 Earliest known lowland inscription – found at Tikal	889 The last monuments are erected at Tikal
	400 BC	AD I	AD 400	AD 800

Komchen
Dzibilchaltún
Izamal
Acanceh
feathers slaves
Chichén Itzá
Oxkintok
feathers slaves
Cobá
Uxmal
Mul-Chic
Chacchob
Yaxuná
Jaina
Xcalumkin
Kabah
Loltun
Chacmultún
Tancah
Sayil
Keuic
Labná
Xcochob
Xcichmook
Yucatán Peninsula
Xtampak
Dzibilnocac
Huntichmul
Edzná
Gulf of Mexico
Hochob
NORTHERN AREA

Isla de Cozumel

Pechal
cacao
Becan
Xpuhil
Hormiguero
Pasión del Cristo
Rio Bec
Cohunlich
Cerros
Uaacbal
Candelaria
Oxpemul
La Muñeca
Nohmul
Cuello
Calakmul
El Palmar
Colhá
Bellote
Naachlún
Altamira
Altun Ha
Comalcalco
Ucal
Balakbal
Jonuta
Rio Azul
Lamanaí
cacao
Balancán
El Mirador
La Honradez
Morales
Xulún
San José
CENTRAL AREA
Nakum
Baking Pot
Tortuguero
Pomoná
1 **4**
Uaxactún
Naranjo
PETÉN
El Perú
Tikal
Palenque
Chinikhá
El Porvenir
Uolaritún
Xunantunich
Piedras Negras
Yaxhá
Mountain Cow
La Mar
El Cayo
Mótul de San José
3
Lago Peten Itzán
Caracol
Pomona
Toniniá
Lacanhá
cacao
San Augustin
Chiapa de Corzo
Agua Escondida
Yaxchilán
Itzán
El Caribe
Sacul
Nimli Punit
7
Bonampak
La Armelia
Seibal
Ixtutz
Santa Cruz
Santa Elena
Poco Uinic
Altar de Sacrificios
Ixtutz
Lubaantún
Dos Pilas
Machaquitá
Pusihá
Grijalva
Chinkultic
Aguateca
Cancuén
marine products and shells
Quen Santo
Salinas de los Nueve Cerros
feathers obsidian salt
cacao
Lagartero
Chamá
cacao
Lago de Izabal
Santa Rica
Nebaj
Quirigua
Los Higos
La Lagunita
San Agustin Acasaguastián
El Paraiso
cacao feathers
SOUTHERN AREA
Motagua
cacao jade
Copán
Guatemalan Highlands
Izapa
jade
5
Takalik
Lago de Atitlán
obsidian
Kaminaljuyú
jade
Chucumuk
Yarumela
El Jobo
El Baul
Asuncion Mita
Amatitlán
Salinac la Bianca
Tiquisate
Pantaleon
Obero
Chalchuapa
Lempa
Monti Alto
Finca Arizona
Tazumal
obsidian
2
Lake Ilopango
PACIFIC OCEAN
Usulutan

The civilization of the Classic Maya was not uniform: several regional decorative styles are known, and there was considerable variation in architectural styles. The Maya were highly skilled craftsmen, producing monumental stone sculpture, jade carving, pottery, paintings and obsidian tools of the highest quality. A few gold and copper objects have been found at Mayan sites, but metals were little used before Postclassic times.

The Classic period came to an end around the beginning of the 9th century, when the city-states of the central lowlands began to collapse. The population declined dramatically, new building ceased, and the tradition of erecting commemorative *stelae* was abandoned. The last monuments were erected at Palenque in 799, at Yaxchilan in 808, at Quirigua 810, at Copán in 822 and Tikal in 889. By 950 all the major central Mayan cities lay in ruins. The "long count" calendar fell out of use.

The collapse is thought to be an indirect consequence of the fall of Teotihuacán around 750. Mayan rulers competed, through warfare and by commissioning more and more ambitious building projects, to fill the power vacuum created by the fall of Teotihuacán. Pressures on the peasantry to supply food and labor increased to such a point that the agricultural economy collapsed; malnutrition, population decline and political collapse followed. Classic Mayan civilization did not die out, but continued to flourish in the semiarid north of the Yucatán peninsula until around 1000, when the area was invaded by the Toltecs, from central Mexico.

See also 17 (first civilizations of Mesoamerica);
55 (Toltecs and late Maya)

The years between AD 600 and 800 saw the final breakup of the world of classical antiquity and the dramatic rise of an Arab Islamic civilization. Islam has its origins in the teachings of Muhammad (c.570–632). Islam united the Arabs and created a theocratic state. Despite civil war after the prophet's death, the caliph or "successor" Umar turned Arab energies outward in campaigns of conquest and conversion (▷ 37).

Circumstances were favorable to Arab expansion. From 602 to 627 the Persian Sasanian empire and the surviving eastern half of the Roman empire were locked in total war. The Romans emerged triumphant but the reforms introduced by the emperor Heraclius created an essentially new Greek state, known as the Byzantine empire. Neither Persia nor Byzantium was thus in a fit state to withstand the sudden invasions of Arab armies, which began with the capture of Damascus in 635. By 642 the Arabs had captured Syria, Palestine and Egypt from the Byzantines and completely destroyed the Sasanian empire. A second wave of conquests began after the Umayyad dynasty came to power in 661. In 698 Byzantine Carthage fell and in 711 the Arabs crossed the Straits of Gibraltar and conquered the Visigothic kingdom of Spain. In the east Arab armies reached the Indus and Samarkand. Failure to take Constantinople in 717 and defeat by the Franks at Poitiers in 732 marked the end of the Arab victories. The unity of the Arab world ended in 749–50 when the Umayyads were overthrown and slaughtered by the Abbasids, except for one who escaped to Spain and founded an independent state. By 800 the Abbasids had also lost control of Morocco and Tunisia.

In 600 the Frankish kingdom was the leading state in western Europe, but dynastic instability led to a decline in the late 7th century (▷ 38). Frankish power recovered under the Carolingian dynasty, named for Charlemagne, who controlled most of Christian western Europe and expanded into the pagan lands of eastern Europe. He was crowned Roman emperor by the pope in Rome on Christmas Day, 800. In the British Isles, the Anglo-Saxons confined the Celts to the hilly west. The Scandinavians were beginning state formation, a by-product of which was the onset of Viking raids on western Europe.

China, divided for almost four centuries, was reunited by the Sui dynasty in 589 (▷ 43). The Sui's ambitions overstretched the empire's resources and they were overthrown by the Tang dynasty in 618. China flourished under the early Tang emperors and campaigns in central Asia extended

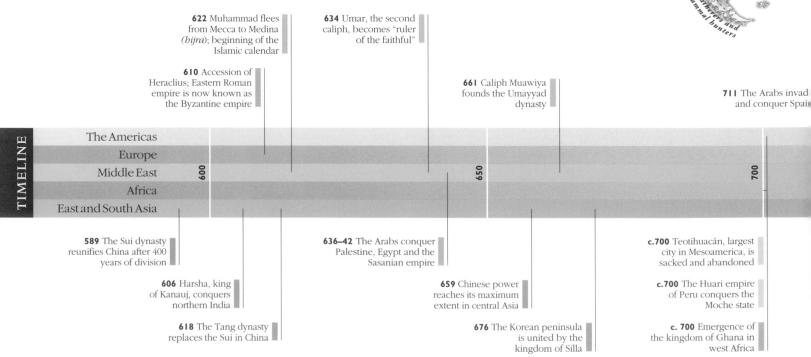

622 Muhammad flees from Mecca to Medina (*hijra*); beginning of the Islamic calendar

634 Umar, the second caliph, becomes "ruler of the faithful"

610 Accession of Heraclius; Eastern Roman empire is now known as the Byzantine empire

661 Caliph Muawiya founds the Umayyad dynasty

711 The Arabs invad and conquer Spai

	600		650		700
The Americas					
Europe					
Middle East					
Africa					
East and South Asia					

TIMELINE

589 The Sui dynasty reunifies China after 400 years of division

636–42 The Arabs conquer Palestine, Egypt and the Sasanian empire

c.700 Teotihuacán, largest city in Mesoamerica, is sacked and abandoned

606 Harsha, king of Kanauj, conquers northern India

659 Chinese power reaches its maximum extent in central Asia

c.700 The Huari empire of Peru conquers the Moche state

618 The Tang dynasty replaces the Sui in China

676 The Korean peninsula is united by the kingdom of Silla

c. 700 Emergence of the kingdom of Ghana in west Africa

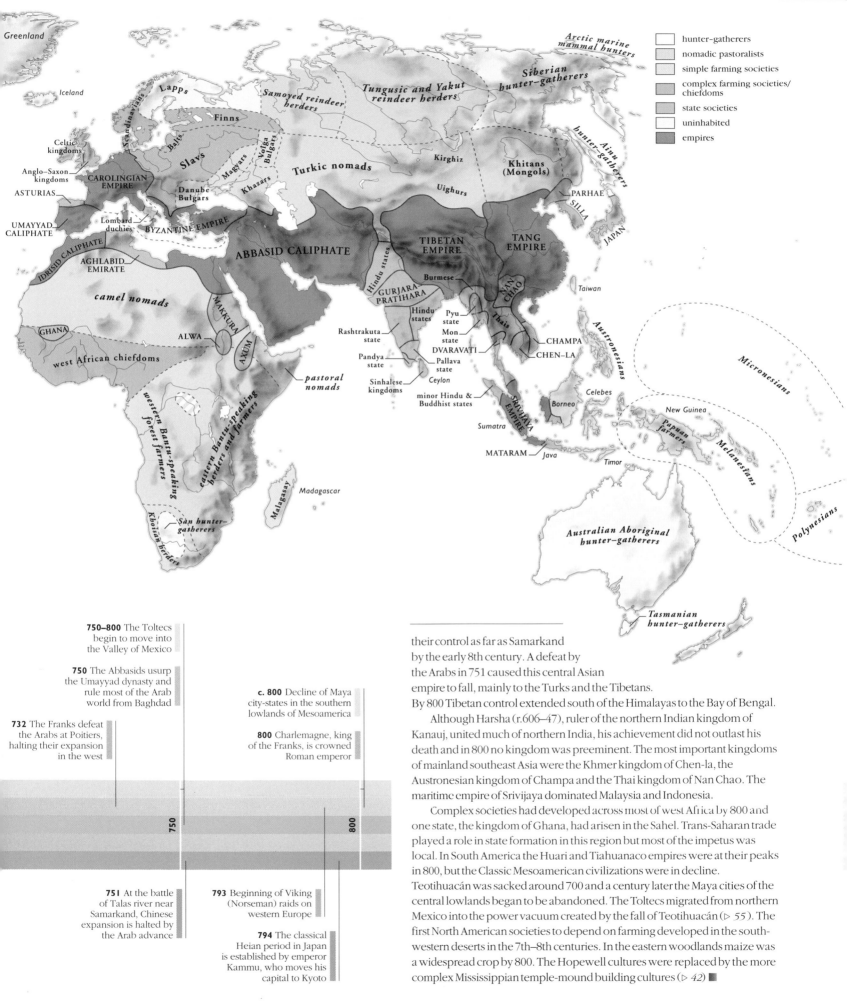

Map legend:
- hunter-gatherers
- nomadic pastoralists
- simple farming societies
- complex farming societies/chiefdoms
- state societies
- uninhabited
- empires

Map labels:

Greenland

Iceland

Lapps

Arctic marine mammal hunters

Samoyed reindeer herders

Tungusic and Yakut reindeer herders

Siberian hunter-gatherers

Ainu hunter-gatherers

Scandinavians

Celtic kingdoms

Finns

Balts

Slavs

Magyars

Volga Bulgars

Kirghiz

Khitans (Mongols)

Anglo-Saxon kingdoms

CAROLINGIAN EMPIRE

ASTURIAS

Danube Bulgars

Khazars

Turkic nomads

Uighurs

PARHAE

SILLA

UMAYYAD CALIPHATE

Lombard duchies

BYZANTINE EMPIRE

TIBETAN EMPIRE

TANG EMPIRE

JAPAN

IDRISID CALIPHATE

ABBASID CALIPHATE

Hindu states

AGHLABID EMIRATE

camel nomads

MAKKURA

GURJARA PRATIHARA

Burmese

NAN CHAO

Taiwan

GHANA

ALWA

AXUM

Rashtrakuta state

Hindu states

Pyu state

Mon state

Thais

CHAMPA

Austronesians

Micronesians

west African chiefdoms

Pandya state

Pallava state

DVARAVATI

CHEN-LA

pastoral nomads

Sinhalese kingdoms

Ceylon

minor Hindu & Buddhist states

SRIVIJAYA EMPIRE

Borneo

Celebes

New Guinea

Papuan farmers

Melanesians

eastern Bantu-speaking herders and farmers

western Bantu-speaking forest farmers

Sumatra

MATARAM

Java

Timor

Madagascar

Malagasay

Australian Aboriginal hunter-gatherers

Polynesians

San hunter-gatherers

Khoisan herders

Tasmanian hunter-gatherers

Timeline:

750–800 The Toltecs begin to move into the Valley of Mexico

750 The Abbasids usurp the Umayyad dynasty and rule most of the Arab world from Baghdad

732 The Franks defeat the Arabs at Poitiers, halting their expansion in the west

c. 800 Decline of Maya city-states in the southern lowlands of Mesoamerica

800 Charlemagne, king of the Franks, is crowned Roman emperor

750

800

751 At the battle of Talas river near Samarkand, Chinese expansion is halted by the Arab advance

793 Beginning of Viking (Norseman) raids on western Europe

794 The classical Heian period in Japan is established by emperor Kammu, who moves his capital to Kyoto

their control as far as Samarkand by the early 8th century. A defeat by the Arabs in 751 caused this central Asian empire to fall, mainly to the Turks and the Tibetans. By 800 Tibetan control extended south of the Himalayas to the Bay of Bengal.

Although Harsha (r.606–47), ruler of the northern Indian kingdom of Kanauj, united much of northern India, his achievement did not outlast his death and in 800 no kingdom was preeminent. The most important kingdoms of mainland southeast Asia were the Khmer kingdom of Chen-la, the Austronesian kingdom of Champa and the Thai kingdom of Nan Chao. The maritime empire of Srivijaya dominated Malaysia and Indonesia.

Complex societies had developed across most of west Africa by 800 and one state, the kingdom of Ghana, had arisen in the Sahel. Trans-Saharan trade played a role in state formation in this region but most of the impetus was local. In South America the Huari and Tiahuanaco empires were at their peaks in 800, but the Classic Mesoamerican civilizations were in decline. Teotihuacán was sacked around 700 and a century later the Maya cities of the central lowlands began to be abandoned. The Toltecs migrated from northern Mexico into the power vacuum created by the fall of Teotihuacán (▷ 55). The first North American societies to depend on farming developed in the southwestern deserts in the 7th–8th centuries. In the eastern woodlands maize was a widespread crop by 800. The Hopewell cultures were replaced by the more complex Mississippian temple-mound building cultures (▷ 42) ■

The Vikings – pagan raiders from Denmark and Norway – burst upon western Europe at the end of the 8th century as a bolt from the blue. The targets for their attacks were defenseless coastal monasteries which offered rich plunder. Their first known raid was against the monastery at Lindisfarne, the center of Northumbrian Christianity, in 793. Six years later they raided the Frankish coast, prompting Charlemagne to set up coastal defenses. But the full weight of Viking raids came in the 830s, when they arrived each year in ever greater numbers and began to sail up navigable rivers like the Rhine to sack inland ports such as Dorestad. Viking activity entered a new phase in 865 when the Danish "Great Army" invaded England with permanent settlement rather than plunder in mind. Much of eastern and northern England was overrun and settled (the area known as the Danelaw, with its capital at York) but the Wessex king Alfred (r.871–99) resisted the Danish advance. By 954 Alfred's successors had conquered the Scandinavian settlements and in the process created a united English kingdom. Traders and farmers as well as pirates, the Vikings also established colonies in Normandy, the Shetland and Orkney Islands, Ireland, the Faroe Islands and Iceland. A migration across the Atlantic in about 1000 led to the colonization of Greenland and the first European exploration in the Americas. In eastern Europe, Swedish venturers known as Rus pioneered trade routes along the rivers of Russia to the Black and Caspian Seas, giving their name to the Russian state, which developed at Novgorod around 862.

The Viking raids and settlements were prompted by developments within Scandinavia itself. By the late 8th century power was becoming centralized, creating an intensely competitive society. For many, pirate raids overseas became a means to acquire wealth, a reputation and an armed following to support their ambitions at home. Others, denied the chance to rule at home, sought to conquer lands for themselves and their followers abroad. Trade and

land hunger, caused by a rising population, were other important factors in the Viking phenomenon.

During the 10th century Denmark and Norway emerged as stable territorial states, a process completed in Sweden by the 12th century. The same period saw the start of the Scandinavians' conversion to Christianity. Denmark's hegemony briefly included England and Norway under Cnut (r.1016–35). In the east the Slavs assimilated the Rus ruling class and by 1000 Kievan Rus was a powerful Slavic state, strongly influenced by the Byzantines who introduced Orthodox Christianity. In Normandy the

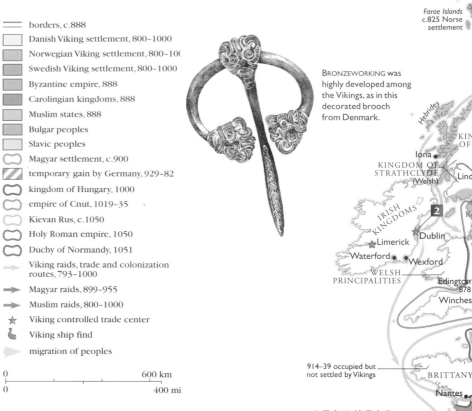

borders, c.888
Danish Viking settlement, 800–1000
Norwegian Viking settlement, 800–100
Swedish Viking settlement, 800–1000
Byzantine empire, 888
Carolingian kingdoms, 888
Muslim states, 888
Bulgar peoples
Slavic peoples
Magyar settlement, c.900
temporary gain by Germany, 929–82
kingdom of Hungary, 1000
empire of Cnut, 1019–35
Kievan Rus, c.1050
Holy Roman empire, 1050
Duchy of Normandy, 1051
Viking raids, trade and colonization routes, 793–1000
Magyar raids, 899–955
Muslim raids, 800–1000
Viking controlled trade center
Viking ship find
migration of peoples

0   600 km
0   400 mi

BRONZEWORKING was highly developed among the Vikings, as in this decorated brooch from Denmark.

Vikings adopted French culture and language by 1000, but remained effectively independent of the French monarchy, which had passed from the Carolingian line when Hugh Capet became king in 987.

The Viking invasions occurred at a time when the Carolingian empire was weakened by internal squabbles. The emperor Louis the Pious (r.814–40) was not willing, as Charlemagne had been, to contemplate the equal division of the empire between his sons. Louis' younger sons and many of the Franks regarded the settlement as unjust and in 827 civil war broke out. The succession was not resolved until the Treaty of Verdun (843) which saw the empire divided into three parts. By this time royal authority was weakened and defenses against the Vikings had collapsed. Charles the Fat briefly reunited the Carolingian empire from 885–87, but it broke

TIMELINE

The Viking world

830s Viking raids on English and Frankish coast increase

845 The Franks buy off raiders by paying Danegeld

859–62 Viking raiders in the Mediterranean

878 Alfred, king of Wessex, defeats the Danes at Edington

882 Oleg makes Kiev capital of the Rus state

911 Charles the Simple allows Viking settlement in Normandy

954 Fall of Viking kingdom of York

965 Harald Bluetooth of Denmark is baptised first Christian king in Scandinavia

986 Erik the Red founds Norse settlements in Greenland

c.1000 Norse Greenlanders found shortlived settlement in Newfoundland

1014 Danes under Svein Forkbeard conquer England

1016–35 Cnut reigns in England, Denmark and Norway

Western Christendom

840 Death of Louis the Pious

843 Treaty of Verdun divides Carolingian empire into three

846 Muslim pirates sack the Vatican

889 Final breakup of the Carolingian empire

898–99 Magyars invade Italy and sack Pavia

910 Cluny abbey is founded in Burgundy, initiating period of monastic reform

911 End of Carolingian rule in Germany and accession of Henry the Fowler, founder of Saxon dynasty

962 Otto I crowned Roman emperor in Rome: Holy Roman empire founded

1002 Umayyad caliphate collapses into petty states

1027 Arrival of Norman mercenaries in southern Italy

1043 Edward the Confessor is crowned king of England

900 ... 1000

Trondheim

NORWAY

Svear
(Swedes)

Oseberg · Tune · Sigtuna
Kaupang · Birka
Hafrsfjord 885 · Gokstad · Vänern

Åskerkärr

Götar

DENMARK · Paviken
Gotland

Arhus · Lund
Skuldelev · Roskilde · Grobin
Ribe · Ladby

EARLDOM OF
NORTHUMBRIA · Hedeby

Baltic Sea · Balts

Abodrites · Wolin · Pomeranians
Hamburg · Kolobrzeg · Elbing
Bremen · Gniezno · Prus
Utrecht · Saxony · Poles
Dorestad · Magdeburg · Vistula · Oder

EAST FRANCIA
(GERMANY)

Dyle 891 · Cologne
Lorraine · Frankfurt
Mainz · Franconia
Metz · Regensburg · Prague
Swabia · Danube · Bohemians
Luxeuil · Lechfeld 955 · Vienna · Gran · Pest
Bavaria · Salzburg · Slovaks
BURGUNDY · St Gall · Pannonia
Sluny · Moravians
Riade 933 · 924 · 915

Finns · Lake Onega · Finns

Beloozero
Staraja Ladoga
Lake Ladoga

Novgorod · Yaroslavl

Izborsk · Pskov
Lake Peipus

KIEVAN RUS

Volga · Bulgar

6 Volga
Bulgars

Gnezdovo · Western Dvina
Viatchians

Derevlians · Chernigov
Kiev · Severyans

Magyars · Dnieper · Don

KHAZAR KHANATE

Sarkel · Volga · Itil

Pechenegs

Goths · Tmutorokan

CARPATHIAN · 896–907

BULGAR
KHANATE

Belgrade · Pliska
Serbs · Danube

Black Sea

Milan · Aquileia · Venice
Pavia · 899
KINGDOM OF ITALY
Patrimony
of St. Peter
CROATIA

ALPS · Lyon

PROVENCE · Marseille · Pisa
Fraxinetum
890–972 Muslim
pirate base · 997
Corsica · 921
Rome · 921
846 · DUCHY OF
BENEVENTO · Otranto
Bari
840–71 Muslim
pirate base

Constantinople 860

ANATOLIA

BYZANTINE EMPIRE

Euphrates · Tigris

Sardinia · 827 · Sicily

Tunis · Malta

AGHLABID
EMIRATE

Mediterranean Sea

Crete

Cyprus

ABBASID
CALIPHATE

up finally in 889 into five kingdoms: West Francia (France), East Francia (Germany), Italy, Burgundy and Provence.

The Vikings were not the only threat facing western Christendom. Muslim pirates from Spain and Tunisia raided the Mediterranean coast and preyed on travelers over the Alpine passes. In the east a nomadic people, the Magyars, crossed the Carpathians around 900 to settle in the Danube plain in the old Roman province of Pannonia, from where they raided Italy, Germany and France. By 1000, however, the Muslim and Magyar threats had ended and Viking activity was limited mainly to the British Isles. Leading the recovery was Germany. With the ending of Carolingian rule there in 911, power passed into the hands of the Saxon kings. Under Otto I (r.936–73) the Magyars were defeated at the

battle of Lechfeld (955) and were converted to Christianity. Expansion against the Slavs continued, and Otto annexed the kingdom of Italy in 951–61. Crowned Roman emperor in 962, he founded what became known as the Holy Roman empire. By the 11th century the German emperors had emerged as the clear leaders of western Christendom.

1 The monastery of Luxeuil was sacked successively by Viking raiders, Muslim pirates and Magyars between 886 and 924.

2 The Viking raids damaged Ireland's monastic culture, but also founded its first towns at Dublin, Wexford, Waterford and Limerick in the 9th century.

3 Paris first rose to prominence as a result of its determined resistance to a Viking siege in 885-86.

4 Conversion of the Poles to Christianity began in 966: the first Polish archbishopric, at Gniezno, was founded in 1000.

5 German protectorates from 935, Burgundy and Provence were united in a single kingdom in 948 and absorbed into the Holy Roman empire in 1033.

6 Rus traders traveled down the river Volga to Bulgar to trade slaves and furs with Arab merchants.

7 Strategically placed, Gotland was an important center of Baltic trade: over 40,000 Arab, 38,000 Frankish and 28,000 Anglo-Saxon silver coins have been found there.

See also 38 (Carolingians);
42 (North America); 44 (world religions)

The initial settlement of North America began around 12,000 years ago as bands of Paleo-indians, the ancestors of modern Native Americans, spread south from Alaska. At first, Paleoindian culture was relatively homogeneous, but adaptation to particular environments led to the emergence of well defined regional cultures by the end of the first millennium BC. From early times hunter–gatherers in many areas of North America had cultivated favored food plants on a small scale. Some native plant species, such as sunflowers, had been domesticated by the end of the first millennium BC and maize and beans had been introduced from Mexico. As wild food sources remained abundant, true farming communities were slow to develop.

The first mainly agricultural North American societies developed in the southwest deserts in about AD 300. Maize, beans, squash and cotton were first cultivated close to permanent water sources, but by about 900 elaborate irrigation systems were in use. By the 9th century three main cultural traditions had developed – the Hohokam, Mogollon and Anasazi – together with two subsidiary cultures, the Patayan and the Fremont. In some areas (such as Chaco Canyon) these cultures developed considerable social complexity. Their most distinctive remains are the multi-roomed dwellings known as pueblos, and their fine pottery. Droughts caused their decline from around 1300.

True farming began to emerge in the eastern woodlands once hardier strains of maize and beans appeared after 700. The resulting growth in food production stimulated the rise of North America's first towns, in the Mississippi basin, by the 12th century. These centered around large earthwork temple mounds. The Mississippian cultures shared a common religion known as the Southern Cult, and were hierarchical. Their rulers were buried in mound-top mortuaries with rich grave goods and even human sacrifices. Large Mississippian towns, such as Cahokia, were the centers of powerful chiefdoms. By the 15th century, Mississippian culture was declining and its heartland was depopulated (the so-called "vacant quarter"). By about 1000 permanent farming villages were established throughout the eastern woodlands. Warfare spread and by the time of European contact, defensive tribal confederacies, such as the Iroquois league, were forming.

Elsewhere in North America hunting, fishing and gathering remained the dominant way of life. On the

cultural areas

- Arctic marine mammal hunters
- sub-Arctic forest hunter-gatherers
- northwest coast salmon fisher-hunter-gatherers
- plateau fisher-hunter-gatherers
- Great Basin hunter-gatherers
- southwest desert farmers
- California fisher-hunter-gatherers
- Great Plains buffalo hunters
- eastern woodland farmer-hunter-gatherers
- Caribbean farmers
- Mesoamerican farming cultures

- uninhabited
- desert
- origin of Thule Inuit culture, 200 BC–AD 800
- Aleut site, AD 600–1500
- Inuit site, AD 600–1800
- Norse settlement, c.AD 1000
- spread of Thule Inuit AD 1000–1500
- Mississippian temple-mound cultures, AD 800–1500
- temple-mound
- the "vacant quarter", c.AD 1450
- Northern Iroquoian territory, c.AD 1000
- site of major bison kill
- Plains farming village, AD 900–1800
- spread of farming

southwest farming cultures

- Anasazi, AD 700–1500
- Fremont, AD 400–1300
- Hohokam, AD 400–1450
- Mogollon, AD 300–1450
- Patayan, AD 875–1450

- Pueblo
- ballcourt
- other important site, AD 600–1500

Pacific coast, ocean resources were so abundant that relatively dense populations and permanent village settlements emerged, with a level of social and cultural complexity far beyond that normally achieved by hunter–gatherer peoples. The Great Plains and the sub-Arctic forests were sparsely populated, though the advent of the bow and arrow in the first millennium AD made big-game hunting more efficient. At the time of European contact buffalo hunting was gradually giving way to farming, but the introduction of the horse (native American horses died out around 10,000 years ago), led many settled Plains peoples to abandon farming for nomadism.

The Paleoindians did not for the most part settle in Arctic North America. The region was uninhabited until about 2500–1900 BC, when the ancestors of

the modern Inuit peoples arrived in Alaska from Siberia. Early Inuit cultures became increasingly well adapted to the Arctic environment, culminating in the Thule tradition which survived to the modern age. This originated during the Old Bering Sea Stage (200 BC–AD 800) among specialized marine mammal hunters on St Lawrence and other Bering Sea islands, from where it spread along Alaska's west coast and north to Point Barrow. From there Thule Inuit migrated east, displacing or assimilating the earlier Dorset Inuit until they reached Greenland in the 13th century. Here they made contact with Norse settlers, with whom they traded and fought. The Norse were not well adapted to life in the Arctic, and by about 1500 their settlements had died out and been occupied by the Thule.

TIMELINE

	800	1100	1400
Eastern woodlands	**800–900** Maize farming becomes an important source of food	**c.1200** Construction of temple-mounds at Moundville, Alabama	
		1050–1250 Growth of towns and large ceremonial centers in Mississippi Basin	**c.1450** Depopulation causes decline of Mississippian towns
SW desert		**c.900** Hohokam culture begins irrigation-based farming	**c.1300** Southwest farming cultures in decline after period of drought
Other areas	**550–600** Bow and arrow adopted by Plains hunters	**c.900** Farming villages begin to spread onto Great Plains	**1492** Columbus reaches the West Indies
		c.1000 Thule Eskimos begin to migrate into eastern Arctic	**c.1500** Extinction of Norse Greenland colony
	800	1100	1400

1 Here a cliff was used as a "jump" over which buffalo were stampeded to their deaths, from c.5400 BC to European contact.

2 A small Norse settlement occupied for about twenty years c.AD 1000 is the only sure evidence that Europeans reached the Americas before Columbus.

3 Ritual ball courts at Snaketown and Casa Grande indicate that the Hohokam culture was influenced by Mesoamerican civilizations.

4 From 900–1300, Chaco Canyon was the hub of a network of 125 planned villages linked by 400 kilometers (250 miles) of roads.

5 Iron ship rivets, textiles and chain mail found at sites at Flagler Bay show contact between the Thule Inuit and the Norse Greenlanders.

6 Sub-Arctic hunters typically sited their camps at river crossings used by herds of caribou (reindeer).

Greenland

Ellesmere Island

AD 1200–1500

5

Flagler Bay
Inuarfissuaq
Thule
Illummersuit

Inussuk

AD 1200–1500

Sermermiut

Utqiagvik
Birnick
Point Barrow

Beaufort Sea

AD 1000–1200

Bathurst Island
de Blicquy

Devon Island
Maxwell Bay
Nunguvik

Craig Harbour

Melville Island

Resolute

Strathcona Sound
Mittimatalik

Baffin Island

Western Settlement

Illutalik

Kangeq
Middle Settlement
Eastern Settlement

avik

AD 1000–1200

Banks Island

Prince of Wales Island

Victoria Island

Kuujja
Memorana

Jackson

Labrador Sea

Klo-kut

6

Bell
Pembroke
Clark
Maleruakik

Pingitkalik

Lady Franklin Point

Naujan

Crystal II

L'Anse aux Meadows

2

Chimi

Great Bear Lake

Silumiut
Iguligardjuk

Southampton Island

GEOMETRICAL design on pottery was typical of the Mimbres Valley in the south-west's Mogollon culture.

Newfoundland

Indian Point

Hudson Bay

Frank Channel

Great Slave Lake

Mingan

er Bay

Charlot River

Lake Athabasca

Reindeer Lake

Metabetchouan

ROCKY

Peace

Athabasca

Tailrace Bay

Lake Winnipeg

Godard Point

Dodge Island

Queen Charlotte Islands

Saskatchewan

Lake Superior

St. Laurent

APPALACHIAN MTS

Fraser

MOUNTAINS

Nesikep

Old Women's Buffalo Jump

Lake Michigan

Lake Huron

Lake Ontario

Maxon-Derby

Nodwell
Sackett

Vancouver Island

Avonlea

Head-Smashed-In

Missouri

1

Columbia

Big Hidatsa
Molander

ATLANTIC OCEAN

Lake Erie

Ozette
Hoko River

Vore

Great Plains

Arzberger

Mississippi

Proctorville

Fort Ancient
Clay Mound

Netarts Sand Spit

Wakemap Mound

Big Goose Creek
Glenrock

Oneota

Ohio

Angel

Town Creek

Snake

Platte

Old Fort
Cahokia

Kings Mound
Hiwassee Island

Gunther Island

Hogup Cave

Wardell

Medicine Creek

Middle Mississippian

Shiloh
Etowah

Knapp Mounds

Arkansas

Alkali Ridge

San Francisco Bay

Mesa Verde

Lamar

SIERRA NEVADA

Salmon Ruin

Colorado

Pueblo Bonito
Pecos Pueblo
Chaco Canyon

Caddoan

Moundville

South Appalachian Mississippian

Lake Jackson

Santa Barbara

Canyon de Chelly
Montezuma Castle

4

Winterville

Plaquemine Mississippian

Topoc Maze

Mogollon

Emerald Mound

Pueblo Grande

3

Snaketown
Casa Grande

Garnsey

Coles Creek

Safety Harbor

Mimbres Valley

Rio Grande

PACIFIC OCEAN

Casas Grandes

Gulf of Mexico

La Candelaria

Cuba

0   1200 km
0   800 mi

See also 62 (Spanish empire);
70 (European exploration of North America)

The centralized Chinese empire created by Shi Huangdi survived until AD 220, when it split into three rival states. Unity was restored in 589 by Yang Jian, who as emperor Wen (r.589–604) became the founder of the Sui dynasty. Wen, a tyrannical but able ruler, re-established a strong centralized bureaucracy and increased the prosperity of the peasantry through a land redistribution scheme. Granaries were built and the canal system expanded. As a result of Wen's reforms, the economy grew and the state amassed large reserves of cash and commodities. These were squandered on building projects and opulent court life by Wen's successor, Yang (r.604–17). Moreover, a disastrous war against the Korean kingdom of Koguryo caused the peasants of the northeast to rebel. The empire was saved only by the coup of Li Yuan, military governor of Taiyuan, who captured the Sui capital at Luoyang in 617 and became, after Yang's murder in 618, the first emperor of the Tang dynasty (as Gaozong, r.618–26). Gaozong was then deposed by his son Taizong (r.626–49), one of Chinese history's ablest rulers.

Taizong based his government loosely on the Han model but without the feudal elements. At its head was the emperor, whose authority (in theory if not always in practice) was absolute. The central administration consisted of three bodies, the Imperial Chancellery, the Imperial Secretariat and the Department for State Affairs. This latter department supervised the six ministries – officials, finances, religious rites, the army, justice and public works – while a Board of Censors oversaw the actions of officials. The empire was divided into 15 administrative regions or "circuits", under an inspecting commissioner. The examination system became more important for selecting bureaucratic staff, yet the cost of education precluded all but the rich landowning classes from pursuing a career in administration. The

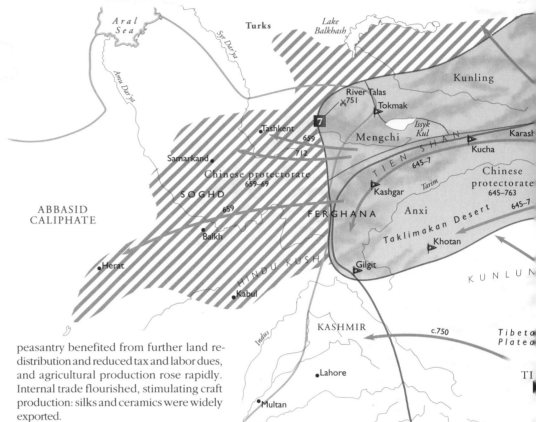

peasantry benefited from further land redistribution and reduced tax and labor dues, and agricultural production rose rapidly. Internal trade flourished, stimulating craft production: silks and ceramics were widely exported.

The Sui had regained the strategic Gansu Corridor. When Turkish nomad power declined after their Uighur subjects rebelled in 627–28, Taizong began to extend Chinese control into central Asia, creating a military protectorate in the Tarim basin. This expansion brought the first extensive contacts between China and Tibet, which had emerged as a powerful centralized kingdom under Sron-btsan-sgampo (r.605–49). Gaozong

TIMELINE

Political change

589 Yang Jian unites China and founds Sui dynasty

c. 600 Emergence of Tibet and Nan Chao states

611–14 A Sui attempt to conquer Koguryo defeated with heavy loss

618 Li Yuan becomes the first emperor of the Tang dynasty

640–59 The Chinese expand into central Asia

676 Silla becomes the leading Korean kingdom

751 Arab victory over the Tang at the River Talas

755–63 Rebellion of An Lushan leads to breakdown of central administration

780 Collapse of the kingdom of Silla

791 Chinese lose control of Gansu corridor after defeat of Chinese–Uighur army by Tibetans at Tingzhou

907–60 The Five Dynasties and Ten Kingdoms

907 Final collapse of the Tang dynasty

936 Foundation of the kingdom of Koryo (Korea)

939 Annam becomes independent of China

960–79 Song Taizu reunites China

874–84 Major peasant rebellions: decline of the Tang dynasty

Cultural change

606–09 The Grand Canal from Beijing to Yue is built

635 Nestorian Christian missionaries reach China

c. 700–800 Earliest text produced by block printing

c. 701–761 Life of the poet Li Po

713–68 Life of the poet Du Fu

780 Lu Yu's *The Classic of Tea* describes tea use

c.825 Chamber lock in use on Chinese canals

845 Persecution of non-Chinese religions including Buddhism and Christianity

c.850 Possible earliest use of gunpowder

Legend

- ——— border, 750
- ——— "circuits" of Tang empire, 742
- civil administration
- military government
- temporary expansion, 7th century
- Abbasid caliphate, c.751
- maximum extent of Tibetan kingdom, c.800
- capital
- seat of circuit-inspecting commissioner, 742
- seat of government-general, 800
- Chinese garrison
- non-Chinese capital
- outbreak of An Lushan's rebellion, 755
- other rebellion against the Tang
- concentration of pottery kilns
- Sui campaign
- Tang campaign
- Tibetan expansion
- frontier wall
- major migration
- major canal
- modern coastline and drainage where altered

0   800 km
0   500 mi

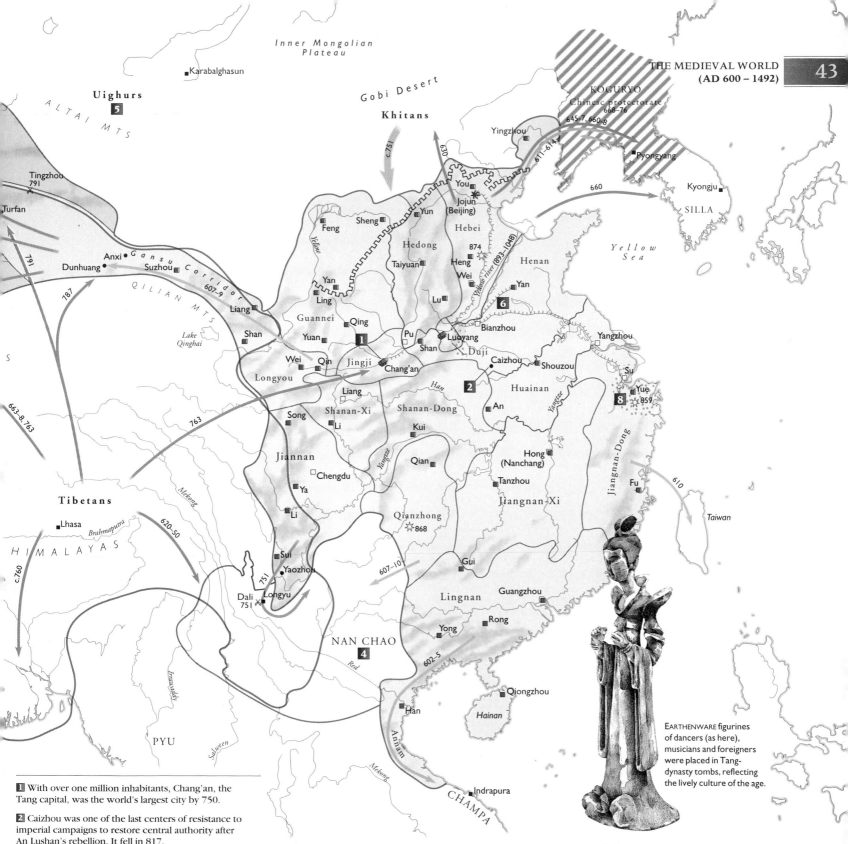

Inner Mongolian Plateau

Karabalghasun

Uighurs
5

ALTAI MTS

Gobi Desert

Khitans

KOGURYO
Chinese protectorate
668–76
645–7, 660–8

Tingzhou
791

Turfan

Yingzhou

You

Jojun
(Beijing)

Pyongyang

Kyongju

SILLA

660

Gansu Corridor
607–9

Anxi

Dunhuang

Suzhou

QILIAN MTS

791

787

Liang

Shan

Wei

Qin

Lake
Qinghai

Feng

Sheng

Yan

Ling

Guannei

Yuan

Qing

Pu

Yun

Hedong

Taiyuan

Hebei

874

Heng

Wei

Lu

Yan

6

Bianzhou

Henan

Luoyang

Yangzhou

Yellow
Sea

663–8, 763

763

Jingji

Chang'an

1

Duji

Shan

Caizhou

2

Han

Shanan-Dong

Shouzou

Su

Yue

859

8

Longyou

Liang

Song

Li

Shanan-Xi

An

Huainan

Yangtze

Tibetans

Lhasa

Brahmaputra

HIMALAYAS

620–50

c.760

Mekong

Jiannan

Chengdu

Ya

Li

Kui

Qian

Qianzhong

868

Jiangnan-Xi

Hong
(Nanchang)

Tanzhou

Jiangnan-Dong

Fu

610

Taiwan

Sui

Yaozhou

751

Dali
751

Longyu

607–10

Gui

Lingnan

Guangzhou

Yong

Rong

NAN CHAO
4

Red

602–5

Qiongzhou

Irrawaddy

Salween

PYU

Han

Hainan

Mekong

Annam

Indrapura

CHAMPA

EARTHENWARE figurines
of dancers (as here),
musicians and foreigners
were placed in Tang-
dynasty tombs, reflecting
the lively culture of the age.

1 With over one million inhabitants, Chang'an, the Tang capital, was the world's largest city by 750.

2 Caizhou was one of the last centers of resistance to imperial campaigns to restore central authority after An Lushan's rebellion. It fell in 817.

3 Tibet emerged as a united kingdom c.600 and reached its greatest extent c.800.

4 Nan Chao, a Thai kingdom in modern Yunnan province, emerged c.600.

5 The Uighurs were a Turkic nomad tribe allied with the Chinese against the Turks and Tibetans.

6 The canal system linked the grain-producing Yangtze valley with the political center of the empire and the northern frontier zone.

7 The decisive battle at the River Talas, which led to the fall of China's central Asian empire, followed an appeal to the Arabs from the ruler of Tashkent for protection against the Chinese.

8 The first true porcelain was made in eastern China during the Tang period.

(r.649–83) brought Ferghana and Soghd under Chinese control in 659. However, these conquests overextended the empire and they were lost by 665. In the east, the Chinese subdued Koguryo in 668 but the Korean kingdom of Silla expelled them in 676.

The Chinese position in central Asia was dealt further blows in 751, with defeats by the Arabs at the River Talas and by the Thai kingdom of Nan Chao at Dali. The Mongol Khitan nomads emerged as a threat in the north in the 8th century. At home, landlord–peasant conflict increased, and the emperors from Gaozong onward proved ineffectual. A rebellion of the general An Lushan in 755 threatened the Tang. It was suppressed in 763 but central authority did not recover and power devolved to around forty semi-independent military governments-general. In 791, the empire lost control of the Gansu Corridor to

the Tibetans following their victory over a Chinese and Uighur army at Tingzhou. In 859, 868 and 874–84 peasant rebellions broke out. The emperor's authority was damaged beyond repair and power was again seized by provincial warlords. The Tang struggled on until 907, finally collapsing in a period of disunity known as the Five Dynasties and Ten Kingdoms (907–960).

The Tang period is regarded as the golden age of Chinese poetry. The dynasty also presided over major achievements in historiography and painting, and restored Confucianism as the state ideology after it had declined during the Period of Disunion.

See also 26 (early imperial China);
44 (the world religions)

The birth of Islam, the most recent of the world religions, dominated the era known to Europeans as the Middle Ages, and it deeply affected all the established world religions.

Islam originated in the teachings of the prophet Muhammad. From 610 Muhammad received a series of revelations which are recorded in the sacred book of Islam, the *Koran*. Islam drew much from Judaism and, to a lesser extent, Christianity. The *Koran* asserts that Muhammad is the last of a line of prophets that included Adam, Abraham, Noah, Moses and Jesus.

By the time of Muhammad's death in 632, Arabs had generally acknowledged him as their religious and political leader and had accepted Islam. Muhammad had no male heir and the decades following his death were marked by prolonged disputes over his successor, which erupted into civil war during the caliphate of Muhammad's son-in-law Ali (r.656–61). When Ali was murdered in 661, his supporters recognized his son Husain as successor (caliph) in preference to Muawiya, founder of the Umayyad dynasty. Husain's death in battle at Karbala in 680 led to his martyrdom, and the development among his supporters of the Shiite tradition of Islam.

Shiism has continued to be distinguished from the majority Sunni tradition by its stress on martyrdom and its radically different theories of religious leadership. In the 9th century doctrinal disputes resulted in the secession from Shiism of the Ismaili sect. Until the 13th century, the Ismailis (who are also known as the Assassins) habitually murdered their enemies. Moreover, the spread of both the Sunni and Shiite Islamic traditions was promoted by the growth, from the 8th century onward, of the mystical movement known as Sufism, which laid a heavy emphasis on piety and zeal.

The rise of Islam halved the area under Christian domination between 600 and 750. Islam tolerated Christians but the social and financial advantages of conversion were great and Christianity soon declined in the areas conquered by the Arabs. However, freedom from Orthodox persecution enabled some minority Christian sects, such as the Nestorians, to spread widely in Asia. Although it regained some ground through missionary work and military conquest – most notably the Crusades that temporarily restored Christian

Map labels

ATLANTIC OCEAN

Nidaras (Trondheim)
Glasgow
SCANDINAVIA Christianity, c.950–1100
Uppsala
Lincoln York
Salisbury London
Canterbury
Roskilde
Rouen Paris
Saxons Christianity, 785
Novgorod
Santiago de Compostela
Chartres Amiens
Cologne
LITHUANIA Christianity, 1386
León Bourges Reims
Danzig
Moscow
Burgos
Strasbourg Ulm
Prague
Poles Christianity c.1000
SPAIN Christianity, 750–1492
Freiburg Regensburg
Russians Christianity, 989
Toledo
Milan Vienna
Seville Córdoba
Kiev
Fez
Magyars (Hungarians) Christianity, c.1000
Tlemcen
Rome
KHAZAR KHANATE Jewish ruling dynasty, c.800–1242
Bulgars Christianity, 890
Mt Athos
Constantinople
Black Sea
TEKRUR Islam, c.1030
BYZANTINE EMPIRE Islam, 1071–1453
GEORGIA
Caspian Sea
Konya
Barda
Niger
GHANA Islam, 1076
Timbuktu
Nisibis
Arbela
Kirkuk
MALI Islam, c.1250
Masyaf
Bethlehem
Damascus Baghdad
Tanta Cairo
Jerusalem
Seleucia
Kaskar
Karbala
AIR Islam, c.1350
Umm Abida
Basra
Rev-Ardashir
Shiraz
Nile
Medina
Humaithira
Mecca
MAKKURA Islam, 1317
Red Sea
ALWA
Axum
CONGO Christianity, 1490
Lalibela
Socotra
Debre Libanos
ETHIOPIA
Harer
Somalis Islam, c.1100
Kilwa

Timeline

		700	1000	1300
TIMELINE	**South and east Asia**	**600–700** Beginning of the Bakhti revival of Hinduism in India **600–800** Spread of Chan and Pure Land Buddhism in China **c.700** Persian Zoroastrians settle in India: origin of Parsis **762** Uighur nomads adopt Manichaeanism as religion	**791** Buddhism becomes the state religion in Tibet **843** Manichaeanism in China is destroyed by persecution **845** Buddhists face persecution in China **900–1000** Pilgrimages are established as an important expression of Hindu devotion	**1191** Zen (Chan) Buddhism is introduced to Japan **1200–1300** Buddhism dies out in northern India
	Middle East	**622** Muhammad's flight (*hijra*) from Mecca to Medina **700–800** Growth of the Sufi mystical movement in Islam	**c.970** Turks convert to Islam **c.1070** Islam spreads to sub-Saharan Africa	**1258** Mongols destroy the Abbasid caliphate of Baghdad
	Europe	**726–843** Iconoclast controversy: destruction of religious images in Byzantine empire	**965** Harald Bluetooth of Denmark is baptized: the first Christian king of Scandinavia **1054** Roman–Orthodox schism becomes permanent **1095–99** The First Crusade is called; Jerusalem is taken	**1209–29** Crusades are launched against Cathar (Manichaean) heretics **1232** The Church sets up the Inquisition to fight heresy **1378–1417** Great Schism damages papal authority
		700	1000	1300

SHIVA, one of the major deities of Hinduism, is seen in his form as Nataraja (Lord of Dance).

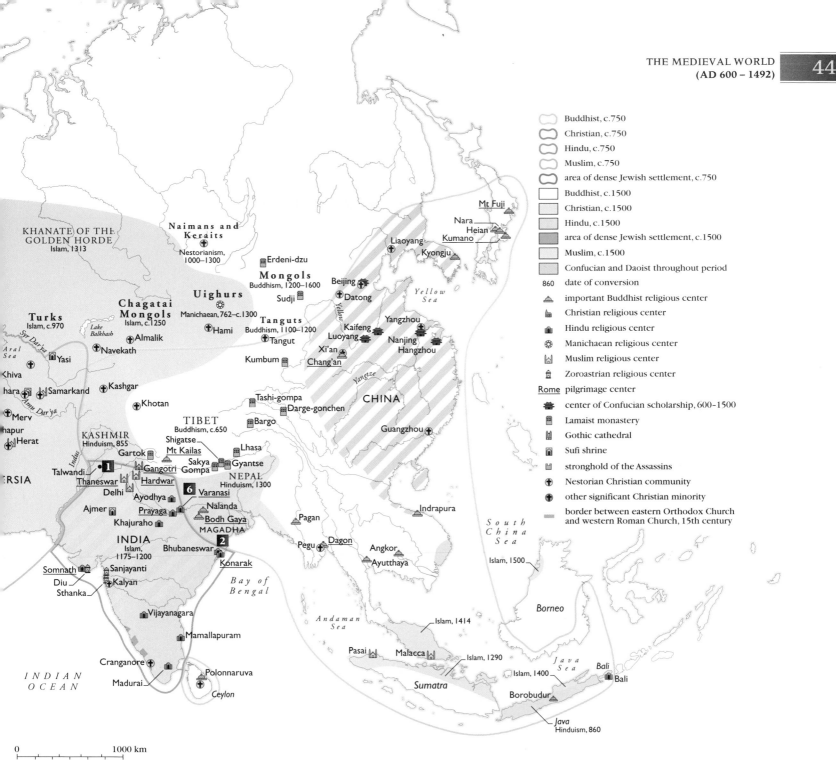

Buddhist, c.750
Christian, c.750
Hindu, c.750
Muslim, c.750
area of dense Jewish settlement, c.750
Buddhist, c.1500
Christian, c.1500
Hindu, c.1500
area of dense Jewish settlement, c.1500
Muslim, c.1500
Confucian and Daoist throughout period
860   date of conversion
▲   important Buddhist religious center
🏛   Christian religious center
🏛   Hindu religious center
✷   Manichaean religious center
🏛   Muslim religious center
🏛   Zoroastrian religious center
Rome   pilgrimage center
✿   center of Confucian scholarship, 600–1500
🏛   Lamaist monastery
🏛   Gothic cathedral
🏛   Sufi shrine
🏛   stronghold of the Assassins
✠   Nestorian Christian community
✠   other significant Christian minority
—   border between eastern Orthodox Church and western Roman Church, 15th century

control to the Holy Land – Christianity was again in retreat by the 15th century. At this time the Muslim Ottoman Turks overran the Byzantine empire and moved into the Balkans.

The Arab conquests destroyed Zoroastrianism in its Persian homeland, but small communities of emigrants established themselves on India's west coast, where the religion still survives among the Parsis.

The Bakhti (devotional) revival movement in the 7th century caused Hinduism to reassert itself against Buddhism, which had been dominant in the preceding centuries. The 8th-century philosopher Shankara gave impetus to Hinduism's recovery by including popular aspects of Buddhist devotion into Hinduism. An important aspect of the Bakhti revival was the great increase in the popularity of pilgrimages to sacred sites such as Varanasi on the River Ganges. A number of Hindus, especially from the lower castes, converted to Islam following the Muslim conquest around 1200, yet Hinduism remained India's principal religion.

Indian Buddhism, however, was destroyed by the Muslim conquest, continuing to flourish only in Ceylon. Buddhism also declined in southeast Asia following the introduction there of Islam in the 13th century. Chinese Buddhism reached the peak of its influence in the 7th and 8th centuries as a result of patronage by the Tang court. The period saw the spread of the meditative school of Chan (known in Japan as Zen) Buddhism, and the populist Pure Land school, which promised its adherents rebirth in paradise. Some 40,000 Buddhist temples and monasteries, all with tax-exempt estates, sprang up. They proved a severe drain on state income by 800. A brief imperial persecution in 845 closed many of these monasteries and forced 250,000 monks back into secular life. Buddhism recovered but never regained its former prestige.

The most important new converts to Buddhism in this period were the Tibetans. Here elements of Tibetan shamanism were incorporated into Buddhism to form the distinctive tradition of Lamaism.

1 Talwandi was the birthplace in 1469 of Guru Nanak, founder of the Sikh religion.

2 Buddhism declined in its original heartland of Magadha after 600 and had been supplanted by Hinduism and Islam by the 13th century.

3 Jerusalem, site of Jesus' crucifixion, was believed by medieval Christians to be the center of the world.

4 Jews were tolerated in Muslim Spain but faced expulsion or forcible conversion after the Christian reconquest.

5 Constantinople, the greatest Christian city of the East, became a leading center of Islamic culture after its conquest by the Ottoman Turks in 1453.

6 Varanasi is Hinduism's most holy site: pilgrimages to bathe in the Ganges had become popular by 1050.

See also 27 (world religions in 600);
43 (China); 48 (the Crusades)

In the 9th century Christian Europe was under attack from Viking raiders from Scandinavia, Muslim pirates from Spain and north Africa, and steppe nomads, the Magyars and Bulgars (▷ 41). The cultural and economic revival fostered by the Carolingian empire collapsed under the impact of the attacks and the empire itself broke up between 843 and 889. However, by 1000 European civilization was expanding and many of the states of medieval Europe had begun to emerge as stable political units. France was a decentralized, weak feudal kingdom but the German kings built a strong state based on their control of the church. In 962 the German king Otto I adopted the title Roman emperor, founding the Holy Roman empire. He ended the Magyar threat in 955, after which the Magyars founded the Christian kingdom of Hungary. Viking attacks on the British Isles were a catalyst in the formation of the kingdoms of England and Scotland, and by 1000 stable kingdoms had developed in Scandinavia itself. Swedish Vikings founded the first Russian state about 862, but by 1000 this had lost its Scandinavian character and was a Slavic state under Byzantine influence.

The Arab world continued to fragment and by 1000 the Abbasid caliphs were no more than spiritual figureheads. Persia passed under the control of native dynasties; Egypt, Syria and Palestine became independent under the Tulunid emirs in 868; most of Arabia was lost around 900; and the Christian Armenians recovered their independence in 886. Abbasid power revived in the early 10th century and control over Egypt and southern Iran was recovered, but it collapsed for good when the Persian Buwayhids seized Baghdad in 945: they ruled in the name of the caliph who was retained only for his spiritual authority. Between 967 and 973 the Tunisian Fatimid dynasty conquered Egypt, Palestine and Syria and were the most powerful Muslim rulers in 1000. Despite the disunity, the Muslim world continued to expand in the 9th and 10th centuries, the most important gain being the conversion of the Ghuzz Turks.

Despite the collapse of the Tibetan empire around 850, the Tang Chinese empire continued to decline in the 9th century (▷ 43). The government's fiscal problems led to persecutions and expropriation of property belonging to Buddhists, Nestorian Christians and Manichaeans. Landlords began to reverse the earlier Tang land reforms, leading to a peasant uprising in 874–84, which broke the authority of the dynasty. Power devolved to provincial warlords and the empire split into several states. In 916 the far north was conquered by the nomad Khitans (a Mongol people), who founded the

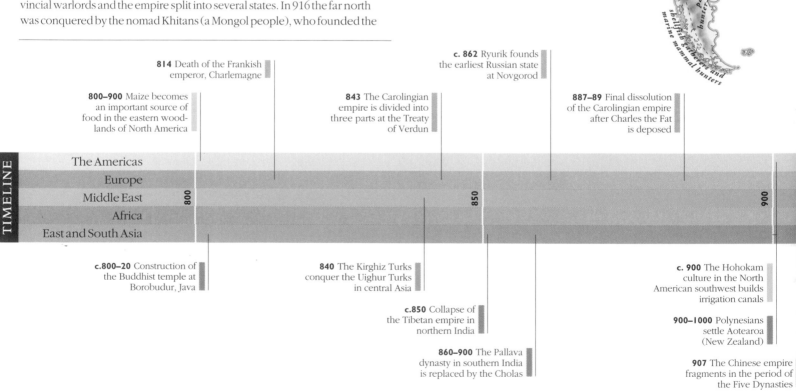

TIMELINE

814 Death of the Frankish emperor, Charlemagne

800–900 Maize becomes an important source of food in the eastern woodlands of North America

c. 862 Ryurik founds the earliest Russian state at Novgorod

843 The Carolingian empire is divided into three parts at the Treaty of Verdun

887–89 Final dissolution of the Carolingian empire after Charles the Fat is deposed

The Americas
Europe
Middle East
Africa
East and South Asia

800

850

900

c.800–20 Construction of the Buddhist temple at Borobudur, Java

840 The Kirghiz Turks conquer the Uighur Turks in central Asia

c. 900 The Hohokam culture in the North American southwest builds irrigation canals

c.850 Collapse of the Tibetan empire in northern India

900–1000 Polynesians settle Aotearoa (New Zealand)

860–900 The Pallava dynasty in southern India is replaced by the Cholas

907 The Chinese empire fragments in the period of the Five Dynasties

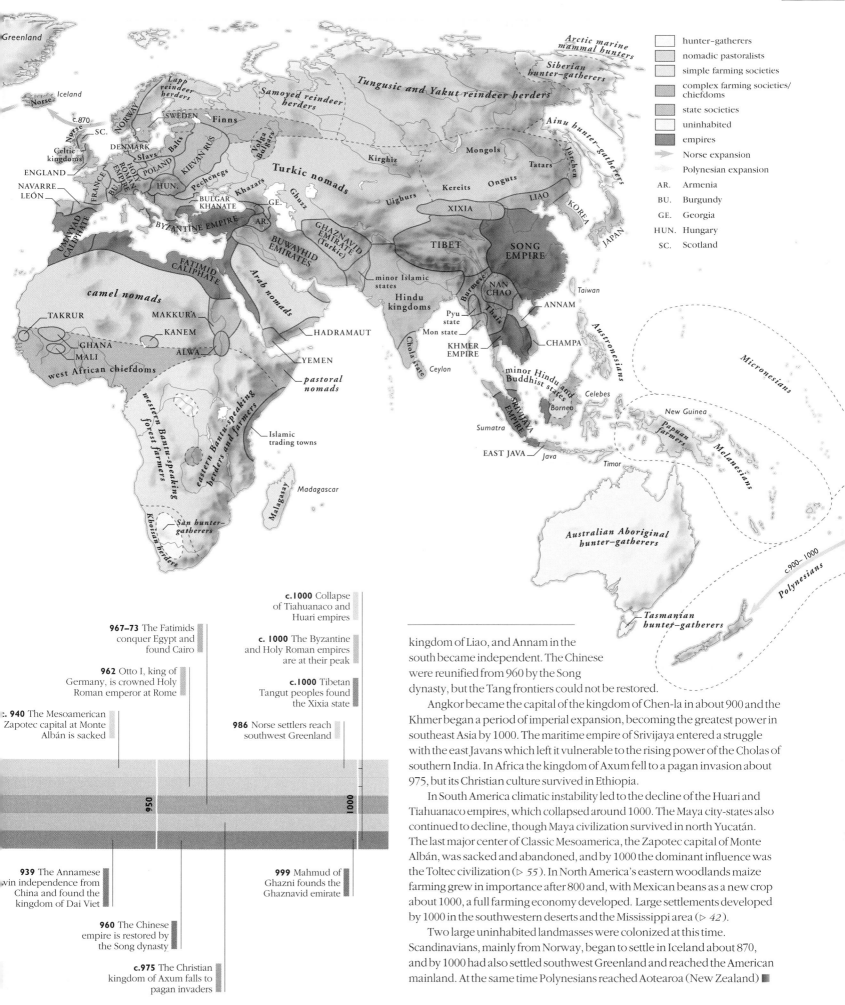

hunter-gatherers
nomadic pastoralists
simple farming societies
complex farming societies/
chiefdoms
state societies
uninhabited
empires
Norse expansion
Polynesian expansion
AR.   Armenia
BU.   Burgundy
GE.   Georgia
HUN. Hungary
SC.   Scotland

967–73 The Fatimids
conquer Egypt and
found Cairo

c.1000 Collapse
of Tiahuanaco and
Huari empires

962 Otto I, king of
Germany, is crowned Holy
Roman emperor at Rome

c.1000 The Byzantine
and Holy Roman empires
are at their peak

c. 940 The Mesoamerican
Zapotec capital at Monte
Albán is sacked

c.1000 Tibetan
Tangut peoples found
the Xixia state

986 Norse settlers reach
southwest Greenland

939 The Annamese
win independence from
China and found the
kingdom of Dai Viet

999 Mahmud of
Ghazni founds the
Ghaznavid emirate

960 The Chinese
empire is restored by
the Song dynasty

c.975 The Christian
kingdom of Axum falls to
pagan invaders

kingdom of Liao, and Annam in the
south became independent. The Chinese
were reunified from 960 by the Song
dynasty, but the Tang frontiers could not be restored.

Angkor became the capital of the kingdom of Chen-la in about 900 and the
Khmer began a period of imperial expansion, becoming the greatest power in
southeast Asia by 1000. The maritime empire of Srivijaya entered a struggle
with the east Javans which left it vulnerable to the rising power of the Cholas of
southern India. In Africa the kingdom of Axum fell to a pagan invasion about
975, but its Christian culture survived in Ethiopia.

In South America climatic instability led to the decline of the Huari and
Tiahuanaco empires, which collapsed around 1000. The Maya city-states also
continued to decline, though Maya civilization survived in north Yucatán.
The last major center of Classic Mesoamerica, the Zapotec capital of Monte
Albán, was sacked and abandoned, and by 1000 the dominant influence was
the Toltec civilization (▷ 55). In North America's eastern woodlands maize
farming grew in importance after 800 and, with Mexican beans as a new crop
about 1000, a full farming economy developed. Large settlements developed
by 1000 in the southwestern deserts and the Mississippi area (▷ 42).

Two large uninhabited landmasses were colonized at this time.
Scandinavians, mainly from Norway, began to settle in Iceland about 870,
and by 1000 had also settled southwest Greenland and reached the American
mainland. At the same time Polynesians reached Aotearoa (New Zealand) ∎

Feudalism was a contractual system by which a lord granted a fief (or estate) to a vassal, usually a knight or nobleman, in return for sworn homage and military service. The Carolingian kings used the system to bind the nobility in loyalty to the crown, but under a weak ruler it could undermine royal authority and decentralize power. By the late 11th century feudalism had been introduced to England and Sicily by the Normans and was highly developed in Spain. It was present, though less dominant, in Scotland, Scandinavia, northern Italy and eastern Europe. By 1200 the military importance of feudalism was in decline, as kings could raise money to hire professional soldiers, and vassals could make a cash payment in lieu of military service. Fiefs had become heritable and were treated by vassals as family estates.

Decentralization was most extreme in France, where the royal lands (the demesne) were confined in the 11th century to the area around Paris and Orléans, while powerful vassals like the dukes of Normandy and the counts of Anjou and Aquitaine were semi-independent rulers of vast fiefs. When William of Normandy became king of England by conquest in 1066, he became more powerful than his feudal lord, the French king. In the 1150s Henry Plantagenet of Anjou accumulated, through inheritance and marriage, fiefs covering half of France, dwarfing the royal demesne. In 1154 he inherited the English throne to become, as Henry II, the most powerful ruler in Europe. Yet he tried to avoid open warfare with the French king, feeling he should not set a bad example to his own vassals. Philip Augustus (r.1180–1223) revived the French monarchy and recovered all the Angevin fiefs except Gascony. In 1214 he repulsed a German invasion at Bouvines, making France the strongest power in Europe.

The German kings and emperors avoided the problems of the French monarchy by granting land as fiefs to the church. Literate priests and abbots were well equipped to administer its fiefs, and celibate churchmen could not found dynasties, so the lands returned into the gift of the king. As long as the king retained control over ecclesiastical appoint-

ments, this system offered a counterweight to the territorial nobility. But when emperor Henry III died in 1056, leaving his son Henry IV (r.1056–1106) in the control of a weak regency, the papacy asserted itself. The ensuing Investiture Contest (1075–1122), a dispute over who had the right to nominate to vacant sees (bishoprics), gave the popes greatly enhanced authority. A sign of their new prestige was the summoning of the First Crusade in 1095, which led to the capture of Jerusalem in 1099.

The Hohenstaufen emperor Frederick Barbarossa (r. 1152–90) found his authority challenged in Germany by powerful territorial princes, such as Henry the Lion of the Welf family. He tried to compensate by tightening imperial control in Italy but was defeated by the Lombard league of cities in 1176. His successors did little better. Though the Hohenstaufens won control of the Norman kingdom of Sicily in 1194, they failed to assert their authority over the German princes, and the Holy Roman empire disintegrated into a loose federation of states. The emperor Frederick II (r.1210–50) attempted to consolidate his

HAROLD II, last Anglo-Saxon king of England (r.1066), is shown here being crowned in the Bayeux Tapestry (c.1080).

Map labels

Faroe Islands
Earldom of Orkney
Orkney Islands
Hebrides
SCOTLAND
Perth
Edinburgh
North Sea
Kingdom of Man
IRISH KINGDOMS & CHIEFDOMS
Dublin
York
Stamford Bridge 1066
ENGLAND
Norwich
WELSH PRINCIPALITIES
Oxford
London
Hastings 1066
Canterbury
Bruges
Bouvines 1214
Bayeux
Normandy
Rouen
Paris
Brittany
Maine
Orléans
Loire
Tours
Anjou
FRANCE
ATLANTIC OCEAN
Clermont
Aquitaine
Bordeaux
Gascony
County of Toulouse
Toulouse
LEÓN
León
NAVARRE
Douro
ARAGON
CASTILE
Barcelona
Coimbra
PORTUGAL
Tagus
Toledo
Valencia
Lisbon
Guadiana
Las Navas de Tolosa 1212
Córdoba
Granada
EMIRATE OF MALLORCA
ALMOHAD CALIPHATE until 1230
1

TIMELINE

Political change

	1100	1200	1300
1047–90 Normans conquer southern Italy and Sicily	**1128** Portugal becomes independent of León	**1194** Henry VI conquers Norman kingdom of Sicily	**1253–99** Commercial rivalry leads to war between Genoa and Venice
1066 William the Conquerer, Duke of Normandy, invades and conquers England	**1154** Henry II becomes the first Angevin king of England	**1212** Christian victory at Las Navas de Tolosa breaks Muslim power in Spain	**1254–73** Interregnum in Germany inaugurates period of political chaos
1075–1122 Investiture Contest with popes damages authority of the Holy Roman emperors	**1170** Murder of Thomas Becket, archbishop of Canterbury	**1215** King John of England signs the Magna Carta	
1095 Pope Urban II calls the First Crusade at Clermont		**1187** Defeat of crusading army by Saladin at the Horns of Hattin leads to fall of Jerusalem to the Muslims	**1230** Union of the kingdoms of Castile and León
1099 Crusaders take Jerusalem			**1237–41** Mongols invade Russia and eastern Europe

Cultural change

1079–1142 Peter Abelard: theologian and philosopher	**c.1136** Geoffrey of Monmouth's *History of the Kings of Britain* popularizes Arthurian romances	**c.1200–75** Sagas (fictionalized family histories of early settlers) written in Iceland	**c.1270–1300** Invention of the mechanical clock
c.1095 "Song of Roland", *chanson de geste*, celebrates chivalric ideals	**c.1140** Abbey church of St Denis near Paris, regarded as first building in Gothic style	**c.1220–92** Roger Bacon: philosopher and early advocate of scientific experiment	**1298** Marco Polo's account of his travels in Asia between 1271 and 1295 becomes an instant success

NORWAY

Trondheim

Bergen

Christiania

Uppsala

SWEDEN

Vänern

Vättern

Visby

Finns

Lake Onega

Lake Ladoga

River Neva 1240

Ladoga

Beloozero

REPUBLIC OF NOVGOROD

Novgorod

PRINCIPALITY OF VLADIMIR

Bulgar

Volga Bulgars

Åbo

Revel

Estonians

Lake Peipus 1242

Livs

Riga

Western Dvina

Pskov

Vladimir

Moscow

Murom

Volga

Árhus

DENMARK

Roskilde

Lund

Schleswig

Holstein

Hamburg

Bremen

Saxony

Magdeburg

Cologne

Thuringia

GERMANY

Frankfurt

Mainz

Franconia

Nuremberg

Swabia

Bavaria

Milan

legnano 1176

Aquileia

Venice

VENICE

KINGDOM OF ITALY

Genoa

Pisa

PISA

Bologna

Florence

Corsica

Rome

PAPAL STATES

Sardinia

Benevento 1266

Naples

Palermo

Sicily

KINGDOM OF SICILY

Tunis

MOHAD LIPHATE until 1230

Malta

Baltic Sea

Danzig

Wends

Stettin

Königsberg

Prus

Vistula

Brandenburg

Breslau

Elbe

Oder

POLAND

Krakow

Prague

BOHEMIA

Salzburg

Vienna

Austria

Styria

Carinthia

Gran

Pest

HUNGARY

Belgrade

Sava

Zara

Ragusa

Danube

Bari

Lithuanians

Polotsk

PRINCIPALITY OF POLOTSK

Minsk

PRINCIPALITY OF SMOLENSK

Smolensk

PRINCIPALITY OF CHERNIGOV

PRINCIPALITY OF MUROM-RYAZAN

Ryazan

Murom-Ryazan

PRINCIPALITY OF TUROV-PINSK

Pinsk

Chernigov

Kiev

PRINCIPALITY OF KIEV

PRINCIPALITY OF PEREYASLAV

Pereyaslav

PRINCIPALITY OF NOVGOROD-SEVERSK

Don

Cumans (Turkic)

Volga

PRINCIPALITY OF VOLHYNIA

Galich

PRINCIPALITY OF GALICIA

Dnieper

Cumans (Turkic)

to Kiev

Alans

to Kiev

GEORGIA

Black Sea

Constantinople

BYZANTINE EMPIRE

Dyrrachium

Thessalonica

Mediterranean Sea

Crete

0   600 km

0   400 mi

Duchy of Normandy, 1066

Norman gains in England and southern Italy by 1154

Holy Roman empire, c.1175

Hohenstaufen demesne

Welf demesne

Church land

other

borders, c.1175

effective Angevin (Anjou) control, c.1175

nominal Angevin control, c.1175

French royal demesne, c.1175

Angevin fiefs in France after 1214

Byzantine empire, 1175

Norwegian territory, 1175

Swedish territory, 1175

Holy Roman empire, 1175

expansion of German settlement, 12th–13th centuries

Lombard league city, 1167

German city founded in 13th century

ARAGON fief of the Papacy during the pontificate of Innocent III, 1198–1216

German and Danish crusades against the pagan Slavs and Balts, 12th–13th centuries

Swedish expansion, 12th–13th centuries

western limit of Mongol conquests, 1240

Spanish states, 1300

Aragon

Castile

emirate of Granada

Portugal

controlled by the Teutonic Knights, c.1300

Russian states

pagan area

position in Italy but, faced with the hostility of the papacy and the Lombard cities, his reign ended in failure and the dynasty was overthrown in 1266. Despite the political fragmentation of the empire, the 13th century saw German influence expand to the east through the establishment of peasant settlements and new towns, and the activities of traders and the crusading order of the Teutonic Knights in the Baltic.

The Slavic state of Kievan Rus broke up into several principalities in 1132, most of which were overrun by the Mongols in 1237–41. Alexander Nevsky (r.1236–63), ruler of Novgorod, submitted voluntarily to the Mongol invasion, and was therefore able to concentrate his resources on resisting incursions by Swedish forces and the Teutonic Knights. In 1252, he added the principality of Vladimir to his possessions.

1 Lisbon was captured from the Muslims by a fleet from northern Europe *en route* to the Second Crusade in the Holy Land in 1147.

2 Alexander Nevsky's victory at the river Neva in 1240 halted further Swedish expansion eastward.

3 Austria was founded as a duchy by Frederick Barbarossa in 1156 to counter Welf power in Bavaria.

4 The wealthy cities of Lombardy formed defensive leagues in 1167 and 1226 to resist imperial attempts to restrict their freedoms.

5 A major concern of the Papacy was to prevent a political union between the Holy Roman empire and the kingdom of Sicily.

6 Sicily passed to the Normans (1091); to emperor Henry IV (1194); to the Angevin dynasty (1266); to the Aragonese (1282); to independence (1295).

See also 41 (Viking age Europe);
48 (Crusades); 49 (Mongol empire)

Turkish power in the Middle East grew rapidly after the Seljuk invasion of the Ghaznavid emirate in 1037. Three years later, under Toghril Beg (r.1038–63), they had occupied the emirate's western provinces. In 1054–55 the Seljuks, heeding an appeal for help by the Abbasid caliph of Baghdad, drove the Buwayhids from the city. As Sunni Muslims, the Seljuks accorded the caliph greater respect than had the Shiite Buwayhids, but they were no less firm in ruling the city. Under Toghril Beg's successor, Alp Arslan (r.1063–72), the Seljuks overran Syria and routed the Byzantines at Manzikert. Alp Arslan was killed in 1072 repelling a Qarakhanid Turk invasion at Berzem, but in the reign of his successor Malik Shah (r.1072–92), Byzantine Anatolia was occupied and the Fatimids were expelled from Palestine.

Malik Shah's death sparked civil war and the Seljuk sultanate began to fragment. By 1095 the sultanate of Rum and the Danishmend emirate in Anatolia had seceded, and by 1100 there were dozens of independent Seljuk states. The main beneficiaries were the Byzantine empire and the First Crusade, which between them deprived the Seljuks of western Anatolia and northern Syria, and the Fatimids, who retook Palestine in 1098, only to lose it again almost at once to the Crusaders.

Turkish power in the west began to recover under Zangi, the *atabeg* (governor) of Mosul (r.1127–46), who united northern Syria and recaptured Edessa from the Crusaders in 1144. Zangi's son Nur al-Din (r.1146–74) conquered the rest of Muslim Syria and destroyed the Shiite Fatimid caliphate of Egypt. After his death, Saladin, Kurdish governor of Egypt, rebelled against the Zangids and by 1177 controlled the emirate. The Ayyubid dynasty founded by Saladin held power until 1250 when the Mamlukes, a caste of mainly Turkish slave soldiers, seized power. This military elite continued to rule Egypt and Syria until 1517, surviving as a class until 1811. The Seljuks of Rum also recovered their power and

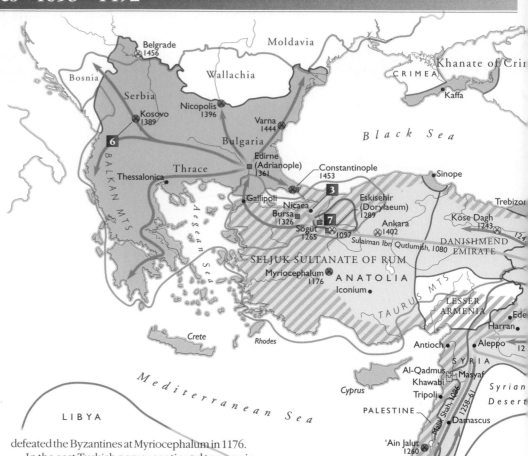

defeated the Byzantines at Myriocephalum in 1176.

In the east Turkish power continued to wane in the 12th century and in 1156 the Abbasid caliphate enjoyed a revival. Although its political authority extended only to Iraq, its spiritual authority enabled it to arbitrate in disputes between the Seljuk states. Then, in the early 13th century, the eastern Seljuk states were absorbed by a new Turkish power, the shahdom of Khwarizm. However, its growth was abruptly halted by the Mongol invasion of 1219. With one stroke, Chingis Khan broke the shahdom's

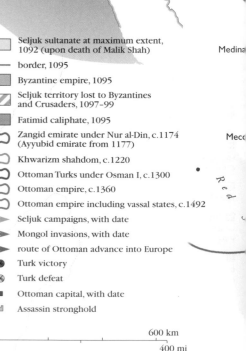

TIMELINE

Political change

1100	1250	1400
1038–40 The Seljuks conquer Khorasan	**1187** Saladin recaptures Jerusalem from the Crusaders	**1354** The Ottomans capture Gallipoli
1055 Seljiks capture Baghdad	**1210** Foundation of the Khwarizm shahdom	**1370–1405** Timur the Lame terrorizes the Middle East
1071 The Seljuks defeat Byzantines at Manzikert	**1243** Seljuk Sultanate of Rum becomes Mongol vassal state	**1389** The Ottoman armies crush the Serbs at Kosovo
1092 Death of Malik Shah; Seljuk sultanate disintegrates	**1258** The Mongols execute the last Abbasid caliph at Baghdad	**1396** The Ottomans defeat the Crusaders at Nicopolis
1099 The First Crusade captures Jerusalem	**c.1280** Foundation of the Ottoman Turkish state	**1402** The Ottomans defeated by Timur at Ankara
1127–46 Zangi, emir of Mosul, unites Turkish emirates of Syria	**1291** The Crusaders are expelled from the Holy Land	**1453** The Ottomans take Constantinople, end of the Byzantine empire
1169–71 Saladin conquers Egypt for the Zangid emirate		

Cultural change

1100	1250	1400
1027–1123 Omar Khayyam: Persian scientist and poet	**1198** Death of Ibn Rushd (Averröes): philosopher	**1352** Ibn Battuta explores the Sahara Desert
1065–67 Nizamayeh academy (Baghdad) is founded	**1273** Death of Djelaleddin Rumi, founder of the order of Dervishes	**1454** Construction of the Topkapi palace is begun at Constantinople
c.1080 Construction of the Friday Mosque in Isfahan	**1347** The Black Death reaches Baghdad	

Map legend

Seljuk sultanate at maximum extent, 1092 (upon death of Malik Shah)
— border, 1095
Byzantine empire, 1095
Seljuk territory lost to Byzantines and Crusaders, 1097–99
Fatimid caliphate, 1095
Zangid emirate under Nur al-Din, c.1174 (Ayyubid emirate from 1177)
Khwarizm shahdom, c.1220
Ottoman Turks under Osman I, c.1300
Ottoman empire, c.1360
Ottoman empire including vassal states, c.1492
Seljuk campaigns, with date
Mongol invasions, with date
route of Ottoman advance into Europe
⊛ Turk victory
⊗ Turk defeat
■ Ottoman capital, with date
Assassin stronghold

0 ——— 600 km
0 ——— 400 mi

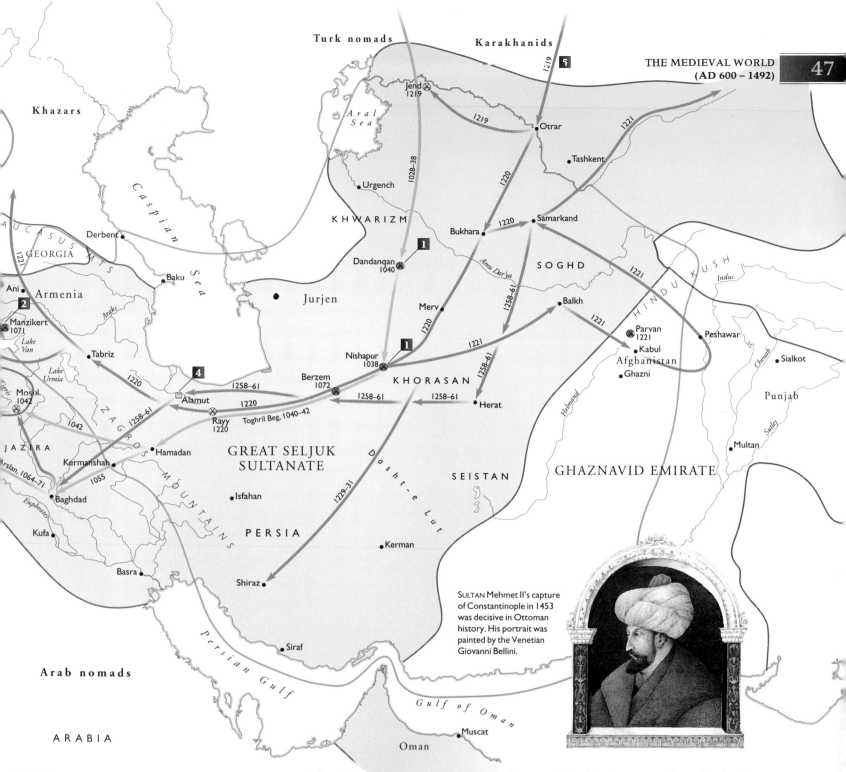

Turk nomads

Karakhanids

5

1219

Khazars

Aral Sea

Jend 1219

Otrar

1219

1221

Tashkent

1028-38

Urgench

1

KHWARIZM

1220

Bukhara

1220

Samarkand

SOGHD

Derbent

GEORGIA

1221

C a s p i a n   S e a

Baku

Dandanqan 1040

1

Jurjen

Merv

1258-61

1221

Balkh

Amu Dar'ya

H I N D U   K U S H

Indus

Ani

Armenia

2

Araks

Manzikert 1071

Lake Van

Tabriz

1220

4

1220

Nishapur 1038

1

Berzem 1072

KHORASAN

1221

1258-61

1258-61

Herat

Parvan 1221

Kabul

Afghanistan

Ghazni

Peshawar

Chenab

Sialkot

Lake Urmia

Mosul 1042

1258-61

Alamut

1258-61

1220

Rayy 1220

Toghril Beg, 1040-42

1258-61

Punjab

Sutlej

JAZIRA

1042

Arslan, 1064-71

Kermanshah

1055

Z A G R O S   M O U N T A I N S

Hamadan

GREAT SELJUK SULTANATE

D a s h t - e   L u t

SEISTAN

GHAZNAVID EMIRATE

Multan

Baghdad

Euphrates

Kufa

Isfahan

Helmand

Kerman

Basra

PERSIA

1229-31

Shiraz

Siraf

P e r s i a n   G u l f

SULTAN Mehmet II's capture of Constantinople in 1453 was decisive in Ottoman history. His portrait was painted by the Venetian Giovanni Bellini.

Arab nomads

G u l f   o f   O m a n

Muscat

Oman

ARABIA

1 The Ghaznavids lost their western territories to the Seljuks after defeats at Nishapur and Dandanqan.

2 Sultan Alp Arslan's victory over the Byzantines at Manzikert began the Seljuk conquest of Anatolia.

3 Nicaea became the capital of the Seljuk sultanate of Rum ("Rome", from *Romaivi*, as the Byzantine Greeks called themselves) in 1080; when it fell to the Crusaders in 1097, the capital was moved to Iconium.

4 Alamut was the main stronghold of the Shiite Ismaili Nizari sect (the Assassins).

5 The Mongol invaders of the 13th century occupied or imposed vassalage on all the Middle East except Palestine, Egypt, Syria and Arabia.

6 Their defeat by the Ottomans at Kosovo is deeply ingrained on the Serbian national consciousness; for many, it justified the "ethnic cleansing" of Muslims in the Bosnian civil war of 1992-95.

7 The Ottoman state is named after Osman I (r.1280-1324), a Turkish chieftain who ruled Sögüt.

power. The Seljuks of Rum were reduced to vassals in 1243, the Abbasid caliphate was destroyed, this time for good, in 1258, and in 1260 the Mongols drove the Mamlukes out of Syria. Though the Mamlukes recovered much of this territory after their victory over the Mongols at 'Ain Jalut later that year, the Mongols remained the dominant power in the Middle East until Timur the Lame's death in 1405.

Following the Mongol conquests, the Seljuk sultanate of Rum broke up. The Byzantine empire was now too weak to benefit, while the Serbs, Bulgars and the Latins were busy arguing over the remains of the dying empire. The Ottoman state began its growth under the minor Anatolian chief Osman I, and by the death of Orhan (r.1324–60) the Ottomans occupied most of northwest Anatolia and had begun to expand into Europe, capturing Gallipoli in 1354. In 1361 Murad I (r.1360–89) captured Adrianople and, renaming it Edirne, transferred the capital there. Timur the Lame's invasion in 1402, and his victory at Ankara, led to the temporary collapse of the sultanate but the Ottomans rallied quickly, expanding

again by 1430. Constantinople, and with it the Byzantine empire, fell in 1453. Although further expansion into central Europe was checked by the Hungarians at Belgrade in 1456, the Ottoman sultanate was still a rising power in 1492.

A major factor in Ottoman success was the weakness of the neighboring Christian and Turkish states. The divisions in Europe caused by the Hundred Years' War and the Great Schism precluded a concerted Christian resistance, while the Seljuks were weakened by the Mongols, who subsequently withdrew from Anatolia. Religious zeal was another vital element. Osman I had been a *ghazi*, an Islamic warrior, and commitment to spreading the faith through holy war motivated the Ottoman armies. This was especially true of its elite Janissary corps which was composed of the children of Christians, who were raised as devout Muslims.

See also 48 (the Crusades);
59 (the peak of the Ottoman empire)

The Crusades were holy wars fought to defend the Catholic church and the Christian people against those who were regarded as external and internal enemies of Christendom. Although the main crusading effort was directed against the Muslims in the Holy Land, Crusades were also conducted against the pagan Slavs of the Baltic, Muslim Spain, the Ottoman Turks in the Balkans and heretics, such as the Cathars, within western Christendom itself. Though considered peripheral at the time, it was these campaigns, particularly those in Spain and the Baltic, that were ultimately the most successful. The movement did not die out completely until the 18th century. However, the main period of crusading activity lasted from 1096 to 1291, which saw eight major campaigns and dozens of smaller expeditions.

The Crusaders saw their role as part of the pilgrimage tradition. Pilgrimages to holy places were undertaken as penance and to acquire spiritual merit. The ultimate pilgrimage was to Jerusalem, and when the Turks began to harass pilgrims in the 11th century, an armed pilgrimage to restore Christian control was thought fully justified. This appealed both to the piety and the adventurous spirit of the feudal knightly class, who saw themselves as protectors of Christendom. As an inducement the papacy offered Crusaders spiritual and legal privileges, most important of which was remission of the penances due for sin. This was popularly interpreted as a guarantee of immediate entry to heaven if the Crusader were to die on the expedition.

The First Crusade was called by Pope Urban II at the Council of Clermont in 1095 in response to an appeal from the Byzantine emperor Alexius I Comnenus for military help against the Seljuk Turks. The first army to set out, a motley band of poorly armed pilgrims, was wiped out near Nicomedia. However, the main army, mostly French and Norman knights, fought its way across Anatolia to Antioch and on to Jerusalem, which was taken in 1099. The First Crusade was the most successful, thanks in part to divisions in the Muslim world. Four Crusader states were set up in Syria and Palestine: the Kingdom of Jerusalem, the County of Tripoli, the Principality of Antioch and the County of Edessa.

Muslim unity began to be restored by Zangi, governor of Mosul, who retook Edessa in 1144. This loss prompted the Second Crusade (1147–49), which was badly mauled crossing Anatolia and achieved nothing. The loss of Jerusalem after Saladin's victory at Hattin in 1187 led to the calling of the Third Crusade under Richard I (Lionheart) of England and Philip II Augustus of France. Although this failed to recover Jerusalem, by retaking the coast of Palestine it ensured the survival of the Crusader states.

In the 13th century, Crusaders showed an increasingly sophisticated strategic approach to defense of the Holy Land. It was realized that Christian control of the region could never be secure so

long as Egypt remained the center of Muslim power. The Fourth Crusade (1202–04) was the first called with the intention of attacking Egypt but it never reached its destination. Assembled in Venice, the Crusaders were unable to pay for their transit to Egypt, and so agreed to help the Venetians capture the Hungarian city of Zara. Thereafter, the Crusade was diverted to Constantinople in support of a claimant for the Byzantine throne who promised support for the expedition. When this was not forthcoming, the Crusaders sacked Constantinople and made it the center of a Latin Empire. The Fifth Crusade (1217–21) took Damietta at the mouth of the Nile but was defeated by river flooding as it

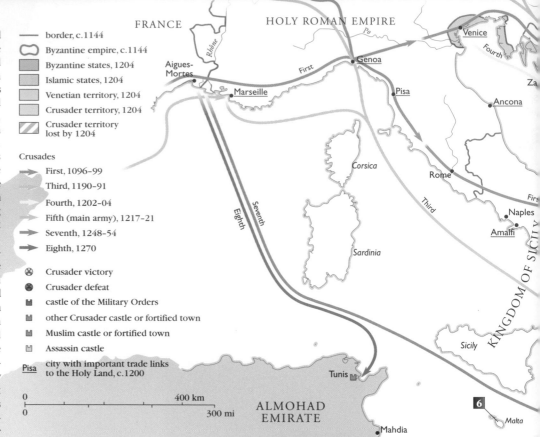

border, c.1144
Byzantine empire, c.1144
Byzantine states, 1204
Islamic states, 1204
Venetian territory, 1204
Crusader territory, 1204
Crusader territory lost by 1204

Crusades
→ First, 1096–99
→ Third, 1190–91
→ Fourth, 1202–04
→ Fifth (main army), 1217–21
→ Seventh, 1248–54
→ Eighth, 1270

⊗ Crusader victory
⊛ Crusader defeat
🏰 castle of the Military Orders
🏰 other Crusader castle or fortified town
🏰 Muslim castle or fortified town
🏰 Assassin castle
Pisa   city with important trade links to the Holy Land, c.1200

0   400 km
0   300 mi

TIMELINE

Eastern Mediterranean

1095 Pope Urban II calls the First Crusade at Clermont

1098 Crusaders take Edessa and Antioch

1099 Crusaders capture Jerusalem. Defeat of Egyptian relief army at Ascalon

1113 Founding of Order of the Hospital of St John in Jerusalem (Hospitallers)

1118 Founding of the Order of the Knights Templar

1144 Zangi, governor of Mosul takes Edessa

1149 The Second Crusade ends in failure

1187 Saladin defeats Christians at Hattin and recaptures Jerusalem

1190–92 Third Crusade under Richard I: Cyprus captured

1204 The Fourth Crusade takes Constantinople; founding of the Latin Empire

1217–21 The Fifth Crusade attacks Egypt

1228–29 The Sixth Crusade secures Jerusalem

1248–54 Louis IX leads the Seventh Crusade in Egypt

1261 Byzantines recapture Constantinople: fall of the Latin Empire

1270 Louis IX (St Louis) dies besieging Tunis on the Eighth Crusade

1291 Mamlukes capture Acre: fall of Kingdom of Jerusalem

1302 Fall of Ruad. Crusaders are expelled from Holy Land

1310 The Hospitallers are established on Rhodes

1312 The Order of the Knights Templar is dissolved

1396 The Ottomans defeat Burgundian–Hungarian Crusade at Nicopolis

1456 Crusaders defend Belgrade against the Ottomans

Other Crusades

1096 Urban II offers privileges to Crusaders fighting the Spanish Muslims

1147 Crusades against the pagan Wends (Slavs) in the Baltic. Crusaders take Lisbon

1208 Pope Innocent III calls a Crusade against the Cathar heretics in southern France

1227 The Teutonic Knights begin crusading against the pagan Prussians

1309 The Teutonic Knights launch a permanent Crusade against the pagan Lithuanians

1420 A Crusade is proclaimed against the Hussite heretics in Bohemia

1492 The fall of Granada completes the Christian reconquest of Spain

1200   1300   1400

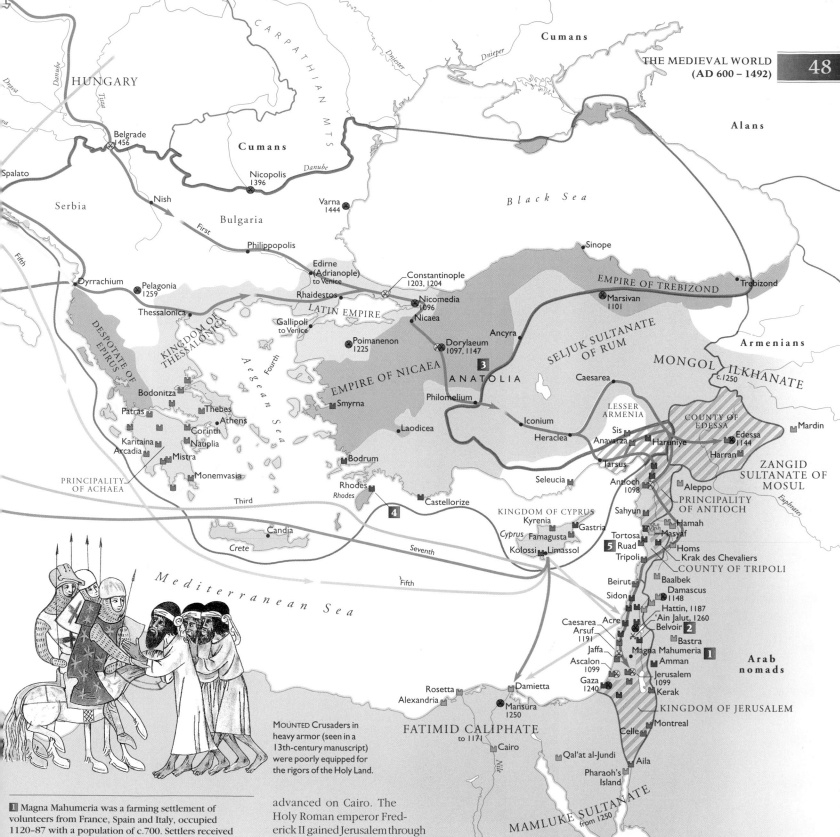

Map labels

HUNGARY
Spalato
Belgrade 1456
Serbia
Nish
Danube
Drava
Tisza
CARPATHIAN MTS
Dniester
Dnieper
Cumans
Cumans
Alans
Black Sea
Nicopolis 1396
Varna 1444
Philippopolis
Edirne (Adrianople) to Venice
Rhaidestos
Constantinople 1203, 1204
Nicomedia 1096
Nicaea
Sinope
EMPIRE OF TREBIZOND
Trebizond
Marsivan 1101
Armenians
MONGOL ILKHANATE c.1250
Mardin
Harran
Edessa 1144
COUNTY OF EDESSA
ZANGID SULTANATE OF MOSUL
First
Fifth
Dyrrachium
Pelagonia 1259
Thessalonica
LATIN EMPIRE
Gallipoli to Venice
Poimanenon 1225
Dorylaeum 1097, 1147
ANATOLIA
SELJUK SULTANATE OF RUM
Ancyra
Caesarea
LESSER ARMENIA
Sis
Anavarza
Haruniye
Tarsus
Aleppo
PRINCIPALITY OF ANTIOCH
Euphrates
DESPOTATE OF EPIRUS
KINGDOM OF THESSALONICA
EMPIRE OF NICAEA
Smyrna
Philomelium
Iconium
Heraclea
Laodicea
Seleucia
Antioch 1098
Sahyun
Hamah
Masyaf
Bodonitza
Thebes
Athens
Patras
Corinth
Nauplia
Karitaina
Arcadia
Mistra
Monemvasia
PRINCIPALITY OF ACHAEA
Aegean Sea
Fourth
Bodrum
Rhodes
Rhodes
Castellorize
KINGDOM OF CYPRUS
Kyrenia
Gastria
Cyprus
Famagusta
Kolossi
Limassol
Tortosa
Ruad
Tripoli
Homs
Krak des Chevaliers
COUNTY OF TRIPOLI
Baalbek
Damascus 1148
Beirut
Sidon
Hattin, 1187
'Ain Jalut, 1260
Belvoir
Bastra
Third
Candia
Crete
Seventh
Fifth
Mediterranean Sea
Caesarea
Arsuf 1191
Acre
Jaffa
Ascalon 1099
Magna Mahumeria
Amman
Jerusalem 1099
Kerak
Arab nomads
Rosetta
Alexandria
Damietta
Mansura 1250
Gaza 1240
Celle
Montreal
KINGDOM OF JERUSALEM
FATIMID CALIPHATE to 1171
Cairo
Nile
Qal'at al-Jundi
Pharaoh's Island
Aila
MAMLUKE SULTANATE from 1250

1 **2** **3** **4** **5**

MOUNTED Crusaders in heavy armor (seen in a 13th-century manuscript) were poorly equipped for the rigors of the Holy Land.

Notes

1 Magna Mahumeria was a farming settlement of volunteers from France, Spain and Italy, occupied 1120–87 with a population of c.700. Settlers received land on easy terms in return for military service.

2 The concentric castle was the most important innovation of Crusader military architecture. The earliest, begun in 1168, is at Belvoir.

3 Food and water shortages and Turkish attacks made Anatolia highly dangerous for Crusaders. After the Second Crusade failed, most went to Palestine by sea.

4 Occupied by the Hospitallers in 1310, Rhodes became an major Crusader base for campaigns against the Turks until its capture by the Ottomans in 1522.

5 The fortress island of Ruad was the last Christian stronghold in the Holy Land to fall to the Muslims, being taken by the Mamlukes in 1302.

6 Malta, the last bastion of the Crusading movement, was home to the Hospitallers from 1530 to 1798, when they were expelled by Napoleon.

advanced on Cairo. The Holy Roman emperor Frederick II gained Jerusalem through diplomacy on the Sixth Crusade (1228–29) but did not win enough territory to ensure its defense once the truce broke down, and the city was lost again in 1244. The Seventh Crusade (1248–54) under Louis IX of France was an exact repeat of the Fifth. The Eighth Crusade (1270), also led by Louis IX and directed against Tunis with the intention of using it as a base for further attacks on Egypt, was also a costly failure. Far more significant than the Crusades in ensuring the survival of the Crusader states in the 13th century were the Mongol attacks on the Muslim world. After decisively defeating the Mongols at 'Ain Jalut in 1260, the Mamlukes turned their full attention to the Crusader states, which finally fell in 1291.

Throughout their existence the Crusader states suffered from a critical shortage of manpower.

Attempts to attract settlers foundered on the extreme inhospitability of the region. Instead, castle building became highly sophisticated; these castles were often garrisoned by military monastic orders, such as the Knights Templars and the Knights Hospitallers, founded to help defend the Holy Land.

The Crusades had considerable effects on the Islamic world, where they briefly revived the concept of the *jihad* (holy war). Nevertheless, Arab historians of the time gave them only scanty attention, and saw the Mongols as a far more potent threat to Islamic civilization.

See also 44 (the world religions); 47 (the medieval Turkish empires)

The dramatic expansion of the Mongols that began under Temujin was the most important event in world history in the 13th century. The son of a minor Mongol chief, Temujin's brilliant leadership in inter-tribal warfare enabled him to unify the Mongol peoples in a ruthless two-year campaign.

To mark his success he was proclaimed Chingis ("universal") Khan in 1206. During his unification campaign, he created what has often been called the finest cavalry army that the world has ever seen. If the army was not to break up, and his khandom with it, he had to find work for it to do and wealth with which to reward it. He therefore adopted a policy of all-round aggression, and by his death in 1227 he had conquered an empire that included most of central Asia and northern China.

His successors, his son Ogedai and grandsons Küyük and Möngke, continued his expansionist policy and by 1259 they had carried the Mongol conquests into Europe and the Middle East. In China, only the southern Song empire stood out against the Mongols, though it too would fall within 20 years. However, Mongol unity was fragile and already the achievement of Chingis Khan had started to unravel.

The Mongol conquests formed the largest land empire in history. The achievement is all the more remarkable in that the Mongols had few governmental institutions and did not even possess basic metalworking skills. They were fortunate in being able to exploit existing disunity among their enemies. China was divided into three hostile kingdoms. The powerful Turkish empires of Kara-Khitai and Khwarizm were mutually hostile and had dynastic problems. Russia, like most of Europe, was a mosaic of quarrelsome states which cooperated only reluctantly and ineffectually against the common enemy.

The key factor in the Mongol success, however, was the magnificent army that Chingis created. Unlike the armies of their opponents, where birth usually determined rank, promotion in the Mongol

army was by merit only. The discipline and mobility of the Mongol army enabled it to execute complex battlefield maneuvers, giving it decisive advantages over any opponent. A frequent tactic was the feigned retreat, used to lure rash pursuers into ambushes on unfavorable ground where they could be destroyed. The Mongols had an excellent long-range weapon in the composite bow, which enabled them to inflict casualties while keeping out of danger themselves. The Mongols also committed horrific atrocities, systematically creating terror to sap their enemies' will to resist. This persuaded many Turks, Uighurs, Kipchaks and Chinese to defect to the Mongols rather than risk defeat.

The Mongol military machine had its limitations. Except in China, the boundaries of the Mongol empire were very close to those of the Eurasian

TIMELINE

The Mongol world

1220	1240	1260
c1167 Birth of Temujin (Chingis Khan)	1227 Death of Chingis Khan on a campaign in the Jin empire	1241 Death of Ogedai
1204–06 Temujin unites the Mongol tribes and is proclaimed Chingis Khan	1229 Ogedai, second son of Chingis, is elected Great Khan	
	1235 Ogedai establishes the Mongol capital at Karakorum	

Eastern conquests

1209 The Mongols attack Xixia and Uighurs	1226 The conquest of Xixia is complete	
1211 The first Mongol attacks on China (Jin empire)	1234 The Jin capital Kaifeng falls to the Mongols	
1215 The Mongols capture Dadu (Beijing)		1252 The conquest of the Song empire (southern China) begins
1218 Kara-Khitai empire is conquered by the Mongols		

The West

1219–21 Chingis Khan invades Khwarizm shahdom	1237–41 The Mongols invade Russia and eastern Europe	1258 Baghdad falls to the Mongols, and the last Abbasid caliph is executed
1220–23 Chingis Khan sends a force to Russia		1260 The Mongols are defeated by the Mamlukes at 'Ain Jalut

| 1220 | 1240 | 1260 |

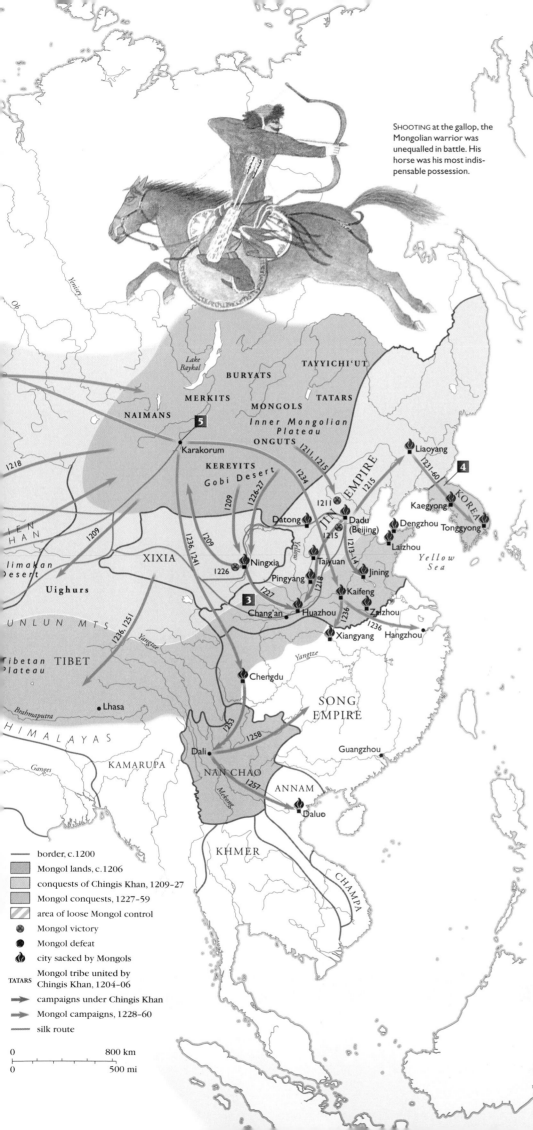

SHOOTING at the gallop, the Mongolian warrior was unequalled in battle. His horse was his most indispensable possession.

steppes and grasslands, which alone could provide the necessary grazing for the vast herds of horses that accompanied every Mongol army. The defeat suffered by the Mongols at the hands of the Mamlukes at 'Ain Jalut in 1260 was to some extent the result of poor grazing in the Syrian desert. This, rather than the strength of local resistance, was probably also the reason the Mongols never returned to Europe after their invasion of 1241–42. The army also needed plenty of room TO maneuver, so it was less effective in forested, mountainous or intensively farmed areas than it was in open country. This helps to explain, for example, the relative slowness of the conquest of China.

The period of the Mongols' expansion had few beneficial results: they destroyed far more than they built. The most sophisticated civilizations of the time – the Muslim and the Chinese – suffered the worst. The Abbasid caliphate of Baghdad, spiritual, cultural and (for much of the time) political leader of the Muslim world since the 8th century, was overthrown. The ancient cities of central Asia were devastated and never recovered their former prosperity. Depopulation and the neglect of irrigation channels meant that most of Iraq and west Persia was reduced to desert for centuries. Northern China suffered depopulation and the Mongol conquest isolated Russia from the mainstream of European development for almost two centuries. The impact of the Mongols on the rest of Christendom was fleeting, and by disrupting the Muslim world they granted a brief stay of execution to the Crusader states and allowed a shortlived revival of the crumbling Byzantine empire. Eventually, Christendom benefited from the Mongol conquests in Asia, as Muslim control of the silk route ended and the way was opened for westerners such as Marco Polo to travel to east Asia for the first time.

1 The governor of Otrar provoked Chingis Khan's invasion of the Khwarizm shahdom by executing merchants and envoys from the Mongols in 1218.

2 Chingis Khan divided his army at Samarkand, despatching a smaller force to pursue the Khwarizm Shah and then cross the Caucasus to gather intelligence in Europe.

3 Chingis Khan died here in 1227 on campaign against the Jin empire.

4 Fighting in unfavorable mountainous terrain, it took the Mongols 30 years to force the Koreans to submit. Thereafter the Koreans became close allies.

5 Karakorum, favorite campsite of Chingis, became the capital of the Mongol empire in 1235.

6 Using frozen rivers as highways, the Mongols launched the only successful winter invasion in Russian history in 1238-39. The Russians paid tribute to the Mongols for two centuries.

7 The combined armies of eastern Europe were routed at Legnica and Mohi in 1241. The Mongols withdrew on news of Ogedai Khan's death.

8 The fall of Baghdad was followed by the massacre of 200,000 captives (20 percent of the population).

9 The first major defeat of the Mongols was at the hands of the Mamlukes at 'Ain Jalut in 1260.

border, c.1200
Mongol lands, c.1206
conquests of Chingis Khan, 1209-27
Mongol conquests, 1227-59
area of loose Mongol control
⊗ Mongol victory
● Mongol defeat
🔥 city sacked by Mongols
TATARS Mongol tribe united by Chingis Khan, 1204-06
➤ campaigns under Chingis Khan
➤ Mongol campaigns, 1228-60
— silk route

0 ———— 800 km
0 ———— 500 mi

See also 46 (Europe);
47 (Muslim world)

The early states of Japan and Korea were strongly influenced by Chinese civilization. By 600 Chinese administrative practices and political ideologies were being introduced by Japanese and Korean rulers as they attempted to build centralized states. These endeavors had been largely successful in Korea by the 15th century, but in Japan initial success was followed by progressive decentralization of authority and, in the 15th century, the growth of feudalism. The elite culture of Korea was heavily influenced b that of China in this period. There were similar fc in Japan but also a much greater retention of dist tively Japanese ideas and practices.

In Japan, the attempt to build a centralized state on Chinese lines began late in the Yamato period (AD 300–710). Prince Shotoku (r.593–622) introduced a constitution in 604 asserting the power of the emperor over the nobility. The Taika reforms that followed in 646 brought all land into imperial ownership and instituted a tax system. In 702 the Taiho laws – new civil and penal codes – were introduced. Buddhism was promoted as a way of increasing imperial authority. Finally in 710 a permanent administrative capital, modeled on Chang'an, was established at Nara. Yet the achievement of the Yamato period reformers was superficial and the centralized state was never able to consolidate its authority.

Nara became an important religious center and the Buddhist clergy soon began to exert strong political influence over the emperors. To escape this interference, emperor Kammu moved the court to a new capital at Heian (modern Kyoto) in 794. Here the emperors came under the sway of the aristocratic Fujiwara family, who skillfully strengthened their political influence by marrying into the imperial family. Buddhist monasteries and great families such as the Fujiwara were able to amass extensive landholdings at imperial expense by obtaining *shoen* (private tax-free estates) as rewards for good service.

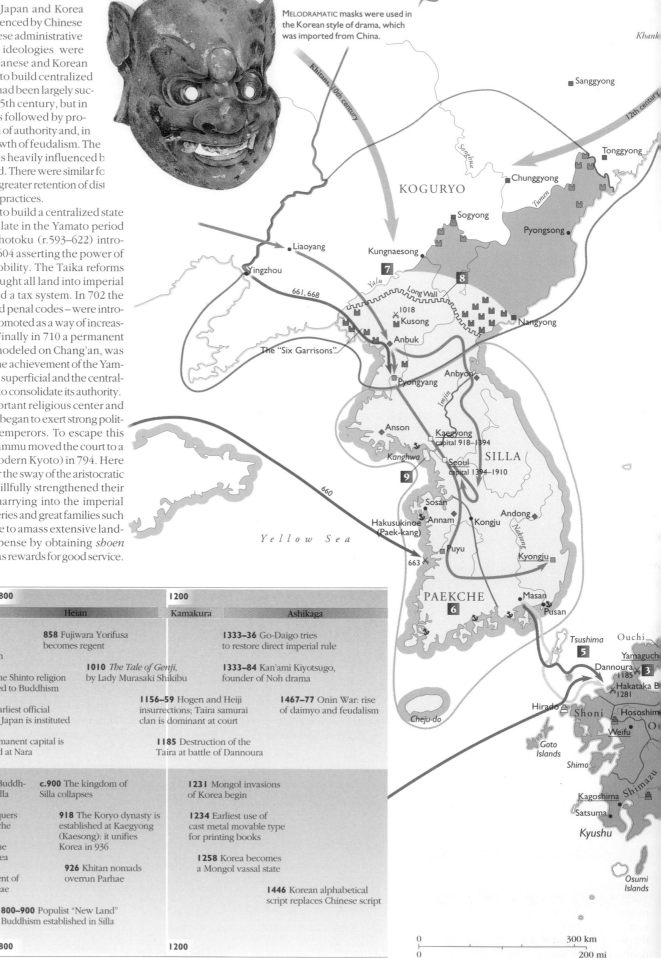

MELODRAMATIC masks were used in the Korean style of drama, which was imported from China.

Yellow Sea

TIMELINE

	800	1200	
	Yamato	Heian	Kamakura	Ashikaga

Japan

604 Prince Shotoku introduces Chinese-influenced constitution

858 Fujiwara Yorifusa becomes regent

1333–36 Go-Daigo tries to restore direct imperial rule

700–800 The Shinto religion is assimilated to Buddhism

1010 *The Tale of Genji*, by Lady Murasaki Shikibu

1333–84 Kan'ami Kiyotsugo, founder of Noh drama

708 The earliest official coinage in Japan is instituted

1156–59 Hogen and Heiji insurrections; Taira samurai clan is dominant at court

1467–77 Onin War: rise of daimyo and feudalism

710 A permanent capital is established at Nara

1185 Destruction of the Taira at battle of Dannoura

Korea

600–700 Chan (Zen) Buddhism is established in Silla

c.900 The kingdom of Silla collapses

1231 Mongol invasions of Korea begin

660–68 China conquers Koguryo and Paekche

918 The Koryo dynasty is established at Kaegyong (Kaesong): it unifies Korea in 936

1234 Earliest use of cast metal movable type for printing books

676 Silla expels the Chinese from Korea

926 Khitan nomads overrun Parhae

1258 Korea becomes a Mongol vassal state

694 Establishment of the state of Parhae

1446 Korean alphabetical script replaces Chinese script

800–900 Populist "New Land" Buddhism established in Silla

800 | 1200

0 _____ 300 km
0 _____ 200 mi

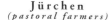

Jürchen
(pastoral farmers)

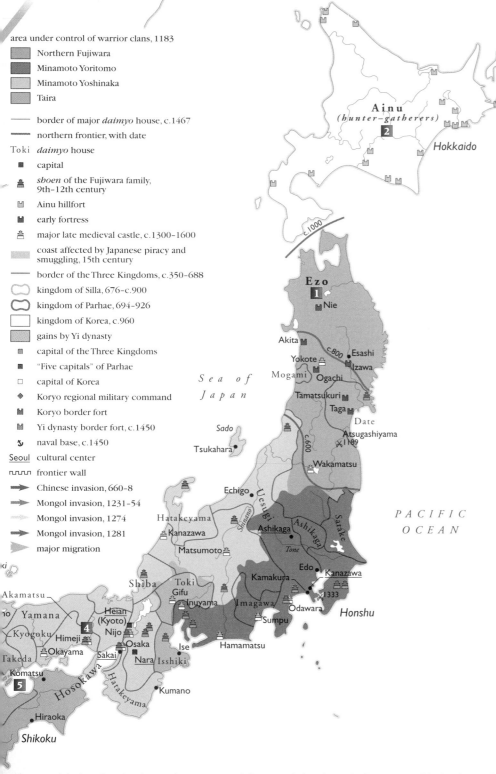

area under control of warrior clans, 1183

- Northern Fujiwara
- Minamoto Yoritomo
- Minamoto Yoshinaka
- Taira

— border of major *daimyo* house, c.1467

— northern frontier, with date

Toki *daimyo* house

- ■ capital
- *shoen* of the Fujiwara family, 9th-12th century
- Ainu hillfort
- early fortress
- major late medieval castle, c.1300-1600
- coast affected by Japanese piracy and smuggling, 15th century
- border of the Three Kingdoms, c.350-688
- kingdom of Silla, 676-c.900
- kingdom of Parhae, 694-926
- kingdom of Korea, c.960
- gains by Yi dynasty
- ▣ capital of the Three Kingdoms
- ■ "Five capitals" of Parhae
- □ capital of Korea
- ◆ Koryo regional military command
- Koryo border fort
- Yi dynasty border fort, c.1450
- naval base, c.1450

Seoul cultural center

ᴧᴧᴧᴧ frontier wall

→ Chinese invasion, 660-8
→ Mongol invasion, 1231-54
→ Mongol invasion, 1274
→ Mongol invasion, 1281
→ major migration

1 The Ezo people of Honshu, related to the Ainu, fiercely resisted Japanese expansion but were conquered by the 12th century.

2 The Ainu were an aboriginal hunter-gatherer people, linguistically and physically unrelated to any other east Asian peoples, who were only brought under Japanese rule in the 17th century.

3 The destruction of the Taira at the battle of Dannoura was made the subject of the *Tale of the Heike*, the major literary work of 13th-century Japan.

4 One of the best preserved Japanese medieval castles is White Heron Castle at Himeji (14th century).

5 Fishing villages in the Inland Sea and on Tsushima became bases for smugglers and pirates, breaking tight Korean and Chinese restrictions on trade.

6 The kingdom of Paekche fell after its Japanese allies were defeated by Silla in a naval battle in 663.

7 The Koryo dynasty extended its control to the Yalu River c.960, since when it has remained Korea's northwestern border.

8 The Long Wall was built in 1033-44 to defend Korea against Khitan and Jürchen invasions.

9 During the Mongol invasions, the Korean royal court moved to the greater safety of Kanghwa Island.

almost 400 effectively independent states. The emperors continued to reign in Heian (Kyoto) but they were powerless and impoverished figureheads.

In Korea three kingdoms – Koguryo, Silla and Paekche – had emerged by 600. In 660 the expansionist Chinese Tang dynasty invaded the peninsula and in alliance with Silla conquered Paekche and Koguryo. On finding that it was not to share in the spoils, Silla drove the Chinese from the peninsula in 676. Silla occupied Paekche and southern Koguryo: northern Koguryo remained in chaos until a successor state, Parhae, emerged in 694. Both Korean states developed as centralized kingdoms on the Tang model. In 780 a struggle between the monarchy and the aristocracy broke out in Silla and in the 9th century the kingdom broke up. A new kingdom was created in 918–36 by Wang Kon (r.918–45), founder of the Koryo dynasty from which Korea gets its name. Parhae was extinguished about the same time by the Khitan nomads. Despite Khitan opposition, Korea had established a heavily fortified frontier on the Yalu River by the early 11th century.

A coup in 1170 deprived the monarchy of real power, leaving Korea leaderless until the military Choe family seized power in 1196. The Choe led resistance to the Mongols but unrest grew more widespread as the wars dragged on. The dynasty was overthrown in 1258 and Korea became a Mongol vassal state. The end of Mongol rule in 1356 brought a return to political instability and the Koryo dynasty was eventually overthrown with Chinese help by the general Yi Songgye (r.1392–98), founder of the Yi dynasty (1392–1910). Under the Yi, Confucianism replaced Buddhism as Korea's main ethical code and was made the basis of the bureaucratic and educational systems. The Yi resumed expansion to the northeast, and by the 15th century the country's modern borders had been established.

The exquisitely refined culture of Heian court life contrasted with growing disorder in the provinces. In the absence of a centralized military system, monasteries and aristocratic houses formed private armies and a class of rural warriors – the *samurai* – developed. Sporadic warfare increased, and with it arose the culture of the warrior.

In the 12th century samurai clans became involved in court politics and Fujiwara influence declined. Following the Gempei war (1180–85) between the Taira and Minamoto clans, Minamoto Yoritomo founded the Kamakura shogunate, beginning a period of military government that would last until 1868. The Kamakura shogunate was overthrown in 1333 and replaced five years later by the Ashikaga shogunate. The shoguns ruled in alliance

with the *shugo* (military constables), who gradually became powerful regional rulers, undermining the authority of the shoguns. When a dispute over the shogunal succession escalated into a fullscale civil war between 1467–77, the shugo lost control of their regional power bases. Control of the provinces fell to new feudal warlords, or *daimyo*. The daimyo feuded almost constantly among themselves, deploying armies of samurai vassals who held small estates in return for military service. The castles of the daimyo became the main centers of government and of warrior culture. Castles attracted craftsmen and merchants and many became a focus for urban development. Though the Ashikaga shogunate survived until 1573, the civil war destroyed its remaining authority and by 1500 Japan had fragmented into

See also 44 (the world religions);
49 (Mongol invasion); 63 (later Japan)

Western Europe's confidence grew in the 11th and 12th centuries, as shown in its Gothic cathedrals and in crusades against the Muslims in the Holy Land and the pagan Slavs in eastern Europe (▷ 48). Spain's Christian kingdoms expanded until by 1279 the Muslims were confined to Granada. The Holy Roman empire looked impressive, but disputes with the papacy undermined its authority. By the mid-13th century the empire was becoming a confederation of semi-independent states. In contrast, England and France had become strong centralized kingdoms (▷ 46).

Although Islam lost ground in Europe it continued to expand elsewhere. The Ghaznavid emirate conquered northwest India and in 1206 a Muslim sultanate was founded at Delhi. By 1279 it was the largest state in India since the fall of the Gupta empire. Islam was spread by merchants to west Africa in the 11th century, and by the 13th century, Timbuktu, the capital of the kingdom of Mali, was a center of Muslim culture. Trade with the Muslim world was a factor in the emergence of the first powerful chiefdom of southern Africa at Great Zimbabwe around 1200.

The dominant Muslim power in the 11th century was the Seljuks (▷ 47). Originally a clan of Ghuzz Turk mercenaries who rebelled against their employer, the Ghaznavid emir, in 1037, the Seljuks overran Persia, the Abbasid caliphate, Syria and the Holy Land, and in 1071 won control of Anatolia. Although the First Crusade, which captured Jerusalem in 1099, allowed the Byzantines to reclaim some lost territory, the empire never fully recovered. By this time Seljuk political unity had broken down, and hostility between them and the Fatimids of Egypt meant that Muslim counterattacks against the Crusaders were ineffective. The Crusaders were put on the defensive after the Seljuk Zangid sultanate of Aleppo overthrew the Fatimids 1169–71 and seized Egypt, but the Zangids were themselves overthrown five years later by Saladin, who retook Jerusalem in 1187. The Crusader states were finally destroyed in 1291 by the Mamlukes who had seized power in Egypt in 1250.

The nomadic Mongol peoples had been gradually expanding westward since the breakup of the Turkish steppe empire in the 8th century. Though superb cavalry fighters, they did not threaten the settled civilizations of Eurasia until they were

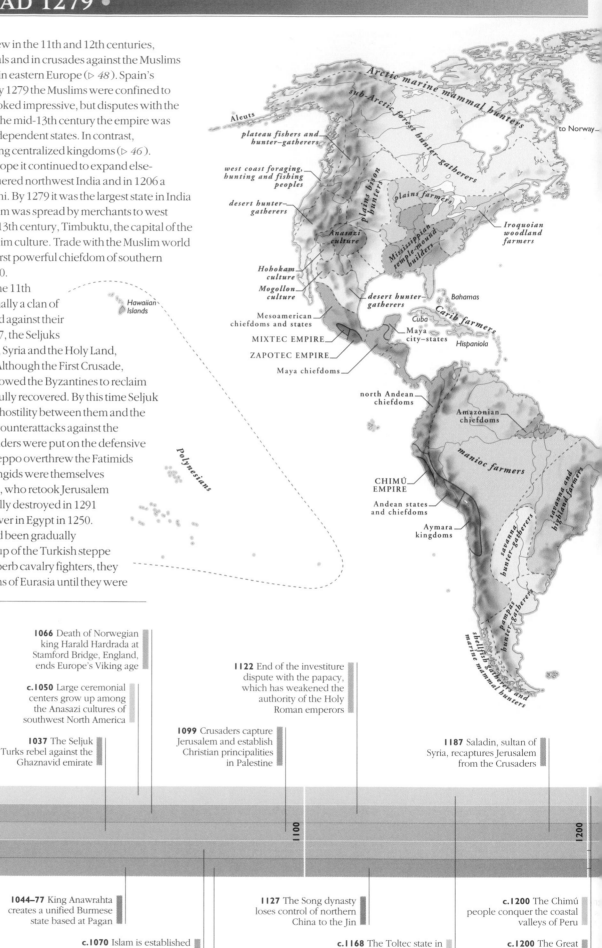

1066 Death of Norwegian king Harald Hardrada at Stamford Bridge, England, ends Europe's Viking age

c.1050 Large ceremonial centers grow up among the Anasazi cultures of southwest North America

1037 The Seljuk Turks rebel against the Ghaznavid emirate

1122 End of the investiture dispute with the papacy, which has weakened the authority of the Holy Roman emperors

1099 Crusaders capture Jerusalem and establish Christian principalities in Palestine

1187 Saladin, sultan of Syria, recaptures Jerusalem from the Crusaders

TIMELINE				
The Americas				
Europe				
Middle East	1000		1100	1200
Africa				
East and South Asia				

1044–77 King Anawrahta creates a unified Burmese state based at Pagan

c.1070 Islam is established in west Africa, carried by trans-Saharan traders

1071 The Byzantine empire is defeated by the Seljuk Turks at Manzikert

1127 The Song dynasty loses control of northern China to the Jin

c.1168 The Toltec state in Mesoamerica falls after its capital Tula is sacked

c.1200 The Chimú people conquer the coastal valleys of Peru

c.1200 The Great Enclosure is built at Zimbabwe in southern Africa

c.1200 The first chiefdoms develop in Polynesia

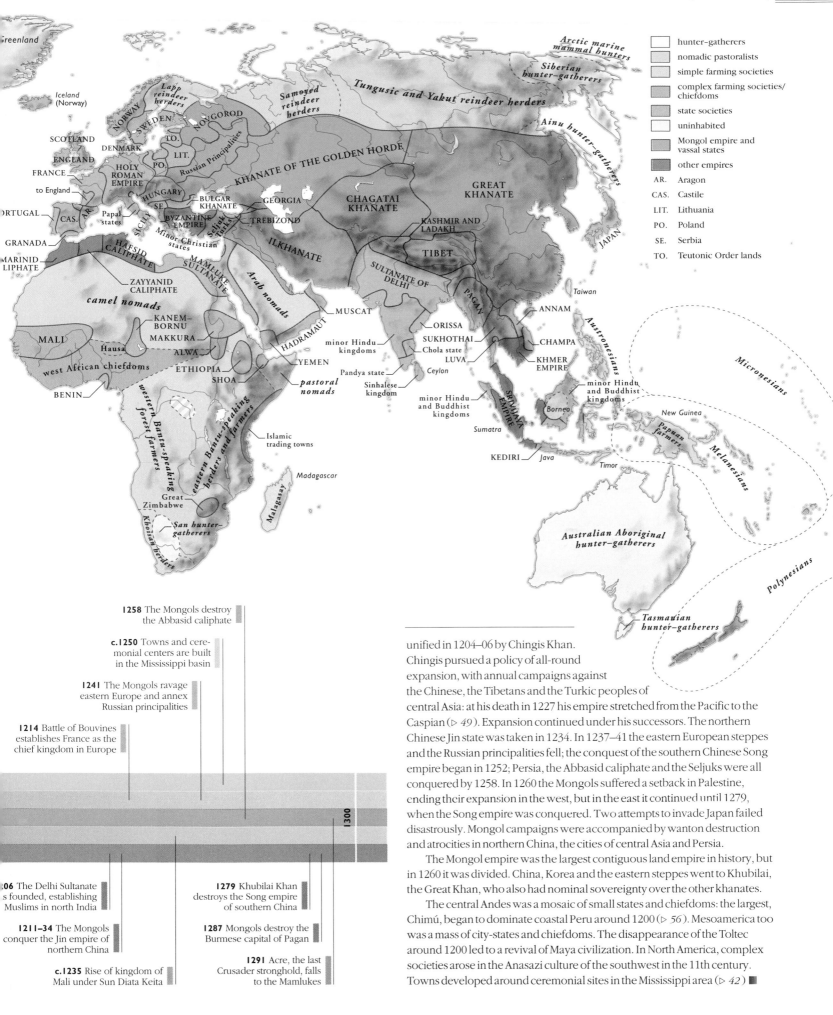

Greenland

Iceland
(Norway)

	hunter-gatherers
	nomadic pastoralists
	simple farming societies
	complex farming societies/ chiefdoms
	state societies
	uninhabited
	Mongol empire and vassal states
	other empires

AR. Aragon
CAS. Castile
LIT. Lithuania
PO. Poland
SE. Serbia
TO. Teutonic Order lands

Arctic marine mammal hunters
Siberian hunter-gatherers
Tungusic and Yakut reindeer herders
Ainu hunter-gatherers

Lapp reindeer herders
NORWAY
SWEDEN
NOVGOROD
Samoyed reindeer herders

SCOTLAND
DENMARK
ENGLAND
TO.
LIT.
PO.
Russian Principalities
KHANATE OF THE GOLDEN HORDE

FRANCE
HOLY ROMAN EMPIRE
HUNGARY
SE.
BULGAR KHANATE
GEORGIA
CHAGATAI KHANATE
GREAT KHANATE
JAPAN

to England
CAS.
AR.
Papal states
SICILY
BYZANTINE EMPIRE
Seljuk Turks
TREBIZOND
ILKHANATE
KASHMIR AND LADAKH

PORTUGAL
GRANADA
MARINID CALIPHATE
HAFSID CALIPHATE
Minor Christian states
MAMLUKE SULTANATE
TIBET
Taiwan

ZAYYANID CALIPHATE
Arab nomads
SULTANATE OF DELHI
PAGAN
ANNAM

camel nomads
MUSCAT
ORISSA
SUKHOTHAI
Chola state
LUVA
CHAMPA
Austronesians
Micronesians

KANEM-BORNU
MAKKURA
Hausa
ALWA
HADRAMAUT
minor Hindu kingdoms
KHMER EMPIRE

MALI
ALWA
YEMEN
Pandya state
Ceylon
minor Hindu and Buddhist kingdoms

west African chiefdoms
ETHIOPIA
SHOA
pastoral nomads
Sinhalese kingdom
SRIVIJAYA EMPIRE
Borneo
New Guinea
Papuan farmers
Melanesians

BENIN
western Bantu-speaking forest farmers
eastern Bantu-speaking herders and farmers
Islamic trading towns
minor Hindu and Buddhist kingdoms
Sumatra

KEDIRI
Java
Timor

Madagascar
Malagasy

Great Zimbabwe
San hunter-gatherers
Khoisan herders

Australian Aboriginal hunter-gatherers

Polynesians

Tasmanian hunter-gatherers

1258 The Mongols destroy the Abbasid caliphate

c.1250 Towns and ceremonial centers are built in the Mississippi basin

1241 The Mongols ravage eastern Europe and annex Russian principalities

1214 Battle of Bouvines establishes France as the chief kingdom in Europe

1300

206 The Delhi Sultanate is founded, establishing Muslims in north India

1279 Khubilai Khan destroys the Song empire of southern China

1211–34 The Mongols conquer the Jin empire of northern China

1287 Mongols destroy the Burmese capital of Pagan

1291 Acre, the last Crusader stronghold, falls to the Mamlukes

c.1235 Rise of kingdom of Mali under Sun Diata Keita

unified in 1204–06 by Chingis Khan. Chingis pursued a policy of all-round expansion, with annual campaigns against the Chinese, the Tibetans and the Turkic peoples of central Asia: at his death in 1227 his empire stretched from the Pacific to the Caspian (▷ 49). Expansion continued under his successors. The northern Chinese Jin state was taken in 1234. In 1237–41 the eastern European steppes and the Russian principalities fell; the conquest of the southern Chinese Song empire began in 1252; Persia, the Abbasid caliphate and the Seljuks were all conquered by 1258. In 1260 the Mongols suffered a setback in Palestine, ending their expansion in the west, but in the east it continued until 1279, when the Song empire was conquered. Two attempts to invade Japan failed disastrously. Mongol campaigns were accompanied by wanton destruction and atrocities in northern China, the cities of central Asia and Persia.

The Mongol empire was the largest contiguous land empire in history, but in 1260 it was divided. China, Korea and the eastern steppes went to Khubilai, the Great Khan, who also had nominal sovereignty over the other khanates.

The central Andes was a mosaic of small states and chiefdoms: the largest, Chimú, began to dominate coastal Peru around 1200 (▷ 56). Mesoamerica too was a mass of city-states and chiefdoms. The disappearance of the Toltec around 1200 led to a revival of Maya civilization. In North America, complex societies arose in the Anasazi culture of the southwest in the 11th century. Towns developed around ceremonial sites in the Mississippi area (▷ 42) ■

The authority of the papacy – already in decline in the face of royal attempts to build centralized nation-states – faced a further setback in 1303 when it fell under the domination of the French monarchy. In 1309 the papacy took up residence at Avignon. It returned to Rome in 1377, but a disputed papal election led to the Great Schism in 1378, with rival popes at Rome and Avignon. The schism stayed unresolved until 1417 as neither pope would submit to the judgment of a church council. It divided Europe and exacerbated existing political differences. France supported the Avignon papacy, for example, so England – then involved in the Hundred Years War (1337–1453) with France – gave its allegiance to the Roman papacy, while Scotland, antagonistic to England, joined the French party.

The Hundred Years War had been sparked off by French attempts to recover English lands in France. After English victories at Crécy (1346) and Poitiers (1356), the French ceded Aquitaine and Gascony at the treaty of Bretigny (1360). But fighting broke out again and when a 28-year truce was made in 1396 the English held less land in France than they had in 1337. In 1363, the French monarchy stored up future trouble by granting the duchy of Burgundy from the royal desmesne to Philip the Bold, the younger son of John II. Through marriage to the heiress of the Count of Flanders (1369), Philip later added the imperial county of Burgundy (the Franche-Comté) and the wool towns of Flanders to his possessions.

War was endemic throughout the Holy Roman empire. The powerful city-states of northern Italy, where imperial control was now purely nominal, engaged armies of mercenaries to fight one another. The German princes were occupied in dynastic struggles to gain primacy and thus win control of imperial elections. The Wittelsbachs gained the upper hand from the Habsburgs in 1325, only to lose it to the Luxembourgs (1346–1438). From 1377–89 the princes formed a united front to reduce the independence of the cities of south Germany and the Rhineland. In 1388, after a century of rebellion, the Swiss confederation of eight cantons secured their independence from the dukes of Habsburg. In eastern Europe in 1354, the Ottoman Turks took

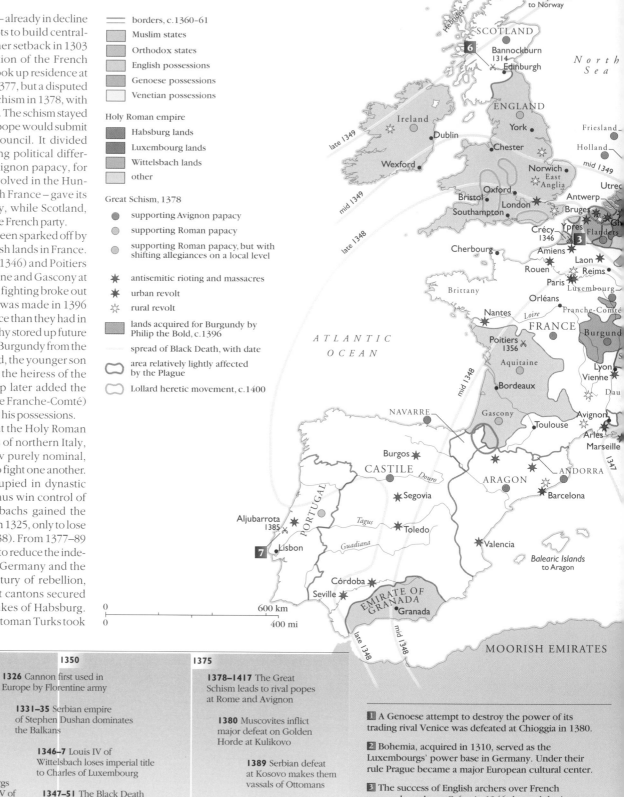

— borders, c.1360–61
☐ Muslim states
☐ Orthodox states
☐ English possessions
☐ Genoese possessions
☐ Venetian possessions

Holy Roman empire
☐ Habsburg lands
☐ Luxembourg lands
☐ Wittelsbach lands
☐ other

Great Schism, 1378
● supporting Avignon papacy
● supporting Roman papacy
● supporting Roman papacy, but with shifting allegiances on a local level

✴ antisemitic rioting and massacres
✴ urban revolt
☆ rural revolt

☐ lands acquired for Burgundy by Philip the Bold, c.1396
— spread of Black Death, with date
area relatively lightly affected by the Plague
Lollard heretic movement, c.1400

0 — 600 km
0 — 400 mi

	1325	1350	1375	
Political change	**1302** Territorial expansion of Muscovy begins	**1326** Cannon first used in Europe by Florentine army	**1378–1417** The Great Schism leads to rival popes at Rome and Avignon	
	1309–77 The papacy is resident at Avignon	**1331–35** Serbian empire of Stephen Dushan dominates the Balkans	**1380** Muscovites inflict major defeat on Golden Horde at Kulikovo	
	1310 John of Luxembourg becomes king of Bohemia	**1346–7** Louis IV of Wittelsbach loses imperial title to Charles of Luxembourg	**1389** Serbian defeat at Kosovo makes them vassals of Ottomans	
	1314–25 War between Wittelsbachs and Habsburgs ends in victory for Louis IV of Wittelsbach	**1347–51** The Black Death devastates Europe	**1397** Union of Calmar unites Scandinavia under the Danish crown	
	1323 Wars between Scotland and England ends; confirmed by treaty of Edinburgh (1328)	**1356** Charles IV issues the Golden Bull ending papal role in imperial elections		
Cultural change	**1305** Frescoes of the Arena Chapel, Padua painted by Giotto	**1348–53** Boccaccio writes the *Decameron*	**1386–1400** Geoffrey Chaucer writes the *Canterbury Tales*	
	c.1314–21 Dante writes the *Divine Comedy*	**1351** Petrarch, Italian poet, moves from Rome to Provence and begins his *Rime*		
	1325	1350	1375	

1 A Genoese attempt to destroy the power of its trading rival Venice was defeated at Chioggia in 1380.

2 Bohemia, acquired in 1310, served as the Luxembourgs' power base in Germany. Under their rule Prague became a major European cultural center.

3 The success of English archers over French armored cavalry at Crécy in 1346 showed the increasing importance of infantry in late medieval warfare.

4 Moscow owed its independence to Prince Daniel (r.1263–1304) who began its territorial expansion.

5 The Lithuanians, Europe's last pagans, resisted the attempt of the Teutonic Knights to convert them by force, but voluntarily adopted Christianity in 1386.

6 Defeat at Bannockburn in 1314 forced the English to recognize Scottish independence in 1328, but both kingdoms continued to raid each other's territory.

7 A Castilian invasion of Portugal was defeated in 1385, securing its future as an independent state.

BLACK DEATH victims – shown in this French wall-painting – were buried immediately, often in unconsecrated ground.

Gallipoli on the European shore of the Dardanelles; by the end of the century they had overrun most of the Balkans. Political conflicts and the paralysis of the papacy ensured that there was no purposeful response to the Ottoman threat apart from the unsuccessful Crusade of Nicopolis, led by John the Fearless of Burgundy to support Hungary in 1396.

But the event that dominated the 14th century was the Black Death, a combined epidemic of bubonic and pneumonic plague that broke out on the east Asian steppes in the 1330s and spread along the Silk Road to reach the Genoese port of Kaffa in the Crimea in late 1346. From here it was carried (by the parasitic fleas that infested ships' rats) to Venice, Genoa and Marseille, all ports with strong links to the east, and then spread amazingly quickly along the main trade routes of Europe. One factor explaining the Black Death's rapid inroads may lie in the series of crop failures earlier in the century, which caused extensive famines in areas where overpopulation was rife. The effects of malnutrition probably weakened resistence to the disease. The impact of the Black Death was catastrophic: even in the most lightly affected areas, ten to fifteen percent of the population died, and in the areas worst affected (Tuscany, East Anglia and Norway) mortality may have been fifty percent or more. Overall, around a third of Europe's population died between 1346 and 1351. The plague remained endemic in Europe for 250 years and many cities had still not regained their pre-plague population levels by the 16th century.

Outbreaks of the plague were often accompanied by religious hysteria, and blame fell on Jews and foreigners who were subjected to attacks. Depopulation caused prices and rents to fall and wages to rise, loosening the traditional bonds of service. Social disruption increased and urban and rural uprisings such as the Jacquerie wars in northern France (1358), and the English peasants' revolt of 1381, were frequent. Mob violence was mainly directed at landlords, tax officials and rich urban oligarchies, and there was often an element of anticlericalism, found also in the rise of heretical movements such as the Lollards in England. In eastern Europe, in contrast, a largely free peasantry had serfdom imposed upon them by lords who were anxious not to lose tenants.

See also 46 (Feudal Europe); 47 (the Turkish empires); 53 (the medieval economy)

Over 90 percent of the population of medieval Europe were peasant farmers. The manorial system – by which a lord divided up an estate (the manor) between individual peasants who farmed it – was widespread, though there were regional variations. The lord was expected to protect his peasants in times of war, provide relief in times of famine and administer justice in return for payments of produce, labor and money. Many peasants were unfree serfs or villeins, tied for life to the land on which they worked and passing their servile status onto their descendants, but they were not slaves and had certain established rights. By the end of the Middle Ages serfs had been replaced by tenant farmers and wage laborers in the British Isles, Italy and Iberia, but serfdom survived into the 18th century in some parts of western Europe and in Russia until 1861.

A number of agricultural improvements took place in the early Middle Ages. Most important was the widespread adoption around the year 700 of a three-field system of crop rotation, in which one field was used for cereals, one for vegetables such as beans and the third left fallow, to preserve soil fertility. The introduction of the wheeled plow, and later of the padded shoulder collar that enabled horses – 50 percent more efficient than oxen – to be used for plowing, allowed the heavy soils of northern Europe to be worked more efficiently. In these ways productivity was boosted far beyond the levels achieved in Roman times and peasant prosperity increased steadily. Most surplus agricultural produce was sold at local markets but wool, hides, wine, dairy products, salt, fish and grain were traded in large quantities over long distances. Moving goods by land was slow and expensive, so most bulk trade went by sea or river boat. Various industrial activities such as mining, ore smelting, logging, charcoal burning, quarrying and salt extraction were also important in the countryside. Both agriculture and rural industry benefited from technological improvements that

TIMELINE

Trade and commerce

1100	1200	1300	1400
1081 Venetians negotiate trade privileges in Constantinople	**1155** Earliest recorded fire insurance (in Iceland)	**c.1300** Italian merchants develop double-entry book-keeping: basis of modern accountancy	**1414** The Medici of Florence become papal bankers
c.1100 Guilds of artisans and craftsmen begin to develop in towns	**1230** Lübeck and Hamburg form alliance – the beginning of the Hanseatic league	**c.1350** Marine premium insurance begins in Genoa	**1441** Portuguese slave trade with west Africa begins
1133 St Bartholomew's Fair, London founded (until 1853)	**1242** Earliest recorded use of convoy system to protect merchant ships from piracy	**1380** Hans Fugger founds a banking concern at Augsburg; Europe's largest financial house by 1500	**1455** First European printing shop is set up at Mainz
	1253 Florence and Genoa introduce gold coinage		

Society

1100	1200	1300	1400
c.1000 European population is about 42 million	**c.1180** Windmills in common use in Europe	**1300** European population is approximately 73 million	**c.1435** Three-masted square-rigged ships, capable of oceanic voyaging, come into use
1086 Domesday Book provides a detailed survey of English agriculture and land ownership	**c.1240** Water-powered sawmills come into use in Europe	**1346–51** Around 24 million die in the Black Death	**c.1450** European population is about 50 million

LÜBECK was a center of the Hanseatic trade in the Baltic, using sturdy ships called cogs, as shown on this seal of 1258.

made possible greater use of water and wind power to mill grain and work pumps, bellows and sawmills.

Except in Italy, urban life declined dramatically in western Europe during the late Roman empire and did not fully recover until the 11th century. Italy remained the most urbanized region of Europe throughout the Middle Ages. Compared with contemporary towns in the Arab world and China, medieval European towns were small and, outside northern Italy and Flanders, rarely had populations above 10,000. They were unhygienic places and, as deaths exceeded births, they relied on immigration from the countryside to maintain their populations. Townspeople were free of servile obligations but

citizenship, and with it a right to participate in local government, was normally restricted to property owners. The trade and craft activities of towns were regulated by associations of merchants or craftsmen known as guilds. These dictated standards of quality and training and provided members with welfare benefits, but their principal function was to protect their members by excluding outside competition. Manufactured goods produced in towns were generally intended for the local market but production of high-quality goods for export was important in some areas, such as Flanders, where there was a flourishing woolen textile industry. Seasonal trade fairs were important commercial events, attracting merchants from a far wider area than the weekly town markets; some, for example the Champagne fairs, developed into major centers of international business.

One of the most powerful trade associations of the Middle Ages was the Hanseatic league, membership of which extended to 37 north German and Baltic towns at its peak in the 14th century. The league negotiated trading privileges for its members, prepared navigational charts, suppressed piracy and even waged war. It maintained offices called *kontors* in London, Bergen, Bruges and Novgorod, where its merchants lived and traded permanently, as well as subsidiary depots in many other cities. The league's power declined at the end of the Middle Ages, when it was faced with greater competition from England and the Netherlands. In the Mediterranean, maritime trade was dominated by Venice and Genoa. Both took advantage of the Crusades to build up trade links with Asia, the source of luxury products such as silks, spices and gems, and maintained a bitter rivalry between them.

By the 13th century merchants were assuming the role of capitalists to finance craft production, so that productivity increased but craftsmen lost their independence. International banking houses such as the Medici and the Fuggers emerged, and the principles of modern insurance and accountancy were established.

1 Flanders was a leading center of Europe's growing textile industry; its prosperity was enshrined in grand town halls, as at Ghent.

2 England's prosperity resulted from it being Europe's main source of wool for cloth-making.

3 The Arabs introduced papermaking to Europe at Valencia in the 12th century.

4 The church's prohibition on eating meat on fast days maintained demand for salted fish from the Baltic and North Seas.

5 The fairs of Champagne flourished as centers of north–south trade in the 12th and 13th centuries.

6 The importance of the Black Sea as a trading area increased after the 13th-century Mongol invasions improved access to the east for European traders.

See also 52 (war, revolt and plague);
66 (European economy 1500–1800)

population density per sq km, early 14th century
- over 30
- 21–30
- 11–20
- 10 or under

- ■ city with population over 10,000, c.1300
- ○ branch of Fugger bank
- ● branch of Medici bank
- Kiev city with important trade fair
- ■ major Hanseatic league member
- ● other Hanseatic league member
- ★ Hanseatic *kontor* (foreign depot)
- ★ Genoese trading center
- ★ Venetian trading center
- grain exporting area
- wine exporting area
- woollen cloth producing area
- *furs* main trade commodity

- ━━ borders, c.1325
- ━━ Hanseatic trade route
- ━━ Genoese trade route
- ━━ Venetian trade route
- ━━ Gascon wine trade route
- ━━ other trade route

0   600 km
0   400 mi

The Renaissance, the great cultural movement of 15th-century Europe, had its origins in the revival of interest in classical philosophy, science and literature that first emerged during the 12th century. But its immediate roots lay in 14th-century Italy in the work of artists such as Giotto and humanist scholars such as Petrarch. By the early 15th century, men like Masaccio and Donatello in Florence were evolving new styles of painting and sculpture, while Brunelleschi was leading the revival of classical forms of architecture. In the course of the century Italy's city-states came to be ruled by dynastic princes. Italian Renaissance rulers – whether the powerful Medici family in Florence or the heads of ducal courts such as Mantua or Urbino – dispensed patronage as an arm of government, to secure prestige and influence. In Venice, a large urban aristocracy was keen to publicize its wealth and status. The technology of printing, developed in Germany in the mid-1450s, aided the spread of the new arts and learning outside Italy. By the early 16th century these arts were beginning to find their place in the courts of Europe's "new monarchs", who were emerging from periods of dynastic rivalry and civil war with strong centralized governments.

In the early 15th century France was divided by the rivalry between the Burgundian and Armagnac families, who disputed control of mad king Charles VI (r.1380–1422). Henry V of England (r.1413–22), anxious to secure the legitimacy of the Lancastrian dynasty established by his father Henry IV in 1399, seized the opportunity to reopen the Hundred Years War. His major victory at Agincourt (1415) and conquest of northern France led to his recognition as Charles VI's heir in 1420. After Henry's death and the revival of French morale under the leadership of Joan of Arc, English fortunes declined. By 1453 they had lost all their French possessions except Calais. Defeat provoked dynastic wars in England (the Wars of the Roses) until Henry VII (r.1485–1509), founder of the Tudor dynasty, restored stable government.

The dukes of Burgundy profited from France's troubles to enhance their own position by forming an alliance with the English which lasted until 1435. Under Philip the Good (r.1419–67) they acquired further territory in the Netherlands. His successor Charles the Bold wanted to establish an indepen-

dent kingdom and tried to build a corridor of lands to link his southern and northern possessions, but died in battle against the Swiss at Nancy in 1477. When his heiress Mary married Maximilian of Habsburg, the Burgundian lands descended to the Habsburgs. They had ruled the Holy Roman empire since 1438, having already united their lands with those of Luxembourg. Louis XI (r.1461–83) seized and retained the lands of the duchy of Burgundy in France. Franche-Comté was ceded to France on the betrothal of the *dauphin* (later Charles VIII) to Mary's daughter in 1482, but reverted to the Habsburgs when the engagement was revoked.

borders, 1429-33
Burgundian territory, 1429
English territory, 1429
nominally English territory, 1429
Aragonese territory, 1430
Byzantine empire, 1430
Genoese territory, 1430
Habsburg territory, 1430
Hungarian territory, 1430
Muscovy, 1430
Ottoman empire, 1430
Poland–Lithuania, 1430
Venetian territory, 1430
Polish acquisition, 1466
Habsburg acquisition, 1477
temporary Hungarian gain under Matthias Corvinus, 1477-90
maximum extent of Burgundian kingdom under Charles the Bold, 1477
kingdom of Aragon & Castile, 1492
kingdom of France, 1492
Muscovy, 1492
Ottoman empire, 1492
Portuguese base
printing center, with date
Milan   early Renaissance cultural center
Tatar campaign
Hussite movement, 1415-36

0 _____ 600 km
0 _____ 400 mi

TIMELINE

	1425		1450	1475
Political change	**1405–06** Florence captures Pisa, giving it an outlet to the sea	**1429** Joan of Arc relieves the siege of Orléans: turning point of Hundred Years War	**1453** Ottoman Turks capture Constantinople, bringing the Byzantine empire to an end	**1478** Foundation of the Spanish Inquisition
	1417 The Council of Constance ends the Great Schism of the papacy	**1434** Cosimo de' Medici becomes the ruler of Florence (d.1464)	**1455–85** The Wars of the Roses in England	**1492** Fall of Granada. Columbus' first voyage to the New World
	1419 John the Fearless, Duke of Burgundy, murdered during peace conference with Armagnacs	**1438** Albert II of Austria, a Habsburg, is elected Holy Roman emperor: the office remains with the Habsburgs until it is abolished in 1806	**1463–79** Venice loses Euboea and the Greek islands to the Ottomans	**1494** Beginning of the Italian Wars between France and the Habsburgs
			1469 Ferdinand of Aragon marries Isabella of Castile	**1497–98** Vasco da Gama sails to India
Cultural change	**1411–66** fl. Donatello, Florentine sculptor	**1435** Rogier van der Weyden's *Descent from the Cross* (wooden altarpiece) painted	**1455** First commercially printed book, the *Gutenberg Bible*, is published at Mainz	**1476** William Caxton sets up the first printing press in London
	1420–36 Brunelleschi builds dome on Florence cathedral		**1456–57** Botticelli, Florentine painter, completes *Primavera*	**1495–97** Leonardo da Vinci paints *The Last Supper* in Milan
	1422–40 fl. Jan van Eyck, Netherlandish painter			

1425   1450   1475

Norway

KINGDOM OF DENMARK
(Union of Calmar) 1

Bergen

Christiania

Vänern

Sweden

Stockholm
1483

Vättern

Calmar

Denmark

Copenhagen
1493

Holstein

Bremen

Lübeck

Hamburg
1491

Stettin

Haarlem

Amsterdam

Deventer
1477

Utrecht
1472

Cologne
1466

Antwerp
1470

Luxembourg

Frankfurt

HOLY ROMAN
EMPIRE

Brandenburg

Berlin

Leipzig
1481

Bamberg
1460

Mainz
1455

Nuremberg
1470

Bohemia

Prague
1478

Breslau

Nancy
1477

Basel
1462

Strasbourg
1460

Augsburg
1468

Munich
1470

Constance 3

Franche-Comté

Zürich

Innsbruck

Salzburg

Vienna
1482

Austria

Tyrol

Swiss
Confederation

Geneva
1478

Savoy

Milan
1470

Milan

Mantua

Venice
1469

VENICE

Genoa

Ferrara 7

Rimini

Urbino

Pisa

Florence
1471

Florence

Siena

PAPAL
STATES

Subiaco
1465

Rome
1467

Corsica

Sardinia

NAPLES
1442 to Aragon

Naples

BENEVENTO

Otranto

Palermo

Reggio
1480

Sicily

Tunis

Malta

Åbo

Helsinki

Revel

PRINCIPALITY OF
NOVGOROD
1478 to Muscovy

Novgorod

*Lake
Ladoga*

*Lake
Peipus*

Pskov

Riga

Vilna

Smolensk

MUSCOVY 4

1463–74
to Muscovy

Yaroslavl

Rostov

Tver
1483 to Muscovy

Moscow

Ryazan

RYAZAN

Kazan

1408, 1447, 1451, 1465, 1472, 1480

KHANATE OF THE
GOLDEN HORDE
Tatars

Sarai

TEUTONIC KNIGHTS

Königsberg

Danzig 2

Tannenberg
1411

POLAND–LITHUANIA

Vistula

Warsaw

Oder

Elbe

Western Dvina

Dnieper

Krakow

Lemberg

MOLDAVIA

GERMAN and Italian armorers
brought plate armor to its
highest development in the
15th century. This finely-
crafted plumed helmet was
made for Ferdinand of Aragon.

Buda

Pest

HUNGARY

Zagreb

Sava

Belgrade

Serbia

Nish

WALLACHIA

Danube

1444

Varna

Danube

Montenegro

Sofia

Zara

Split

Bosnia

RAGUSA

ALBANIA

OTTOMAN

EMPIRE

Constantinople
1488
1453 to Ottomans

Adrianople

Ankara
1402

Kaffa
1475 to Ottomans

Black Sea

GEORGIA

Trebizond

TREBIZOND

TURKISH
EMIRATES

Otranto

ATHENS

Euboea

Morea

KNIGHTS OF
ST JOHN

Rhodes

CYPRUS
1489 to Venice

Cyprus

Crete

MAMLUKE
SULTANATE

*Mediterranean
Sea*

In the Iberian peninsula a century or more of rivalry between Castile and Aragon (which added the kingdom of Naples to its extensive Mediterranean empire in 1442), came to an end in 1469 with the marriage of Ferdinand of Aragon to Isabella of Castile. Under their joint leadership, Granada, the last Muslim state in Spain, was conquered in 1485–92. Portugal, prevented from expanding in the peninsula by Castile, turned its attention to North Africa, beginning with the capture of Ceuta in 1415. In the 1430s Portuguese navigators began to explore the African coast and in 1487 entered the Indian Ocean. Even more significant was the voyage of Columbus, commissioned by Isabella of Castile, which led to the discovery of the New World in 1492.

Eastern Europe saw the creation of a strong but short-lived kingdom: Poland–Lithuania, under Casimir IV (r.1447–92) the largest state in Europe.

Hungary, which resisted Ottoman expansion in the Balkans, dominated central Europe under Matthias Corvinus (r.1477–90). By the end of the century Muscovy had absorbed most of the other Russian principalities. With the fall of the Byzantine empire in 1453, it was left as the only significant Orthodox state. Ivan III married a Byzantine princess in 1472, adopting the title of *czar* (caesar).

1 The Union of Calmar, proclaimed in 1397, was unpopular in Sweden, where it led to several revolts before its final collapse in 1523.

2 The defeat by Poland–Lithuania of the Teutonic Knights at Tannenberg saw the start of their decline.

3 The burning for heresy of the Bohemian religious reformer Jan Hus at Constance in 1415 sparked a 20-year revolutionary uprising by his followers.

4 In 1480 Ivan III of Muscovy ceased paying tribute to buy off the Golden Horde, by now a shadow of its former strength.

5 In 1492, after their victory over the Muslims, Ferdinand and Isabella expelled from Spain around 150,000 Jews who refused to convert to Christianity.

6 England's preoccupation with war in France in the 15th century allowed much of Ireland to achieve effective independence.

7 The patronage of the wealthy Medici family made Florence the leading cultural center of the age, as well as a center for banking and trade, and the dominant political entity of central Italy.

See also 53 (economy of medieval Europe);
58 (Reformation Europe)

The destruction of Teotihuacán in the 8th century left a power vacuum in central Mexico, which allowed new peoples to migrate to the region. The Chichimeca and the Nonoalca settled to the north of the Valley of Mexico, where they merged to form the Toltec nation. By around 900 a Toltec state was established around Tula, from where they expanded over the Valley of Mexico. Little is known of the history of the Toltecs, but their legends feature prominently in the traditions of the Aztecs, who claimed descent from them. The most important legend concerns the Toltec ruler Topiltzin-Quetzalcóatl, a real person born in 935 or 947, who soon came to be identified with the god Quetzalcóatl ("feathered serpent"). His opposition to human sacrifice offended the god Tezcatlipoca, who overthrew him: Topiltzin-Quetzalcóatl fled east overseas, vowing to return one day to reclaim his kingdom. Intriguingly, Mayan records show that in 987 a man called Kukulcán ("feathered serpent" in Mayan) conquered Yucatán. Whether or not this was the Toltec Quetzalcóatl, archeological evidence confirms that in about 1000 the main Mayan city of Chichén Itzá was occupied by Toltecs.

Tula was sacked in about 1168 and the Toltec empire was supplanted by many rival city-states. Around 1200 the Aztecs, a farming people from the west, moved into the Valley of Mexico, eventually founding a permanent settlement at Tenochtitlán in 1325. First serving as mercenaries for Tezozomoc, ruler of Azcapotzalco, the Aztecs allied with Texcoco to destroy Azcapotzalco after Tezozomoc's death in 1426. Two years later Itzcóatl established a strong Aztec monarchy. In 1434 Tenochtitlán, Texcoco and Tlacopan formed the Triple Alliance, imposing tributary status on the other states of the Valley of Mexico. Expansion continued under Itzcóatl's successors; by 1500 the alliance ruled over some 10 million people. The empire peaked under Moctezuma II (r.1502–20) but was abruptly ended by Hernán Cortés' invasion of 1519–21. Though Cortés had great advantages in weaponry and armor, these were not decisive against overwhelming Aztec superiority of numbers.

Moctezuma vacillated, believing Cortés to be the returning Quetzalcóatl, whom the legends described as fair-skinned and bearded. The Mesoamerican custom of taking prisoners for sacrifice also hampered the Aztecs against the conquistadors, who fought to kill. Moreover, Cortés found willing allies in the Tlaxcallans, the Aztecs' main source of sacrificial victims. Finally, diseases such as smallpox, brought by the Spanish, decimated the Aztecs.

At the time of the conquest, Aztec society was a class-based hierarchy. Relatives of the king formed the aristocracy, while the commoners (the largest class) comprised members of 20 clans. Each clan had its own quarter of the city with its own schools, temples and communal farms. The lowest class were conquered peoples, who served the aristocracy as farmers and laborers. There were also slaves, usually war captives, and a merchant class, the *pochteca*.

After the Classic Maya cities of the Petén lowlands were abandoned in about 800, Mayan civilization continued in northern Yucatán. Around 850–900 the Putún or Itza Maya settled at Chichén Itzá, which quickly became the dominant Maya center. Around 1000 Yucatán was conquered by the Toltecs, whose rule ended in 1221 with the fall of Chichén Itzá to Hunac Ceel, ruler of Mayapán. The Cocom dynasty he founded dominated Yucatán for over 200 years. When the Spanish landed on Yucatán in 1517, the northern Maya were divided into 16 rival states. This made them harder to subdue than the Aztecs, as there were no key institutions. Thus, Tayasal, the last independent Maya state, did not fall until 1697.

TIMELINE

Toltecs and Aztecs

1000	1200	1400
c.800 Toltec migration into Valley of Mexico	**c.1168** Tula is destroyed, and the Toltec state in Mexico collapses	**1428–40** Reign of Itzcóatl; beginning of Aztec expansion
c.900 The Toltecs found a state with capital at Tula	**c.1200–1300** The Aztecs enter the Valley of Mexico	**1434** Triple Alliance between Tenochtitlán, Texcoco and Tlacopan
c.940 The Mixtecs sack the Zapotec capital Monte Albán	**1325** The Aztecs found Tenochtitlán	**1502–20** Zenith of the Aztec empire under Moctezuma II
	1365 Aztecs mercenaries for Tezozomoc of Azcapotzalco	**1519–21** Conquest of the Aztecs by Cortés

Maya

1000	1200	1400
c.850 Foundation of Chichén Itzá	**1221** Hunac Ceel, founder of Cocom dynasty Mayapán, conquers Chichén Itzá	**1480** Civil wars rage in northern Maya states
c.900 The lost-wax method of gold casting is introduced to Mesoamerica from South America	**1275–1300** Quiché Maya conquers Pokomam Maya	**1524–1697** Spanish conquest of the Maya
987 Kukulcán conquers Chichén Itzá		**1425–75** Quiché Maya dominates Guatemala highlands under Quicab
1000	1200	1400

Inset map (Valley of Mexico)

Citlaltepec
Tizayucan
Coyotepec
Xoloc
Teoloyucan
Lake Zumpanco
Teotihuacan
Cuautitlán
Lake Xaltocan
Chiconautla
Tepexpan
VALLEY OF MEXICO
Ecatepe
Tenayuacan
Lake Texcoco
Xaloztoc
Texcoco
Azcapotzalco
8
Tepeyacac
Tlacopán
Chalpultepec
Tenochtitlán
5
Culhuacán
Chimalpan
Coyohuacán
Ixtapalucan
Zapotitlan
Lake Xochimilco
Xico
Xochimilco
Lake Chalco
Chalco
Atlapulco
Tezompa

0   30 km
0   20 mi

Main map

AH KIN CHEL
CEH PECH
Motul
CHIKINCHEL
Isla Mujeres
CUPUL
TASÉS
CHAKAN
Dzibilchaltún
Izamal
HOCABÁ
Tihoo
Chichén Itzá
ECAB
Balankanché
San Miguel
Mayapán
6
Isla de Cozumel
SOTUTA
Cobá
3
Tancah
4
AH CANUL
Mani
Tulum
Uxmal
Muyil
TUTUL XIUH
COCHUAH
Chacmóol
CANPECH
Yucatán Peninsula
HUAYMIL
CHAMPUTÚN
Cilvituk
Ichpaatun
Tzibanché
Santa Rita
Gulf of Mexico
CHETUMAL
Mixtlan
Atazta
Xicallanco
Lamanai
TABASCO
1519
PUTÚN MAYA (ITZA)
Itzamkanac
Candelaria
Tolteca-Nonoalca
MAYA
PETÉN
TAYASAL
Topoxté
Tayasal
Chiapa de Corzo
Usumacinta
Sierra Madre
Wild Cane Cay
Grijalva
Lago de Izabal
Nito
Naco
Xoconochco
1
MAM MAYA
Zacaleu
QUICHÉ MAYA
CAKCHIQUEL MAYA
Quirigua
Huiztlan
Mazatlan
Utalán
Motagua
Mixco Viejo
Iximché
Lago de Atitlán
POKOMAM MAYA

HIEROGLYPHS were most fully developed among the Maya; this example is from a Mixtec manuscript.

Legend

- Toltec empire, c.1200
- Aztec empire under Itzcóatl, 1427–40
- expansion under Moctezuma I, 1440–68 and Axayacatl, 1469–81
- expansion under Ahuitzotl, 1486–1502 and Moctezuma II, 1502–20
- late Postclassic Maya states
- borders, c.1520
- major Postclassic Maya site
- other Postclassic Maya site
- major Toltec site
- other Toltec site
- major Aztec site
- other Aztec site
- other major Postclassic site
- other site
- Aztec garrison
- Tlacopán city of the Triple Alliance
- Putún Maya trade route
- migration, c.900
- Toltec migration, c.980–1200
- route of Cortés, April to November 1519

1 Xoconochco was a rich province of the Aztec empire, conquered for its cocoa.

2 The Aztecs allowed Tlaxcallan to remain independent so that they could raid it for sacrificial victims.

3 Chichén Itzá: founded by the Putún Maya c.850, it was the Toltec capital of Yucatán c.987–1221. Many of its buildings were modeled on the old Toltec capital of Tula.

4 Isla de Cozumel was settled by the Putún Maya, who used the island as a storage depot for their coastal trade routes.

5 The key to Aztec power was intensive agriculture on fertile reclaimed swampland, or *chinampas*, on the southern shores of Lake Texcoco.

6 The Maya Cocom dynasty, founded by Hunac Ceel, ruled Yucatán from Mayapán from 1283 until their empire broke up in 1441.

7 The Toltec state, founded at Tula c.900, became the model for the later Mesoamerican states of the Aztecs and northern Maya.

8 With a population of 500,000 at the time of the Spanish conquest, Tenochtitlán ("place of the high priest Tenoch") was far larger than most contemporary European cities. Its site is now buried under Mexico City.

See also 39 (early Mesoamerica);
62 (Spanish empire)

The collapse of the highland Tiahuanaco and Huari empires in about 1000 ushered in a long period of political fragmentation in the Andean civilizations. Both in the highlands and on the coast many local states emerged, most of which, like the Sicán state of Lambayeque, controlled no more than a single valley. Around 1200 the Chimú state, centered on Chan Chan in the Moche valley, began a period of gradual imperial expansion, until in the 15th century, it controlled over a thousand kilometers (620 miles) of the Peruvian coast. Around the same time that the Chimú began to expand, a semi-legendary figure, Manco Capac, founded the Inca state at Cuzco in the Killke cultural area of the highlands. For most of its history the Inca state controlled little more than the valley around Cuzco, but in the 15th century it became the greatest of all the empires of the pre-Columbian Americas. It was also destined to be the last.

At its peak in around 1500, the Inca empire encompassed much of modern Peru and Bolivia, together with sizable portions of Chile, Argentina and Equador, and ruled over some 12 million people. The Incas' remarkable territorial expansion took place almost entirely during the reigns of Pachacutec (r.1438–71) and his equally able son Tupac Yupanqui (r.1471–93). The Incas overcame the Chimú, their only serious rivals as an imperial power, with little difficulty, capturing their capital Chan Chan in 1470. By the end of Tupac's reign the Inca empire was reaching the practicable limits of its expansion. The Amazonian rainforest to the east and the southern Andes had sparse, mobile populations that would have proved difficult to control and had environments that were unsuited to the settled intensive agriculture that might make their conquest and colonization worthwhile.

Some new territorial gains were made in the north under Huayna Capac (r. 1493–1525), but on his death a bloody civil war broke out between his sons Atahuallpa and Huáscar. Atahuallpa finally triumphed in 1532, but he had no opportunity to restore the weakened empire. In the same year the Spanish conquistador Francisco Pizarro invaded and captured Atahuallpa in a daring assault on Cajamarca. In 1533 the Spanish executed Atahuallpa and installed a puppet ruler at Cuzco. However, when he rebelled in 1536, they assumed direct rule. Inca resistance continued from inaccessible mountain strongholds but was finally crushed in 1572.

There are many reasons for the Incas' spectacular rise and equally rapid decline. They were fortunate in having able generals as rulers. Inca nobles were brought up in the art of war and a standing army was maintained, so the empire was able to react quickly to any threat. Uniquely among Andean states, the Incas built a network of strategic roads estimated to have been more than 20,000 kilometers (12,500 miles) long – second only in size to the Roman empire's among pre-industrial civilizations – which allowed troops to move quickly to quell trouble on the borders or in the provinces. Conquests were ensured by deporting rebellious populations to the heart of the empire where they could be supervised, while their lands were resettled by loyal Inca subjects.

Probably the main factor in Inca success, however, was their complex administrative system. It was maintained without any type of writing, and with record-keeping done using an elaborate system of knotted strings known as *quipu*, which allowed them to marshal the empire's human resources with great efficiency. Inca society was highly centralized and rigidly hierarchical. At its head was the semidivine emperor. Below the emperor, and directly answerable to him, were the prefects of the

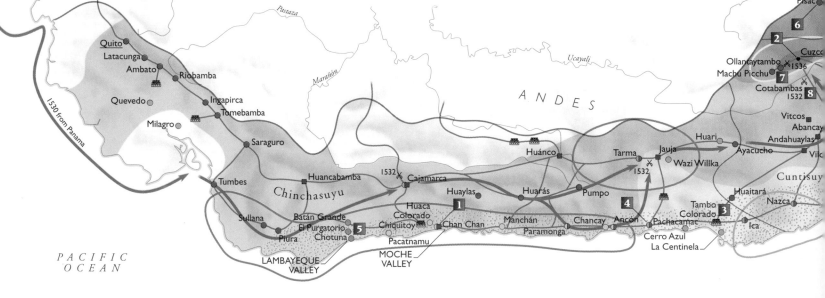

		750		1000		1250		1500
Other Andean states	c.600 Tiahuanaco and Huari empires at their peak		c.850 Foundation of Chimú capital Chan Chan			c.1200 Beginning of Chimú imperial expansion		1470 Chimú empire conquered by Incas
			c.900 Naymlap founds Sicán state				1370 Sicán state conquered by Chimú	
				c.1000 Tiahuanaco and Huari abandoned				
Inca empire					c.1200–1230 Manco Capac founds the Inca state at Cuzco		c.1438 Emperor Pachacutec begins rapid Inca expansion	
							1525 Death of Huayna Capac: Inca empire at its height	
							1525–33 Inca empire collapses after civil war and Spanish invasion	
		MIDDLE HORIZON PERIOD			LATE INTERMEDIATE PERIOD			LATE HORIZ.

TIMELINE

Four Quarters, and below them provincial governors, followed by district officers, local chiefs and, at the bottom, foremen each responsible for supervising ten families. Farmland was divided into thirds, for the support of the state, the gods and the people. All Inca men and women contributed taxation in the form of labor on those parts of the land allocated to the state and the gods. Able-bodied men also paid tax through a labor draft known as *mit'a*. This could last for months and range from military service to work on major construction projects, such as roads and fortresses, or agricultural improvements, such as terracing steep hillsides. This system enabled the empire to raise and supply large armies and keep them in the field for long campaigns.

Although Pizarro was fortunate in having his invasion coincide with the end of a long and destructive civil war, the centralized hierarchy of the Inca empire was also partly responsible for its swift demise. No major decision could be taken without the emperor, whch meant that the empire was paralyzed once Atahuallpa had been captured. Diseases also contributed to the Incas' defeat; as in Mesoamerica, the indigenous population had no resistance to epidemics brought by the Spanish. Indeed, the civil war that first weakened the Inca empire was indirectly caused by a disease introduced from Europe: Huayna Capac died of a smallpox epidemic that spread south from the Spanish base at Panama.

1 Chan Chan was the capital of the Chimú empire from c.850-1470: at the heart of the city were ten walled palace-mausoleum compounds.

2 The Inca capital Cuzco was regarded as the center of the universe, from which radiated the "Four Quarters" of the world. In the Quechua language of the Incas (still widely spoken in the Andes), *cuzco* means "navel".

3 *Tambos*, roadside hostels and storehouses, were sited at intervals of one day's journey on all the empire's roads; one of the largest and best preserved is Tambo Colorado.

4 The oracle of the god Pachacamac, dating to around AD 200, was a major pilgrimage center and rival to the Incas' state solar cult.

5 The Lambayeque valley was the center of the wealthy Sicán state from c.900 until its conquest by the Chimú in c.1370.

6 The Inca increased the area of farmland by terracing mountainsides: many, as at Pisac, are still farmed today.

7 Machu Picchu, the most famous Inca site, was a remote mountain-top religious center and frontier outpost.

8 The victory of Atahuallpa's forces over his rival Huáscar at Cotabambas ended the Inca civil war.

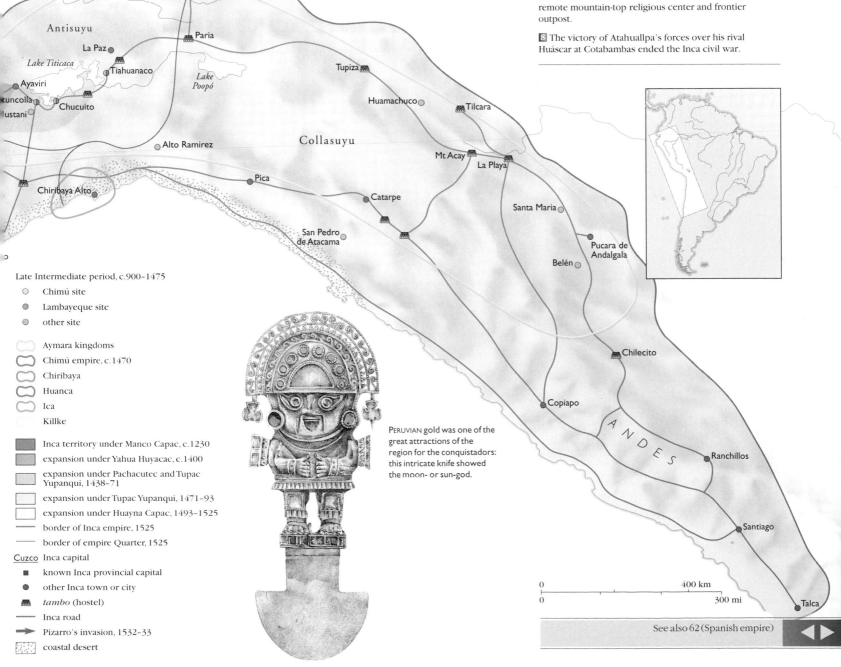

Late Intermediate period, c.900-1475
- ○ Chimú site
- ○ Lambayeque site
- ○ other site

- Aymara kingdoms
- Chimú empire, c.1470
- Chiribaya
- Huanca
- Ica
- Killke

- Inca territory under Manco Capac, c.1230
- expansion under Yahua Huyacac, c.1400
- expansion under Pachacutec and Tupac Yupanqui, 1438-71
- expansion under Tupac Yupanqui, 1471-93
- expansion under Huayna Capac, 1493-1525
- border of Inca empire, 1525
- border of empire Quarter, 1525
- Cuzco   Inca capital
- ■ known Inca provincial capital
- ● other Inca town or city
- 🏛 *tambo* (hostel)
- Inca road
- → Pizarro's invasion, 1532-33
- ░ coastal desert

PERUVIAN gold was one of the great attractions of the region for the conquistadors: this intricate knife showed the moon- or sun-god.

0   400 km
0   300 mi

See also 62 (Spanish empire)

A t the end of the 13th century Islam began to spread through Malaya and the islands of southeast Asia, gradually supplanting Hinduism and Buddhism. At the same time, the Mongols tried to expand into southeast Asia, but with little success. Their vast empire broke up in the 14th century. In China they were overthrown by the native Ming dynasty in 1368, following peasant rebellions and internal power struggles. The Ming ruled in the tradition of the Tang dynasty and reasserted Chinese power in southeast Asia. One of their first acts was to forbid Chinese from traveling abroad. This isolated China, ruined Chinese trade and led to a fateful neglect of maritime matters just as the Europeans were about to begin their own oceanic exploration. By the time the interdict was lifted in 1567, the initiative had passed irretrievably to the Europeans.

The Mongols remained a power on the eastern steppes and the khanates of the Chagatai and the Golden Horde survived at the end of the 15th century, but their mainly Turkic subjects had already reasserted their independence. In the Middle East the Mongols converted to Islam and were assimilated by their Persian and Turkic subjects. Fragmentation followed and by 1350 the Ilkhanate had dissolved into a number of Turkish, Persian and nominally Mongol states. One of these, the Ottoman Turk sultanate, had by 1400 conquered most of Anatolia and the Balkans and reduced the Byzantine empire to its capital Constantinople (▷ 47). Attempts to build a united Christian front to counter this new Muslim threat to Europe foundered amid international rivalries. The Ottomans, however, were defeated in 1402 by Timur the Lame (r.1361–1405), ruler of Samarkand, who claimed Chingis Khan as his ancestor. Timur saw himself as restorer of the Mongol empire, though he was culturally more Turk than Mongol. In a devastating reign of terror, Timur rebuilt the Ilkhanate, broke the power of the Delhi sultanate and was only prevented from invading China by his death. His empire broke up shortly after.

Ottoman power revived after Timur's death and the advance into Europe began again. In 1453 Constantinople fell after an epic siege and the Byzantine empire finally died. In 1475 the Ottomans crossed the Danube and pushed west. Although Byzantium had fallen, much of its heritage survived in the

c.1300 Decline of the Anasazi and other farmers of southwestern deserts

c.1300 The Renaissance begins in Italy as Classical forms in art, architecture and literature are revived

1293 Osman I, a Turkish chief in Anatolia, founds the Ottoman dynasty

1346 The Black Death bubonic plague epidemic (begun in east Asia 1331) reaches Europe

1337 Outbreak of the Hundred Years War between England and France: hostilities continue sporadically until 1453

c.1325 Arrival of the Aztecs in Mexico

1397 The Swedish, Norwegian and Danish crowns are united

1378 The "Great Schism" in the Catholic church begins, with popes in both Rome and Avignon

1428 The Aztec empire is founded by Itzcóatl (r.1428–40)

TIMELINE

The Americas
Europe
Middle East
Africa
East and South Asia

1300

1400

1290 Merchants introduce Islam into Indonesia and Malaysia

1317 Christian Makkura is overthrown by Muslim Arab nomads

c.1330 The sultanate of Delhi reaches its maximum extent under Muhammad ibn Tughluk

1361–1405 From his capital at Samarkand Timur the Lame leads a resurgence of Mongol power in the Middle East

1368 The establishment of the Ming dynasty ends Mongol rule in China

1370 The kingdom of Vijayanagara dominates southern India

1415 The Portuguese take Ceuta in Morocco, their first African possession

Aleuts
sub-Arctic forest hunter-gatherers
Arctic marine mammal hunters
plateau fishers and hunter-gatherers
west coast foraging, hunting and fishing peoples
remnant bison hunters
Plains farmers
Iroquoian woodland farmers
desert hunter-gatherers
Pueblo farmers
Mississippian temple-mound builders
Columbus, 1492
Hawaiian Islands
Mesoamerican chiefdoms
Arawakan farmers
Bahamas
Cuba
Hispaniola
AZTEC EMPIRE
MIXTEC EMPIRE
Maya chiefdoms
Maya city-states
Carib farmers
north Andean chiefdoms
Amazonian chiefdoms
Polynesians
Arawakan manioc farmers
INCA EMPIRE
savanna hunter-gatherers
Tupi-Guarani savanna and highland farmers
pampas hunter-gatherers
shellfish gatherers and marine mammal hunters

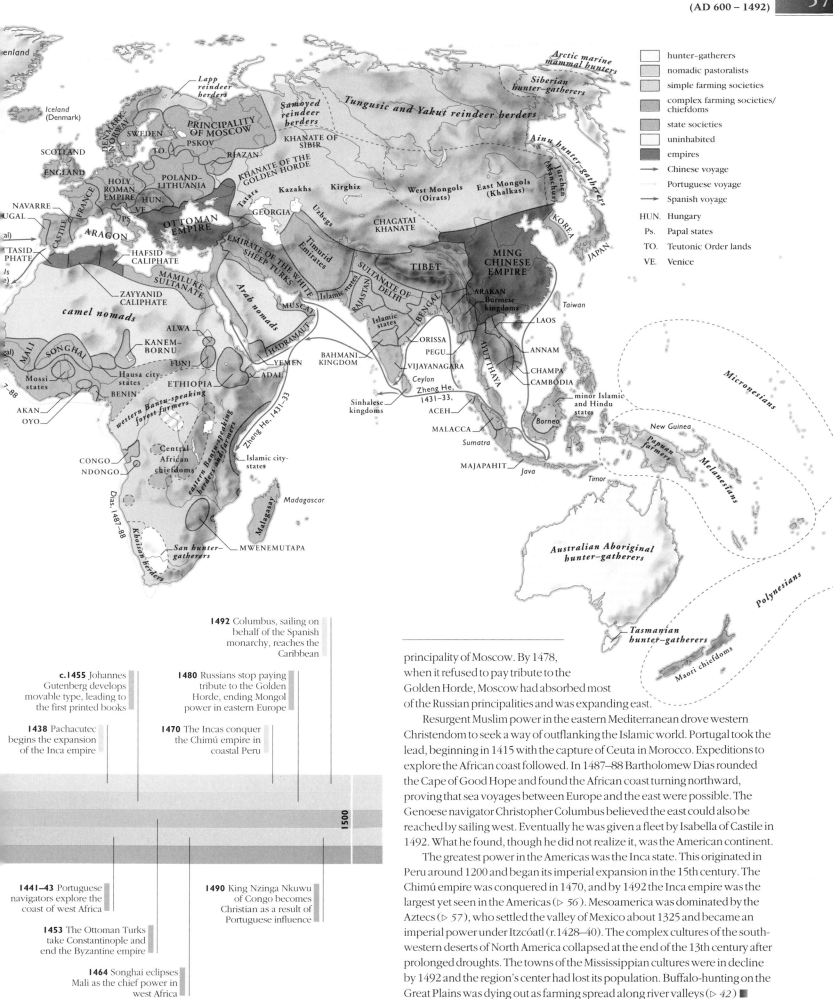

hunter-gatherers
nomadic pastoralists
simple farming societies
complex farming societies/chiefdoms
state societies
uninhabited
empires
→ Chinese voyage
→ Portuguese voyage
→ Spanish voyage
HUN. Hungary
Ps. Papal states
TO. Teutonic Order lands
VE. Venice

1492 Columbus, sailing on behalf of the Spanish monarchy, reaches the Caribbean

c.1455 Johannes Gutenberg develops movable type, leading to the first printed books

1480 Russians stop paying tribute to the Golden Horde, ending Mongol power in eastern Europe

1438 Pachacutec begins the expansion of the Inca empire

1470 The Incas conquer the Chimú empire in coastal Peru

1500

1441–43 Portuguese navigators explore the coast of west Africa

1490 King Nzinga Nkuwu of Congo becomes Christian as a result of Portuguese influence

1453 The Ottoman Turks take Constantinople and end the Byzantine empire

1464 Songhai eclipses Mali as the chief power in west Africa

principality of Moscow. By 1478, when it refused to pay tribute to the Golden Horde, Moscow had absorbed most of the Russian principalities and was expanding east.

Resurgent Muslim power in the eastern Mediterranean drove western Christendom to seek a way of outflanking the Islamic world. Portugal took the lead, beginning in 1415 with the capture of Ceuta in Morocco. Expeditions to explore the African coast followed. In 1487–88 Bartholomew Dias rounded the Cape of Good Hope and found the African coast turning northward, proving that sea voyages between Europe and the east were possible. The Genoese navigator Christopher Columbus believed the east could also be reached by sailing west. Eventually he was given a fleet by Isabella of Castile in 1492. What he found, though he did not realize it, was the American continent.

The greatest power in the Americas was the Inca state. This originated in Peru around 1200 and began its imperial expansion in the 15th century. The Chimú empire was conquered in 1470, and by 1492 the Inca empire was the largest yet seen in the Americas (▷ 56). Mesoamerica was dominated by the Aztecs (▷ 57), who settled the valley of Mexico about 1325 and became an imperial power under Itzcóatl (r.1428–40). The complex cultures of the southwestern deserts of North America collapsed at the end of the 13th century after prolonged droughts. The towns of the Mississippian cultures were in decline by 1492 and the region's center had lost its population. Buffalo-hunting on the Great Plains was dying out as farming spread along river valleys (▷ 42) ■

Part 4

THE EARLY

T he three centuries between 1492 and 1783 saw the different parts of the world interact as never before, and at the same time witnessed a decisive rise of European power. The period (often called the "early modern period") began with the European "discovery" of the New World by Christopher Columbus, and ended, ironically, with the throwing off by Britain's North American colonies of European rule.

The rise of Europe and the shrinking of the world were linked. First Spain and Portugal, and later England, France and the Dutch all conquered and settled important portions of North and South America. It was through the projection of Portuguese naval power that European military strength began to make its impact in the Indian Ocean; again, the other powers, notably the Dutch and British but also the French and Spanish, soon followed in their wake.

The result was a shift in global power. For much of the preceding millennium, Europe had been fairly insignificant on the world stage. In the fifteenth century Europeans had been unable to prevent the advance of the Ottoman Turks into the Balkans, a process that had led to the fall of Constantinople, last bastion of the old Roman empire, to Mehmet II in 1453. At that time, no European king matched Mehmet's power. And at the same date, Chinese ships dominated Asian waters; and Chinese fleets, far larger than any contemporary European one, sailed the Indian Ocean.

Over the next 150 years, the impact of Europe on the rest of the world grew enormously. Spain made dramatic gains in the New World in the early decades of the sixteenth century, overthrowing the Aztecs of Mexico and the Incas of Peru. The supply of precious metals from these two regions sustained

THE GREAT WALL OF CHINA, built to keep out the nomads of central Asia.

MODERN WORLD

the European economy throughout the century. When Spain began to take control of the Philippines in the 1570s, King Philip II of Spain – for whom the islands were renamed – became the world's first ruler of an empire on which the sun never set. Meanwhile Portuguese warships destroyed the leading Indian fleets of Calicut and Gujarat, and those of Egypt and Turkey; Portugal also laid claim to the coast of Brazil.

The tide of transoceanic European maritime activity and territorial expansion was maintained through the next two centuries. England and France set up colonies – initially little more than fragile footholds but eventually growing to lay claim to much of the eastern seaboard – in North America, while the Dutch took over some of the spice-producing regions of the East Indies, regions that brought with them a fantastically profitable trade. Russian power too expanded across Siberia to the Pacific, as a result of which even China acquired a land-frontier with a European state.

In the New World in the eighteenth century, the Portuguese pressed into the interior of Brazil, the Spaniards expanded into California and the English and French competed for supremacy in the Great Lakes region. In India, the British took over Bengal and became the leading power on the southeast coast. Europe's only serious defeat occurred in North America, where the Thirteen Colonies fought their way into independence from Britain. Yet, even this defeat was at the hands of people of European descent, armed with European weapons and allied to a European state, France.

Europeans were not victorious everywhere. Their control in Africa was still limited, even though the demands of the slave trade to the New World had political and demographic ramifications deep in the interior of the continent. In east Asia the most expansive state in the eighteenth century was still China. The Persians resisted the Russians spiritedly while the Turks showed great resilience against Austria.

But the world was increasingly one where the crucial links were controlled or created by Europeans. A "world economy" developed as distant regions traded with one another under European auspices. Thus the British shipped tea from India to North America or the Dutch moved Chinese porcelain to Europe. This trade was to the profit of the European maritime powers that controlled it, and maritime rivalry was the source of several conflicts between Britain, France and the Netherlands. Eventual British dominance in this trade helped make London the world's dominant financial center and ensured that Britain was well placed for the rapid economic growth that would lead to the Industrial Revolution.

The theme of European expansion might appear exaggerated. Much of the world had never seen a European. European maps of central Asia or of inland Africa were either blanks or full of errors. To talk of European power would have seemed curious in Tibet, conquered by China in 1720; in Mombasa, whence the Omani Arabs expelled the Portuguese in 1698; or in west Africa where the kingdom of Dahomey dominated European trading posts from 1720.

Yet, however limited their impact in some respects, Europeans were to be found off the coast of Asia, not Asians off that of Europe. Europeans charted the oceans, explored their dark side of the world – the Pacific – and acquired the knowledge that helped them to profit from their strength. The world was renamed by Europeans. Many of the consequences of European ambition were unattractive, most obviously the slave trade. Today we can consider the rise of Europe without applauding it; but it is difficult to challenge its importance. At this era Europeans remolded the world, and created new political, economic, religious and cultural spaces, forging links that still affect our world today ■

As the 15th century neared its close, the monarchies of western Europe consolidated their positions and brought civil wars within their territories to an end. Louis XI of France (r.1461–81) overcame his Burgundian rivals, Henry Tudor brought England's long Wars of the Roses to an end in 1485, and Ferdinand of Aragon and Isabella of Castile oversaw the unification of their kingdoms and the final conquest of Moorish Granada in 1492. As feudal relationships continued to break down, the near-independence of the great nobles in times of weak kings was gradually curtailed by the rise of administrators and financiers. Europe's monarchs became distributors of patronage in a world where finance was beginning to count for more than fealty.

The territorial kingdoms of 16th-century Europe were very different from the monolithic states of today. Material conditions, slow communications and the stubborn survival of local customs, economies and even laws limited royal power. The nation-state was still a novelty.

The old notion of a secular empire transcending the state endured. Charles VIII of France invaded Italy in 1494 in pursuit of such an aim, prompting a long struggle in which French, Spanish and German armies rampaged through the peninsula, almost destroying the achievements of the Italian Renaissance. In 1519, Charles of Habsburg, grandson both of Ferdinand of Aragon and Emperor Maximilian I, became Emperor Charles V. The empire itself was weak and fragmented, but Charles now held the Austrian Habsburg lands in Spain, the Netherlands, Franche-Comté and much of Italy, as well as Spain's new overseas possessions, creating a power bloc that dominated Europe until the late 17th century.

Alarmingly, though, the defeat of Louis II of Hungary by the Ottomans at Mohács in 1526 raised the specter that the empire that would unify Europe might not even be a Christian one. In both central Europe and the Mediterranean (where Barbarossa's

major faith, 1550

- Anglican
- Catholic
- Calvinist
- Lutheran
- Muslim
- Orthodox
- mixed

- ● state with significant Catholic minority, 1550
- ● state with significant Protestant minority, 1550
- ── borders, 1560
- ◠ territory controlled by Christian military orders, 1500
- Austrian Habsburg land
- ◠ Spanish Habsburg land
- ◠ Ottoman empire, 1492
- European territory lost to Ottomans by 1560
- ⊗ Christian defeat by Ottomans
- ⊓ major Ottoman siege
- → Ottoman advance against Christian Europe
- popular uprising, with date
- 📖 major printing center, 15th–16th centuries
- 🏰 Spanish *presidio* fort

Italian wars
- ⊗ French victory
- ⊗ Spanish Habsburg victory
- ⊗ Venetian victory
- → invasion route of Charles VIII of France, 1494

0 _____ 600 km
0 _____ 400 mi

ATLANTIC OCEAN

Ireland

Irish Pale
Dublin

1549, Western Rebellion

Britta 1491 to F

La Roc

Bo

La Coruña

Santander

Burgos

Pamplona
Nav

1521–22, Comunero revolt

Douro

SPAIN

Ar 1479

Madrid

Tagus

PORTUGAL

Castile 1479 to Spain

Lisbon

Valenc

Córdoba

Seville

Granada

Granada 1492 to Spain

Car

Tangier
Asilah

Ceuta

Oran 1509 to Spain

Melilla
1497 to Spain

LUTHER was caricatured as the Devil's plaything in this typically grotesque woodcut of 1525.

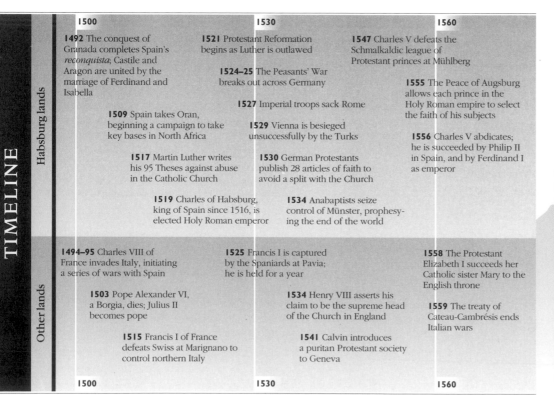

1500

1492 The conquest of Granada completes Spain's *reconquista*; Castile and Aragon are united by the marriage of Ferdinand and Isabella

1509 Spain takes Oran, beginning a campaign to take key bases in North Africa

1517 Martin Luther writes his 95 Theses against abuse in the Catholic Church

1519 Charles of Habsburg, king of Spain since 1516, is elected Holy Roman emperor

1494–95 Charles VIII of France invades Italy, initiating a series of wars with Spain

1503 Pope Alexander VI, a Borgia, dies; Julius II becomes pope

1515 Francis I of France defeats Swiss at Marignano to control northern Italy

1530

1521 Protestant Reformation begins as Luther is outlawed

1524–25 The Peasants' War breaks out across Germany

1527 Imperial troops sack Rome

1529 Vienna is besieged unsuccessfully by the Turks

1530 German Protestants publish 28 articles of faith to avoid a split with the Church

1534 Anabaptists seize control of Münster, prophesying the end of the world

1525 Francis I is captured by the Spaniards at Pavia; he is held for a year

1534 Henry VIII asserts his claim to be the supreme head of the Church in England

1541 Calvin introduces a puritan Protestant society to Geneva

1560

1547 Charles V defeats the Schmalkaldic league of Protestant princes at Mühlberg

1555 The Peace of Augsburg allows each prince in the Holy Roman empire to select the faith of his subjects

1556 Charles V abdicates; he is succeeded by Philip II in Spain, and by Ferdinand I as emperor

1558 The Protestant Elizabeth I succeeds her Catholic sister Mary to the English throne

1559 The treaty of Cateau-Cambrésis ends Italian wars

1500   **1530**   **1560**

victory at Prevesa in 1538 ensured Ottoman and Barbary corsair domination), Charles V shouldered the responsibility for halting the Ottoman advance.

Against this background of imperial commitments, the greatest event of the 16th century, the Reformation, was played out. What began as a challenge by a monk, Martin Luther, to corrupt practices in the church became an expression of German nationalism, and then of local interests asserted against the emperor. The Peasants' Wars, uprisings partly fueled by religious unrest, were vigorously put down by the German nobility, who then began to adopt the reformed faith themselves, often for political reasons. Charles won a crushing victory at Mühlberg over the Protestant nobles, but otherwise did little to halt the spread of reform.

The papacy faced Luther's challenge hamstrung

Map labels (within image):

Christiania · SWEDEN · Stockholm · Revel · ESTONIA · Novgorod · LIVONIA · Lake Peipus · Pskov 1510 to Russia · Riga · COURLAND · Western Dvina · Polotsk · RUSSIA · Moscow · Smolensk · North Sea · Vänern · Vättern · Gotland · Baltic Sea · Königsberg · PRUSSIA · Danzig · ROYAL PRUSSIA · Vilna · Minsk · Lithuania · Gomel · Kiev · Ukraine · Hamburg · Emden · Bremen · Amsterdam · Deventer · HOLY ROMAN EMPIRE · Leiden · Utrecht · Münster · Netherlands · Berlin · Brandenburg · Stettin · Elbe · Vistula · Warsaw · POLAND · Antwerp · Cologne · Leipzig · Wittenberg · Lusatia · Lemberg · Brussels · Bonn · Saxony · Dresden · Silesia · Krakow · Mühlberg 1547 · Prague · Frankfurt · Mainz · Bamberg · Bohemia · Moravia · Picardy 1482 to France · Luxembourg · Worms · Nuremberg · 1526 to Austrian Habsburgs · MOLDAVIA 1504 Ottoman Vassal · Jedisan 1526 to Ottoman empire · Paris · 1524–25 Peasants War · Augsburg · Bavaria · Danube · 1529 · Vienna · Jassy · Strasbourg 1482 to France · Ulm · Austria · Gran · TRANSYLVANIA 1541 to Ottoman empire · Orléans · Basel · Rhine · Munich · Guns 1532 · Buda · Swiss Confederation · Tyrol · HUNGARY 1541 to Ottoman empire · Franche Comté · Zürich · Berne · Trent · Mohács 1526 · Bourbon · Geneva · Savoy · Pieve di Cadore 1509 · IMPERIAL HUNGARY · Lyon · Marignano 1515 · Venice · WALLACHIA · Bucharest · 1527 to France · Pavia 1525 · Milan · Parma · Belgrade · Saluzzo 1559 to France · Genoa · Modena · PAPAL STATES · Danube · Avignon · Ravenna 1512 · URBINO · Nish · Bulgaria · Black Sea · Provence 1481 to France · Florence · Montenegro · Sofia · Roussillon 1493 to Spain · Piombino · Siena · Ragusa · Perpignan · ANDORRA · Corsica to Genoa · Orbetello · Rome · Subiaco · Adrianople · OTTOMAN · Constantinople · Barcelona · NAPLES · Gariglano 1503 · Naples · Cerignola 1503 · Thessalonica · BENEVENTO · Rumelia · ANATOLIA · EMPIRE · Sardinia · SARDINIA · Cagliari · Izmir · Balearic Islands · Palermo · Messina · Reggio · Corfu 1537 · Prevesa 1538 · Athens · SICILY · Sicily · Morea · BARBARY COAST · Algiers 1510 to Spain 1541 to Ottoman empire · Bougie 1510 to Spain · Tunis 1535 to Spain · Mediterranean Sea · MALTA 1551 1530 to Knights of St John · Monemvasia · Rhodes 1522 · Crete to Venice · Candia · DENMARK-NORWAY · Copenhagen

1536, Pilgrimage of Grace · 1549, Ket's Rebellion · Norwich · 1549, Wyatt's Rebellion · London · Calais 58 to France · FRANCE

---

by a decline in the need for a unified church (literacy, once the church's preserve, had become more widely diffused in the previous two centuries) and by the widespread perception that the pope was merely a cynical participant in the complex web of Italian politics. The authority of the church was challenged even by rulers with no particular religious motive. First by Ferdinand of Aragon, who threatened in 1508 to withdraw his kingdoms from obedience to the pope; by Gustavus Vasa's 1527 seizure of church lands in Sweden; and by Henry VIII of England, who repudiated papal authority in 1532.

The Reformation was driven by a shift in religious sensibilities, as the spread of printing gave the new demands for a more personal spirituality an unprecedented mobility and resilience. Even as political compromise between the faiths was agreed in

1555 within the empire (the Peace of Augsburg) and between France and Spain in Italy in 1559 (the treaty of Cateau-Cambrésis), the Catholic response to church reform was taking shape. The Council of Trent formulated a statement of Catholic doctrine and the Jesuit Order was adopted by the papacy as the spearhead of a new pastoral effort.

1 A defeat at the hands of the English at Flodden ensured Scotland did not interfere in English affairs for most of the Tudor period.

2 Martin Luther, an Augustinian monk, nailed his *95 Theses* to the Wittenberg cathedral door in 1517, challenging church abuses and initiating the Reformation.

3 The château of Chambord, built by Francis I from 1519, is a classic of French Renaissance architecture.

4 The Christian stronghold of Rhodes fell to the Ottomans in 1522, after vigorous defense by the Knights of St John.

5 The unexpected defeat and capture of Francis I of France by Spanish forces at Pavia in 1525 was the climax of the Italian wars.

6 The brutal sack of Rome in 1527 by Spanish and German mercenaries in the service of Charles V shocked the whole of Europe.

7 In three sessions from 1545, the Council of Trent decrees laid the basis of modern Catholicism in doctrines directly opposing Protestantism.

See also 54 (Renaissance Europe);
59 (Ottoman empire)

The rise of the Ottoman Turkish state from a regional power in Asia Minor in the mid-15th century to the greatest empire in Europe and the Middle East by the mid-16th was a dramatic one. In less than a century, the house of Osman had destroyed Byzantium and become unquestioned leaders of the Islamic world, wealthy patrons of a confident culture and rulers of an empire stretching from the Atlas Mountains to the Caspian Sea.

The key moment in this transformation is often considered to be the capture of Constantinople by Mehmet II in 1453, but the second decade of the 16th century perhaps has a better claim. Between 1516 and 1520 the armies of Selim I (r.1512–20) drove the Safavid Persians out of Kurdistan, destroyed the empire of the Mamlukes on the battlefields of Marj Dabiq and al-Raydaniyya, and secured from the *sharif* of Mecca recognition of their sultan as caliph, or leader of the Islamic faithful.

The conquest of Syria and Egypt from the Mamlukes made the Ottoman territories an integral part of a vast network of overland caravan routes from Morocco to the gates of Beijing. At one end of this network were the spices, drugs, silks and (later) porcelain of the east. At the other end were the traders in gold dust, slaves, gems and other products of the African interior, and the shipments of textiles, glass, hardware, timber and currency from Europe.

Christian Europe responded ambivalently to the Ottomans. Venice was anxious to retain as great a share as possible of trade with the Levant – even, ultimately, at the expense of Venetian territory – while Francis I of France openly allied himself with

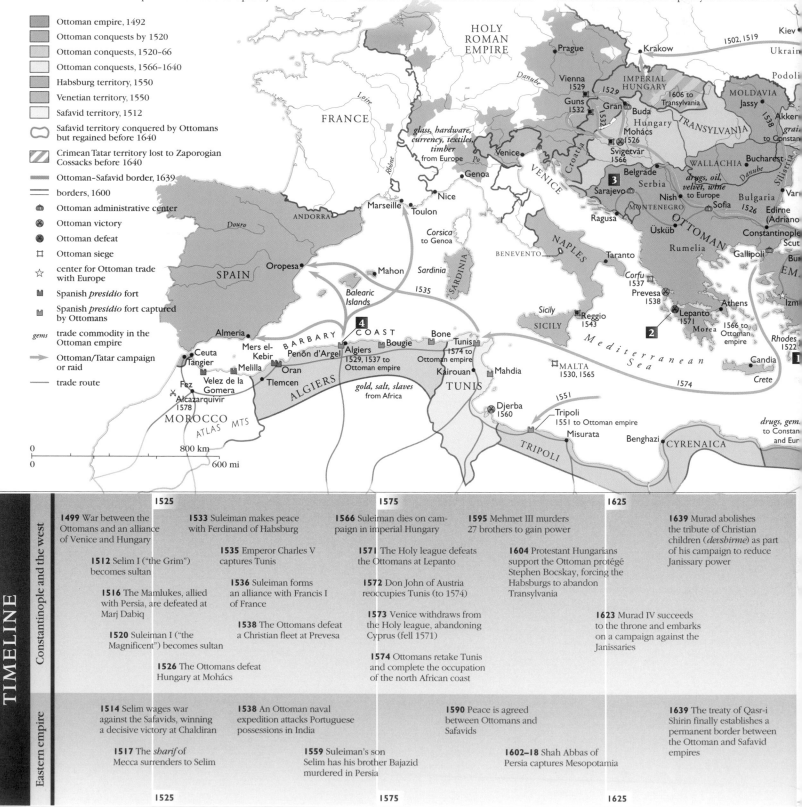

Legend:
- Ottoman empire, 1492
- Ottoman conquests by 1520
- Ottoman conquests, 1520-66
- Ottoman conquests, 1566-1640
- Habsburg territory, 1550
- Venetian territory, 1550
- Safavid territory, 1512
- Safavid territory conquered by Ottomans but regained before 1640
- Crimean Tatar territory lost to Zaporogian Cossacks before 1640
- Ottoman-Safavid border, 1639
- borders, 1600
- ⬢ Ottoman administrative center
- ⊗ Ottoman victory
- ⊗ Ottoman defeat
- ⊡ Ottoman siege
- ☆ center for Ottoman trade with Europe
- Spanish *presidio* fort
- Spanish *presidio* fort captured by Ottomans
- *gems* trade commodity in the Ottoman empire
- → Ottoman/Tatar campaign or raid
- — trade route

0 —— 800 km
0 —— 600 mi

1 Rhodes was captured by the Ottomans in 1522, when help from Europe failed to arrive for the defending Knights of St John (Hospitallers).

2 At the Battle of Lepanto, Ali Pasha's Ottoman fleet was defeated by a Don John of Austria. Casualties included writer Miguel de Cervantes, who lost an arm.

3 The Ottomans were initially welcomed by many of the inhabitants of the Balkans; in Bosnia, descendants of the Bogomil heretics voluntarily converted to Islam.

4 After the Spanish fort of Peñon d'Argel was taken by the Ottoman admiral Khaireddin in 1529, Algiers became a major base for Barbary corsairs.

5 The deployment of artillery – which their opponents lacked – was decisive in the Ottoman victories of Chaldiran and at al-Raydaniyya.

6 An expedition to Muscat in 1551 secured Ottoman control of Oman and raided Portuguese bases in India, but the Ottomans failed to expel the Portuguese from the Indian Ocean or to dominate the region's trade.

Suleiman the Magnificent (r.1520–66) against the Habsburgs. Reformation and Counter-Reformation helped to weaken the crusading spirit that had once united Europe against Islam. Suleiman reduced Hungary to vassal status after his victory at Mohács in 1526, then conquered a swathe of European territory from Croatia to the Black Sea. His siege of Vienna in 1529 was broken more by the winter weather and the length of Ottoman supply lines than by Habsburg action. Ultimately, though, it was the Ottoman commitment to a savage and apparently endless religious war with Safavid Persia that saved Habsburg central Europe.

The Ottoman–Christian frontier on the Danube achieved a kind of equilibrium after the death of Suleiman. In the Mediterranean, Ottoman conquest of the north African coast was facilitated by the naval victory at Prevesa, but Charles V's initially successful offensive at Tunis (1535) and the Christian victory at Lepanto (1571) restored the *status quo*. A rough division of the sea was made along a line through Italy, Sicily and Tunisia. The Ottoman fleet was quickly rebuilt, but there was no new naval confrontation.

The wars between Ottomans and Christians never entirely halted trade between Europe and the Levant. European merchant ships continued to arrive at Iskanderun or Tripoli in Syria, or at Alexandria, and to unload cargoes of European goods and quantities of Spanish–American gold and silver destined for Asia. These cargoes were carried through the Ottoman and Safavid empires in caravans forbidden to Europeans, meticulously organized, secure, regular and often faster than the European sea routes. The same system of caravans brought Asian goods back for export to Europe from Mediterranean ports. Until the mid-17th century, this trade flourished, enriching the Ottoman empire and ensuring that European technology remained available to the sultan.

The most costly of the Ottoman–Safavid wars broke out in 1602; the reorganized and re-equipped armies of the Persians reversed almost all the Ottoman gains of the previous century before a peace came. Constantinople was devastated by plagues and economic crises. The empire was further weakened by instability, which derived both from the lack of a clear custom of succession (fratricide often settled the matter) and from the growing independence and political influence of the Janissaries. These were originally an elite military and administrative caste recruited from the *devshirme* system, by which children of Balkan Christians were surrendered as tribute to Constantinople. This caste increasingly played the role of the empire's kingmakers. From the mid-16th century, too, the caravan routes' profitability began to wane under pressure from alternative routes to the East through Russia and around the Cape of Good Hope. By the death of Murad IV (r.1623–40), the Ottoman empire was starting to fall behind its European rivals in military technology, in wealth and even in political unity.

SULEIMAN I was renowned as a lawgiver, soldier and art patron. The Venetian artist Titian painted his portrait.

Map labels:

RUSSIA
Moscow
Volga
Kazan
1571–2
Cossacks
Dnieper
1521
Cossacks
1527, 1543
Astrakhan
Azov
KHANATE OF THE CRIMEA
...dware,
...xtiles
...Europe
Russia
Kaffa
1579–80
CAUCASUS MTS
Derbent
Caspian Sea
carpets, gems, skins, tobacco to Europe and Russia
Georgia
...ck Sea
Sinope
Batum
Tiflis
Shirvan
Baku 1583 to Ottoman empire
Trabzon
Kars
Yerevan
...masra
Samsun
Armenia 1578
Tokat
Chaldiran 1514
Azerbaijan
Ankara
Sivas
Tabriz 1514 to Ottoman empire
Kayseri
Diyarbakir
5
ANATOLIA
Urfa
Mardin
Kurdistan
ZAGROS
silk from Asia
Konya
Tarsus
Adana
MESOPOTAMIA
Mosul
Marj Dabiq 1516
Iskanderun
Aleppo 1516 to Ottoman empire
Hamadan
drugs, gems, spices to Europe
Euphrates
Tigris
Qasr-i-Shirin
SAFAVID EMPIRE
Famagusta 1571
Syria
Luristan
PERSIA
Cyprus ...71 to Ottoman empire
Tripoli
Desert Route
Baghdad 1534 to Ottoman empire
Damascus 1516 to Ottoman empire
Iraq
MTS
...xandria
Basra 1546 to Ottoman empire
al-Raydaniyya 1517
currency from Europe
Cairo 1517 to Ottoman empire
Suez
Bandar Abbas 1551
Hormuz 1514–1622 to Portugal
Egypt
El Hasa
Bahrain 1554
gems, rice, spices from southeast Asia
Hejaz
Arabs
Muscat 1551
currency to Asia
Asyut
Nile
6 OMAN
Quseir
...dain
El Kharga
Aswan
Medina
Jiddah
Mecca 1517 to Ottoman empire
Red Sea
Suakin
drugs, gems, gold, slaves, spices from Asia and Africa
...ma
Sana
Massawa
YEMEN
FUNJ
Mocha
Aden 1538 to Ottoman empire
ETHIOPIA

See also 47 (rise of the Ottomans); 58 (16th-century Europe)

The early 16th century brought dramatic changes to the political and economic order of the world. Ottoman expansion and the collapse of the established power of the Lodis in north India led to a series of decisive military clashes in Europe and south Asia, while Portuguese and Spanish maritime expansion overthrew empires and trading networks worldwide.

The most dynamic empire in the late 15th century was the Ottoman. After capturing Constantinople in 1453, Ottoman armies completed their conquest of the Balkan peninsula and established their authority over the Crimean Tatars, ensuring Turkish domination of the Black Sea for nearly two centuries (▷ 59). The greatest Ottoman advances, though, came in Asia and north Africa. In 1514 the armies of the new Safavid dynasty of Persia were destroyed at Chaldiran, leading to temporary Ottoman control of western Persia. The defeat of Mamluke Egypt in 1516–17 opened the way for further advances into Arabia and north Africa, as well as bringing the wealth of Egypt to the sultan. In 1521 Suleiman the Magnificent resumed the Ottoman drive into Europe, overrunning Hungary after Mohács in 1526. When he laid siege to Vienna in 1529 the Ottomans seemed irresistible.

Partly drawn by a weakening Ming China, the Turkic nomads of central Asia began to move east around 1500, after nearly three centuries of westward pressure. The Mughals of Ferghana moved south from Afghanistan, destroying the armies of the Lodi sultanate at Panipat in 1526.

The energy with which the Ming emperors had rebuilt China after the Mongol invasions was beginning to wane. In the early 15th century Chinese maritime expeditions had ranged as far as the east African coast, spreading a network of Chinese trade routes. In 1421, however, the Mings had moved their capital from Nanjing to Beijing, facing the resurgent Mongols on the northern frontier. Both the Ming empire and the wider economy centered on it turned away from the sea. In 1500, with India, the East Indies and southeast Asia fragmented, the Indian Ocean trade lay open to new exploitation.

The opportunity was seized by the explorers and traders of Portugal. Pedro da Covilhã had reached India via the Red Sea in 1488 and

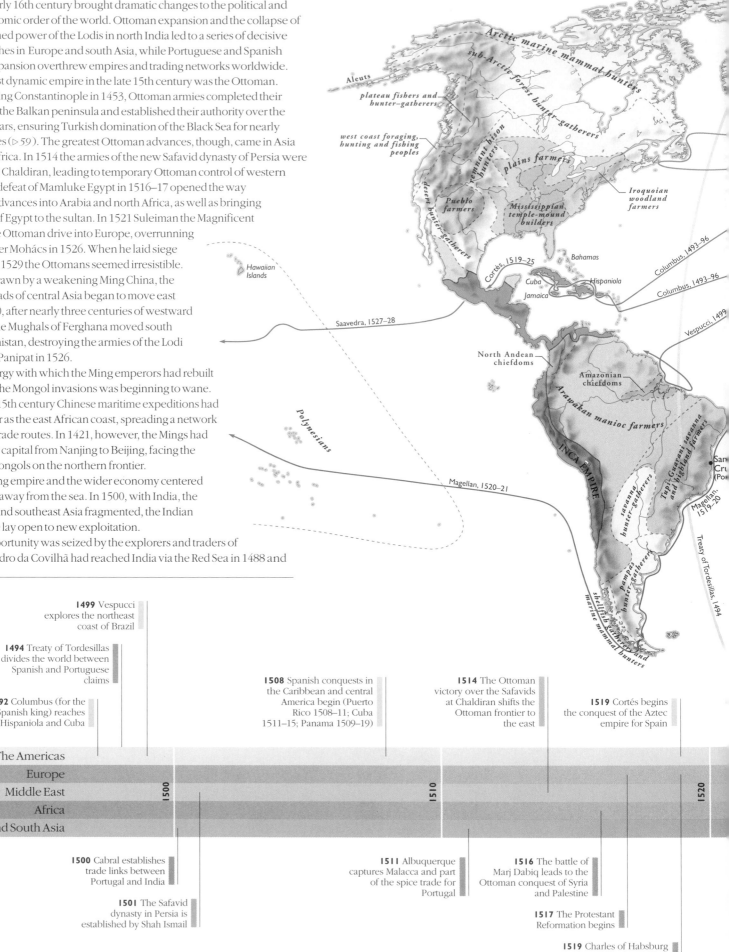

TIMELINE

1499 Vespucci explores the northeast coast of Brazil

1494 Treaty of Tordesillas divides the world between Spanish and Portuguese claims

1492 Columbus (for the Spanish king) reaches Hispaniola and Cuba

1508 Spanish conquests in the Caribbean and central America begin (Puerto Rico 1508–11; Cuba 1511–15; Panama 1509–19)

1514 The Ottoman victory over the Safavids at Chaldiran shifts the Ottoman frontier to the east

1519 Cortés begins the conquest of the Aztec empire for Spain

	1500	1510	1520
The Americas			
Europe			
Middle East			
Africa			
East and South Asia			

1500 Cabral establishes trade links between Portugal and India

1501 The Safavid dynasty in Persia is established by Shah Ismail

1511 Albuquerque captures Malacca and part of the spice trade for Portugal

1516 The battle of Marj Dabiq leads to the Ottoman conquest of Syria and Palestine

1517 The Protestant Reformation begins

1519 Charles of Habsburg is elected Charles V, Holy Roman emperor

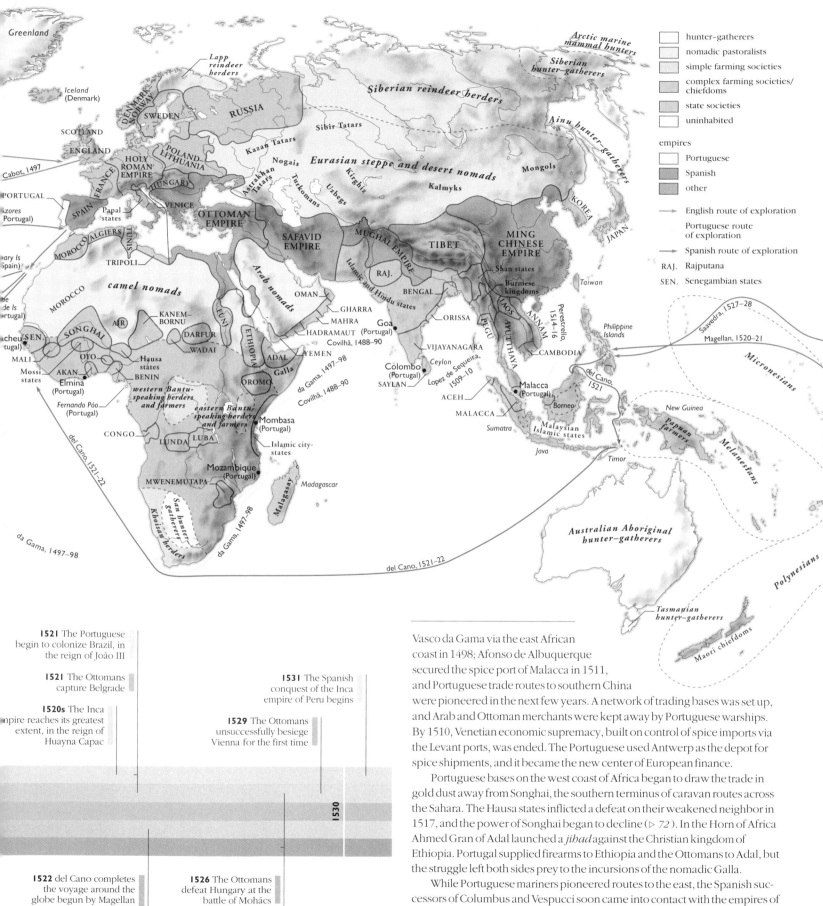

Greenland

Iceland
(Denmark)

Arctic marine mammal hunters

Siberian hunter-gatherers

Lapp reindeer herders

SCOTLAND

ENGLAND

DENMARK NORWAY

SWEDEN

RUSSIA

Siberian reindeer herders

Ainu hunter-gatherers

Cabot, 1497

HOLY ROMAN EMPIRE

POLAND LITHUANIA

HUNGARY

FRANCE

Sibir Tatars

Eurasian steppe and desert nomads

Kazan Tatars

Nogais

Mongols

PORTUGAL

Azores
(Portugal)

SPAIN

Papal states

VENICE

OTTOMAN EMPIRE

Astrakhan Tatars

Turkomans

Uzbegs

Kirghiz

Kalmyks

KOREA

MOROCCO ALGIERS TUNIS

TRIPOLI

camel nomads

Arab nomads

SAFAVID EMPIRE

MUGHAL EMPIRE

TIBET

MING CHINESE EMPIRE

JAPAN

ary Is
(Spain)

MOROCCO

AIR

KANEM-BORNU

OMAN

Islamic and Hindu states

RAJ.

BENGAL

Shan states

Burmese kingdoms

Taiwan

de Is
rtugal)

SONGHAI

OYO

Hausa states

DARFUR

WADAI

FUN

GHARRA

MAHRA

HADRAMAUT

ETHIOPIA

ADAL

Goa
(Portugal)

Covilhã, 1488–90

ORISSA

VIJAYANAGARA

LAOS

ANNAM

PEGU

AYUTTHAYA

Perestrello, 1514–16

Philippine Islands

Saavedra, 1527–28

Magellan, 1520–21

cheu SEN
tugal)

MALI

Mossi states

AKAN

Elmina
(Portugal)

Fernando Póo
(Portugal)

BENIN

western Bantu-speaking herders and farmers

OROMO

YEMEN

Galla

da Gama, 1497–98

Covilhã, 1488–90

Colombo
(Portugal)

SAYLAN

Ceylon

Lopez de Sequeira, 1509–10

ACEH

MALACCA

Malacca
(Portugal)

del Cano, 1521

CAMBODIA

Micronesians

CONGO

LUNDA LUBA

eastern Bantu-speaking herders and farmers

Mombasa
(Portugal)

Islamic city-states

Sumatra

Borneo

Java

Malaysian Islamic states

New Guinea

Papuan farmers

Melanesians

del Cano, 1521–22

MWENEMUTAPA

Mozambique
(Portugal)

Madagascar

Timor

da Gama, 1497–98

San hunter-gatherers

Khoisan herders

da Gama, 1497–98

Malagasay

da Gama, 1497–98

del Cano, 1521–22

Australian Aboriginal hunter-gatherers

Tasmanian hunter-gatherers

Maori chiefdoms

Polynesians

Legend:

- hunter-gatherers
- nomadic pastoralists
- simple farming societies
- complex farming societies/chiefdoms
- state societies
- uninhabited

empires
- Portuguese
- Spanish
- other

→ English route of exploration
→ Portuguese route of exploration
→ Spanish route of exploration

RAJ. Rajputana
SEN. Senegambian states

1521 The Portuguese begin to colonize Brazil, in the reign of João III

1521 The Ottomans capture Belgrade

1520s The Inca empire reaches its greatest extent, in the reign of Huayna Capac

1531 The Spanish conquest of the Inca empire of Peru begins

1529 The Ottomans unsuccessfully besiege Vienna for the first time

1530

1522 del Cano completes the voyage around the globe begun by Magellan in 1519

1526 The Ottomans defeat Hungary at the battle of Mohács

1526 The Mughal leader Babur defeats the Lodis at Panipat and overruns northern India

Vasco da Gama via the east African coast in 1498; Afonso de Albuquerque secured the spice port of Malacca in 1511, and Portuguese trade routes to southern China were pioneered in the next few years. A network of trading bases was set up, and Arab and Ottoman merchants were kept away by Portuguese warships. By 1510, Venetian economic supremacy, built on control of spice imports via the Levant ports, was ended. The Portuguese used Antwerp as the depot for spice shipments, and it became the new center of European finance.

Portuguese bases on the west coast of Africa began to draw the trade in gold dust away from Songhai, the southern terminus of caravan routes across the Sahara. The Hausa states inflicted a defeat on their weakened neighbor in 1517, and the power of Songhai began to decline (▷ 72). In the Horn of Africa Ahmed Gran of Adal launched a *jihad* against the Christian kingdom of Ethiopia. Portugal supplied firearms to Ethiopia and the Ottomans to Adal, but the struggle left both sides prey to the incursions of the nomadic Galla.

While Portuguese mariners pioneered routes to the east, the Spanish successors of Columbus and Vespucci soon came into contact with the empires of the Americas. The Aztec state collapsed in the face of Hernán Cortés in 1519–24, and in Peru the Incas, divided by a succession struggle, were ill-prepared to resist the expedition being organized by Francisco Pizarro in 1530. Spain was on the verge of a huge territorial expansion, and about to tap a source of silver that would drive the world's economy for over a century (▷ 62) ■

The eastward migration of Mongols and Tatars in the late 15th and early 16th centuries meant that the Mughals, a people descended from Timur's Mongols, were driven out of the principality they had established in Ferghana. Under their leader Babur (r.1501–30), the Mughals conquered an area around Kabul in 1504, and made the first of several exploratory invasions of India in 1519, culminating in a fullscale attempt in 1526. The Indian subcontinent at the time was a patchwork of warring Muslim and Hindu states. Among these the Rajput lands southwest of Delhi, the ancient Hindu kingdom of Vijayanagara in the south and the Afghan Lodi sultanate of Delhi were the most powerful. Babur's force of 12,000 men, supported by artillery, overcame the army of Ibrahim Shah Lodi at Panipat in 1526. Mughal conquest thereafter was swift; by Babur's death, all the former Lodi lands had been subdued, while his son Humayun (r.1530–40; 1555–56) invaded Gujarat in 1535, taking the fortress of Champanir. In the 1540s, however, a rebellion of the Afghan Sur dynasty of south Bihar against their new masters almost spelled the end of the Mughal dynasty. The Surs captured the Gangetic plain and Delhi, and forced Humayun to take refuge in Persia. Only in 1555 did Humayun succeed in reoccupying Delhi, but his reconquest was cut short by his death.

Babur's grandson Akbar (r.1556–1605) not only managed to regain all the lands lost to the Surs, but created one of the world's most powerful states. In 1572 the conquest of Gujarat brought access to the sea, while control of Bengal in 1576 secured India's richest region for the Mughals. By 1605 their advance into the Deccan had begun with the subjugation of Khandesh and Berar, with the loyalty of the Rajputs assured by military force and dynastic intermarriage. Akbar's reign brought administrative efficiency and social reform. The empire was divided into provinces (subahs) which were administered by professional civil servants who were appointed on merit. Moreover, though himself a devout Muslim, the sophisticated Akbar promoted religious toleration throughout his empire.

Other external powers also arrived in India after 1500. The Portuguese acquired trading bases at Goa, Daman and Diu in the early 16th century. Conflict ensued; the Portuguese defeated a combined Indian and Mamluke Egyptian fleet off Diu in 1509, and repulsed an Ottoman-Gujarati attack on the same base in 1538. In general, though, the Indians found mercantile benefits in cooperating with Europeans. By 1500 Indian banking and credit facilities supported a commercial network that covered most of Asia and east Africa, and extended as far as Moscow. Since Roman times Europeans had exchanged silver or gold for Indian silks, cottons, spices and dyes, and European access to the silver mines of Latin America made possible a huge increase in this trade. Trading links with European companies became more and more important in the Mughal economy.

Mughal agriculture was highly efficient (cereal yields were higher than those of Europe until the 19th century), and cash crops (indigo, cotton, sugar, opium, pepper and later tobacco) were developed within a centrally controlled internal market. Indian industry, based on cheap labor and proven, low-level technology, included both the world's largest textile industry (whose products were exported worldwide) and an iron industry producing high-quality steel and cannon the equal of any in Europe. The Mughals kept a standing army of about one million men who were equipped with weapons that, until the 18th century, rivaled European arms. Yet the vast Mughal empire was already fragmenting by the death of the last great emperor, Aurangzeb (r.1658–1707). Religious intolerance had grown under Akbar's successors Jahangir, Shah Jahan and Aurangzeb himself, leading to increasingly frequent revolts, even as the empire reached its greatest territorial extent with the conquest of Ahmadnagar (1636), Bijapur (1686) and Golconda (1687). As bases of the Dutch and English East India companies spread in the later 17th century, largely displacing the Portuguese, the Hindu Marathas of the Western Ghats were already asserting their independence of the Mughal empire.

Map legend:

- Mughal territory, 1525
- territorial gain by Babur and Humayun to 1539
- territorial gain after Akbar's campaigns to 1605
- territorial gain by Jahangir, Shah Jahan or Aurangzeb to 1707
- Mughal territory lost to Marathas by 1707
- other Mughal territory lost by 1707
- maximum extent of Suri territory, 1553
- Maratha territory upon death of Shivaji, c.1680
- maximum extent of Maratha influence in the Deccan under Shivaji
- Bidar   Mughal *subah*
- ■   *subah* capital
- —   border of *subah*
- TIBET   independent state or region
- *Surs*   dynasty habitually opposed to Mughal rule

European trading base, 1707
- ★   English
- ☆   Danish
- ☆   Dutch
- ★   French
- ★   Portuguese
- 🔥   Maratha raid, with date
- 🕌   mosque
- —   trade route

Map labels: Bukhara, Samarkand, Amu Darya, Merv, Mashhad, to Persia & the Levant, SAFAVID PERSIA, Herat, HIND, to Safavid Persia, 158, Kandahar 1649, 1652, 4, BALUCHIST, to Persia & Arabia, Arabian Sea

Mughal empire

1525	1600	1675
1504 The Mughals under Babur are expelled from Ferghana by the Uzbegs	**1556** Mughals under Akbar rout the Suri army at Panipat	**1598** The Mughal capital is moved to Agra	**1659–70** The Hindu Maratha leader Shivaji defeats Bijapur and sacks Surat
1526 Babur defeats Shah Ibrahim Lodi of the sultanate of Delhi at Panipat	**1568–69** Akbar captures the Rajput fortresses of Chittaurgarh and Rathambhor	**1632** Shah Jahan begins the Mughal conquest of Deccan	**1669–78** Religious persecution prompts rebellions by the Jats and Sikhs
1535 Humayun invades Gujarat	**1571** Construction of new capital Fatehpur Sikri begins		**1679–1709** War between the Mughals and Hindu Rajputs
1539 Suri Afghans of Bihar under Sher Shah rebel and reconquer much Mughal territory	**1572** Conquest of Gujarat gives the Mughals a seaport		**1707** Death of Aurangzeb marks the start of the disintegration of the Mughal empire
	1576 The Mughal conquest of Bengal is completed		

Europeans in India

1525	1600	1675
1498 A Portuguese expedition under Vasco da Gama reaches the Malabar Coast	**1608** The English East India Company receives its first trading concessions in India	**1661** The English East India Company gains a base at Bombay
1509 The Portuguese under Francisco de Almeida defeat Egyptian–Indian fleet at Diu	**1612** The English East India Company defeats a Portuguese fleet at Surat	**1664** The French East India Company is founded
1538 The Portuguese defeat an attack on Diu by Ottoman and Gujarati forces		**1685** The English are expelled from Surat by Aurangzeb

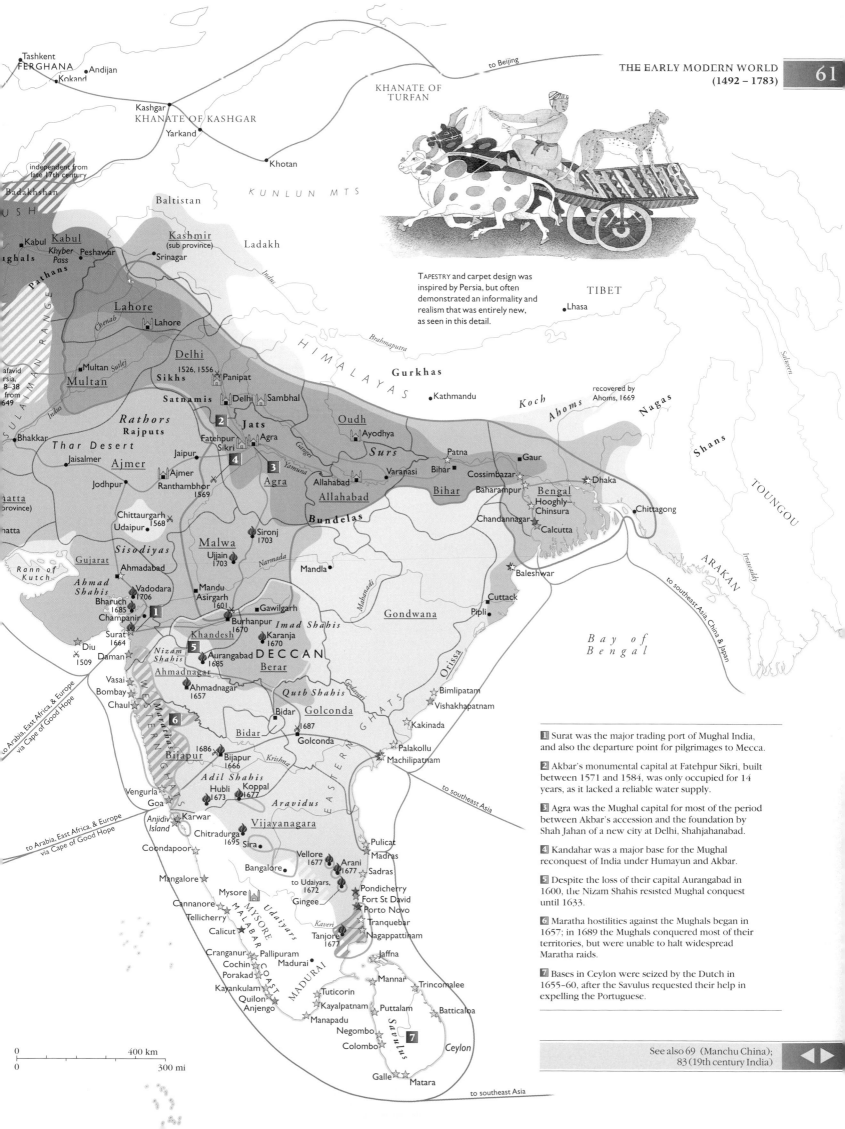

Tashkent
FERGHANA
Andijan
Kokand

to Beijing

KHANATE OF TURFAN

Kashgar
KHANATE OF KASHGAR
Yarkand

Khotan

KUNLUN MTS

independent from
late 17th century

Badakhshan

KUSH

Baltistan

Kashmir
(sub province)
Srinagar

Ladakh

TAPESTRY and carpet design was
inspired by Persia, but often
demonstrated an informality and
realism that was entirely new,
as seen in this detail.

TIBET

Lhasa

Kabul
Khyber Pass
ghals
Peshawar

Kabul

Indus

Lahore
Lahore
Chenab

afavid
rsia
8–38
from
649

Multan
Multan
Sutlej

Delhi
1526, 1556
Panipat
Sikhs

HIMALAYAS

Brahmaputra

Gurkhas

Koch

Ahoms

Nagas

recovered by
Ahoms, 1669

Shans

TOUNGOU

Satnamis
Delhi
Sambhal

Kathmandu

Salween

Bhakkar

Rathors
Rajputs

2 Jats
Fatehpur
Sikri
Agra

Oudh
Ayodhya

Thar Desert

Jaisalmer

Ajmer

Jaipur

4

Ganges

Surs

Patna

Gaur
Dhaka

Jodhpur

Ajmer
Ranthambhor
1569

3
Agra

Yamuna

Allahabad
Allahabad

Varanasi

Bihar
Bihar

Cossimbazar
Baharampur

Bengal
Hooghly–
Chinsura

Chittagong

hatta
province)

Chittaurgarh
Udaipur
1568

Bundelas

Chandannagar

Calcutta

ARAKAN

hatta

Sisodiyas

Malwa
Ujjain
1703

Sironj
1703

Narmada

Mandla

Gondwana

Baleshwar

to southeast Asia, China & Japan

Irrawaddy

Rann of
Kutch

Gujarat
Ahmadabad

Ahmad
Shahis

Vadodara
1706

Bharuch
1685
Champanir

1

Mandu
Asirgarh
1601

Mahanadi

Cuttack

Pipli

Bay of
Bengal

Surat
1664
Diu
1509
Daman

Khandesh

Gawilgarh

Burhanpur
1670

Karanja
1670

Imad Shahis

Orissa

Godavari

Nizam
Shahis

5
Aurangabad
1685

DECCAN

Berar

Qutb Shahis

Bimlipatam

Vishakhapatnam

Vasai
Bombay
Chaul

Ahmadnagar
Ahmadnagar
1657

WESTERN GHATS

Marathas

6

Bidar
Bidar

Golconda
Golconda
1687

Krishna

Kakinada

EASTERN GHATS

Palakollu
Machilipatnam

to Arabia, East Africa, & Europe
via Cape of Good Hope

Vengurla

Bijapur
Bijapur
1666

Adil Shahis

Hubli
1673

Koppal
1677

Goa

to southeast Asia

Anjidiv
Island

Karwar

Aravidus

Chitradurga
1695

Sira

Coondapoor

Vijayanagara

Pulicat

to Arabia, East Africa, & Europe
via Cape of Good Hope

Mangalore

Vellore
1677

Arani
1677

Madras

Sadras

Bangalore

Mysore
Mysore

to Udaiyars,
1672

Gingee

Pondicherry
Fort St David
Porto Novo
Tranquebar
Nagappattinam

Cannanore

Udaiyars

MALABAR

MYSORE

Tellicherry
Calicut

Kaveri

Tanjore
1677

Cranganur
Cochin
Porakad
Kayankulam
Quilon
Anjengo

Pallipuram
Madurai

Jaffna

MADURAI

COAST

Mannar

Tuticorin
Kayalpatnam

Trincomalee

Manapadu
Negombo
Colombo

Puttalam

Batticaloa

Savulus

7

Ceylon

Galle
Matara

to southeast Asia

0 ____ 400 km
0 ____ 300 mi

1 Surat was the major trading port of Mughal India,
and also the departure point for pilgrimages to Mecca.

2 Akbar's monumental capital at Fatehpur Sikri, built
between 1571 and 1584, was only occupied for 14
years, as it lacked a reliable water supply.

3 Agra was the Mughal capital for most of the period
between Akbar's accession and the foundation by
Shah Jahan of a new city at Delhi, Shahjahanabad.

4 Kandahar was a major base for the Mughal
reconquest of India under Humayun and Akbar.

5 Despite the loss of their capital Aurangabad in
1600, the Nizam Shahis resisted Mughal conquest
until 1633.

6 Maratha hostilities against the Mughals began in
1657; in 1689 the Mughals conquered most of their
territories, but were unable to halt widespread
Maratha raids.

7 Bases in Ceylon were seized by the Dutch in
1655–60, after the Savulus requested their help in
expelling the Portuguese.

See also 69 (Manchu China);
83 (19th century India)

Spanish conquest in the New World profoundly affected both the region itself and Europe. Spain's empire was the largest in world history to date other than that of the Mongols. It destroyed ancient cultures and decimated native populations, who proved disastrously vulnerable to diseases introduced from the Old World. Meanwhile, the mining of huge silver deposits financed Spanish Habsburg ambitions and underpinned the whole of European trade. Nor was the traffic in disease all one-way: syphilis, caught by Spanish sailors in the Caribbean, became a feared killer in Europe from the early 16th century.

Spain's incursion in the Americas began with royal sponsorship of the voyages of the Italian navigator-merchants Christopher Columbus and Amerigo Vespucci at the end of the 15th century. In particular, Columbus' discovery of the West Indies for Spain soon led to permanent settlements. Colonization of the Caribbean islands began on Santo Domingo (Hispaniola) and provided a foretaste of Spanish rule on the mainland. Administrative, legal, and religious structures were rapidly put in place, while the aboriginal Arawak and Carib peoples fell victim to maltreatment and disease.

The Spanish empire was territorial from the outset, concerned with the government, economic exploitation and religious conversion of its native subjects. It was perhaps less careless of the welfare of its subject peoples than were some other colonial empires. Paradoxically, its rapid growth depended on existing political structures and communications networks. Hernán Cortés and Francisco Pizarro encountered, in the Aztec and Inca empires respectively, centralized, populous and formidable states, yet internal divisions helped them swiftly to destroy any resistance. Beyond their boundaries, the population was sparse and the environment hostile and virtually impenetrable to Europeans. These hinterlands were still only partially conquered by 1800.

The prosperity of the empire was built above all on Mexican and Peruvian gold and silver. These precious metals had been extracted on a modest scale by the Aztecs and Incas for use in ceremonial artifacts, but were now mined and shipped in huge quantities by the Spanish. This enterprise required regular commercial fleets with permanent naval escorts, linking Seville and Veracruz on the east coast of Mexico, and Peru and the west coast of the Central American isthmus. The maintenance and protection of these fleets was one of the great maritime and commercial achievements of the age.

Challenges by Spain's European rivals to the Spanish–American empire itself were frequent but largely unsuccessful; indeed, Spanish America proved more resilient than Spain's European territories to challenges from the other powers. From the 1570s, major ports were subjected to numerous assaults. The English capture of Jamaica in 1655 was an important strategic loss, but the empire remained largely secure until the Seven Years War (1756–63). In 1762, the British occupied Havana; Spain only regained control by ceding Florida. However, the demise of France as a colonial power in America allowed Spain to acquire Louisiana while, in the American War of Independence, it regained Florida and checked British expansion on the Mississippi.

Spain was not the only significant colonial power in South America. In 1494, Spain and Portugal

Legend:
- Portuguese territory, 1650
- Portuguese territory, 1750
- Portuguese frontier land, 1750
- Spanish territory, 1650
- Spanish territory, 1750
- Spanish frontier land, 1750
- Jesuit mission state to 1767
- Dutch Brazil, 1630-54
- British territory, 1750
- Dutch territory, 1750
- French territory, 1750
- concentration of African slaves in the 18th century

early settlement or trading post, with date of foundation
- ○ Portuguese
- ● Spanish
- ⊕ Portuguese or Spanish archbishopric, with date of foundation
- Cuzco Spanish university founded between 1523 and 1750
- ☆ sustained native resistance
- ⊗ military action
- - - Treaty of Tordesillas, 1494
- Spanish trade route
- → route of explorer
- → slaving expedition of the *Paulistas*
- Ute native American peoples

HERNAN CORTÉS took Aztec Mexico with only a few hundred men, using a blend of ruthlessness, daring and guile.

TIMELINE

Spanish America

1508–15 Puerto Rico (San Juan), Jamaica (Santiago) and Cuba are colonized by Spain

1519–24 Hernán Cortés conquers the Aztec empire

1531–35 Francisco Pizarro completes the conquest of the powerful Inca empire

1538 Spanish control is established in Colombia

1565 Forts are built in Florida to defend Spanish fleets

1569 Francisco de Toledo establishes a stable Spanish government in Peru

1577–80 Francis Drake raids Spanish settlements on the Pacific coast

1655 An English expedition captures Jamaica during Oliver Cromwell's war against Spain

1670 The English freebooter Henry Morgan sacks Panama

1716 Spain occupies part of modern Texas in response to French expansion from Louisiana

1739 A British expedition sacks Porto Bello, but in 1741 fails to take Cartagena

1762 A British expeditionary force captures Havana

1780–81 Spanish forces recapture west Florida and the Bahamas from Britain

Portuguese America

1530–32 The first major Portuguese colony is established in the Americas at São Vicente

1534 The first African slaves are landed in Brazil

1565–67 Rio de Janeiro is founded by Portuguese

1615 A French attempt to colonize Maranhão is thwarted by the Portuguese

1624 A Dutch fleet takes Bahia (recaptured 1625)

1630 The Dutch briefly overrun most of north-eastern Brazil

1680 Portugal bans the enslavement of Brazilian native peoples

1708–09 Portugal suppresses the *Paulistas*

1711 The French sack Rio de Janeiro during the War of the Spanish Succession

1750 Treaties of Madrid and San Ildefonso (1777) update the Treaty of Tordesillas

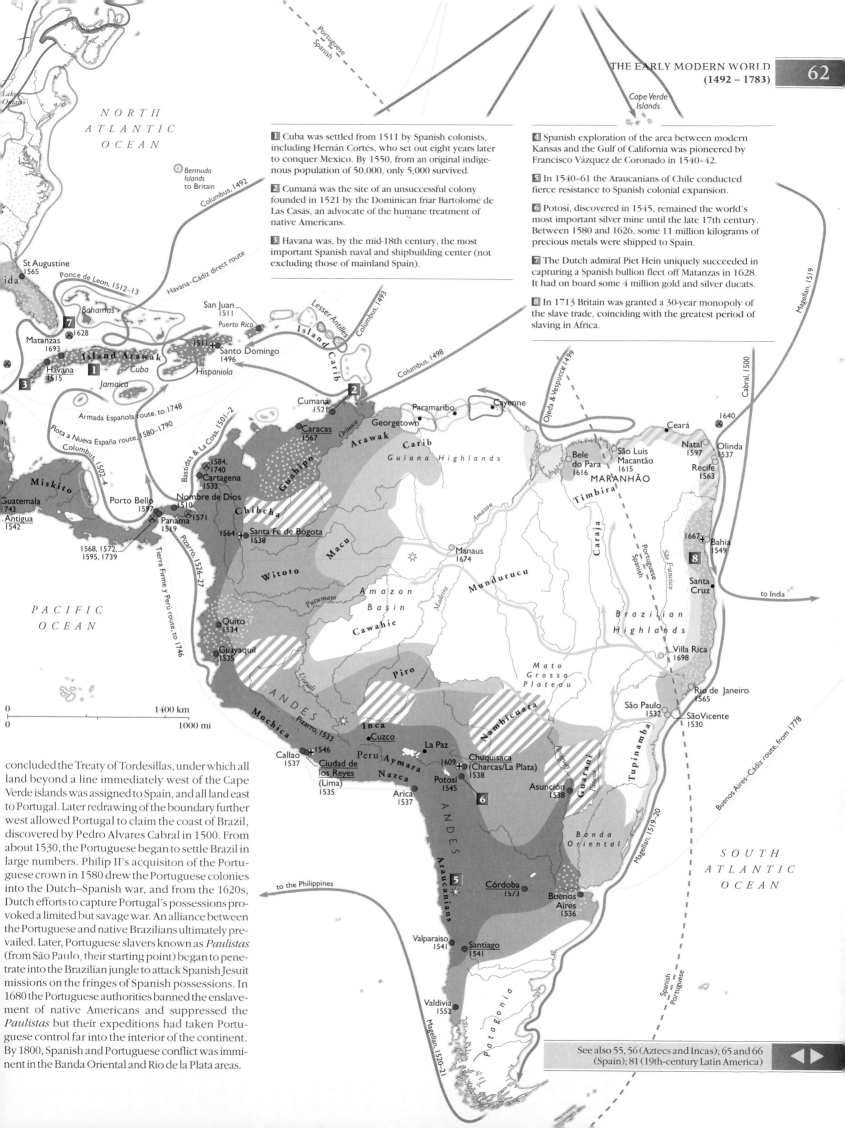

NORTH ATLANTIC OCEAN

1 Cuba was settled from 1511 by Spanish colonists, including Hernán Cortés, who set out eight years later to conquer Mexico. By 1550, from an original indigenous population of 50,000, only 5,000 survived.

2 Cumaná was the site of an unsuccessful colony founded in 1521 by the Dominican friar Bartolomé de Las Casas, an advocate of the humane treatment of native Americans.

3 Havana was, by the mid-18th century, the most important Spanish naval and shipbuilding center (not excluding those of mainland Spain).

4 Spanish exploration of the area between modern Kansas and the Gulf of California was pioneered by Francisco Vázquez de Coronado in 1540-42.

5 In 1540-61 the Araucanians of Chile conducted fierce resistance to Spanish colonial expansion.

6 Potosí, discovered in 1545, remained the world's most important silver mine until the late 17th century. Between 1580 and 1626, some 11 million kilograms of precious metals were shipped to Spain.

7 The Dutch admiral Piet Hein uniquely succeeded in capturing a Spanish bullion fleet off Matanzas in 1628. It had on board some 4 million gold and silver ducats.

8 In 1713 Britain was granted a 30-year monopoly of the slave trade, coinciding with the greatest period of slaving in Africa.

Cape Verde Islands

Portuguese / Spanish

Bermuda Islands to Britain

Columbus, 1492

St Augustine 1565
Ponce de Leon, 1512–13
Bahamas
Havana–Cádiz direct route

San Juan 1511
Puerto Rico
Lesser Antilles
Columbus, 1493
Island Carib

7 1628
Matanzas 1693
3 Havana 1515
Island Arawak
Cuba
1511
Santo Domingo 1496
Hispaniola
Jamaica

Armada Española route, to 1748
Flota a Nueva España route, 1580–1790
Columbus, 1502–4

Columbus, 1498
Cumaná 1521 **2**

Magellan, 1519
Cabral, 1500

1640
Ceará
Natal 1597
Olinda 1537
Recife 1563

PACIFIC OCEAN

Miskito
Guatemala 743
Antigua 1542

Porto Bello
1568, 1572, 1595, 1739
Nombre de Dios 1510
Panama 1519 1571
Cartagena 1533
Bastidas & La Cosa, 1501–2
1584, 1740
Caracas 1567
Orinoco
Arawak
Guahippo
Chibcha
1564 Santa Fe de Bogotá 1538
Paramaribo
Georgetown
Cayenne
Ojeda & Vespucci 1499

Carib
Guiana Highlands

Bele do Para 1616
São Luis Macantão 1615
MARANHÃO
Timbira
Caraja

Tierra Firme y Perú route, to 1746
Pizarro, 1526–27

Macu
Witoto
Putumayo
Amazon Basin
Cawahie

Amazon
Manaus 1674
Madeira
Mundurucu

Portuguese Spanish
São Francisco

1667 Bahia 1549 **8**

to India

Quito 1534
Guayaquil 1535

ANDES
Mochica
Pizarro, 1533
Inca
Cuzco
Peru
Callao 1546
1537
Ciudad de los Reyes (Lima) 1535
Aymara
Nazca
Arica 1537

Ucayali
Piro

Mato Grosso Plateau

Santa Cruz

Villa Rica 1698

Brazilian Highlands

Rio de Janeiro 1565
São Paulo 1532
São Vicente 1530

Buenos Aires–Cádiz route, from 1778

0 ——— 1400 km
0 ——— 1000 mi

La Paz
1609 Chuquisaca (Charcas/La Plata) 1538
Potosí 1545 **6**

Nambicuara
Paraguay
Asunción 1538
Guarani
Tupinamba

concluded the Treaty of Tordesillas, under which all land beyond a line immediately west of the Cape Verde islands was assigned to Spain, and all land east to Portugal. Later redrawing of the boundary further west allowed Portugal to claim the coast of Brazil, discovered by Pedro Alvares Cabral in 1500. From about 1530, the Portuguese began to settle Brazil in large numbers. Philip II's acquisiton of the Portuguese crown in 1580 drew the Portuguese colonies into the Dutch–Spanish war, and from the 1620s, Dutch efforts to capture Portugal's possessions provoked a limited but savage war. An alliance between the Portuguese and native Brazilians ultimately prevailed. Later, Portuguese slavers known as *Paulistas* (from São Paulo, their starting point) began to penetrate into the Brazilian jungle to attack Spanish Jesuit missions on the fringes of Spanish possessions. In 1680 the Portuguese authorities banned the enslavement of native Americans and suppressed the *Paulistas* but their expeditions had taken Portuguese control far into the interior of the continent. By 1800, Spanish and Portuguese conflict was imminent in the Banda Oriental and Rio de la Plata areas.

to the Philippines

Araucanians **5**
Córdoba 1573

Banda Oriental

Buenos Aires 1536

Valparaiso 1541
Santiago 1541

SOUTH ATLANTIC OCEAN

Magellan, 1519–20

Spanish / Portuguese

Valdivia 1552

Patagonia

Magellan, 1520–21

See also 55, 56 (Aztecs and Incas); 65 and 66 (Spain); 81 (19th-century Latin America)

The last century of the Ashikaga shogunate (1338–1573) in Japan was dominated by the political fragmentation arising from the Onin war of 1467–77. Following this protracted civil conflict, real power devolved to small, feudal units subject to the changing allegiances of local lords (*daimyo*), while the authority of the emperor and his military commander, the *shogun*, was only nominal. Instability was heightened by ever more frequent popular uprisings, often fomented by the powerful Buddhist monasteries. Both this tradition of religious militancy and the independent merchant guilds provided an alternative focus for popular loyalty.

The lack of political stability did not, however, prevent the steady growth of Japanese trade and industry throughout the later 15th and early 16th centuries, although the proliferation of local customs boundaries did preclude a truly national economy. Japan also remained culturally vibrant, with many great *daimyo* patronizing such diverse art forms as *noh* drama, poetry, the tea ceremony and painting. At the same time, traveling balladeers, preachers and dancers helped create a popular culture that transcended Japan's political fragmentation.

In 1568, the first of a series of leaders powerful enough to attempt the political unification of Japan emerged. Nobunaga, lord of the Oda clan, captured the imperial capital Kyoto in that year, and embarked on the destruction of the Buddhist temples and slaughter of the monks. Warfare in Japan had been transformed by the introduction of firearms by the Portuguese in 1542: muskets were copied in large numbers, and sophisticated new tactics developed to utilize this firepower. Even more significant was the construction by Nobunaga of an entirely new type of castle at Azuchi. In contrast to earlier mountain strongholds, Azuchi was built to dominate the rice fields and communications of the plain, and was an administrative center as well as a fortress. Its importance was such that the age of national

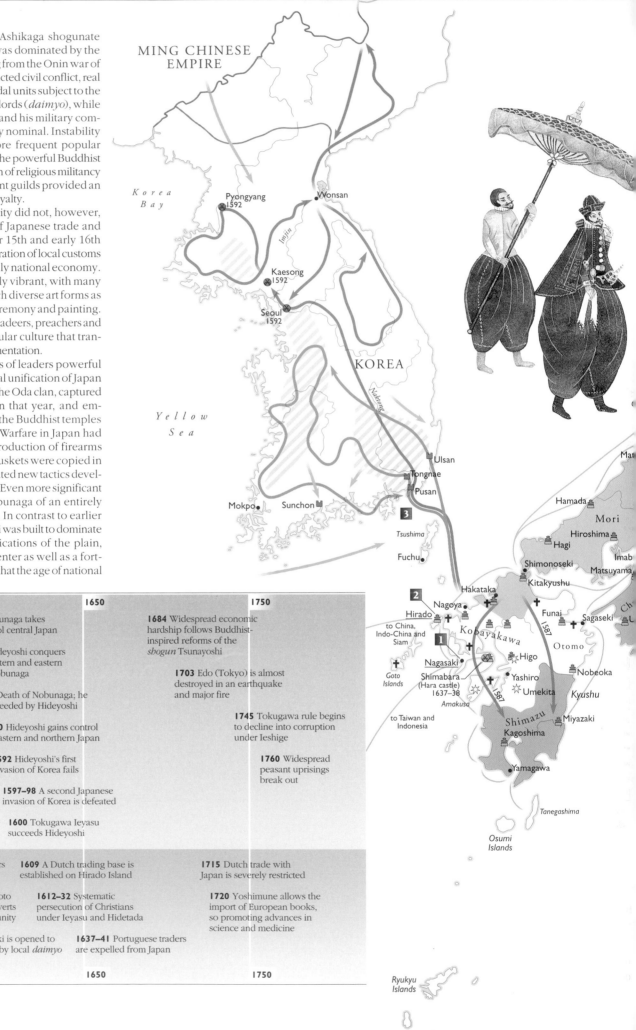

TIMELINE

Unification of Japan

1568 Oda Nobunaga takes Kyoto to control central Japan

1571–82 Hideyoshi conquers lands in western and eastern Japan for Nobunaga

1582 Death of Nobunaga; he is succeeded by Hideyoshi

1590 Hideyoshi gains control of eastern and northern Japan

1592 Hideyoshi's first invasion of Korea fails

1597–98 A second Japanese invasion of Korea is defeated

1600 Tokugawa Ieyasu succeeds Hideyoshi

1684 Widespread economic hardship follows Buddhist-inspired reforms of the *shogun* Tsunayoshi

1703 Edo (Tokyo) is almost destroyed in an earthquake and major fire

1745 Tokugawa rule begins to decline into corruption under Ieshige

1760 Widespread peasant uprisings break out

Foreign influences

1542 First Portuguese traders arrive on Tanegashima

1548–51 Mission to Kyoto and western Japan converts first Japanese to Christianity

1570 Nagasaki is opened to foreign trade by local *daimyo*

1609 A Dutch trading base is established on Hirado Island

1612–32 Systematic persecution of Christians under Ieyasu and Hidetada

1637–41 Portuguese traders are expelled from Japan

1715 Dutch trade with Japan is severely restricted

1720 Yoshimune allows the import of European books, so promoting advances in science and medicine

Sea of Japan

EUROPEAN traders (seen in this Japanese painting) and missionaries were initially welcomed, but repression increased in the 1630s.

JAPAN

Honshu

Shikoku

Sado

Tsukahara

Hokkaido

Hakodate
Miyuma
Hirosaki
Hachinohe
Noshiro
Akita
Morioka
Miyako
Senpoku
Honjo
Ichinoseki
Shinjo
Shonai
Ozaki
Tsuruoka
Sendai
Yamagata
Yonezawa
Niigata
Shibata
Fukushima
Aizu
Nagaoka
Iwaki
Wajima
Takata
Shirakawa
Uesugi
Nikko
Toyama
Zenkoji
Utsunomiya
Kanazawa
Sasa
Takeda
Takasaki
Maeda
Hojo
Choshi
Fukui
Edo
Shibata
Iida
Odawara 1590
Obama
Sekigahara 1600
Nagoya
Numazu
Tottori
Akechi
Azuchi
Yoshida
Shimoda
Fukuchiyama
Kyoto
Momoyama
Himeji
Kobe
Osaka 1614-15
yama
Sakai
Ise
Toba
akamatsu 1584-85
Tokushima
Tanabe
Shingu
Oshima

Osaka–Edo route

eastward coastal route
ward coastal route
Oshu Kaido
Nakasendo
Koshu Kaido
Nikko Kaido
Tokaido

PACIFIC OCEAN

Map key:
- Oda land, 1560
- area conquered by Nobunaga and Hideyoshi by 1582
- main *daimyo* house opposed to Hideyoshi, 1582
- Mori *daimyo* house, 16th–17th centuries
- campaigns of Hideyoshi, 1584–90
- Hideyoshi's first invasion of Korea, 1592
- Hideyoshi's second invasion of Korea, 1597–98
- Korean and Ming Chinese counteroffensives
- main areas of Korean resistance to Hideyoshi
- Japanese base in Korea retained after 1593
- Hideyoshi victory
- castle town
- Japanese peasant revolt against Hideyoshi's land survey
- victory of Tokugawa Ieyasu or his successors
- area with significant number of Christian converts
- Hirado trading port used by Europeans
- "Five Highways" of Tokugawa Japan
- coastal shipping route

0 _____ 200 km
0 _____ 150 mi

1 Nagasaki was an unimportant fishing village until it was developed as Japan's main port for foreign trade by the local lord Omura in 1570.

2 The Dutch East India Company base on Hirado Island was moved to Deshima Island, near Nagasaki, in 1641. The Dutch officials had to undergo various symbolic indignities to retain their trading privileges.

3 Hideyoshi's invasion of Korea was commanded by Kato Kiyomasa and Konishi Yukinaga. Konishi took Pusan in 1592, but the Ming navy almost destroyed the Japanese fleet, leaving the army cut off.

4 Azuchi castle, on the shores of Lake Biwa, was begun by Oda Nobunaga in 1576. This pioneering castle was widely imitated by other *daimyo* over the next few decades.

5 Edo (Tokyo) became the administrative and military base of Tokugawa Ieyasu in 1590. In the 1600s it became a rival to the ancient capital, Kyoto.

6 Osaka castle, stronghold of Hideyoshi's son Hideyori, became a center for opposition to the rule of Ieyasu, until Ieyasu's forces sacked it in 1614–15.

7 The Five Highways (*gokaido*) formed an efficient transport network converging on the *shogun*'s court; *daimyo* traveling to the court had their travel papers checked at control points on the highways.

---

unification is known in Japan as the Azuchi–Momoyama period, after Nobunaga's castle and its counterpart built by his lieutenant Hideyoshi.

Hideyoshi, who acquired the surname Toyotomi ("the Wealthy"), was a military genius of humble origins. Under his leadership, Oda forces overran the lands of their rivals in central Japan, the Akechi, Shibata and Mori, and then expanded eastward into Takeda and Uesugi territory. After Nobunaga's death in 1582, Hideyoshi became ruler of most of central Japan in alliance with Tokugawa Ieyasu, his most dangerous rival. Campaigns against rival daimyo on the islands of Shikoku and Kyushu followed, and in 1590 Hideyoshi's capture of the Hojo clan's castle at Odawara also gave him control of eastern Japan.

Hideyoshi's conquests were accompanied by political changes designed to prevent further unrest. He disarmed the peasantry and insisted that the *samurai* (warrior-class) live in castle towns, which ensured that potentially rebellious farming communities could no longer rely on local samurai support. Taxation was reformed in an unpopular land survey, which initially caused widespread unrest. Trade was brought under government control, and steps were taken to suppress Christianity, which had spread from the Portuguese base at Nagasaki (founded 1572) but which now seemed alien and subversive.

Ieyasu succeeded Hideyoshi after two Japanese invasions of Korea in the 1590s were beaten back by

the Koreans with the help of Ming China. He continued the policies of his predecessor, as did subsequent *shoguns* of the Tokugawa dynasty which he founded in 1603. Christianity, persecuted under Hidetada (r.1605–23), was eradicated by the massacre of 37,000 Japanese Christians at Hara castle (1638). Social and economic stability were maintained by strict segregation of farming and trade, a ban on private investment and official discouragement of any contact between different parts of the country that did not use the closely controlled Five Highways. Portuguese ships were banned from Japan in 1639, export restricted to Dutch and Chinese bases at Nagasaki, and Japanese citizens were forbidden to travel abroad (while those long resident in ports throughout Asia were forbidden to return). The construction of large ships was banned in 1638 to prevent the Japanese from traveling abroad.

Despite these repressive measures, the early Edo period (1603–1867) was remarkable for its economic prosperity and agricultural productivity (led by growing demand from the booming cities), and for its technological advancement. The population grew rapidly in the 17th and early 18th centuries to nearly 30 million, and a vigorous merchant class had its heyday in the late 17th century. However, economic and social ills did begin to accumulate. By the mid-18th century many peasants had left the land, many samurai had fallen into debt, and unrest was again becoming common. Lifting both of the social strictures and of the ban on European books under the enlightened shogun Yoshimune (r.1716–45) brought some relief, but famine, natural disasters and government corruption provoked frequent peasant uprisings after 1760. The late 18th century saw the growth of an opposition movement around the emperor to the rule of the Tokugawa shoguns, and a new Japanese awareness of the threat from expanding European influence in Asia.

See also 50 (medieval Japan); 93 (19th-century Japan)

By 1600, Europe and Asia had enjoyed a century of population growth. European prosperity was matched by a rise in living conditions in Asia, India and the Middle East. African populations and material conditions stayed stable, but in the Americas the Europeans brought demographic catastrophe.

Spanish and Portuguese penetration of the Americas was slow after the collapse of the Inca empire. Beyond the highly-organized Inca and Aztec states, populations were sparse, distances huge and political structures lacking, and the conquistadors had little incentive to explore. Instead they exploited their conquests (▷62). In 1545 production began at the rich mines of Potosí; silver was shipped to Seville and spread through Europe, as the Genoese backers of Spain's voyages multiplied its value by sophisticated credit mechanisms. Spanish silver was also used by Europe's merchants to buy into other trading networks around the world. Antwerp's reign as financial capital of Europe had ended by 1576 when it was sacked by Spanish mutineers: from 1557 Genoa called the tune in Europe's economy (▷66).

Spanish political and military power reached its peak in the 1580s when Philip II seized the crown of Portugal. For sixty years the two crowns were united, although Portuguese overseas possessions were still administered from Lisbon. As the Netherlands began a campaign of conquest against the Portuguese trading bases worldwide, Portuguese power in Asia declined.

European politics spilled over into the Spanish empire. Dutch and English pirates raided the Spanish–American cities and attempted to seize bullion fleets. French Huguenot (Protestant) colonists reached Florida and the mouth of the Amazon. They were driven from the former by Spanish forces, but the Portuguese could not dislodge them from the latter for over a century. French explorers such as Jacques Cartier penetrated North America via the St Lawrence river, while the Spaniard Francisco Coronado pioneered routes north from Mexico (▷70).

In Africa, the Ottomans steadily reduced the Spanish footholds in North Africa, while Morocco's stunning defeat of a major Portuguese expedition at Alcazarquivir in 1578 led directly to the union of Portugal with Spain. The Moroccans then mounted an even more spectacular expedition across the Sahara in 1590–91 to overthrow the weakened Songhai empire at Tondibi. In sub-Saharan Africa, the Muslim empire of Kanem-Bornu emerged as the most

1552–56 Russia conquers Kazan and Astrakhan from the Tatars and begins expansion into Siberia

1535 Pizarro completes the conquest of Peru for Spain (begun 1531)

1545 The Potosí silver mines in Peru begin production

1566 The Dutch begin a rebellion against Spanish rule (to 1648)

1565 St Augustine is founded by Spain to prevent French Huguenots from colonizing Florida

1580 Philip II of Spain claims the throne of Portugal

TIMELINE

The Americas
Europe
Middle East
Africa
East and South Asia

1540 · 1560 · 1580

1538 The Ottoman Turks overrun the entire Red Sea coast of Arabia

1539–56 The Mughals are driven from northern India by the Afghan Sur dynasty

1542 Portuguese traders land at Tanegashima, Japan

1557 A Portuguese trading base is established at Macao, China

1568 Japanese unification under the control of Nobunaga begins

1570 Kanem-Bornu begins to reach the peak of its power under Idris III Aloma

1571 A combined Christian fleet defeats the Ottoman navy at Lepanto

1577–80 Drake's circumnavigation of the world includes raids on Pacific Spanish America

1578 The Moroccans defeat and kill Sebastian I of Portugal at al-Qasr al-Kabir (Alcazarquivir)

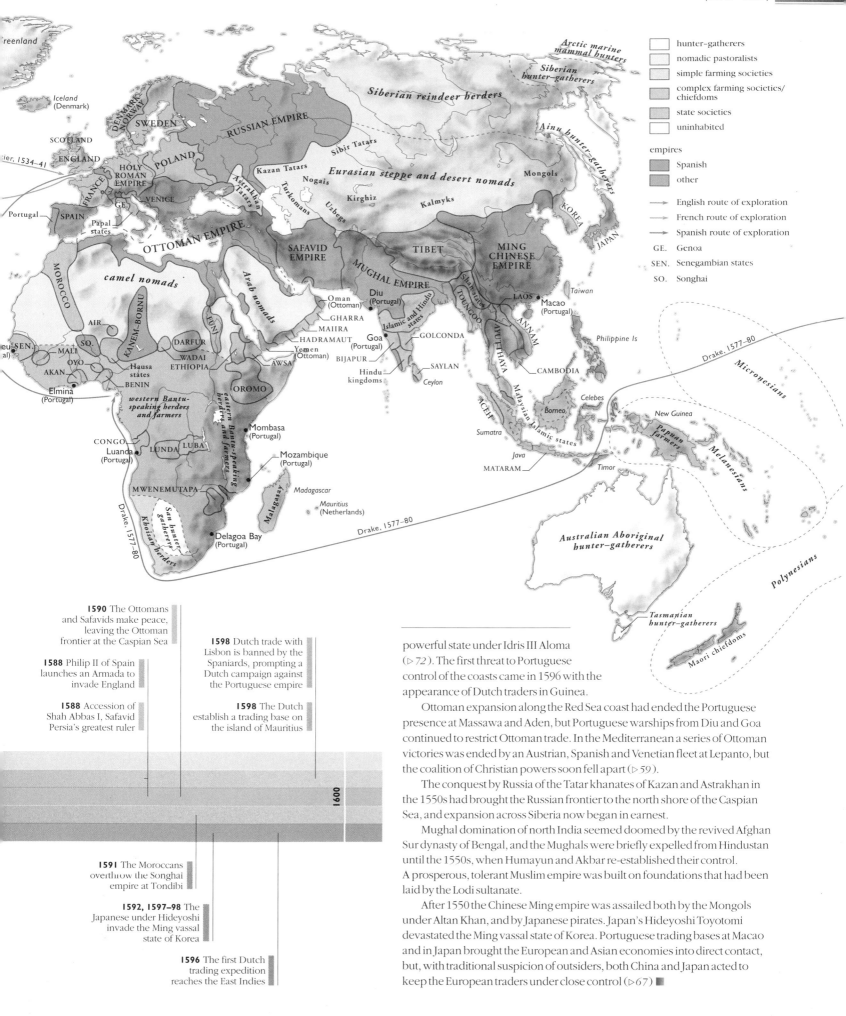

hunter-gatherers
nomadic pastoralists
simple farming societies
complex farming societies/chiefdoms
state societies
uninhabited

empires
Spanish
other

→ English route of exploration
→ French route of exploration
→ Spanish route of exploration

GE.   Genoa
SEN. Senegambian states
SO.   Songhai

1590 The Ottomans and Safavids make peace, leaving the Ottoman frontier at the Caspian Sea

1588 Philip II of Spain launches an Armada to invade England

1588 Accession of Shah Abbas I, Safavid Persia's greatest ruler

1598 Dutch trade with Lisbon is banned by the Spaniards, prompting a Dutch campaign against the Portuguese empire

1598 The Dutch establish a trading base on the island of Mauritius

1600

1591 The Moroccans overthrow the Songhai empire at Tondibi

1592, 1597–98 The Japanese under Hideyoshi invade the Ming vassal state of Korea

1596 The first Dutch trading expedition reaches the East Indies

powerful state under Idris III Aloma
(▷ 72). The first threat to Portuguese
control of the coasts came in 1596 with the
appearance of Dutch traders in Guinea.

Ottoman expansion along the Red Sea coast had ended the Portuguese
presence at Massawa and Aden, but Portuguese warships from Diu and Goa
continued to restrict Ottoman trade. In the Mediterranean a series of Ottoman
victories was ended by an Austrian, Spanish and Venetian fleet at Lepanto, but
the coalition of Christian powers soon fell apart (▷ 59).

The conquest by Russia of the Tatar khanates of Kazan and Astrakhan in
the 1550s had brought the Russian frontier to the north shore of the Caspian
Sea, and expansion across Siberia now began in earnest.

Mughal domination of north India seemed doomed by the revived Afghan
Sur dynasty of Bengal, and the Mughals were briefly expelled from Hindustan
until the 1550s, when Humayun and Akbar re-established their control.
A prosperous, tolerant Muslim empire was built on foundations that had been
laid by the Lodi sultanate.

After 1550 the Chinese Ming empire was assailed both by the Mongols
under Altan Khan, and by Japanese pirates. Japan's Hideyoshi Toyotomi
devastated the Ming vassal state of Korea. Portuguese trading bases at Macao
and in Japan brought the European and Asian economies into direct contact,
but, with traditional suspicion of outsiders, both China and Japan acted to
keep the European traders under close control (▷ 67) ■

The "crisis of the 17th century" brought social upheaval, religious violence and economic hardship from Portugal to Russia. Monarchs tried to increase their power at the expense of the nobility, local corporations and the peripheral regions.

Religious tensions abounded, heightened by the uncompromising stances of both Calvinism and Counter-Reformation Catholicism. Religion was, however, seldom the overriding factor in conflict. In England and France it gave an edge to political and social struggles, while in the shifting alliances of the Thirty Years War, religious affiliation was often little more than a kind of badge for armies recruited indiscriminately from all faiths, or for princes prepared to change religion to further a political advantage.

After the assassination of Henry IV in 1610, France underwent a period of weak government until Cardinal Richelieu became chief minister in 1624. Plots against him by the brother of Louis XIII led to a renewal of hostilities between the administration and the nobility. The Huguenots demanded concessions and rose in revolt again. Richelieu laid siege to their chief stronghold, La Rochelle; the defenders were starved into submission. Thereafter Richelieu concentrated on dismembering the Habsburg empire. Offensives against the strategic route to Flanders were narrowly defeated by Spanish and imperialist forces. In the1640s Richelieu and his successor Mazarin brought the scheme to fruition, with military success in Flanders, the Rhineland, Italy and the Pyrenees, and French-sponsored revolts in Portugal, Catalonia, Sicily and Naples. Spain's empire appeared doomed, but unrest in France showed the cost of these efforts.

Contemporaries recognized the war that broke out in 1618 as one which subsumed all Europe's other conflicts. The Thirty Years War consisted of several stages. First, the Bohemian–Palatinate war (1618–23) in which a Bohemian Protestant and Transylvanian threat to Habsburg Vienna was defeated and the Calvinist Lower Palatinate was conquered by imperial and Spanish troops. Second, the Danish war (1625–29) in which an intervention on behalf of the German Protestants by Denmark was shattered at Lutter, and the Edict of Restitution strengthened the position of the Catholics in Germany. Third, the Swedish war (1630–35) in which Sweden briefly carried the war to the the heart of Catholic southern Germany. Fourth, the French–Swedish war (1635-48), in which the French defeated successive Spanish invasions and undertook counter-offensives against all the Spanish possessions, Sweden defeated the imperialists and various armies spread unprecedented devastation over much of Germany before peace was made.

Spain's role as Catholic champion of Europe was the greatest casualty of the war. The years of relative peace in the early 17th century were wasted and the reform program initiated after 1621 by the chief minister Olivares could not be sustained, as the cost of financing a war effort across the continent escalated while silver revenues dwindled. With the revolts of Catalonia and Portugal in 1640, Spain was forced to divert resources to deal with domestic difficulties.

James VI and I of Scotland and England planted Ulster with Protestant settlers, but avoided commitment to the Protestant cause on Europe's mainland. Constitutional and religious opposition to his son Charles I led to war in Scotland (1639–40), to a massacre of the Ulster Protestants, and then to civil war in England. The victory of his Parliamentary enemies did not end unrest. The king was executed in 1649 (though few sought such a radical solution) and a Commonwealth established under Oliver Cromwell.

The Dutch alone gained from Europe's long, grim war. By weathering years of Spanish assaults they preserved their trading empire and won their independence. They now set about commercial expansion. By 1650 Amsterdam's financiers dominated the entire European economy.

Legend:

- Austrian Habsburg territory, 1618
- Spanish Habsburg territory, 1618
- Habsburg allies, 1618
- France, 1618
- German Protestant states
- United Provinces, 1609
- Sweden, 1618
- other state hostile to Habsburgs
- borders, 1648
- French offensive
- Protestant offensive
- Spanish offensive
- Swedish offensive
- Habsburg and imperialist victory
- Habsburg and imperialist defeat
- major siege
- town sacked
- major revolt or unrest
- major Dutch fortifications built 1605–06
- Spanish blockade of Dutch trade, 1624–27
- major Habsburg strategic route
- major Dutch trade route
- Spanish naval patrol
- British settlement in Ireland, 1613
- "Plantations" of James I, 1613-25
- Eastern Association of pro-Parliamentary counties, 1643
- royalist victory
- royalist defeat

(map labels: Irel..., Limerick, Tralee, Cork, ATLANTIC OCEAN, to the Atlantic and East Indies, to Spanish Netherlands, La Coruña, San..., Valladolid, Oporto, PORTUGAL, SPAIN, Tagus, Portuguese revolt, 1640, 1640, Lisbon, to the Americas, Córdoba, Seville, Tangier, Ceuta, Me..., 0 400 km, 0 300 mi)

TIMELINE

British Isles

1603 James VI of Scotland becomes James I of England, creating a personal union of the kingdoms

1605 A plot to blow up James and Parliament is foiled

1613–25 Ulster, forfeited to the crown after Tyrone's rebellion, is planted by Protestant settlers

1627 Charles I undertakes an abortive expedition to relieve the siege of La Rochelle

1629–40 Charles attempts to rule without Parliament

1637 Scots "covenant" to defend Calvinism

1642–46 In the 1st Civil War, Parliament defeats the King

1648 Cromwell defeats the Scots Covenanters at Preston

1649 Charles executed; the Commonwealth is set up

1639-40 Charles is defeated by the Scots in Bishops' Wars

Western Europe

1609 A twelve-year truce is agreed between Spain and the United Netherlands

1627–28 The Huguenot stronghold of La Rochelle is besieged and captured

1628 French offensives against Spanish and imperialist territories begin

1640 France supports revolts against Spain in Catalonia (to 1652) and Portugal

1643 The French defeat the Spanish at Rocroi

Germany/Empire

1609 Bavaria and Spain set up the Catholic league

1618 Thirty Years War begins as Protestant Bohemia rejects imperial authority

1620 Spain conquers the Lower Palatinate

1625–29 Christian IV of Denmark intervenes

1629 The Edict of Restitution promotes the Catholic position in the empire

1632 Gustavus Adolphus dies at Lützen (Swedish victory)

1644–45 The French drive imperial forces from Alsace

1648 Treaty of Westphalia ends the war; religious freedom granted to Calvinists

(timeline axis years: 1610, 1630, 1650)

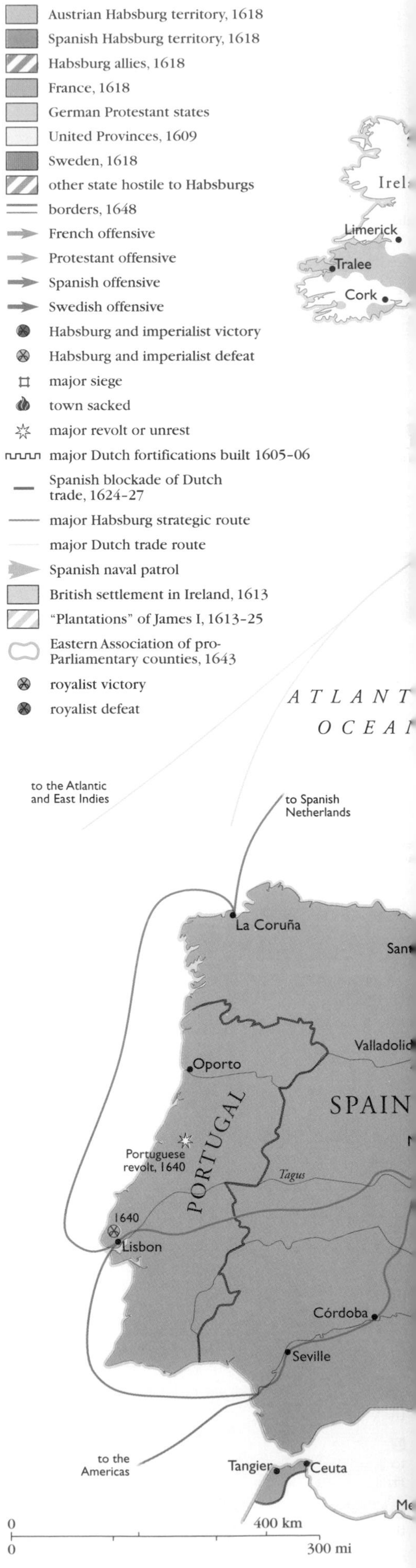

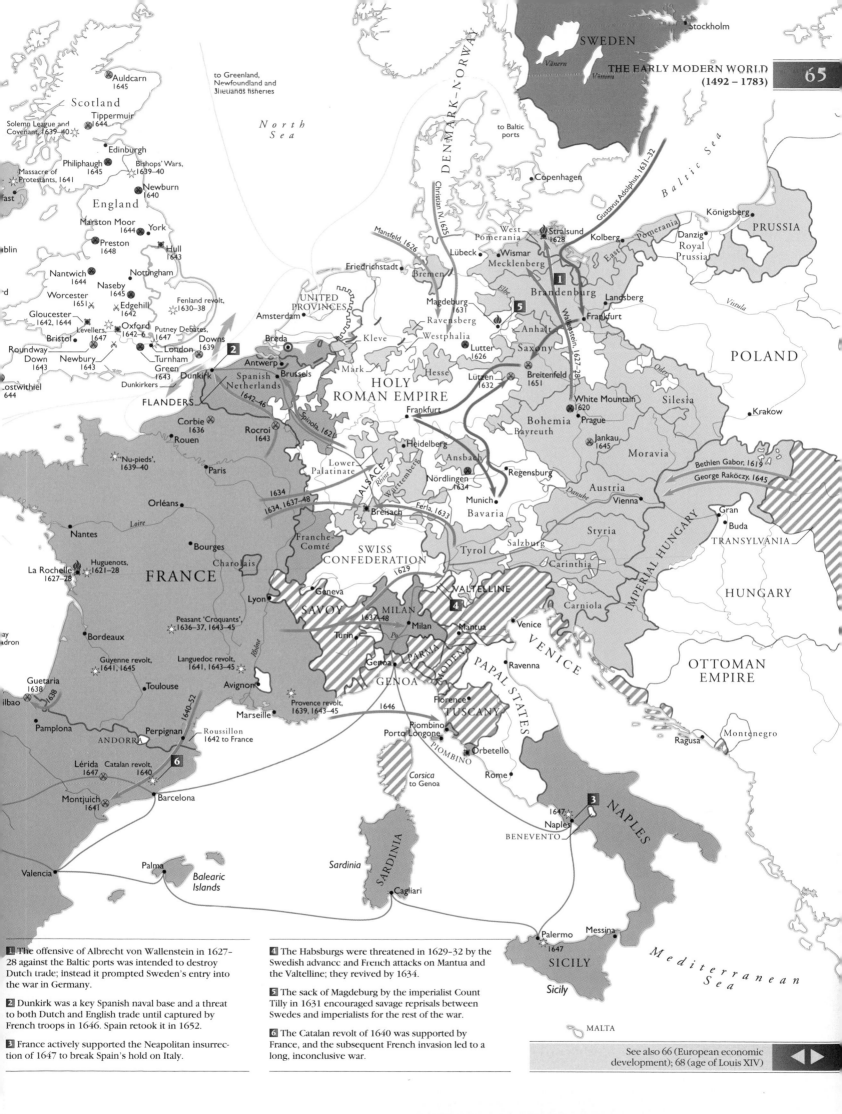

Scotland

Auldcarn
1645

Tippermuir
1644

Solemn League and
Covenant, 1639–40

to Greenland,
Newfoundland and
3hetlands fisheries

North
Sea

Edinburgh

Philiphaugh
1645

Bishops' Wars,
1639–40

Massacre of
Protestants, 1641

Newburn
1640

England

Marston Moor
1644

York

Preston
1648

Hull
1643

Nantwich
1644

Nottingham

Naseby
1645

Fenland revolt,
1630–38

Worcester
1651

Edgehill
1642

Gloucester
1642, 1644

Oxford
1642–6

Putney Debates,
1647

Levellers,
1647

Bristol

Roundway
Down
1643

Newbury
1643

Turnham
Green
1643

London

Downs
1639

ostwithiel
644

Dunkirkers

Dunkirk

FLANDERS

Corbie 1636

Rouen

Rocroi
1643

Amsterdam

UNITED
PROVINCES

Breda

Antwerp

Brussels

Kleve

Mark

Spanish
Netherlands

1642–46

Spinola, 1621

Westphalia

Mansfeld, 1626

Friedrichstadt

Bremen

Lübeck

DENMARK–NORWAY

Christian IV, 1625

Copenhagen

SWEDEN

Stockholm

Vänern

Baltic
Sea

to Baltic
ports

Gustavus Adolphus, 1631–32

West
Pomerania

Stralsund
1628

Wismar

Mecklenberg

Kolberg

East
Pomerania

Königsberg

Danzig
Royal
Prussia

PRUSSIA

Magdeburg
1631

Ravensberg

Elbe

Brandenburg

Frankfurt

Landsberg

Vistula

Anhalt

Wallenstein, 1627–28

Saxony

Lutter
1626

Hesse

Lützen
1632

HOLY
ROMAN EMPIRE

Frankfurt

Heidelberg

Lower
Palatinate

ALSACE

Rhine

Württemberg

Breisach

1634

1634, 1637–48

Ansbach

Nördlingen
1634

Ferla, 1633

Regensburg

Munich

Bavaria

Breitenfeld
1631

White Mountain
1620

Prague

Bohemia

Bayreuth

Jankau
1645

Moravia

Silesia

Krakow

POLAND

Oder

Danube

Austria

Vienna

Bethlen Gabor, 1619

George Raköczy, 1645

Gran

Buda

TRANSYLVANIA

to Greenland

Amsterdam

FRANCE

Paris

Orléans

Loire

Bourges

'Nu-pieds',
1639–40

La Rochelle
1627–28

Huguenots,
1621–28

Charolais

Franche-
Comté

SWISS
CONFEDERATION

1629

Geneva

SAVOY

Lyon

Rhône

Milan
1637–48

Turin

Milan

Mantua

Venice

Ravenna

VENICE

Tyrol

Salzburg

Carinthia

Styria

Carniola

IMPERIAL HUNGARY

HUNGARY

OTTOMAN
EMPIRE

Nantes

Bordeaux

Peasant 'Croquants',
1636–37, 1643–45

Guyenne revolt,
1641, 1645

Languedoc revolt,
1641, 1643–45

Guetaria
1638

ilbao

adron

Toulouse

Avignon

Marseille

Provence revolt,
1639, 1643–45

1646

Genoa

PARMA

MODENA

GENOA

PAPAL
STATES

Florence

TUSCANY

Riombino

Porto Longone

PIOMBINO

Orbetello

Rome

Corsica
to Genoa

Montenegro

Ragusa

Pamplona

Perpignan

ANDORRA

Roussillon
1642 to France

Lérida
1647

Catalan revolt,
1640

Montjuich
1641

Barcelona

Valencia

Palma

Balearic
Islands

Sardinia

SARDINIA

Cagliari

1647

Naples

BENEVENTO

NAPLES

Palermo
1647

SICILY

Sicily

Messina

Mediterranean
Sea

MALTA

1 The offensive of Albrecht von Wallenstein in 1627-28 against the Baltic ports was intended to destroy Dutch trade; instead it prompted Sweden's entry into the war in Germany.

2 Dunkirk was a key Spanish naval base and a threat to both Dutch and English trade until captured by French troops in 1646. Spain retook it in 1652.

3 France actively supported the Neapolitan insurrection of 1647 to break Spain's hold on Italy.

4 The Habsburgs were threatened in 1629-32 by the Swedish advance and French attacks on Mantua and the Valtelline; they revived by 1634.

5 The sack of Magdeburg by the imperialist Count Tilly in 1631 encouraged savage reprisals between Swedes and imperialists for the rest of the war.

6 The Catalan revolt of 1640 was supported by France, and the subsequent French invasion led to a long, inconclusive war.

See also 66 (European economic development); 68 (age of Louis XIV)

Europe's economy in 1783 still rested on a base of semi-subsistence agriculture, poor transport, local economies based partly on barter, lack of development capital and the slow adoption of technological advances. Important developments in agriculture, industry and commerce had taken place since the 16th century, most importantly in Britain and France, but their social impact was still slight.

The population growth of the 16th century had brought pressure on resources, resulting in rising prices and falling wages. Population stagnation in the 17th allowed a slight rise in living standards; but renewed population growth in the later 18th century was not matched by an equivalent increase in production and so brought hardship again. This contributed to the revolutionary explosion at the end of the century. Overall, however, Europe's population doubled between 1500 and 1800. The cities grew most: London and Paris exceeded 250,000 inhabitants by 1700.

It was in the cities that a higher level of economic activity took place. Sophisticated banking and credit systems emerged, providing finance not only for long-distance trade but also for monarchs and governments. Although neither standards of living nor technology were markedly superior in Europe to those in Asia or the Middle East, this new merchant capitalism made possible Europe's transformation into the economic powerhouse of the world.

The economic area dependent on European capitalism underwent an extraordinary expansion after 1492, reaching across the Atlantic to incorporate the Americas and spreading a galaxy of trading bases across south and east Asia. Its center of gravity, having see-sawed between Flanders and northern Italy, finally settled in the north, at Amsterdam in the 17th century and London in the late 18th. A succession of financially dominant cities took European capitalism progressively closer to world domination, in a contest between the nimble city-states of the past and the nation-states of the future; Britain's precocious national economy centered on London finally proved too powerful for its predecessors.

In the late 15th century, the dominant financial powers were still Venice and the Hanseatic league, each controlling a network of trade routes. Flemish and English incursions into Hanseatic areas, and the arrival of Portuguese ships with East Indies spices at Antwerp (bypassing the Venetian spice route through the Levant), resulted in the collapse of their partnership. From 1501 to 1568 European capitalism was dominated by the bankers of Antwerp. The distribution of the American silver flooding into Seville was handled from Flanders, while Dutch and Flemish ships dominated the Baltic grain trade to southern Europe – and reduced the Mediterranean to a peripheral area. In 1557 the pendulum swung back to the south. The first Spanish state bankruptcy damaged the Antwerp banking system, and the Genoese seized their chance. For the next seventy years Europe's finances were managed from Genoa, while the Netherlands subsided into religious war.

Whereas Antwerp and Genoa competed for dominance during the economic upswing of the 16th century, as the downturn gathered pace in the 1620s and silver remittances from Spanish America reduced, Amsterdam emerged as Europe's capitalist powerhouse. Maritime expertise combined with a stable, subtle and flexible credit system led to Dutch control of much European and Asian trade.

The foremost nation-states, Britain and France, made strenuous efforts to compete. The advantages of a stable banking system and an established system of national debt – and the benefit of huge investments after 1688 from the Dutch themselves – finally told in Britain's favor.

Legend

population density per sq km, c.1620

- over 40
- 20–40
- under 20

- city with static population of over 40,000
- city with significant population growth, 1500–1800
- port for European external trade, 18th century
- Genoa   city dominating the European financial system at date shown
- pioneering development in steam power
- important development in iron manufacture and use
- important development in the mechanization of the textile industry
- commercial center for linen industry
- area of coastal or marsh reclamation
- textile area in the 18th century
- grain exporting area in the 16th century
- grain importing area in the 16th century
- coalfield exploited by the late 18th century
- advanced agricultural techniques practiced by the late 18th century
- area of iron working in the 18th century
- major metallurgical area in the 18th century
- copper
- lead and zinc
- silver
- tin
- migration
- major canal built by 1770

The counterpart to this struggle for the heights of European capitalism was the beginning of a transformation of the European economy itself. New agricultural techniques (notably the enclosure by private landlords of common land, improved crop rotation and animal husbandry techniques, and the drainage of marginal lands) in the 18th century spread across Britain and the Netherlands. At the same time, transportation was revolutionized by the construction of canal networks, and energy use by the exploitation of coalfields once bulk transport on the canals became possible. Thomas Newcomen's steam

TIMELINE

Trade and finance

1501 Portuguese ships carrying East Indies spices begin arriving at Antwerp

1535 Antwerp becomes the distribution center for silver from Spanish America

1556 Hanseatic trading privileges end in England

1557 A Spanish state bankruptcy damages the German and Antwerp bankers

1585 Antwerp is sacked by Spain; its merchants and bankers move to Amsterdam

1609 The Exchange Bank of Amsterdam is founded

1620 Spanish silver shipments from the Americas begin to decline sharply

1627 A new Spanish bankruptcy ends Genoa's financial domination of Europe

1664 France tries to impose national tarrifs against Dutch trade (and in 1667 against English trade)

1693 The British National Debt is instituted; in 1694 the Bank of England is set up

1720 Crashes of the South Sea Company in London and Mississippi Company in Paris shake both economies

1730s The Dutch commercial system in Europe begins to decline

1739 Britain and Spain clash over trading rights in the Americas

1783 The power of the British economy is confirmed by the "Eden Treaty" with France

Technology

1520s Coal is increasingly used as a fuel in Britain and the Low Countries

1556 Agricola (Georg Bauer) writes a survey of mining

1620s Dutch engineers assist in the drainage of lowland areas of east England

1709 Abraham Darby (Britain) devises a blast furnace

1712 Thomas Newcomen designs a low-pressure steam pump for mines

1733 John Kay initiates a period of mechanical development in the textile industry in England

(Map labels)

ATLANTIC OCEAN

Oporto   Douro   Vall

Tagus

Guadiana

Lisbon

Moriscoes

Seville

Cádiz

Ceuta

SELECTIVE breeding contributed to the agricultural revolution of the 18th century. This British illustration shows a prize pig.

engine, which was developed in 1712 in England as a means of pumping water from mines (and soon imitated in Europe), was turned into a source of mechanical power by the Scottish inventor James Watt and his partner Matthew Boulton in 1776. Metallurgy was revolutionized by Abraham Darby and others. Above all, the mechanization of the textile industry initiated by John Kay, Samuel Crompton and Richard Arkwright led directly to the first modern-style factories – and the beginnings of the transformation of work itself in what became known as the Industrial Revolution.

1 Portugal broke Venetian control of the spice trade in the early 1500s, but Venice was a center of trade, finance and manufacturing until the late 18th century.

2 English and Dutch merchant ships entered the Mediterranean in the 1570s to break the dominance of Venice and Genoa.

3 After the golden years of the empire, Spain's economy stagnated, with low investment, little technological innovation and entrenched local interests.

4 The North Sea and Atlantic fishing and whaling fleets contributed greatly to Dutch prosperity.

5 Steam pumps in a mine at Jemappe and the Paris water works at Passy were among the first to be used.

6 Agricultural advances transformed Ireland from a subsistence economy into an efficient supplier of butter and meat for Britain in the 18th century.

7 Urbanization, transport and metallurgical advances gave 18th-century Germany a dynamic economy.

See also 53 (medieval economy); 74 (world trading networks); 90 (Industrial Revolution)

The first half of the 17th century saw a downturn in material conditions in Eurasia so widespread that many historians consider a global climatic change to be the only sufficient explanation. The population growth of the 16th century was sharply reversed amid widespread famine, plague and warfare. Even Europe's exploration of the wider world came to a halt, with the exception of Tasman's voyage to Australia and New Zealand.

All the great empires were shaken, but the greatest casualty of the "crisis of the 17th century" was Ming China, in 1600 still the most powerful in the world. Mongol and Japanese attacks at the end of the 16th century added to taxation and economic pressures, and from the 1620s peasant revolts and military rebellions threatened the dynasty. In 1644 it was swept away by a nomad people from the north, the Manchus, and by 1650 northern and central China were under Manchu control (▷ 69).

Although Shah Jahan extended Mughal territory in mid-century, religious intolerance and political instability grew rapidly in his reign. Safavid Persia had enjoyed a period of prosperity under Shah Abbas I, but after 1629 the Ottomans retook Mesopotamia and the Safavid empire began to decline rapidly. The Ottoman empire itself was shaken by a series of revolts during the reign of Murad IV, and made little progress in wars with Austria and Venice.

Russia fell into renewed chaos during the early 17th century, with civil strife and military intervention by Poland and Sweden. Russian merchants spread through Siberia, creating an empire tyrannized by its own vast size, but the Russian sphere of influence remained open to exploitation by traders from both Europe and Asia.

In Europe, the tensions of the Protestant Reformation had already brought widespread bloodshed to France, Germany and the Netherlands, and several other regions. The outbreak of the Thirty Years War in 1618, however, devastated much of Europe. Contemporaries were horrified at the scale of destruction. The predominance of Spain was ended, and the Holy Roman empire was torn apart (▷ 65). There were few winners on the Protestant side either: the German Protestant states were ruined, and their backers Denmark and Sweden were exhausted by their military efforts.

The only states to emerge strengthened from the war were France (by its victories over its rivals, the Habsburgs) and the United Provinces

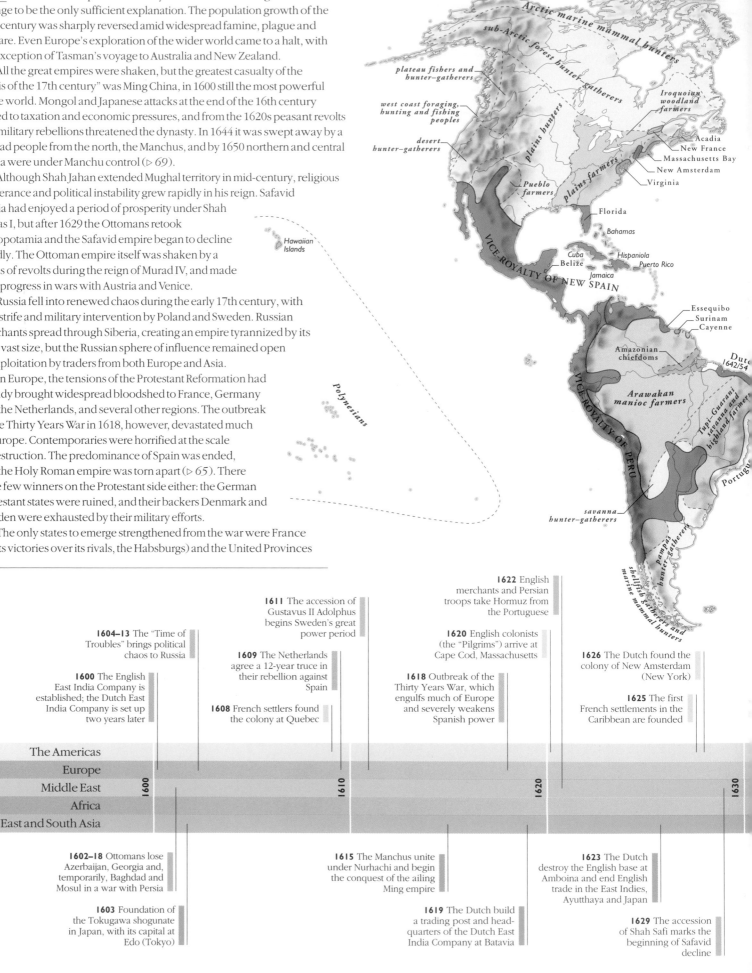

1604–13 The "Time of Troubles" brings political chaos to Russia

1611 The accession of Gustavus II Adolphus begins Sweden's great power period

1622 English merchants and Persian troops take Hormuz from the Portuguese

1600 The English East India Company is established; the Dutch East India Company is set up two years later

1609 The Netherlands agree a 12-year truce in their rebellion against Spain

1620 English colonists (the "Pilgrims") arrive at Cape Cod, Massachusetts

1626 The Dutch found the colony of New Amsterdam (New York)

1608 French settlers found the colony at Quebec

1618 Outbreak of the Thirty Years War, which engulfs much of Europe and severely weakens Spanish power

1625 The first French settlements in the Caribbean are founded

The Americas			
Europe			
Middle East	1600	1610	1620	1630
Africa			
East and South Asia			

1602–18 Ottomans lose Azerbaijan, Georgia and, temporarily, Baghdad and Mosul in a war with Persia

1615 The Manchus unite under Nurhachi and begin the conquest of the ailing Ming empire

1623 The Dutch destroy the English base at Amboina and end English trade in the East Indies, Ayutthaya and Japan

1603 Foundation of the Tokugawa shogunate in Japan, with its capital at Edo (Tokyo)

1619 The Dutch build a trading post and head-quarters of the Dutch East India Company at Batavia

1629 The accession of Shah Safi marks the beginning of Safavid decline

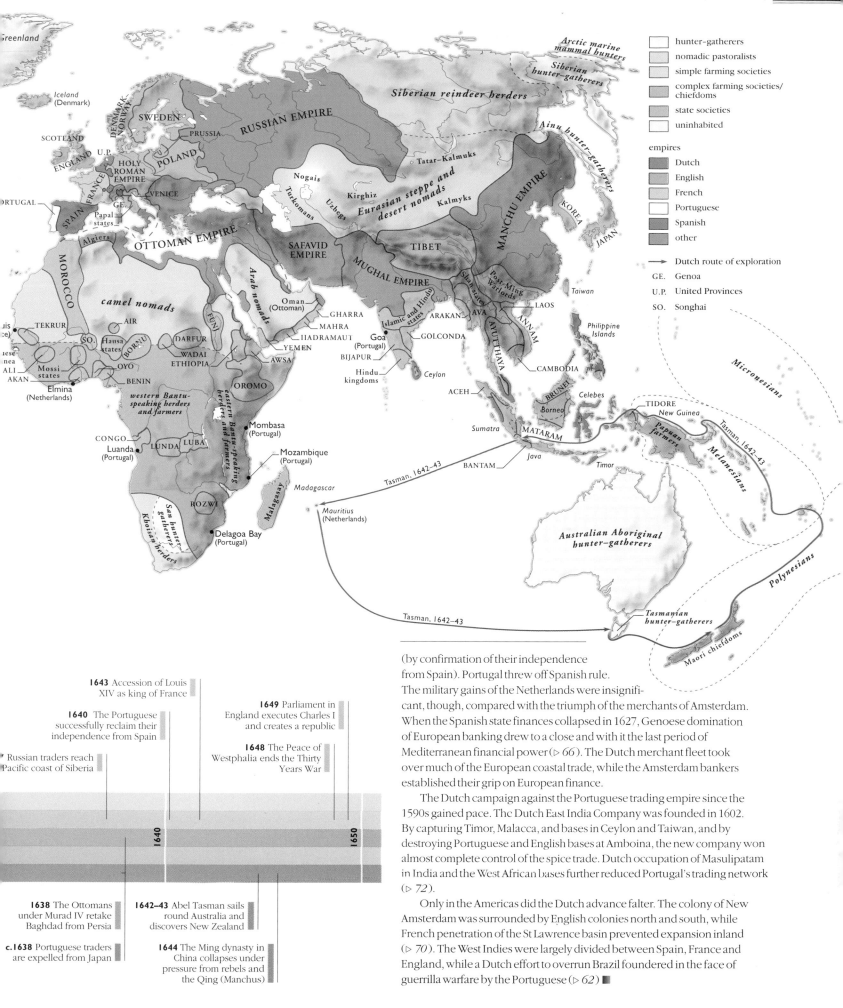

1643 Accession of Louis XIV as king of France

1640 The Portuguese successfully reclaim their independence from Spain

Russian traders reach Pacific coast of Siberia

1649 Parliament in England executes Charles I and creates a republic

1648 The Peace of Westphalia ends the Thirty Years War

1640

1650

1638 The Ottomans under Murad IV retake Baghdad from Persia

c.1638 Portuguese traders are expelled from Japan

1642–43 Abel Tasman sails round Australia and discovers New Zealand

1644 The Ming dynasty in China collapses under pressure from rebels and the Qing (Manchus)

(by confirmation of their independence from Spain). Portugal threw off Spanish rule. The military gains of the Netherlands were insignificant, though, compared with the triumph of the merchants of Amsterdam. When the Spanish state finances collapsed in 1627, Genoese domination of European banking drew to a close and with it the last period of Mediterranean financial power (▷ 66). The Dutch merchant fleet took over much of the European coastal trade, while the Amsterdam bankers established their grip on European finance.

The Dutch campaign against the Portuguese trading empire since the 1590s gained pace. The Dutch East India Company was founded in 1602. By capturing Timor, Malacca, and bases in Ceylon and Taiwan, and by destroying Portuguese and English bases at Amboina, the new company won almost complete control of the spice trade. Dutch occupation of Masulipatam in India and the West African bases further reduced Portugal's trading network (▷ 72).

Only in the Americas did the Dutch advance falter. The colony of New Amsterdam was surrounded by English colonies north and south, while French penetration of the St Lawrence basin prevented expansion inland (▷ 70). The West Indies were largely divided between Spain, France and England, while a Dutch effort to overrun Brazil foundered in the face of guerrilla warfare by the Portuguese (▷ 62) ▪

The Thirty Years War concluded the conflicts that had threatened Europe since the Reformation and brought a revulsion against religious and social extremism. Only in Britain, where Cromwell's regime faced mounting discontent until it collapsed in 1660, did the radical opponents of the existing social order achieve power. Instead there was a general extension of royal control over the affairs of the state, and the doctrine of the absolute power of the monarch emerged. The long struggle between kings and territorial magnates was at last resolved, nowhere more so than in France, Europe's most populous and most influential state. Local administration was put in the hands of officials while aristocrats were required to dance attendance on the king at his court, and representative institutions were stripped of the power to criticize the government.

The seven decades after 1648 saw Louis XIV systematically pursue his ambition of supplanting Habsburg Spain as Europe's dominant power. The Netherlands, formerly banker and mainstay of the anti-Habsburg cause, allied itself with Spain against the growing threat of France and England. Under Cromwell and the later Stuart kings, England took a pro-France, anti-Spain stance, leading it into a series of damaging naval wars with the Netherlands. The dramatic accession of the Dutchman William of Orange to the English throne in 1688–89 reversed this pattern and Anglo-French enmity again became a feature of European history. Austria, once a junior partner in Habsburg Europe, emerged as a power while Spanish might waned. Sweden, France's partner against the Habsburgs in the 1630s and 40s, suffered a defeat at Fehrbellin while supporting Louis XIV against the Netherlands, and thereafter shrank from direct involvement in western Europe. In Italy, Savoy eclipsed Habsburg Milan, while the Spanish possessions in the south survived the French-supported revolts of the 1640s and

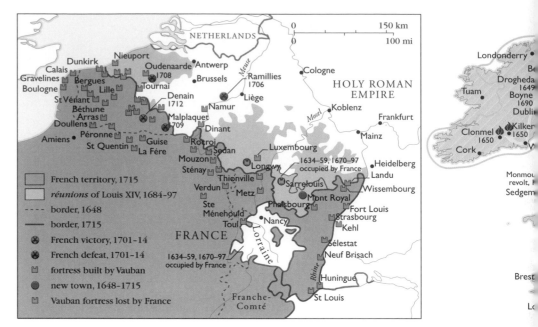

passed to Austrian control after 1713 as Spain's European territories were shared out between the new Bourbon king of Spain, Philip V, and the Austrian Habsburgs.

Louis' military aggressiveness raised a coalition of hostile powers against him. He achieved much in modernizing the French state, but failed to control and centralize the economy, ultimately ensuring social upheaval and economic collapse for his successors. Furthermore his revocation of the Edict of Nantes led to the flight of 200,000 Huguenots and ended any hope of again enlisting the Protestant German states against the Habsburgs.

Louis relied for most of his reign on a small group of competent ministers: Colbert (responsible for

economic and financial policy, and building up the armed forces), Louvois (minister of war), Vauban (an engineer whose fortresses secured the northern and eastern frontiers for the first time since the Roman era), and a group of exceptional generals (Turenne, Condé, Luxembourg and Villars). France fought four major wars in his reign, making substantial territorial gains and dominating Europe's seas for thirty years. The widespread imitation of Louis' palace at Versailles throughout Europe in the 18th century is a testament to the influence of France during his reign.

In Britain, the accession of William of Orange had other effects than the realignment of foreign policy. In 1714 the equally Protestant George I, Elector of Hanover, came to the British throne, keeping the Catholics from power and involving

TIMELINE

France and Spain

1650	1675	1700
1643 Louis accedes to the French throne aged five; Mazarin runs the government	**1672** Louis attacks the Netherlands (except Holland), and occupies most by 1678	**1701** Outbreak of the War of the Spanish Succession after death of Charles II of Spain
1648 The Fronde, a noble and parliamentary revolt, causes widespread disorder	**1681** France annexes Strasbourg	**1710** Madrid is briefly occupied by the anti-Bourbon alliance
1661 Louis XIV's personal rule begins	**1685** Revocation of the Edict of Nantes ends Huguenot toleration in France	**1713** The Treaty of Utrecht divides Spanish territories between Philip V of Bourbon and the Austrian Habsburgs
1667–68 French War of Devolution against the Spanish Netherlands	**1688–97** War of the League of Augsburg: Sweden, Spain, the Palatinate, Bavaria and Saxony oppose France	

Rest of Europe

1650	1675	1700
1649 Execution of Charles I of England and establishment of the Commonwealth	**1675** The Swedes, allies of Louis, are defeated by Brandenburg at Fehrbellin	**1699** Treaty of Karlowitz cedes most of Hungary to Austria
1651 England's Navigation Act leads to the 1st Anglo-Dutch war (1652–54); 2nd war 1665–67; 3rd war 1672–74)	**1683** The Ottoman siege of Vienna is defeated	**1707** Act of Union unites Scotland and England as Great Britain
1660 Restoration of the English monarchy under Charles II	**1688** In England's Glorious Revolution, Stuart King James II is replaced by William III of Orange and Queen Mary	**1714** The Elector of Hanover becomes King George I of Britain
1665 Great Plague in London, followed by the Great Fire in 1666	**1688** Death of Frederick William, "Great Elector" of Brandenburg since 1640	

Map labels

Christiania
Drottningholm
Stockholm
Vänern
Gotland
Vättern
SWEDEN
Revel
Estonia
Livonia
Lake Peipus
Riga
Courland
Memel
Königsberg
Danzig
Thorn
Bialystok
Poznan
POLAND
Lazienki
Lublin
Krakow
Galicia

DENMARK–NORWAY
North Sea
Baltic Sea
Copenhagen
West Pomerania
Bremen-Verden until 1714
Brandenburg
PRUSSIA
Fehrbellin 1675
Berlin (Charlottenburg)
Potsdam (Sans Souci)
Elbe
Oder
Vistula

Aberdeen
Glasgow
Edinburgh
Dunbar 1650
Jacobite revolt, 1715 1650-51
York
GREAT BRITAIN
49-50
Worcester 1651
Norwich
Woodstock (Blenheim)
London
mpton Court
rixham
La Hogue 1692

NETHERLANDS
Amsterdam
Texel 1652
Southwold Bay 1672
Utrecht
Het Loo
Bremen
Wilhelmshöhe
Hanover after 1714
Münster
HOLY ROMAN EMPIRE
Leipzig
Saxony
Dresden
Prague
Bohemia
Moravia
Schleissheim

Medway 1667
Dunes 1658
Dunkirk
Beloeil
Fleurus 1690
1667, 1673-74, 1684, 1690
Luxembourg
Fronde, 1648-53 1683-84
Paris (Versailles)
Lorraine
Rouen
Koblenz
Mainz
Mannheim
Schwetzingen
Karlsruhe
Stuttgart
Bonn
Brühl (Poppelsdorf)
Frankfurt
Bayreuth (L'Ermitage)
Alsace
Blenheim 1704
Munich (Nymphenburg)
Austria
Vienna 1683
Styria
Salzburg
Carinthia

Orléans
Tours
antes
Bourges
FRANCE
Limoges
Charolais
1667 1674
SWISS CONFEDERATION
Franche-Comté
Tyrol
Carniola
Venice
Luzzara 1702
Carpi 1701
VENICE
Ravenna
Budapest
Buda 1686
TRANSYLVANIA
HUNGARY
Karlowitz
Mohács 1687
Zenta 1697
Banat of Temesvar
Slankamen 1691
Belgrade
Bosnia
Serbia
Rakoczy revolt, 1702-11
Nish 1689

Bordeaux
Camisards, 1702-07
al du Midi, 1664-84
1674, 1684, 1694, 1697
Toulouse
Avignon
Nice
Marseille
Toulon
Lyon
Geneva
Turin 1706
SAVOY-PIEDMONT
Milan
Parma (Colorno)
Genoa
MODENA
Corsica to Genoa
STATO DEI PRESIDII
Rome
TUSCANY
PAPAL STATES
OTTOMAN EMPIRE
MONTENEGRO
Ragusa
Cattaro
Rhône

Minorca 1713 to Britain
Balearic Islands
Barcelona
Catalonia
goza
ncia
Sardinia
SARDINIA
Cagliari
Naples (Caserta)
NAPLES
BENEVENTO
Mediterranean Sea
Ionian Islands to Venice
Messina
SICILY
Sicily
MALTA
Crete to Venice 1669 to Ottoman empire

Legend

- British territory, 1648
- French territory, 1648
- Austrian Habsburg territory, 1648
- Spanish Habsburg territory, 1648
- Russian territory, 1648
- Savoy-Piedmont territory, 1648
- Ottoman territory, 1648
- Venetian territory, 1648
- British territorial gains by 1715
- French territorial gains by 1715
- Austrian Habsburg territorial gains by 1715
- Spanish Bourbon territory, 1715
- Savoy-Piedmont territorial gains by 1720
- Venetian territorial gains by 1715
- borders, 1715
- French and Bourbon victory
- French and Bourbon defeat
- Ottoman victory
- Ottoman siege
- town sacked
- revolt
- fortress built by Vauban
- French naval base
- palace modeled on Versailles built in 18th century
- French strategic offensive, 1648-97
- Spanish Habsburg invasion of Portugal, 1657-68
- Ottoman campaign
- relief of Vienna, 1683
- Marlborough's campaign, 1704
- major Habsburg strategic route
- state generally in alliance with Louis XVI
- state generally opposed to Louis XVI
- campaign of Oliver Cromwell, 1649-51
- area granted to veterans of Cromwell's army, 1651
- advance of William of Orange, 1688

0   400 km
0   300 mi

Britain deeply in European politics for the remainder of the century. The deposed Stuart royal family became a focus of political discontent for several decades, with the threat of a counter-coup first manifested in the Earl of Mar's revolt in 1715.

After a series of reforms under Kara Mustafa, the Ottomans advanced a huge army against Vienna in 1683, but the city was relieved by a German and Polish army. Austrian Habsburg forces swiftly reconquered Hungary before Turkish resistance stiffened.

The War of the Spanish Succession (1701–14), fought on the death of the last Habsburg king of Spain, exemplified the changes that had taken place since 1648. Once Europe's predominant power, Spain was now little more than a battleground for French, Austrian, British and Portuguese armies,

while Britain, Holland and the Austrian Habsburgs lined up against the house of Bourbon, who claimed the throne with Louis' backing. The Bourbons ultimately succeeded despite several major French defeats, confirming the power-base Louis had built.

1 Cromwell's alliance with France against Spain allowed England to capture Dunkirk (1658); Charles II kept the alliance but sold the port to Louis (1662).

2 The Duchy of Hanover and Great Britain were temporarily united in 1714, when dynastic links allowed George of Hanover to succeed Queen Anne.

3 In 1656 English admiral Robert Blake captured a Spanish bullion fleet off Cadiz, a feat achieved before only by Dutchman Piet Hein in the Caribbean (1628).

4 The Netherlands were saved from occupation at the hands of Louis, Turenne and Condé (1672) by William of Orange, who flooded much of the country.

5 In 1704 an anti-Bourbon army led by Marlborough and Eugene of Savoy succeeded in knocking France's ally Bavaria out of the War of the Spanish Succession.

6 Louis XIV's naval base at Toulon played a major role in French naval campaigns against the Habsburgs.

7 The War of the Spanish Succession was most bitter in Spain itself; pro-Bourbon Castile prevailed against pro-Habsburg Catalonia.

See also 65 (Thirty Years War); 66 (European economic development)

The Manchus originated as one of the Jürchen tribes – themselves part of a larger group of Tungusic (Siberian) peoples – from the area to the north of the Korean peninsula adjoining the Han Chinese enclave of Liaodong. They began to emerge as a political force under the leadership of Nurhachi (r.1586–1626). Nurhachi imposed a Mongol-style military administration on his people in 1615, and took the title Jin Khan the following year to indicate continuity with the Jürchen Jin (or Ruzhen) dynasty that had ruled northern China in the 12th century.

In the 1620s and 1630s, the peoples united by Nurhachi profited from Ming weakness to establish their control over the Mongol lands just north of the Wall, the Liaodong basin and the Ming vassal state of Korea. Although Nurhachi died in battle, his son Dorgun (r.1628–50) gained control of Beijing in 1644 and acted as regent to his nephew who was installed as the first Manchu (Qing) emperor of China, under the name Shunzhi, in the same year. Over the next 15 years, Ming resistance was suppressed, with the far southwestern province of Yunnan the last to fall.

The Manchus adopted a more subtle approach to administrative reform than that of China's previous conquerors, the Mongols. Manchu officials were given senior posts in existing Ming institutions, and military garrisons were set up in the major provincial cities, but new structures were not imposed whole-sale. The Manchus were initially quick to require cultural changes (such as their characteristic shaven head and pigtail), but their numerical inferiority to the Han Chinese meant that, by the 18th century, their culture had become fully assimilated. Their most significant contribution was to inject an unprecedented dynamism and efficiency into Chinese political and military life.

Resistance to Manchu rule was rekindled in 1674. An attempt by the Beijing government to assert its authority over the southern province of Guangdong, which had been allowed considerable autonomy since its subjugation, prompted a popular revolt led by Wu Sangui, governor of Yunnan and Guizhou. Wu, supported by Shang Zhixin of Guangdong and Geng Jingzhong of Fujian (the "Three Feudatories"), was only defeated after five years of campaigning. At the same time, the government was confronted with a rebellion by the Ming-loyalist warlord Zheng Jing, whose father Zheng Cheng-gong (Koxinga) had expelled the Dutch from Taiwan in 1662.

After this, only the uprising of non-Han tribal peoples in Yunnan in 1726–29 disrupted more than

Legend

Manchu homeland, early 17th century

Manchu territorial expansion

to 1644, with date of acquisition

1644–97, with date of acquisition

1697–1783, with date of acquisition

vassal state acquired before 1644, with date

vassal state acquired or confirmed after 1697, with date

area affected by Wu Sangui's rebellion, 1674–81

area held by Ming loyalists, 1662–83

☀ rebellion of non-Han people against Manchu rule

Manchu national capital

■ Manchu provincial capital

— trade route of the Manchu empire

area of extensive coastal trade

silk   major export from Manchu China

rice   major import to Manchu China

➤ migration of Kalmyk Tatars, mid-17th century

migration of Oirat Mongols, late 17th to early 18th centuries

internal migration of Han Chinese, 18th century

═ borders, c.late 18th century

� Great Wall

ᾮ Willow Palisade

⋯⋯ Grand Canal

⎯⎯ modern coastline and drainage where altered

Map labels

Semipalatinsk

Lake Balkhash

Dzungars 1765

Oirat Mongols 1750–57

Ili Protectorate 1755–57

Ili

DZUNGARIA

Issyk Kul

Dzungars

territory ad to Gansu l

4

Urumqi

TIEN SHAN

Turfan

KASHGARIA Aksu 1759

Kashgar   ☀ Muslims 1758–59

gems, silk, tea to Middle East

Yarkand

4

Xinjiang 1724–60

EASTERN TURKESTAN

Khotan

gems, silk, tea to Middle East

LADAKH 1783

Leh

KUNLUN MTS

Xizang 1718–20

TIBET

HIMALAYAS

NEPAL 1792

Lhasa

Tashilumpo

SIKKIM

Darjeeling

BHUTAN 1730

Brahm

Ab

Timeline

	1650	1700	1750
Northern China	1643–46 The Amur region is explored by Russian pioneers	1689 Treaty of Nerchinsk: Russians exchange the Amur region for trade with China	1727 The Kyakhta treaty fixes the Chinese–Russian frontier
	1645–59 Manchu forces advance from the north, completing the conquest of China proper	1690 Imperial forces defend Khalka against Dzungars	1755 A revolt in Dzungaria leads to Chinese conquest
		1696 Dzungar forces under Galdan are crushed at Ulan Bator	1758–59 Kashgaria comes under Chinese control after a Muslim revolt
Southern China	1653 The pirate leader Zheng Cheng-gong takes Xiamen	1717–18 Mongol forces attack Manchu puppet regime in Tibet and destroy a large Chinese army	1765–69 Inconclusive Chinese invasions of (Mian) Burma lead to nominal Burmese acceptance of Manchu suzerainty
	1661–62 Zheng Cheng-gong captures Fort Zeelandia on Taiwan from the Dutch	1720 Chinese expeditions from Gansu and Sichuan restore a popularly acceptable Dalai Lama and garrison Tibet	
	1674–81 Imperial viceroy Wu Sangui rebels in south		1747–79 Extensive Chinese military campaigns pacify the Tibetan border region
	1675 Zheng Jing's forces again attack Fujian province		1751 Chinese invade Tibet, establishing control over the succession of the Dalai Lama
	1676 Guangzhou falls to rebel forces		
	1683 Imperial forces overrun Taiwan		
	1650	1700	1750

1 The name "Manchu" is thought to derive from Manjusri, a Buddhist *bodhisattva* recognized in Mongolia from 1579; the term was not used until 1652.

2 The Willow Palisade around the Liaodong region was retained after the Manchu conquest of China as a barrier to Han Chinese settlement in Manchuria.

3 The province of Gansu was created in 1715; the large area of former Mongol territory added to the province in 1759 was directly administered by the imperial bureaucracy in Beijing.

4 The Ili (Dzungaria) and Xinjiang regions remained under military control throughout the Manchu period.

5 Manchu administrative reforms resulted in the creation of the new provinces of Anhui (1662) and Hunan (1664), as well as Gansu.

6 The Russian fort built at Albazin in 1651 was ceded to China in return for trade concessions that created a large market for Russian furs in Beijing.

7 The vast population growth of China in the 18th century stimulated internal migration to outlying areas; Sichuan and Yunnan provinces experienced extensive Han Chinese immigration.

8 The Manchu conquest of 1683 brought imperial Chinese control to Taiwan for the first time, but the inhospitable eastern side of the island was barely settled by Han Chinese until the late 19th century.

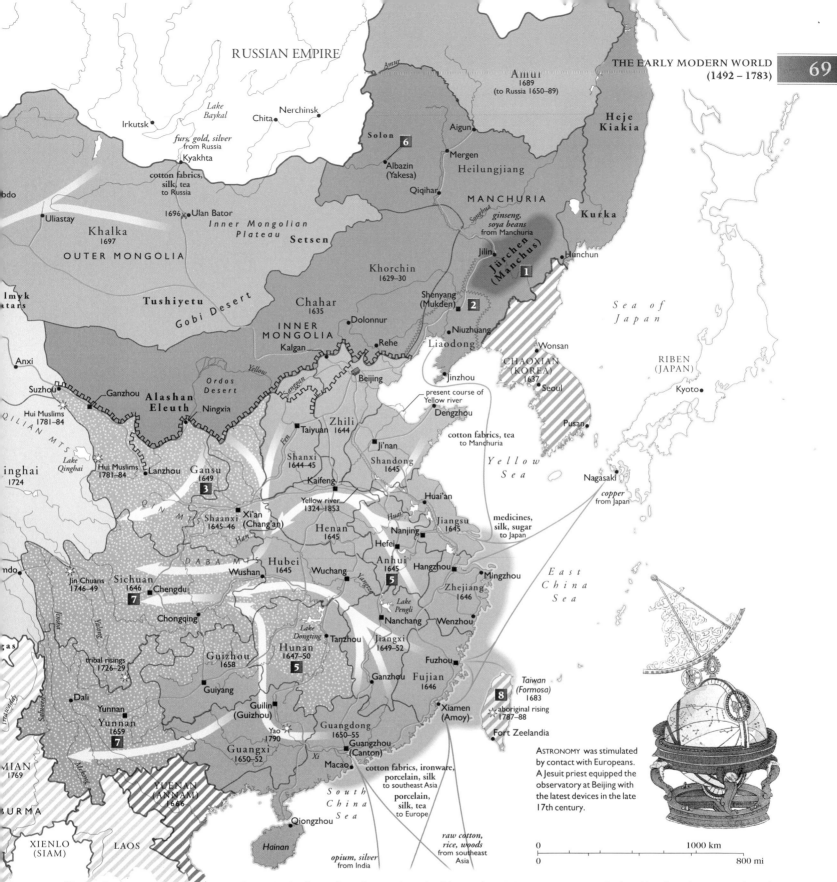

RUSSIAN EMPIRE

Amur
1689
(to Russia 1650–89)

Irkutsk

Lake Baykal

Chita   Nerchinsk

Amur

He je
Kiakia

Solon 6

Aigun

furs, gold, silver
from Russia

Kyakhta

Mergen   **Heilungjiang**

cotton fabrics,
silk, tea
to Russia

Albazin
(Yakesa)

Qiqihar

MANCHURIA

Kurka

Uliastay   1696 × Ulan Bator

Inner Mongolian
Plateau

Setsen

Songhua   *ginseng,*
soya beans
from Manchuria

Jilin

Khalka
1697

OUTER MONGOLIA

Khorchin
1629–30

Jürchen
(Manchus)
1

Hunchun

mlyk
atars

Tushiyetu

Gobi Desert

Chahar
1635

Dolonnur

Shenyang
(Mukden)   2

Niuzhuang

Sea of
Japan

Anxi

Alashan
Eleuth

Ngxia

Yellow

INNER
MONGOLIA

Kalgan

Rehe

Liaodong

Jinzhou

CHAOXIAN
(KOREA)
1637   Seoul   Wonsan

RIBEN
(JAPAN)

Suzhou

Ganzhou

Ordos
Desert

Beijing

present course of
Yellow river

Dengzhou

Pusan

Kyoto

QILIAN MTS

Hui Muslims
1781–84

Lanzhou

Ningxia

Yangzen

Zhili
1644

Taiyuan   1644

Ji'nan

cotton fabrics, tea
to Manchuria

Yellow
Sea

Nagasaki

copper
from Japan

inghai   *Lake*
Qinghai

Hui Muslims
1781–84

Gansu
1649

3

Shanxi
1644–45

Fen

Shandong
1645

Kaifeng

Yellow river
1324–1853

Huai'an

Huai

medicines,
silk, sugar
to Japan

Qinghai
1724

Shaanxi
1645–46

Xi'an
(Chang'an)

Han

Henan
1645

Nanjing

Jiangsu
1645

ndo

QIN MTS

Hefei

DABA MTS

Hubei
1645

Wuchang

Anhui
1645   5

Hangzhou

Mingzhou

East
China
Sea

Jin Chuans
1746–49

Sichuan
1646   7

Wushan

Chengdu

Yangtze

Lake
Pengli

Zhejiang
1646

Wenzhou

Insha

Chongqing

Lake
Dongting

Nanchang

Yalong

tribal risings
1726–29

Guizhou
1658

Hunan
1647–50   5

Tanzhou

Jiangxi
1649–52

Fuzhou

Saween

Dali

Guiyang

Guilin

Xi

Ganzhou

Fujian
1646

Taiwan
(Formosa)
1683

8

Irrawaddy

Yunnan
1659   7

Guizhou

Yao
1790

Guangdong
1650–55

Xiamen
(Amoy)

aboriginal rising
1787–88

Fort Zeelandia

as

Guangxi
1650–52

Xi

Guangzhou
(Canton)

ASTRONOMY was stimulated
by contact with Europeans.
A Jesuit priest equipped the
observatory at Beijing with
the latest devices in the late
17th century.

MIAN
1769

YUENAN
(ANNAM)
1666

Macao

cotton fabrics, ironware,
porcelain, silk
to southeast Asia

porcelain,
silk, tea
to Europe

BURMA

XIENLO
(SIAM)   **LAOS**

Qiongzhou

South
China
Sea

Hainan

opium, silver
from India

raw cotton,
rice, woods
from southeast
Asia

0   1000 km

0   800 mi

---

a century of internal peace and stability for Manchu
China. An aggressive campaign of territorial expansion, however, resulted in the creation of the greatest
Eurasian land empire since the Mongols. Russian
incursions into the Amur region were ended by the
Treaty of Nerchinsk in 1689. The Manchus then embarked on a sustained campaign to end the Mongol
menace. Military expeditions of great ferocity finally
subdued the formidable Dzungars (West Mongols).
By 1783 Manchu colonial administration had been
extended to Tibet and – nominally at least – its vassal
states (Bhutan, Sikkim and Ladakh) and the former
Turkic khanates of eastern Turkestan. (This extension of Chinese authority brought its own problems,

in the form of a widespread revolt of the Muslim Hui
people in 1781–84.) Burma and Laos were reduced
to nominal vassal status, and Manchu troops were
poised to invade Nepal and Annam.

Following the conflicts and plagues that had
afflicted the region during the 17th century, peace
and prosperity caused a demographic explosion
within the Manchu empire. The Chinese population
swelled from 100 million in 1650 to 300 million in
1800. This expansion created growing tensions. A
ban imposed by the Manchus on the settlement of
Han Chinese north of the Wall led to largescale internal migrations in the late 17th and 18th centuries
from the overpopulated Yangtze basin and south-

east to new agricultural lands in the west and southwest. The authorities maintained Chinese external
trade, but were able to restrict foreign merchants to
Guangzhou in the south and Kyakhta in the north.
The export of Chinese luxury goods for silver continued to ensure a strong monetary economy. At the
end of the 18th century, however, Manchu China's
decline was about to begin, with growing government corruption, social unrest and the start of the
European opium trade to China.

See also 63 (Tokugawa Japan);
94 (19th-century China)

The exploration of North America was unlike other achievements of the age of European expansion. Even though many of the cultures and civilizations encountered in other continents had had little recent contact with Europeans, they were not all wholly alien. Moreover, many had dynamic economies willing to supply in bulk products that Europe lacked. Even in Mexico and Peru, whose cultures were entirely new to Europeans, strong centralized states, a relatively dense population and an available fund of gold and silver were familiar elements. Only the Caribbean islands and the vast, empty interior of South America provided a foretaste of what confronted the first explorers of North America. From the first landing of John Cabot in 1497 until the 18th century, North America remained enigmatic; its true scale was not appreciated for a long time, nor did it offer any immediate returns on the investments of explorers and their backers.

Explorers were driven by a number of pervasive myths, and dogged by a sense of disappointment once their lack of substance was revealed. The earliest chanced upon North America while seeking a route to China; Columbus died convinced that he had found an island off the Asian mainland. After Giovanni da Verrazano had explored the length of the Atlantic seaboard and the first colonial ventures had encountered a densely wooded interior and native peoples hostile to exploration inland, the search began for a route around the continent. A possible northern passage remained an English obsession: Hudson, Davis and Baffin endured hardships in the Canadian north to find a northwest sea passage to China. Even James Cook, mapping the Alaskan coast in 1778–79, felt compelled to explore major inlets in search of the elusive seaway.

French exploration of the St Lawrence river was stimulated by the idea of a sea passage through the heart of the continent. Cartier, Champlain, the Jesuit fathers, the de la Vérendryes and generations of fur trappers progressed down the St Lawrence and through the Great Lakes, fueling the myth of a route westward to the Pacific. This myth finally evaporated in the endless expanse of the Great Plains beyond Lake Manitoba. The supreme French achievement, La Salle's descent of the Mississippi in 1682, did reveal a north–south passage, yet his disappointment at finding the Gulf of Mexico, rather than the Pacific, at the mouth of the river was profound.

Initial Spanish exploration of North America from Mexico and the Caribbean under leaders such as de Soto and Coronado was mounted in a spirit of conquest, gold-lust and missionary zeal. Large military expeditions were equipped to build forts, establish missions and despoil the cities that reputedly lay to the north. After epic journeys, survivors of these expeditions returned exhausted and empty-handed. By the early 17th century, Spanish New Mexico was little more than a string of outposts in the *pueblo* villages around Santa Fé, surrounded by desert. Florida, which the Spaniards initially believed to be an island, was explored (and defended) for strategic reasons to protect the bullion fleet route to Europe. Similarly, the Spaniards began to venture up the Californian coast in the 17th century in response to a British and Russian threat.

By the 1650s the Caribbean and, to a lesser extent, the Atlantic seaboard had attracted settlers in number, but it was in the north that the true wealth of the American continent—rich farmland—began to be exploited. From the outset, the Dutch New Netherland colony encouraged settlement by farmers, while the English colonies quickly developed a European-style agricultural economy. The native peoples welcomed settlers for the trade they brought, but they prevented expansion inland; the Appalachian mountains also remained a formidable barrier. It was 180 years after Cabot's landing before English traders and explorers penetrated the basin of the Ohio, after European diseases and the erosion of native cultures had weakened resistance. In the years following the British conquest of French America, the trickle of pioneers across the Appalachians and into the fertile lands of Kentucky and Tennessee became a flood, marking a new era of truly profitable exploration.

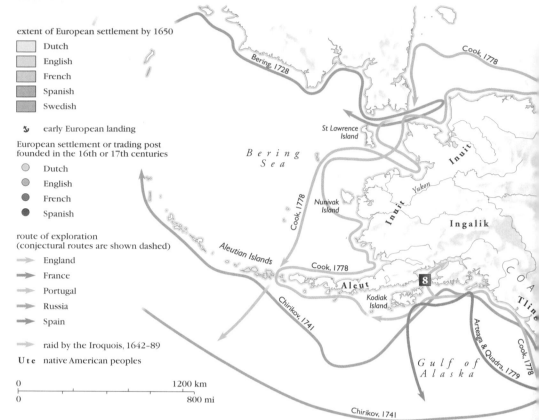

extent of European settlement by 1650
- Dutch
- English
- French
- Spanish
- Swedish

⤸ early European landing

European settlement or trading post founded in the 16th or 17th centuries
- ○ Dutch
- ○ English
- ● French
- ● Spanish

route of exploration
(conjectural routes are shown dashed)
- → England
- → France
- → Portugal
- → Russia
- → Spain

→ raid by the Iroquois, 1642–89

Ute native American peoples

0   1200 km
0   800 mi

TIMELINE

French North America

1524 Giovanni da Verrazano explores the Atlantic coastline of North America for France

1534–41 Voyages of Jacques Cartier lead to the first (unsuccessful) French attempt to settle the St Lawrence

1608 Champlain refounds Québec, then explores the area around Lake Champlain

1613–15 First French fur trading route opens

1630–70 French Jesuits explore the Great Lakes

1681–82 La Salle explores the length of the Mississippi

1731–40 The de la Vérendryes inaugurate the lower Saskatchewan fur trade

1739–40 The Mallet brothers reach Santa Fé from the east

British North America

1497 John Cabot makes the first European landfall of modern times in North America, in Newfoundland

1584–90 Raleigh's Roanoke colony fails

1607 Jamestown colony; first permanent English settlement

1620 The Pilgrim colonists arrive at Cape Cod

1626 The Dutch settle New Amsterdam (later New York)

1671 English explorers are the first Europeans to cross the Appalachians

1678–92 Henry Kelsey travels to western Canada for furs

1685–92 Fur traders reach Great Lakes and Ohio valley

Spanish/West coast

1513 Ponce de Léon begins Spanish exploration of Florida

1540–42 Coronado leads an army northeast from Mexico

1741 Bering and his lieutenant, Chirikov, explore the south coast of Alaska

1778–79 James Cook charts the Pacific coast

1550   1650   1750

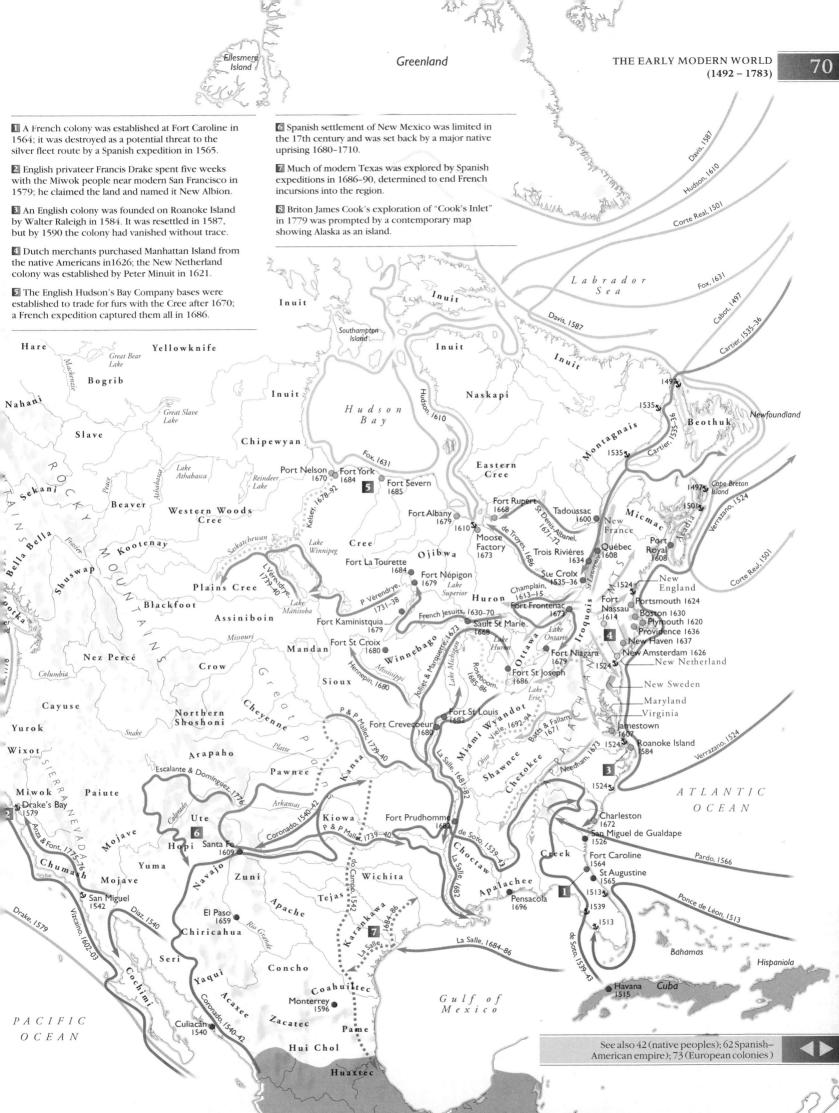

1 A French colony was established at Fort Caroline in 1564; it was destroyed as a potential threat to the silver fleet route by a Spanish expedition in 1565.

2 English privateer Francis Drake spent five weeks with the Miwok people near modern San Francisco in 1579; he claimed the land and named it New Albion.

3 An English colony was founded on Roanoke Island by Walter Raleigh in 1584. It was resettled in 1587, but by 1590 the colony had vanished without trace.

4 Dutch merchants purchased Manhattan Island from the native Americans in 1626; the New Netherland colony was established by Peter Minuit in 1621.

5 The English Hudson's Bay Company bases were established to trade for furs with the Cree after 1670; a French expedition captured them all in 1686.

6 Spanish settlement of New Mexico was limited in the 17th century and was set back by a major native uprising 1680–1710.

7 Much of modern Texas was explored by Spanish expeditions in 1686–90, determined to end French incursions into the region.

8 Briton James Cook's exploration of "Cook's Inlet" in 1779 was prompted by a contemporary map showing Alaska as an island.

See also 42 (native peoples); 62 Spanish–American empire); 73 (European colonies)

The global demographic crisis became less severe after about 1670. The bubonic plague, which had appeared in India in 1616 and Turkey in 1661 spread as far as London by 1665, then declined – one of the last great plagues in Eurasian history. A great famine of 1709 also proved to be Europe's last. In Asia, the population of China reached 100 million by 1650, and began to expand at a rate that would take it to nearly 300 million by 1800.

Dutch domination of European worldwide trade survived three damaging wars with England. France under Louis XIV, though, was Europe's greatest power, its population in 1700 as large as that of the Spanish and Austrian Habsburg lands combined (▷ 68). But Louis XIV failed to break the hold of the Amsterdam bankers on French trade, revealing the enduring financial power of the last great European city-state.

Dutch might was built on control of trade within Europe, but trade with the rest of the world also grew. As silver production in Spanish America fluctuated and Asia's demand for silver was partially assuaged, the Dutch took over the Asian coastal trade. Bills of exchange from Amsterdam underpinned credit transactions worldwide.

The rise of France pursuing a consistently anti-Habsburg policy upset the balance between Austria and Turkey in the Balkans. After a near-disastrous campaign against Crete (1645–69), Ottoman reforms led to a new, though unsuccessful, siege of Vienna (1683). This, however, was followed by a Russian and Austrian onslaught on Ottoman territory, while in Africa the corsair rulers of Algiers confirmed their independence. After taking Azov from the Turks in 1696, Peter the Great of Russia embarked on war with Sweden. His victory at Poltava marked the end of Sweden's dominance of northern Europe and Russia's rise to the status of great power.

The campaigns of Aurangzeb against the Hindu Marathas extended Mughal frontiers into the Deccan, but his empire began to fall apart on his death in 1707. By 1715 the Marathas were the most powerful of the successor states within the empire's nominal borders. The foundation of British trading bases at Bombay and Calcutta, and French at Pondicherry, however, established both Britain and France as future players in Indian affairs.

Manchu control over southern China was finally confirmed. The Ming warlord Zheng Cheng-gong had driven the Dutch from Taiwan in 1661–62,

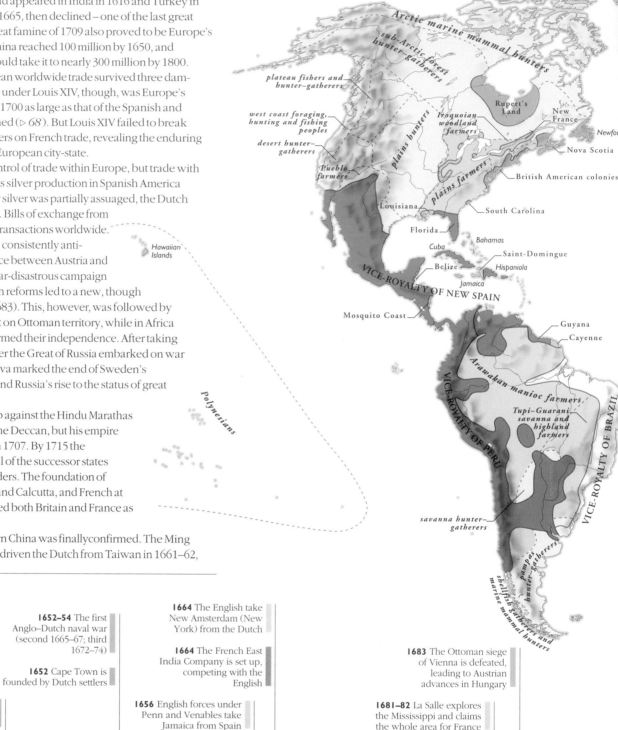

TIMELINE

1652–54 The first Anglo–Dutch naval war (second 1665–67; third 1672–74)

1652 Cape Town is founded by Dutch settlers

1643 Louis XIV succeeds to the French throne (to 1715)

1664 The English take New Amsterdam (New York) from the Dutch

1664 The French East India Company is set up, competing with the English

1656 English forces under Penn and Venables take Jamaica from Spain

1683 The Ottoman siege of Vienna is defeated, leading to Austrian advances in Hungary

1681–82 La Salle explores the Mississippi and claims the whole area for France

The Americas		
Europe		
Middle East		
Africa		
East and South Asia		

1650   1670   1690

1636 The Mughals begin to expand into the Deccan

1655 The Dutch expel the Portuguese from their trading posts in Ceylon

1661 An English East India Company base is set up in Bombay, India

1661–62 Jeng Cheng-gong takes Taiwan

1686 France claims Madagascar after the establishment of Fort Dauphin

1689 The Russians withdraw from the Amur basin following the Treaty of Nerchinsk with China

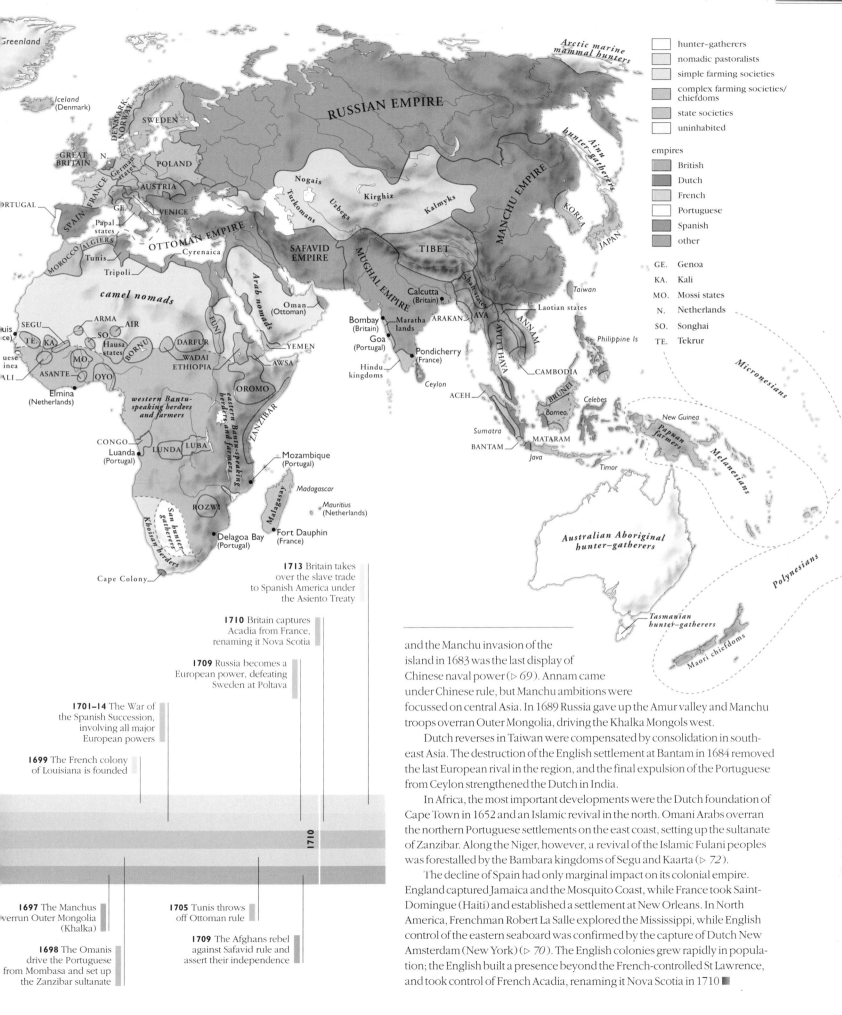

hunter-gatherers
nomadic pastoralists
simple farming societies
complex farming societies/
chiefdoms
state societies
uninhabited

empires
British
Dutch
French
Portuguese
Spanish
other

GE.   Genoa
KA.   Kali
MO. Mossi states
N.   Netherlands
SO.   Songhai
TE.   Tekrur

Greenland

Iceland
(Denmark)

DENMARK-NORWAY

SWEDEN

GREAT
BRITAIN

N.

German
states

POLAND

RUSSIAN EMPIRE

Arctic marine
mammal hunters

hunter-gatherers

Ainu

FRANCE

AUSTRIA

GE.

VENICE

Papal
states

SPAIN

PORTUGAL

ALGIERS

MOROCCO

Tunis

Tripoli

OTTOMAN EMPIRE

Cyrenaica

camel nomads

Nogais

Turkomans

Uzbegs

Kirghiz

Kalmyks

SAFAVID
EMPIRE

MUGHAL EMPIRE

TIBET

MANCHU EMPIRE

KOREA

JAPAN

Taiwan

SEGU

Louis
(France)

TE.

KA.

ARMA

AIR

SO.

Hausa
states

BORNU

DARFUR

WADAI

ETHIOPIA

MO.

ASANTE

OYO

Elmina
(Netherlands)

ALI

uese
inea

Arab nomads

Oman
(Ottoman)

YEMEN

AWSA

OROMO

eastern Bantu-
speaking herders
and farmers

western Bantu-
speaking herders
and farmers

CONGO

Luanda
(Portugal)

LUNDA

LUBA

ZANZIBAR

Mozambique
(Portugal)

Madagascar

Mauritius
(Netherlands)

Malagasy

ROZWI

San hunter-
gatherers

Khoisan
herders

Cape Colony

Delagoa Bay
(Portugal)

Fort Dauphin
(France)

EUNT

Shah-states

Calcutta
(Britain)

Bombay
(Britain)

Maratha
lands

Goa
(Portugal)

Pondicherry
(France)

Hindu
kingdoms

ARAKAN

AVA

ANNAM

AYUTHAYA

Laotian states

CAMBODIA

Ceylon

ACEH

BRUNEI

Celebes

Sumatra

Borneo

Philippine Is

Micronesians

New Guinea

Papuan
farmers

Melanesians

MATARAM

BANTAM

Java

Timor

Australian Aboriginal
hunter-gatherers

Polynesians

Tasmanian
hunter-gatherers

Maori chiefdoms

1713 Britain takes
over the slave trade
to Spanish America under
the Asiento Treaty

1710 Britain captures
Acadia from France,
renaming it Nova Scotia

1709 Russia becomes a
European power, defeating
Sweden at Poltava

1701–14 The War of
the Spanish Succession,
involving all major
European powers

1699 The French colony
of Louisiana is founded

1710

1697 The Manchus
overrun Outer Mongolia
(Khalka)

1698 The Omanis
drive the Portuguese
from Mombasa and set up
the Zanzibar sultanate

1705 Tunis throws
off Ottoman rule

1709 The Afghans rebel
against Safavid rule and
assert their independence

and the Manchu invasion of the
island in 1683 was the last display of
Chinese naval power (▷ 69). Annam came
under Chinese rule, but Manchu ambitions were
focussed on central Asia. In 1689 Russia gave up the Amur valley and Manchu
troops overran Outer Mongolia, driving the Khalka Mongols west.

Dutch reverses in Taiwan were compensated by consolidation in southeast Asia. The destruction of the English settlement at Bantam in 1684 removed
the last European rival in the region, and the final expulsion of the Portuguese
from Ceylon strengthened the Dutch in India.

In Africa, the most important developments were the Dutch foundation of
Cape Town in 1652 and an Islamic revival in the north. Omani Arabs overran
the northern Portuguese settlements on the east coast, setting up the sultanate
of Zanzibar. Along the Niger, however, a revival of the Islamic Fulani peoples
was forestalled by the Bambara kingdoms of Segu and Kaarta (▷ 72).

The decline of Spain had only marginal impact on its colonial empire.
England captured Jamaica and the Mosquito Coast, while France took Saint-
Domingue (Haiti) and established a settlement at New Orleans. In North
America, Frenchman Robert La Salle explored the Mississippi, while English
control of the eastern seaboard was confirmed by the capture of Dutch New
Amsterdam (New York) (▷ 70). The English colonies grew rapidly in popula-
tion; the English built a presence beyond the French-controlled St Lawrence,
and took control of French Acadia, renaming it Nova Scotia in 1710 ■

The arrival of Europeans in sub-Saharan Africa caused dislocations in old patterns of trade and cultural exchange that were unresolved by 1800. Nonetheless, outside influence was nowhere so extensive or systematic that it overwhelmed indigenous culture: several important African states emerged in this period.

The geographical barriers of the oceans and the Sahara, and Africa's abundance of natural resources, had inhibited the growth of an African seafaring or long-distance trading culture. Even coastal trade was minimal until it was developed by the Portuguese and the Dutch. Nevertheless the empires of the Sahel (the southern fringe of the Sahara), notably Songhai, traded gold, ivory and slaves in exchange for salt, glass and other luxuries. Other states flourished and traded with one another along the great river routes, especially those of west Africa.

Portuguese navigators first appeared off west Africa in the mid-15th century; the coastal bases they established drew trade away from the upper Niger. Following a long struggle with the Hausa people to the east, the Songhai empire was overthrown in 1591 by a Moroccan mercenary army at the battle of Tondibi, and a Moroccan *pashalik* (governorship) was established on the Niger. Neither Morocco nor the new African states on the upper Niger – the short-lived Manding empire and the Bambara kingdoms of Segu and Kaarta – could match the power of Songhai at its height.

The early 16th century saw the emergence of other states to the south of the Sahara, including the Mossi around Ouagadougou and, later, the Oyo states of the Niger delta. Asante and Dahomey emerged in the 17th century, first in the interior and later dominating the coast. By the late 18th century both of these were centralized, bureaucratic kingdoms. South of the Equator was the culturally dynamic Congo kingdom, where rivalry with Ndongo allowed the Portuguese to establish a colony in Angola after 1575, which was to become a major base for the transatlantic slave trade. Nevertheless, Ndongo's Queen Njinga (r.1624–63) prevented any further European expansion here. Further inland, the powerful Lunda empire arose in the mid-18th century, and pressed westward.

1 The Funj were pagan nomadic cattle-herders who overran the Islamic state of Nubia in the early 16th century, but then converted to Islam themselves.

2 The Portuguese force sent to support Christian Ethiopia against Ahmad Gran was commanded by Cristoforo da Gama, son of the explorer Vasco.

3 The Songhai empire rose to prominence under Sonni Ali (r.1464–92); its trading towns, notably Timbuktu, were celebrated centers of Islamic culture.

4 The Dutch traded on the Guinea coast in 1595 as part of a campaign against Portuguese trading bases; by 1637 the Portuguese had gone.

5 The Gold Coast–Benin area was the hub of the west African slave trade; in the 18th century 35,000 slaves a year were transported from here.

6 By 1783 the Dutch colony in the Cape region was the largest concentration of Europeans in Africa.

European influence in the states of the southern edge of the Sahara was minimal, and here Islam made its greatest progress. From 1570, Idris Aloma of Kanem-Bornu created the most purely Islamic state in Africa, and built up its power by importing firearms from the Ottomans. Its conversion of the pagan Wadai and Bagirmi states to the east was one of the few genuine territorial advances of Islam during this period. An Islamic revival, though, took place in Senegambia in the late 18th century.

In east Africa, a direct conflict arose between Islam and Christianity, mainly because of the survival of the ancient Christian kingdom of Ethiopia. The conversion of the Funj to Islam was accompanied by a rebellion of Adal, an alliance of Islamic states, against Ethiopian rule in 1527. Ahmed Gran, an Adali *imam*, ravaged Ethiopia for thirteen years before being killed by a Portuguese–Ethiopian force. On the east African coast, Portugal established a string of bases from Delagoa Bay to Socotra to dominate Indian Ocean trade. These were largely successful until the end of the 17th century, when the sultanate of Oman, semi-independent of the Ottoman empire, capitalized on a fierce conflict between the Portuguese and the Dutch by occupying most of the northern bases. Omani and Indian

arms, cotton, fabrics, guns, hardware from Europe

Banu Hassan Arabs
Idjil
Cape Blanc
salt
Ouadane
Ber
Arguin
to Portugal,
1617 to Netherlands,
1678 to France
Chinguetti
Cape Verde Islands
1495 to Portugal
salt
St Louis
1626 to France
WALO
Kaédi
Ou
CAYOR
Gorée
1617 to Netherlands,
1677 to France
BAOL
KAAR
gole
Fort James
1618 to Britain
Gambia
Fulani
M
Cacheu
1460 to Portugal
MANDING
Bamako
Portuguese
Guinea
FULA
N
FUTA JALON
Kan
Bunce Island
Mitomba
SUSU
iror
Brazil
gold
iro
ivory
ko
ATLANTIC OCEAN
Little Cestos
L
Ca
Palm
Dutch & Portuguese traders

West Indies, Central & North America

Brazil, West Indies, Central & North Ameri

trade across the Indian Ocean revived as a result.

The most dramatic impact of the Europeans on Africa was the transatlantic slave trade, which began early in the 16th century. A trade in slaves within Africa had been known long before; but the demand for labor in the plantations in the Americas and the willingness of many African states to deal with Europeans led to a true explosion of the trade in the 17th century. States such as Dahomey used the provision of slaves as part of their own political processes – waging war in their traditional manner to obtain slaves, or enslaving and selling parts of their own populations. The human cost of transporting some ten million people to the Americas is incalculable.

TIMELINE

	1550		1650		1750
Southern Sahara	**1512** Askia Mohammed of Songhai defeats Hausa states	**1570** Idris III Aloma establishes Kanem-Bornu as the greatest power between the Nile and the Niger		**1660** Bambara kingdoms of Kaarta and Segu rise to prominence over Manding empire	
	1529 The Songhai empire dominates the region				
		1591 Moroccan expeditionary force overthrows Songhai			
West Africa	**1517** Regular slave trade instituted from west Africa to the Americas by Spain	**1575** Portuguese settlement of Angola begins at Luanda	**1626** The French set up St Louis (at mouth of Senegal)	**1701** The kingdom of Asante emerges under Osei Tutu	**1747** Dahomey finally submits to Oyo
		1588 The English Guinea Company is founded	**1637** The Dutch capture Elmina from Portugal	**1713** British slave trade to Spanish America begins	**1758–83** Britain and France clash over control of Senegal
		1592 British participation in transatlantic slavery begins		**1724** Dahomey grows as partner of European slavers	
E. & S. Africa	**1508** Portuguese colonization of Mozambique begins	**1555** Portuguese Jesuit missions to Ethiopia instituted	**1626** French settlement of Madagascar begins	**1698** Omanis establish sultanate of Zanzibar	
	1527 Adali chief Ahmed Gran attacks Ethiopia		**1598** Portuguese colonists settle in Mombasa	**1652** Cape Town founded by Dutchman Jan van Riebeck	
	1550		1650		1750

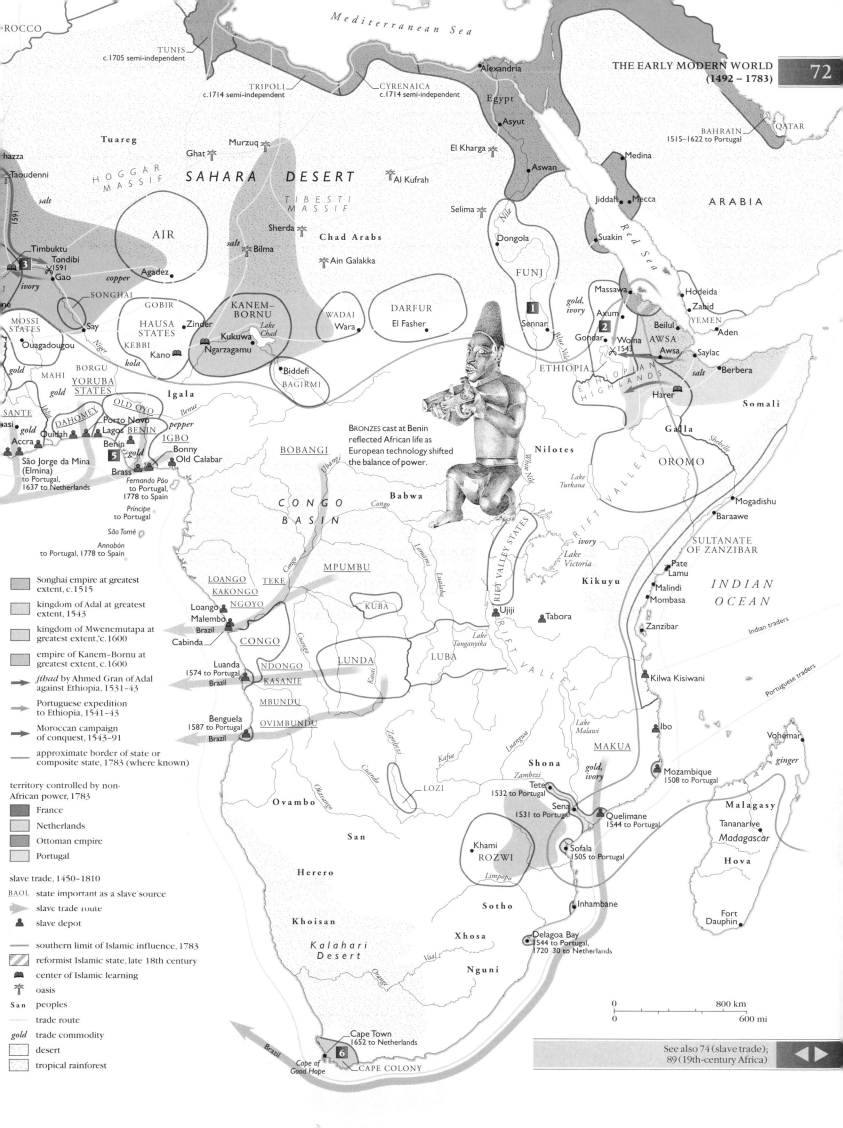

Mediterranean Sea

ROCCO

TUNIS
c.1705 semi-independent

TRIPOLI
c.1714 semi-independent

CYRENAICA
c.1714 semi-independent

Alexandria

Egypt

Asyut

BAHRAIN
1515–1622 to Portugal

QATAR

Tuareg

Murzuq

Ghat

El Kharga

Medina

hazza

Taoudenni

HOGGAR
MASSIF

SAHARA DESERT

TIBESTI
MASSIF

Aswan

ARABIA

salt

AIR

salt
Bilma

Sherda

Chad Arabs

Ain Galakka

Selima

Nile

Jiddah   Mecca

Red Sea

Timbuktu
Tondibi
×1591
Gao

Agadez

copper

SONGHAI

Dongola

FUNJ

Suakin

Hodeida
Zabid
YEMEN

ivory

Say

GOBIR

HAUSA
STATES

Zinder

KANEM-
BORNU

Lake
Chad

WADAI
Wara

DARFUR
El Fasher

Sennar

gold,
ivory

Massawa

Axum

Gondar

2

Woina
×1543

Beilul

AWSA

Aden

Massif

MOSSI
STATES

Ouagadougou

KEBBI

Kukuwa
Ngarzagamu

Kano

1

ETHIOPIA

Awsa

Saylac

Berbera

gold

Niger

kola

BORGU

Biddefi

BAGIRMI

ETHIOPIAN
HIGHLANDS

Harer

salt

MAHI

YORUBA
STATES

Igala

Harer

Somali

gold

SANTE

DAHOMEY

OLD OYO

Porto Novo

BENIN

Benne

pepper

IGBO

Galla

Shebelle

OROMO

asi

Accra

Ouidah

Lagos

Benin

5

gold

Bonny
Old Calabar

São Jorge da Mina
(Elmina)
to Portugal,
1637 to Netherlands

Brass

Fernando Póo
to Portugal,
1778 to Spain

Príncipe
to Portugal

São Tomé

Annobón
to Portugal, 1778 to Spain

BOBANGI

Ubangi

Congo

Babwa

CONGO
BASIN

Nilotes

White Nile

Lake
Turkana

Mogadishu

Baraawe

BRONZES cast at Benin
reflected African life as
European technology shifted
the balance of power.

Lamani

RIFT VALLEY

SULTANATE
OF ZANZIBAR

Pate
Lamu

INDIAN
OCEAN

Songhai empire at greatest
extent, c.1515

kingdom of Adal at greatest
extent, 1543

kingdom of Mwenemutapa at
greatest extent, c.1600

empire of Kanem-Bornu at
greatest extent, c.1600

jihad by Ahmed Gran of Adal
against Ethiopia, 1531–43

Portuguese expedition
to Ethiopia, 1541–43

Moroccan campaign
of conquest, 1543–91

approximate border of state or
composite state, 1783 (where known)

territory controlled by non-
African power, 1783

France

Netherlands

Ottoman empire

Portugal

slave trade, 1450–1810

BAOL   state important as a slave source

slave trade route

slave depot

southern limit of Islamic influence, 1783

reformist Islamic state, late 18th century

center of Islamic learning

oasis

San   peoples

trade route

gold   trade commodity

desert

tropical rainforest

LOANGO

TEKE

KAKONGO

NGOYO

Loango

KUBA

MPUMBU

Malembo

Brazil

Cabinda

CONGO

Luanda
1574 to Portugal

Brazil

NDONGO

KASANJE

LUNDA

Kasai

LUBA

Kwango

MBUNDU

Benguela
1587 to Portugal

OVIMBUNDU

Brazil

Ovambo

San

Herero

Kalahari
Desert

Khoisan

Okavango

Cuando

Zambezi

Kafue

LOZI

Luangwa

Shona

ROZWI

Khami

Limpopo

Sotho

Xhosa

Vaal

Nguni

Orange

Cape Town
1652 to Netherlands

6

Brazil

Cape of
Good Hope

CAPE COLONY

Ujiji

Tabora

Lake
Victoria

Kikuyu

RIFT VALLEY STATES

ivory

Lake
Tanganyika

Malindi
Mombasa

Zanzibar

Kilwa Kisiwani

Lake
Malawi

Ibo

MAKUA

gold,
ivory

Mozambique
1508 to Portugal

Tete
1532 to Portugal

Sena
1531 to Portugal

Quelimane
1544 to Portugal

Sofala
1505 to Portugal

Inhambane

Delagoa Bay
1544 to Portugal,
1720–30 to Netherlands

MALAGASY

Tananarive

Madagascar

HOVA

Fort
Dauphin

ginger

Indian traders

Portuguese traders

Vohémar

0   800 km

0   600 mi

See also 74 (slave trade);
89 (19th-century Africa)

From the 1650s most major European wars were also fought in North America. First the smaller colonies were eliminated. After the Netherlands turned against France, the Dutch in 1655 took New Sweden (Delaware) from Louis XIV's European ally. Likewise, the New Netherland colony (in the Hudson River region) was overrun by English forces during the Anglo-Dutch naval wars (1664).

The main rivalry was between the French and the British. Early exploration had created distinct areas of influence on the St Lawrence and the eastern seaboard respectively. As these grew to include claims in the Mississippi basin, Georgia and the Appalachian foothills, some native peoples were drawn into the hostility between the colonists. Sporadic fighting erupted into the conflict known as King William's War (an extension of the War of the League of Augsburg in Europe), when a French expedition sacked English trading forts on Hudson Bay (1686), and French and Huron raids ravaged New England, despite England's alliance with the Iroquois.

Britain seized the opportunity of Queen Anne's War (the War of the Spanish Succession) to overrun the French territory of Acadia in 1710. Renamed Nova Scotia, the peninsula was confirmed as a British possession (together with Newfoundland) by the Treaty of Utrecht in 1713, while the Ile St Jean and Ile Royale remained French. However, the area remained the scene of regular skirmishes for fifty years. In King George's War – the War of the Austrian Succession – the French naval base at Louisbourg on Ile Royale was sacked (1745), a French naval expedition to reconquer Acadia was destroyed by a storm (1746), and an unsuccessful British and Iroquois attack on New France led to widespread French and Huron raids (1746–48). Hostilities continued after the war in the Ohio basin, where the French tried to halt British expansion westward by destroying the advanced post at Pickawillany.

The decisive phase of Anglo-French conflict came with the French and Indian War (1755–63), the American counterpart of the Seven Years War. The European population of New France and Louisiana was only one-tenth that of the British colonies, and despite strategically sited forts and alliances with the indigenous peoples, the French could no longer offset this imbalance. Though France had achieved naval parity after 1748, the Royal Navy was able to blockade both trade and military reinforcements from France. Initially Britain suffered defeat at Fort Duquesne, failed to take Crown Point (1755), and endured successful French counterattacks (1756) and defeat at Ticonderoga (1758). Thereafter, the war swung in Britain's favor. James Wolfe's victory over the Marquis de Montcalm on the Plains of Abraham near Québec in 1759 secured British supremacy. By 1760 the whole of New France was in British hands. At the same time, British naval forces captured all French possessions in the West Indies except Saint-Domingue. When France coerced Spain to enter the war, the British occupied Florida and Havana. In the Treaty of Paris (1763) Britain's control of the whole of North America east of the Mississippi was confirmed. French territories beyond the Mississippi passed to Spain, which also regained Havana in exchange for Florida.

Contact with Europeans initially brought some benefits to indigenous peoples. In the southwest, the Plains peoples reverted to buffalo-hunting after acquiring Spanish horses, while, in the mid-17th century, the Huron people of the Great Lakes were saved by their military alliance with France from destruction by the Iroquois. However, native Americans experienced a steady loss of their traditional lands. King Philip's War of 1675–76 ended native resistance to European encroachment in the northeast. The Tuscarora and Yamassee peoples were driven out of the Carolinas in 1711 and 1715 respectively; and from 1730 to 1755 the Shawnee and Delaware fled west down the Ohio. Only in the west, where French traders encountered the Sioux nation of the Plains, was European impact minimal.

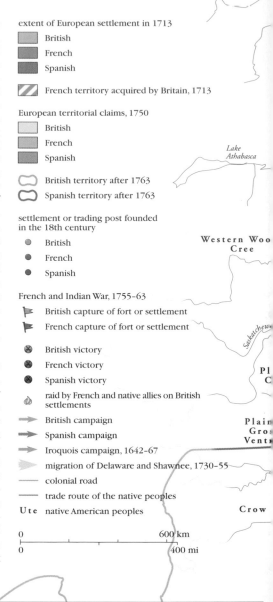

extent of European settlement in 1713
- British
- French
- Spanish

French territory acquired by Britain, 1713

European territorial claims, 1750
- British
- French
- Spanish

- British territory after 1763
- Spanish territory after 1763

settlement or trading post founded in the 18th century
- British
- French
- Spanish

French and Indian War, 1755–63
- British capture of fort or settlement
- French capture of fort or settlement
- British victory
- French victory
- Spanish victory
- raid by French and native allies on British settlements
- British campaign
- Spanish campaign
- Iroquois campaign, 1642–67
- migration of Delaware and Shawnee, 1730–55
- colonial road
- trade route of the native peoples

Ute native American peoples

0   600 km
0   400 mi

Lake Athabasca

Western Woo
Cree

Saskatchewa

Plain
Gros
Vent

Crow

TIMELINE

French–English conflict

1675	1700	1725	1750
	1686–97 King William's War: the Iroquois and English ally against the French and most peoples of Canada and Maine		**1743–48** King George's War; the British capture Louisbourg and the French raid New York
	1704 The French and allies raid widely in Connecticut		**1755** The French and Indian War begins
	1710 British colonial troops take Port Royal and Acadia (renamed Nova Scotia)		**1756** Montcalm captures major British forts
	1711 A British–Iroquois assault on Québec and Montreal fails		**1759** Wolfe defeats Montcalm; French resistance ends
			1763 Treaty of Paris confirms British control of French America and cedes trans-Mississippi areas to Spain

Other colonial history

1651–63 English legislation enforces strict mercantilist control over colonial trade	**1681–82** William Penn's Pennsylvania colony founded	**1711** British settlers suppress Tuscarora in North Carolina	**1733** The British colony of Georgia is chartered
1664 New Amsterdam surrenders to English forces and is renamed New York		**1713** The Treaty of Utrecht confirms the British hold on Nova Scotia and Newfoundland	**1733** British trade with other countries' colonies curbed
	1675–76 Native Americans revolt against the Europeans	**1715** The Yamassee of South Carolina are defeated	**1739–41** Hostilities between Georgia and Spanish Florida
			1749 British naval base is set up at Halifax (Nova Scotia)
			1763 The widespread Native American Pontiac's rebellion overruns many western British forts

| 1675 | 1700 | 1725 | 1750 |

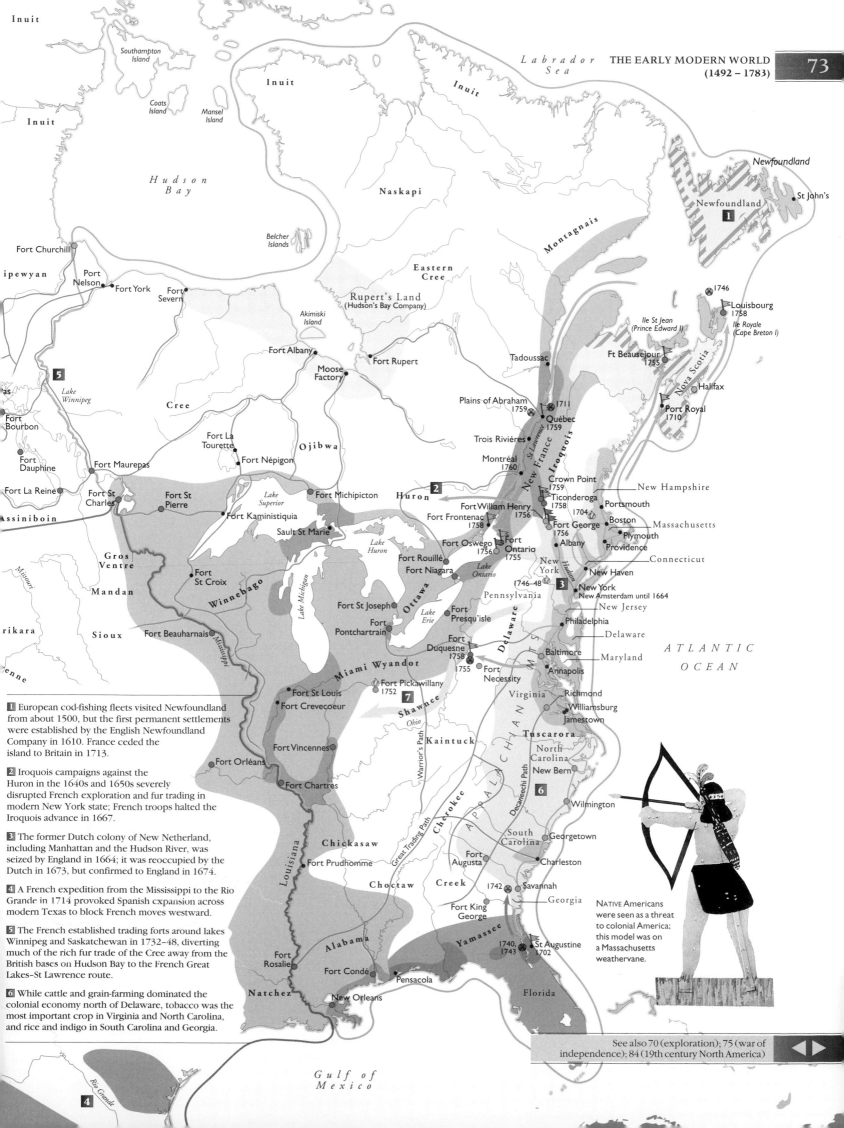

Inuit

Southampton Island

Inuit

Coats Island *Mansel Island*

Inuit

Inuit

Labrador Sea

Newfoundland

Newfoundland **1**

St John's

H u d s o n B a y

Naskapi

Montagnais

⊗ 1746

Louisbourg 1758

1ipewyan

Fort Churchill

Port Nelson

Fort York

Fort Severn

Belcher Islands

Eastern Cree

Rupert's Land
(Hudson's Bay Company)

Akimiski Island

Ile St Jean
(Prince Edward I)

Ile Royale
(Cape Breton I)

Tadoussac

Ft Beausejour 1755

5

Lake Winnipeg

1as

Fort Bourbon

Fort Albany

Moose Factory

Fort Rupert

Plains of Abraham 1759 ⊗

1711 ⊗

Québec 1759

Nova Scotia

Halifax

Port Royal 1710

C r e e

Trois Riviéres

Fort Dauphine

Fort La Reine

Fort La Tourette

Fort Maurepas

Fort Népigon

O j i b w a

Montréal 1760

New France

Iroquois

2

Crown Point 1759

New Hampshire

1ssiniboin

Fort St Charles

Fort St Pierre

Fort Kaministiquia

Fort Michipicton

Lake Superior

H u r o n

Fort William Henry 1756

Ticonderoga 1758

1704

Portsmouth

Boston

Massachusetts

G r o s
V e n t e

Sault St Marie

Fort Frontenac 1758

Fort George 1756

Plymouth

Missouri

Fort St Croix

Lake Huron

Fort Rouillé

Fort Oswego 1756

Fort Ontario 1755

Albany

Providence

Connecticut

M a n d a n

W i n n e b a g o

Lake Michigan

Fort Niagara

Lake Ontario

1746–48 ⚔ **3**

New York
New Amsterdam until 1664

New Haven

1rikara

S i o u x

Fort St Joseph

Fort Beauharnais

Mississippi

O t t a w a

Lake Erie

Fort Presqu'isle

Pennsylvania

New York

New Jersey

Philadelphia

Delaware

1enne

Fort Pontchartrain

Delaware

Baltimore

Maryland

A T L A N T I C
O C E A N

M i a m i W y a n d o t

Fort Duquesne 1758 1755

Fort Necessity

Annapolis

Fort St Louis

Fort Pickawillany 1752

7

S h a w n e e

Richmond

Virginia

Williamsburg

Fort Crevecoeur

Ohio

Jamestown

A P P A L A C H I A N M T S

Fort Vincennes

K a i n t u c k

Warrior's Path

T u s c a r o r a

North Carolina

New Bern

6

Fort Orléans

L o u i s i a n a

Great Trading Path

C h e r o k e e

Decaheechi Path

Wilmington

Fort Chartres

South Carolina

Georgetown

C h i c k a s a w

Fort Prudhomme

Fort Augusta

Charleston

C h o c t a w

C r e e k

1742 ⊗

Savannah

A l a b a m a

Fort King George

Georgia

Fort Rosalie

N a t c h e z

Fort Condé

Y a m a s s e e

1740, 1743 ⊗

St Augustine 1702

Florida

Pensacola

New Orleans

Rio Grande

4

*G u l f o f
M e x i c o*

1 European cod-fishing fleets visited Newfoundland from about 1500, but the first permanent settlements were established by the English Newfoundland Company in 1610. France ceded the island to Britain in 1713.

2 Iroquois campaigns against the Huron in the 1640s and 1650s severely disrupted French exploration and fur trading in modern New York state; French troops halted the Iroquois advance in 1667.

3 The former Dutch colony of New Netherland, including Manhattan and the Hudson River, was seized by England in 1664; it was reoccupied by the Dutch in 1673, but confirmed to England in 1674.

4 A French expedition from the Mississippi to the Rio Grande in 1714 provoked Spanish expansion across modern Texas to block French moves westward.

5 The French established trading forts around lakes Winnipeg and Saskatchewan in 1732–48, diverting much of the rich fur trade of the Cree away from the British bases on Hudson Bay to the French Great Lakes–St Lawrence route.

6 While cattle and grain-farming dominated the colonial economy north of Delaware, tobacco was the most important crop in Virginia and North Carolina, and rice and indigo in South Carolina and Georgia.

NATIVE Americans were seen as a threat to colonial America; this model was on a Massachusetts weathervane.

See also 70 (exploration); 75 (war of independence); 84 (19th century North America)

Trade between the Mediterranean and the east was of very ancient origin. The "Silk Route" linked the Middle East with China from classical times (▷ 49). Ancient Rome, like 16th-century Europe, imported goods from China and paid for them in gold and silver. India developed a money-based economy before the Christian era, despite a lack of local precious metals, by attracting gold through the sale of cheap cotton textiles (▷ 31). Credit facilities for merchants, which made long-distance trade possible, developed at an early date in both China and India, and achieved roughly their modern form in Europe by 1200.

The period 1500–1800, however, brought three new developments in world trade, all of them originating in Europe. First was the establishment of regular routes around Africa from Europe to India and China. These routes, and the permanent bases along them, meant that European traders no longer had to rely on the overland caravan routes and Islamic middlemen.

The second development resulted from the Spanish conquests in the Americas. By the second half of the 16th century, as the gold mines of southern Germany and Hungary were nearing exhaustion, vast shipments of silver from Peru and Mexico began to arrive at Seville. Much of the Spanish–American silver found its way into the general European economy, where it made possible a huge increase in the credit available to European merchants, and helped avert financial collapse during the grim 17th century (▷ 66).

American silver bought European access to the other world markets. Until 1750, only in shipbuilding did European technology enjoy the superiority over its world rivals that was to characterize the 19th century, and European manufactured goods had little allure for Indian or Chinese merchants. Europeans could only obtain the goods they desired – southeast Asian spices, Indian cottons or Chinese silks and porcelain – by paying in gold or silver. The huge quantities of American silver flowing into Europe after about 1550 therefore flowed out again to the east almost as quickly – some via the Ottoman empire (the old trade routes never completely closed), some (after the opening of Siberia) via Russia, and some by sea. Meanwhile large quantities of American silver were reaching the Asian economies from the Americas, via the Philippines. In the hands of the Dutch, and then their British successors, Spanish–American silver became the means of establishing a permanent

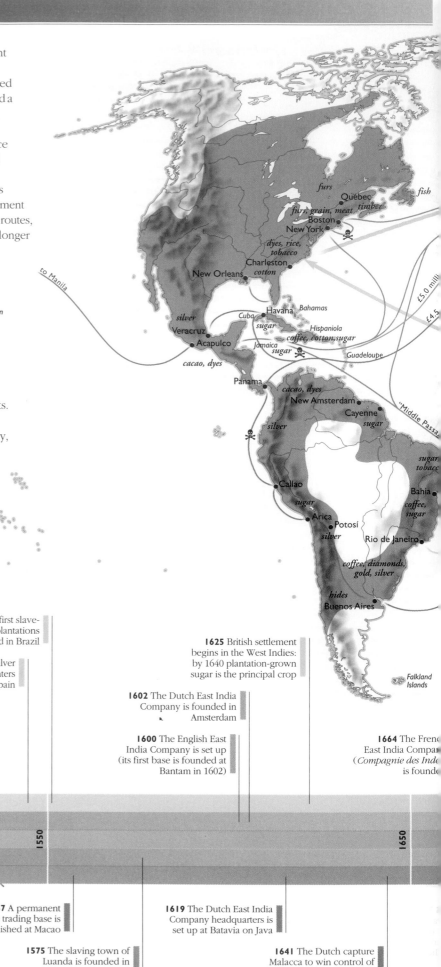

c.1550 The first slave-worked sugar plantations are established in Brazil

1545 The Potosí silver mine in Peru enters production for Spain

1521 Lisbon and Oporto are licensed as monopoly ports for trade with Brazil

1503 The Spanish office of American trade is set up at Seville

1625 British settlement begins in the West Indies: by 1640 plantation-grown sugar is the principal crop

1602 The Dutch East India Company is founded in Amsterdam

1600 The English East India Company is set up (its first base is founded at Bantam in 1602)

1664 The French East India Compan (*Compagnie des Inde* is founde

TIMELINE		1550		1650
The Americas				
Europe				
Middle East				
Africa				
Asia and Australasia				

1498 Vasco da Gama reaches Calicut, initiating European maritime trade links with India

1557 A permanent Portuguese trading base is established at Macao

1619 The Dutch East India Company headquarters is set up at Batavia on Java

1575 The slaving town of Luanda is founded in Portuguese Angola to supply slaves for Brazil

1641 The Dutch capture Malacca to win control of the East Indies trade

1661–62 The Dutch lose Formosa (Taiwan) to the Chinese

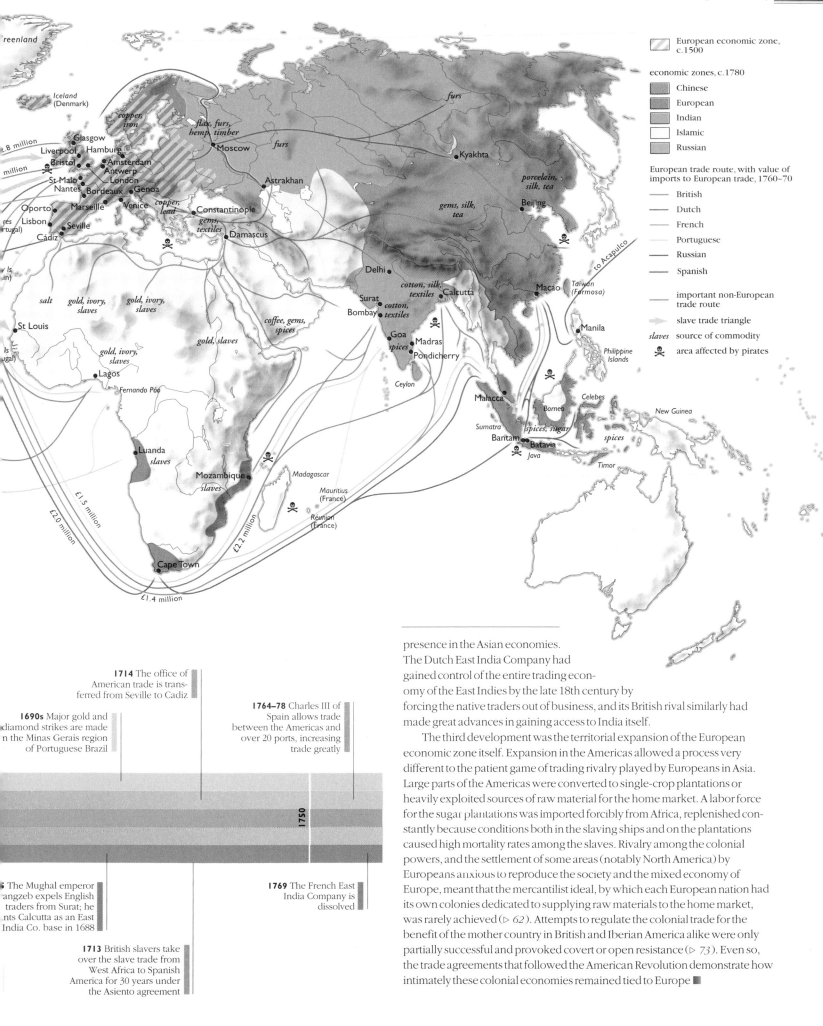

European economic zone,
c.1500

economic zones, c.1780

Chinese

European

Indian

Islamic

Russian

European trade route, with value of
imports to European trade, 1760–70

—— British

—— Dutch

—— French

—— Portuguese

—— Russian

—— Spanish

—— important non-European
    trade route

slave trade triangle

slaves source of commodity

area affected by pirates

Greenland

*Iceland
(Denmark)*

2.8 million

million

Glasgow
Liverpool Hamburg
Bristol Amsterdam
St Malo Antwerp
Nantes London
Bordeaux Genoa
Oporto Marseille Venice
Lisbon
Seville
Cádiz

*copper,
iron*

*flax, furs,
hemp, timber*
Moscow *furs*

furs

Kyakhta

*porcelain,
silk, tea*

Beijing

*copper,
lead* Constantinople
*gems,
textiles* Damascus

*gems, silk,
tea*

to Acapulco

salt *gold, ivory,
slaves* *gold, ivory,
slaves*

St Louis

*gold, ivory,
slaves*

*coffee, gems,
spices*

gold, slaves

Delhi

Surat *cotton, silk,
textiles* Calcutta
Bombay *cotton,
textiles*

Goa Madras
spices Pondicherry

Macao *Taiwan
(Formosa)*

Manila

*Philippine
Islands*

Lagos

Fernando Póo

Ceylon

Malacca *Celebes*

New Guinea

Sumatra *spices, sugar*
Bantam Batavia *spices*
Java

Timor

Luanda
slaves

Mozambique
slaves

Madagascar

*Mauritius
(France)*

*Réunion
(France)*

£1.5 million

£2.0 million

£2.2 million

Cape Town

£1.4 million

presence in the Asian economies.
The Dutch East India Company had
gained control of the entire trading economy of the East Indies by the late 18th century by
forcing the native traders out of business, and its British rival similarly had
made great advances in gaining access to India itself.

The third development was the territorial expansion of the European
economic zone itself. Expansion in the Americas allowed a process very
different to the patient game of trading rivalry played by Europeans in Asia.
Large parts of the Americas were converted to single-crop plantations or
heavily exploited sources of raw material for the home market. A labor force
for the sugar plantations was imported forcibly from Africa, replenished constantly because conditions both in the slaving ships and on the plantations
caused high mortality rates among the slaves. Rivalry among the colonial
powers, and the settlement of some areas (notably North America) by
Europeans anxious to reproduce the society and the mixed economy of
Europe, meant that the mercantilist ideal, by which each European nation had
its own colonies dedicated to supplying raw materials to the home market,
was rarely achieved (▷ 62). Attempts to regulate the colonial trade for the
benefit of the mother country in British and Iberian America alike were only
partially successful and provoked covert or open resistance (▷ 73). Even so,
the trade agreements that followed the American Revolution demonstrate how
intimately these colonial economies remained tied to Europe ■

1714 The office of
American trade is trans-
ferred from Seville to Cadiz

1690s Major gold and
diamond strikes are made
in the Minas Gerais region
of Portuguese Brazil

1764–78 Charles III of
Spain allows trade
between the Americas and
over 20 ports, increasing
trade greatly

1750

The Mughal emperor
angzeb expels English
traders from Surat; he
nts Calcutta as an East
India Co. base in 1688

1769 The French East
India Company is
dissolved

1713 British slavers take
over the slave trade from
West Africa to Spanish
America for 30 years under
the Asiento agreement

The 18th century witnessed a great increase in the colonial population of North America, particularly with the end of the struggle for supremacy between Britain and France in 1763. In just five years between 1769 and 1774, 152 ships from Irish ports alone brought over 44,000 new colonists. By 1774 Europeans in North America numbered two million – over a quarter of Britain's population. This growth altered the nature of the colonies and the allegiances of their inhabitants. In Pennsylvania, a flood of German and Irish Protestant immigrants in the 1720s outnumbered the original English Quakers. German soldiers sent to the colonies by the Hanoverian dynasty ruling Britain further swelled the non-British populace; Scots and Irish settlers, many with Jacobite (anti-Hanoverian) sympathies, also arrived. After 1775 loyalist support was concentrated in those longer-established colonies whose inhabitants could claim English ancestry. Even so, Virginia and the Carolinas, which attracted few non-British immigrants and were developing a distinctive plantation economy based on mass importation of slaves, showed little enthusiasm for the loyalist cause.

The influx of new immigrants, together with a rising birthrate in the colonies, are evidence of a booming economy. Agriculture was by far the most important activity, but it was commerce (particularly that of New England) that caused Britain most concern. Mercantilist theory maintained that colonial possessions should be developed to supply goods or raw materials unavailable in the home country, that these commodities should be paid for in manufactured goods for the colonists, and that the colonies should be discouraged from engaging in any other form of external trade. From the mid-17th century onward, these theories were imposed on the British colonies through a range of legislation, including the 1651 and 1673 Trade and Navigation Acts and the 1663 Staple Act. Yet the introduction of European-style agriculture into North America compromised the first of these conditions, while application of the second caused a currency shortage that rendered useless any attempts to restrict independent colonial trade. By the 18th century, the economy relied on smuggling: that is, trade other than with Britain. Merchants traded in fish, whale oil, horses, beef and timber to the Spanish, Dutch and French Caribbean in exchange for sugar, molasses, rum and silver coin. By the 1750s, they had begun to export dried fish, grain and flour to Europe in their own vessels, competing with British shippers and often bypassing British ports. In response, customs administration was tightened and a succession of laws passed in Britain from 1763 sought to curb this trade, including the 1764 Sugar Act. Along with the imposition of direct taxation in the Stamp Act of 1763, these caused great resentment in America.

At the same time, the costs that had been incurred in the war to gain control of the French colonies proved a severe drain on Britain's finances. In 1763–65 prime minister George Grenville forced the colonies to bear a greater share of this cost by imposing a series of taxes and other obligations. One that caused particular resentment was the Quartering Act of 1765, providing for the quartering of soldiers in colonial public buildings; it was seen as irrelevant once the French threat had dissipated.

Finally, the British attempted to forestall further hostilities over land with the indigenous peoples by setting limits to colonial expansion. The 1763 Proclamation Line defined a theoretical western boundary to the growth of the colonies. This aroused opposition (and was largely disregarded) in America, where the open frontier had already become an essential element in economic growth and the absorption of new immigrants. The 1774 Quebec Act, which provided for the government of former French colonies and extended Quebec's boundaries to the Ohio and Mississippi, was widely seen as a further attempt to restrict colonial freedom.

These issues combined to produce escalating tension and finally open war between colonists and British troops in 1775. Despite early reverses, the British commanders Sir William Howe and his brother Admiral Lord Howe had regained the initiative by the second year of the war, by capitalizing on the strategic mobility that their naval supremacy afforded. Subsequent campaigns confirmed the difficulty of holding large territories against an increasingly hostile population, but the intervention of France ultimately proved decisive. The victory of a French fleet over the Royal Navy off the Chesapeake Capes forced the surrender of a besieged British army at Yorktown. Although Britain saved the the economically vital West Indies by defeating a French invasion fleet in the eastern Caribbean in 1782, the American colonies were lost irretrievably. The Treaty of Paris of 1783 confirmed the independence of the new United States of America.

Lake Winnipeg

Fort Népigon

Fort William

Winnipeg

Fort St Charles

Mississippi

TIMELINE

Military campaigns

1770 The Boston Massacre; Bostonians are killed in fracas with British soldiers

1773 Boston Tea Party; protest against British tea-dumping in America

1775 Fighting erupts near Boston between British and colonial forces; Americans take Montréal but fail to capture Québec

1776 Declaration of Independence; British vacate Boston; Howe captures New York

1777 British advances on the Hudson are halted; Howe occupies Philadelphia

1778 France gives Americans military support; British forces secure Savannah

1779 Spain declares war on Britain and retakes Florida

1780 Charleston falls; Netherlands declares war on Britain

1781 British surrender after the siege at Yorktown

1782 British defeat French at The Saintes in West Indies

1783 The Treaty of Paris confirms US independence

Legislation

1763 Direct taxation is imposed on America

1765 The Stamp Act imposes the first direct taxation on the Brritish colonies

1766 The Declaratory Act affirms Britain's right to legislate in the colonies

1774 Massachusetts Government Act removes many rights; Quebec Act ends the growth of several colonies

1774 The First Continental Congress meets in Philadelphia

1776 Congress adopts the Declaration of Independence

1777 Congress adopts the Articles of Confederation, setting up the United States of America

1770   1780

1 The seizure of the vessel *Liberty* for smuggling at Boston in 1768 provoked a riot, followed by the refusal of the citizens to billet British troops.

2 The First Continental Congress met at Philadelphia on 5 September 1774; in 1776, the Second Congress proclaimed the Declaration of Independence.

3 Bunker Hill, the first engagement of the American revolution, was a British victory. However, as colonial forces inflicted heavy casualties on the British at little cost to themselves, the battle raised American morale.

4 Colonial forces besieged Québec in 1775–76, but withdrew when their commander was killed.

5 New York remained a loyalist stronghold after its capture by Sir William Howe in 1776, replacing Boston as the main British base in North America.

6 George Washington's Continental Army wintered in great hardship at Valley Forge in 1776–77, after its retreat across New Jersey from New York.

7 After British commander Samuel Hood's failure to prevent the French capture of St Kitts in 1782, George Rodney defeated de Grasse off The Saintes islands.

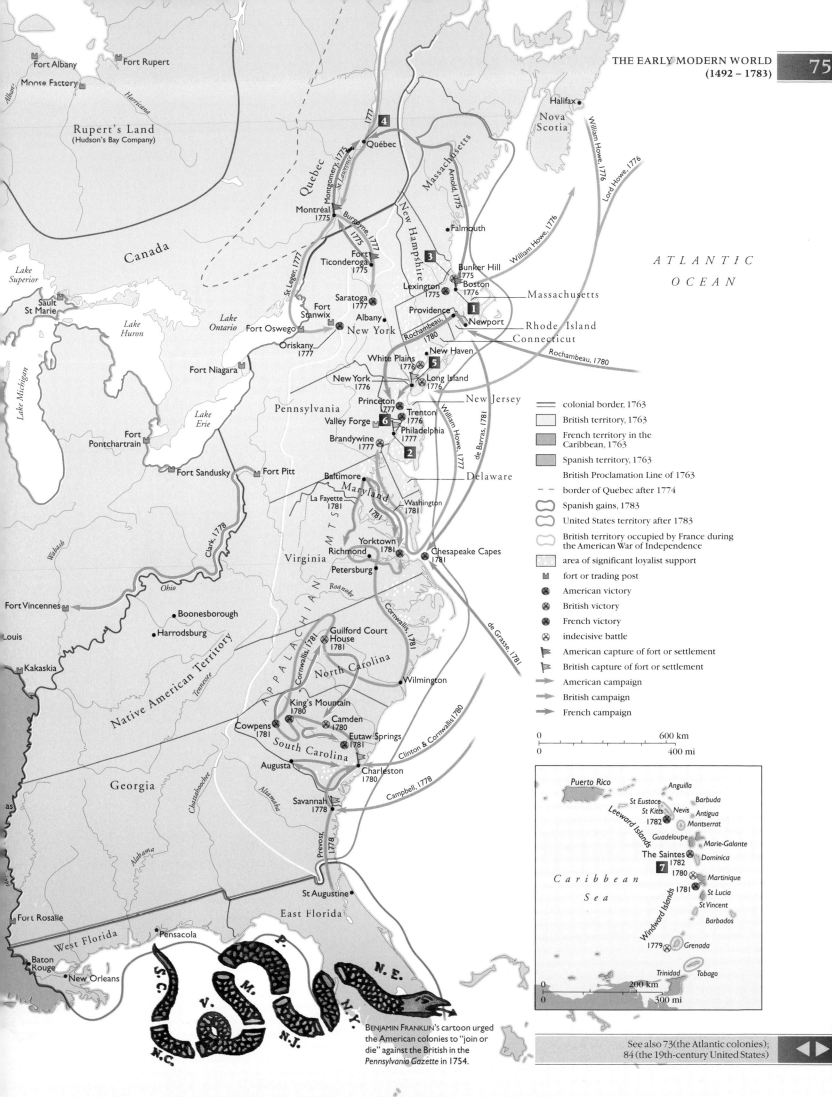

Fort Albany
Fort Rupert
Moose Factory

Halifax

Nova
Scotia

Rupert's Land
(Hudson's Bay Company)

William Howe, 1776

Québec

ATLANTIC
OCEAN

Montgomery, 1775

Montréal
1775

Burgoyne, 1777

Canada

St Leger, 1777

Arnold, 1775

William Howe, 1776

Lord Howe, 1776

Lake
Superior

Sault
St Marie

Lake
Huron

Lake
Ontario

Fort
Ticonderoga
1775

Fort
Stanwix

Saratoga
1777

Albany

Fort Oswego

New York

Oriskany
1777

Fort Niagara

Falmouth

New Hampshire

4

Massachusetts

3

Bunker Hill
1775
Boston
1776

Lexington
1775

Providence

Newport

Rochambeau, 1780

1

Massachusetts

Rhode Island

Connecticut

New Haven

Rochambeau, 1780

Lake
Michigan

Lake
Erie

Fort
Pontchartrain

Fort Sandusky

Fort Pitt

Pennsylvania

White Plains
1776

5

Long Island
1776

New York
1776

Princeton
1777

Trenton
1776

Valley Forge

6

Philadelphia
1777

2

Brandywine
1777

William Howe, 1777

de Barras, 1781

New Jersey

Delaware

colonial border, 1763

British territory, 1763

French territory in the
Caribbean, 1763

Spanish territory, 1763

British Proclamation Line of 1763

border of Quebec after 1774

Spanish gains, 1783

United States territory after 1783

British territory occupied by France during
the American War of Independence

area of significant loyalist support

fort or trading post

American victory

British victory

French victory

indecisive battle

American capture of fort or settlement

British capture of fort or settlement

American campaign

British campaign

French campaign

Baltimore

La Fayette
1781

Maryland

Washington
1781

Clark, 1778

Fort Vincennes

Boonesborough

Harrodsburg

Louis

Kakaskia

Wabash

Ohio

Native American Territory

Tennessee

APPALACHIAN MTS

Yorktown
1781

Richmond

Virginia

Petersburg

Roanoke

Cornwallis, 1781

Chesapeake Capes
1781

de Grasse, 1781

Guilford Court
House
1781

Cornwallis, 1781

North Carolina

Wilmington

King's Mountain
1780

Camden
1780

Cowpens
1781

Eutaw Springs
1781

South Carolina

Augusta

Charleston
1780

Clinton & Cornwallis 1780

Savannah
1778

Campbell, 1778

Georgia

Chattahoochee

Altamaha

Alabama

Prevost, 1778

St Augustine

East Florida

Fort Rosalle

West Florida

Pensacola

Baton
Rouge

New Orleans

as

0   600 km
0   400 mi

Puerto Rico

Anguilla

St Eustace
St Kitts
1782

Nevis
Montserrat

Barbuda

Antigua

Leeward Islands

Guadeloupe

Marie-Galante

The Saintes
1782

7

1780

Dominica

Caribbean

Martinique
1781

St Lucia

St Vincent

Sea

Barbados

Windward Islands

1779

Grenada

Trinidad

Tobago

0   200 km
0   300 mi

BENJAMIN FRANKLIN's cartoon urged
the American colonies to "join or
die" against the British in the
Pennsylvania Gazette in 1754.

S.C.

V.

M.

N.E.

N.Y.

N.J.

N.C.

See also 73(the Atlantic colonies);
84 (the 19th-century United States)

After more than a century of worldwide famine, plague, warfare and hardship, recovery took place in the course of the 18th century. In China, the population rose from 120 million in 1680 to nearly 300 million by 1790. In Europe, perhaps 100 million in 1650 had become 187 million by 1800. Even in the Americas, 13 million inhabitants in 1650 had doubled by 1800. Only in Africa did the overall population of 100 million stay unchanged: here several million were forcibly moved under the slave trade.

It is often said that medical and sanitation advances gave humankind the means to escape the tyranny of plague and high infant mortality. Such advances were indeed made in parts of Europe, but nowhere else. A more general cause may have been climatic, with a gradual rise in the temperature of the planet leading to improved harvests and greater resistance to disease.

Politically, the 18th century brought the struggle between the most dynamic nation-states of western Europe, France and Great Britain, to the world stage. British gains in the Americas were extended during the War of the Austrian Succession (1740–48), but French successes in India and in Europe meant that the Treaty of Aix-la-Chapelle (1748) simply restored the pre-war status quo. In the Seven Years War (1756–63), however, British naval superiority was decisive. James Wolfe's victory at Quebec in 1759 delivered New France to Britain, and all French possessions in the West Indies except Saint-Domingue were taken in 1762. In the same year, British forces captured Havana, heart of the Spanish–American empire, and twelve months later Florida was ceded. In India, the English East India Company, struggling to reverse the French gains of 1748, won a decisive victory at Plassey (1759) over France's ally Siraj ud-Daulah of Bengal. By 1763, France held only Pondicherry in India, and had lost all footholds in North America east of the Mississippi.

Britain's attempts to tighten fiscal control over colonial America and its concern at illicit trade between its American subjects and French, Dutch and Spanish colonies led to war with its largest colonial possession. France, supporting the colonials, sent troops and a fleet to threaten British North America and the economically valuable West Indies. By 1783 Britain had secured the West Indies but lost America (▷ 75).

New powers emerged elsewhere in the world in the 18th century. In Europe, the Prussia of Frederick the Great mounted

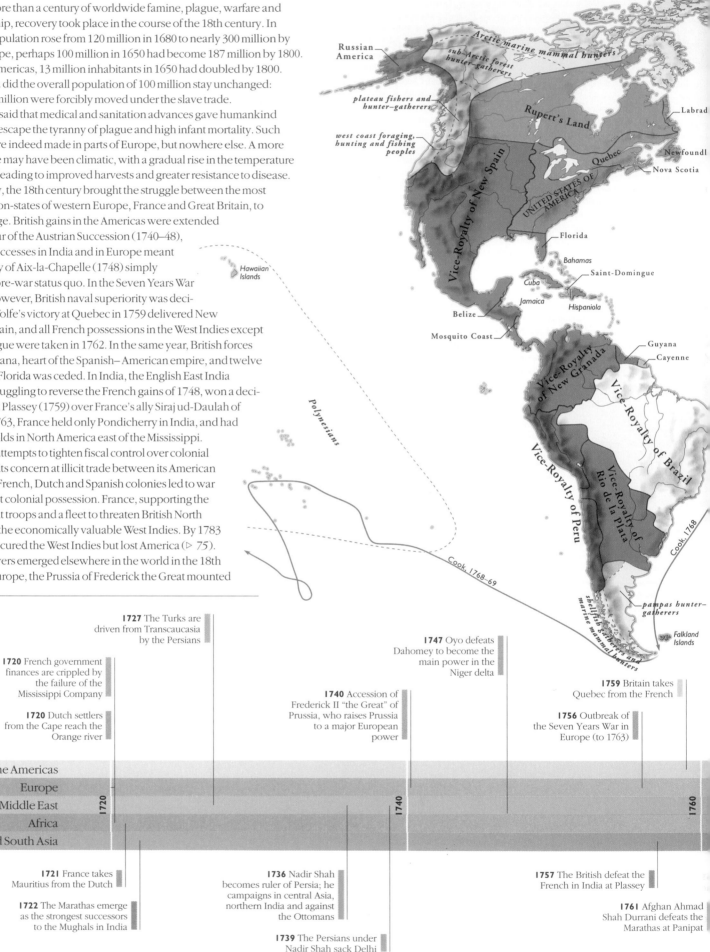

TIMELINE

1727 The Turks are driven from Transcaucasia by the Persians

1720 French government finances are crippled by the failure of the Mississippi Company

1720 Dutch settlers from the Cape reach the Orange river

1747 Oyo defeats Dahomey to become the main power in the Niger delta

1740 Accession of Frederick II "the Great" of Prussia, who raises Prussia to a major European power

1759 Britain takes Quebec from the French

1756 Outbreak of the Seven Years War in Europe (to 1763)

The Americas
Europe
Middle East
Africa
East and South Asia

1720
1740
1760

1721 France takes Mauritius from the Dutch

1722 The Marathas emerge as the strongest successors to the Mughals in India

1736 Nadir Shah becomes ruler of Persia; he campaigns in central Asia, northern India and against the Ottomans

1739 The Persians under Nadir Shah sack Delhi

1757 The British defeat the French in India at Plassey

1761 Afghan Ahmad Shah Durrani defeats the Marathas at Panipat

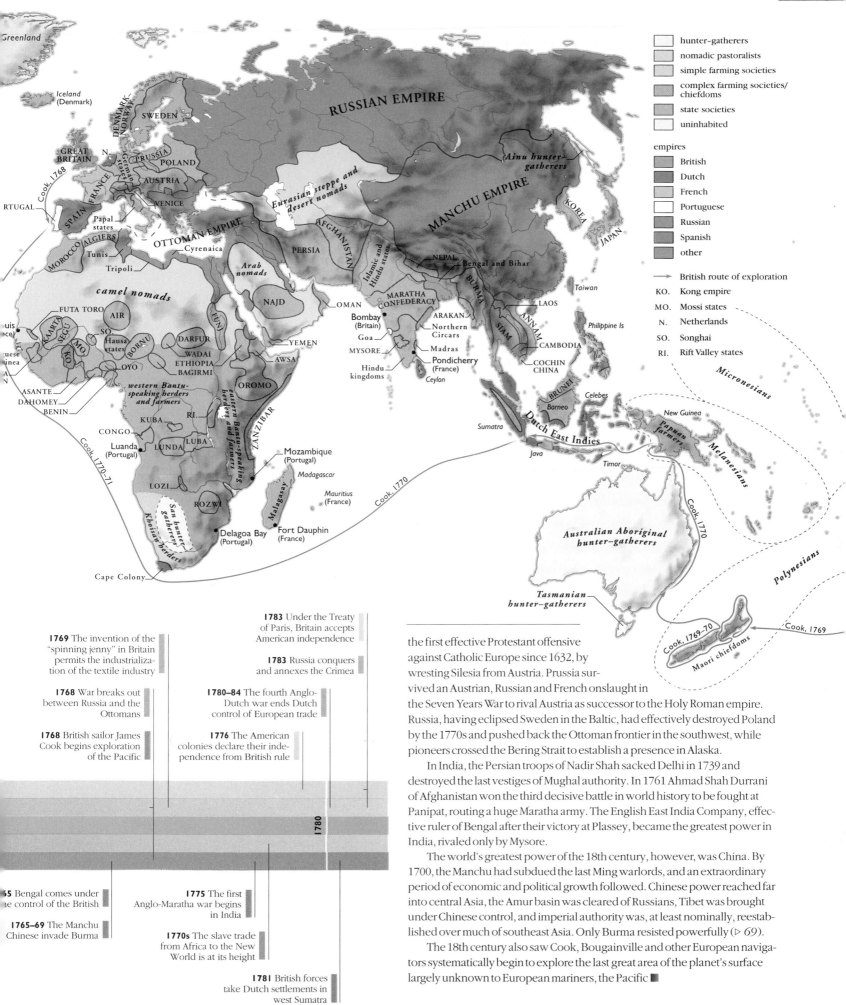

hunter–gatherers
nomadic pastoralists
simple farming societies
complex farming societies/
chiefdoms
state societies
uninhabited

empires
British
Dutch
French
Portuguese
Russian
Spanish
other

→ British route of exploration
KO. Kong empire
MO. Mossi states
N. Netherlands
SO. Songhai
RI. Rift Valley states

1769 The invention of the "spinning jenny" in Britain permits the industrialization of the textile industry

1768 War breaks out between Russia and the Ottomans

1768 British sailor James Cook begins exploration of the Pacific

1783 Under the Treaty of Paris, Britain accepts American independence

1783 Russia conquers and annexes the Crimea

1780–84 The fourth Anglo-Dutch war ends Dutch control of European trade

1776 The American colonies declare their independence from British rule

1780

65 Bengal comes under the control of the British

1765–69 The Manchu Chinese invade Burma

1775 The first Anglo-Maratha war begins in India

1770s The slave trade from Africa to the New World is at its height

1781 British forces take Dutch settlements in west Sumatra

the first effective Protestant offensive against Catholic Europe since 1632, by wresting Silesia from Austria. Prussia survived an Austrian, Russian and French onslaught in the Seven Years War to rival Austria as successor to the Holy Roman empire. Russia, having eclipsed Sweden in the Baltic, had effectively destroyed Poland by the 1770s and pushed back the Ottoman frontier in the southwest, while pioneers crossed the Bering Strait to establish a presence in Alaska.

In India, the Persian troops of Nadir Shah sacked Delhi in 1739 and destroyed the last vestiges of Mughal authority. In 1761 Ahmad Shah Durrani of Afghanistan won the third decisive battle in world history to be fought at Panipat, routing a huge Maratha army. The English East India Company, effective ruler of Bengal after their victory at Plassey, became the greatest power in India, rivaled only by Mysore.

The world's greatest power of the 18th century, however, was China. By 1700, the Manchu had subdued the last Ming warlords, and an extraordinary period of economic and political growth followed. Chinese power reached far into central Asia, the Amur basin was cleared of Russians, Tibet was brought under Chinese control, and imperial authority was, at least nominally, reestablished over much of southeast Asia. Only Burma resisted powerfully (▷ 69).

The 18th century also saw Cook, Bougainville and other European navigators systematically begin to explore the last great area of the planet's surface largely unknown to European mariners, the Pacific ■

Part 5

THE NINETEENTH WORLD

I n 1783 Britain disconsolately accepted the independence of its thirteen colonies in North America. Yet, in the century and a quarter after the emergence of the United States, European powers still dominated the world. Their armies spread their authority, their navies charted the seas and their merchants built a network of trade and investment. A genuinely global economy was the result.

The only part of the world effectively to resist the European powers was North America, but the United States itself was a state ruled by people of European descent, its economy closely linked to and partly financed by Europe, and its culture shaped by European influences. The railroads that effectively made the United States by linking the Atlantic and Pacific coasts owed much to British investment and technology. By 1900, though, the United States had challenged and overtaken much of Europe's economic and technological lead, and was poised to become the most powerful state in the world.

The United States was sustained by migration. Between 1815 and 1901, the United States took over eight million immigrants from the British Isles alone, and many more from Germany, Scandinavia and eastern and southern Europe. European migrants also totally altered the politics, economy and ethnic composition of Australasia and Canada.

Europeans were not the only people to move, but those non-whites who journeyed long distances in pursuit of work – Chinese, Japanese, Indians, Malays as well as Africans – did so only with the consent of the European or North American states. Unlike Europeans who were generally welcomed, despite their poverty, to assist in populating the new lands and building a new society, these non-Europeans were often contract laborers or worse, controlled by strict racial barriers.

THE FRONTIERLANDS of North America drew settlers from Europe.

CENTURY

The age of migrations reflected the potency of the new technologies of the age. Thanks to the steamship, the oceans shrank; long voyages became faster, safer, cheaper, more comfortable. Barbed wire, invented in the United States in 1873, made possible the fencing in of the prairies and thus the establishment of vast ranches on what had been virgin land. Refrigerated shipholds allowed fresh meat grown on these ranches to be shipped to cities on the other side of the globe. Railroads, too, brought foodstuffs and other raw materials quickly and efficiently to the urban centers.

Trade was not restricted to raw materials. The heavy industry, light engineering, chemicals and textile manufacture that now drove Europe's economy also provided products for the rest of the world. European investment capital acted as the engine of this global economy, financing the creation of the infrastructure for the new trade on every continent. The British empire, which encompassed more than a fifth of the Earth's landmass by 1914 (its political and financial influence pervaded much of the rest) was dominant in this flow of capital, though increasingly challenged by its cultural and political offspring, the United States. As a result English became the international language of business across most of the globe.

The spread of European influence was not always peaceful. There was violent resistance, especially in Africa and China. Yet there was frequently also emulation. This was most apparent in Japan, which embarked on an effective process of westernization from the 1870s. Similar choices were made in Egypt, Persia and Siam, all more or less independent states which saw the benefits of adopting western ways.

The formal European empires ensured that their colonies were educated in European ways of government, law and culture as much as in technology and commerce. This cultural imperialism was often conducted with little thought for the indigenous civilizations, and was barely questioned by the Europeans. The *pax Britannica* was maintained across the globe by a combination of British gunboats and diplomats, but the introduction of British education, religion and the political institutions of Westminster was thought to bring undeniable benefits to the "poor benighted heathen". Although advantages undoubtedly accrued, the forcible imposition of western civilization built up resentments that would grow throughout the first half of the twentieth century and explode after 1945.

In the nineteenth century, humanity sought to use advances in knowledge to mould the environment. Science – conducted mainly in Germany, France, Britain and the United States – made massive advances and its power to change the world became undeniable. Scientific breeding and a thorough knowledge of the needs of plants and animals transformed national economies: Malaya, for example, was changed utterly when the British introduced the rubber tree from South America. Science seemed to hold the key to the future, to the creation and use of goods, new sources of power (electricity, turbines, internal-combustion engines) and new materials (alloys, dyes, fertilizers, explosives). Equally revolutionary were the telegraph, telephone and radio, which shrank distance even more than had railroad and steamships: in 1901 Marconi transmitted radio signals across the Atlantic. Two years later the Wright brothers made the world's first heavier-than-air flight, giving the industrial countries access to a new medium that would have great implications, civil and military.

Every such innovation helped dissolve former certainties, and in 1914, when Europe began the conflict that engulfed the continent, the assumptions of the previous century were destroyed. To survive, the powers drew on the resources of their old colonies in ways that changed the relationships between them for ever ■

Enlightenment thinkers of the mid-18th century often emphasized people's right to self-determination through a system of representative government. In this they expressed a hostility to the repressive forces – clerics, aristocrats and absolute monarchs – that still reigned supreme throughout Europe in the 18th century. Fueled by poverty, inflation and food shortages, and inspired by the successful revolution of American colonists against the British, this discontent was soon to erupt.

Uprisings occurred in 1784, when the Patriot party in the Dutch Netherlands tried to democratize government, and in 1787, when citizens of the neighboring territory of the Austrian Netherlands (Belgium) attempted to establish an independent republic. Neither insurrection achieved its goals.

A more widely based protest began against the *ancien régime* (autocratic royal government) in France when Louis XVI tried to raise taxes to avert state bankruptcy. He summoned the Estates-General – a periodic assembly of deputies from the three "Estates" (clergy, nobility, and commoners) – to approve his plans. However, Louis was faced with a political crisis when the Third Estate (made up of the rising middle class) withdrew to found a National Assembly and institute reform. Parisians feared an attack on the Assembly by Louis' forces and, on 14 July 1789, stormed the Bastille fortress, symbol of Bourbon tyranny. The rebellion spread rapidly .

In August 1789 the Assembly abolished the feudal system and issued its *Declaration of the Rights of Man*. That proclaimed freedom of conscience, property and speech, and established the principle that sovereign power resided in the nation rather than the king. After failing to escape from the country in 1791, Louis was compelled to approve a constitution that divested him of most of his power. By this stage, aristocrats who had managed to flee France had persuaded Prussia and the Habsburg

empire (Austria) to intervene on Louis' behalf. Opposition to revolutionary France soon crystallized into the First Coalition of European powers. The ensuing Revolutionary Wars (1792–1802) saw the French repulse an initial invasion and then go on the attack. The king and queen and many of aristocratic supporters were executed, counter-revolutionary risings were suppressed, internecine struggles broke out among the revolutionaries (the "Terror"), and the French tried to export revolution to their hostile neighbors the Netherlands, Spain and Britain (where they fomented rebellion in Ireland).

The First Coalition was broken by a series of French victories in 1794–95, culminating in a

	borders, 1783
	border of Holy Roman empire, 1783
	Austrian Habsburg territory, 1783
	France, 1783
	Brandenburg–Prussia, 1783
	Great Britain & Hanover, 1783
	Ottoman empire, 1783
	Spanish Bourbon territory, 1783
	Russian empire, 1783
	Russian gains by 1795
	Brandenburg–Prussian gains by 1795
	Austrian Habsburg gains by 1797
	French gains by 1800
Roman Republic	state established by Revolutionary France
	extent of the "Great Fear" within France, 1789
	French counter-revolution, 1793
	French campaign, 1796–98
	Russian campaign, 1798–1800
	town bombarded by Russian Black Sea fleet
	Naval mutiny in Great Britain
	major revolt, riot or disorder

THE SANS-CULOTTE, "man without breeches", symbolized the radical republicans of France in 1790.

successful invasion of the Netherlands (ruled by France as the Batavian Republic until 1806). Prussia and Spain sued for peace, leaving Britain and the Habsburg empire isolated. Britain, though, maintained naval supremacy with victories over France, and latter its Dutch and Spanish allies, from 1794–97. In 1798 a Second Coalition was formed.

Napoleon Bonaparte now began to emerge as the greatest of the French commanders through his brilliant campaigns in Italy and Austria. By late 1797, he had forced Austria to cede the Austrian Netherlands to France, in exchange for Venice, in a peace treaty that also created French-ruled states in northern Italy. As a prelude to his planned invasion

TIMELINE

Revolts

1790	1795	1800
1784–87 Revolts occur in Dutch and Austrian Netherlands	**1793** Execution of Louis XVI; a royalist rebellion begins in the Vendée	**1797** Mutinies in the British Royal Navy at Spithead and the Nore
1788 Louis XVI of France summons the Estates-General	**1794** Tadeusz Kosciuszko leads a national rebellion in Poland	**1798** United Irishmen rebel in a vain effort to win independence from Britain
1789 French Revolution begins; the Bastille is stormed		

Revolutionary wars

	1792 The Prussians are checked at Valmy; Austrians are defeated at Jemappes	**1798** The French defeat the Mamlukes at the Battle of the Pyramids but are defeated by British at Battle of the Nile
	1793 France blocks Anglo-Hanoverians at Hondschoote; defeats Austrians at Wattignies	**1799** Bonaparte returns to France and seizes power
	1794 Britain beats France at the Battle of the First of June	**1800** Bonaparte defeats the Austrians at Marengo

Alliances & treaties

1783 Britain recognizes the independence of the United States in the Treaty of Paris	**1792** Austria and Prussia ally against France: start of the French revolutionary wars	**1797** Treaty of Campo Formio follows the French defeat of Austria
	1793 Second Partition of Poland; Spain, Holland, Britain and the empire join First Coalition against France	**1798** Second Coalition against France
	1795 Third Partition of Poland	

| 1790 | 1795 | 1800 |

North Sea

SWEDEN

Christiania

DENMARK–NORWAY

Göteborg

Vänern

Stockholm

Vättern

Gotland to Sweden

Baltic Sea

Helsinki

Svenskund 1789, 1790

St Petersburg

Revel

Riga

Western Dvina

Lake Peipus

RUSSIAN EMPIRE

Samogitia

Copenhagen

Swedish Pomerania

Danzig

West Prussia

Königsberg

East Prussia

Ermland

New East Prussia from 1795

Minsk

Lithuania

Black Russia

1795–1806 *Batavian Republic*

Camperdown 1797

Amsterdam

Nore

Hamburg

Bremen

Hanover

Pomerania

Stettin

Brandenburg

Berlin

Netze

PRUSSIA

Mazovia

Warsaw

POLAND

4 ✪1794

1787

NETHERLANDS

1784

Brussels

Neerwinden 1793

Liège 1789

Fleurus 1794

Great Poland
South Prussia from 1793

Oder

Saxony

Dresden

Prague

Little Poland
West Galicia from 1795

Podlesia

Volhynia

oote 1793

mappes 1792

ignies 1793

Paris

Versailles 1789

Valmy 1792

Saarwerden

Salm

Frankfurt

Nuremberg

Wissembourg 1793

Bohemia

Vistula

Moravia

Austrian Silesia

Galicia and Lodomeria

Red Russia

Orléans

Montbeliard 1792–93

Rauracian Republic

RANCE

1

Geneva

Lyon

Zürich 1799

Bavaria

Munich

Hohenlinden 1800

Danube

Austria

Vienna

Salzburg

Leoben

HABSBURG EMPIRE

Bukovina

Jassy

Moldavia

Bessarabia

Sebastopol

SWISS CONFEDERATION 1798–1803 *Helvetic Republic*

Tyrol

Carinthia

Styria

Hungary

✪1790

Transylvania

SARDINIA–PIEDMONT

Turin

Marengo 1800

Milan

Castiglione 1796

Rivoli 1797

Mantua

Arcole 1796

1797–1802 *Cisalpine Republic*

Campo Formio 1797

Venice

VENICE

Carniola

Croatia

Sava

Slavonia

Banat

Wallachia

Danube

Varna

Black Sea

enaissin
apal States

Mondovi 1796

Genoa

GENOA 1797–1805 *Ligurian Republic*

Fano

TUSCANY

PAPAL STATES

Herzegovina

Bosnia

Serbia

Bulgaria

Russian Black Sea fleet, 1798–1800

Avignon 1796

Nice

Toulon

1798

1798–99 *Roman Republic*

RAGUSA

MONTENEGRO

Üsküb

Edirne

Rumelia

Constantinople

Marseille

Trouillas 1793

Vernet 1793

Corsica 1794–96 to Britain

Ajaccio

Civitavecchia

Rome

Naples

1798–99 *Parthenopean Republic*

Naples

Albania

Janina

ANATOLIA

elona

SARDINIA–PIEDMONT

Minorca 1798 to Britain

Sardinia

✪1793

KINGDOM OF NAPLES AND SICILY

Ionian Islands
Venetian, 1797 to France, 1799 to Russia

Morea

Athens

OTTOMAN EMPIRE

Balearic Islands

Palermo

Messina

Sicily, 1799 independent of Naples

Rhodes

Cyprus

Igiers

Tunis

Bonaparte, 1798

Cythera Venetian, 1797 to France, 1799 to Russia

Crete

ALGIERS

Tunis

Malta
Knights of St John, 1798 to France, 1800 to Britain

Mediterranean Sea

Acre

Mount Tabor ✕ 1798

Jaffa

Tripoli

Cyrene

Aboukir Bay
(Battle of the Nile)
1798

Palestine

Bonaparte, 1798

Alexandria

Cairo

Battle of the Pyramids 1798

Egypt

Nile

1 In July and August 1789, a series of panics known as the "Great Fear" swept the French countryside, caused by rumors of brigands in the pay of aristocrats.

2 The Jacobin Maximilien Robespierre came to power in Paris in July 1793, initiating the revolutionary "Terror" and executing over a thousand people in the following twelve months.

3 The main counter-revolutionary revolt took place in the Vendée region of western France in 1793, and was brutally suppressed.

4 The Polish uprising against Russian rule in 1794 was led by Tadeusz Kosciuszko. Defeated and exiled, he refused to support subsequent attempts by France and Russia to grant Poland nominal independence.

5 Despite victories over France and its allies, harsh conditions in Britain's Royal Navy caused low morale, which led to two serious mutinies in 1797.

6 The French were persuaded by Wolfe Tone to support Irish risings against British rule. The rising of 1798 failed, and Tone committed suicide in prison.

of Britain, Bonaparte threatened Britain's trade route to India by attacking Egypt in 1798. Though victorious against Egypt's Mamluke rulers, his fleet was defeated by the British admiral Nelson at the Battle of the Nile. In response to reverses in Italy and on the Rhine, Bonaparte returned to France, overthrew the committee that had ruled France since 1795 (the "Directory") and installed himself as military dictator.

French military fortunes proceeded to rise; Napoleon's generals blocked an Anglo-Russian expedition to the Batavian Republic and defeated the Russians at Zürich, while he himself masterminded the defeat of the Austrians at Marengo (1800). Yet though his forces were all-powerful on land, his lack

of naval superiority meant that he could not prevent raids from the Russian Black Sea fleet in 1798–1800, or – more importantly – deliver a decisive blow against the Second Coalition.

In eastern Europe, Poland embarked on a course of constitutional reform modeled on Enlightenment ideas in the 1790s. Russia under Catherine II, which had annexed part of the country in 1772, responded by invading in 1792. Further regions were annexed by Russia and Prussia in the Second Partition (1793). A rebellion against the foreign overlords ended with the fall of Warsaw in 1794, and the Third Partition (1795) saw the disappearance of Poland as a sovereign country for over 120 years.

0   600 km

0   400 mi

See also 68 (*ancien regime* Europe);
78 (Napoleonic Europe)

◄ ►

French victories in 1800 virtually secured the defeat of Austria, but British naval power still frustrated Napoleon Bonaparte. His army in Egypt was forced out by the British in 1801, while the Danish fleet he hoped would keep Britain from the Baltic was destroyed at Copenhagen in the same year. A respite from war was confirmed by the Treaty of Amiens in 1802, enabling Britain to implement the Act of Union which incorporated Ireland into the United Kingdom, improving the islands' security.

War broke out again, however, in the spring of 1803. Napoleon revived his plan to invade Britain, which now stood alone against France, but he was unable to put it into action because of the undiminished strength of the Royal Navy. Britain's comprehensive naval victory at Trafalgar (1805), and the formation of the Third Coalition later that year, focussed Napoleon's attention back on the armies of Austria, overwhelming them at Ulm and Austerlitz. In 1806, Napoleon proclaimed the dissolution of the Holy Roman empire, united all the German states (apart from Austria and Prussia) into the Confederation of the Rhine, and then moved north to smash the Prussians at Jena–Auerstädt.

As in his earlier campaigns, Napoleon's generalship was unsurpassed and his army irresistible. The Treaty of Tilsit that followed his defeat of a Russian army at Friedland in 1807 broke the Third Coalition and placed Napoleon at the height of his power. He now turned to blockading all legitimate trade with Britain. The so-called "Continental System," established in Napoleon's Berlin and Milan decrees (1806, 1807), was designed to force the British to buy over-priced smuggled goods, thus depleting their gold reserves. Britain retaliated by prohibiting all French trade between one port and another.

Between 1804 (when he declared himself emperor) and 1814, Napoleon imposed his administrative and political ideas upon a conquered Europe while countering British attempts to probe the weak points in the continental blockade. In all his vassal states, he introduced the *Code Napoléon*, the French civil code that enshrined the revolutionary principles of equality and liberty, and provided the protection of private property.

A new phase of the Napoleonic wars opened in 1808, when a French army marched across the Iberian peninsula to force Portugal to adopt the Continental System. This sparked a uprising in Spain against the French, while the British under the command of Wellington established a base in Portugal. In a war of shifting fortunes, a number of hard-fought battles drained the reserves of both sides. At the same time, Napoleon was obliged to conduct another campaign against the Austrians, finally overcoming them at Wagram (1809) to reassert his position as master of Europe. Although this victory allowed Napoleon to concentrate his forces on Spain and temporarily reverse his setbacks suffered there, his decision to attack Russia in 1812 – again to enforce the Continental System – radically altered the situation. The campaign was a huge drain on men and supplies; after hunger, winter and Russian resistance forced a withdrawal from Moscow in late 1812, Napoleon's enemies seized the opportunity to create a Fourth Coalition. For the first time since 1795, a united Europe front opposed France.

Even the retreat from Russia did not break Napoleon's power. In 1813, his forces were still able to resist the new coalition at Lützen, Bautzen and Dresden, but suffered heavy casualties in doing so. The loss of troops in Russia, combined with the huge international force ranged against him, finally proved decisive. At Leipzig – in the "Battle of the Nations" – Napoleon suffered his first major defeat and was forced to quit Germany. At the same time, Wellington managed to push north to Toulouse and conclude the Peninsular War. Allied armies pressed home their attack from Germany, and threatened Paris in 1814. Napoleon now abdicated and was sent

into exile on the Mediterranean island of Elba.

While the victorious allies were redrawing the map of Europe at the Congress of Vienna, Napoleon escaped from exile and re-entered France in a final attempt to rebuild his empire. In his so-called "Hundred Days," he reformed his armies and challenged the combined British, Dutch and Prussian forces at Waterloo. The ensuing battle was closely contested, but ended in final defeat for Napoleon. He abdicated for a second time and was exiled to St Helena in the south Atlantic, where he died. Europe was finally at peace after twenty-three years of war.

Map key:

- borders, 1812
- French empire, 1812
- state dependent on France, 1812
- French ally, 1812
- Ottoman empire, 1812
- Russian empire, 1812
- United Kingdom of Great Britain and Ireland, 1812
- Confederation of the Rhine
- France, 1815
- Spanish guerrilla activity
- French victory
- French defeat
- Austrian campaign
- British campaign
- French campaign
- Napoleon's escape from Elba, and the Waterloo campaign, 1815
- Prussian campaign
- Russian campaign

TIMELINE

Napoleonic wars

1801 British and Turks defeat the French army at Aboukir

1802 The Treaty of Amiens is signed by Britain and France

1803 War is resumed with Britain over Malta

1805 British victory at Trafalgar; Austrians beaten at Ulm; Russian and Austrian armies routed at Austerlitz

1806 Prussia is defeated at Jena-Auerstädt

1807 At second battle of Copenhagen, Britain captures Danish fleet; Peace of Tilsit leaves Napoleon dominant

1808 Spanish national uprising against the French; start of Peninsular War

1812 Napoleon's invasion of Russia ends in retreat

1813 Napoleon is defeated at Battle of the Nations at Leipzig

1815 Final defeat of Napoleon by British under Wellington and Prussians under Blücher at Waterloo

Political developments

1800 The Act of Union unites British and Irish legislatures

1801 Napoleon restores state–church relations in the Concordat with the Pope

1802 Napoleon is made First Consul for life

1804 Napoleon is made emperor; the *Code Napoléon* applied in continental Europe

1806 Napoleon replaces the Holy Roman empire with the Confederation of the Rhine

1807 "Continental System" is completed

1808 Napoleon installs his brother as Spanish king

1810 Napoleon marries Marie Louise, daughter of Emperor of Austria, to provide an heir

1813 Fourth Coalition against France (Prussia, Russia, Britain, Sweden, Austria)

1814 Napoleon abdicates and is exiled to the island of Elba

1815 Napoleon's "Hundred Days"; final exile to St Helena, where he dies (1821)

THE LÉGION D'HONNEUR, an award for all ranks for notable service to France, was created by Napoleon in 1802.

1 By the Treaty of Amiens (March 1802), Britain and France both agreed to return most conquests made since 1793. Peace, though, lasted barely a year.

2 The Battle of Trafalgar, in which the French lost over half of their ships, ended Napoleon's plans to invade Britain. British commander Lord Nelson died of injuries sustained in the action.

3 Borodino was a costly victory for Napoleon, who lost a quarter of his men. Only 30,000 troops of an original French force of 600,000 survived the Russian campaign.

4 Napoleon planned to invade England from Boulogne in 1804, and assembled a fleet of 2,000 ships; he failed, however, to control the Channel.

5 Naval bombardment forced Denmark to surrender its fleet to Britain in 1807, further weakening French opposition to British sea power.

6 Napoleonic armies lived off the land in invaded countries, a strategy that brought disaster in the severe Russian winter of 1812–13. In contrast, British success in the Peninsular War was based on sustaining strong defensive positions with supplies from home.

0   600 km
0   400 mi

See also 77 (revolutionary Europe); 80 (mid-19th-century Europe); 90 (Industrial Revolution)

The early 19th century saw Europe continue to open new markets and exploit new sources of raw materials worldwide. Another aspect of European expansion – colonialism – led many countries to expend considerable resources on the conquest and administration of new territories. Europeanization would influence every other culture in the world in some measure. Some, as in India, were long established and highly sophisticated; others, as in Africa, were at critical stages in their evolution. Many native cultures in North America, Australia and New Zealand would face the threat of displacement or extermination.

Both the United States of America and imperial Russia expanded their continental empires. The United States purchased Louisiana from France in 1803 and expeditions pioneered routes to the Pacific in 1805–12 (▷ 84). Russia and Britain also promoted their North American interests, in Alaska and Vancouver respectively. American commerce grew after the revolution, first with China and then with Europe. Disruption to this trade, by Barbary pirates and the British blockade of Napoleonic Europe, met with a military response. American forces attacked Tripolitania in 1804 and British positions around Lakes Erie and Ontario in 1812.

The Ottomans still claimed authority over Egypt, Tripolitania, Tunis and Algiers, though all were now virtually independent. European penetration of Africa was mainly confined to the voracious demands of the slave trade. Portuguese traders at the mouth of the Congo and the Zambezi made great profits from slavery. British involvement in the trade was also intense until its abolition in 1807, by which time opponents of slavery had founded the state of Sierra Leone as a home for freed slaves.

Africa was in a state of turmoil that was to worsen in the course of the 19th century. In west Africa, the Asante and Fulani empires were dominant; the Omani were rebuilding their trading empire on the east coast; and central African states were jostling for power. Further south, the Lozi and Kazembe empires controlled east–west trade along the Zambezi. Madagascar, gradually being absorbed by Merina, supplied slaves (as did Angola) to Brazil and the United States. Dutch settlers at the Cape were joined by the English (1795), who established a naval base at Simonstown in 1806. Before long they would

Map labels:
Russian America
Arctic marine mammal hunters
sub-Arctic forest hunter–gatherers
plateau fishers and hunter–gatherers
Rupert's Land
Red River colony
Newfoundland
west coast foraging, hunting and fishing peoples
1795
1812
1805
Louisiana purchase
Upper & Lower Canada
Nova Scotia
New Brunswick
UNITED STATES
Vice-Royalty of New Spain
Florida
Bahamas
Cuba
HAITI
Jamaica
Puerto Rico
British Honduras
Mosquito Coast
British Guiana
Hawaiian Islands
Galapagos Islands
Vice-Royalty of New Granada
Vice-Royalty of Peru
Vice-Royalty of Brazil
PARAGUAY
Polynesians
Marquesas Islands
Tuamotu Archipelago
Pitcairn Island
first trade link between United States and China 1784
United Provinces of La Plata
pampas hunter–gatherers
shellfish gatherers and marine mammal hunters
Falkland Islands (Spain)

Timeline

1792 France becomes a republic; French Revolutionary Wars begin

1792 The first white settlers land at Bay of Islands, New Zealand

1791 Slave revolt led by Toussaint L'Ouverture on Haiti (St Domingue)

1789 French revolution; the *ancien régime* is overthrown

1798 Failed nationalist rebellion in Ireland led by Wolfe Tone

1798 Napoleon Bonaparte occupies Egypt

1805 Napoleon defeats Austro-Russian armies at Austerlitz

1803 Louisiana Purchase; USA buys extensive territories from France

TIMELINE		1790		1800	
The Americas					
Europe					
Middle East					
Africa					
Asia and Australasia					

1787 First freed slaves settle in Sierra Leone; becomes a colony 1808

1788 Sydney, Australia, is founded as a British convict settlement

1793 A British trade delegation to China is rebuffed by the Manchu

1795 First British settlers land at the Cape of Good Hope; Cape Colony under British control from 1806

1804 Napoleon proclaims himself emperor of France

1804 Usman dan Fodio begins *jihad* in Hausaland (northern Nigeria), which results in large Islamic state

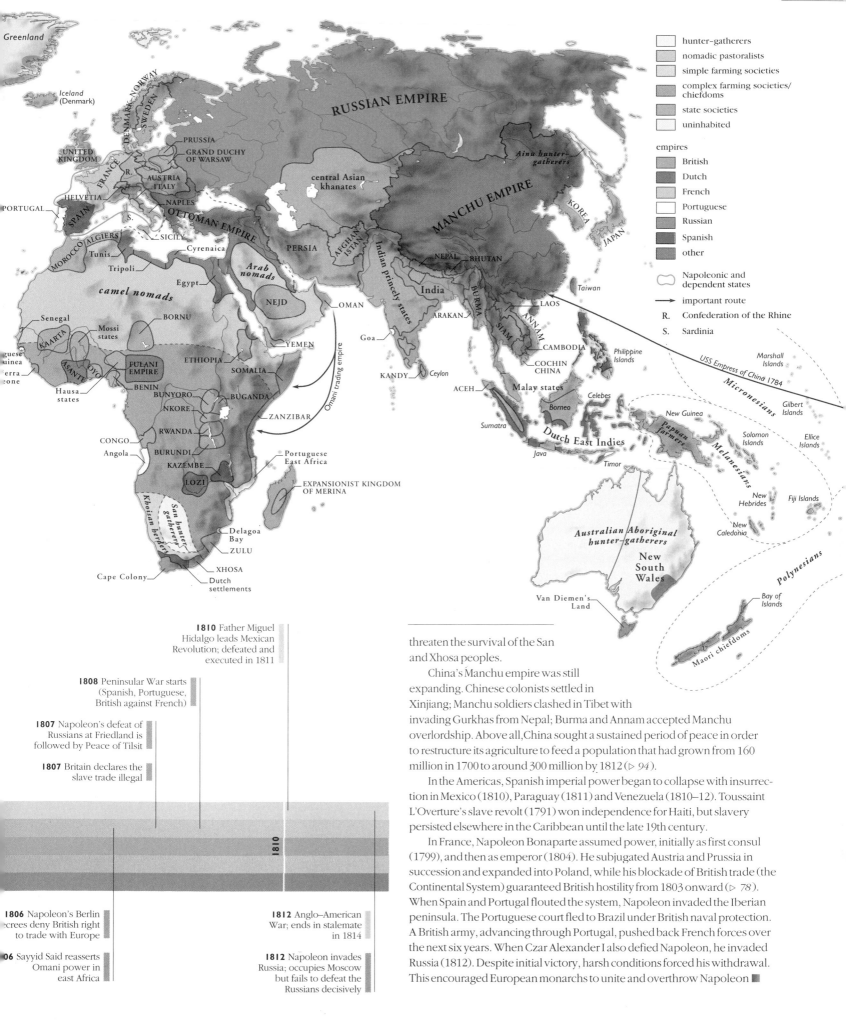

Legend:

- hunter-gatherers
- nomadic pastoralists
- simple farming societies
- complex farming societies/chiefdoms
- state societies
- uninhabited

empires

- British
- Dutch
- French
- Portuguese
- Russian
- Spanish
- other

- Napoleonic and dependent states
- important route
- R. Confederation of the Rhine
- S. Sardinia

Map labels:

Greenland, Iceland (Denmark), UNITED KINGDOM, DENMARK-NORWAY, SWEDEN, PRUSSIA, GRAND DUCHY OF WARSAW, RUSSIAN EMPIRE, FRANCE, R., AUSTRIA, ITALY, HELVETIA, NAPLES, PORTUGAL, SPAIN, SICILY, S., OTTOMAN EMPIRE, central Asian khanates, Ainu hunter-gatherers, MANCHU EMPIRE, KOREA, JAPAN, MOROCCO, ALGIERS, Tunis, Tripoli, Cyrenaica, PERSIA, AFGHANISTAN, NEPAL, BHUTAN, Taiwan, Egypt, Arab nomads, camel nomads, NEJD, OMAN, Indian Princely states, India, BURMA, ARAKAN, LAOS, Senegal, BORNU, YEMEN, Goa, SIAM, ANNAM, CAMBODIA, COCHIN CHINA, Philippine Islands, Marshall Islands, Mossi states, KAARTA, Hausa states, ASANTE, OYO, FULANI EMPIRE, BENIN, ETHIOPIA, SOMALIA, KANDY, Ceylon, ACEH, Malay states, Celebes, Gilbert Islands, Guinea, Sierra Leone, BUNYORO, BUGANDA, NKORE, ZANZIBAR, Borneo, New Guinea, Papuan farmers, Solomon Islands, Ellice Islands, CONGO, RWANDA, Sumatra, Dutch East Indies, Java, Timor, Angola, BURUNDI, KAZEMBE, LOZI, Portuguese East Africa, EXPANSIONIST KINGDOM OF MERINA, New Hebrides, Fiji Islands, New Caledonia, San hunter gatherers, Khoisan herders, Delagoa Bay, ZULU, Cape Colony, XHOSA, Dutch settlements, Australian Aboriginal hunter-gatherers, New South Wales, Van Diemen's Land, Bay of Islands, Maori chiefdoms, Micronesians, Melanesians, Polynesians, USS Empress of China 1784, Omani trading empire

Timeline:

1810 Father Miguel Hidalgo leads Mexican Revolution; defeated and executed in 1811

1808 Peninsular War starts (Spanish, Portuguese, British against French)

1807 Napoleon's defeat of Russians at Friedland is followed by Peace of Tilsit

1807 Britain declares the slave trade illegal

1810

1806 Napoleon's Berlin decrees deny British right to trade with Europe

1806 Sayyid Said reasserts Omani power in east Africa

1812 Anglo–American War; ends in stalemate in 1814

1812 Napoleon invades Russia; occupies Moscow but fails to defeat the Russians decisively

threaten the survival of the San and Xhosa peoples.

China's Manchu empire was still expanding. Chinese colonists settled in Xinjiang; Manchu soldiers clashed in Tibet with invading Gurkhas from Nepal; Burma and Annam accepted Manchu overlordship. Above all, China sought a sustained period of peace in order to restructure its agriculture to feed a population that had grown from 160 million in 1700 to around 300 million by 1812 (▷ 94).

In the Americas, Spanish imperial power began to collapse with insurrection in Mexico (1810), Paraguay (1811) and Venezuela (1810–12). Toussaint L'Overture's slave revolt (1791) won independence for Haiti, but slavery persisted elsewhere in the Caribbean until the late 19th century.

In France, Napoleon Bonaparte assumed power, initially as first consul (1799), and then as emperor (1804). He subjugated Austria and Prussia in succession and expanded into Poland, while his blockade of British trade (the Continental System) guaranteed British hostility from 1803 onward (▷ 78). When Spain and Portugal flouted the system, Napoleon invaded the Iberian peninsula. The Portuguese court fled to Brazil under British naval protection. A British army, advancing through Portugal, pushed back French forces over the next six years. When Czar Alexander I also defied Napoleon, he invaded Russia (1812). Despite initial victory, harsh conditions forced his withdrawal. This encouraged European monarchs to unite and overthrow Napoleon ∎

The decades after 1815 saw the emergence of nationalism in the aftermath of Napoleon's imperial rule. Liberals and democrats demanded nation-states that embraced a common racial and linguistic identity and embodied constitutionally guaranteed rights for their citizens. Only a few nation-states were actually created in the early 19th century: Belgium, the Netherlands, Switzerland and Greece. More often, the monarchies restored after the fall of Napoleon (Prussia, Austria and Russia) stifled the nascent democracies. The strongest states to emerge – Italy and the German second empire – did so not through popular nationalist uprisings, but by growing around dynamic existing monarchies (Sardinia–Piedmont and Prussia respectively).

The Congress of Vienna (1814–15), convened at Napoleon's defeat, was intended to create a balance of power. Under the leadership of the conservative Austrian foreign minister Clemens Metternich, the Congress restored hereditary monarchies, created new enlarged kingdoms by unifying Norway with Sweden and Belgium with Holland, and established the "concert of Europe": congresses to deal with threats to political stability. A few concessions were made to nationalism: the Turkish sultan granted a measure of self-government to Serbia (1817) and to Moldavia and Wallachia (1829). However, when revolutions broke out in Naples, Spain and Portugal, the congresses at Troppau, Laibach and Verona authorized intervention. France sent troops to help conservatives suppress a liberal regime in Spain in 1823.

The Greek revolt against Ottoman rule broke out in 1821. The Greeks won control of the Peloponnese (Morea) by early 1822 when they declared Greece a sovereign state, but Turkish forces, bolstered by Egyptian troops, reinvaded in 1825. The conservative nature of the Greek rebellion, combined with strategic machinations against the crumbling Ottoman empire, led the European powers to approve an autonomous Greek state. A British, French and Russian naval force destroyed the Turkish–Egyptian fleet at Navarino, and the Ottomans conceded Greek independence in 1832.

Revolutions in Modena, Parma, the Papal States, Poland and some areas of Germany broke out in 1830–31, but were all suppressed. The reactionary regime of Bourbon Charles X in France was ended by the July Revolution of 1830, though this lead not to a new republic but to the accession of the "citizen-king" Louis-Philippe. In the same year, Belgium began its struggle for independence from the Dutch.

The Congress of Vienna had replaced Napoleon's German state with an alliance of 39 states headed by Austria and Prussia, known as the German Confederation. Prussia gradually gained ascendancy, partly by forming the *Zollverein* free trade zone from 1819–44, isolating protectionist Austria.

The most serious challenge to Metternich came in 1848, the "Year of Revolutions". The catalyst was the fall of Louis-Philippe's regime to republicans in February. Unrest spread to Hungary, Croatia, and the Czech lands, where liberal governments were installed and democratic constitutions were drafted. Metternich was forced to resign and flee abroad. Republics were proclaimed throughout Italy and a

borders, 1815
Austrian empire, 1815
France, 1815
Ottoman empire, 1815
Prussia, 1815
Russian empire, 1815
United Kingdom & Hanover, 1815
German Confederation, 1815
French territorial gain by 1860
Prussian territorial gain by 1866
Belgium, 1830
Greece, 1830
Italy, 1861
German second empire, 1871
"Concert of Europe" congress
nationalist revolt or unrest, 1815–49
revolt or unrest in the United Kingdom, with movement involved
route of Garibaldi, 1860

| 0 | | 600 km |
| 0 | | 400 mi |

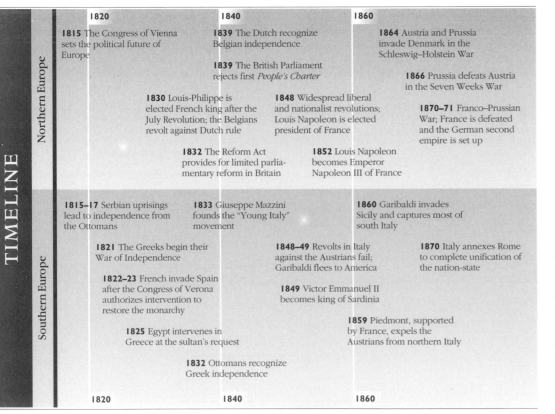

TIMELINE

	1820	1840	1860
Northern Europe	**1815** The Congress of Vienna sets the political future of Europe	**1839** The Dutch recognize Belgian independence	**1864** Austria and Prussia invade Denmark in the Schleswig–Holstein War
		1839 The British Parliament rejects first *People's Charter*	**1866** Prussia defeats Austria in the Seven Weeks War
	1830 Louis-Philippe is elected French king after the July Revolution; the Belgians revolt against Dutch rule	**1848** Widespread liberal and nationalist revolutions; Louis Napoleon is elected president of France	**1870–71** Franco–Prussian War; France is defeated and the German second empire is set up
		1832 The Reform Act provides for limited parliamentary reform in Britain	**1852** Louis Napoleon becomes Emperor Napoleon III of France
Southern Europe	**1815–17** Serbian uprisings lead to independence from the Ottomans	**1833** Giuseppe Mazzini founds the "Young Italy" movement	**1860** Garibaldi invades Sicily and captures most of south Italy
	1821 The Greeks begin their War of Independence	**1848–49** Revolts in Italy against the Austrians fail; Garibaldi flees to America	**1870** Italy annexes Rome to complete unification of the nation-state
	1822–23 French invade Spain after the Congress of Verona authorizes intervention to restore the monarchy	**1849** Victor Emmanuel II becomes king of Sardinia	
	1825 Egypt intervenes in Greece at the sultan's request	**1859** Piedmont, supported by France, expels the Austrians from northern Italy	
	1832 Ottomans recognize Greek independence		
	1820	1840	1860

1 The reunification of the northern and southern Netherlands in 1815 under the Protestant Dutch monarchy caused resentment in Catholic Belgium.

2 Ferdinand VII, king of Spain (r.1808-33) brutally suppressed liberal opposition after his return from exile in 1814. In 1820, the army he had assembled to reassert his rule in Latin America rose against him.

3 An early challenge to the rule of Louis-Philippe occurred in Lyon in 1831, when 600 protestors were killed in rioting.

4 A Roman republic was established by radicals (including Garibaldi) in 1848-49, but was ended when French troops restored Pope Pius IX to power

5 The head of the Bonaparte dynasty, Louis Napoleon, was elected French president in 1848. He became emperor Napoleon III after a coup (1851), but was exiled after defeat by Prussia in 1871.

NORWAY
Union from 1815
Christiania

SWEDEN
Göteborg
Vänern
Vättern
Stockholm
Gotland

Helsinki
Revel
St Petersburg 1825
Riga
Lake Peipus

North Sea

DENMARK
Copenhagen

Schleswig 1865 to Prussia
Holstein 1865 to Austria, 1866 to Prussia
Hamburg
Bremen
Oldenburg
HANOVER 1866 to Prussia
BRUNSWICK
1830
1830
Amsterdam
NETHERLANDS
Brussels 1830, 1848
Belgium
Aix-la-Chapelle 1848
Frankfurt 1833, 1848
1830
HESSE
Westphalia

Baltic Sea

MECKLENBURG-SCHWERIN
Königsberg
Danzig
Pomerania
Stettin
PRUSSIA
Brandenburg
Berlin 1848
East Prussia
Vistula
Poznan 1848
Warsaw 1830-31, 1848
Poland
Dresden 1848
Silesia
Oder
1847 to Austrian empire
Krakow 1846, 1848
Lvov (Lemberg) 1848
Galicia and Lodomeria
Dniester

RUSSIAN EMPIRE

5 Luxembourg
Paris 1830, 1832, 1848
Palatinate 1815 to Bavaria
Alsace-Lorraine 1871 to German empire
1849
BADEN
WÜRTTEMBERG
Hohenzollern
Munich 1848
Rhine
Zürich
Berne
SWITZERLAND
Geneva
FRANCE
Milan 1848
Savoy
Lyon 1831, 1834, 1848
3 1860 to France
Magenta 1859
Turin 1815-30
Piedmont to Sardinia
Genoa 1834
Avignon 1815-48 to Sardinia 1848 to France
MONACO 1861 independent
Brescia
Lombardy
Parma
1831
MODENA
LUCCA
Florence 1849
Tuscany
ANDORRA

Prague 1848
Bohemia
Moravia
Brünn (Brno) 1848
1815
Troppau 1820
Linz 1848
Vienna 1848
Austria 1848
Salzburg
Salzburg
Tyrol
Styria
Carinthia
Cariola
Venetia 1866 to Italy
Verona 1822
Venice 1848
Solferino 1859
AUSTRIAN EMPIRE
Pressburg 1848
Buda 1848
Debrecen 1848
Koloszvar 1848
Transylvania
Blaj 1848
Temesvár 1849
Hungary
Danube
Laibach 1821
Agram 1848
Slavonia
Croatia
Belgrade
Sava
Dalmatia
Bosnia
SERBIA 1817 autonomous
Herzegovina
MONTENEGRO
WALLACHIA 1829 autonomous
Bucharest 1848
Danube
Bulgaria
Varna
MOLDAVIA 1829 autonomous
Jassy 1848
Ochakov
Sebastopol

Black Sea

Barcelona 1820

Avignon
ulouse
Corsica
Talamone
1870 to Italy
PAPAL STATES
Rome 1848
Macerata 1831
4
Volturno 1860
Naples 1820, 1848
BENEVENTO
Bari 1815-30
Salerno 1815-30
Sardinia
SARDINIA
Palermo 1848-49
Catalfimi 1860
KINGDOM OF THE TWO SICILIES
Reggio 1815-30
Milazzo 1860
Sicily

OTTOMAN EMPIRE
Üsküb
Macedonia
Albania
Janina
Missolonghi 1826
Morea
Navarino 1827
Athens
Ionian Islands 1815-63 to Britain 1863 to Greece
Cythera 1815-63 to Britain 1863 to Greece

learic Islands to Spain

ers
Tunis
ALGIERS
occupied by France from 1830 but not fully subjugated until 1848
Tunis
Malta to Britain
Mediterranean Sea

LORD BYRON, the British Romantic poet, was inspired by the cause of Greek independence and died at Missolonghi in 1824.

parliamentary assembly met in Frankfurt with the aim of uniting Germany. Yet internal divisions prevailed, and by late 1849 the Habsburgs regained control in Austria, Italy and Hungary (the latter with Russian help). The German assembly collapsed under pressure from Prussia, which consolidated its power by means of swift victories over Denmark, Austria and France.

In Italy, revolutionary movements from 1820 onward, such as the Carbonari, had failed to expel the Austrians or unite the country. In mid-century an unlikely champion of the unification movement (*Risorgimento* or "resurrection") arose: the rich industrial state of Sardinia–Piedmont. The Piedmontese king Victor Emmanuel II and his prime minister Camillo di Cavour instituted liberal domestic reforms and secured the help of Napoleon III's France to drive the Austrians from northern Italy in 1859. The liberal constitutional monarchy sought by Piedmont was threatened when the revolutionary Giuseppe Garibaldi and his "redshirts" took Sicily and overran much of the southern mainland. Yet Garibaldi passed his conquests to Victor Emmanuel II, who effectively became king of a united Italy.

Britain was less affected by nationalist agitation, though the Chartists – supporters of a "People's Charter" – sought universal manhood suffrage after limited parliamentary reform was conceded in 1832. Irish nationalism was given urgency by the famine of 1845–47, and the Irish Republican Brotherhood (Fenians), precursor of the movement that won Irish independence in 1921, was set up in 1858.

See also 78 (Napoleonic Europe); 90 (Industrial Revolution)

Napoleon's invasion of the Iberian peninsula in 1808–09 was the catalyst to the independence movements in the American colonies of Spain and Portugal. In the Spanish territories, wars of liberation broke out when Napoleon's brother Joseph Bonaparte took the Spanish throne. Brazil played host to Portugal's prince regent, later João VI, who fled there in 1807 after the French occupied Portugal. When he returned home in 1822, his son Pedro became emperor of an independent Brazil. The new state was recognized by Portugal in 1825.

Mexico's war of independence, led by the priest Miguel Hidalgo, began in 1810. Hidalgo was executed, but his conservative successor Agustín Iturbide united Mexican society and in 1822–23 formed the Mexican empire with himself as emperor. At the same time, the Spanish colonies in Central America proclaimed a Confederation of the United Provinces, which lasted until 1838, when its constituent parts became individual sovereign states.

The principal figure of South American independence, Simón Bolívar (the "Liberator"), began his fight to free his native Venezuela and adjoining territories from Spanish rule in 1811. Bolívar's victory at Boyacá in 1819 heralded the proclamation of the Republic of Gran Colombia, and his defeat of the royalists at Carabobo in 1821 led to the fall of Caracas and to Venezuelan independence. In Argentina, revolutionary forces were led by José de San Martín, a veteran of the Peninsular War. San Martín trained an army and led it across the Andes in 1817 to take Lima in 1821. He proclaimed Peru's independence, then gave up control to Bolívar who established a revolutionary government at Lima. With the final battle of the wars of liberation at Ayacucho in 1824, all Spanish possessions in the Americas were independent, except Cuba and Puerto Rico.

The new states not only inherited the frontiers of the former Spanish and Portuguese administrative regions; their social divisions also remained intact. There was no tradition of pluralistic government, and color was still decisive. Spanish-born whites or *peninsulares* (and *reinóis*, the Portuguese equivalent in Brazil) were dominant. The majority of the people (*mestizos* or Indian–Europeans) had limited

Map legend

- Portuguese colony c.1800
- Spanish colony c.1800
- Republic of Gran Colombia, 1819–30
- united with Mexico 1821-23, independent as United Provinces of Central America 1823-38
- Confederation of Peru & Bolivia 1836-39
- **1838** date of independence as a nation-state
- territory gained by former Spanish colony since independence, with date
- territory gained by the United States from Mexico, with date
- campaign by Simón Bolívar 1819-24
- campaign by José de San Martín 1817-22
- campaign by United States forces, 1846-48
- ⊗ battle fought by José de San Martín
- ⊗ battle fought by Bolívar or de Sucre
- ⊗ battle during the Mexican–American War, 1846-48
- ⊗ battle during the Paraguayan War (War of the Triple Alliance), 1864-70
- ⊗ battle during the War of the Pacific 1879-83
- border c.1840
- - - - other border
- railroad within Latin America by 1914
- *oil* trade commodity
- movement of peoples

SIMON BOLIVAR was a remarkable military leader, and is the only individual to have a state named for him today.

Galapagos Islands 1832 to Ecuador

Map labels

Fort Leavenworth 1845 · St Louis · UNITED STATES 1783 · Atlanta · Birmingham · Jacksonville · Memphis · Denver · Kearney 1845 · Arkansas · Mississippi · New Orleans · Florida 1810/19 to US · Miam[i] · Bah[amas] · to B[ritain]

Salt Lake City · Fremont 1846 · Fremont 1845-46 · Colorado · 1848 to US under Treaty of Guadalupe Hidalgo · 1836-45 sold to Texas; 1850 sold to US · 1836-45 to Texas · *cattle* · Texas 1836-45 independent republic; 1845 to US · 2

Sacramento · San Francisco · Monterey · Stockton 1846 · Santa Barbara · Los Angeles · San Diego · Mexicali · 1853 sold to US under Gadsden Purchase · Sloat 1846

Ciudad Juárez · *cattle* · Alamo 1836 · San Jacinto 1836 · San Antonio · Scott 1846 · Gulf of Mexico · Havana · CUB[A] 1898, 1902 US con[trol] · *sugar*

Doniphan 1847 · Chihuahua 1847 · Resaca de la Palma · Taylor 1846 · Palo Alto 1846 · Fort Brown · *oil*

Ciudad Obregón · Monterrey · Buena Vista 1847 · Padilla

Mazatlán · San Luis Potosí · *silver* · *sugar* · *oil* · Tampico · Scott 1847 · Mérida · Yucatan 1835–48 independent · British Honduras to Britain

Cerro Gordo 1847 · Veracruz · Mexico City · Chapultepec 1847 · MEXICO 1821 · *coffee* · *coffee* · GUATEMALA 1838 · HONDURAS 1838 · Mos[quito] Coas[t] to Br[itain] · *coffee* · Tegucigalpa 1838 · *coffee* · *bananas* · 1859 Nica[ragua] Hond[uras]

Guatemala City · EL SALVADOR 1838 · San Salvador · Managua · NICARAGUA 1838 · San José · COSTA RICA 1838 · PANAMA 1821 to Colombia, 1903

TIMELINE

Wars and revolutions

1810–11 Miguel Hidalgo leads an unsuccessful popular revolt in Mexico

1810–14 An attempted revolution in Chile is defeated

1819 Simón Bolívar routs the Spanish at Boyacá and founds Republic of Gran Colombia

1821 Battle of Carabobo; independence of Venezuela

1836 Texas gains its independence from Mexico at the Battle of San Jacinto

1836–39 Bolivia and Peru form a brief confederation

1846–48 Mexican–American War following US annexation of Texas (1845); Mexico loses all its northern territories

1863 Ill-fated attempt by Mexican conservatives and French to install emperor (Maximilian I; executed 1867)

1864–70 War of the Triple Alliance is fought by Paraguay against Argentina, Uruguay and Brazil.

1879–83 War of the Pacific between Chile and Bolivia and Peru

1903 A revolution in Panama brings independence from Colombia

1910 The Mexican Revolution begins; forces under Francisco Madero oppose dictatorship of Porfirio Diaz (1876–1911)

1914 United States Marines occupy Veracruz to safeguard US interests

Social and political change

1807 The Braganzas (Portuguese royal family) flee to Brazil under British escort

1823 US recognizes newly independent states and proclaims the "Monroe Doctrine"

1829–52 Dictatorship of Juan Manuel Rosas in Argentina

1831 Emperor Pedro I of Brazil abdicates and his son Pedro II succeeds

1853 Mexico sells the Mesilla Valley to the United States in the "Gadsden Purchase"

1870–88 Liberal Guzman Blanco is president in Venezuela; many social and political reforms are instituted

1879 French company under Ferdinand de Lesseps is set up to build the Panama Canal

1889 The Brazilian empire is succeeded by Republic of the United States of Brazil

1904 US engineers begin cutting the Panama Canal (completed 1914)

power, while the *mulattoes* (African–Europeans), *zambos* (Indian–Africans), blacks and Indians all suffered discrimination. Sectional interests, such as the military, the church, industrialists, bankers and landlords were often in conflict, and power was frequently seized by *caudillos*, dictators who ruled through patronage and private armies.

The *caudillo* José Francia helped lead Paraguay's struggle for independence and was "el supremo" 1814–40. Bernardo O'Higgins was prominent in Chile's revolution and became "supreme director" 1817–23. The Mexican Antonio de Santa Anna, after a period as an elected president (1833–36), intermittently took dictatorial powers. During his rule Mexico fought, largely unsuccessfully, against the United States, and ceded large tracts of land by 1850.

Intervention by European powers in Latin American affairs was effectively preempted by the Monroe doctrine of 1823, which signaled US hostility toward any attempt to colonize the region. Most territorial changes that occurred did so as a result of wars between the new sovereign states. Major conflicts of the period were the War of the Pacific, in which Chile defeated Peru and Bolivia, and the War of the Triple Alliance), involving Paraguay, Brazil, Argentina and Uruguay. The 1910–11 Mexican revolution led to chaos, mass slaughter and eventual US intervention, as US president Wilson supported General Huerta, who exterminated the nationalist Zapata rebels while Pancho Villa's bandits ran riot in the north. Wilson sent warships to Tampico and troops to Veracruz in 1914.

Economic change came swiftly to Latin America. Foreign capital funded railroad and harbor construction. The Panama Canal was completed by US engineers in 1914 after an earlier French venture had failed. British firms exploited the natural phosphates and nitrates of Peru and northern Chile, for use in fertilizers and explosives. US investment turned coffee exports into a vital element in Brazil's economy. In Argentina, revenue from wool, leather and beef exports brought a sharp rise in the standard of living. Meat exports grew after refrigerated sea transport was introduced in the 1880s; but a decline in world trade in the 1890s ended the boom years. Immigrants were among the region's greatest assets. Initially they entered Chile and Argentina (which saw a huge influx of Italian immigrants from the 1850s), but Brazil became the preferred destination after slavery was abolished there in 1888. Over one million Europeans arrived in Brazil by 1898. They were favored over the original inhabitants for educational and work opportunities. Chinese and Japanese laborers were also imported in large numbers to work on the railroads and in the mines.

1 Peruvian *guano* (seabird droppings used as fertilizer) was a major source of foreign revenue after independence, but deposits were exhausted in 20 years.

2 At the Alamo in 1836, during the Texan War of Independence from Mexico, 180 defenders resisted Mexican forces but were eventually overcome.

3 The War of the Triple Alliance was the bloodiest conflict in Latin American history. Paraguay lost over 60 percent (300,000) of its population.

4 Costa Rica was the first Central American republic to export coffee beans. The United Fruit Company developed the country, building its railroad and port facilities. The first elections were held there in 1885.

5 Manaus, in the Amazon basin, saw great prosperity in the rubber boom of 1890–1920. The town's lavishly appointed opera house was built in 1896.

6 Mechanization (railroads, steam excavators) and medical provision against malaria were crucial in the success of the US Panama Canal project (1904–14).

See also 62 (the Spanish–American empire);
84 (expansion of the United States)

The Congress of Vienna (1814–15) dismembered Napoleon's empire and transformed the map of Europe (▷ 78). The German Confederation was formed, an alliance of states dominated by Austria and Prussia. Wholly new nations also arose. Greece wrested sovereignty from the Ottoman empire from 1821–28; Belgium rebelled against Dutch rule (1830) and won international recognition of its independence in 1839. Yet the restoration of autocratic monarchies by the Congress in the name of stability bred resentment, which erupted in a series of revolutions that swept the continent in 1848 (▷ 80). Only Britain and Russia stayed unaffected. Elsewhere, liberals and nationalists exploited economic hardship to foment revolts demanding representative forms of government. Internal divisions caused the revolutions to fail and conservative forces soon regained power.

In contrast, revolutions succeeded in toppling the Spanish and Portuguese empires in Central and South America. Brazil proclaimed an independent empire after King João VI returned to Portugal in 1822. The collapse of Spain during the Napoleonic Wars led to a succession of uprisings against Spanish rule in the Americas. Eleven independent states were formed by 1826 (▷ 81). The disparate nature of the region's cultures and the diversity of the revolutionaries' aspirations prevented the development of the envisaged Hispano–American state. Simón Bolívar's Gran Colombia (comprising modern Venezuela, Colombia, and Ecuador) fragmented in 1830, only eleven years after its formation.

Spain's fall benefited the United States, which gained the territories of East and West Florida in 1819–22. US foreign policy was outlined in the Monroe Doctrine of 1823, which stipulated separate spheres of interest for Europe and the Americas to forestall any renewal of European ambition in the region. The transcontinental expansion of the United States also accelerated during this period, with the annexation of Oregon in 1844, and Texas in 1845 (▷ 84). War with Mexico (1846–48) led to the United States gaining California, where gold deposits were discovered soon after.

In Russia, Czar Alexander I and his successor Nicholas I maintained an implacable opposition to reform at home and abroad. An insurrection in Poland against Russian rule was suppressed (1830–31), while Russian troops were also sent to help Austria quell a Hungarian nationalist uprising in 1848–49. Russian forces

1823 Monroe Doctrine warns against further European expansion in the Americas

1822 Brazil declares independence from Portugal

1818 Border between Canada and United States is defined as 49th Parallel

1830–31 Polish revolt against Russian rule

1839–42 Britain fights the First Afghan War to stop the southern spread of Russian influence

1815 Defeat of Napoleon by British and Prussian forces at Waterloo

1828 Greeks win War of Independence (Ottomans recognize Greece 1832)

TIMELINE

The Americas
Europe
Middle East
Africa
Asia and Australasia

1820

1830

1816–20 Argentina declares its independence from Spain; war of liberation lasts for four years

1820 British settlers begin to arrive at the Cape in large numbers

1833 Falkland Islands are occupied by Britain

1837 Natal Republic is founded by Afrikaners

1816 Shaka, king of the Zulu, begins to expand the Zulu empire

1824–26 British fight two unsuccessful wars against the Asante of west Africa

1833 The Ottoman empire recognizes the independence of Egypt

1839 Belgian independence is international guarantee

1816 Britain begins to recruit Gurkha soldiers from Nepal

1839–42 First Opium War is fought betwee Britain and Chin

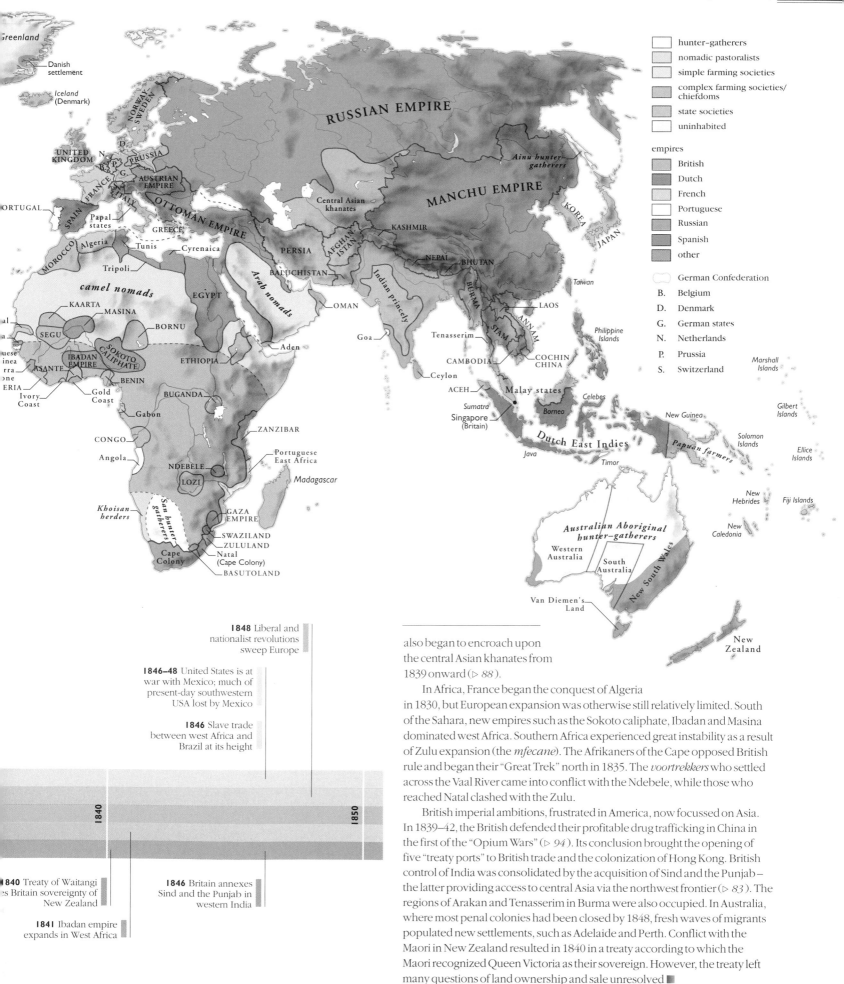

Map legend:

hunter-gatherers
nomadic pastoralists
simple farming societies
complex farming societies/chiefdoms
state societies
uninhabited

empires
British
Dutch
French
Portuguese
Russian
Spanish
other

German Confederation
B. Belgium
D. Denmark
G. German states
N. Netherlands
P. Prussia
S. Switzerland

Timeline:

1848 Liberal and nationalist revolutions sweep Europe

1846–48 United States is at war with Mexico; much of present-day southwestern USA lost by Mexico

1846 Slave trade between west Africa and Brazil at its height

1840

1850

1840 Treaty of Waitangi gives Britain sovereignty of New Zealand

1846 Britain annexes Sind and the Punjab in western India

1841 Ibadan empire expands in West Africa

also began to encroach upon the central Asian khanates from 1839 onward (▷ 88).

In Africa, France began the conquest of Algeria in 1830, but European expansion was otherwise still relatively limited. South of the Sahara, new empires such as the Sokoto caliphate, Ibadan and Masina dominated west Africa. Southern Africa experienced great instability as a result of Zulu expansion (the *mfecane*). The Afrikaners of the Cape opposed British rule and began their "Great Trek" north in 1835. The *voortrekkers* who settled across the Vaal River came into conflict with the Ndebele, while those who reached Natal clashed with the Zulu.

British imperial ambitions, frustrated in America, now focussed on Asia. In 1839–42, the British defended their profitable drug trafficking in China in the first of the "Opium Wars" (▷ 94). Its conclusion brought the opening of five "treaty ports" to British trade and the colonization of Hong Kong. British control of India was consolidated by the acquisition of Sind and the Punjab – the latter providing access to central Asia via the northwest frontier (▷ 83). The regions of Arakan and Tenasserim in Burma were also occupied. In Australia, where most penal colonies had been closed by 1848, fresh waves of migrants populated new settlements, such as Adelaide and Perth. Conflict with the Maori in New Zealand resulted in 1840 in a treaty according to which the Maori recognized Queen Victoria as their sovereign. However, the treaty left many questions of land ownership and sale unresolved ■

Despite its territorial acquisitions toward the end of the 18th century, the British East India Company still saw its role in the subcontinent as primarily commercial. This was enshrined in the India Act passed by the British Parliament in 1784, which forbade further annexation. Nevertheless, British rule (*raj*) in India continued to grow, as successive governors-general felt obliged to occupy hostile territory or form protectorates to prevent disruption to trade. Thus, when Tipu Sultan of Mysore attacked Travancore in 1789, he saw half his dominions annexed by Lord Cornwallis (governor-general 1786–93) in the ensuing war. Warfare was resumed against the Marathas of central India in 1803.

The fear of an assault on India by Napoleon radically altered British policy. A far more aggressive approach was adopted, in which independent principalities such as Hyderabad were reduced to dependencies by the stationing of British troops there. After the French threat had passed, Company interest turned toward countering Burmese aggression in the east and guarding against Russian incursions from the north. Assam, Arakan, and Tenasserim were acquired from Burma in 1824–26. On the northwest frontier, the First Afghan War (1839–42) was begun against Dost Muhammed. In both this and a later conflict (1878–80), the British occupied Kabul but failed to dominate the country. An attack on Sind secured the Bolan Pass in 1843, while two bloody wars against the Sikhs brought control of the Punjab. Lord Dalhousie (governor-general 1848–56) now evolved the doctrine of "lapse" (when a Hindu prince had no natural heirs his lands passed to the Company) and, on the pretext of ineffective government, annexed Muslim Oudh in 1856.

The East India Company also instituted administrative reforms. These began with revision of land revenue collection (the principal source of public finance) and a reorganization of the judicial system along British lines. Despite a Parliamentary directive urging respect for the people's rights and customs, the Company often disregarded religious and cultural sensitivities – particularly under governor-general Lord Bentinck (1828–35) who tried to ban *suttee* (the immolation of Hindu widows), *thuggee* (ritual robbery and murder) and infanticide. Continuing

Christian conversion efforts, plans to extend roads and railroads and an insistence on English as the language of education and commerce all threatened the traditional ways of life of both Hindus and Muslims.

Opposition to British rule was not, however, anticipated among the Company's *sepoy* (native) armies. Three such armies had been raised in India; those based at Madras and Bombay were largely untroubled by questions of caste and religion. But the Bengal *sepoys* – high-caste Hindus and Shi'ite Muslims – were offended by a rumor that new rifle cartridges (which had to be bitten before use) were greased with pork and beef fat. This violated the dietary proscriptions of their religions. Thus began the most serious challenge to British rule in India.

The Indian mutiny (also known as the First War of Independence) arose in January 1857 among troops stationed at Meerut and rapidly spread through north central India. The army revolt acted as a catalyst to a number of other grievances, and the mutineers were supported by peasant uprisings and some isolated *jihads*. The capture of Delhi and the besieging of the cities of Kanpur and Lucknow were serious blows to British authority. However, the Bombay and Madras armies remained largely loyal, and there was no strategy for a national revolt.

Though brief, the mutiny changed the face of British India; suspicion was now widespread on both sides. The 1858 Government of India Act transferred sovereignty from the East India Company to the British monarch and ended the doctrine of lapse, but other reforms were never instituted. Theoretically, racial impartiality operated in recruitment to the Indian civil service; in practice few Indians were admitted. The insular community of Anglo-Indians shunned contact with the local population and became ever more prosperous, partly through investment in plantations in southeast Asia and Africa. Gurkha and Sikh troops from the northwest of India now formed the backbone of the army.

The British policy in frontier regions continued to be determined by fear of Russian expansion. This led to the Second Afghan War of 1878–80, which ended with the recognition that Afghanistan could not be incorporated within the Indian empire. Similarly, in 1903 the British under Colonel

Younghusband invaded Tibet. After a year's conflict Tibet agreed not to concede territory to a foreign power.

Excluded from the administration of their country, educated Indians turned increasingly toward nationalism. The Indian National Congress was founded in 1885 and Gopal Gokhale, its president in 1905, worked for peaceful constitutional progress towards responsible government. The All-India Muslim League, a similarly constitutional organization, was founded in 1906. The Morley–Minto constitutional reforms (1909) brought in a measure of representative government, but Indians were still

Map legend

- territory under direct Maratha rule, 1785
- British territory, 1805
- British territorial gains by 1838
- British territorial gains by 1857
- British territorial gains by 1914
- British sphere of influence, 1914
- princely state or protectorate, 1914
- border of princely state or protectorate
- border, 1914
- ⊗ battle in the second Maratha War, 1803–05
- disruption to British administration during the Indian mutiny, 1857–59
- Ⓜ *Sepoy* army base remaining loyal to Britain, 1857
- ☼ center of rebellion
- ⚓ naval station
- *coal* source of commodity
- → British campaign
- railroad by 1914

AFGHANISTAN
Kandahar
Quetta

PERSIA

1893 to Britain

Bola Pas

Baluchistan
1876 British protectorate

TIMELINE

Political & social change

1800	1850	1900
1784 The India Act declares that "territorial expansion" is repugnant to the nation	**1836** Major road-building program begins	**1905** Bengal is partitioned into Bengal, East Bengal and Assam
1798 Ceylon becomes a Crown Colony	**1853** The first railroad in India is opened in Bombay	**1906** The All-India Muslim League is founded in Dhaka
1813 Christian missionaries are licensed to preach	**1857** The first Indian doctors graduate in Agra	**1909** The Morley–Minto reforms give India a first taste of representative government
	1877 Queen Victoria is proclaimed Empress of India in Delhi	
1835 English language made the medium of instruction	**1858** Queen Victoria assumes sovereignty of India as East India Company is wound up	**1885** The Indian National Congress is formed in Bombay
		1911 King George V attends coronation *Durbar* in Delhi

Military developments

1800	1850	1900
1799 Tipu Sultan is defeated by Cornwallis and killed	**1839–42** Disastrous Afghan War is fought to counter a perceived Russian threat	**1878–80** Second Afghan War; Britain fails to subdue Afghanistan	**1903–04** British military expedition to Tibet forces trade agreement
1803 Second Maratha War begins (lasts until 1818)	**1843–49** Forcible annexation of Sind and the Punjab	**1886** Upper Burma is annexed by the British	**1912** Viceroy of India is wounded by terrorist bomb
1816 The Nepalese end their war with the British	**1857** Mutiny begins with the capture of Delhi and sieges of Lucknow and Kanpur	**1897** A Pathan uprising on the northwest frontier is put down with difficulty	

1800   1850   1900

1 Tipu Sultan of Mysore, the East India Company's greatest adversary in south India from the early 1780s, tried to ally himself with the French and was killed at the siege of Seringapatam in 1799.

2 Gurkha warriors from the hill tribes of Nepal fought fiercely against the British from 1814–16. From 1860 to the present day, Gurkhas have been recruited to form an elite infantry unit of the British Army.

3 The First Afghan War ended with a humiliating retreat from Kabul to Jalalabad (1842); only 121 men of the entire 20,000-strong British force survived.

4 Atrocities were committed by both sides during the mutiny; British reprisals included executing mutineers by strapping them to the muzzles of artillery pieces.

5 Tea has been cultivated as a major commercial crop since the mid-19th century, particularly in the fertile, rainy upper Brahmaputra valley in Assam.

6 The northwest frontier of India proved the most troublesome to defend for the British. In 1897, 35,000 troops were needed to quell a rising by Pathan tribes.

7 The British briefly invaded Tibet in 1903–04, to counter Russian influence there by imposing a trading agreement on the Dalai Lama.

8 Bombay was the site of the Gateway to India, an arch erected in Mughal style in 1911.

RUSSIAN EMPIRE

Kashgar
Yarkand
Khotan

silk
Northwest Frontier Province
wheat
6
Pass
1842
Jalalabad
Peshawar
Rawalpindi
Kashmir
1846 British protectorate
Jammu
sugar
Punjab
1846/49 to Britain
cotton
Amritsar
Lahore
Jullundur
Firozpur
tobacco
Ambala
Saharanpur
HIMALAYAS
Lhasa
1903–04
7
TIBET
Sikkim
1817 British protectorate
Northeast Frontier Agency 1913/14 to Britain
tea
Bhutan
Assam from 1824 to Britain
5
Carchar
1868–82 British protectorate

wheat
HINDU KUSH RANGE
Khairpur
cotton
wheat
Bahawalpur
Thar Desert
Bikaner
Meerut
Delhi
1803
Bareilly
Sitapur
sugar
NEPAL
Kathmandu
2 Gurkha War 1814–16
Darjeeling
rice
Manipur
1813 to Burma, 1886 British protectorate
Tripura
Upper Burma
1886 to Britain

Sind
43 to Britain
on
barley
Laswari 1803
Jaipur
Agra
wheat
Mainpura
Farrukhabad 1804
barley
Oudh
1856 to Britain
Lucknow 1857–58
Kanpur
rice
Danupur
tea
tobacco
jute
sugar
Dhaka
rice
Chittagong
Mandalay
Burma
Chinese tributary until 1886

Ajmer
Nasirabad
Gwalior
Kalpi
4 Fatehpur
Allahabad
sugar
silk
Benares (Varanasi)
maize
Azamgarh
Patna
oil seed
Baharampur
1857
sugar
Bengal
Dum-Dum
Calcutta
jute

Rajputana
1818 British protectorate
Udaipur
Erinpura
Nimach
Jhansi
Bundelkhand
wheat
Bhopal
Narmada
Jabalpur
Orissa
Arakan 1826 to Britain

Rann of Kutch
cotton
Ahmadabad
tobacco
Baroda
Indore
Mhow
rice
wheat
Nagpur
Burhanpur
Cuttack
Lower Burma
created 1862 incorporating Arakan, Pegu and Tenasserim

Gujarat
Surat
Diu
to Portugal
Daman
to Portugal
cotton
rice
wheat
tobacco
Bombay
8
Poone
Argaon 1803
Amravati
linseed
Assaye 1803
DECCAN
Aurangabad
Godavari
cotton
Bastar
Northern Circars
Pegu
1852 to Britain
Rangoon
Tenasserim 1826 to Britain

cotton
Hyderabad
Hyderabad
cotton
Yanam
to France
cotton
Krishna
Bijapur
rice
Goa
Goa
to Portugal
tobacco
coffee
cotton
EASTERN GHATS
WESTERN GHATS
Mysore
1831 British protectorate
Bangalore
Seringapatam 1799
1
Mysore
rice
Tellicherry
Mahé
to France
tea
Cochin
coconuts
Madras
cotton
rice
Vellore
Sepoy mutiny, 1806
groundnuts
Kaveri
Pondicherry
to France
Karikal
to France
Madurai
Jaffna
Mannar
Trincomalee
Anjengo
Trivandrum
Travancore
tobacco
Tuticorin
cotton
1815, 1818
Ceylon
1798 to Britain
Kandy
coconuts
Colombo
rice *tea*

Bay of Bengal

Laccadive Islands

Andaman Islands
1857 to Britain

Nicobar Islands
1869 to Britain

MEMBERS of the British Raj (rule) saw themselves as dispensing even-handed justice and the benefits of European civilization to grateful natives.

See also 61 (Mughal India);
103 (Indian nationalism before 1947)

0 ————— 400 km
0 ————— 300 mi

Two decisions made by the Congress of the embryonic United States of America set up the decisive conflict between white settlers and native Americans. In 1787 the indigenous peoples were promised that their lands and property could only be ceded with their consent. In 1791, however, George Washington authorized expansion westward along the Ohio. Initially the growth of the United States was limited by Spain's (from 1800, France's) possession of lands beyond the Mississippi. Even at this stage, however, trade links existed between the thirteen eastern states of the Union and the Pacific. By 1795, the pattern of territorial gains by the whites and displacement of native Americans to the west was set, a process hastened by Thomas Jefferson's purchase of Louisiana from France in 1803, when the territory of the United States was doubled.

In the ensuing decades further territories were gained by the United States, through purchase or conflict: Florida, Texas, Oregon, the Mexican cession and the Gadsden Purchase. Some 400,000 native people were confronted by the westward thrust of settler culture across the Great Plains.

In Florida, the Seminole people conducted a sustained resistance which was only ultimately suppressed in the 1840s. The forcible removal of the Cherokee to the unsettled "Indian Territory" of Oklahoma in 1838–39, after gold was found in their original homelands, cost four thousand lives (the "Trail of Tears"). The Delaware, Wichita and many others suffered a similar fate. Congress offered free land in return for minimal investment, encouraging claims to be staked to territories on the Great Plains. Railroads further threatened the Plains peoples' main food source, the vast buffalo herds.

The Kiowa, Comanche and Arapaho accepted reservation status at the Medicine Lodge Creek Conference (1867), while Sitting Bull's Dakota Sioux

ceased hostilities in return for permanent occupation of the Black Hills reservation. However, gold prospector incursions in 1874 provoked resistance by the Sioux and Northern Cheyenne in 1876–77. They annihilated General Custer and 200 troopers at the Battle of the Little Bighorn, but their leaders were eventually forced to surrender. Other native peoles in Wyoming, Montana, Oregon and Idaho met similar fates. Cochise and Geronimo of the Chiricahua Apaches in Arizona and New Mexico

conducted guerrilla campaigns until forced to surrender (1872 and 1886 respectively).

Geronimo's surrender marked the end of the Indian Wars. Despair at their situation, however, led many native Americans to follow the cult of the ghost dance which was supposed to make initiates immune to gunfire. The US Seventh Cavalry massacred Sioux ghost dancers and their families at Wounded Knee Creek in December 1890.

Throughout this period the United States thrived. The northeast saw a stream of immigrants from Europe, and new industries arose to feed, house and clothe the growing population. In the south, the high export prices of cotton brought the development of large plantations. The invention of the cotton gin in 1792 to separate cotton fiber from seeds stimulated production. Yet the plantation system relied on slavery, a growing point of contention between North and South. In the 1820s, many had hoped to liberate the slaves, but three decades later the rising value of slaves made this less attractive. California was allowed to join the Union as a "free" state in 1850 in return for harsh laws against fugitive slaves, but the issue exploded into civil war.

Canada's population changed in the late 18th century as a result of Britain's loss of its other colonies. White loyalists from New York and South Carolina, as well as the Mohawks who had fought alongside the British, settled in Nova Scotia, New Brunswick, Cape Breton and Prince Edward Island. Expansion westward began when the Red River Colony, nucleus of what later became Manitoba, was founded in 1812, though further growth was hampered by the rocky terrain of the Canadian Shield.

A United States invasion of Canada in 1812 was followed by a British attack on Washington (1814) and the Battle of New Orleans (1815). Thereafter, border issues were settled peacefully: the 1818 agreement on the 49th Parallel created an undefended US–Canadian frontier from the Lake of the Woods to the Rockies, which the 1846 Oregon Treaty then extended to Vancouver.

Legend

expansion of the United States
- the original Thirteen Colonies
- 1783 settlement and Native American cessions
- Louisiana Purchase, 1803
- British cession, 1818 and 1842
- Florida, 1813–19
- Texas, 1845
- Oregon Country, 1846
- Mexican cession, 1848
- Gadsden Purchase, 1853
- Alaska, 1867

expansion of Canada
- Canadian provinces, 1867
- territory added 1870
- province added by 1873
- territory added 1880

- **1787** admission of state to US, or provincial status achieved within Canada
- **Fox** Native American nation, 1783
- "reservation" within the US, 1875
- Native American battle
- massacre of Native Americans
- Métis rebellion under Louis Riel
- Anglo-American conflict, 1812-15

exploration route
- Hearne, 1770–71
- Mackenzie, 1789–93
- Thompson, 1789-1811
- Lewis & Clark, 1804-06
- goldfield
- trail route
- railroad by 1914
- borders, 1914
- national capital

0 ____ 900 km
0 ____ 600 mi

St Lawrence Island
Nome
Inuit
Alaska
1912 US territory
3
Fairb
Bering Sea
Tinneh
Anchorage
Aleutian Islands
Aleut
Tling
Kodiak Island
Gulf of Alaska

TIMELINE

	1800	1850	1900
The United States	**1787** The Northwest Ordinance sets rules for new state government formation	**1849** California gold rush attracts over 100,000 settlers	**1880** The United States of America is comprised of 38 states
	1804–06 Lewis and Clark explore beyond the Mississippi and reach the Pacific	**1849** California joins the Union as a free state	**1890** The government declares that the western frontier no longer exists
	1815 Reopening of European markets boosts cotton exports	**1861** Nevada, Dakota and Colorado are organized as US territories	**1890** Massacre at Wounded Knee
	1819 Spain cedes Florida to the United States	**1863–68** New US territories created in Idaho, Arizona, Montana and Wyoming	
	1830 President Andrew Jackson's Indian Removal Act is passed by Congress	**1869** The first trans-American railroad link is completed	
Canada	**1784** New Brunswick is founded to accommodate British loyalists	**1839** Lord Durham, governor-general of British North America, plans a unified state	**1869–70** Métis revolt under Louis Riel fails in Manitoba
	1791 Representative government is established in Ontario and Quebec	**1842** The Ashburton Treaty defines the southern limits of Quebec and New Brunswick	**1885** Métis revolt fails in Saskatchewan
	1812 The Red River Colony is founded	**1846** Oregon Treaty is signed and the Pacific coast frontier extended along 49th Parallel	**1885** Completion of the Canadian Pacific Railway
			1896 Discovery of gold in the Yukon
	1818 Agreement is reached on siting the US–Canadian frontier on the 49th Parallel	**1867** Dominion of Canada is set up: Quebec, Ontario, New Brunswick and Nova Scotia	
	1800	1850	1900

1 Meriwether Lewis and William Clark were commissioned by Thomas Jefferson to explore beyond the Mississippi in 1804.

2 The "Five Civilized Tribes" of the southeast United States – Choctaw, Cherokee, Chickasaw, Creek, and Seminole – were socalled for their adaptation to white culture. Even so, they were forcibly relocated in 1830.

3 Alaska was bought from czarist Russia in 1867 for US$7.2 million.

4 In 1869, the Union Pacific and the Central Pacific railroads met at Promontory Point in Utah.

5 In 1866–70, the Fenian Brotherhood, an American arm of the Irish Republican Brotherhood, carried out raids in Canada, trying to change British policy on Irish independence. The first attack was at Fort Erie.

The American Civil War proved a decisive factor in Canadian unification. The Federal victory in 1865, attacks by the Fenian Brotherhood on Canadian territory (1866–70) and the westward expansion of the United States together caused Canada to press for a coast-to-coast union to ensure national security. In 1867 Nova Scotia, New Brunswick, Quebec and Ontario were united in the Dominion of Canada. Manitoba joined in 1870, British Columbia in 1871 and Prince Edward Island in 1873. The first government of the new dominion promoted a "national policy" aimed at peopling the Canadian Shield and the Far West, building a transcontinental railroad and introducing tariffs to protect farm prices.

The long-promised Canadian Pacific Railway was completed in 1885. The railroad consolidated the western frontier, created new towns along its route and provided a tangible link between British Columbia and the east.

Canada continued to expand to the north. In 1912 Manitoba advanced to the 60th Parallel (to match Saskatchewan and Alberta). In the same year Quebec and Ontario were extended to the Hudson Bay and the Arctic. Another frontier developed as Canada's northernmost territories, home to the Inuit, were encroached upon first by fur-trappers and then thousands of gold prospectors. Oil reserves, too, were found in Alberta in 1912–14.

See also 85 (American Civil War); 87 (the United States in the later 19th century)

The demand for cotton as an export crop made the economy of the states south of the Mason–Dixon line (the border between Pennsylvania and Maryland) dependent on the systematic exploitation of humanity. On plantations and farms and in cities and towns, four million black slaves were denied their rights to a family, education and citizenship. Slavery became a political issue during the westward expansion of the United States. In deference to southern interests, the Constitutional Convention of 1787 prohibited the importation of slaves, but protected slavery in the states from federal interference. In the Missouri compromise of 1820, which admitted Maine and the Louisiana Purchase lands (except Missouri) as free and proclaimed all states above latitude 36° 30' as free, a convention of balancing abolitionist and slave-owning interests was established.

Attitudes toward slavery were polarized; some demanded complete and immediate abolition, while others saw good economic and racial reasons for its retention. The issue was made even more divisive by a number of legislative decisions in the 1850s. The 1850 compromise admitted California as a free state, but took no action to curb slavery in the other territories ceded by Mexico after the war of 1846–48 (Utah and New Mexico). The Kansas–Nebraska Act (1854) gave settlers the right to decide whether or not to permit slavery in a new territory, a situation that led to open warfare between rival groups in "bleeding Kansas." Finally a Supreme Court ruling of 1857 – the "Dred Scott" decision – declared that neither Congress nor the people of a territory could abolish slavery in the territories. This meant the Missouri compromise was unconstitutional and destroyed the artificial balance between free and slave states. This decision threatened the democratic foundation of the Union. Meanwhile, fugitive slaves escaped to the north via the "Underground Railroad" (a network of abolitionist households). In the 1860 presidential elections all the free states – except New Jersey – returned the Republican Abraham Lincoln, who refused to extend slavery to new territories.

On 20 December 1860, South Carolina seceded from the Union. Georgia, Alabama, Texas, Florida, Mississippi and Louisiana soon followed, creating a Confederacy and electing Jefferson Davis as their president. On 12 April 1861, Confederate forces began hostilities with a bombardment of Fort Sumter. Lincoln called for 75,000 northern volunteers, prompting Virginia, North Carolina, Tennessee and Arkansas to join the Confederacy. Yet not all the slave states seceded: Kentucky declared itself neutral; Delaware, Maryland and Missouri remained loyal, as did the northwestern counties of Virginia (which became the state of West Virginia in 1863).

The civil war that erupted was a devastating conflict: a quarter of all those who saw combat lost their lives. Confederate strategy was to defend itself and win international recognition as an independent state. The Union government thus had no option but to attack the south and restore the rebel states to the Union. The Union had a larger population, less vulnerable railroads and far greater industrial resources than the Confederacy. Lincoln was confident of achieving his two main objectives: to blockade the Confederate coastline and capture Richmond, the Confederate capital. However, superior Confederate generalship caused Union armies several early setbacks, notably their defeat at the two Battles of Bull Run, and their failure to take the key town of Fredericksburg. In January 1863, Lincoln espoused abolition of slavery in his emancipation proclamation, freeing all slaves in the Confederacy. Meanwhile, Confederate armies pushed north into Pennsylvania to take the war to the enemy. This aim was thwarted at the Battle of Gettysburg in July 1863, which marked a turning point in Union fortunes.

At the same time, Union armies were victorious in the west. Under the command of Ulysses Grant, they advanced down the Mississippi. After gaining

control of the area through the battle of Shiloh and the siege of Vicksburg, the North succeeded in cutting off Arkansas, Louisiana and Texas from the Confederacy. William Sherman's campaign in Georgia saw the destruction of Atlanta and the capture of Savannah. Grant fought a series of battles (Wilderness, Spotsylvania, Cold Harbor and Petersburg) against the Confederate commander Robert E. Lee, which left the south with barely 60,000 troops. Richmond fell on 3 April 1865 and Lee surrendered the Confederate army at Appomattox Court House on 9 April. Five days later, Lincoln was assassinated.

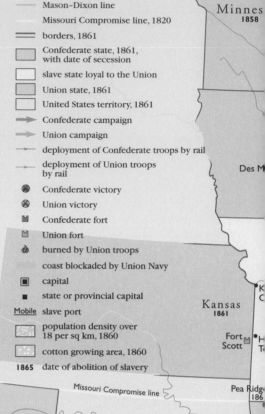

Northwest Territory (slavery forbidden, 1787)
Mason–Dixon line
Missouri Compromise line, 1820
borders, 1861
Confederate state, 1861, with date of secession
slave state loyal to the Union
Union state, 1861
United States territory, 1861
Confederate campaign
Union campaign
deployment of Confederate troops by rail
deployment of Union troops by rail
Confederate victory
Union victory
Confederate fort
Union fort
burned by Union troops
coast blockaded by Union Navy
capital
state or provincial capital
Mobile slave port
population density over 18 per sq km, 1860
cotton growing area, 1860
1865 date of abolition of slavery

TIMELINE

Abolition of slavery

1855	1860	1865
1831 The first issue of the abolitionist journal *The Liberator* is published	**1859** Commercial convention at Vicksburg demands the resumption of slave imports	**1863** The formal Emancipation Proclamation liberates slaves in the Confederacy
1854 The Kansas–Nebraska Act repeals the Missouri compromise of 1820	**1859** John Brown tries to seize the Federal arsenal at Harper's Ferry	**1864** Lincoln is re-elected as US president
1856 Slave-holders and abolitionists clash in Kansas	**1860** Lincoln becomes US president	**1865** Ratification of the Thirteenth Amendment abolishing slavery
	1857 The Dred Scott decision outlaws restrictions on slavery in the territories	

Secession and civil war

	1860 President Buchanan denies any state may secede	**1864** Sherman's southern campaign destroys Atlanta and Savannah
	1861 Civil War begins when Confederate forces fire on Fort Sumter	**1865** Confederates surrender at Appomattox
	1861 "Stonewall" Jackson wins First Battle of Bull Run	
	1862 Battle of Antietam checks Confederate advance; Lee falls back to Virginia	
	1863 Gen. Meade repels the south's army at Gettysburg	
1855	1860	1865

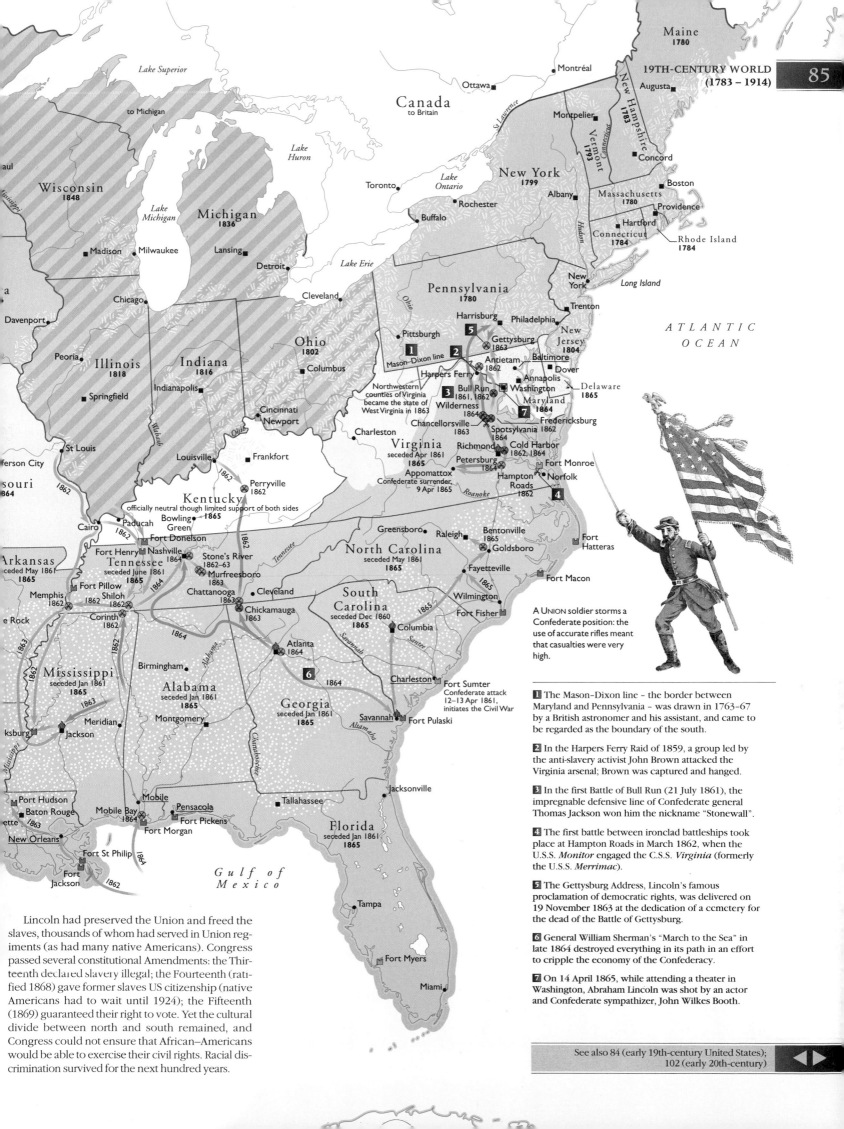

Maine
1780

New Hampshire
1783

Vermont
1793

New York
1799

Massachusetts
1780

Connecticut
1784

Rhode Island
1784

Pennsylvania
1780

New Jersey
1804

Ohio
1802

Indiana
1816

Illinois
1818

Wisconsin
1848

Michigan
1836

Delaware
1865

Maryland
1864

Virginia
seceded Apr 1861
1865

Northwestern counties of Virginia became the state of West Virginia in 1863

Kentucky
officially neutral though limited support of both sides
1865

Tennessee
seceded June 1861
1865

Arkansas
ceded May 1861
1865

North Carolina
seceded May 1861
1865

South Carolina
seceded Dec 1860
1865

Mississippi
seceded Jan 1861
1865

Alabama
seceded Jan 1861
1865

Georgia
seceded Jan 1861
1865

Florida
seceded Jan 1861
1865

1 Mason–Dixon line

Appomattox
Confederate surrender,
9 Apr 1865

Fort Sumter
Confederate attack
12–13 Apr 1861,
initiates the Civil War

A UNION soldier storms a Confederate position: the use of accurate rifles meant that casualties were very high.

1 The Mason–Dixon line – the border between Maryland and Pennsylvania – was drawn in 1763–67 by a British astronomer and his assistant, and came to be regarded as the boundary of the south.

2 In the Harpers Ferry Raid of 1859, a group led by the anti-slavery activist John Brown attacked the Virginia arsenal; Brown was captured and hanged.

3 In the first Battle of Bull Run (21 July 1861), the impregnable defensive line of Confederate general Thomas Jackson won him the nickname "Stonewall".

4 The first battle between ironclad battleships took place at Hampton Roads in March 1862, when the U.S.S. *Monitor* engaged the C.S.S. *Virginia* (formerly the U.S.S. *Merrimac*).

5 The Gettysburg Address, Lincoln's famous proclamation of democratic rights, was delivered on 19 November 1863 at the dedication of a cemetery for the dead of the Battle of Gettysburg.

6 General William Sherman's "March to the Sea" in late 1864 destroyed everything in its path in an effort to cripple the economy of the Confederacy.

7 On 14 April 1865, while attending a theater in Washington, Abraham Lincoln was shot by an actor and Confederate sympathizer, John Wilkes Booth.

Lincoln had preserved the Union and freed the slaves, thousands of whom had served in Union regiments (as had many native Americans). Congress passed several constitutional Amendments: the Thirteenth declared slavery illegal; the Fourteenth (ratified 1868) gave former slaves US citizenship (native Americans had to wait until 1924); the Fifteenth (1869) guaranteed their right to vote. Yet the cultural divide between north and south remained, and Congress could not ensure that African–Americans would be able to exercise their civil rights. Racial discrimination survived for the next hundred years.

See also 84 (early 19th-century United States);
102 (early 20th-century)

Growing urbanization and industrialization, and a dramatic increase in population, were evident throughout the world by 1880. European cities developed rapidly, as ever more people were drawn away from rural life by factory work (▷ 90). Technological advances, especially in communications, impelled industrial development and promoted colonial expansion. By the 1850s, the British had installed the first railroads and telegraph systems in India. Politically, while some ancient entities such as the Tokugawa shogunate in Japan did not survive the advent of the modern age, others – the Chinese Manchu dynasty, the Ottoman empire and czarist Russia – lingered into the 20th century, though torn by internal dissent.

Dynamic new nation-states arose as the 19th century progressed, changing the balance of power in Europe. In Italy, nationalist groupings in the north and south combined to bring about the unification of the country (▷ 80). The struggle for domination in the German Confederation between Austria and Prussia resulted in conflict in 1866, from which Prussia emerged victorious. Another crushing Prussian military victory in 1870–71 against France destroyed the empire of Napoleon III and led to Prussia forming the nucleus of the German "second empire".

Warfare was in the process of being radically altered by mechanization. The American Civil War (1861–65) was the first conflict to utilize the greatly enhanced mobility and firepower afforded respectively by railroads and the mass production of munitions (▷ 85). Fought between the North and the South over the question of slavery and the extent of federal jurisdiction, the war exacted a huge toll in human lives. The North's far superior manpower and industrial capacity eventually allowed it to prevail. Despite the damage caused by the war, however, the United States was fast becoming the dominant power in the Western Hemisphere. Expansion continued with the purchase of the Gadsden Strip from Mexico (1853) and Alaska from Russia (1867). The inauguration of a transcontinental electric telegraph was swiftly followed by the linking of the Union Pacific and the Central Pacific railroads to form a coast-to-coast route in 1869 (▷ 84). In the 1870s and 1880s, the construction of another railroad across the North American continent played a vital role in unifying Canada, joining the new western territory of British Columbia to the eastern provinces that had declared the Dominion of Canada in 1867.

Central and South America were beset by armed conflict. France undertook an imperial adventure in Mexico in 1863–67, which ended disastrously.

1861–65 American Civil War; northern states fight to preserve Union against secessionist South

1861 Czar Alexander II undertakes reform by emancipating Russian serfs

1854–56 Crimean War; Britain and France oppose Russian expansion into Ottoman territories

1860 Abraham Lincoln elected US president on anti-slavery ticket

1867 Russia sells Alaska to the United States

1852 French second empire: Louis Napoleon emperor (Napoleon III)

1858 Piedmontese premier Camillo Cavour and Napoleon III plan Italian unification

1866 Austro-Prussian War; Prussia defeats Austria

TIMELINE

The Americas

Europe

Middle East — 1850

Africa

Asia and Australasia

1860

1851–53 Gold rush in Australia

1857–58 Indian Mutiny; Muslims and Hindus rebel against British rule

1863 Asante people of west Africa defeat British in Third Asante War

1868 Japanese Tokugawa shogunate ends; Meiji dynasty restored

1853 US Commodore Matthew Perry opens up Japan to western trade

1869 Suez Canal, built by the French, opens

1870 Unification of Ita as Rome becomes pa of the kingdo

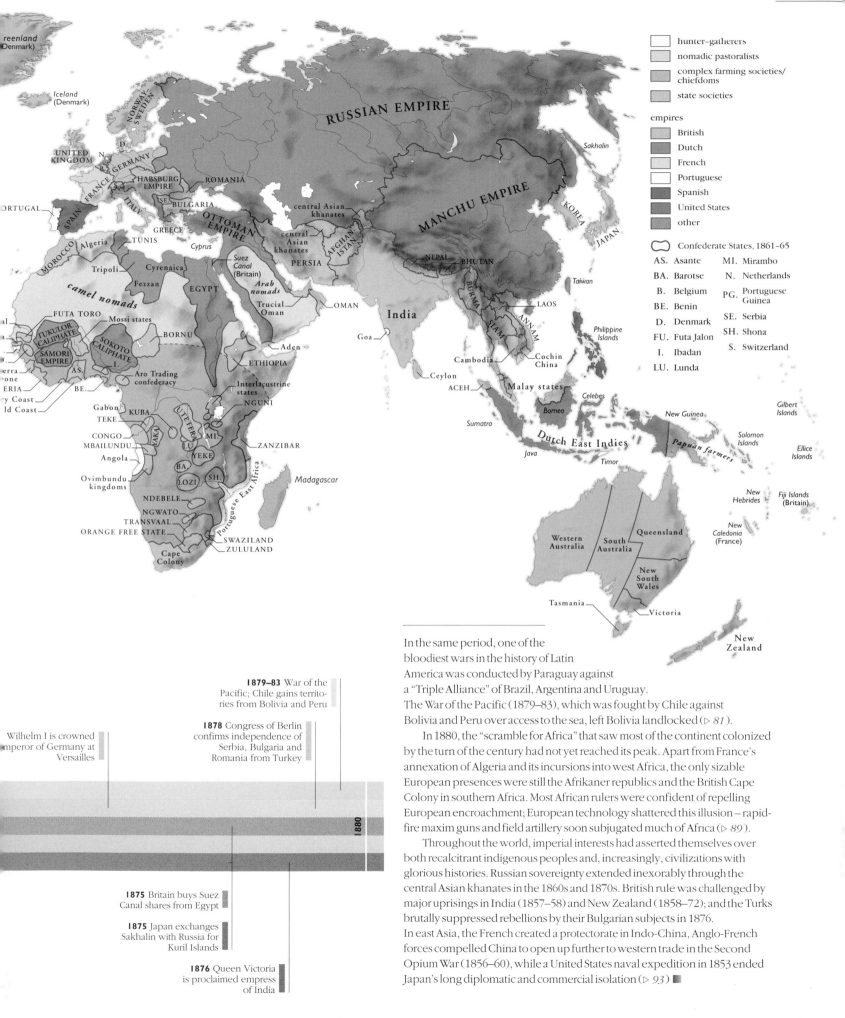

Legend:

- hunter-gatherers
- nomadic pastoralists
- complex farming societies/chiefdoms
- state societies

empires
- British
- Dutch
- French
- Portuguese
- Spanish
- United States
- other

Confederate States, 1861–65

AS.	Asante	MI.	Mirambo
BA.	Barotse	N.	Netherlands
B.	Belgium	PG.	Portuguese Guinea
BE.	Benin		
D.	Denmark	SE.	Serbia
FU.	Futa Jalon	SH.	Shona
I.	Ibadan	S.	Switzerland
LU.	Lunda		

Map labels:

Greenland (Denmark), Iceland (Denmark), NORWAY SWEDEN, RUSSIAN EMPIRE, Sakhalin, UNITED KINGDOM, D., N., B., GERMANY, FRANCE, HABSBURG EMPIRE, ROMANIA, PORTUGAL, SPAIN, ITALY, SE., BULGARIA, GREECE, OTTOMAN EMPIRE, central Asian khanates, central Asian khanates, MANCHU EMPIRE, KOREA, JAPAN, Taiwan, MOROCCO, Algeria, TUNIS, Cyprus, Suez Canal (Britain), PERSIA, AFGHAN-ISTAN, NEPAL, BHUTAN, Tripoli, Cyrenaica, Arab nomads, BURMA, LAOS, Fezzan, EGYPT, Trucial Oman, India, SIAM, ANNAM, camel nomads, OMAN, Aden, Goa, Philippine Islands, FUTA TORO, Mossi states, BORNU, ETHIOPIA, Cambodia, Cochin China, TUKULOR CALIPHATE, SOKOTO CALIPHATE, Ceylon, ACEH, Malay states, SAMORI EMPIRE, AS., Aro Trading confederacy, Interlacustrine states, Celebes, New Guinea, Gilbert Islands, erra one, BE., Gabon, TEKE, KUBA, NGUNI, Sumatra, Borneo, Solomon Islands, y Coast, ld Coast, CONGO, MBAILUNDU, UTETERA, LU., MI., ZANZIBAR, Dutch East Indies, Java, Papuan farmers, Ellice Islands, Angola, YAKA, YEKE, BA., LOZI, SH., Madagascar, Timor, Ovimbundu kingdoms, NDEBELE, New Hebrides, Fiji Islands (Britain), NGWATO, TRANSVAAL, ORANGE FREE STATE, Portuguese East Africa, New Caledonia (France), SWAZILAND, ZULULAND, Cape Colony, Western Australia, South Australia, Queensland, New South Wales, Tasmania, Victoria, New Zealand

Timeline:

Wilhelm I is crowned emperor of Germany at Versailles

1879–83 War of the Pacific; Chile gains territories from Bolivia and Peru

1878 Congress of Berlin confirms independence of Serbia, Bulgaria and Romania from Turkey

1880

1875 Britain buys Suez Canal shares from Egypt

1875 Japan exchanges Sakhalin with Russia for Kuril Islands

1876 Queen Victoria is proclaimed empress of India

Body text:

In the same period, one of the bloodiest wars in the history of Latin America was conducted by Paraguay against a "Triple Alliance" of Brazil, Argentina and Uruguay. The War of the Pacific (1879–83), which was fought by Chile against Bolivia and Peru over access to the sea, left Bolivia landlocked (▷ 81).

In 1880, the "scramble for Africa" that saw most of the continent colonized by the turn of the century had not yet reached its peak. Apart from France's annexation of Algeria and its incursions into west Africa, the only sizable European presences were still the Afrikaner republics and the British Cape Colony in southern Africa. Most African rulers were confident of repelling European encroachment; European technology shattered this illusion – rapid-fire maxim guns and field artillery soon subjugated much of Africa (▷ 89).

Throughout the world, imperial interests had asserted themselves over both recalcitrant indigenous peoples and, increasingly, civilizations with glorious histories. Russian sovereignty extended inexorably through the central Asian khanates in the 1860s and 1870s. British rule was challenged by major uprisings in India (1857–58) and New Zealand (1858–72); and the Turks brutally suppressed rebellions by their Bulgarian subjects in 1876. In east Asia, the French created a protectorate in Indo-China, Anglo-French forces compelled China to open up further to western trade in the Second Opium War (1856–60), while a United States naval expedition in 1853 ended Japan's long diplomatic and commercial isolation (▷ 93) ■

A t the end of the Civil War, the northern states experienced unprecedented prosperity as American and foreign speculators rushed to invest in a new wave of industrialization. Railroad construction drove the economy. The completion of the first transcontinental link in 1869 encouraged the development of other lines across America; three more were in operation by 1883. Urban centers and rural areas alike benefited. Millions of cattle were transported to slaughterhouses in the new cities of Chicago and Kansas City. By opening up the west to profitable farming, railroads also hastened political change. By 1890 most of the western territories had been admitted as states of the Union. Yet the railroad boom was not without its negative aspects. Corrupt share-dealing provoked a panic and withdrawal of foreign capital in 1873.

The south had been devastated by the civil war. Its principal towns lay in ruins and its economic life destroyed. Opinion in the north was divided on how the rebel states should be treated. President Andrew Johnson (Lincoln's successor) favored reconciliation, while hardliners counseled repression. After a period of radical administration, conservatives reasserted white rule in the south, circumventing the constitutional rights guaranteed by Congress to freed blacks. Reconstruction proceeded slowly, and states were gradually readmitted to the Union.

Towns and cities grew with astonishing rapidity. By 1914, the United States had an urban population of 45 million, most of whom were immigrants. On five occasions the annual total of immigrants – from every corner of Europe – exceeded one million. Desperate for work and willing to take low-paid employment, the newcomers were quickly absorbed into the factories of New York, Chicago, Buffalo, Pittsburgh, Cleveland, Milwaukee, Cincinnati and St Louis. Appalling conditions prevailed in the crowded cities, polluted factories, primitive mining communities and harsh lumber camps. Immigrants often faced discrimination; as early as 1871, the Chinese who had entered through California to work in mining and on the railroads were the

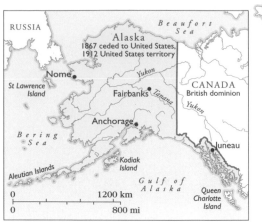

population density per sq km, c.1900
- over 18
- 2–18
- under 2

- ■ city with population over 1 million, c.1900
- ▪ city with population of between 250,000 and 1 million, c.1900
- Boston immigrant entry port
- ✳ start of great labor strike, 1877
- ✸ other industrial conflict
- oilfield
- coalfield
- iron ore deposits
- center of steel production
- Goodnight–Loving cattle trail
- western cattle trail
- Chisholm cattle trail
- Shawnee or eastern cattle trail
- Sedalia cattle trail, later abandoned
- railroad
- borders, 1914

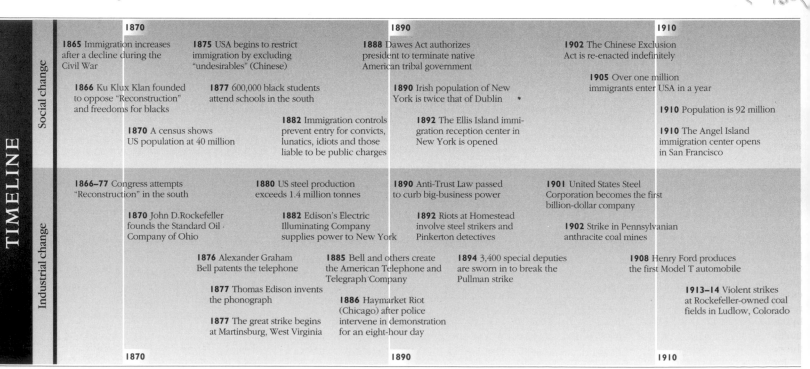

TIMELINE

Social change

1870

1865 Immigration increases after a decline during the Civil War

1866 Ku Klux Klan founded to oppose "Reconstruction" and freedoms for blacks

1870 A census shows US population at 40 million

1875 USA begins to restrict immigration by excluding "undesirables" (Chinese)

1877 600,000 black students attend schools in the south

1882 Immigration controls prevent entry for convicts, lunatics, idiots and those liable to be public charges

1890

1888 Dawes Act authorizes president to terminate native American tribal government

1890 Irish population of New York is twice that of Dublin

1892 The Ellis Island immigration reception center in New York is opened

1910

1902 The Chinese Exclusion Act is re-enacted indefinitely

1905 Over one million immigrants enter USA in a year

1910 Population is 92 million

1910 The Angel Island immigration center opens in San Francisco

Industrial change

1866–77 Congress attempts "Reconstruction" in the south

1870 John D. Rockefeller founds the Standard Oil Company of Ohio

1876 Alexander Graham Bell patents the telephone

1877 Thomas Edison invents the phonograph

1877 The great strike begins at Martinsburg, West Virginia

1880 US steel production exceeds 1.4 million tonnes

1882 Edison's Electric Illuminating Company supplies power to New York

1885 Bell and others create the American Telephone and Telegraph Company

1886 Haymarket Riot (Chicago) after police intervene in demonstration for an eight-hour day

1890 Anti-Trust Law passed to curb big-business power

1892 Riots at Homestead involve steel strikers and Pinkerton detectives

1894 3,400 special deputies are sworn in to break the Pullman strike

1901 United States Steel Corporation becomes the first billion-dollar company

1902 Strike in Pennsylvanian anthracite coal mines

1908 Henry Ford produces the first Model T automobile

1913–14 Violent strikes at Rockefeller-owned coal fields in Ludlow, Colorado

1870   1890   1910

victims of race riots. Further Chinese immigration was blocked by the Chinese Exclusion Act of 1882.

The depression that affected Europe in the late 19th century had little effect on the vibrant US economy. This period saw the rise of magnates who made the United States into the world's great industrial power. John D. Rockefeller dominated the oil industry while Philip D. Armour controlled a meat-packing empire. The financier J. Pierpont Morgan underwrote railroads, and Andrew Carnegie was the leading figure in the steel industry. These men took advantage of low interest rates, cheap labor and a largely unregulated market. However, though employers used ruthless business methods and dealt summarily with discontent among their workforces, the age of American capitalism had its benefits. The essential symbol of American enterprise and democracy was the Model T automobile, first made in 1908 by the Detroit mechanic Henry Ford. Also some multimillionaires, such as Carnegie, were philanthropists who gave away part of their fortunes.

Industrial growth brought labor problems. The job losses resulting from the 1873 economic crisis made labor unions hostile to further immigration. Strikes were common, the most damaging in 1877. Railroad employees, enraged by a pay cut, withdrew their labor and were supported in their grievances by a large army of unemployed. Unrest spread to Pittsburgh, Chicago, St Louis, Kansas City, Galveston and San Francisco before militiamen were called out to suppress it. Although this dispute, the first general strike in American history, involved millions and even spread to Canada, its most significant feature was the Federal administration's use of troops. In 1892, workers at the Carnegie steel mill in Homestead were beaten by the state militia. Two years later president Cleveland sent soldiers to put down a strike of railroad workers in Chicago.

The economy, though, stayed buoyant. By 1914, with a population over 97 million, the United States led the world in the manufacture of steel and lumber products, in meat-packing and precious metal extraction, and had more telephones, telegraphs, electric lights and automobiles than anywhere else.

1 Between 1867 and 1871, about 1.5 million head of cattle were herded on "long drives" along the Chisholm Trail to the railhead at Abilene, Kansas.

2 Atlanta had been razed by fire during the Georgia campaign of the civil war, but became the center of Federal government activity during reconstruction.

3 During the great strike of 1877, Pittsburgh was devastated by three days of rioting that destroyed much railroad property and almost leveled the city.

4 Oklahoma was opened to settlement in 1889; settlers raced across the prairie to stake their claims.

5 Ellis Island in New York Bay became the country's principal immigration station from 1892 onward.

6 Utah was admitted to the Union as a state in 1896, after its Mormon inhabitants had promised to relinquish the practice of polygamy.

See also 85 (American Civil War);
102 (the Americas in the early 20th century)

The Russian empire, though ostensibly mighty, had structural weaknesses. Above all, its sheer size made it difficult to govern and prevented ready use of its abundant resources. As a result, corruption was rife and the country remained economically underdeveloped. Territorially, Russia continued to expand throughout the 18th and 19th centuries. Catherine the Great's energetic foreign policy added much of Poland and extended Russia's empire in the south. Czar Alexander I (r.1801–25) suffered Napoleon's invasion of 1812, but secured a share of the spoils after the defeat of France. The Congress of Vienna ceded the remainder of Poland to Russia, thus augmenting its recent acquisitions in Finland and Bessarabia.

Territorial expansion left Russian rulers with a permanent fear of rebellion by conquered peoples. During the 1828–29 war with the Turks, Nicholas I (r.1825–55) was able to field barely 180,000 troops, as half a million frontline soldiers were committed to maintaining security in the Baltic provinces and the Caucasus. In 1830, an uprising in Poland against Russian rule was only suppressed with difficulty. Internal dissent at autocratic rule began to grow. The "Decembrist" revolt of progressive army officers early in Nicholas I's reign was ruthlessly put down.

The principal aim of Nicholas' foreign policy was dominance over the Ottomans to ensure that Russia's grain exports had free passage across the Black Sea and through the Dardanelles to the Mediterranean. Russia endeavored to absorb Turkey's Balkan possessions and to encourage fellow Slavs to rebel against Ottoman rule in Europe. This policy brought Russia into conflict with the western powers. Britain saw its trade with India threatened by Russian expansion into the eastern Mediterranean, while France was concerned in its role as protector of the Catholic church within Turkish territories. Nicholas' decision to occupy the Ottoman

provinces of Moldavia and Wallachia in 1853 provoked Britain and France to invade the Crimea (1854). Once again, mustering sufficient manpower to resist the invaders proved a severe problem.

Russia's defeat in the Crimean War, its withdrawal from Moldavia and Wallachia and the requirement that it "neutralize" the Black Sea compelled Alexander II (r.1855–81) to review his power base. Russian rulers had always depended on the conscription of serfs, but this force was no match for the modern armies of France and Britain. The nobility, whose wealth was grounded in serfdom, was reluctant to innovate or invest in modern industry. To forestall revolution from below, Alexander reformed from above, emancipating the serfs and moving Russia toward a capitalist economy. Even so, millions of former serfs had to pay redemption fees for the lands they tilled. Massive discontent remained, held in check only by conscripts and the secret police. The czar was assassinated in 1881.

Alexander II had begun to tap the vast resources of Siberia, had extended the empire in central Asia and had secured a warm-water port in east Asia. The territory of Alaska was sold to the United States to concentrate development efforts on eastern Siberia and Vladivostok. Alexander's armies gradually sub-

TIMELINE

Domestic developments

1796 Death of Catherine II; brief reign of her son Paul I ends in assassination

1801 Alexander I ascends the throne; kingdom of Georgia voluntarily unites with Russia

1812 Napoleon invades Russia and occupies Moscow, but is forced to withdraw

1825 Accession of Czar Nicholas I; Decembrist revolt of army officers fails

1855 Alexander II becomes czar and institutes reform

1861 Russian serfs are emancipated by the "Czar Liberator" Alexander

1881 Assassination of Alexander II in St Petersburg; Alexander III becomes czar and reasserts autocratic rule

1894 Nicholas II, the last czar, ascends the throne

1905 Major uprisings sweep the country and lead to limited constitutional reform

1911 Pyotr Stolypin, reforming prime minister under the first *dumas*, is assassinated

Foreign policy

1810–50 Russia extends its dominion in central Asia

1815 Congress Poland is united with Russian empire, but retains its government

1830–31 Insurrection in Poland is brutally suppressed

1849 Russian troops are sent to crush Hungarian liberals

1854–56 Crimean War; British and French halt Russian Black Sea expansion

1860–70 Russian expansion into Turkestan

1867 Alaska is sold to the United States for US$7.2 million

1877–78 Last of a series of Russo-Turkish wars; creation of the vassal state of Bulgaria

1904–05 Russo-Japanese War; Russian forces are humiliated

1914 Russia mobilizes its army against Germany; on the outbreak of war it suffers a major defeat at the Battle of Tannenberg

1 Catherine II annexed the Crimea in 1783 and ordered the construction of a huge naval facility at Sevastopol; this base was besieged by Anglo-French forces in 1854–56.

2 Congress Poland, so-called because it was awarded to Russia by the Congress of Vienna in 1815, lost its constitution after the 1830 revolt, and was entirely absorbed by Russia after another rebellion in 1863.

3 A strip of mountainous country known as Wakhan was appended to Afghanistan in 1905 to separate conflicting Russian and British interests in the region.

4 The revolution of 1905 spread to the armed forces; sailors of the battleship *Potemkin* seized control of the ship in Odessa and sought asylum in Romania.

5 Count Sergei Witte, Minister of Finance 1892–1903, was the driving force behind the Russian rail network and industrial expansion.

6 The loop of the Trans-Siberian railroad around Lake Baykal was completed in 1915, and the eastern Siberian link in 1916.

7 Thousands of political dissidents were sent to Siberian labor camps by the czarist regime, including the Bolsheviks Lenin (Shushenskoye), Stalin (Kureika), and Trotsky (Verkholensk).

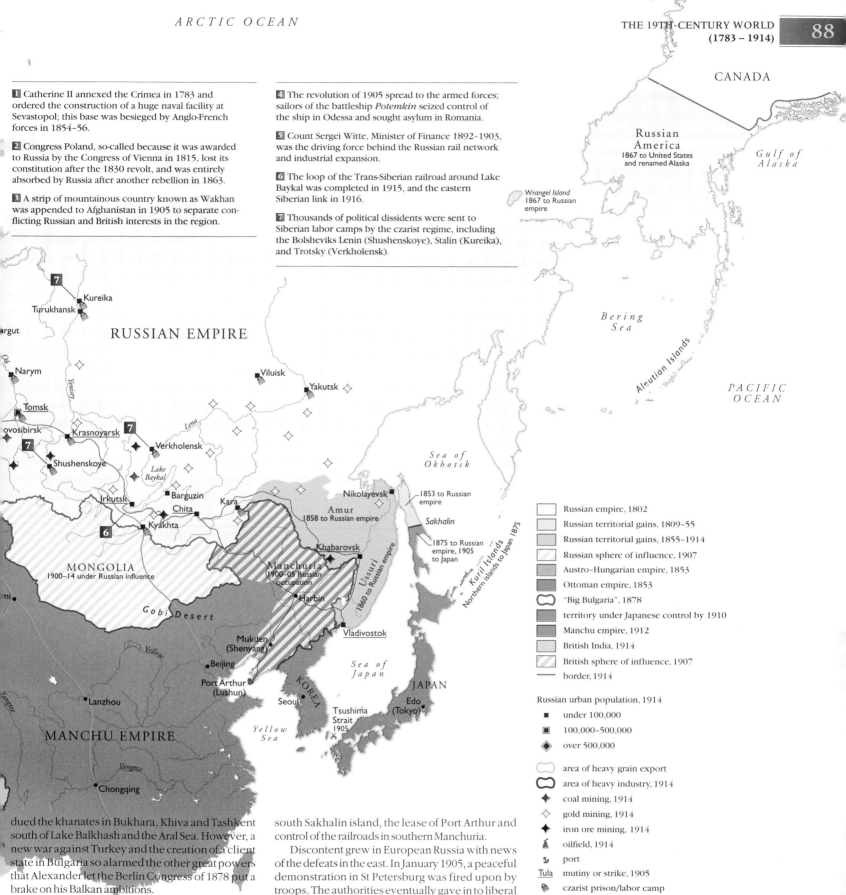

dued the khanates in Bukhara, Khiva and Tashkent south of Lake Balkhash and the Aral Sea. However, a new war against Turkey and the creation of a client state in Bulgaria so alarmed the other great powers that Alexander let the Berlin Congress of 1878 put a brake on his Balkan ambitions.

Under his successor, Alexander III (r. 1881–94), Russia was poised to exploit trade routes in east Asia. The Trans-Siberian Railroad was begun, giving greater access to the mineral wealth of Siberia and central Asia and helping Russian entrepreneurs to penetrate Manchuria and Korea. This expansion brought Russia into collision with Britain and Japan. When antagonism erupted over the Russian occupation of Port Arthur, Japan humiliated the forces of czar Nicholas II (r. 1894–1917) in 1904–05. Russia lost south Sakhalin island, the lease of Port Arthur and control of the railroads in southern Manchuria.

Discontent grew in European Russia with news of the defeats in the east. In January 1905, a peaceful demonstration in St Petersburg was fired upon by troops. The authorities eventually gave in to liberal demands and allowed an elected national assembly (*duma*) with limited powers. In its foreign relations, Russia agreed to "spheres of influence" in Persia with Britain in 1907. However, Russian interest revived in seeking access to the Mediterranean through the Balkans. Pan-Slavic Russian involvement with militant Serb groups opposing Austrian domination fueled the Balkan crisis of 1914 that sparked World War I. Within three years, Russia was beaten and the empire of the Russian czars had collapsed.

See also 93 (Russo-Japanese war);
100 (Russian revolution)

In 1884–85 representatives of fifteen European nations met in Berlin to settle rival claims to Africa. The Berlin Conference did not designate specific regions as colonies; rather it established the broad principles of the "scramble for Africa." The hinterland of a coast occupied by a European power was defined as a sphere of influence. To claim it, a power had to show itself capable of protecting "existing rights" and "freedom of trade and transit." This doctrine of "effective occupation" meant the process of colonization was conducted violently. Although the partition of Africa occurred quickly, it was the climax of years of activity by traders, administrators, soldiers and missionaries.

Africans were confronted with sudden piecemeal colonization. Some European governments worked through commercial ventures such as the Portuguese Niassa Company, the German South West and East Africa Companies, the Imperial East Africa Company, the Royal Niger Company and the British South Africa Company. By crudely imposing western practices – abolishing existing currencies, introducing hut taxes and removing middlemen from established trade patterns – these companies sowed the seeds of confrontation and armed resistance. In other cases companies conquered territory without reference to their governments. Sometimes, though, Africans invited the Europeans in, then found them impossible to remove.

The Europeans brought changes in modes of life and work. To pay the new taxes, Africans had to undertake wage labor. Imperial enterprises created a vast demand for unskilled labor: railroads, rubber, sugar and cocoa estates, and mining operations in central and southern Africa were all highly labor-intensive. By forcing Africans into these jobs, Europeans took away their culture and independence.

The response was varied. Some – such as the Bugandans who helped the British take over the states between the Great Lakes and form Uganda in 1903 – collaborated with the invaders. Others put their faith in religion: in the Sudan, Muhammad Ahmed (the *Mahdi*) rebelled against Anglo-Egyptian rule and founded a strict Islamic state. Yet apart from

1 The British general Charles Gordon, appointed governor of the Sudan by Khedive Ismail Pasha in 1873, was killed when Mahdist forces overran Khartoum in 1885.

2 In an uprising in 1905–07, Kinkjikitele Ngwale promised his followers that magic water (*maji-maji*) would protect them against machine-guns.

3 The Uganda railroad was built from 1896–1901, and was the most important factor in opening up the landlocked but fertile area north of Lake Victoria.

4 German colonization of Africa was characterized by foreign minister Bernard von Bülow in 1897 as the country claiming its right to "a place in the sun".

5 In 1898, at Fashoda on the White Nile, a confrontation between a French expeditionary force sent from west Africa and British troops almost led to war. The French ultimately withdrew.

the Mahdist revolt and the defiance of the west African Asante, most African resistance was short-lived. Artillery and rapid-fire maxim guns brought many uprisings to a swift end: the Ijebu surrendered in 1892, the Matabele in 1896, the Mandinka (under Samori Toure) in 1898 and the Zulu in 1908.

The Swazi branch of the Zulu nation was never defeated in battle; their state was guaranteed independence by the Transvaal and the British, before becoming a British protectorate in 1905. Only one state successfully defied the Europeans: Ethiopia, led by a modernizing Emperor Menelik II, crushed the Italian army at the Battle of Adowa in 1896. The freed-slave state of Liberia also survived despite losing parts of its territory to Britain and France.

By 1914, virtually the whole continent had come under European control. African raw materials and human resources were exploited for the benefit of European industry and commerce. Portugal shipped thousands of indentured laborers to the cocoa plantations on São Tomé and Príncipe, where they lived and died in appalling conditions. Leopold II of Belgium, who took the Congo Free State as his personal possession in 1885, amassed a fortune in revenues from rubber and ivory. By 1908 when the

Belgian state annexed the Congo, its population was half what it had been in 1891. Conditions then improved only marginally: thousands of people were moved forcibly to work the copper mines.

With footholds in the west, south and north of Africa, Britain was well placed to acquire half of the new colonies and protectorates during the "scramble". Its Gold Coast colony was the world's top rubber producer by 1895. Threatened by competitors in southeast Asia, the colony switched to cocoa and became world leader in this crop by 1914.

Germany came late to colonization. Among its African possessions was Togoland, where medical reforms, support for missionary schools, new roads and rail links brought some benefits of modern life.

QUEEN VICTORIA of Britain, as visualized by a Yoruba craftsman in Nigeria in the late 19th century.

Madeira

Ifni 1912 Spanish protectorate

Canary Islands
1912 Spanish protectorate

Rio de Oro 1884 Spanish protectorate

Spanish Saha

Mauritan

Cape Verde Islands

St Louis   Kaédi
Dakar
Senegal   *1881*   *1891*
Gambia   Kayes   *1883*
Fort James
Cacheo
Portuguese Guinea   French Guinea   Bamak
Bai Bureh's war   Samori's resistance, 1881–92
Conakry
Sierra Leone
Freetown

Monrovia   LIBERI

TIMELINE

European colonial policy

1881 Bey of Tunis accepts a French protectorate	**1889** Italy establishes its first colony in Eritrea	**1898** Britain creates the West African Frontier Force	**1906** Control of Morocco split between Spain and France
1883 French culture is imposed on African colonies	**1890** Britain gives Germany Heligoland in exchange for Pemba and Zanzibar	**1904** *Entente Cordiale* settles the Anglo-French disputes over Morocco, Egypt, the Suez Canal and Madagascar	**1912** Italy annexes Tripolitania and Cyrenaica
1883 France begins its conquest of Madagascar	**1894** Britain occupies Uganda		**1914** Amalgamation of Northern and Southern provinces into Nigeria
1884 The Berlin Conference on Africa opens		**1904** France creates a federal structure for its African empire, based at Dakar	

Wars and conflicts

1884 Samori Toure proclaims his Islamic theocracy	**1892** France destroys the Tukulor empire (Mali)	**1900** Death of Samori Toure, two years after his capture	**1911** German gunboat *Panther* creates international incident at Agadir
1885 British relieve Khartoum from Mahdist attack	**1893** French suppress the Fon warriors of Dahomey	**1900** Britain finally subjugates the Asante of west Africa	**1914** European warfare transfers to all the German colonies in Africa
1889 Chief Abushiri, leader of the Swahili peoples, is executed	**1896** Ndebele massacre whites and their African supporters in Matebeleland	**1905–07** Maji-Maji rebellion in German East Africa leads to an estimated 75,000 deaths	
1890 Hendrik Witbooi leads the first Nama rebellion against Germans in South-West Africa	**1898** Kitchener defeats the Mahdists at Omdurman and defuses the Fashoda incident	**1906–08** Chief Bambata leads the last Zulu revolt	

1890   1900   1910

From the last quarter of the 18th century to the outbreak of World War I, Europe was transformed from a series of traditional agrarian communities into a collection of modern industrial nations. Radical changes in the methods by which goods were produced – the widespread adoption of capitalism, mechanization and the factory system – gave rise to a period of unparalleled economic growth, though interrrupted by cyclical depressions. There was also a rapid increase in population and an influx of people from the countryside into the towns and cities that sprang up around the new workplaces.

The Industrial Revolution, as this transformation came to be known, had its origins in Britain. Its effects were first seen in the cotton and woollen industries in the north of the country. Mechanical innovations improved the speed and efficiency of weaving, and required new factories powered first by waterwheels and later by steam engines. These factories brought together the various operations involved in textile manufacture. Britain was ideally placed to pioneer and develop mass production. If possessed abundant natural resources to power the new machinery, favorable terrain on which to construct extensive transport networks (canals in the late 18th and early 19th centuries, and rail from the 1830s onward), and a ready market for manufactured goods. By 1815, Britain's industrialists had already made it the "workshop of the world", with coal mining, textile production and pig-iron smelting exceeding the output of the rest of Europe combined. Industrialization had spread to mainland Europe at the end of the 18th century (for example, in the Belgian armaments industry or cotton weaving in Saxony and northern France). But Britain's embargo on the emigration of skilled artisans and the export of machinery during the Napoleonic period prevented a wider adoption of the new methods of production.

Beginning in the 1820s in Belgium, however, coal mining and the textile and metal industries took root in continental Europe. As in Britain, the new rail network played a prime role in promoting economic expansion. Rail transport allowed rapid distribution of goods, and its con-

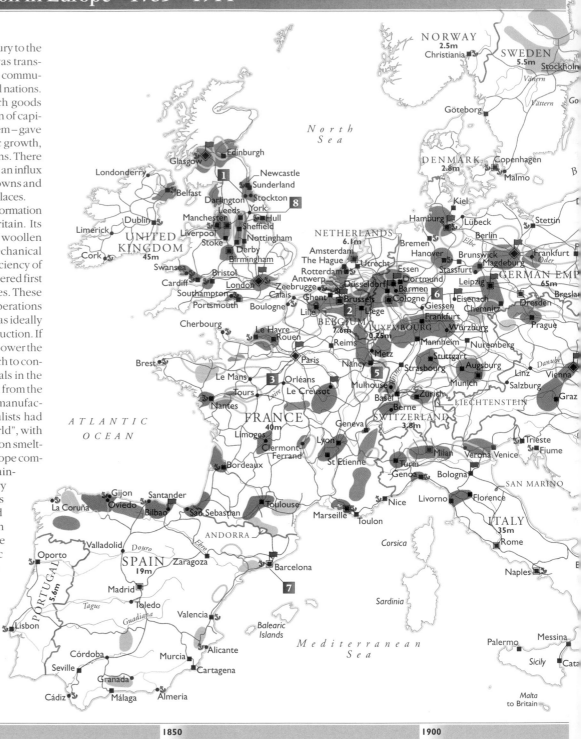

Map legend

— border, 1914

▨ heavy industrial or mining area

▢ major textile manufacturing area

▨ other large coal deposit

▨ other large iron ore deposit

urban population, 1914
- • under 100,000
- ▪ 100,000–500,000
- ▪ 500,000–1,000,000
- ◆ over 1,000,000

⚲ oilfield, 1914

🛥 port

🚩 center of socialism

Berlin research and development center for the chemical industry

19m national population (million) where known, 1914

— railroad constructed by 1870

— railroad constructed 1870–1914

0 ——— 600 km
0 ——— 400 mi

Lake Onega

Lake Ladoga

Vyborg

Helsinki
Revel
Narva
St Petersburg

Riga
Libau
Memel
Lake Peipus

Königsberg
Vilna
Minsk

RUSSIAN EMPIRE
171m

Warsaw
Western Dvina

Kiev
Dnieper

Vistula
rakow
Lvov (Lemberg)
Dniester

USTRO-
NGARIAN
MPIRE
51m
pest
Szeged
4
Ploisti
Bucharest
Danube
ROMANIA
7.1m
Belgrade

Odessa

SERBIA
3.2m
Sofia
BULGARIA
4.3m
Varna

MONTENEGRO
0.6m
Edirne

ALBANIA
Constantinople

Thessalonica

GREECE
Izmir

Ankara
ANATOLIA

OTTOMAN EMPIRE
Konya

Athens

Black Sea

CHILD-LABOR was common in the mines of early 19th-century Britain, but was banned in 1842.

Damascus
Acre
Jerusalem

---

more hazardous. Employers exploited the large pool of child and female labor to depress wages. Living conditions deteriorated in the vastly expanding new cities, where sanitation failed to keep pace with population growth. Cholera and typhus epidemics were common. A second bout of industrialization after 1870, based on steel and the new power source of electricity, did little to alleviate these problems.

To challenge the effects of capital, both the industrial working classes and the rural peasantry (serfdom did not end in Russia until 1861) organized themselves into trade unions. These efforts met opposition from the state as well as the capitalists. Ideas for alternative ways of structuring society arose during this period. Socialist parties were formed to argue for a more equal distribution of wealth, becoming particularly strong in Germany and France. Karl Marx and Friedrich Engels published their *Communist Manifesto* in 1848, arguing for a class-based revolution in highly industrialized states such as Britain. Anarchists advocated the violent abolition of the state, while syndicalists sought worker-control of industry through general strikes. To forestall social upheaval, some governments enacted legislation to alleviate the worst effects of industrialization. Compulsory free state education was widely instituted; labor in factories and mines was gradually regulated; working hours were cut and wages rose (as did inflation); improved housing also became slowly available. The first decade of the 20th century was marked by widespread unrest, but the old problem of unemployment would be briefly solved by the demands of World War I.

For many people, the solution to poverty was to emigrate. Nearly half a million Poles moved west to find jobs in the industrialized Ruhr, and Italian farmers took harvest work in Germany, France and Austria. Yet far more people left Europe, emigrating in their millions to Australia and New Zealand, but above all to the Americas.

---

1 The world's first railroad to use steam locomotive traction was opened for coal traffic in 1825 between Stockton and Darlington in northeast England.

2 The new country of Belgium, flat and densely populated, was the first continental European state to complete its rail network, in the 1840s.

3 A major early corporate investment bank was Crédit Mobilier, founded in Paris in 1852; ill-advised speculation led to the bank's collapse in 1867.

4 In 1856, one of the world's first oil refineries opened in Ploisti. Foreign investment brought rapid expansion of the Romanian oilfields from 1895.

5 The major iron-ore deposits in Lorraine were a serious loss to France's nascent steelmaking industry after the area was annexed by Germany in 1871.

6 The German Social Democratic Party was the strongest prewar socialist party, despite laws banning it. The party claimed 1.5 million members in 1890.

7 Barcelona and Bilbao were the two main industrial centers of 19th-century Spain; Barcelona's powerful anarcho-syndicalist movement was set up in 1910.

8 A Luddite (machine-wrecker) revolt (1811–12) ended when its leaders were hanged in York 1813.

---

sumption of materials stimulated further growth. By 1890, nearly all the main rail routes across Europe had been completed.

Private investment lay behind the success of many major industrial ventures, such as some early railroads, but spectacular bankruptcies showed the need for a new method of funding capital projects. Especially in continental Europe, joint stock limited liability companies, supported by development banks, were founded to provide credit. Free trade (the abolition of import tariffs protecting local producers from competition) was another crucial factor in industrial expansion. Britain lifted its high import duties on corn in 1846. Agreements with France, the Prussian *Zollverein* and Belgium in the 1860s further encouraged the reduction of tariffs. By 1870, most

European countries had expanded foreign trade and industrial production by lowering or abolishing their tariffs – though the position gradually reversed after the Franco-Prussian War (1870–71).

The social effects of the Industrial Revolution were as radical as its technological and financial consequences. The years of growth between 1840–70 also witnessed periodic financial crises and bouts of widespread unemployment. Harvests were critical, causing wild fluctuations in the price of food. Later, the import of cheap foodstuffs from Canada, the United States and Russia undercut agriculture in the industrializing states. New production methods threatened traditional skills, sometimes leading to machine-wrecking by disgruntled workers. As mechanization spread, working conditions became

See also 66 (18th-century European economy);
91 (world trade); 92 (migration)

Between 1830 and 1914 world trade was dominated by the industrialized nations of Europe and the United States. These countries traded manufactured goods and foodstuffs with each other and, increasingly, with the traditional societies of Latin America, Asia and Africa.

The growth in production in the industrialized nations was accompanied by a rise in foreign trade, which had risen from 10 percent of all earnings in 1830 to 33 percent in 1914. This was based in large part on the systematic exploitation of traditional societies and their raw materials. The trade passing through the major ports constructed in China, Latin America and Africa hardly benefited the economies of the host countries. As a result, rural economies were often destroyed – as in Africa, India and the Dutch East Indies – and replaced by westernized agricultural patterns that dictated the nature of the crops grown, and the manner in which they were marketed. Accompanied by colonial warfare, this exploitation was the ultimate expression of imperialism between 1830 and 1914.

The infrastructure of global trade was financed by the industrialized nations. For example, the economic development of Africa required railroads to carry exports to the coast (▷ 89). Rail links were vital, as the continent's great rivers were often ill suited to the mass transportation of freight, especially in sub-Saharan Africa. Similarly, investment by the industrialized nations built harbors, provided ships and established coaling stations worldwide. To handle the new commerce, port facilities were transformed in the industrialized countries themselves as well as in the colonies. Existing harbors, for example those in New York and Barcelona, were enlarged, while entirely new ports were built at Trieste in Italy and Le Havre in France.

Ship design also underwent radical change, with the advent of steam propulsion in 1833, iron hulls in 1837 and steel hulls in 1856. Sailing-ships reached their peak in the fast, elegant "clippers" that competed to transport commodities such as tea from China in record time. Yet by mid-century, purpose-built steamships with efficient engines were beginning to provide stiff competition for sailing vessels. Sail was dealt a further blow when the new canals cut at Suez, Kiel and Panama spared the need for long and often treacherous voyages around land-masses (▷ 81). Between 1850 and 1914 the world's merchant fleet expanded from 9 million net tons to over 35 million tons in 1914.

Increased global trade required changes in the way the world's economy

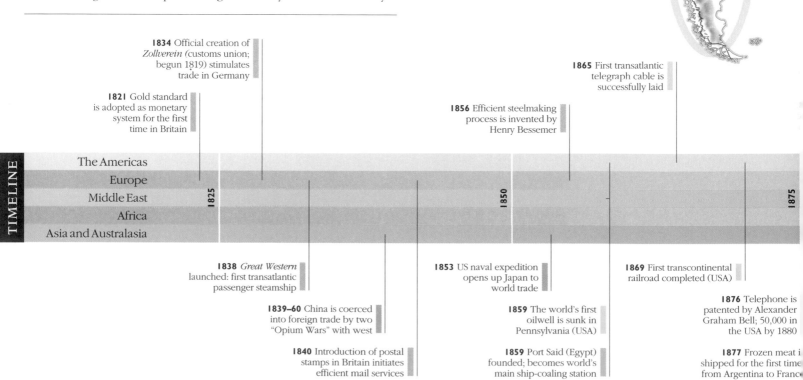

1834 Official creation of *Zollverein* (customs union; begun 1819) stimulates trade in Germany

1821 Gold standard is adopted as monetary system for the first time in Britain

1865 First transatlantic telegraph cable is successfully laid

1856 Efficient steelmaking process is invented by Henry Bessemer

TIMELINE	The Americas		
	Europe		
	Middle East		
	Africa		
	Asia and Australasia		

1825 1850 1875

1838 *Great Western* launched: first transatlantic passenger steamship

1839–60 China is coerced into foreign trade by two "Opium Wars" with west

1840 Introduction of postal stamps in Britain initiates efficient mail services

1853 US naval expedition opens up Japan to world trade

1859 The world's first oilwell is sunk in Pennsylvania (USA)

1859 Port Said (Egypt) founded; becomes world's main ship-coaling station

1869 First transcontinental railroad completed (USA)

1876 Telephone is patented by Alexander Graham Bell; 50,000 in the USA by 1880

1877 Frozen meat is shipped for the first time from Argentina to France

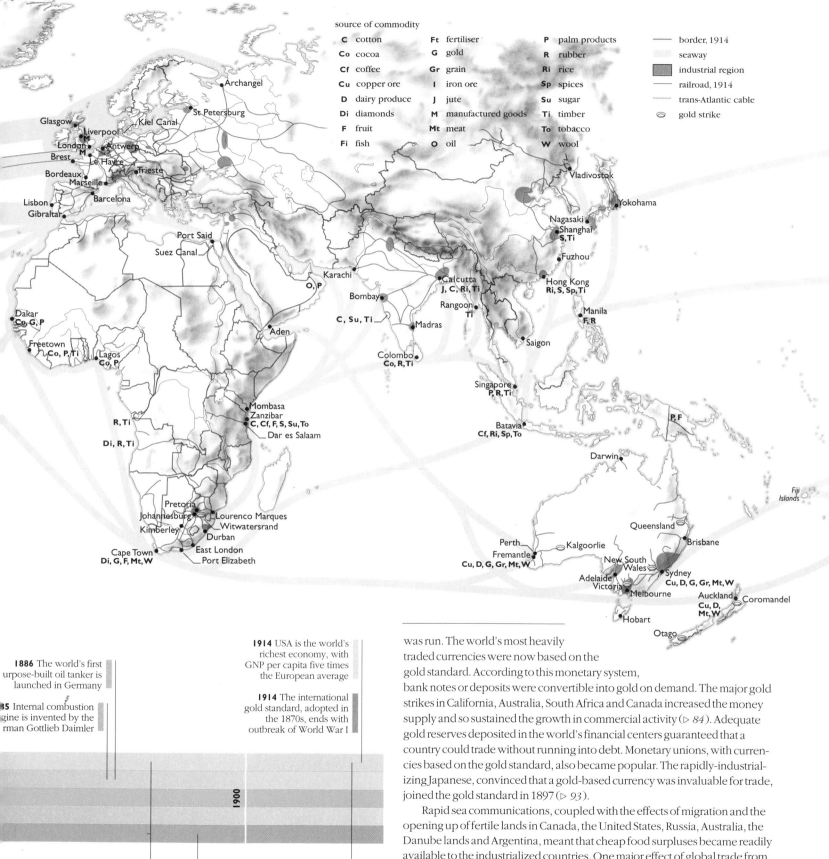

source of commodity

C	cotton	**Ft**	fertiliser	**P**	palm products	— border, 1914
Co	cocoa	**G**	gold	**R**	rubber	seaway
Cf	coffee	**Gr**	grain	**Ri**	rice	industrial region
Cu	copper ore	**I**	iron ore	**Sp**	spices	railroad, 1914
D	dairy produce	**J**	jute	**Su**	sugar	trans-Atlantic cable
Di	diamonds	**M**	manufactured goods	**Ti**	timber	gold strike
F	fruit	**Mt**	meat	**To**	tobacco	
Fi	fish	**O**	oil	**W**	wool	

1886 The world's first purpose-built oil tanker is launched in Germany

85 Internal combustion engine is invented by the German Gottlieb Daimler

1890–1914 Natural nitrates are exported from Chile in large quantities, for use in fertilizers and explosives

1890–1910 Cheap cotton goods produced in China, India and Japan undercut European cotton industry

1895 Malayan rubber plantations begin production

1914 USA is the world's richest economy, with GNP per capita five times the European average

1914 The international gold standard, adopted in the 1870s, ends with outbreak of World War I

1900

1913 Henry Ford introduces conveyor-belt mass production techniques in his automobile plants

was run. The world's most heavily traded currencies were now based on the gold standard. According to this monetary system, bank notes or deposits were convertible into gold on demand. The major gold strikes in California, Australia, South Africa and Canada increased the money supply and so sustained the growth in commercial activity (▷ 84). Adequate gold reserves deposited in the world's financial centers guaranteed that a country could trade without running into debt. Monetary unions, with currencies based on the gold standard, also became popular. The rapidly-industrializing Japanese, convinced that a gold-based currency was invaluable for trade, joined the gold standard in 1897 (▷ 93).

Rapid sea communications, coupled with the effects of migration and the opening up of fertile lands in Canada, the United States, Russia, Australia, the Danube lands and Argentina, meant that cheap food surpluses became readily available to the industrialized countries. One major effect of global trade from the 1870s onward, therefore, was to reduce drastically the price of wheat and most other staple foodstuffs.

Another important result of global trade was the growth in the sales of modern technology to traditional societies. This was frequently in the form of transport technology, such as railroads and engines, or factory machinery, but also increasingly came to include advanced military hardware. The balance of power in regional conflicts was radically altered by this development ■

The world's population grew from around 950 million in 1830 to around 1,600 million in 1914. This increase was the result of many factors: improved food production and diet; a greater awareness of hygiene and the start of public health programs; and new labor opportunities in industrialized regions that allowed people to escape rural hardship. Yet in spite of these improvements, millions still lived in abject poverty; the biggest migrations ever recorded began in the 19th century. The reasons were diverse and complex. Europe experienced increased cycles of emigration after each economic depression, as emigrants tried to escape unemployment, poverty and poor housing. Substantial numbers from Russia and Ireland also fled from persecution or starvation. In all, over 40 million people left Europe between 1830 and 1914, yet during the same period the population of the continent increased by some 76 percent.

Migrants looked above all to the Americas as lands of unlimited opportunities. While the first of them to venture west did so aboard any cargo vessels that would take them, by mid-century passenger lines with purpose-built steamships were running regular services that offered cheap transatlantic passages in reasonable accommodation.

Up to 1895, immigrants to the United States and Canada tended to come from Scandinavia, Germany, Britain and Ireland (▷ 5.10). Among those who endured the greatest hardship were the Irish, a trend dramatized by famine when the potato crop failed in 1845–47. Many prospective immigrants suffered from cholera and typhoid, and did not survive the passage. After 1895 most immigrants were of central and southern European origin. As a result of the huge influx (especially between 1900 and 1914), some regions of the United States were chiefly composed of either first- or second-generation European immigrants by 1914 (▷ 84).

European imperial acquisitions also attracted their own immigration, with Italians moving to Libya, and French to north Africa (▷ 89). The territories gained by Germany in inhospitable equatorial zones proved less inviting to emigrants from the home country. Many British people, especially Scots and Welsh, willingly emigrated to Canada, South Africa, Australia and New Zealand in order to find work.

The Chinese emigrated in great numbers in this period; as early as 1850, Australian employers began shipping in Chinese "coolies" to undertake the

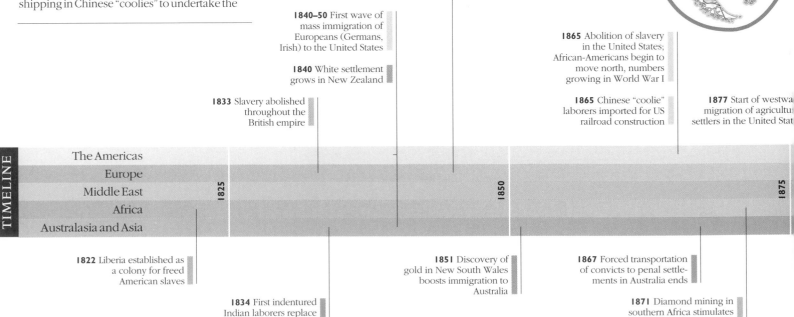

from Japan

from China

CANADA

UNITED STATES

MEXICO

Bahamas
CUBA
Jamaica
HAITI
Puerto Rico
DOMINICAN REPUBLIC

British Guiana
Dutch Guiana
French Guiana

PERU

BRAZIL

CHILE

URUGUAY

ARGENTINA

Hawaiian Islands

Newfoundland

1845–51 Irish potato crop blight drives many to emigrate to the United States and Britain

1840–50 First wave of mass immigration of Europeans (Germans, Irish) to the United States

1840 White settlement grows in New Zealand

1833 Slavery abolished throughout the British empire

1865 Abolition of slavery in the United States; African-Americans begin to move north, numbers growing in World War I

1865 Chinese "coolie" laborers imported for US railroad construction

1877 Start of westwa migration of agricultu settlers in the United Stat

TIMELINE		1825		1850		1875
The Americas						
Europe						
Middle East						
Africa						
Australasia and Asia						

1822 Liberia established as a colony for freed American slaves

1834 First indentured Indian laborers replace slave labor in West Indies

1851 Discovery of gold in New South Wales boosts immigration to Australia

1867 Forced transportation of convicts to penal settlements in Australia ends

1871 Diamond mining in southern Africa stimulates European immigration and African migrant labor

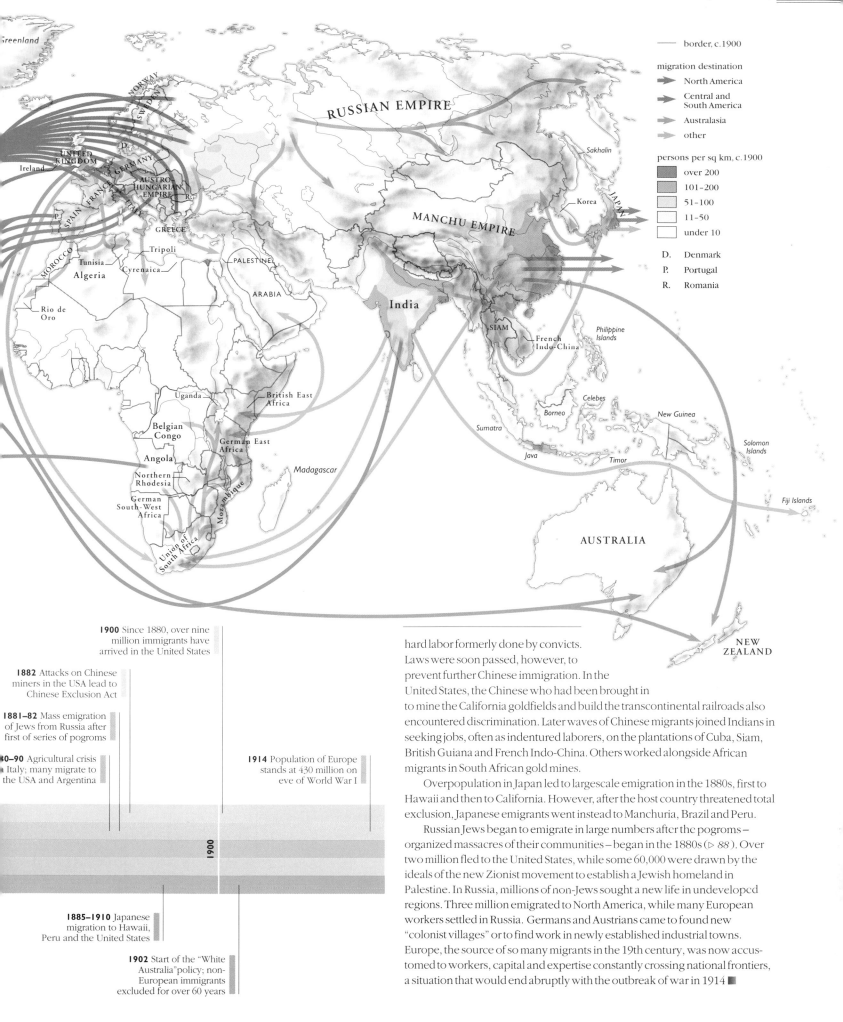

border, c.1900

migration destination

North America

Central and
South America

Australasia

other

persons per sq km, c.1900

over 200

101–200

51–100

11–50

under 10

D. Denmark
P. Portugal
R. Romania

1900 Since 1880, over nine
million immigrants have
arrived in the United States

1882 Attacks on Chinese
miners in the USA lead to
Chinese Exclusion Act

1881–82 Mass emigration
of Jews from Russia after
first of series of pogroms

[8]0–90 Agricultural crisis
[in] Italy; many migrate to
the USA and Argentina

1914 Population of Europe
stands at 430 million on
eve of World War I

1900

1885–1910 Japanese
migration to Hawaii,
Peru and the United States

1902 Start of the "White
Australia" policy; non-
European immigrants
excluded for over 60 years

hard labor formerly done by convicts.
Laws were soon passed, however, to
prevent further Chinese immigration. In the
United States, the Chinese who had been brought in
to mine the California goldfields and build the transcontinental railroads also
encountered discrimination. Later waves of Chinese migrants joined Indians in
seeking jobs, often as indentured laborers, on the plantations of Cuba, Siam,
British Guiana and French Indo-China. Others worked alongside African
migrants in South African gold mines.

Overpopulation in Japan led to largescale emigration in the 1880s, first to
Hawaii and then to California. However, after the host country threatened total
exclusion, Japanese emigrants went instead to Manchuria, Brazil and Peru.

Russian Jews began to emigrate in large numbers after the pogroms –
organized massacres of their communities – began in the 1880s (▷ 88). Over
two million fled to the United States, while some 60,000 were drawn by the
ideals of the new Zionist movement to establish a Jewish homeland in
Palestine. In Russia, millions of non-Jews sought a new life in undeveloped
regions. Three million emigrated to North America, while many European
workers settled in Russia. Germans and Austrians came to found new
"colonist villages" or to find work in newly established industrial towns.
Europe, the source of so many migrants in the 19th century, was now accustomed to workers, capital and expertise constantly crossing national frontiers,
a situation that would end abruptly with the outbreak of war in 1914 ■

The military bureaucracy (*bakufu*) that had been established at Edo by Tokugawa Ieyasu at the beginning of the 17th century held sway over Japan until the mid-19th century. Under this system, the governor (*shogun*) exercised absolute power and kept close control of the provincial barons (*daimyo*) and the increasingly poverty-stricken *samurai* warrior class. The emperor remained a remote, divine figurehead, residing at Kyoto some 480 kilometers (280 miles) from Edo.

Contact with foreigners was abhorred by this closed society. Russian and American ships that attempted to trade with Japan in 1791–92 were repelled. However, the opening up of California and the 1849 gold rush made the United States conscious that the Pacific offered unexplored commercial opportunities. The arrival at Uraga in 1853 of US Commodore Matthew Perry's "black ships" – a naval expedition to open trade with Japan – brought the question of contact with the outside world to the fore. Perry's return to Edo Bay the following year with a squadron of warships and 4,000 marines forced the *bakufu*'s hand, and the first limited concessions were granted to westerners to trade through the small ports of Shimoda and Hakodate.

The years following Perry's expedition saw resistance to foreign influence, organized by young samurai. Attacks on shipping caused a multinational naval force to bombard the forts at Kagoshima and Shimonoseki in 1863–64. Anti-foreign sentiment grew into concerted opposition to the shogunate. During 1867–68 civil war led to the the shogun being replaced with the emperor, in a development known as the Meiji ("enlightened rule") restoration. The emperor moved to Edo, now renamed Tokyo.

Under the new imperial regime, Japan resolved to compete with the west by industrializing, building a modern army and navy and adopting an aggressive foreign policy. In this way, it was intended that Japan should become the dominant power in east Asia. A pragmatic line was now taken toward foreign influence. Western expertise was harnessed to build Japan's first light industrial enterprise, a silk-reeling factory. The growth of heavy industry also required the import of western plant and materials – steel, steam engines, and railroad rolling stock were all purchased from overseas. Through the offices of a samurai financier, Masayoshi Matsukata, the Japanese government borrowed money from the four giant *zaibatsu*, (financial organizations) that dominated banking, industry and commerce – Mitsui, Mitsubishi, Sumitomo and Yasuda.

Between 1871 and 1914 Japan achieved dominance in east Asia; the country acquired the Ryukyu Islands, the Bonin Islands (Ogasawara), southern Sakhalin and the Kuril Islands. In 1894 the Tonghak revolt in Korea reflected a growing socio-economic crisis at home, but this provoked Chinese and Japanese intervention, with war erupting between the two powers the same year. Japanese ships destroyed the Chinese navy at the Battle of the Yellow Sea, while its army crushed the Chinese in Manchuria. The Japanese took Taiwan and the Pescadores; Korea briefly became independent. Yet intervention by the great powers subsequently deprived Japan of Port Arthur and the Liaodong Peninsula. When Russia was granted a lease of Port Arthur by China and attempted to expand its influence in Korea, Japanese fears grew stronger. Japan negotiated an alliance with Britain in 1902 that effectively neutralized Russia's ally, France, in the event of war, and then resolved to confront and overcome its chief rival in the region.

In 1904 Japanese troops landed in Korea and moved north toward the Yalu. Japanese warships attacked and then blockaded the Russian fleet at Port Arthur. On 1 January 1905 the Russian base surrendered. At Mukden Japan defeated the Russian army. Meanwhile the Russian Baltic Fleet, having sailed halfway around the world, arrived in Tsushima Straits too late to relieve Port Arthur. In one of the most important sea victories in history, Admiral Togo annihilated the obsolescent Russian fleet. In 1905 by the Treaty of Portsmouth (USA), Russia surrendered south Sakhalin and leases on Port Arthur and the South Manchurian railroad (completed in 1904). In 1910 Japan annexed independent Korea. By 1914 Japan had a major sphere of influence in east Asia.

- border, c.1850
- Japanese territory, c.1850
- Japanese territorial gain by 1914
- Japanese sphere of influence by 1914
- Manchu empire, c.1850
- Republic of China, 1914
- Russian empire, c.1850
- Russian territorial gain by 1914
- Russian sphere of influence by 1914
- Russian occupation, 1897–1905
- area allied against *Bakufu*, 1868
- area leased by China to a foreign power
- Commodore Perry's visits to Japan, 1853 and 1854
- Japanese campaign, Sino–Japanese war, 1894–95
- Japanese campaign, Russo–Japanese war, 1904–05
- Russian campaign, 1904–05
- ★ Japanese trading port by 1860
- bombardment by western powers, 1863–64
- battle, 1894–95
- battle, 1904–05
- peasant protest or riot, 1780–1850
- Tonghak revolt, 1894
- Japanese industrial area by 1914
- railroad, c.1914

0   400 km
0   400 mi

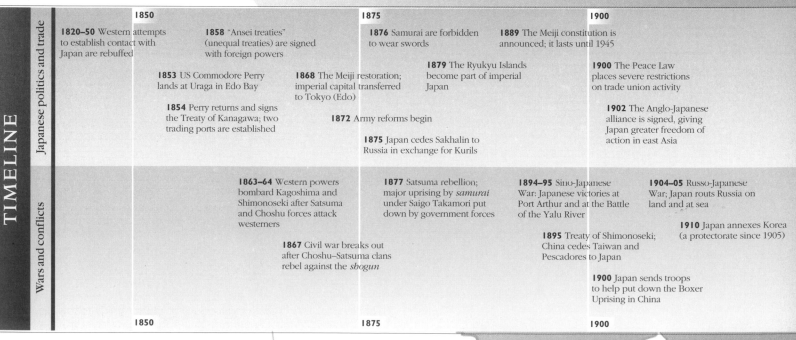

Japanese politics and trade

1850

1820–50 Western attempts to establish contact with Japan are rebuffed

1858 "Ansei treaties" (unequal treaties) are signed with foreign powers

1853 US Commodore Perry lands at Uraga in Edo Bay

1854 Perry returns and signs the Treaty of Kanagawa; two trading ports are established

1875

1876 Samurai are forbidden to wear swords

1879 The Ryukyu Islands become part of imperial Japan

1868 The Meiji restoration; imperial capital transferred to Tokyo (Edo)

1872 Army reforms begin

1875 Japan cedes Sakhalin to Russia in exchange for Kurils

1900

1889 The Meiji constitution is announced; it lasts until 1945

1900 The Peace Law places severe restrictions on trade union activity

1902 The Anglo-Japanese alliance is signed, giving Japan greater freedom of action in east Asia

Wars and conflicts

1863–64 Western powers bombard Kagoshima and Shimonoseki after Satsuma and Choshu forces attack westerners

1867 Civil war breaks out after Choshu–Satsuma clans rebel against the *shogun*

1877 Satsuma rebellion; major uprising by *samurai* under Saigo Takamori put down by government forces

1894–95 Sino-Japanese War: Japanese victories at Port Arthur and at the Battle of the Yalu River

1895 Treaty of Shimonoseki; China cedes Taiwan and Pescadores to Japan

1900 Japan sends troops to help put down the Boxer Uprising in China

1904–05 Russo-Japanese War; Japan routs Russia on land and at sea

1910 Japan annexes Korea (a protectorate since 1905)

1850   **1875**   **1900**

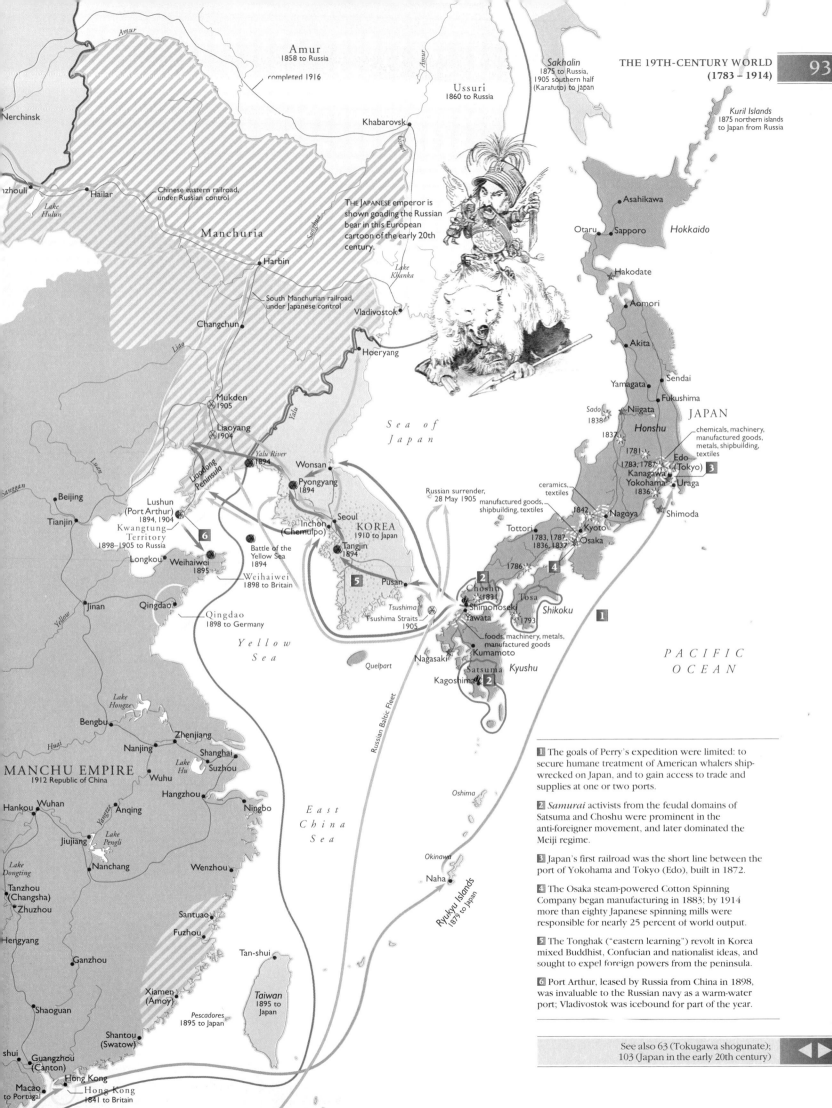

Amur
1858 to Russia

completed 1916

Ussuri
1860 to Russia

Sakhalin
1875 to Russia,
1905 southern half
(Karafuto) to Japan

Kuril Islands
1875 northern islands
to Japan from Russia

Nerchinsk

Amur

Khabarovsk

nzhouli

Lake Hulun

Hailar

Chinese eastern railroad,
under Russian control

Manchuria

Harbin

Changchun

Liao

South Manchurian railroad,
under Japanese control

Vladivostok

Lake Khanka

THE JAPANESE emperor is
shown goading the Russian
bear in this European
cartoon of the early 20th
century.

Hoeryang

Mukden
1905

Liaoyang
1904

Liaodong
Peninsula

Yalu River
1894

Wonsan

Sea of Japan

Hokkaido

Asahikawa

Otaru   Sapporo

Hakodate

Aomori

Akita

Yamagata   Sendai

Fukushima

Sado
1838

Niigata

1837

JAPAN

Honshu

chemicals, machinery,
manufactured goods,
metals, shipbuilding,
textiles

1781

1783, 1787

1842

Kanagawa
Yokohama
1836

Edo
(Tokyo) 3

Uraga

Shimoda

Pyongyang
1894

Beijing

Tianjin

Lushun
(Port Arthur)
1894, 1904

Kwangtung
Territory
1898–1905 to Russia

Longkou Weihaiwei
1895

Weihaiwei
1898 to Britain

Jinan

Qingdao

Qingdao
1898 to Germany

Yellow Sea

6

Battle of the
Yellow Sea
1894

Inchon
(Chemulpo)

Seoul

KOREA
1910 to Japan

Tangjin
1894

5

Pusan

Russian surrender,
28 May 1905

ceramics,
textiles

manufactured goods,
shipbuilding, textiles

Tottori

1783, 1787,
1836, 1837

1786

Kyoto

Osaka

4

Nagoya

Shikoku

2

Choshu
1831

Shimonoseki
Yawata

1793

Tosa

1

*PACIFIC
OCEAN*

Tsushima

Tsushima Straits
1905

Quelpart

foods, machinery, metals,
manufactured goods

Kumamoto

Nagasaki

Satsuma

Kagoshima   2

Kyushu

MANCHU EMPIRE
1912 Republic of China

Lake Hongze

Bengbu

Zhenjiang

Nanjing

Shanghai

Wuhu   *Lake Hu*   Suzhou

Hankou Wuhan

Anqing   Hangzhou

Jiujiang   *Lake Pengli*

Ningbo

Lake Dongting

Nanchang

Oshima

Wenzhou

East China Sea

Tanzhou
(Changsha)

Zhuzhou

Santuao

Hengyang

Fuzhou

Okinawa

Naha

Ryukyu Islands
1879 to Japan

Ganzhou

Tan-shui

Xiamen
(Amoy)

Pescadores
1895 to Japan

Taiwan
1895 to Japan

Shaoguan

Russian Baltic Fleet

shui

Shantou
(Swatow)

Guangzhou
(Canton)

Hong Kong

Hong Kong
1841 to Britain

Macao
to Portugal

1 The goals of Perry's expedition were limited: to
secure humane treatment of American whalers ship-
wrecked on Japan, and to gain access to trade and
supplies at one or two ports.

2 *Samurai* activists from the feudal domains of
Satsuma and Choshu were prominent in the
anti-foreigner movement, and later dominated the
Meiji regime.

3 Japan's first railroad was the short line between the
port of Yokohama and Tokyo (Edo), built in 1872.

4 The Osaka steam-powered Cotton Spinning
Company began manufacturing in 1883; by 1914
more than eighty Japanese spinning mills were
responsible for nearly 25 percent of world output.

5 The Tonghak ("eastern learning") revolt in Korea
mixed Buddhist, Confucian and nationalist ideas, and
sought to expel foreign powers from the peninsula.

6 Port Arthur, leased by Russia from China in 1898,
was invaluable to the Russian navy as a warm-water
port; Vladivostok was icebound for part of the year.

See also 63 (Tokugawa shogunate);
103 (Japan in the early 20th century)

Under the expansionist Manchu (Qing) dynasty, China enjoyed unrivaled power in east Asia. By 1783, emperor Qianlong (r. 1736–96) had settled colonists in Xinjiang and imposed tributary status on Burma and Annam. He restricted foreign merchants to Guangzhou and shunned the industrial innovations offered by western "barbarian" traders. After his abdication, however, imports of opium from British India increased steadily, and eventually led to two "Opium Wars" with China (1839–42; 1856–60). The outcome of the first was the 1842 Treaty of Nanjing, which confirmed Britain's gain of Hong Kong and right to trade through five "treaty ports". The second resulted in two agreements (in 1858 and 1860) for more western commercial footholds.

Russian ambitions focussed on obtaining strategically important Chinese territory. Russian forces annexed the valuable Ili region and advanced into Xinjiang, from which they withdrew in return for cash compensation in 1881. Russia also annexed eastern Siberia (1858–60) to secure ice-free waters in the Sea of Japan. A similar policy of territorial acquisition was adopted by Britain, France and Japan, which began to encroach on the tributary states beyond the Manchu borders. Britain moved into Lower Burma in 1852 and annexed the entire country in 1886. France, entrenched in southern Indo-China, was anxious to open trade with the southern Chinese province of Yunnan. It therefore fought a brief war with China to establish a protectorate over Tongking by 1885. Between 1875 and 1880, Japan annexed the Chinese tributary of the Ryukyu islands and began to weaken Chinese influence in another tributary, Korea. Taiwan and the Pescadores were also lost by China in 1894–95. These concessions and defeats represented unprecedented humiliation for the Qing dynasty.

While foreign powers eroded its frontiers, China faced even greater dangers from within. Official corruption, high taxation and continuing internal migration caused local uprisings. Many were caused by secret societies with political aspirations. The White Lotus sect vowed to overthrow the Qing and restore the Ming dynasty. Their rebellion raged through central China 1796–1804, though some unrest continued to 1813. After 1850 these revolts became so serious as to threaten the survival of the Qing. Hong Xiuquan led the Taiping rebellion, proclaiming the end of Manchu rule and the advent of the "Heavenly Kingdom of the Great Peace." This insurrection and its suppression by Qing forces cost up to 20 million lives. Disaffection with Manchu rule also brought rebellion in Taiwan, Muslim revolts in Xinjiang and Yunnan, Nian peasant risings in Henan and Miao tribal unrest in Guizhou.

The short-lived "self-strengthening movement" instigated by the statesman Li Hongzhang in the 1860s attempted to construct a modern military and industrial state. Yet his plan to purchase foreign armaments and build arsenals and factories met with little support from the dowager empress Cixi (r. 1862–1908) and her court at Beijing. Meanwhile, the western clamor for land concessions, mining rights, railroad, building and trade facilities continued. In Cixi's reign, anti-western sentiment took on a republican flavor, and crystallized into the nationalist movement led by Sun Yixian (Sun Yat-sen).

The shame of further territory losses in 1898 led to the Boxer Uprising of 1900–01. This major revolt engulfed several provinces but concentrated chiefly on attacking the foreign legations in Beijing. The outcome of this rebellion, which was supported by the dowager empress, was the International Protocol of 1901, which gave the powers yet more trade concessions and a huge indemnity payment from the Qing. Western soldiers guarded the civilian settlements, while gunboats patrolled the rivers. Merchant and missionary activity increased. Foreign

RUSSIAN EMPIRE

Lake Balkhash

Ili
1854 annexed by Russia
DZUNGARIA

Ili
1871–81
to Russia

TIEN SHAN

Tarim

Xinjiang
1

KUNLUN MTS

TRADITIONAL ways of life, including the use of head stocks (known since Han times) for criminals, survived throughout the Manchu era.

1 With acquisitions of new territories such as Xinjiang by the Manchu, the Chinese population rose to over 400 million by the mid-19th century.

2 Opium was imported to China not as a narcotic, but as a pharmaceutical. Its addictive properties led to imperial decrees against its import and cultivation from 1800 onward.

3 Hong Kong was ceded to Britain by China in 1841 (confirmed in 1842); in 1898, the British signed a 99-year lease on the territory.

4 Shanghai was one of the first treaty ports, opened to western trade in 1842. In these ports, westerners were free from all aspects of Chinese jurisdiction, including taxation.

5 The Taiping rebellion of 1850–64 took its egalitarianism from Christianity brought by western missionaries. Its leader Hong Xiuquan claimed to be the younger brother of Jesus Christ.

6 The Boxers – or "League of Righteous Harmonious Fists" – were an anti-foreigner, anti-Christian secret society originating in the Shandong peninsula.

7 Germany sent a force to occupy the port of Qingdao in 1897. Thereafter the site was heavily industrialized; with the outbreak of war in 1914, Japan (an Allied country) captured the city.

TIMELINE

Trade and politics

1800	1850	1900
1793 Emperor Qianlong snubs a British trade mission under Lord Macartney	**1839** Imperial commissioner Lin Zexu sent to Guangzhou to stop opium trade	**1885** Chinese troops defeat a French force at Langson
1796 Qianlong abdicates in order not to rule longer than his grandfather	**1839–42** First Anglo-Chinese War opens up "treaty ports"	**1886** Britain completes its annexation of Burma
1816 Expulsion of British Lord Amherst's trade mission	**1844** France and the United States sign trade agreements with China	**1894–95** Sino-Japanese War: China is defeated and loses Taiwan and the Pescadores
1830 Anglo-American illicit supply of opium increases	**1856–60** Second Anglo-Chinese War	**1896** China, through Li Hongzhang, permits Russia to build a railroad across Manchuria
	1860 An Anglo-French force destroys the imperial palace at Beijing	**1901** An International Protocol is imposed on China

Rebellions

1800	1850	1900
1796–1804 The White Lotus rebellion disrupts most of central China	**1850** The Taiping rebellion (*Taiping*: "heavenly kingdom") begins in Jintian; it is crushed by 1864	**1895** Sun Yixian's attempt at revolution in Guangzhou fails
	1855–57 The Miao rebellion against Manchu in Guizhou	**1900** Boxer Uprising against foreign influence
	1855–57 The Christian, nationalist Hakka rebel against their Manchu overlords	**1908** Death of the dowager empress Cixi
		1911 Chinese revolution begins
	1863–73 Muslim rebellion in Gansu, Qinghai and Shanxi	**1912** Yuan Shikai president of the new Chinese Republic

| 1800 | 1850 | 1900 |

Krasnoyarsk

Angara

Trans-Siberian railroad

completed 1916

Lena

Amur

Nikolayevsk
founded 1850

Amur
1858 annexed by Russia

Amur

Sakhalin
1875 to Russia,
1905 southern half
to Japan

Lake Baykal

Irkutsk

Chita

Nerchinsk

Manzhouli

completed 1915

Khabarovsk
founded 1858

Aigun

Manchuria
1900–05 under Russian influence,
1905–45 under Japanese influence

Ussuri
1860 annexed by Russia

Lake Khanka

Songhua

Harbin

Suifenhe

Hunchun

Vladivostok
founded 1860

Kuril Islands
1875 northern islands to Japan

Sapporo

Hokkaido

Hakodate

Tannu Tuva
protectorate
1911 independent,
1914 to Russia

Selenga

Ulan Bator

Inner Mongolian
Plateau

MONGOLIA
1912 independent

Gobi Desert

Changchun

Sea of
Japan

Honshu

Mukden
(Shenyang)

Niuzhuang

KOREA
1905 Japanese protectorate,
1910 Japanese colony

Tokyo
Yokohama

JAPAN

slim rebellion
1862–73

Gansu

Kwangtung Territory
1898–1905 to Russia,
1905 to Japan

Beijing
capital city,
focus of Boxer
Uprising

Qinhuangdao

Tianjin

Lushun
(Port Arthur)

Dalian

Weihaiwei
1895

Dandong

Yalu River
1894

Seoul

Pusan

Shimonoseki

Shikoku

Ganzhou

Pingluo

Yulin

*Ordos
Desert*

Shanxi

Dengzhou

Longkou

Chefoo

Weihaiwei
1898 to Britain

Nagasaki

Kyushu

TILIAN MTS

ghai

*Lake
Qinghai*

Hezhou

Hegang

Muslim rebellion
1862–73

Yellow

Jinan

Shandong

Qingdao
1898 to
Germany

Qingdao

Weihaiwei
1898 to Britain

Yellow
Sea

Kagoshima

QIN MTS

Henan

Nian rebellion
1853–68

IMPERIAL CHINA

Yanguan

Han

Huai

Zhenjiang

Shanghai

Suzhou

Nanjing

Taiping rebellion
1850–64

Wuhu

DABA MTS

Yangtze

Wanxian

Yichang

Lichuan

Hankou

Wuhan

Wuchang

Shasi

Anqing

Hangzhou

Ningbo
(Mingzhou)

Mingshan

Chongqing

Yeuyang

Jiujiang

Taiping
rebellion
1850–64

Wenzhou

Assam
1826 annexed by
Britain

Luzhou

Mianning

Nanchang

Tanzhou

*Lake
Dongting*

*Lake
Pengli*

Santuao

Fuzhou

Tan-shui

Upper Burma
1886 annexed by Britain

Guizhou

Miao rebellion
1855–57

Taiping
rebellion
1850–64

Dali

Tengyueh

Muslim
rebellion
1855–73

Yunnan

Xiamen
(Amoy)

Pescadores
1895 to Japan

Aboriginal
rebellion
1862–63

Tainan

Taiwan
1895 to Japan

dalay

Mengzi

Manhao

Simao

Hakka rebellion
1855–57

Jintian

Wuzhou

Guangzhou
(Canton)

Shantou
(Swatow)

Linan

Nanning

Sanshui

Macao
to Portugal

Kowloon

Hong Kong

RMA
o Britain

Longzhou

Langson

Pakhoi

Zhanjiang

Hong Kong
1841 to Britain

Tongking
1884–85 French protectorate

Hanoi

Zhanjiang
1898 to France

Laos
1899 French
protectorate

Qiongzhou

Hainan

Lower Burma
created 1862

Mekong

FRENCH
INDO-CHINA
1887–98 united by
France

Annam
1883–85 French
protectorate

South
China
Sea

Philippine Islands
1571–1898 to Spain,
1898 to United States

Manila

SIAM

Legend

Manchu empire, mid-19th century

former Manchu tributary state

British India, mid-19th century

Japanese empire, mid-19th century

Russian empire, mid-19th century

borders, c.1912

Manchu /Chinese empire, 1912

former Manchu state gaining independence

Manchu territory lost to Britain by 1912

Manchu territory lost to France by 1912

Manchu territory under Japanese control
at some time before 1912

Manchu territory lost to Russian empire by 1912

temporary Russian territorial gain

area leased by China to foreign power

spheres of influence

British

French

German

Japanese

port open to foreign trade under the
Treaty of Nanjing, 1842

treaty port opened from 1858

Taiping marches, 1850–64

anti-Manchu rebellion, with date

center of Boxer Uprising, 1900–01

railroad by 1914

Trans-Siberian railroad sector completed in 1915

Trans-Siberian rail link to Vladivostok,
completed 1916

0   1000 km

0   800 mi

banks virtually ran China's economy, funding such projects as the rail link across Manchuria between the Trans-Siberian railroad and Vladivostok.

In 1911, an army mutiny in the industrial conurbation of Wuhan was exploited by Sun Yixian's Revolutionary Alliance Party, or Guomindang (KMT), which proceeded to seize power in central and southern China and overthrow the Qing dynasty. Sun Yixian returned from overseas exile to Shanghai, proclaimed the Three Principles of the republican revolution—nationalism, democracy and

people's livelihood—and was duly appointed provisional president of China. On 1 January 1912, the Chinese Republic was founded. However, when the Manchu boy-emperor Pu Yi abdicated on 13 February, General Yuan Shikai was named as president. For the sake of national unity, Sun Yixian voluntarily relinquished the presidency. Yet Yuan Shikai's desire to found a new imperial dynasty led to suppression of the Guomindang. In 1913, Sun Yixian established the first of a series of provisional governments at Guangzhou.

See also 69 (the rise of Manchu China);
88 (19th-century Russia)

Southeast Asia had suffered extensive foreign intervention by the end of the 18th century. While the Dutch seaborne empire in island southeast Asia remained the major European presence, British entrepreneurs had also set up bases for trade with China. French missionaries and traders, interested in Vietnam since the 17th century, were given more leeway through a 1787 treaty. However, the first major French expedition did not occur until 1858–59, when the empire-building aspirations of Napoleon III resulted in the capture of Saigon. Despite resistance in the Mekong delta area, the French made further gains, establishing a protectorate over the Buddhist state of Cambodia and opening Hanoi and Tourane (Da Nang) as treaty ports. In an undeclared war with China (1883–85), France tried to win control of the whole of Indo-China, a goal achieved in 1887 with the merging of Cochin China, Cambodia, Annam and Tongking as the Indo-Chinese Union (French Indo-China). In 1893 it was extended to include Laos.

At first the French in Indo-China concentrated on modernizing and maximizing profits. Peasants were urged to sell land to boost rice production, so undermining traditional large viable villages. Landless peasants took jobs in salt and opium factories or worked for landlords.

British involvement in mainland southeast Asia began with the purchase of the island of Penang from the sultan of Kedah in 1786. During the Napoleonic Wars (when the Netherlands was under French control), Britain attacked Batavia to win control of Java and safeguard its trade routes to China through the island channels. The administrator Sir Stamford Raffles founded the free port of Singapore in 1819, which rapidly became the commercial center of the region, stimulating demand for British cotton manufactures in southeast Asia and China. In 1824 Britain ceded Benkulen and its claims to Sumatra in exchange for Dutch recognition of British sovereignty over Penang, Port Wellesley, Singapore and Malacca (collectively known as the Straits Settlements). Britain became involved in combating piracy and slavery, and settling disputes among the Malay princely states and sultanates on

Legend:
- sultanate of Aceh, 1873
- Federated Malay States, 1896
- Unfederated Malay States, 1909
- borders, 1914
- British territory, 1914
- British sphere of influence
- Dutch East Indies, 1914
- French Indochina, 1914
- German territory, 1914
- Portuguese territory, 1914
- United States territory, 1914
- area of piracy
- ☆ area of resistance by indigenous peoples
- → British campaign
- → French campaign
- → United States campaign
- *gold* source of commodity
- — trade route through Malacca Straits

0   600 km
0   400 mi

TIMELINE

Indo-China

1782–1809 Rama I founds Bangkok and increases Siam's influence in Chiangmai, the Lao states and Cambodia

1786 Britain acquires Penang from Sultan of Kedah

1795 Britain takes Malacca from the Dutch

1802 Nguyen Anh unifies Vietnam and rules from Hue as the first Nguyen emperor

1819 Founding of Singapore by Sir Stamford Raffles

1820–42 Vietnamese emperor Minh-Manh revives Confucianism and persecutes Christians

1824 The Anglo-Dutch Treaty confirms British dominance in Malaya (and Singapore)

1824–25 The British take Rangoon in First Burmese War

1852–53 Second Burmese War; British gains reduce Burma to an inland state

1855 King Mongkut (r.1851–68) opens Siam to British trade

1858–59 French and Spanish naval force bombards Tourane and occupies Saigon

1873 France begins the occupation of Tongking

1883 The Treaty of Hué leads to the creation of French protectorates in Annam and Tongking

1886 Britain annexes Upper Burma in Third Burmese War

1887 The Indo-Chinese Union is created by France

1896 Malay states of Perak, Selangor, Negri Sembilan and Pahang are federated

1909 Anglo-Siamese Treaty; Britain controls Kedah, Perlis, Kelantan and Trengganu

1914 100,000 Vietnamese go to France to serve in labor battalions in World War I

Island southeast Asia

1811 The Dutch surrender Java to a British invasion force

1814–16 The Netherlands regains Sumatra and Java

1841 The sultan of Brunei cedes Sarawak to Brooke

1859 The Dutch and Portuguese agree to partition island of Timor

1873 The Dutch attack the Aceh sultanate (to 1907)

1884 Germany annexes northern New Guinea and the Bismarck Archipelago

1898–99 US takes Philippines in the Spanish-American War

1901 Filipino leader Emileo Aguinaldo is captured

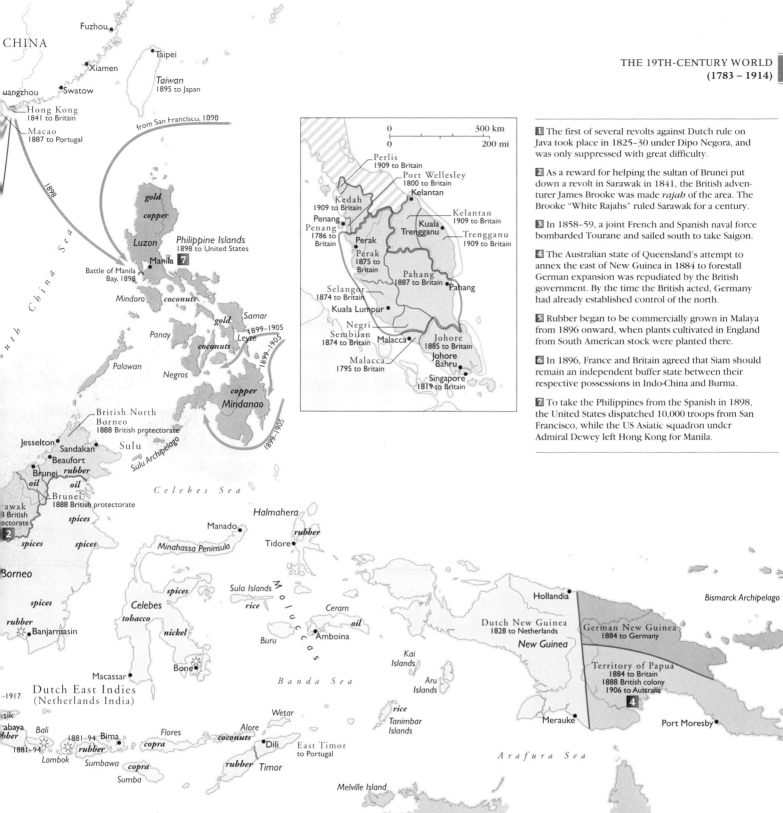

CHINA

Fuzhou

Taipei

Xiamen

uangzhou
Swatow

Taiwan
1895 to Japan

Hong Kong
1841 to Britain

Macao
1887 to Portugal

from San Francisco, 1898

1898

gold

copper

Luzon

Philippine Islands
1898 to United States

Manila **7**

Battle of Manila
Bay, 1898

S o u t h   C h i n a   S e a

Mindoro   *coconuts*

gold   Samar

Panay   *1899–1905*

Leyte   *1899–1905*

coconuts

Palawan   Negros

copper
Mindanao

British North
Borneo
1888 British protectorate

Jesselton
Sandakan
Beaufort   *Sulu*

Brunei   *rubber*

oil   *oil*

Brunei
1888 British protectorate

Sulu Archipelago

rawak
B British
ectorate

2   *spices*

spices   *spices*

C e l e b e s   S e a

Borneo

spices

rubber
Banjarmasin

spices   *rice*
Manado

Minahassa Peninsula

rubber
Tidore

Halmahera

Celebes   *spices*

tobacco   Sula Islands

nickel   Buru   Ceram   *oil*

Macassar   Bone   Amboina

Dutch East Indies
(Netherlands India)

–1917

sik
abaya
bber   Bali   1881–94   Bima   *copra*
1881–94   *rubber*
Lombok   Sumbawa   *copra*
Sumba

Flores   Alore   *coconuts*
Dili
Wetar   *rubber*   Timor

rice
Tanimbar
Islands

rice
Kai
Islands

Aru
Islands

B a n d a   S e a

East Timor
to Portugal

A r a f u r a   S e a

Melville Island

M o l u c c a s

Hollandia

Dutch New Guinea
1828 to Netherlands

New Guinea

Merauke

German New Guinea
1884 to Germany

Bismarck Archipelago

Territory of Papua
1884 to Britain
1888 British colony
1906 to Australia

4

Port Moresby

Inset map (Malay Peninsula):

0   300 km
0   200 mi

Perlis
1909 to Britain

Port Wellesley
1800 to Britain

Kelantan

Kedah
1909 to Britain

Kelantan
1909 to Britain

Penang

Penang
1786 to
Britain

Kuala
Trengganu

Trengganu
1909 to Britain

Perak

Perak
1875 to
Britain

Pahang
1887 to Britain

Pahang

Selangor
1874 to Britain

Kuala Lumpur

Negri
Sembilan
1874 to Britain

Malacca

Malacca
1795 to Britain

Johore
1885 to Britain

Johore
Bahru

Singapore
1819 to Britain

1 The first of several revolts against Dutch rule on Java took place in 1825–30 under Dipo Negora, and was only suppressed with great difficulty.

2 As a reward for helping the sultan of Brunei put down a revolt in Sarawak in 1841, the British adventurer James Brooke was made *rajah* of the area. The Brooke "White Rajahs" ruled Sarawak for a century.

3 In 1858–59, a joint French and Spanish naval force bombarded Tourane and sailed south to take Saigon.

4 The Australian state of Queensland's attempt to annex the east of New Guinea in 1884 to forestall German expansion was repudiated by the British government. By the time the British acted, Germany had already established control of the north.

5 Rubber began to be commercially grown in Malaya from 1896 onward, when plants cultivated in England from South American stock were planted there.

6 In 1896, France and Britain agreed that Siam should remain an independent buffer state between their respective possessions in Indo-China and Burma.

7 To take the Philippines from the Spanish in 1898, the United States dispatched 10,000 troops from San Francisco, while the US Asiatic squadron under Admiral Dewey left Hong Kong for Manila.

the peninsula. In 1896 Federated Malay States was set up under a British resident-general. Thirteen years later other states were acquired from Siam; these formed the Unfederated Malay States. Tin exports increased after mining was mechanized in the early 1900s. Rubber also became a major export; by 1911 nearly half a million hectares of rubber was being grown, mainly on large, European-owned estates. The 1824 treaty had also provided a case for the "white rajah" James Brooke to gain British protection for the state he created in Sarawak in 1841. In North Borneo commercial competition for concessions from Brunei and Sulu led eventually to an 1881 royal charter for a British North Borneo Company, which undertook the exploitation of the territory.

To protect India's borders, Britain also annexed Burma in the course of three brief wars. The first (1824–26) was in response to a Burmese invasion of Bengal, and resulted in Burma surrendering large

tracts of territory. Lower Burma was secured by the British in the second war (1852–53), and Upper Burma in the third (1885–86). The British administered the country as part of India.

Germany and the United States were late beginning their colonial ventures in southeast Asia. Rival claims to the eastern part of New Guinea eventually saw Germany occupy the northeast and the adjacent islands (renamed the Bismarck Archipelago), and a British protectorate over the southeast of the island. A crown colony in 1888, British New Guinea became a territory of the Australian Commonwealth in 1906. The United States acquired its first and most important southeast Asian colony in 1898, when Admiral Dewey destroyed a Spanish fleet in Manila Bay to secure the Philippines. Filipino nationalists, who had been encouraged by the United States to fight for their independence against Spanish rule, now felt betrayed by US actions and fierce fighting

ensued on Mindanao during 1902–05. The conflict wrecked the fragile economy and, in addition to military casualties, 100,000 people died from famine.

After the withdrawal of the British from Sumatra, the Dutch faced opposition from indigenous people in the East Indies. Prince Dipo Negoro's rebellion led to the Java War of 1825–29; Tuanku Imam, Minangkabau's militant leader, fought the Dutch 1830–39; and persistent attacks on merchant shipping by the state of Aceh led the Dutch to declare war in 1873. Thirty years of conflict drained the Dutch reserves so that effective occupation of the islands was still incomplete by 1914, although the governor-general J.B. Van Heutsz (1904–09) strove relentlessly to govern the East Indies as a single state from Batavia.

See also 103 (southeast Asia 1914–41)

Bismarck, who initiated the complex web of alliances that developed after the Franco–Prussian War, now had as his ultimate objective the preservation of peace on the continent. He aimed to prevent France from launching a war of revenge by isolating it from any potential ally.

Bismarck's first step was to form the league of Three Emperors (*Dreikaiserbund*) between Germany, Austria–Hungary and Russia in 1873. In doing so, he had to reconcile a number of conflicting interests. Since the Crimean War, Russia had tried to reassert its position in Europe by championing the cause of Slav freedom from Austrian and Turkish rule. This brought Austria and Russia into conflict, as both empires cherished ambitions to secure the Balkan lands of the moribund Ottoman empire. The loose alliance that Bismarck forged was designed to stabilize southeast Europe, as its members agreed to act in concert against subversive movements in the region. In 1878, however, the Congress of Berlin forced Russia to renounce some of the excessive Balkan gains it had wrested from Turkey in 1877–78.

The chief beneficiary of the Berlin Congress was Austria, which negotiated a secret, defensive Dual Alliance with Germany (who, in World War I, were known as the Central powers). This relationship was to be the main focus of Bismarck's subsequent diplomacy. He publicly renewed the *Dreikaiserbund* in 1881 and distracted France by encouraging its colonial ambitions in north Africa, but secretly created a Triple Alliance between Germany, Austria and Italy.

When the *Dreikaiserbund* expired in 1887, Bismarck replaced it with a bilateral Reinsurance Treaty, which recognized the Balkans as a Russian sphere of influence and confirmed that Russia and Germany would stay neutral unless Germany attacked France, or Russia attacked Austria. This represented the pinnacle of Bismarck's diplomacy, which

sought to secure German predominance in central Europe and avoid dangerous adventurism.

In 1890, a change occurred in the politics of European alliances, when growing antagonism between the headstrong new emperor Wilhelm II and Bismarck brought the latter's resignation. The Reinsurance Treaty was allowed to lapse without renewal and the Russian harvest failed the same year. France offered aid to Russia, so laying the groundwork for a military alliance. This was duly signed in 1894, with the critical provision that if a Triple Alliance country mobilized its armies then Russia and France would do likewise. Mobilization of any armed forces was thus likely to lead to war.

— border proposed by the Treaty of San Stefano, 1878
═ borders, 1912
▮ Allied powers, Aug 1914
▯ Central powers, Aug 1914

Schlieffen plan, 1905
▲ German army position
→ route of German attack

▯ fortress of the Central powers
▯ fortress of the Allied powers
▯ Belgian fortress
↯ major naval base
⚓ major armaments center
○ league of Three Emperors, 1873–87
○ Triple Alliance, 1882–1915
● *Entente Cordiale*, 1904
● Triple Entente, 1907
— key railroad line for transferring German troops to Russian front
➜ anticipated Russian attack
▫ Slavic language in central Europe

EUROPEAN royalty in the early 20th century had close family ties; Britain's King George V (shown here with Queen Mary) was cousin to Wilhelm II.

Britain had stood aloof from these alliances but after the death of Queen Victoria in 1901 the new king Edward VII made overtures to France that culminated in the *Entente Cordiale* of 1904. A similar agreement was made with Russia in 1907, forming a Triple Entente (of what became known as the "Allied powers" in 1914) to balance the Triple Alliance.

Several international incidents occurred that tested the commitment of the European powers to peace. Germany's claims to Morocco ran into opposition from both Britain and France, and resulted in the Tangier crisis (1905), settled at the Algeciras conference, and the Agadir crisis of 1911, which resulted in German recognition of France's claim to Morocco. The Balkans, too, continued to provide a highly charged arena. The Balkan peoples tried to organize

TIMELINE

Alliances and ententes

1873 Bismarck negotiates the League of the Three Emperors (*Dreikaiserbund*)

1879 Dual Alliance: Germany and Austria-Hungary

1882 Italy joins the Dual Alliance, thus creating the Triple Alliance

1887 German Reinsurance Treaty with Russia

1890 Bismarck resigns over differences with Kaiser Wilhelm II

1894 Franco-Russian military alliance is announced after France aids Russian famine

1902 The Anglo-Japanese Naval Alliance guarantees naval security in east Asia

1904 *Entente Cordiale* signed between Britian and France

1907 Agreement between Britain and Russia results in a Triple Entente in Europe

1914 Germany pledges total support ("Blank Check") for Austrian actions in Balkans

Crises and rearmament

1875–78 Eastern crisis begins when Bosnia and Herzegovina rebel against Turks

1877–78 Russo-Turkish War ends; Russia gains much from the Treaty of San Stefano

1878 The Congress of Berlin compels Russia to reduce its recent gains in the Balkans

1885–86 Tension between Austria and Russia over Bulgaria destroys the *Dreikaiserbund*

1889 Britain guarantees dominance of the Royal Navy

1898 Fashoda crisis: a clash between French and British military missions in Sudan causes mutual hostility

1900 Second German Naval Law (First 1898) confirms growth of the Imperial Navy

1905–06 German colonial ambitions spark the first Morocco crisis

1906 HMS *Dreadnought* revolutionizes warship design

1908 Austria–Hungary annexes Bosnia–Herzegovina

1911 The visit of a German gunboat to Agadir causes the second Morocco crisis

1914 The Sarajevo crisis leads to Austrian bombardment of Belgrade, Russian mobilization and war

1 The Treaty of San Stefano concluded between Russia and Turkey in 1878 envisaged the creation of a large new Bulgarian state beholden to Russia.

2 In France in 1886–89, a vociferous *revanche* ("revenge") movement arose over Alsace–Lorraine, headed by war minister Georges Boulanger.

3 From 1887–89, British prime minister Lord Salisbury resisted Bismarck's requests for an Anglo-German alliance. Salisbury described Britain's disdain for alliances as "splendid isolation".

4 One of the greatest European industrial complexes was the Skoda Works in Pilsen, built to produce a new machine-gun for the Austrian army in 1890.

5 Britain transferred sovereignty of the North Sea island of Heligoland (Helgoland) to Germany in return for Zanzibar in 1890. Germany developed Helgoland into a major naval base.

6 The *Entente Cordiale* was tested in 1905, when Wilhelm II spoke in Tangier in favor of Moroccan independence. The Algeçiras conference in 1906 upheld French claims to the territory.

into nation-states and the Balkan Wars of 1912 and 1913 radically transformed the map of southeast Europe, arousing the hostility of Austria–Hungary.

Throughout this period, plans were made for war. The most ambitious was devised by the German chief of staff, Alfred von Schlieffen, for a war on two fronts. The Schlieffen plan required a surprise push through neutral Holland, Belgium and Luxembourg to isolate Paris from the coast and encircle the French armies. Troops would then be transferred by rail to reinforce the eastern front against Russia, which was expected to attack near Königsberg.

Rapid developments were also made in armaments. Germany produced medium and heavy artillery of high quality, France excelled in rapid-fire field guns, while all countries were perfecting the

machine-gun. At sea, the British *Dreadnought* class of battleship, begun in 1906, inaugurated a new era of naval design. Heavily armored, equipped entirely with big guns and driven by steam turbines, these ships started a race to build ever more powerful fleets. Wilhelm II was especially keen to develop the navy to challenge the might of Britain's Royal Navy.

Conscription swelled the size of the continent's armies. Most German youth served for three years in the army corps; French conscripts served for two. Both these countries (and Italy) could mobilize a million men within days. Austria and Russia could call on three times this number, though more slowly. The threat of war had loomed for so long over Europe that by 1914 all countries had arsenals and forces of unparalleled size and efficiency.

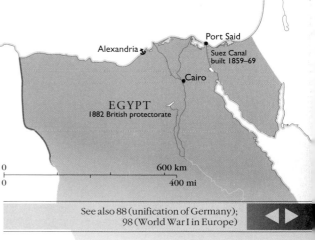

See also 88 (unification of Germany); 98 (World War I in Europe)

By 1914 the dominion of European peoples had spread throughout the world – the imperial system was at its peak, and expeditions had explored both polar regions. Colonization was most extensive in Africa. The "scramble for Africa" that had begun among European powers after 1870 was formalized at the Berlin Conference of 1884–85, which divided virtually all of the continent between rival claimants (▷ 89). Africans resisted the despoliation of their homelands, but usually to no avail. The Ethiopians successfully repulsed Italian invaders in 1896, but other peoples fought in vain against European troops equipped with superior weapons. Colonial forces also clashed; France and Britain disputed control of the upper Nile, and Germany's vigorous late pursuit of an African empire presaged the conflict to come in Europe. The Second Anglo-Boer War (1899–1902) was the culmination of decades of tension between settlers of Dutch and British origin in southern Africa. The British gained supremacy in a bitter struggle, but their failure to attract mass settlement left the Afrikaners dominant in the new Union of South Africa.

The United States emerged as an imperial power, while the empires of Russia and Britain continued to grow. The British empire reached the height of its power, with important colonial possessions in every continent. The transoceanic remnants of Spain's empire – Cuba, Puerto Rico, Guam and the Philippines – fell to the United States in the Spanish–American War of 1898. In Central America, US technology succeeded in cutting the Panama Canal, which opened for navigation in 1914. The extension of the railroad network throughout the United States by the end of the 19th century was instrumental in opening up new territories. As the 20th century dawned, American engineers pioneered important new forms of transport. The first powered heavier-than-air flight was made in 1903, and mass automobile ownership was a fact by 1914.

Russia's expansion to the east brought it into conflict with Japan (▷ 88). The industrializing and ambitious Japan routed Russian forces in 1904–05 and annexed Korea in 1910. Russia's humiliation sparked the first of a series of revolutions that led to the fall of the imperial regime in 1917.

Britain's prime interest was to protect its trade through the Suez Canal, including the new resource of oil which Britain received from the Persian Gulf. To this end, bases were developed in the Mediterranean. Egypt was also occupied in 1882. Further east, British

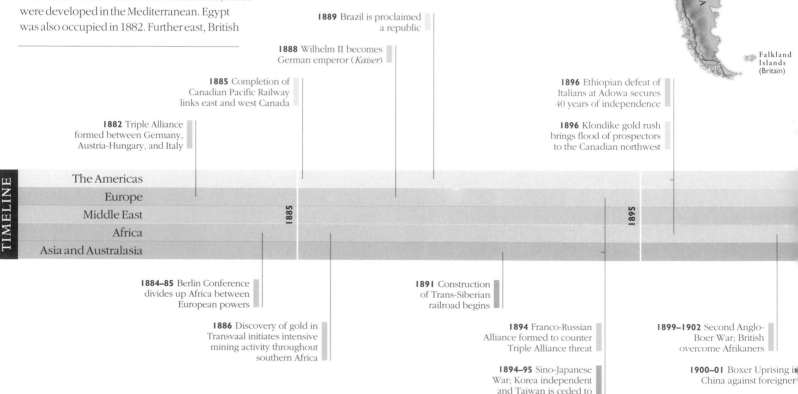

Hawaiian Islands (United States)

Marquesas Islands (France)

Tuamotu Archipelago (France)

Easter Island (Chile)

1889 Brazil is proclaimed a republic

1888 Wilhelm II becomes German emperor (*Kaiser*)

1885 Completion of Canadian Pacific Railway links east and west Canada

1882 Triple Alliance formed between Germany, Austria-Hungary, and Italy

1896 Ethiopian defeat of Italians at Adowa secures 40 years of independence

1896 Klondike gold rush brings flood of prospectors to the Canadian northwest

TIMELINE

The Americas
Europe
Middle East
Africa
Asia and Australasia

1885

1895

1884–85 Berlin Conference divides up Africa between European powers

1886 Discovery of gold in Transvaal initiates intensive mining activity throughout southern Africa

1891 Construction of Trans-Siberian railroad begins

1894 Franco-Russian Alliance formed to counter Triple Alliance threat

1894–95 Sino-Japanese War; Korea independent and Taiwan is ceded to Japan on Chinese defeat

1899–1902 Second Anglo-Boer War; British overcome Afrikaners

1900–01 Boxer Uprising in China against foreigner

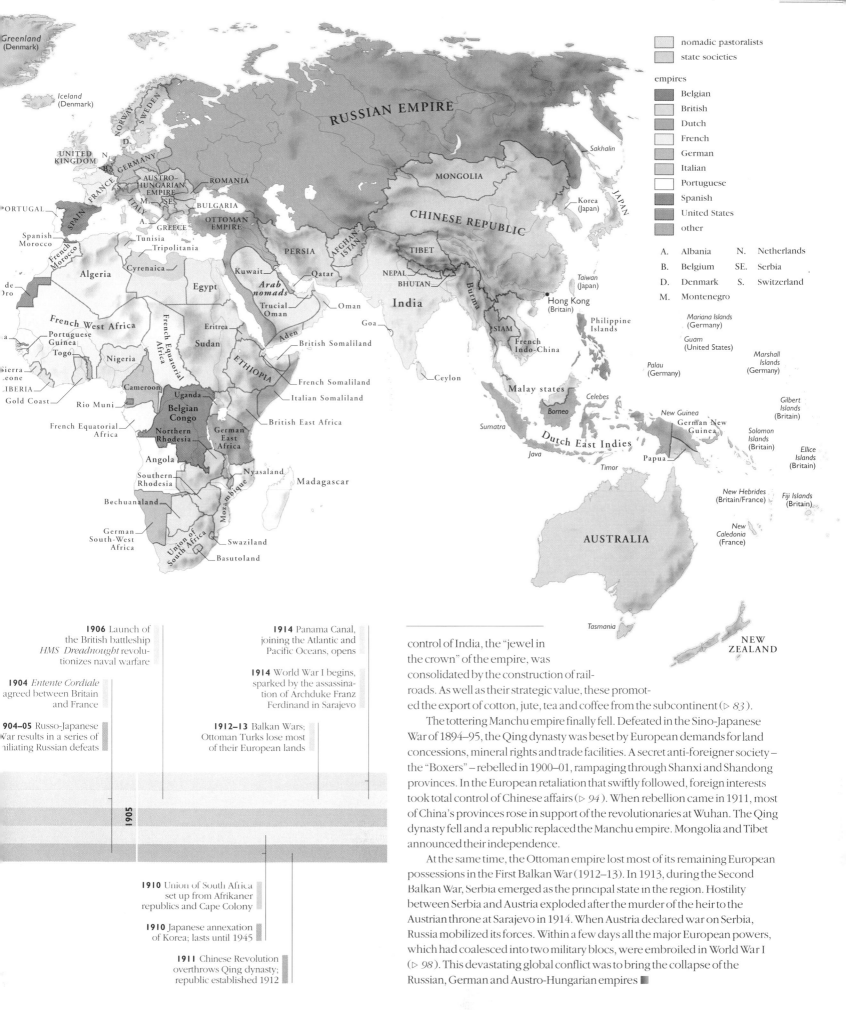

1906 Launch of the British battleship *HMS Dreadnought* revolutionizes naval warfare

1904 *Entente Cordiale* agreed between Britain and France

904–05 Russo-Japanese War results in a series of humiliating Russian defeats

1914 Panama Canal, joining the Atlantic and Pacific Oceans, opens

1914 World War I begins, sparked by the assassination of Archduke Franz Ferdinand in Sarajevo

1912–13 Balkan Wars; Ottoman Turks lose most of their European lands

1905

1910 Union of South Africa set up from Afrikaner republics and Cape Colony

1910 Japanese annexation of Korea; lasts until 1945

1911 Chinese Revolution overthrows Qing dynasty; republic established 1912

control of India, the "jewel in the crown" of the empire, was consolidated by the construction of railroads. As well as their strategic value, these promoted the export of cotton, jute, tea and coffee from the subcontinent (▷ 83).

The tottering Manchu empire finally fell. Defeated in the Sino-Japanese War of 1894–95, the Qing dynasty was beset by European demands for land concessions, mineral rights and trade facilities. A secret anti-foreigner society – the "Boxers" – rebelled in 1900–01, rampaging through Shanxi and Shandong provinces. In the European retaliation that swiftly followed, foreign interests took total control of Chinese affairs (▷ 94). When rebellion came in 1911, most of China's provinces rose in support of the revolutionaries at Wuhan. The Qing dynasty fell and a republic replaced the Manchu empire. Mongolia and Tibet announced their independence.

At the same time, the Ottoman empire lost most of its remaining European possessions in the First Balkan War (1912–13). In 1913, during the Second Balkan War, Serbia emerged as the principal state in the region. Hostility between Serbia and Austria exploded after the murder of the heir to the Austrian throne at Sarajevo in 1914. When Austria declared war on Serbia, Russia mobilized its forces. Within a few days all the major European powers, which had coalesced into two military blocs, were embroiled in World War I (▷ 98). This devastating global conflict was to bring the collapse of the Russian, German and Austro-Hungarian empires ■

Part 6

THE MODERN

Many of those who went into battle in August 1914 thought the war would be short and glorious. World War I, though, tested human endurance to the limit. The combatant states had the ideological, bureaucratic and technological capabilities, as well as the nationalistic fervor, to mobilize vast human and material resources.

The postwar settlement was built on the principle of national self-determination. But this settlement was partial: totalitarian governments appeared in Germany, Italy and Russia, using the state's resources to foster a virulent nationalism, and committed to revising the precarious status quo.

Germany's invasion of Poland in September 1939 led to a war that soon became truly global and total. Each side sought the unconditional surrender of the other, and the distinction between soldier and civilian collapsed as air power provided the means to strike at the enemy's heartland. This strategy culminated in the atomic destruction of the Japanese cities of Hiroshima and Nagasaki, and the devastation of the social and economic fabric of Germany. Meanwhile six million Jews perished in the Holocaust, a demonstration of the modern totalitarian state's ability to combine ideology, technology and bureaucracy in systematic mass extermination.

The two wars had one positive outcome: the recognition that the propensity of states to destroy one another had to be restrained by means of international institutions to reinforce the rule of law. The League of Nations, created in 1919, failed, but its successor the United Nations raised expectations that a concert of victorious powers could deter and defend against aggressive states.

The Cold War between the United States and the Soviet Union was perhaps a product of misperception: each assumed

SINGAPORE's high rise blocks symbolized the global economy of the 1990s.

WORLD

the other was bent on aggression. A precarious order ensued, at times threatened by crises in which nuclear disaster was sometimes only narrowly averted. There were, though, other trends in the postwar years whose influence shaped international relations for many years.

First, the United States committed itself to restoring western Europe's battered economies, and equally to the defense of Europe – a reversal of its isolationism after 1919. NATO gave western Europe the confidence to begin economic integration; the European Economic Community was set up in 1957–58. Second, the independence of India, Pakistan and Ceylon from British imperial rule set a precedent for anticolonial struggle elsewhere. By 1968 fifty African states had joined the United Nations. China, too, began a long march to great power status after the Communist victory in 1949. Third, the principle of domestic jurisdiction slowly dissolved, bringing an expansion in the legal competence of bodies such as the UN to intervene when human rights were abused. South Africa's policy of *apartheid* was the catalyst, as new norms entered the vocabulary of inter-state discourse.

The relative stability provided by the threat of "mutually assured destruction" was bought at the expense of the Third World. Nehru in India, Sukarno in Indonesia, Nkrumah in Ghana and Nasser in Egypt hoped to build a third force in international affairs, mediating between east and west, and committed to redressing the inequalities between the rich northern states and the poorer south. Some victories were won: the legal establishment of human rights; the isolation of *apartheid*-ridden South Africa; the recognition that Third World states needed aid and technical assistance to provide a decent life for their peoples.

But the Cold War years also saw wars by proxy fought in Third World states such as Angola, Ethiopia, Somalia and Vietnam, as the superpowers vied to support rival factions in civil wars. And as détente, or relaxation of superpower tension, took hold, the influence of the "nonaligned movement" began to wane, especially as many Third World states failed to deliver social and economic benefits to their people.

Meanwhile, led by Japan, the "tiger" economies – South Korea, Singapore, Taiwan, Malaysia, Hong Kong – underwent an economic miracle via export-led growth and a mix of government intervention and private enterprise. China, too, encouraged market liberalization, though under the strict control of the ruling Communist Party.

In contrast, the Soviet Union was unable to deliver both "guns and butter" to its people. The economy was hamstrung by obsolete state controls, and the arms race of the 1980s placed great burdens on the economy just when conservative western governments – especially in the United States and Britain – were successfully employing free market solutions to boost productivity. Attempts at reform merely led to revolt in several of the Soviet republics and the satellite states of east and south Europe. The fall of the Berlin Wall – symbol of Cold War division – in 1989 heralded a new era, one in which economic activity was global, and free-market capitalism was enshrined as the chief ideology for economic development throughout the world.

As the millennium approached, all governments were constrained by global economic forces. Conventional attack by a neighbor often seemed less threatening than organized crime, drugs and arms trafficking, illegal migration, terrorism and environmental degradation: dangers a nation-state was ill-equipped to cope with. Pressure mounted for the establishment of wider groupings of states, and it seemed possible that such regional associations would be the building blocks for a "new world order" for the twenty-first century ∎

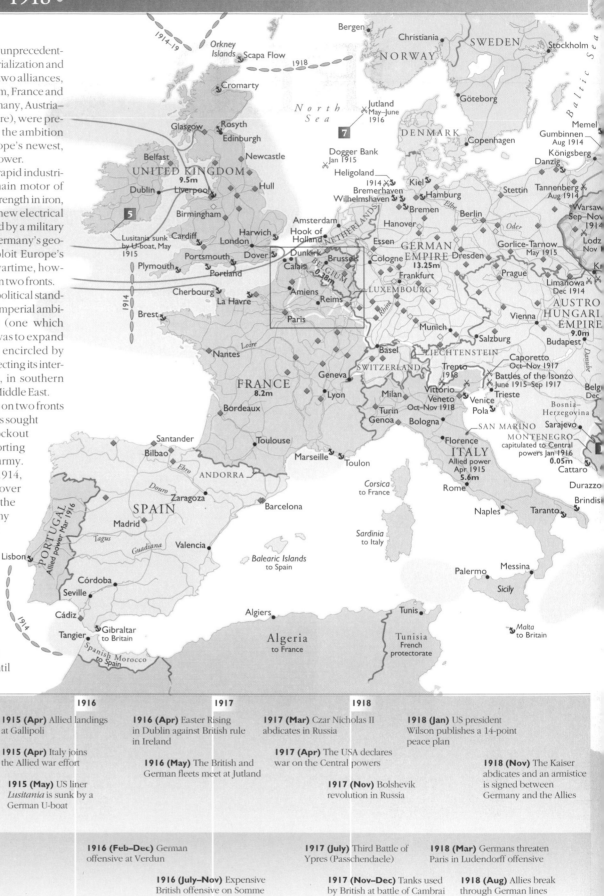

Before 1914, Europe had enjoyed unprecedented prosperity, the fruit of industrialization and a century without a general war. Yet two alliances, the Allied powers (the United Kingdom, France and Russia), and the Central powers (Germany, Austria–Hungary and, later, the Ottoman empire), were preparing for war. The main reason was the ambition and the instability of Germany, Europe's newest, and strongest, industrial and military power.

Germany had enjoyed a period of rapid industrialization, replacing Britain as the main motor of Europe's economy. Furthermore, its strength in iron, steel and coal production, and in the new electrical and chemical industries, was matched by a military machine second to none. In peace, Germany's geographical position enabled it to exploit Europe's extensive rail and sea networks. In wartime, however, it faced the prospect of fighting on two fronts.

Germany's rulers believed that its political standing did not match its commercial and imperial ambitions. One of its oldest ambitions (one which brought it into conflict with Russia) was to expand eastward. Germany believed it was encircled by hostile powers and was intent on protecting its interests, and those of Austria–Hungary, in southern Europe, the Ottoman empire and the Middle East.

In a long war, the strain of fighting on two fronts would inevitably tell. Military planners sought to combat this by launching a knockout blow against France and then transporting troops to the east to face the Russian army. But the plan failed when, in August 1914, war broke out following a crisis over Austrian and Russian influence in the Balkans. The exhausted German army was halted 80 kilometers (50 miles) short of Paris. The French army was swiftly mobilized and the transport network used shrewdly – even the Parisian taxi cabs were pressed into service to take soldiers to the front. Stalemate followed on the Western Front; the war was bogged down in trench warfare, as the defensive capabilities of the machine gun dominated the war until

TIMELINE		1915	1916	1917	1918
	General	1914 (28 June) Assassination of the Austrian Archduke Franz Ferdinand by a Serb nationalist at Sarajevo	1915 (Apr) Allied landings at Gallipoli	1916 (Apr) Easter Rising in Dublin against British rule in Ireland	1917 (Mar) Czar Nicholas II abdicates in Russia	1918 (Jan) US president Wilson publishes a 14-point peace plan
		1914 (Aug) Germany declares war on Russia and France; Britain, France and Russia on Germany and Austria–Hungary	1915 (Apr) Italy joins the Allied war effort	1916 (May) The British and German fleets meet at Jutland	1917 (Apr) The USA declares war on the Central powers	1918 (Nov) The Kaiser abdicates and an armistice is signed between Germany and the Allies
			1915 (May) US liner Lusitania is sunk by a German U-boat		1917 (Nov) Bolshevik revolution in Russia	
	Western Front	1914 (Aug) Germans launch Schlieffen plan		1916 (Feb–Dec) German offensive at Verdun	1917 (July) Third Battle of Ypres (Passchendaele)	1918 (Mar) Germans threaten Paris in Ludendorff offensive
		1914 (Sep) Germans halted at the Battle of the Marne		1916 (July–Nov) Expensive British offensive on Somme	1917 (Nov–Dec) Tanks used by British at battle of Cambrai	1918 (Aug) Allies break through German lines
	Eastern Front	1914 (Aug) The Russian advance into Germany is halted at Tannenberg	1915 (Oct) Austria-Hungary invades Serbia	1916 (Sep) Central powers defeat Romania	1917 (July) Last Russian offensive of the war	1918 (Mar) Treaty of Brest-Litovsk ends war in Russia
				1916 (Oct) The Russian Brusilov offensive ends	1917 (Dec) Bolsheviks sign an armistice with Germany	
		1915	1916	1917	1918	

1 The assassination of the Austrian Archduke Franz Ferdinand on 28 June 1914 by a Serbian began the descent into war. Austria declared war on Serbia; Russia mobilized; Germany declared war on Russia and France, and Britain on Germany, by 4 August.

2 The German offensive in the west began with the reduction of the Belgian fortresses around Liège.

3 The French stopped the German advance on Paris on the Marne in September 1914.

4 The unsuccessful Allied landings at Gallipoli were intended to win control of the Dardanelles and secure a sea route to Russia.

5 The sinking of the passenger liner *Lusitania* by a German U-boat in 1915 did much to turn American sentiment in favor of the Allies.

6 The war on the Eastern Front never declined into trench warfare and strategic mobility was preserved; casualties, though, were as heavy as in the west.

7 Although Britain's fleet suffered heavier losses than Germany's, the Battle of Jutland confirmed Britain's control of the seas.

new offensive tactics, using tanks and artillery more intelligently, were developed in 1917. Despite early victories against the Russians, the Germans now had to cope with war on two fronts.

In the Balkans, victories by the Central powers over Serbia and Romania (and the entry of the Ottomans into the war in 1915) seemed to create the kind of central European political and trading empire that Germany wanted. In 1917 czarist Russia collapsed, its economy and political system exhausted by the demands of the war. Early in 1918, its revolutionary Bolshevik government withdrew entirely from the war, leaving Germany in control of much of the Ukraine and southern Russia. German colonial ambitions in Europe seemed satisfied at last.

Yet the Central Powers could not match the Allies for men, materiel, wealth or opportunities. During 1916 Allied economic power began to assert itself. Britain developed a war economy, supplying munitions and other war materiel manufactured at home or imported from the United States and the British empire. Britain's financial superiority allowed it to bankroll the Allied war effort. The German navy tried to break Allied lines of supply by torpedoing British shipping. When unrestricted submarine warfare began in 1917, the United States was prompted to join the war on the Allied side – though more significantly as a supplier of munitions rather than as a belligerent. The Allies blockaded German ports, intensifying German economic difficulties.

The years 1916–17 saw several desperately costly battles on the Western Front – notably Verdun, the Somme, Ypres – made possible by the huge buildup of arms on the Allied side. The Central powers decided to make a tactical withdrawal on the Western Front and to militarize the economy at home. The result was disastrous. By November 1918, the German army had not retreated to within its own borders (it had in fact made large advances the previous spring), but it was in clear disarray, while food and fuel shortages led to the country collapsing from within. Kaiser Wilhelm II abdicated, as did the emperor of Austria–Hungary. The Allies were clearly in a position to dictate the terms of the peace.

Map labels

Petrograd (St Petersburg)
Moscow
Vitebsk
Vilna
Minsk
RUSSIAN EMPIRE capitulated Dec 1917 13.0m
Brusilov offensive June–Oct 1916
Kiev
Ukraine
Lvov
Odessa
Sevastopol
Feodosiya
Black Sea
ROMANIA 1.0m
Bucharest
Allied Power Aug 1916, capitulated to Central powers Dec 1917
SERBIA capitulated to Central powers Oct–Nov 1915 1.0m
BULGARIA 0.95m
Sofia
Central Power Sep 1915, capitulated to Allied Powers Sep 1918
Edirne
Doiran Apr–May 1917
Constantinople
Thessalonica Sep 1918
GREECE Allied power June 1917 0.2m
Athens
Gallipoli Apr 1915–Jan 1916
Crete to Greece
Rhodes
Dodecanese to Italy
Cyprus to Britain
OTTOMAN EMPIRE capitulated Oct 1918 2.85m
Konya
Tbilisi
Trabzon Apr 1916
Erzurum Feb 1916
Mosul
Aleppo
Damascus Sep 1918
Megiddo Sep 1918
Jerusalem Dec 1917
Baghdad Mar 1917
Kut Dec 1915–Apr 1916, Feb 1917
Basra
Mediterranean Sea
Cyrene
Cyrenaica to Italy
Alexandria
Egypt under British occupation
Cairo
Port Said
Suez Canal
Aqaba July 1917

Legend

borders, 1914
Allied powers and associates, June 1917
Central powers, June 1917
Central power capitulating before Nov 1918
neutral state
furthest advance of Central powers
furthest advance of Russian forces
Armistice line, 11 Nov 1918

Western Front
front line, 5 Sep 1914
front line, 29 Dec 1914
front line, 11 Nov 1918
German offensive, 16 Aug–5 Sep 1914
German offensive, 5 Apr–17 July 1918
furthest extent of German advance, 17 July 1918
Allied counteroffensive, 26 Sep–10 Nov 1918

Russian territory lost at the Treaty of Brest-Litovsk
main area of U-boat activity, 1915-18
naval base
Allied naval blockade
armaments, engineering and metal industry
chemical industry
shipbuilding industry
9.5m maximum mobilized forces (millions)
railroad
shipping route to United States and Canada

0　　　　600 km
0　　　400 mi

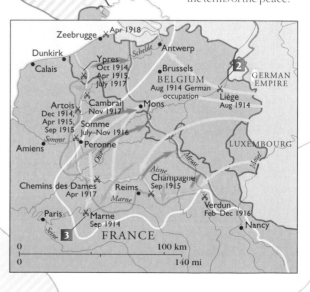

Zeebrugge Apr 1918
Antwerp
Dunkirk
Calais
Ypres Oct 1914, Apr 1915, July 1917
Brussels
BELGIUM Aug 1914 German occupation
Liège Aug 1914
GERMAN EMPIRE
Artois Dec 1914, Apr 1915, Sep 1915
Cambrai Nov 1917
Mons
Somme July–Nov 1916
Peronne
Amiens
Chemins des Dames Apr 1917
Reims
Champagne Sep 1915
Paris
Marne Sep 1914
Verdun Feb–Dec 1916
Nancy
LUXEMBOURG
FRANCE
Schelde *Aisne* *Marne* *Seine* *Oise* *Meuse* *Moselle* *Somme*

0　　　　100 km
0　　　　140 mi

See also 96 (Europe before 1914); 99 (the war outside Europe); 101 (Europe between the wars)

A t the beginning of the 20th century the world was dominated by Europe's imperial powers, many of them in the hands of ancient, autocratic monarchies. World War I shattered much of this, and, by its end, revolutions had swept away several monarchies, to be replaced in some states, such as Germany, by fragile democracies and in others (such as Russia) by revolutionary dictatorships (▷ 98). Among the factors driving change were the introduction of new technologies, particularly in the field of communications. Continental and oceanic transit networks were completed, and wireless telegraphy and radio were developed. Horse- and steam-power began to give way to gasoline- and diesel-driven transportation systems, and the war brought a rapid advance in air transport, both for civilian as well as military purposes.

Challenges to Europe's empires were already evident before 1914. In the east, Japan was industrializing rapidly, had defeated Russia and advanced into Manchuria as the Manchu dynasty in China collapsed (▷ 103). Europe's most formidable challenge, however, came from the United States which, following the defeat of Spain in 1898, became the only power capable of determining the development of the American continent. As a result, the United States built its own informal empire, enforcing its will if necessary by military intervention (▷ 102).

During World War I, Britain and France relied on their colonies and on the United States for men and materiel. When they came to make peace in 1919, they could not dictate the settlement alone. The United States was now the world's leading financial, industrial and, potentially, military power, thanks to the boost given to its industry by Allied orders at a time when the European economies were drastically disrupted. While Britain almost bankrupted itself funding the Allied war effort, the United States took over as the world's banker.

The American president Woodrow Wilson used this power to alter the conduct of international relations. On his initiative the League of Nations was set up, an organization of nation-states dedicated to preventing war by substituting mediation for military action. Wilson was also committed to the principle of national self-determination, and promoted the creation of new states such as Czechoslovakia, Yugoslavia and an independent Poland (▷ 101). He also tried to discourage imperialism, arguing that Germany's colonies should not be seized as the spoils of war. Instead, he persuaded the victorious powers to mandate these territories to Britain (whose empire thereby achieved its greatest territorial extent), France,

A.	Albania
AU.	Austria
B.	Belgium
C.	Czechoslovakia
D.	Denmark
E.	Estonia
H.	Hungary
KS.	Kingdom of Serbs, Croats, and Slovenes
L.	Luxembourg
LI.	Lithuania
N.	Netherlands
PG.	Portuguese Guinea
S.	Switzerland
T.	Transjordan
YE.	Yemen

Kingsford-Smith and Ulm, 1919

Hawaiian Islands (United States)

French Polynesia (France)

Alaska

CANADA

UNITED STATES

Newfoundland

MEXICO

Bahamas (Britain)

British Honduras

CUBA

Jamaica

HAITI

Puerto Rico (United States)

DOMINICAN REPUBLIC

GUATEMALA
EL SALVADOR
HONDURAS
NICARAGUA

COSTA RICA

PANAMA

Canal Zone (United States)

Galapagos Islands (Ecuador)

VENEZUELA

COLOMBIA

British Guiana
Dutch Guiana
French Guiana

ECUADOR

PERU

BRAZIL

BOLIVIA

CHILE

PARAGUAY

ARGENTINA

URUGUAY

Falkland Islands (Britain)

TIMELINE

1914 (Aug) Opening of the Panama Canal under US auspices	1915 (Apr) Italy, formerly a member of the Central Powers, joins the Allies			1918 (Mar) Treaty of Brest-Litovsk yields much of western Russia to Germany
1914 (Aug) Outbreak of general European war as Germany invades France and attacks Russia	1915 (Apr) The Allies attempt to seize control of the Dardanelles by landing at Gallipoli	1916 Battles of Verdun and the Somme on the Western Front	1917 (Apr) The United States declares war on the Central Powers	

The Americas
Europe
Middle East
Africa
Asia and Australasia

1914   1916   1918

1914 Japan takes over many German colonies in the Pacific	1915 Allied armies advance through Mesopotamia	1916 (Jun) An Arab revolt against the Ottomans begins in the Hejaz	1917 (Nov) Bolshevik revolution in Russia, leading to civil war (to 1921)
1914 Australia takes over the German colony of Kaiser Wilhelmsland			1917 (Nov) The Balfour Declaration commits Britain to the creation of a Jewish state in Palestine
			1917 (Dec) British forces occupy Jerusalem

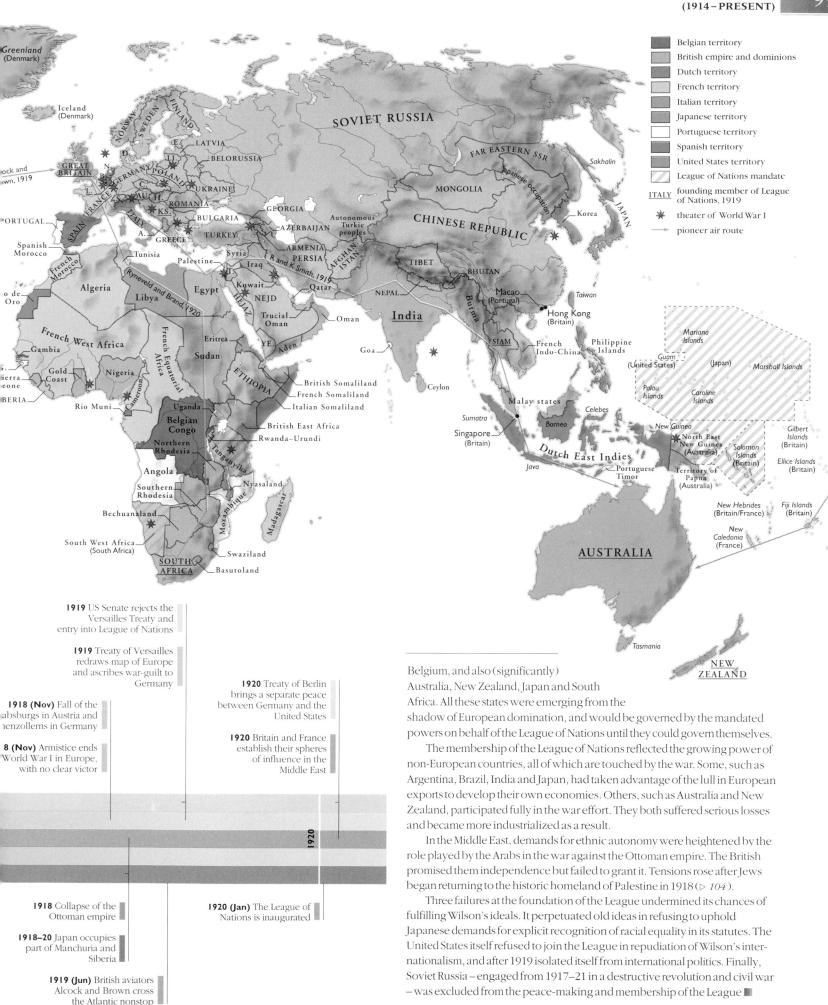

Belgian territory
British empire and dominions
Dutch territory
French territory
Italian territory
Japanese territory
Portuguese territory
Spanish territory
United States territory
League of Nations mandate
ITALY founding member of League of Nations, 1919
theater of World War I
pioneer air route
Greenland (Denmark)
Iceland (Denmark)
SOVIET RUSSIA
FAR EASTERN SSR
Japanese occupation
Sakhalin
MONGOLIA
CHINESE REPUBLIC
Korea
JAPAN
NORWAY
SWEDEN
FINLAND
E.
LATVIA
LI.
BELORUSSIA
D.
GREAT BRITAIN
N.
B.
GERMANY
POLAND
UKRAINE
L.
FRANCE
C.
S.
AU.
H.
ROMANIA
KS.
BULGARIA
ITALY
A.
GREECE
TURKEY
GEORGIA
AZERBAIJAN
ARMENIA
Autonomous Turkic peoples
PERSIA
AFGHANISTAN
R and K Smith, 1919
PORTUGAL
SPAIN
Spanish Morocco
French Morocco
Tunisia
Algeria
Libya
Palestine
Syria
Iraq
Egypt
Ryneveld and Brand, 1920
Kuwait
NEJD
Qatar
HEJAZ
Trucial Oman
Oman
YE.
Aden
TIBET
BHUTAN
NEPAL
India
Goa
Ceylon
Burma
Macao (Portugal)
Hong Kong (Britain)
Taiwan
SIAM
French Indo-China
Philippine Islands
Malay states
Singapore (Britain)
Sumatra
Borneo
Celebes
Java
Dutch East Indies
Portuguese Timor
New Guinea
North East New Guinea (Australia)
Territory of Papua (Australia)
Mariana Islands
Guam (United States)
(Japan)
Marshall Islands
Palau Islands
Caroline Islands
Gilbert Islands (Britain)
Solomon Islands (Britain)
Ellice Islands (Britain)
New Hebrides (Britain/France)
Fiji Islands (Britain)
New Caledonia (France)
AUSTRALIA
Tasmania
NEW ZEALAND
French West Africa
Gambia
Gold Coast
Nigeria
BERIA
Rio Muni
Cameroon
French Equatorial Africa
Sudan
Eritrea
ETHIOPIA
British Somaliland
French Somaliland
Italian Somaliland
Uganda
Belgian Congo
British East Africa
Rwanda-Urundi
Northern Rhodesia
Tanganyika
Angola
Nyasaland
Southern Rhodesia
Mozambique
Madagascar
Bechuanaland
South West Africa (South Africa)
Swaziland
SOUTH AFRICA
Basutoland

1919 US Senate rejects the Versailles Treaty and entry into League of Nations

1919 Treaty of Versailles redraws map of Europe and ascribes war-guilt to Germany

1918 (Nov) Fall of the absburgs in Austria and ienzollerns in Germany

8 (Nov) Armistice ends World War I in Europe, with no clear victor

1920 Treaty of Berlin brings a separate peace between Germany and the United States

1920 Britain and France establish their spheres of influence in the Middle East

1920

1918 Collapse of the Ottoman empire

1918–20 Japan occupies part of Manchuria and Siberia

1919 (Jun) British aviators Alcock and Brown cross the Atlantic nonstop

1920 (Jan) The League of Nations is inaugurated

Belgium, and also (significantly) Australia, New Zealand, Japan and South Africa. All these states were emerging from the shadow of European domination, and would be governed by the mandated powers on behalf of the League of Nations until they could govern themselves.

The membership of the League of Nations reflected the growing power of non-European countries, all of which are touched by the war. Some, such as Argentina, Brazil, India and Japan, had taken advantage of the lull in European exports to develop their own economies. Others, such as Australia and New Zealand, participated fully in the war effort. They both suffered serious losses and became more industrialized as a result.

In the Middle East, demands for ethnic autonomy were heightened by the role played by the Arabs in the war against the Ottoman empire. The British promised them independence but failed to grant it. Tensions rose after Jews began returning to the historic homeland of Palestine in 1918 (▷ *104*).

Three failures at the foundation of the League undermined its chances of fulfilling Wilson's ideals. It perpetuated old ideas in refusing to uphold Japanese demands for explicit recognition of racial equality in its statutes. The United States itself refused to join the League in repudiation of Wilson's internationalism, and after 1919 isolated itself from international politics. Finally, Soviet Russia – engaged from 1917–21 in a destructive revolution and civil war – was excluded from the peace-making and membership of the League ■

World War I imposed unbearable social and economic strain on Russia. The czar, who had assumed personal command of the armed forces in 1915, was held responsible for many of the failures of the war, and abdicated following a revolution in Petrograd in March (February in the Russian calendar) 1917. A provisional government took power but its decision to continue the war combined with fear of counterrevolution led to increasing radicalization. Local *soviets* – committees of workers, soldiers and sailors – sprang up in industrial areas. Many were dominated by the radical socialist parties, among whom the anti-war Bolsheviks (led by Vladimir Ilych Lenin since his return in April from exile in Berne) won growing influence. In November (October) 1917, the Bolsheviks overthrew the government.

The Bolsheviks were heavily outnumbered in the Constituent Assembly by the Socialist Revolutionaries representing the peasantry. Lenin therefore dissolved the Assembly and fought a bloody civil war to secure his position. Non-Bolshevik socialists, liberals, aristocrats, national minorities and the peasantry all opposed the regime, and several foreign powers also intervened. Nevertheless, the "Whites" (anti-Bolshevik forces) were too divided geographically and politically to depose the government. Nineteen independent governments were formed but, although at one point the Whites were within 400 kilometers (250 miles) of Moscow, the Bolsheviks ("Reds") recaptured the Ukraine, Caucasus, central Asia and Siberia. They ceded territory to Poland and recognized the independence of the Baltic states, but in 1923 the Union of Soviet Socialist Republics (USSR) was created, comprising the republics of Russia, Ukraine, Belorussia and Transcaucasia.

During the civil war the Bolsheviks adopted a policy of "war communism" and requisitioned food for the army and cities. This brought an arduous struggle with the peasantry which culminated in widespread revolts in 1920–22 and a famine in the Volga region that killed five million people. With the end of the civil war in 1921 Lenin adopted the "new economic policy" (NEP). This reintroduced limited

TIMELINE

Political change

1920

1917 Ukraine, Finland. Latvia, Lithuania claim independence

1917 (Mar) First revolution; czar abdicates and provisional government is set up

1917 (Nov) The Bolsheviks seize power

1918 (Mar) Bolsheviks sign the Treaty of Brest-Litovsk

1918–21 Civil war between the "Whites" and the "Reds"

1918 The Caucasus states and Estonia declare independence

1920 The Red Army invades Poland

1920–21 Ukraine, the Caucasus states and Turkestan are reconquered; Mongolia expels the Chinese

1922 Treaty of Rapallo: Soviet–German commercial and military agreement

1922–23 Formation of the Union of Soviet Socialist Republics (USSR)

1924 Death of Lenin

1930

1926 The Soviet Union and Germany sign a neutrality pact

1934 Start of the "great terror" after the assassination of Leningrad Party secretary Kirov

1934 The Soviet Union joins the League of Nations

1936–38 Height of the great purges in the Soviet Union

1936 Stalin's constitution is promulgated

1940

1939 Stalin signs the Nazi–Soviet pact with Hitler

1939 The Soviet Union occupies eastern Poland and Finland

1940 The Soviet Union occupies the Baltic states; Finland sues for peace

1941 Germany invades the Soviet Union

1938 Purge of the armed forces by Stalin

Economic change

1918 Depopulation of towns and cities in the civil war

1920–22 Peasant revolts occur throughout Russia

1921 The "new economic policy" is introduced

1928 The first Five Year Plan is announced

1929 The collectivization of agriculture is announced

1932–33 Famine in the Ukraine and central Asia

1933 The second Five Year Plan is announced

1939 The third Five Year Plan is announced

1920   **1930**   **1940**

free trade to encourage the peasants to produce more while the Bolsheviks (soon to be called Communists) tried to modernize the country.

Lenin died in 1924 without leaving an obvious successor, but Joseph Stalin used his post as general-secretary of the Communist Party to secure control of the state. The Communists now had to face the contradiction that they were a workers' government in a peasant country. In 1929 Stalin addressed this issue by ordering the collectivization of agriculture.

Private trade was abolished and peasants forced to give up their private holdings and work on collective farms. Many responded by slaughtering their livestock and planting only enough grain to feed themselves. When this was requisitioned famine ensued, and millions were deported to the *gulag* (prison camps), resulting in around 14.5 million deaths.

Collectivization was intended to cow the peasantry and provide sufficient grain to support a massive program of industrialization as the Soviet

Union was built into a modern economic power. Even during the famine, grain was being used to feed the city population and sold abroad to buy western technology. In 1928 Stalin announced the first Five Year Plan, with which he proposed that the Soviet Union should catch up with the west which, he claimed, was "50 to 100 years ahead". Production grew quickly, especially in the heavy and defense industries as old industrial centers were expanded and new ones created in remote regions.

Industrial development was undermined by the purges that Stalin unleashed in 1934. "Subversives" (in the first instance, old Bolsheviks) appeared in show trials, were convicted of fantastic crimes and shot, while millions of others faced deportation to labor camps. Stalin's war with his own population extended across the Soviet Union as he sought scapegoats for the failures of collectivization and industrialization to achieve the targets set out in the Plan. Fear and suspicion led to mass denunciations and the decimation of the upper levels of bureaucracy and Party.

By 1938 a purge of the army and navy began and the country lost most of its officer corps. The following year Stalin agreed to the Nazi–Soviet pact with Hitler and subsequently occupied eastern Poland and the Baltic states. Stalin apparently believed that Hitler would not invade Russia until France and Britain were defeated. He also thought that fascism, which he saw as the highest form of capitalism, must presage the Communist revolution in Europe.

In 1941, though, Hitler did invade. The Soviet Union was in a better position to resist than Russia had been in 1914, despite the depredations of the purges. Communism had been established against all the odds in what had been Europe's most backward country. Stalin's policies, which were mainly an extension of those used by Lenin to win the civil war, were pursued at massive human cost and allowed the Communist Party to prevail.

New Siberian Islands

Wrangel Island

Ambarchik

Nordvik

Dubinka
Norilsk
arka

Tiksi

Kolymskaya

Anadyr

UNION OF SOVIET
SOCIALIST REPUBLICS
from 1923

kovo

oyarsk

Lena

3

Magadan

POSTERS publicized the Bolshevik cause. This image shows Lenin in typical pose.

Sea of Okhotsk

Petropavlovsk

emkhovo Lake Baykal
Irkutsk
Ulan Ude Chita

Far Eastern Republic
1920–22 independent

Magdagachi Nikolaevsk

1925 to Russia

Aleksandrovsk
Sakhalin

Komsomolsk

Ulan Bator

Sovetskaya Gavan
Khabarovsk

MONGOLIA
1924 Communist state under
Russian influence

Manchuria
Harbin

Kuril Islands

Gobi Desert

Mukden
(Shenyang)

Vladivostok

Yellow

Beijing

Sea of Japan

Lushun
(Port Arthur)

anzhou

CHINA

Yellow
Sea

Korea
Chosen from 1910
to Japan

Tokyo
JAPAN

NORTH

PACIFIC

OCEAN

1 Petrograd (renamed Leningrad in 1924) was imperial Russia's capital and largest city. It was the conduit for revolutionary ideas and the center of events in 1917.

2 The Bolsheviks held the central position in the civil war and control of the rail network centered on Moscow (the capital from March 1918), was vital to their cause.

3 A variety of forces opposed the Bolsheviks: the Czech legion, formed to fight for the Allies during World War I, tried to get home via Vladivostok and in 1918 controlled the trans-Siberian railroad.

4 Magnitogorsk was the showpiece of Soviet industrializiation, a huge industrial plant built in the shadow of the Urals.

5 The Soviet "corrective labor camps", known by their acronym (*gulag*), were originally set up by Lenin. They became a key feature of Stalin's economic policy as well as of the eradication of opposition.

6 Tambov was the focus of violent peasant rebellions in 1920–22.

—	western frontier of Russian empire, 1914
🚩	principal town where Bolsheviks seized power, Nov–Dec 1917
▨	area controlled by Bolsheviks, Aug 1918
➤	advance of anti-Bolshevik armies, 1918–20
◠	area controlled by Bolsheviks, Oct 1919
—	border of temporarily independent area
➤	Japanese Siberian expedition, 1918–22
▢	Union of Soviet Socialist Republics, 1939
—	border, 1939

➤	Russian campaign, 1939
▢	main area of collectivization
◠	area under *gulag* administration
●	new town founded 1925–38
⛽	oilfield
≈	hydroelectric power station
—	railroad

0   800 km
0   500 mi

See also 88 (19th-century Russia);
101 (Europe between the wars)

World War I destroyed the old order in central and eastern Europe: the fall of the Romanovs (Russia), Habsburgs (Austria–Hungary) and Hohenzollerns (Germany) brought political instability that compounded the economic and social dislocation of the war. Extremism flourished across central Europe, with Marxist revolutions in several major cities being countered by a rightwing backlash.

The peace treaties failed to create a lasting settlement, and provided instead the grounds for future discontent. United States president Wilson hoped that ethnically homogeneous nation-states could eradicate the nationalist rivalries and squabbling over territory that appeared to have caused the war; but this proved impossible. Two new states (Czechoslovakia and the Kingdom of the Serbs, Croats and Slovenes – later Yugoslavia) and one reconstituted one (Poland) assembled many ethnic groups within arbitrary borders, and nationalist groups were often disappointed in disputed areas. Everywhere populations were on the move. Italy, its promises from the Allies for territory unfulfilled, set out to take the territory it claimed by force, as did Poland.

The Treaty of Versailles forced Germany to admit guilt for starting the war and to pay huge reparations to the Allies. It was forbidden to ally with Austria and was divided by the Polish Corridor, while three million ethnic Germans remained outside the state.

The League of Nations, set up to resolve the disputes that were bound to arise from the settlement, was hamstrung as the United States, the only power capable of giving weight to its decisions, declined to join. With Russia preoccupied with domestic affairs, Britain and France were left to deal with European issues alone. They were faced with the prospect of a reborn Germany avenging its grievances and filling the power vacuum created by the fall of the imperial monarchies. Both Britain and France were economically weak following the war and they sought to keep Germany weak as well. France occupied the Ruhr in 1923 to enforce payment of reparations, but the hyperinflation that ensued provided fertile ground for extremist groups in Germany. With

Legend

- area temporarily independent
- border, 1921

dictatorships by 1 Sep 1939
- Communist
- fascist
- other
- **1924** date of introduction of dictatorship

democracies, 1939
- British territories and mandates
- French territories and mandates
- other

- German gain, 1935–1 Sep 1939
- Hungarian gain, 1938–39
- Italian gain, Apr 1939
- Turkish gain, 1923
- Nationalist-held Spain, late 1936
- Nationalist gain by Dec 1938
- demilitarized zone, 1919–35
- area of economic revival
- area of economic decline
- SPAIN country experiencing civil war, with date
- ☆ strike, riot or other protest action
- ✳ Communist uprising, 1919–23
- ✳ international incident
- ✳ incident of Polish aggression, 1920
- ✡ city with large Jewish population
- supply route for Spanish civil war
- emigration of more than 200,000 refugees

0 — 600 km
0 — 400 mi

TIMELINE

International affairs

1920	1930	1940
1919–20 Treaties of Versailles, St Germain, Neuilly, Trianon create the postwar settlement in Europe	**1925** The European powers guarantee Germany's eastern European borders at Locarno	**1932** German postwar reparations are abolished	**1936** The Rome–Berlin Axis is formed
1922 Germany and USSR sign a treaty at Rapallo	**1928** The antiwar Kellogg–Briand pact is signed in Paris	**1932** France and the USSR sign a nonaggression treaty	**1938** Munich agreement on Germany's occupation of the Sudetenland
	1924 The Dawes plan reduces German reparations	**1929** Beginning of the Great Depression	**1934** Yugoslavia, Romania, Turkey, Greece sign a Balkan pact against Hitler and Stalin	**1939** The Nazi–Soviet pact is signed

Western Europe

1920 Abortive Communist revolutions in Germany	**1926** General strike in Britain, led by the miners	**1931** The Republicans win a landslide victory in Spanish elections; the king flees	**1936–39** The Spanish Civil War follows an attempted rightwing coup by Franco
1921 The Irish Free State is set up in southern Ireland	**1926** Germany enters the League of Nations	**1933** Adolf Hitler is elected chancellor of Germany	**1939** Britain and France declare war on Germany
1923 France occupies the Ruhr; hyperinflation in Germany	**1929** Lateran treaties between Italy and the Papacy ensure the Vatican's independence		**1936** German army reoccupies the Rhineland

Eastern Europe

1920–22 War between Greece and Turkey	**1924–29** Joseph Stalin consolidates his power in USSR	**1934** Austrian chancellor Dollfuss is murdered by Nazis	**1938** German invasion of Austria (*Anschluss*)
1920–21 Poland and the Soviet Union are at war	**1926** Josef Pilsudski comes to power in Poland	**1934** King Alexander of Macedonia is assassinated	**1939** Germany and Soviet Union invade Poland

alliance system
- ● French
- ● German
- ○ Italian
- ○ Locarno treaty, 1925
- ● Balkan Entente, 1934
- ● Baltic Entente, 1922

Britain and France tried to buy them off by conceding small territorial claims (the policy of "appeasement"), but the dictators demanded more. Italy escaped virtually unpunished for invading Ethiopia in 1935 as Britain and France tried (unsuccessfully) to preserve Mussolini as an ally against Germany. Hitler, as well as initiating his anti-Jewish policies, began to challenge the Treaty of Versailles: in 1935 Germany began to rearm and then reoccupied the Rhineland. Further steps to extend German power and territory followed, with the *Anschluss* with Austria (1938) and the partition of Czechoslovakia (agreed with Britain and France at Munich in 1938).

By now Britain and France had lost all credibility. Germany invaded Czechoslovakia in 1939 and the French and British guaranteed the security of several other European states, but to little avail. A French strategy of fencing the Germans in with the "Little Entente" in eastern Europe had already been weakened by a German–Polish non-aggression treaty in 1934. The democracies failed to secure an alliance with the Soviet Union and Stalin, believing Britain and France to be encouraging Hitler to expand to the east, signed a Nazi–Soviet pact in August 1939. Hitler and Stalin partitioned Poland between them, but Hitler failed to anticipate a sea-change in British and French opinion after his annexation of Czechoslovakia. Unexpectedly he had to fight in the west before pursuing his primary objectives in the east.

---

1 Budapest saw a Communist takeover in March 1919 under Bela Kun. Hungary then invaded Slovakia and Transylvania; Kun fled abroad in August 1919.

2 Following a plebiscite in 1920, Schleswig was divided between Germany and Denmark.

3 Ireland was divided in 1921: the mainly Protestant north elected to stay in the United Kingdom, the south became the Irish Free State. Civil war ensued in the south (1922–23), where many rejected partition.

4 The Saar became a League of Nations mandate under French rule in 1919, but returned to Germany by plebiscite in 1935.

5 The town of Guernica was destroyed by German bombers in the first massive aerial attack on civilians.

6 The Sudetenland of northwest Czechoslovakia, which had a large German minority, was annexed by Hitler following the Munich agreement in 1938.

See also 98 (World War I); 100 (the Soviet Union to 1941); 105 (World War II)

Germany's prosperity essential for European well-being, reparations were reduced and a limited recovery followed, funded by American loans.

Germany's grievances might have been resolved peacefully. The Locarno pact (1925) guaranteed its western borders and showed that foreign minister Stresemann would work peacefully to revise the Treaty of Versailles, while the Kellogg–Briand pact of 1928 officially, if implausibly, renounced war.

The depression of the early 1930s, caused in part by the withdrawal of American loans, shattered the illusion of stability. Democracy was weakly established in many countries: massive unemployment and protest were now seen, followed by a return to authoritarian government. The dictator Pilsudski had upheld Catholicism in Poland since 1926; now Franco did the same in Spain after a three-year civil war. This bloody conflict showed how polarized politics in Europe was, and became a war by proxy between the Soviet-supplied republic and German- and Italian-supported right. Royal dictatorships also flourished in Bulgaria, Romania and Yugoslavia.

The radical new phenomenon of fascism now threatened the peace. Promising national renewal and fueled by grievances over the peace settlement, Mussolini's movement in Italy had established itself as a totalitarian regime in 1925. Fascist parties formed across Europe and in 1933 Hitler's Nazi party won power in Germany, its appeal magnified by mass unemployment and fear of Communism.

The British and French governments continued to be cautious. In Germany the Nazis eliminated unemployment by means of public work schemes, but in Britain the principles of classical economics still applied. Some economists, led by J.M. Keynes, advocated jump-starting the economy through government spending, but heavy industry did not recover until the armaments boom at the end of the 1930s (newer industries, such as electronics, motor and aircraft production, however, showed rapid growth).

The same caution applied to foreign policy. Unwilling to destabilize the international economy with wars or sanctions, the League proved unable to take a firm line with Germany and Italy in the 1930s.

World War I involved many of the American states, despite an original intention to stay out of the conflict. The Caribbean islands and Canada owed direct allegiance to Britain, but most other countries had divided loyalties and were anxious to preserve their own interests. US president Woodrow Wilson advised neutrality. By 1918 Brazil and several Central American states had joined the Allies; the United States itself stayed out until German U-boat (submarine) attacks drove Wilson to declare war in 1917. The nation was put on a war footing: the government took over the railroads and strikers were faced with the draft. Factories and shipyards converted to warwork, and thousands of African–Americans moved north to the munitions factories.

By the end of the war, there was little enthusiasm for any US involvement in Europe's postwar territorial arrangements. The Treaty of Versailles and the League of Nations, Wilson's brainchild, were both rejected by Congress as Americans sought "normalcy". The "jazz age" of the 1920s brought a quest for consumer goods and material comfort, despite a moral backlash in the form of the Volstead Act, which brought Prohibition in 1920, with intoxicating liquor banned across the country. The result was a rise in political corruption and gangsterism.

In 1929, the Wall St stock market crash threw the country into the Great Depression, which had global repercussions as US loans and investments had propped up the world's trade. The shadow of the depression was felt throughout the Western Hemisphere. In the United States itself, the crisis was exacerbated by drought and storms that devastated parts of Texas and the Mid-West, and created a dustbowl on the Great Plains. Some 12 million Americans lost their jobs, and shanty-towns (Hoovervilles) sprang up around many cities. In 1933, Democrat Franklin D. Roosevelt became president, offering a New Deal to alleviate the depression through unprecedented government spending, giving work to millions on infrastructure projects such as dams and airports. The New Deal could not, however, cure all the economic ills of the country. Agriculture and heavy industry recovered only after 1940, mainly due to US contributions to Britain's war effort, followed by

the outbreak of war with Japan in December 1941.

Canada had suffered in the Great War, and lost 60,000 men by 1918. This experience, followed by the prosperity of the 1920s, encouraged a new spirit of independence. But the country was hit hard by the depression, as it was heavily reliant on the export of wheat and lumber. The great drought of 1934 also wrought havoc on the farmers of the prairies. New political groupings suggested nationalization and the redistribution of income as a cure to national ills, while separatists won a large following in Quebec. The rise in world prices after 1937, and closer economic ties with the United States caused both proposals to be shelved for several decades.

The United States claimed the Caribbean and Central America as its "backyard", intervening to maintain its investments (including the Panama Canal and the oil reserves of Mexico and Venezuela) and building a military base at Guantanamo Bay on Cuba. The region was badly hit by the recession, and strikes and demonstrations were common, especially in the British West Indies. Several countries turned to dictatorships: some, such as Lázaro Cárdenas, ruler of Mexico from 1934–40, tried honestly to improve the condition of their people. Cárdenas restored communal lands to the peasants, and nationalized railroads and oil companies. Venezuela was ruled by Juan Vicente Gómez from 1908–35. He took over the Lake Maracaibo oil reserves, but failed to address the weakness of so many Latin American states: the reliance on a single export commodity.

Colombia became the world's second producer of coffee but, like its main rival Brazil (ruled after 1930 by Getúlio Vargas), tried to reduce the economy's dependence on the fragile coffee trade in the 1930s by industrial diversification and import substitution. Argentina, which had flourished since the 19th century on grain and meat exports, now had to endure austerity measures. Chile too suffered with the fall in copper prices, while its nitrate exports were hit by the discovery of new chemical methods of production. Several South American states engaged in border disputes: Chile and Peru clashed over nitrate resources; the Chaco War between Bolivia and Paraguay in the 1930s was the most

violent conflict to take place in the world between 1918 and 1939; and Ecuador lost the Amazonian region to Peru in 1942.

World War II brought full employment and high wages to North America: by 1943 the USA was outproducing all the enemy nations combined. Millions moved to the cities; African–Americans flooded to California, Detroit and New York. Convoys took troops and supplies to all main theaters of war, and brought aid to Britain and the USSR. To counter enemy submarines operating down the Atlantic seaboard and in the Gulf of Mexico, air patrols were maintained far out to sea. For the Latin American countries the war years were eased by Roosevelt's "good neighbor" policy. The Coffee Accords of 1940 guaranteed US markets; in return Roosevelt gained bases and promises of military support.

TIMELINE

North America

1920	1930	1940
1914 Canada enters the war against Germany	**1923** Chinese settlement in Canada is stopped	**1929** Wall St Crash leads to financial chaos in the United States
1917 The United States declares war on Germany		
1919 The US Senate rejects the Treaty of Versailles		**1932** F.D. Roosevelt wins the US election, and introduces New Deal policies (1933)
1919 The United States outlaws intoxicating liquor (1920–33)		**1933** Newfoundland gives up its status as a dominion, but remains within the British empire

1937 Automobile workers strike in Detroit
1945 First atomic explosion takes places in New Mexico
1939 Canada declares war on Germany
1941 The Lend-Lease Act stimulates US industry in support of Allied war effort
1941 The Pearl Harbor attack leads the USA to enter the war

Central and South

1917 A new Mexican constitution embodies the principle of land reform
1925 The United States intervenes in Nicaragua following a civil war
1930 Getúlio Vargas leads a revolution in Brazil
1939 Unions and the military clash in Argentina

1921 Guatemala, Honduras and El Salvador form the Republic of Central America
1929 The United States arbitrates over a border dispute between Chile and Peru
1934 Cárdenas begins his reform program in Mexico
1940 War begins between Ecuador and Peru over the Amazonia region (to 1942)

1935 End of the Chaco War between Paraguay and Bolivia (since 1932)
1940 "Destroyers-for-bases" deal between the United States and Britain leads to new US bases in Caribbean

1920   1930   1940

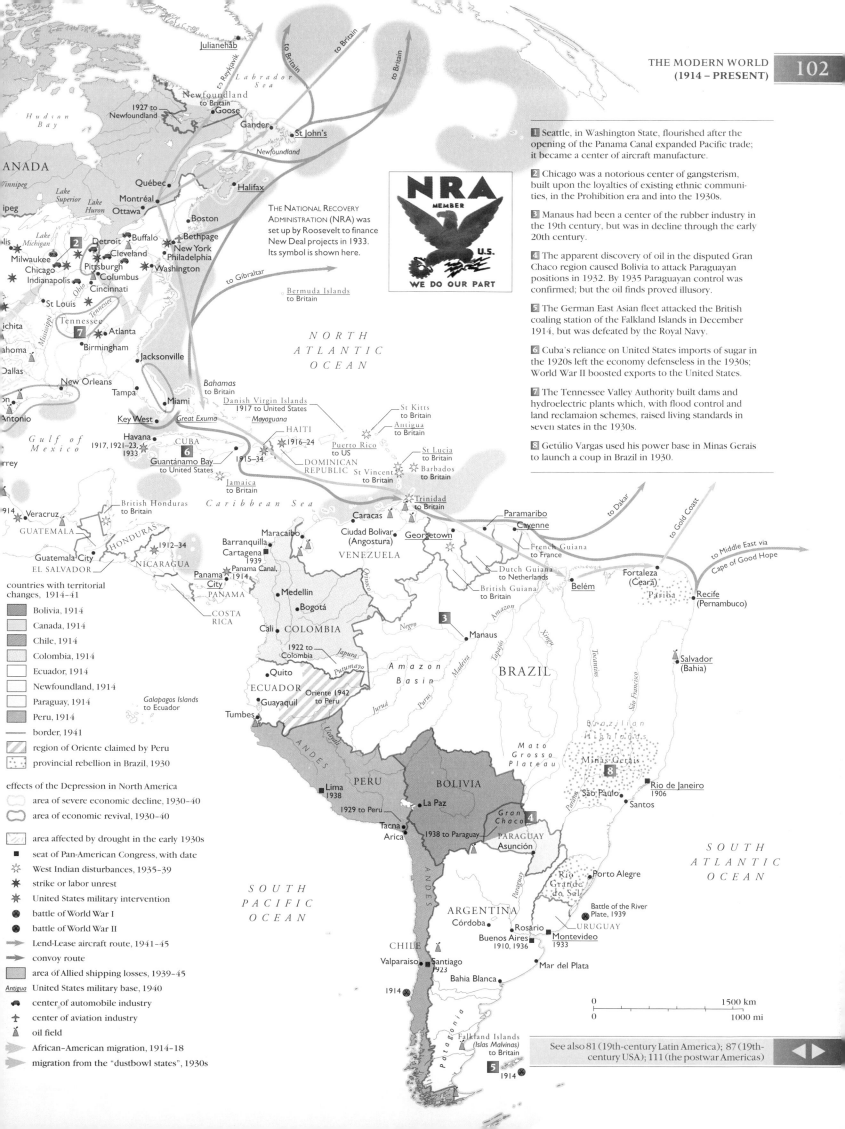

THE NATIONAL RECOVERY ADMINISTRATION (NRA) was set up by Roosevelt to finance New Deal projects in 1933. Its symbol is shown here.

NRA
MEMBER
U.S.
WE DO OUR PART

1 Seattle, in Washington State, flourished after the opening of the Panama Canal expanded Pacific trade; it became a center of aircraft manufacture.

2 Chicago was a notorious center of gangsterism, built upon the loyalties of existing ethnic communities, in the Prohibition era and into the 1930s.

3 Manaus had been a center of the rubber industry in the 19th century, but was in decline through the early 20th century.

4 The apparent discovery of oil in the disputed Gran Chaco region caused Bolivia to attack Paraguayan positions in 1932. By 1935 Paraguayan control was confirmed; but the oil finds proved illusory.

5 The German East Asian fleet attacked the British coaling station of the Falkland Islands in December 1914, but was defeated by the Royal Navy.

6 Cuba's reliance on United States imports of sugar in the 1920s left the economy defenseless in the 1930s; World War II boosted exports to the United States.

7 The Tennessee Valley Authority built dams and hydroelectric plants which, with flood control and land reclamaion schemes, raised living standards in seven states in the 1930s.

8 Getúlio Vargas used his power base in Minas Gerais to launch a coup in Brazil in 1930.

countries with territorial changes, 1914–41

Bolivia, 1914
Canada, 1914
Chile, 1914
Colombia, 1914
Ecuador, 1914
Newfoundland, 1914
Paraguay, 1914
Peru, 1914
border, 1941
region of Oriente claimed by Peru
provincial rebellion in Brazil, 1930

effects of the Depression in North America
area of severe economic decline, 1930–40
area of economic revival, 1930–40
area affected by drought in the early 1930s

■ seat of Pan-American Congress, with date
☆ West Indian disturbances, 1935–39
✳ strike or labor unrest
✴ United States military intervention
⊗ battle of World War I
⊗ battle of World War II
→ Lend-Lease aircraft route, 1941–45
→ convoy route
area of Allied shipping losses, 1939–45
Antigua United States military base, 1940
● center of automobile industry
✦ center of aviation industry
⌂ oil field
→ African-American migration, 1914–18
→ migration from the "dustbowl states", 1930s

See also 81 (19th-century Latin America); 87 (19th-century USA); 111 (the postwar Americas)

The Russo-Japanese War of 1904–05 gave Japan protectorate authority over Korea and the lease of Chinese territory in south Manchuria. From these bases the army looked to consolidate its influence in Manchuria and north China. By this time, a new and increasingly militant anti-imperialist nationalism was developing among young Chinese intellectuals, merchants and soldiers. This development was echoed elsewhere in the region, for example in the growth of Indian and Vietnamese national movements. In the case of China, resentment after 1905 was clearly focussed on Japan as the other western powers were preoccupied with European politics and hoped merely to hold onto their Asian interests.

Tokyo's decision to enter World War I was driven as much by interests in China – where the Manchu dynasty had finally fallen three years earlier – as by the desire to help its ally Britain. In August 1914 Japan issued an ultimatum to Germany to hand over territories in Shandong province. Japan then took the German outpost of Qingdao; the whole province was eventually occupied.

As one of the victorious nations, Japan was invited to attend the Versailles peace conference in 1919 and retained the former German territory in Shandong. However, this conference marked a turning point in the position of the European powers in east Asia – Britain, France, the Netherlands, and, to a lesser extent, Portugal. All had been weakened by the war, while the revolution of 1917 ended Russia's imperialism. The League of Nations, created in the aftermath of war, adopted a policy generally critical of colonialism. In the interwar years Britain, while publicly supporting its empire, privately explored ways to enable the Asian colonies to achieve self-governing Dominion status (like New Zealand, since 1907) or Commonwealth status (like Australia). The Dutch, too, were beginning to consider ways of passing power to the native populations.

Nationalist movements in the colonies were given impetus by the severe effects of the worldwide depression of the 1930s and the collapse of European prestige wrought by the carnage of World War I. In India, the Indian National Congress, led by Jawaharlal Nehru and Mohandas "Mahatma" Gandhi, organized a mass self-rule movement in the 1920s and 1930s. In Burma, which was separated from India and given a form of responsible government in 1937, nationalist demands were heightened by the depression. The Dutch East Indies experienced a Communist uprising in 1926–27, and French Indo-China also saw Communist-inspired strikes and rural unrest with the overall objective of national independence. Neither the French nor the Dutch made significant concessions, and – except in India – the nationalist movements appeared divided and unable to make a lasting impression. The United States, though, appeared to support the nationalists, and in 1935 promised independence for its own colony in the Philippines within ten years.

The general unrest in east and southeast Asia led Japan into further military expansion from 1931. After establishing the puppet state of Manzhouguo in Manchuria, however, Japan was criticized by the League of Nations and quit this body in protest. The resulting international isolation made Japan turn for new allies to Germany and Italy and, in China, to pursue an even more aggressive and uncompromising policy toward the Nationalist government which was already engaged in civil war with Chinese Communists. In mid-1937 Japan and China engaged unofficially in a war which Japanese generals confidently promised would be over by the end of the year. Japan's bombing of cities and the massacre of civilians as its forces took the Nationalist cities of Shanghai and Nanjing brought the war to the attention of the world, heightening criticism in the west.

In 1939 Japanese forces landed in French Indo-China to cut off supply routes to the Chinese Nationalists. After the fall of France to Hitler in 1940, the Japanese went on to occupy most of the colony, while maintaining a French administration. Politically, the Japanese exploited the anti-European feeling among the nationalist groups, promising a form of independence such as Burma had been given. Economic prosperity was similarly promised in the Japanese-sponsored Greater East Asian Co-Prosperity Sphere. Some – such as the Indian leader

TIMELINE

Japan

1904-05 Japan defeats Russia and wins control of Manchuria

1910 Japan annexes Korea

1914 Japan takes the German-leased territory in Shandong province, China

1918–22 Japanese forces invade Siberia as part of an Allied expedition to Russia

1919 Japanese gains in China are confirmed by Treaty of Versailles

1920 Japan is mandated control of the former German Pacific islands by the League of Nations

1932 Japan sets up the puppet state of Manzhouguo in Manchuria

1933 Japan withdraws from the League of Nations

1937 Japanese expansion in China begins

1937 The United States threatens to impose an oil embargo on Japan

1938 Fighting breaks out between Japanese and Soviet forces on Manzhouguo–Soviet border

1940 Japanese control is extended over Indo-China

1941 Japan attacks the United States at Pearl Harbor

Other powers

1915 Australian and New Zealand forces make an important contribution to the Allied attack on Turkey at Gallipoli

1920 Former German territories in the Pacific are mandated to Australia, Britain and Japan by the League of Nations

1920 Mahatma Gandhi takes control of the Indian National Congress

1926 Anticolonial Communist agitation takes place in the Dutch East Indies

1927 Ahmed Sukarno sets up the Indonesian Nationalist Party

1930 Gandhi institutes salt marches to protest against British rule in India

1935 British Government of India Act reforms the Indian administration

1939 The kingdom of Siam is renamed Thailand, celebrating its avoidance of colonial rule

1941 A Communist-nationalist guerrilla organization, the Vietminh, is set up in Indo-China

Map legend

— borders, 1914
British territory, 1914
Dutch territory, 1914
French territory, 1914
German territory, 1914
Japanese territory, 1914
Portuguese territory, 1914
United States territory, 1914

territorial gains from Germany by mandate, 1920
Australian
Japanese

Japanese territorial expansion in Asia
temporary occupation, 1915–25
gains by 1934 (empire of Manzhouguo)
gains by 1937
gains by 7 Dec 1941

under Japanese influence, 1936–40
Chinese Communist headquarters, 1937
strong Indian National Congress support
• Allied base
oil strategic resource
☆ area of anti-colonial agitation
— Burma road
➔ Japanese attack

0   1200 km
0   800 mi

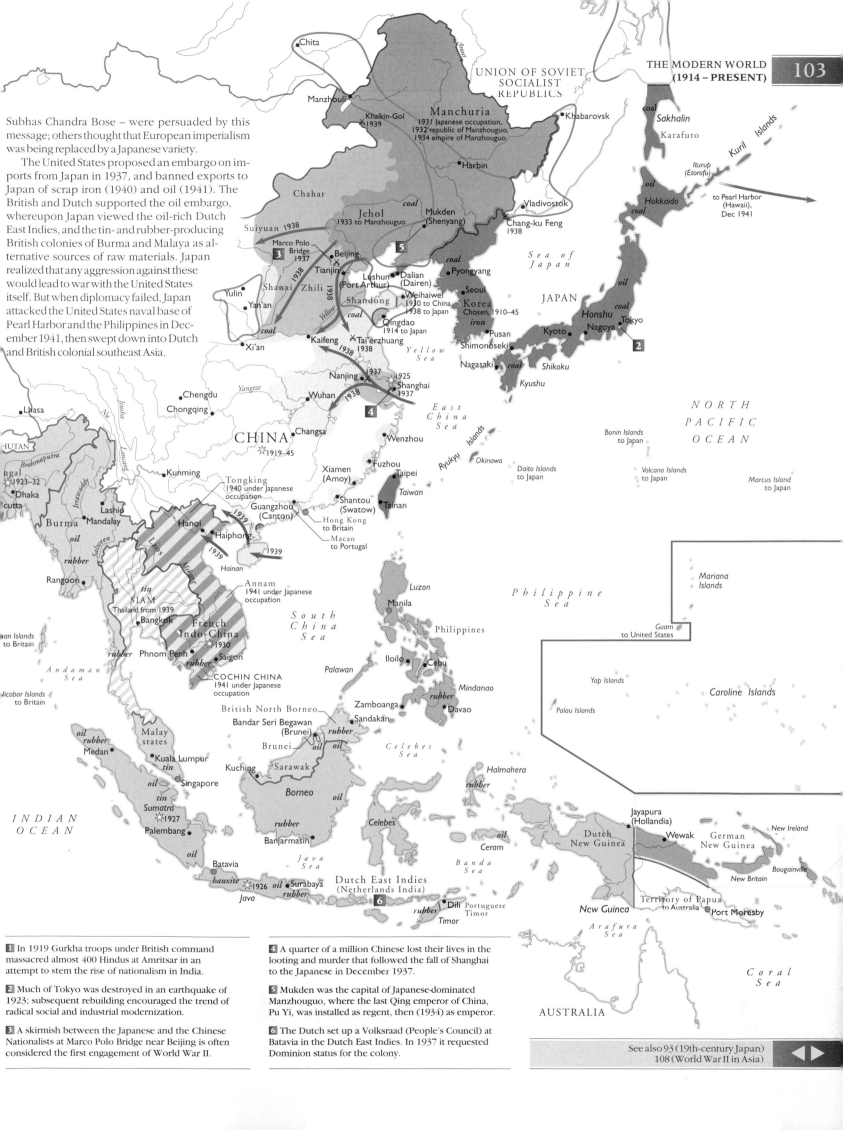

Subhas Chandra Bose – were persuaded by this message; others thought that European imperialism was being replaced by a Japanese variety.

The United States proposed an embargo on imports from Japan in 1937, and banned exports to Japan of scrap iron (1940) and oil (1941). The British and Dutch supported the oil embargo, whereupon Japan viewed the oil-rich Dutch East Indies, and the tin- and rubber-producing British colonies of Burma and Malaya as alternative sources of raw materials. Japan realized that any aggression against these would lead to war with the United States itself. But when diplomacy failed, Japan attacked the United States naval base of Pearl Harbor and the Philippines in December 1941, then swept down into Dutch and British colonial southeast Asia.

1 In 1919 Gurkha troops under British command massacred almost 400 Hindus at Amritsar in an attempt to stem the rise of nationalism in India.

2 Much of Tokyo was destroyed in an earthquake of 1923; subsequent rebuilding encouraged the trend of radical social and industrial modernization.

3 A skirmish between the Japanese and the Chinese Nationalists at Marco Polo Bridge near Beijing is often considered the first engagement of World War II.

4 A quarter of a million Chinese lost their lives in the looting and murder that followed the fall of Shanghai to the Japanese in December 1937.

5 Mukden was the capital of Japanese-dominated Manzhouguo, where the last Qing emperor of China, Pu Yi, was installed as regent, then (1934) as emperor.

6 The Dutch set up a Volksraad (People's Council) at Batavia in the Dutch East Indies. In 1937 it requested Dominion status for the colony.

See also 93 (19th-century Japan)
108 (World War II in Asia)

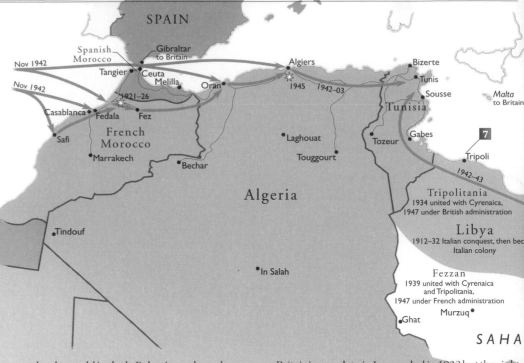

In 1914 the Allies decided to carry the war into every German colony in Africa. Military operations in Togoland, Cameroon and South-West Africa were completed by 1916; the campaigns in German East Africa (later Tanganyika) continued until 1918, a week after the armistice was signed on the Western Front. Turkey's alliance with Germany led to assaults on the Suez Canal and Basra, both repelled by Allied forces. The British supported the Arab revolts against the Turks: they took Jerusalem in 1917, and a more general assault on Turkish control of the Middle East followed as the British raced to occupy the Mesopotamian oilfields. Britain ensured its hold over the oilfields of southern Persia, too, claiming a *de facto* protectorate in 1918.

The Covenant of the League of Nations required the peacemakers to help underdeveloped peoples to cope with the "strenuous conditions of the modern world". The colonies of the defunct German and Turkish empires were administered under the mandate system. Some ex-colonies were scheduled for rapid independence: on this understanding Britain was awarded a mandate over Palestine, Iraq (formerly Mesopotamia) and Transjordan; France gained Syria and Lebanon. Less advanced areas could not expect independence in the near future; these included the Cameroons and Togoland, shared between Britain and France; Britain acquired Tanganyika, Belgium was awarded Ruanda-Urundi.

This redistribution of territory meant that the British and French colonial empires grew substantially; the indigenous peoples were not consulted about their aspirations for independence. The notable exception was in Palestine where, the British government declared in 1917, it favored the establishment of a national home for the Jews. This conflicted with an earlier promise to the Arabs that their

new lands would include Palestine, where the population was 90 percent Muslim. Jewish immigration to the area was limited through the 1920s, but grew substantially in the 1930s, when the British first proposed the division of Palestine into separate Jewish and Arab states. After World War II, with the world horrified by the Holocaust and the Jews and Arabs in Palestine engaged in civil war, the United Nations supported partition and approved the state of Israel which came into being in 1948.

Britain, by 1918 the dominant power in the region, held back from interfering in central Arabia, permitting the Saudi kingdom to emerge in 1932.

Britain's mandate in Iraq ended in 1932 but the right to protect oil and military interests was retained, notably by means of two airforce bases. A native Pahlavi dynasty seized control of Persia in 1925, renaming it Iran in 1935. By the outbreak of war, Iran produced more oil than the rest of the Middle East, and the shah's ties with Nazi Germany led the Allies to occupy the country again in 1941. The shah was forced to abdicate and his son Mohammed Reza Pahlavi installed in his place. The market for Middle Eastern oil grew in the interwar years, but the oilfields were not fully developed until the 1950s. French rule in Syria and Lebanon was benevolent, but was compromised by the fall of France in 1940; both countries were occupied during the war by Free French and British troops, and their independent status was recognized in 1946.

North and east Africa, too, were caught up in the conflicts of the European powers. The British confirmed Egyptian independence in 1922 but maintained the right to use Egypt's facilities in time of war, to defend the Suez Canal and maintain the Anglo-Egyptian joint rule in the Sudan. The British in Egypt and Italians in Libya began a conflict in 1940 which drew in the German army the following year; by 1943 the entire North Africa littoral was involved. Meanwhile indigenous independence movements were beginning to emerge, though most did not bear fruit until after World War II.

Ethiopia had retained its independence from colonial rule since defeating the Italians in 1896, and from 1935 was ruled by Haile Selassie (formerly Ras Tafari), who faced an invasion from Italy's Fascist dictator Mussolini. After using mustard gas on the Ethiopians, the Italians took Addis Ababa in 1936. A resistance movement continued to harry the Italians until World War II, when the British invaded and drove the Italians out once more, restoring Haile Selassie in 1941 and making Ethiopia the first African country to be liberated. Britain now took over the adminstration of the former Italian colonies of Eritrea and Somaliland.

French colonization of north Africa had failed to create a settler class comparable with the traditional peasantry of France. Settlers tended to be large farmers engaged in speculative agriculture for

TIMELINE

	1920		1940	
Middle East	**1916** Arab revolt in the Hejaz against Ottoman rule	**1930** Standard Oil and Texas Oil form Bahrain Petroleum Company		**1946** Transjordan wins independence, annexes the West Bank and becomes kingdom of Jordan
	1917 "Balfour Declaration" promises a national homeland for the Jews in Palestine	**1932** The British mandate in Iraq ends		**1948** Proclamation of the state of Israel
	1918 Iraq is brought under British rule	**1933** Ibn Saud permits Standard Oil to prospect in Saudi Arabia		
	1922 The League of Nations approves Palestinian mandate		**1941** Britain and Soviet Union invade Iran	
	1924 Britain insists on control of Transjordan's affairs			
North Africa	**1914** Egypt is proclaimed a British protectorate	**1928** Muslim Brotherhood founded in Egypt	**1941** Germans conquer north Libya and invade Egypt	
	1921-26 A nationalist revolt against French and Spanish rule in Morocoo	**1934** Formation of Moroccan nationalist party	**1943** Allied forces defeat the Germans in Tunisia	
	1922 Egypt gains independence under King Fuad I	**1936** Britain is granted use of Egyptian facilities in wartime		
Sub-Saharan Africa	**1914** African, French and British forces take Togoland and German East Africa	**1935-36** Italian invasion of Ethiopia		
	1920 Old German colonies mandated to Britain, Belgium, France and South Africa	**1941** Italy surrenders Ethiopia, Eritrea, and Somaliland		
	1920		1940	

GREECE
Athens
Crete

Istanbul ☆1918–23
Ankara ☆1918–23
TURKEY
Ottoman empire until 1923
Izmir ☆1918–23
Konya ☆1918–23
Adana ☆1918–23
Nicosia
Cyprus

Kars
site of massacre, 1915
Lake Van
Ufra
☆1933
☆1937–39
Aleppo ☆1920–21
Latakia ☆1939
Homs
SYRIA 1920–41 French mandate,
1946 independent
LEBANON
1920–41 French mandate,
1946 independent
Beirut ☆1936, 1943
Damascus ☆1925–26, 1945

Caspian Sea

Tabriz
Lake Urmia
1931–32, 1935–36, 1943–44
Mosul
1919, 1922–27, 1930–31
Kirkuk

Tehran
Hamadan

IRAN
Persia until 1935,
1941–42 Allied occupation

1
Isfahan
Kerman

Mediterranean Sea

enghazi
Tobruk
☆1923–32
Cyrenaica
1934 united with
Tripolitania,
1947 under British
administration

1942

PALESTINE
1920–48 British mandate
Tel Aviv
2
Amman
☆1920, 1936–39
Jerusalem ☆1920, 1936–39
☆1929
Alexandria
Aqaba
Suez Canal
Aug–Oct 1918

1920
Baghdad
Habbiniyah
☆1936, 1941
IRAQ
1920–32 British mandate,
1932 independent
☆1920, 1935
An Najaf
Oct 1914 Nov 1918

JORDAN
1920–46 British mandate,
Transjordan until independent 1946
1925–27, 1937–39

Basra
Shaiba
Abadan
Kuwait
Kuwait

Shiraz
Bandar Abbas

EGYPT
1914 British protectorate,
1922 independent
Cairo
Suez
El Kharga
Aswan

Nile

ESERT

SAUDI ARABIA
1916–26 Nejd,
1926–32 Hejaz and Nejd

4
Riyadh

1916 ☆
Medina

Hejaz 1916 independent, 1926 to Nejd

Al Manamah
Bahrain
Doha
Qatar
Abu Dhabi

Persian Gulf

Trucial Oman
Muscat
Oman

Wadi Halfa

Port Sudan
Suakin

Jiddah
Mecca

Asir 1917 independent, 1920 to Nejd

Red Sea

IBN SAUD with a representative
of ARAMCO (Arab-American oil
company) in 1939; from the
1930s oil took on a crucial role
in the region.

Ottoman empire, 1914

colonial powers, 1914

France
Italy
Spain
United Kingdom

mandate territory, 1920

British mandate
French mandate

independent Armenia, 1918–21
area under Greek control, 1922
border, 1948
⛽ oilfield
☆ nationalist revolt or political disturbance
— railroad
→ Allied campaign
→ Italian campaign

Anglo-Egyptian Sudan

Omdurman
Khartoum
Kassala

El Obeid
Sennar
5

White Nile
Blue Nile

Eritrea
1941 under British
administration

Asmera
Massawa
Adowa
Jan–Sep 1941
Oct 1935–May 1936
Gondar
6
1941
Apr 1941
Addis Ababa
Mar–Apr 1941
ETHIOPIA
1936–41 to Italy,
1941 independence restored

Jizan
YEMEN
1919 independent
Sana

West Aden Protectorate
Aden

French Somaliland
Djibouti
3

Harar
Berbera
British Somaliland

Walwal
Apr–May 1936

Shebelle

Italian Somaliland
Italian protectorate until 1941,
1941 under British administration

Mukalla
Hadramaut
(East Aden
Protectorate)

Socotra

INDIAN OCEAN

0   600 km
0   400 mi

export to France. Intensively farmed wheat, olives and vines required capital investment but between 1914 and 1935 these produced spectacular yields, strong exports and brought about the development of the north African workforce. In the same way control of mineral resources by French managers meant that virtually all the production of iron ore and phosphates, and the zinc, lead and cobalt deposits, went to France. The depression of the 1930s led to the collapse of much of this activity, and a rise in unemployment.

Libyan resistance to Italian colonization persisted until 1932. Italy's Fascist government encouraged large estates worked by Italian settlers, but there was little investment in infrastructure and barely 90,000 Italians had settled in Libya by 1939.

British policy toward Egypt and the Sudan was very different, with little or no settlement from

Britain. The British saw Egypt as a major source of cotton, and encouraged Egyptian financial institutions to support local industry and cotton-related projects in the Sudan. By 1939 Egypt was approaching self-sufficiency in a range of manufactured goods; production rose further during the war years.

1 Masjed-Suleyman was the site of the first oil find in the Middle East, in 1908. Oil was found in Libya in the 1920s, and in Kuwait in 1932.

2 Tel Aviv was founded in 1909 by Zionist idealists as a suburb of the ancient city of Jaffa; the Turks cleared the settlement in 1916–17, but it became the focus for Jewish immigration in the 1920s and 1930s.

3 Aden, an important British coaling station on the route to India, was ruled from India until 1937 when it became a crown colony.

4 Abdul Aziz Ibn Saud (r.1901-53) took Riyadh in 1901, consolidated his hold over Nejd by 1906 and Hejaz (1926) and set up the kingdom of Saudi Arabia in 1932. Oil reserves were found there in 1938.

5 The Sennar Dam was completed in 1925, marking the beginning of a plan to irrigate the Sudan and develop the cotton industry for export.

6 Italy's invasion of Ethiopia in October 1935 began with a land and air attack on Adowa, the scene of an Italian defeat in 1896.

7 Tripoli was the center of Mussolini's Libyan industrial program: more than 700 factories were in operation there by 1939.

See also 115 (postwar Middle East);
118 (Africa)

The declaration of war on Germany by Britain and France in 1939 took Hitler by surprise; he was now forced to deal with the threat to Germany's western flank in order to avoid fighting the war on two fronts. His primary objective, though, remained the conquest of the Soviet Union.

Germany and the Soviet Union divided Poland between them as they had agreed in the Nazi–Soviet pact of 1939, both sides deporting large numbers of people. The USSR later absorbed the Baltic states with the exception of Finland, which preserved its independence in the "Winter War" of 1939–40. A "phoney war" ensued, the first break in the inactivity being the German invasion of Denmark and Norway in April 1940. The Allies had planned to seize Narvik to deny Germany access to the only port capable of handling the exports of vital Swedish iron ore; however, the rapid and well-planned German advance resulted in a hurried Allied withdrawal.

Soon after, Winston Churchill took over as British prime minister, but Allied resistance was ineffectual during the German attack on the Low Countries and France in May. France surrendered within six weeks. Germany occupied the north, while a collaborationist regime at Vichy controlled the south; Belgium and the Netherlands became satellites in the German industrial complex. Britain evacuated most of its forces from northern France, but in the Battle of Britain of 1940 (the first decisive battle to be fought in the air) stifled plans for a seaborne invasion by denying air superiority to the Luftwaffe (German air force). Italy chose this point to enter the war. The Mediterranean was closed to British shipping and fighting began in north and east Africa.

While the air offensive continued against Britain and escalated into the Blitz, Hitler turned his attention to the east. By the summer of 1940 he was planning the Barbarossa campaign – an invasion of the Soviet Union which he had planned for the mid-

1940s, but which was now brought forward by the success of the German war effort and the rapid rearmament of the other powers.

In April 1941 German, Bulgarian and Italian forces invaded Greece and Yugoslavia to secure their southern flank for Barbarossa. Italy had been defeated in Greece the previous year but now the Axis forces overran all opposition, driving British troops first to Crete and then to Egypt. German

- Germany, 1 Sep 1939
- territory gained by USSR, 1939–40
- western frontier of USSR, June 1941
- area of population and industry evacuated to Siberia, 1941–42
- borders, June 1942
- Axis power, June 1942
- ally of Axis power, June 1942
- under Axis occupation, June 1942
- Vichy territory, June 1942
- under Allied control, June 1942
- furthest Axis advance, 1941
- front lines, end Nov 1942
- Maginot line
- bombed city, 1940–42
- U-boat base
- siege
- atrocity or mass murder
- Lidice reprisal killing
- death camp
- concentration camp
- Axis airborne operation
- British commando raid
- Allied withdrawal
- Axis offensive
- Allied offensive
- main convoy route, 1941–42

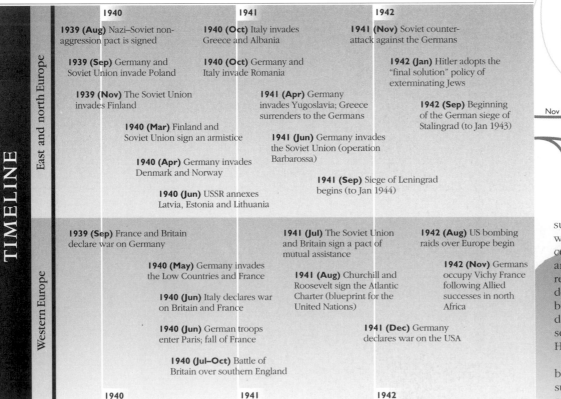

TIMELINE

East and north Europe

1940

1939 (Aug) Nazi–Soviet non-aggression pact is signed

1939 (Sep) Germany and Soviet Union invade Poland

1939 (Nov) The Soviet Union invades Finland

1940 (Mar) Finland and Soviet Union sign an armistice

1940 (Apr) Germany invades Denmark and Norway

1940 (Jun) USSR annexes Latvia, Estonia and Lithuania

1941

1940 (Oct) Italy invades Greece and Albania

1940 (Oct) Germany and Italy invade Romania

1941 (Apr) Germany invades Yugoslavia; Greece surrenders to the Germans

1941 (Jun) Germany invades the Soviet Union (operation Barbarossa)

1941 (Sep) Siege of Leningrad begins (to Jan 1944)

1942

1941 (Nov) Soviet counter-attack against the Germans

1942 (Jan) Hitler adopts the "final solution" policy of exterminating Jews

1942 (Sep) Beginning of the German siege of Stalingrad (to Jan 1943)

Western Europe

1939 (Sep) France and Britain declare war on Germany

1940 (May) Germany invades the Low Countries and France

1940 (Jun) Italy declares war on Britain and France

1940 (Jun) German troops enter Paris; fall of France

1940 (Jul–Oct) Battle of Britain over southern England

1941 (Jul) The Soviet Union and Britain sign a pact of mutual assistance

1941 (Aug) Churchill and Roosevelt sign the Atlantic Charter (blueprint for the United Nations)

1941 (Dec) Germany declares war on the USA

1942 (Aug) US bombing raids over Europe begin

1942 (Nov) Germans occupy Vichy France following Allied successes in north Africa

1940   **1941**   **1942**

success had been based on *blitzkrieg* or lightning war. With limited access to raw materials, Germany could not afford a long war. Tanks, dive-bombers and motorized infantry destroyed defenses before reserves could be mobilized or a war of attrition develop. Barbarossa was expected to last six weeks, but by November 1941 the campaign was bogged down by the weather. Hitler had ignored advice to seize Moscow, preferring to advance on all fronts. His forces were now dangerously stretched.

Stalin launched an offensive in the spring of 1942, but the Germans occupied more territory in the summer. It became clear, however, that they could not launch a knockout blow: the vast size of the

er route to Murmansk and Archangel

1 London and other cities suffered aerial bombardment from September 1940 to May 1941. The "Blitz" failed to break British industry or civilian morale.

2 A surprise amphibious attack in April 1940 allowed Germany to take Norway before British support could arrive. Only in Narvik did the plan falter temporarily.

3 The defense of Greece in April 1941 was poorly coordinated and quickly overrun; the British forces were evacuated to Crete, and soon after to Alexandria.

4 After the Soviet invasion of November 1939, the Finns caused heavy losses but sued for peace in March 1940. Though nominally neutral, Finland favored Germany against the USSR.

5 Vichy, a spa town, was seat of the collaborationist French government from 1940 to November 1942.

6 Britain's strategic naval base at Malta endured more than 1,200 air raids during World War II.

country and its population, and the safety of the industrial areas evacuated east of the Urals meant that the USSR had huge capacity. By the end of 1942, a turning point was approaching.

The United States had already been supplying Britain and the Soviet Union with materiel through the "lend–lease" scheme, and its entry into the war as a full belligerent in December 1941 gave the Allies a major boost. From then on Allied superiority in men and arms, and Hitler's lack of strategic vision were to lead to German defeat.

Disruption of the supply routes from America had become of central concern to the western Allies. The United States was anxious to invade western

Europe as quickly as possible, but U-boat attacks on convoys in the Atlantic hampered the transport of men and materiel. A minor invasion of north Africa, occupied by Italian and Vichy forces backed up by General Rommel's Afrika Korps, met with rapid success. If the Battle of the Atlantic could not be won, though, United States numerical and industrial power would count for little in the battle for Europe.

In eastern Europe the Germans undertook the enslavement and murder of the subject populations. Executions of civilians were commonplace in the invasion of Poland, and during Barbarossa mass murder was a tool of occupation policy. Hitler hoped to create a "new order" based on the Nazi idea of the

"historic conflict" between the Aryans (Germans) and the other "inferior races". Millions of Slavs and Gypsies were shot, deported, starved or enslaved to create a "living space" for Germans. In what was called the "final solution", mass shootings and gassings were used to exterminate the Jews. Death camps were built and by the end of 1942 almost the entire Jewish population of Poland, the Baltic states, and the USSR as far east as the Caucasus – about three million people – had been killed.

See also 101 (Europe between the wars); 107 (World War II to 1945); 108 (World War II in Asia)

The international order which emerged from World War I failed to match the intentions of allowing for national self-determination for all, and left a deep resentment in Germany, which was made to carry the blame for the war. As a result, stability was not achieved, and the post-Versailles order was overturned by extremist powers which by 1942 dominated much of the globe. The Axis powers, Germany and Japan, exploited the political vacuum left by the withdrawal of the United States and Russia from world affairs after the war, and by the effects of the depression on Britain and France. However, although 1942 marked the zenith of Axis power, their attacks on the two nascent superpowers made their eventual victory unlikely.

Soviet Russia emerged from its civil war of the early 1920s and turned in on itself as Stalin tried to build "socialism in one country" (▷ 100). The attempt to entrench Soviet power and catch up with the west was partially successful but extremely costly, as Stalin unleashed famine and terror on the Soviet Union.

In Europe, economic recovery was built on American loans. The US stock market crash of 1929 precipitated the global economic collapse known as the Great Depression. Its effect was to increase the appeal of fascist or extreme rightwing schemes of national regeneration in countries dissatisfied with the outcome of the peace settlements of 1919–23 (notably Germany). Governments everywhere looked to protect their interests by erecting tariff barriers and closed trading blocs, which further depressed the world economy.

The United States became isolated from international affairs as it tried to resolve its internal problems, and Britain and France were left to try to contain fascist expansion. But, although the depression began to lift in the late 1930s, both countries were economically too weak and too preoccupied by their global commitments to act effectively (▷ 101). They feared the prospect of fighting on three fronts – against Germany in Europe, Italy in the Mediterranean, and Japan in Asia. Their empires were potentially unstable – especially British India, where the nationalist Congress Party was growing in strength (▷ 103) – as were their domestic economies and societies.

The League of Nations reacted weakly to a series of crises in the 1930s – an Italian invasion of Ethiopia and German invasions of the Rhineland, Austria, Czechoslovakia – and thereby lost its credibility. France and Britain tried but failed to preserve peace through negotiation, alliances

A.	Albania (Italy)
B.	Belgium
CR.	Croatia
D.	Denmark
DR.	Dominican Republic
H.	Hungary
L.	Luxembourg
M.	Montenegro
N.	Netherlands
PA.	Palestine (Britain)
PG.	Portuguese Guinea (Portugal)
SE.	Serbia
SR.	Southern Rhodesia (Britain)
S.	Switzerland
TO.	Trucial Oman (Britain)
YE.	Yemen

1923 France occupies the Ruhr; hyperinflation results in Germany

1923 Foundation of the modern republic of Turkey

1921 The Russian civil war ends with a Bolshevik victory

1932 US president F.D. Roosevelt initiates the "New Deal"

1932 The kingdom of Saudi Arabia is founded

1931 The Mukden incident: Japan occupies Manchuria

1929 Wall St Crash begins the Great Depression and world trading collapse

1933 Adolf Hitler becomes German chancellor

1938 Munich crisis: Britain accepts German expansion in Czechoslovakia

1937 Japan invades China; Sino-Japanese war begins

TIMELINE

| The Americas |
| Europe |
| Middle East |
| Africa |
| Asia and Australasia |

1920   1930

1922 Mussolini marches on Rome, establishing the first Fascist government

1922 Washington Naval Agreement limits Japanese naval power in the Pacific

1925 Joseph Stalin comes to power in USSR

1927 A Chinese Nationalist government is established under Jiang Jieshi

1928 Russia's first Five Year Plan of industrialization is introduced

1934 Chinese Communists undertake the "Long March" to Yan'an

1935 Mussolini invades Ethiopia to set up an Italian empire

1936 Civil war in Spain after a rightwing uprising against the government

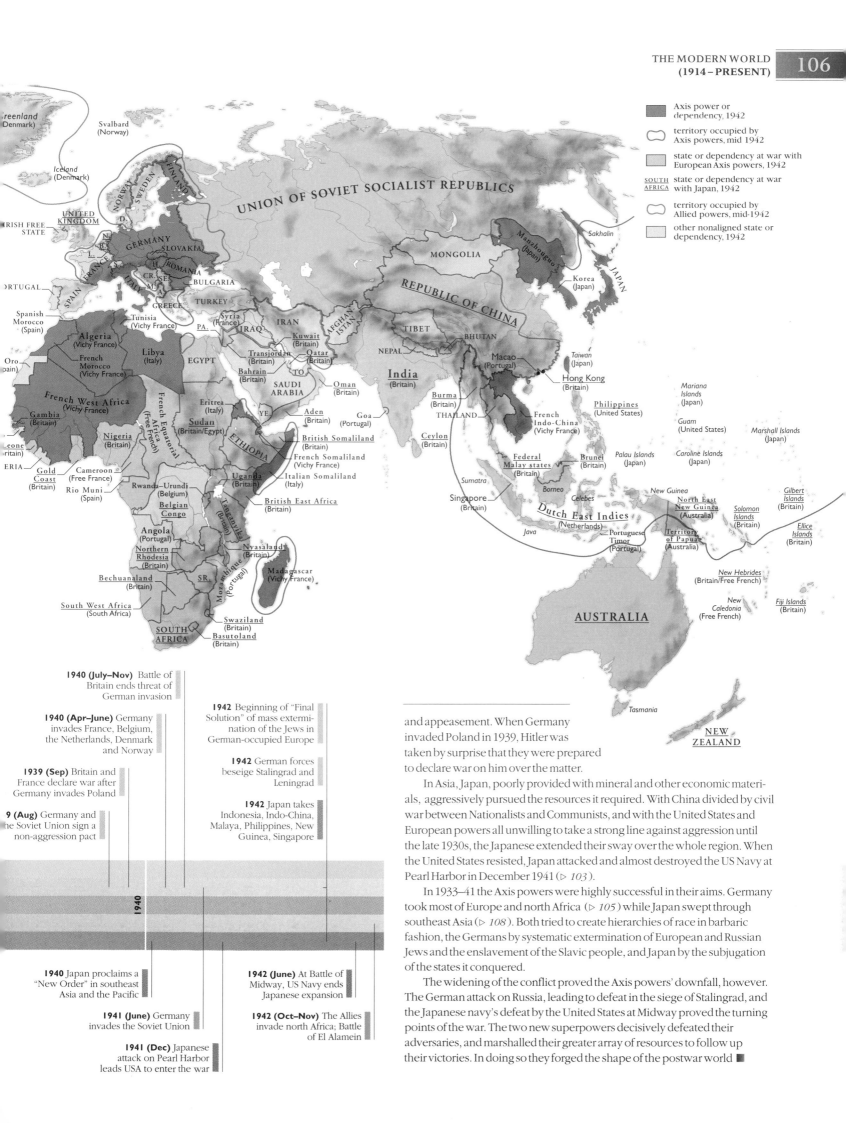

Axis power or dependency, 1942

territory occupied by Axis powers, mid 1942

state or dependency at war with European Axis powers, 1942

SOUTH AFRICA state or dependency at war with Japan, 1942

territory occupied by Allied powers, mid-1942

other nonaligned state or dependency, 1942

Greenland (Denmark)

Svalbard (Norway)

Iceland (Denmark)

IRISH FREE STATE

UNITED KINGDOM

PORTUGAL

Spanish Morocco (Spain)

Oro (Spain)

SPAIN

FRANCE

D.

N.

L.

B.

GERMANY

SLOVAKIA

SWITZERLAND

H.

CR.S S.

M.

ITALY

ROMANIA

BULGARIA

GREECE

TURKEY

PA.

Tunisia (Vichy France)

Algeria (Vichy France)

Libya (Italy)

French Morocco (Vichy France)

French West Africa (Vichy France)

Gambia (Britain)

Sierra Leone (Britain)

LIBERIA

Gold Coast (Britain)

Nigeria (Britain)

Cameroon (Free France)

Rio Muni (Spain)

French Equatorial Africa (Free French)

EGYPT

Syria (France)

IRAQ

IRAN

AFGHANISTAN

Kuwait (Britain)

Qatar (Britain)

Bahrain (Britain)

TO.

SAUDI ARABIA

YE.

Aden (Britain)

Oman (Britain)

Eritrea (Italy)

Sudan (Britain/Egypt)

ETHIOPIA

British Somaliland (Britain)

French Somaliland (Vichy France)

Italian Somaliland (Italy)

Uganda (Britain)

Rwanda–Urundi (Belgium)

Belgian Congo

Tanganyika (Britain)

British East Africa (Britain)

Angola (Portugal)

Northern Rhodesia (Britain)

Nyasaland (Britain)

Mozambique (Portugal)

Madagascar (Vichy France)

Bechuanaland (Britain)

SR.

South West Africa (South Africa)

SOUTH AFRICA

Swaziland (Britain)

Basutoland (Britain)

UNION OF SOVIET SOCIALIST REPUBLICS

MONGOLIA

REPUBLIC OF CHINA

Manzhouguo (Japan)

Sakhalin

Korea (Japan)

JAPAN

Taiwan (Japan)

TIBET

NEPAL

BHUTAN

India (Britain)

Macao (Portugal)

Hong Kong (Britain)

Burma (Britain)

THAILAND

Goa (Portugal)

Ceylon (Britain)

French Indo-China (Vichy France)

Federal Malay states (Britain)

Brunei (Britain)

Singapore (Britain)

Sumatra

Borneo

Celebes

Java

Dutch East Indies (Netherlands)

Portuguese Timor (Portugal)

New Guinea

North East New Guinea (Australia)

Territory of Papua (Australia)

Philippines (United States)

Mariana Islands (Japan)

Guam (United States)

Palau Islands (Japan)

Caroline Islands (Japan)

Marshall Islands (Japan)

Solomon Islands (Britain)

Gilbert Islands (Britain)

Ellice Islands (Britain)

New Hebrides (Britain/Free French)

New Caledonia (Free French)

Fiji Islands (Britain)

AUSTRALIA

Tasmania

NEW ZEALAND

1940 (July–Nov) Battle of Britain ends threat of German invasion

1940 (Apr–June) Germany invades France, Belgium, the Netherlands, Denmark and Norway

1939 (Sep) Britain and France declare war after Germany invades Poland

1939 (Aug) Germany and the Soviet Union sign a non-aggression pact

1940

1940 Japan proclaims a "New Order" in southeast Asia and the Pacific

1941 (June) Germany invades the Soviet Union

1941 (Dec) Japanese attack on Pearl Harbor leads USA to enter the war

1942 Beginning of "Final Solution" of mass extermination of the Jews in German-occupied Europe

1942 German forces beseige Stalingrad and Leningrad

1942 Japan takes Indonesia, Indo-China, Malaya, Philippines, New Guinea, Singapore

1942 (June) At Battle of Midway, US Navy ends Japanese expansion

1942 (Oct–Nov) The Allies invade north Africa; Battle of El Alamein

and appeasement. When Germany invaded Poland in 1939, Hitler was taken by surprise that they were prepared to declare war on him over the matter.

In Asia, Japan, poorly provided with mineral and other economic materials, aggressively pursued the resources it required. With China divided by civil war between Nationalists and Communists, and with the United States and European powers all unwilling to take a strong line against aggression until the late 1930s, the Japanese extended their sway over the whole region. When the United States resisted, Japan attacked and almost destroyed the US Navy at Pearl Harbor in December 1941 (▷ 103).

In 1933–41 the Axis powers were highly successful in their aims. Germany took most of Europe and north Africa (▷ 105) while Japan swept through southeast Asia (▷ 108). Both tried to create hierarchies of race in barbaric fashion, the Germans by systematic extermination of European and Russian Jews and the enslavement of the Slavic people, and Japan by the subjugation of the states it conquered.

The widening of the conflict proved the Axis powers' downfall, however. The German attack on Russia, leading to defeat in the siege of Stalingrad, and the Japanese navy's defeat by the United States at Midway proved the turning points of the war. The two new superpowers decisively defeated their adversaries, and marshalled their greater array of resources to follow up their victories. In doing so they forged the shape of the postwar world ∎

The year 1942 marked a turning point, but two more years of fighting were needed before the war in Europe ended. The German surrender at Stalingrad was a major blow to Hitler, who was committed to holding the city and supplying it by air. In July the Soviet army repulsed the Germans at Kursk in the war's biggest land battle; the Red Army then drove westward, its next victory being at Kharkov.

In May, the Germans capitulated in north Africa. By mid-1943 Germany had also lost the crucial Battle of the Atlantic, where the Allied use of long-range aircraft made Germany's submarine assault on transatlantic convoy routes less effective. The German war effort intensified with the announcement of total war (the complete mobilization of the economy). The Allies invaded Sicily, Mussolini was deposed and the Italians sued for peace. However Germany immediately occupied north and central Italy and made further Allied progress very difficult through the mountainous terrain.

The Allies' Italian campaign was a relatively minor response to success in north Africa, though it dragged on until the end of the war. The main action in the west – the "second front" that Stalin had long demanded – was to be the Allied landing in Normandy, as the Allied leaders had agreed at their meeting in Tehran in November 1943. Even before this was launched, however, Hitler had to withdraw troops from the east to strengthen the western defenses. Allied bombing increased in strength and effectiveness as the US joined the British in attacking German cities in force. The first 1,000-bomber raid took place against Cologne in 1943. The bombing campaign directed German resources from the other fronts and weakened the war economy.

When the Normandy landings finally came in June 1944, they met with stiff resistance. The Allies liberated France and Belgium before halting briefly. Meanwhile in east and southeast Europe the Red Army took advantage of the increased pressure on Germany in the west, and defeated both Romania and Bulgaria. Germany pulled out of Greece but Hungary was kept in the war by a Nazi coup after initially surrendering to the Soviet Union; fierce fighting broke out around Budapest.

Political as well as military considerations had held back United States president Roosevelt from supporting British prime minister Churchill's plan to invade southeast Europe. Unlike Roosevelt, Churchill had little faith in Stalin's postwar intentions, and

made an agreement with Stalin which stipulated the influence that Britain and the Soviet Union would each have in the region. Soviet action in Poland and elsewhere did not engender confidence. As the Red Army advanced toward Warsaw, a fullscale rising against the German forces occurred in the city. Despite surrounding the city, Stalin did not assist the rebels, and when the Germans eventually quashed the revolt, as many as 250,000 people were killed.

Across Europe guerrilla partisan forces fought the Axis powers. Many were divided on ethnic or political lines, and their activities provoked bloody reprisals. A revolt in Slovakia at the same time as the Warsaw rising was brutally put down, but in Yugoslavia the Communist-dominated partisans enjoyed

Map legend:

- borders, 1943
- Axis power or ally
- Axis occupied, Mar 1943
- Allied control, Mar 1943
- front line, Dec 1943
- front line, Aug 1944
- front line, Dec 1944
- front line, Apr 1945
- defensive line
- heavily bombed city
- siege
- area of partisan activity
- German reprisal killing
- death camp
- concentration camp
- Allied airborne operation
- conference of Allied leaders, with date
- London — V-weapon target zone
- 26 Aug 1944 — date of capitulation
- Axis withdrawal
- Axis offensive
- Allied offensive
- Soviet deportation, 1944-45

CIVILIANS, including women, were universally important to the war effort by working in the factories. This poster was from Britain.

Map labels: Reykjavik, ICELAND, Faroe Islands to Denmark, Shetland Islands to Britain, Glasgow, Edinburgh, Belfast, IRELAND, Dublin, UNITED KINGDOM, Liverpool, Manchester, Birmingham, Cambridge, Oxford, Reading, Southampton, Plymouth, Ports, June 1944, NORMANDY, Brest, Falaise Aug 1944, ATLANTIC OCEAN, Nantes, Oradour-sur-Glane, Bordeaux, FRANCE liberated by, Bilbao, Ebro, ANDORRA, Douro, Barcelona, PORTUGAL, Tagus, SPAIN, Madrid, Guadiana, Valencia, Balearic Islands to Spain, Lisbon, Seville, Cádiz, Gibraltar to Britain, Tangier, Oran, Spanish Morocco to Spain, Algeria Free French, Fez, Casablanca Jan 1943, French Morocco Free French

TIMELINE

East and north Europe

1943	1944	1945
1943 (Jan) German army surrenders at Stalingrad	**1944 (Jan)** The siege of Leningrad ends after 900 days	**1945 (Jan)** Red Army enters Budapest, Warsaw, Auschwitz
1943 (Apr) Jews of Warsaw stage a revolt; 60,000 die	**1944 (Apr)** The Red Army retakes the Crimea	**1945 (May)** Berlin surrenders to the Red Army
1943 (June–Aug) Russians defeat a German offensive in a vast tank battle at Kursk	**1944 (July)** Soviet forces enter Poland; (Aug) Warsaw second rising	
1943 (Nov) The Russians retake Kiev	**1944 (Oct)** Soviet troops liberate Belgrade	
	1944 (Oct–Nov) Allied forces liberate Greece	

Western Europe

1943	1944	1945
1942 (Oct) US bombers destroy Lille railyards in northern France	**1943 (July)** Allied forces land in Sicily	**1944 (June)** D-Day: Allied forces land in Normandy	**1945 (Mar)** Allied forces cross the Rhine
	1943 (Sep) Italy surrenders to the Allies; German forces occupy Milan and Rome	**1944 (Aug)** Allied forces liberate Paris	**1945 (May)** Germany surrenders
	1943 (Oct) Italy declares war on Germany		**1945 (Feb)** Huge Allied bombing raid on Dresden

Other

1943	1944	1945
1942 (Oct–Nov) British army defeats Germans at el Alamein	**1943 (Nov)** Roosevelt, Stalin and Churchill meet at Tehran	**1945 (Feb)** Roosevelt, Stalin and Churchill meet at Yalta to discuss the postwar division of Germany
1943 (Jan) Roosevelt and Churchill meet at Casablanca		

1943 — 1944 — 1945

1 Hitler's attack on the Soviet defenses at Kursk (June 1943) led to a conflict between the Soviet light but nimble T-34 tanks, and the heavy German Tiger tanks. Despite huge losses, the Red Army broke through.

2 Some 640 villagers, including 200 women and children, were burned to death in a church at the village of Oradour-sur Glane in June 1944.

3 When the Germans retreated to their prewar defenses – the Siegfried Line – in September 1944, the Allies attacked via the Netherlands. The line was broken in February 1945.

4 Peenemünde was the site of research into rocketry by the Germans under Werner von Braun. Allied intelligence knew of it from 1939.

5 Auschwitz was the largest of the Nazi death camps, established in 1940. Well over a million Jews and Poles died there before liberation in January 1945.

6 Churchill, Stalin and Roosevelt met at Yalta in February 1945 to coordinate strategy and agree to spheres of influence in postwar Europe.

considerable success and formed the basis of Tito's postwar government. In Prague, a popular rising helped the Soviet advance on the city. In Greece, the Communists, who dominated the rural resistance movement, defied the British who sought to reestablish the monarchy after the Germans had withdrawn in October 1944. The result was a civil war which ended only with the collapse of the Communists in 1949. Resistance in Poland and countries incorporated into the Soviet Union also continued after the war, but it was now directed against the USSR.

Hitler always believed that providence would save him. He tried to stop the Allied bomber assault on Germany by firing rocket-powered V-bombs at Britain, but the forces ranged against him were too

great. The last German offensive, through the Ardennes at the end of 1944, was a failure and after Hitler's suicide, Germany surrendered (8 May 1945).

The implementation of Nazi policies of genocide continued right up until the liberation of the death camps by Allied troops. As the Soviets marched westward, many inmates of camps in Poland were moved to Germany to join prisoners-of-war and other forced foreign labor. By 1944 there were almost eight million foreigners at work in Germany. Some Axis countries – Hungary, Bulgaria and Italy – refused to release many or all of their Jewish population to the Nazis, but the attempt to exterminate the Jews of Europe still proceeded. By the end of the war some six million had been killed, along with

millions of other nationalities including Ukrainians, Poles, Balts, Belorussians, Russians and Gypsies.

Of the 5.5 million Soviet soldiers captured by the Germans, 3.3 million had died; as the Red Army advanced it took its revenge. Ten million ethnic Germans were expelled from their homes in central and eastern Europe; perhaps two million died. The USSR deported five million of its subject nationalities for alleged collaboration; returning prisoners-of-war often faced exile or death. By 1945 much of Europe was destroyed, its peoples dead or homeless.

See also 105 (World War II to 1942);
108 (World War II in Asia); 110 (postwar Europe)

In late 1941 the Japanese planned a series of synchronized attacks to secure control in the Pacific and Asia. Prime minister Hideki Tojo and Isoroko Yamamoto, head of the navy and mastermind behind the attack on the United States naval base of Pearl Harbor in Hawaii, sought to create a defense perimeter from the Kurils to the Dutch East Indies and containing all the oil, rubber and rice Japan would need for survival. Yamamoto promised a string of victories in the first six months.

The surprise attack on Pearl Harbor on 7 December 1941 destroyed the US Pacific fleet, but all the large aircraft carriers were at sea. Their survival was to be of crucial significance. By the spring of 1942 Japan had taken the Philippines (attacked the same day as Pearl Harbor), ejected the Dutch from the East Indies, driven the British from Hong Kong, Malaya (including the great naval base of Singapore) and most of Burma, and forced the Americans to surrender Guam, Wake Island, Attu and Kiska. At this point, Japan suffered a setback at the Battle of the Coral Sea as the Japanese attempted to take the Allied base at Port Moresby on New Guinea (thus isolating Australia). Further advances across the Pacific were decisively halted when their fleet was defeated by the US Navy at the Battle of Midway.

Allied strategy for the destruction of Japan's new empire depended upon the immense resources and manpower that the United States could bring to bear. The plan required the British, who had suffered during their long retreat in Burma, to block a Japanese invasion of India, undertake offensives in the Arakan and recapture Rangoon. They would have limited US assistance and cooperation from Chinese Nationalist armies from Yunnan. These forces came under a new southeast Asia command headed by Lord Louis Mountbatten. US forces in the south and southwest Pacific under General Douglas MacArthur

and Admiral William Halsey were planned to retake New Guinea and the Solomons. Admiral Nimitz would assemble fresh task forces at Pearl Harbor and attack Japanese-held islands in the central and north Pacific. Key bases would be established on the islands and in China for an air assault upon Japan.

In the north Pacific, US and Canadian troops attacked in the Aleutians and forced the Japanese back. In the central Pacific, US marines assaulted the tiny coral atoll of Tarawa, 5,000 kilometers (3,000 miles) from Japan. They wiped out its Japanese and Korean defenders, but only after three days of bitter fighting. After this experience, the Americans

decided to ignore unimportant islands and by-pass many Japanese bases. They fought and won the Battle of the Philippine Sea and then targeted Kwajalein and Eniwetok in the Marshalls. They went on to occupy Saipan, Guam and Tinian, the bases from which in 1944–45 US B-29 bombers undertook their raids on Japanese cities.

US forces returned to the Philippines and fought the Battle of Leyte Gulf, during which the Japanese navy was effectively destroyed. The Battle of Iwo Jima, the fiercest of the war, provided the Americans with a base for their fighter aircraft capable of escorting the bombers to Japan and back. About 500,000

Legend:

- ▬▬▬ borders, 7 Dec 1941
- Japanese occupied territory, 7 Dec 1941
- maximum extent of Japanese occupied territory, June 1942
- - - - intended eastern perimeter of Japanese territory
- Japanese occupied territory, 6 Aug 1945
- Japanese occupied territory, Sep 1945
- Allied territory, June 1942
- Nationalist Chinese or warlord territory
- Communist Chinese territory, 1937
- → Japanese advance, with date
- → Allied advance, with date
- → Russian advance, 9 Aug 1945
- ⚐ Japanese base, June 1942
- Japanese air strike outside occupied territory
- US bombing raids on Japan, 1942–45
- nuclear air strike, Aug 1945
- Japanese victory
- ⊗ Allied victory
- *oil* strategic resource vital to Japan

Map labels:

TIBET · Lhasa · BHUTAN · NEPAL · Thimphu · Kathmandu · Southeast Asian Forces Apr–June 1944 · Kohima Apr–June 1944 · Imphal Mar–June 1944 · India to Britain · Calcutta · Burma · Arakan · Bay of Bengal · Rangoon · Vishakhapatnam Apr 1942 · Kakinada Apr 1942 · Trincomalee Apr 1942 · Colombo Apr 1942 · Bay of Bengal Apr 1942 · Andaman Islands · Nicobar Islands · THAILAND · Bangkok 1941 · rubber · Phnom Penh · Indo- · Malaya · Medan · Kuala Lumpur · Sumatra · oil tin · Singapore · Palembang · China · Yellow · Lanzhou 1937 · Xi 1937 · Chengdu Sept 1941 · Chongqing 1937–45 · June · Yunnan · Kunming 1937–45 · Guili Sept 194 · Hanoi · Haiphong coal · Mekong · oil rubber · tin · Fre Indo-

0 ——————— 1500 km
0 ——————— 1200 mi

1 The attack on Pearl Harbor was essential to Japan's plans to control the Pacific. Eight battleships were destroyed but dockyard facilities remained intact.

2 Singapore was Britain's foremost and most recently equipped naval base in the region, but it fell to a surprise land attack in February 1942.

3 The Bataan peninsula in the Philippines was the scene of an incident in April 1942, when the Japanese forced 35,000 men to march 100km (60 miles) in six days; more than 10,000 died.

4 The Japanese invasion of the Dutch East Indies was welcomed by Ahmed Sukarno, leader of the Indonesian Nationalist Party (PNI).

5 Darwin and other north Australian towns were bombed, and the east coast was blockaded by submarines in 1943; the country was a key base for US operations in the southwest Pacific.

6 Saipan was a major air base, used by the US Air Force for bombing Japan from November 1944.

7 Hiroshima suffered the world's first atomic bomb attack on 6 August 1945; 80,000 people died instantly.

TIMELINE

Japan

1943	1945
1941 Japan and the Soviet Union sign a neutrality pact	**1944 (July)** Prime minister Tojo resigns	**1945 (Aug)** Atomic attacks on Hiroshima and Nagasaki
1942 (Apr) B-25 bombers from USS *Hornet* raid Tokyo		**1945 (Sep)** Formal Japanese surrender

Pacific war

1941 (Dec) Japan attacks Pearl Harbor and Philippines	**1943 (Nov)** Tarawa captured by US forces	
1942 (Feb) Japanese troops win the Battle of Java Sea	**1944 (July)** US troops land on island of Leyte	
1942 (May) Battle of the Coral Sea halts Japanese attack on Port Moresby	**1944 (Oct)** The Battle of Leyte Gulf ends Japanese naval power	
1942 (June) Japanese carriers are destroyed at Midway	**1945 (Feb–Mar)** The Battle of Iwo Jima is followed by the invasion of Okinawa	
1942 (Aug) US marines land on Guadalcanal		

Southeast Asia

1941 (Dec) Japan attacks Hong Kong and Malaya	**1943** Nationalists stem the Japanese offensives in China	**1945 (May)** The Burma Road reopened and Rangoon recaptured
1942 (Feb) British forces in Singapore surrender to Japan	**1944** Japanese invasion of India; sieges of Imphal and Kohima (Mar–June)	**1945 (Aug)** The Soviet Union declares war and attacks in Manchuria and Korea
1942 (Mar) The Dutch surrender the East Indies		
1942 British retreat from Burma	**1944** Chinese Communists and Japan stop fighting	

1943   1945

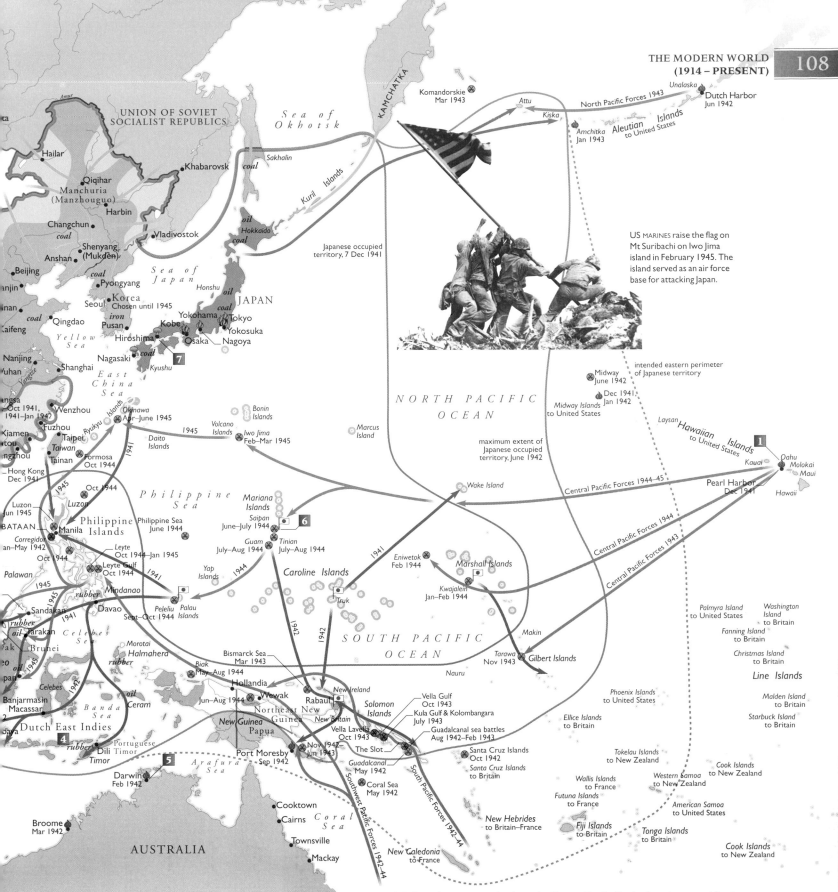

US MARINES raise the flag on Mt Suribachi on Iwo Jima island in February 1945. The island served as an air force base for attacking Japan.

troops were then committed to attack Okinawa; the Japanese defenders employed *kamikaze* aircraft and piloted bombs against American and British ships.

Before and during the Iwo Jima and Okinawa campaigns the Americans subjected Japan to ruthless bombing. Tokyo, Nagoya and Osaka were devastated and the Tokyo firestorm of May 1945 is considered to be the most destructive air raid in history. In the Philippines, the Battle of Luzon was still in progress and in Burma the British, Indian, African, Chinese and US troops, after great battles at Kohima and Imphal, were slowly pushing down the Irrawaddy toward Mandalay and Rangoon.

Despite near universal defeat, the Japanese had no desire to surrender and all sides anticipated a fight to the finish. Allied planning for an amphibious attack on Japan went ahead. Stalin promised that the Soviet Union would enter the war against Japan three months after the total surrender of Nazi Germany. President Truman assessed the likely scale of casualties involved in an invasion (approximately one million fighting men), and compared this with the enemy civilian deaths that would result from the use of the new atomic bomb being tested in New Mexico. He chose the atomic weapon: the bombs fell on Hiroshima and Nagasaki in August 1945. After

the first strike Stalin declared war and Soviet troops invaded Manchuria and Korea. As Japan reeled, carrier aircraft harried Honshu and Kyushu and a giant bombing raid savaged the remains of Tokyo. On 15 August 1945, Emperor Hirohito asked the Japanese people to "endure the unendurable and suffer the insufferable". Japan formally signed the surrender document on the battleship USS *Missouri* on 2 September 1945.

See also 103 (east Asia between the wars); 105, 107 (World War II in Europe)

The United States had entered World War II at the end of 1941 to prevent the domination of Europe and Asia by totalitarian regimes. Yet by 1950 the world was again polarized. The split of the wartime Allies (the United States, the Soviet Union and Britain) created power blocs whose rivalry was consolidated by the outbreak of war in Korea, a conflict by proxy between the democratic capitalist "west" and authoritarian Communist "east".

The Axis powers were in retreat from 1942. Japan was pushed across the Pacific by American military and naval might (▷ 108); Germany was beaten by the Soviet Union at Stalingrad and Kursk. British and American troops landed in Italy and Normandy as their airforces pounded German cities (▷ 107). When the war ended after the dropping of atomic bombs on Hiroshima and Nagasaki, 50 million people, mostly civilians, had died.

As the tide of war turned, the patterns of the postwar world were already laid down. The United Nations Organization (UNO), a new body for resolving international disputes, was set up, but it was clear that the United States and Soviet Union would be the world's strongest powers. The United States and Britain tried to win Soviet trust by allowing Russian troops to occupy east Germany. They also accepted the incorporation of the Baltic states into the Soviet Union, the annexation of Polish territory and the forced repatriation of Soviet prisoners of war.

The Soviet Union soon become involved in the internal affairs of the states of eastern Europe, however, and the wartime lines of demarcation became the boundaries of a divided postwar Europe. The United States supplied massive financial aid to prevent the devastated countries of western Europe from falling to Communism. In response the Soviet Union created Comecon, a system of economic planning designed to strengthen its hold on eastern Europe. Germany remained divided, a division reinforced by the Soviet blockade of the western zones of Berlin in 1947–48, when Britain and the United States kept the city supplied by airlifting supplies (▷ 110).

American aid to Europe followed the Truman doctrine of 1947, which committed the United States to supporting "free peoples" in the struggle against totalitarianism. Initially the struggle against Communism was a European one: in much of Asia, the immediate struggle was for independence from colonial rule.

A.   Albania
AU. Austria (Allied occupied)
B.   Belgium
C.   Czechoslovakia
D.   Denmark
EG. East Germany
H.   Hungary
L.   Luxembourg
N.   Netherlands
PG. Portuguese Guinea (Portugal)
SR. Southern Rhodesia (Britain)
S.   Switzerland
TO. Trucial Oman (Britain)
WG. West Germany (Allied occupied)
YE. Yemen
YU. Yugoslavia

TIMELINE

The Americas
Europe
Middle East
Africa
Asia and Australasia

1944 — 1946 — 1948

1944 (June) D-Day: a huge Allied force invades northern France

1943 June Allied forces land in Italy

1942–43 (Jan) Defeat at Stalingrad ends German expansion to the east

1945 (Oct) The United Nations Organization (UNO) is created

1945 (July) Churchill loses British election; Labour wins power

1945 (May) Germany surrenders, ending war in Europe

1947 (Mar) The "Truman Doctrine" is announced

1947 The United States withdraw from China

1948 (Apr) Organization of American States is founded

1943 (May) Axis forces are evacuated from north Africa

1943 (July) Soviet forces defeat Germans at Kursk

1944 (July) The International Monetary Fund (IMF) is founded

1945 (Aug–Sep) Japan surrenders after atomic bombs are dropped at Hiroshima and Nagasaki

1945 (Sep) North and South Korea independent

1945 (Oct) The Arab league is founded

1946 (July) The Philippines gain their independence

1947 (June) US "Marshall Aid" to assist recovery in western Europe proposed

1947 (Aug) India and Pakistan gain independence from Britain

1948 (Feb) A Communist coup takes place in Czechoslovakia

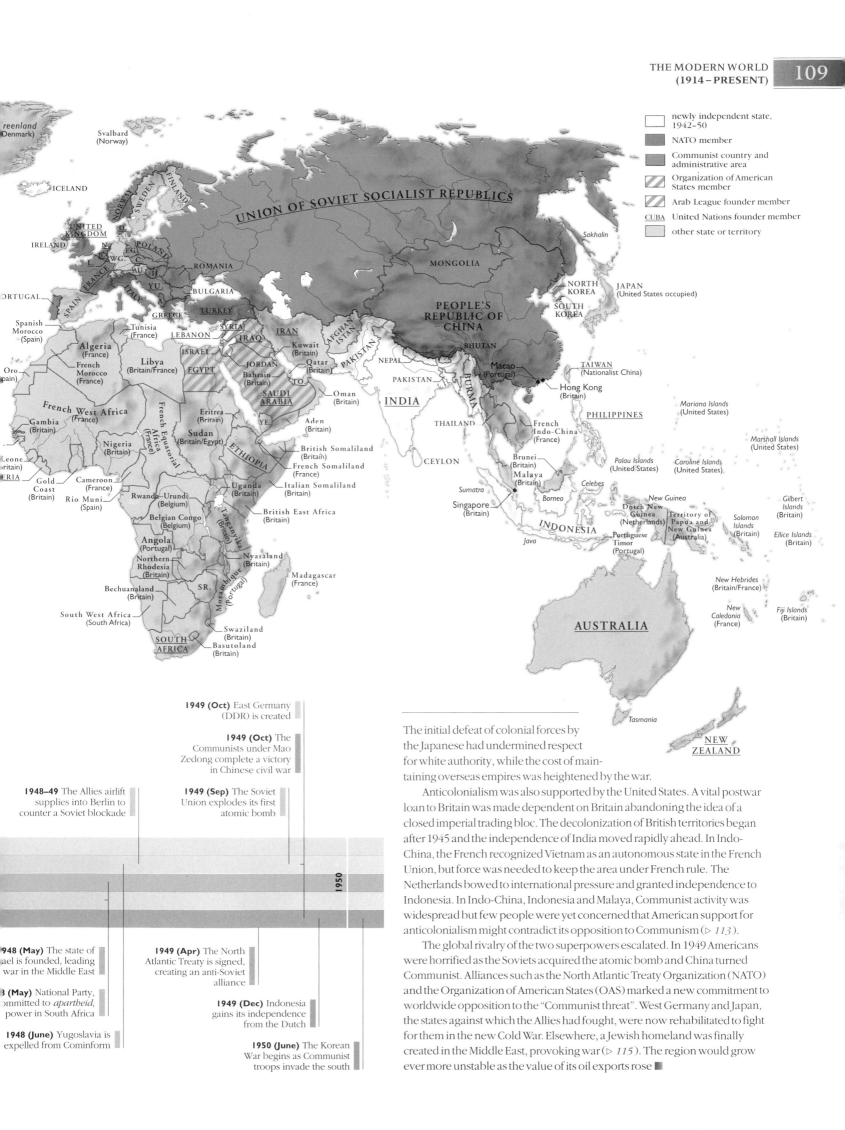

reenland
(Denmark)

Svalbard
(Norway)

ICELAND

SWEDEN

FINLAND

NORWAY

UNITED
KINGDOM

IRELAND

DE.

POLAND

N

L.

B

FR.

WG.

C.

AU.

H.

YU.

ROMANIA

SPAIN

PORTUGAL

IT.

GREECE

BULGARIA

TURKEY

UNION OF SOVIET SOCIALIST REPUBLICS

Sakhalin

MONGOLIA

NORTH
KOREA

SOUTH
KOREA

JAPAN
(United States occupied)

PEOPLE'S
REPUBLIC OF
CHINA

Spanish
Morocco
(Spain)

Tunisia
(France)

SYRIA

LEBANON

ISRAEL

IRAQ

IRAN

AFGHAN-
ISTAN

Algeria
(France)

French
Morocco
(France)

Oro
(pain)

Libya
(Britain/France)

EGYPT

JORDAN

Kuwait
(Britain)

Qatar
(Britain)

Bahrain
(Britain)

TO.

SAUDI
ARABIA

Oman
(Britain)

PAKISTAN

NEPAL

BHUTAN

Macao
(Portugal)

TAIWAN
(Nationalist China)

Hong Kong
(Britain)

PAKISTAN

INDIA

French West Africa
(France)

Gambia
(Britain)

Eritrea
(Britain)

Aden
(Britain)

YE.

BURMA

French
Equatorial
Africa
(France)

Sudan
(Britain/Egypt)

British Somaliland
(Britain)

French Somaliland
(France)

ETHIOPIA

Italian Somaliland
(Britain)

Mariana Islands
(United States)

PHILIPPINES

THAILAND

French
Indo-China
(France)

Marshall Islands
(United States)

Leone
(ritain)

ERIA

Nigeria
(Britain)

Gold
Coast
(Britain)

Cameroon
(France)

Rio Muni
(Spain)

Uganda
(Britain)

CEYLON

Palau Islands
(United States)

Caroline Islands
(United States)

Gilbert
Islands
(Britain)

Rwanda–Urundi
(Belgium)

Belgian Congo
(Belgium)

Angola
(Portugal)

Tanganyika
(Britain)

British East Africa
(Britain)

Sumatra

Brunei
(Britain)

Malaya
(Britain)

Singapore
(Britain)

Borneo

Celebes

INDONESIA

Java

Dutch New
Guinea
(Netherlands)

New Guinea

Territory of
Papua and
New Guinea
(Australia)

Portuguese
Timor
(Portugal)

Solomon
Islands
(Britain)

Ellice Islands
(Britain)

Northern
Rhodesia
(Britain)

Nyasaland
(Britain)

Mozambique
(Portugal)

Madagascar
(France)

Bechuanaland
(Britain)

SR.

South West Africa
(South Africa)

Swaziland
(Britain)

SOUTH
AFRICA

Basutoland
(Britain)

New Hebrides
(Britain/France)

New
Caledonia
(France)

Fiji Islands
(Britain)

AUSTRALIA

Tasmania

NEW
ZEALAND

newly independent state,
1942–50

NATO member

Communist country and
administrative area

Organization of American
States member

Arab League founder member

CUBA United Nations founder member

other state or territory

1949 (Oct) East Germany
(DDR) is created

1949 (Oct) The
Communists under Mao
Zedong complete a victory
in Chinese civil war

1948–49 The Allies airlift
supplies into Berlin to
counter a Soviet blockade

1949 (Sep) The Soviet
Union explodes its first
atomic bomb

1950

948 (May) The state of
ael is founded, leading
war in the Middle East

8 (May) National Party,
ommitted to *apartheid*,
power in South Africa

1948 (June) Yugoslavia is
expelled from Cominform

1949 (Apr) The North
Atlantic Treaty is signed,
creating an anti-Soviet
alliance

1949 (Dec) Indonesia
gains its independence
from the Dutch

1950 (June) The Korean
War begins as Communist
troops invade the south

The initial defeat of colonial forces by
the Japanese had undermined respect
for white authority, while the cost of maintaining overseas empires was heightened by the war.

Anticolonialism was also supported by the United States. A vital postwar
loan to Britain was made dependent on Britain abandoning the idea of a
closed imperial trading bloc. The decolonization of British territories began
after 1945 and the independence of India moved rapidly ahead. In Indo-
China, the French recognized Vietnam as an autonomous state in the French
Union, but force was needed to keep the area under French rule. The
Netherlands bowed to international pressure and granted independence to
Indonesia. In Indo-China, Indonesia and Malaya, Communist activity was
widespread but few people were yet concerned that American support for
anticolonialism might contradict its opposition to Communism (▷ *113*).

The global rivalry of the two superpowers escalated. In 1949 Americans
were horrified as the Soviets acquired the atomic bomb and China turned
Communist. Alliances such as the North Atlantic Treaty Organization (NATO)
and the Organization of American States (OAS) marked a new commitment to
worldwide opposition to the "Communist threat". West Germany and Japan,
the states against which the Allies had fought, were now rehabilitated to fight
for them in the new Cold War. Elsewhere, a Jewish homeland was finally
created in the Middle East, provoking war (▷ *115*). The region would grow
ever more unstable as the value of its oil exports rose ∎

The wartime cooperation of the Allies quickly broke down and two blocs emerged: the western democratic countries which were oriented toward the United States, and the eastern Communist countries dominated by the Soviet Union. Europe lived in the shadow of the superpowers.

Blame for the deterioration of international relations and the drawing of the "iron curtain" across Europe has been laid with both sides, and little is known of Soviet motives. It is clear, however, that US hopes of an "open" Europe were misplaced. Stalin never considered giving up the Soviet Union's new influence in eastern Europe and, though he probably did not envisage invading the west either, there was a real fear that the rest of the continent would succumb to Communism. As a result, with Europe devastated and trying to cope with millions of refugees, the United States produced a massive cash injection ("Marshall Plan") in 1947, becoming the counterweight to Soviet power in the east.

Crucial to the division of Europe was the partition of Germany. The economic and military powerbase of the continent was occupied jointly by the Allies, neither side being willing to risk losing overall control to the other. In 1948 the Soviets blockaded western-occupied West Berlin, and in 1949 the republics of West and East Germany were formally constituted. The same year the North Atlantic Treaty was signed, binding the western states and America in an anti-Soviet alliance (NATO). Comecon was formed to incorporate the east European countries in a system of Soviet-dominated interstate economic planning. In 1950 US troops returned to Europe as part of NATO after the outbreak of war in Korea; the Soviet-led Warsaw Pact was founded five years later.

Thereafter west and east Europe developed on different lines. The western countries soon recovered their prosperity, creating economic areas to increase trade. The Benelux Customs Union of 1948 was followed by the creation of the European Coal and Steel Community (ECSC), which laid the basis for the European Economic Community (EEC) in 1958. A looser affiliation, the European Free Trade Area (EFTA), also existed, but the EEC was the more important, later becoming the European Community (EC), aspiring to a political as well as economic role.

The EEC was intended to transcend national boundaries, prevent the strife that had characterized Europe's history and assist Europe to become an independent player on the world stage. The French president Charles de Gaulle twice vetoed Britain's application to join, on the grounds of Britain's "special relationship" with the United States. De Gaulle deplored US involvement in Europe, and withdrew France from NATO, yet the idea of an independent European Defense Community proved unworkable. The United States encouraged western European integration but American troops remained essential. Britain and France established independent nuclear capability; West German chancellor Willy Brandt negotiated cooperation agreements between West and East Germany. But given the Soviet Union's military might, Europe could not be independent until the iron curtain was raised.

In eastern Europe the influence of the Soviet Union was deeply resented. Eastern European countries did not enjoy the "economic miracle" seen in West Germany, and felt their national identities to be compromised by Soviet interference. Yugoslavia and Albania preserved their traditions of independent Communism as, to a lesser extent, did Romania. Hungary (1956) and Czechoslovakia (1968) tried more radical escapes from the Soviet bloc but were brought back into line by force.

Following the Helsinki agreement of 1975 under which the borders of the German Democratic Republic (East Germany) were recognized and the governments of eastern Europe accepted the principle of observing human rights, dissident activity grew more intense. In 1980 the Polish trade union Solidarity was set up and longstanding popular resentment (kept alive by the Catholic church and the accession of John Paul II as the first Polish pope) was manifested in widespread industrial disputes.

Protest in western Europe was directed both against the United States (over the Vietnam war or the presence of US-controlled nuclear missiles) or against individual governments. The Paris riots of 1968 were part of a general revolt of youth

TIMELINE

Western Europe

1945 Potsdam conference of the great powers agrees the postwar position in Germany

1947 USA provides Marshall Aid to western Europe

1948–49 The Berlin airlift follows a Soviet blockade of the city's western zone

1949 North Atlantic Treaty is signed; NATO is set up

1955 Allies end occupation of West Germany and Austria; West Germany joins NATO

1957 The Treaty of Rome sets up the European Economic Community (EEC), from Jan 1958

1966 France withdraws from NATO

1967 French president de Gaulle vetoes UK entry to EEC for the second time

1968 Students riot in Paris and almost bring down the government; unrest is felt in West Germany and Britain

1974 Turkey invades northern Cyprus

1974 Portugal's rightwing government is overthrown

1977 Spain's first postwar elections take place following the death of Franco in 1975

1979 Conservative leader Margaret Thatcher is elected prime minister in Britain

1986 Portugal and Spain join the EC

Eastern Europe

1947–48 Sovietization of the governments of eastern Europe

1949 Comecon is set up to integrate eastern Europe's economies

1956 An anti-Soviet revolt takes place in Hungary

1961 The Berlin Wall is built to prevent emigration from East to West Germany

1968 Czechoslovak "Prague spring" ends with Warsaw Pact invasion

1970–72 *Ostpolitik* agreements for East and West German cooperation

1975 Helsinki agreement on Germany's borders and human rights in east Europe

1980 Solidarity, Polish trade union, is founded

1989 The Berlin Wall is taken down; regimes in Hungary, Poland, East Germany, Bulgaria, Czechoslovakia, Romania fall

1950   1970   1990

Legend:

- pre-war border of Poland
- North Atlantic Treaty Organization (NATO), established 1949
- Warsaw Pact, established 1955
- zones of occupation of Germany and Austria, 1945–55,
  - American
  - British
  - French
  - Soviet
- borders, 1989
- NATO nuclear-capable base, 1980s
- Warsaw Pact nuclear-capable base, 1980s
- nationalist tension or violence, 1945–89
- civil war, 1945–89
- international dispute, 1945–89
- attempted revolution, 1945–89
- Soviet military intervention
- movement of Germans 1945–50
- movement of Russians 1945–50
- other movement of peoples 1945–50
- mass exodus of refugees, with date
- ITALY founding member of EEC, 1957
- 1945 date of Communist takeover

0   400 km
0   300 mi

against authority, as was the Baader–Meinhof terrorist group in West Germany.

In the 1970s, the economic downturn caused by inflation, high public spending and the rise in oil prices led to unemployment and industrial militancy. British prime minster Margaret Thatcher's response to these problems after 1979 marked a radical departure from the consensus politics of the postwar period, which had stressed cooperation between employers, workers and the state. The introduction of free-market economics and revision of labor legislation brought a year-long miners' strike (1984–85). Elsewhere, terrorism and violence fueled by economic dislocation flared in areas of nationalist tension. Basque separatists mounted a bombing campaign in Spain (where the Catalans gained internal autonomy), and the British province of Ulster simmered on the brink of civil war.

In the late 1980s the disparity in living standards between east and west, and the moral and economic bankruptcy of Communism led the new Soviet leader, Mikhail Gorbachev, to slacken the ties binding eastern Europe in an effort to free up the east's economy. It was soon clear that he had unleashed forces beyond his control. Revolutions ensued, first in Poland and then East Germany, Hungary, Czechoslovakia, Bulgaria and Romania. The old order crumbled, as exhilaration mixed with apprehension at the new shape Europe would take.

1 Divided Berlin was a focus for Cold War tension. In 1948-49 the western zone was supplied by air after Soviet forces surrounded the city; in 1961 the Berlin Wall was built to stop refugees from leaving the East.

2 The Nuremberg war crimes trials of 1946 indicted many leading Nazis but lesser ones were unpunished; a strong West Germany was needed as a cornerstone of the rebuilding of western Europe.

3 Hungary (1956) and Czechoslovakia (1968) looked to break away from the Communist bloc, but both were forced back into line by Warsaw Pact invasions.

4 Yugoslavia remained neutral thanks to its tradition of independent Communism. Its unity was maintained to the 1980s by its Croat leader Tito.

5 The Gdansk shipyards were the center of popular resistance in Poland, which led the way in the later opposition to Communism in eastern Europe.

6 The Treaty of Rome – signed by France, Italy, West Germany, Belgium, the Netherlands and Luxembourg – in 1957 formed the basis for the integration of western Europe under the EEC (later EC and EU).

7 The prolonged attempt by Nikolai Ceauçescu to collectivize the peasantry in Romania was one example of the introduction of Stalinism to eastern Europe, and met with great opposition.

8 The "Forest Brethren" partisans in the Baltic states resisted incorporation into the USSR after 1945.

See also 107 (World War II);
119 (Europe in the 1990s)

The United States was the undoubted victor of World War II. It suffered only sporadic attacks on its territory, while its armed forces played a decisive role in theaters of war from east Asia to western Europe. Its economy was stimulated by the war; and with its unique access to the atomic bomb, the United States looked forward to dominating the postwar world, and to a spell of prosperity at home.

In many ways the domestic dream was realized. American families formed the largest property-owning democracy in the world. They moved in large numbers away from the drudgery of field and factory into the rewarding aerospace, automobile, information technology and service industries. Their ambitions led to continuous relocation in the United States itself, a pattern imitated by hopeful immigrants including Hispanics, Filipinos and east Asians. By 1960 almost 40 percent of American families were in the professional or skilled worker classes and prosperity grew faster than in any other industrialized country. Federal aid supported business, commerce and defense; consumer spending rose and strikes never obstructed production. Yet the United States failed to abolish the poverty that still touched a fifth of the population, to improve health care or to provide real educational opportunity for all. Poverty, especially among the blacks, was a major issue in the Civil Rights campaigns of the 1960s, and resurfaced in the 1980s and 1990s. Though sympathetic, the federal government tried to balance the undoubted needs of the poor with the demands of the United States' role as a superpower.

Nor was it unchallenged in that role, at least until the 1990s. With the start of the Cold War in the late 1940s, a nuclear arms race ensued that developed into the space race of the 1960s, culminating in putting men on the Moon in 1969. Meanwhile, the United States was drawn into costly conflicts across the globe. The Cold War affected Americans at home, too, with the McCarthy "witchhunts" against suspected Communists and sympathizers from 1950.

Latin America was a battleground of the Cold War; nowhere more so than Cuba, a virtual US client since 1898, but one overtaken by socialist–nationalist

revolution in 1959. Soviet support for the new Castro regime led to a crisis in 1962, when the Soviet Union threatened to use the island as a base for nuclear missiles. The United States reasserted its dominance, though at the cost of increasing complaints at its heavy-handed involvement in the affairs of others.

The United States dominated even its northern neighbor, Canada, where economic and cultural life was increasingly dictated by the United States (most of the population lived within a few hundred kilometers of the border). Meanwhile Canada sought to build an independent Pacific role in the later 20th century. At the same time, Quebec's demands for independence grew louder.

South America too was a source of important United States commercial and political involvement, as the governments of the region – which ranged from the more or less democratic to out-and-out military dictatorships – wrestled with the problem of having such a rich and powerful neighbor. In Chile in 1973, an elected Marxist government was replaced, with United States instigation, by a rightwing dictatorship, whose practice of military rule characterized by brutal suppression of opposition was followed in many countries. Occasionally dictatorial methods were put to more constructive ends, notably in Brazil in the 1940s and 1950s. In the 1940s the charismatic Juan and Eva Perón were popular in Argentina until unemployment, strikes and inflation destroyed their appeal and brought the army to power. Argentina's military regime sought to revive its flagging popular appeal by invading the British Falkland Islands in 1982. Failure resulted in the civilian "Peronist" government of Carlos Menem, who sought to reduce inflation, privatize industry and introduce healthcare for workers.

The vested interests of the well-off, combined with the policies of the international banks to whom most countries were in debt, argued against drastic social change. As a result the environmental and social problems associated with a rapidly expanding population worsened (especially in Brazil, where São Paulo and Rio de Janiero were among the world's largest, fastest-growing cities). Indigenous

peoples, like the rainforests that they inhabited, were treated as expendable in the face of land hunger and mineral-prospecting. Several countries, including Peru, endured long and violent revolutionary conflicts; others, such as Colombia, had their economies increasingly dominated by illegal drug trafficking.

Many countries entered into economic organizations: Venezuela and Ecuador were founder members of the Organization of Petroleum Exporting Countries (OPEC) in 1960; the Mercosur or Southern Cone Common Market (1991), Latin American Integration Association (1980) and Andean Pact (1969) were all attempts at economic cooperation. In 1992, to the dismay of many in the United States and Canada who feared the competition of Third World wages, the North American Free Trade Agreement was extended to include Mexico.

TIMELINE

North America

1950	1970	1990
1945 The United States develops the first atom bomb at Los Alamos, New Mexico	**1961** US president Kennedy launches the manned space program	**1974** US president Nixon resigns following revelations in the Watergate affair	**1992** A Canadian referendum rejects limited autonomy for Quebec

1949 Newfoundland becomes a province of the Canadian Federation

1963 John F. Kennedy is assassinated in Dallas, Texas

1982 Britain gives up its last constitutional rights in Canada

1995 A terrorist bomb explodes in Oklahoma City

1968 Martin Luther King is assassinated in Memphis Tennessee; youth and antiwar protests across North America

1988 The North American Free Trade Agreement is signed by the United States and Canada

Latin America

1946 Juan Perón is elected president of Argentina

1959 Castro's Marxist revolutionaries take over in Cuba

1973 Chile's Marxist president Allende is killed in a US-backed coup

1989 Carlos Menem comes to power in Argentina, introducing economic and political reform

1954 The pro-American Alfredo Stroessner becomes president of Paraguay (to 1989)

1967 Bolivian military capture and kill Che Guevara, former associate of Castro

1976–82 The "dirty war" is fought between the Argentinian military and guerrilla forces

1990 Democracy is restored in Chile under Patricio Aylwin

1967 A free-market economic boom in Brazil leads to violent opposition in the early 1970s

1982 An Argentinian invasion launches the Falklands War, in which the British confirm their control over the islands

1950   1970   1990

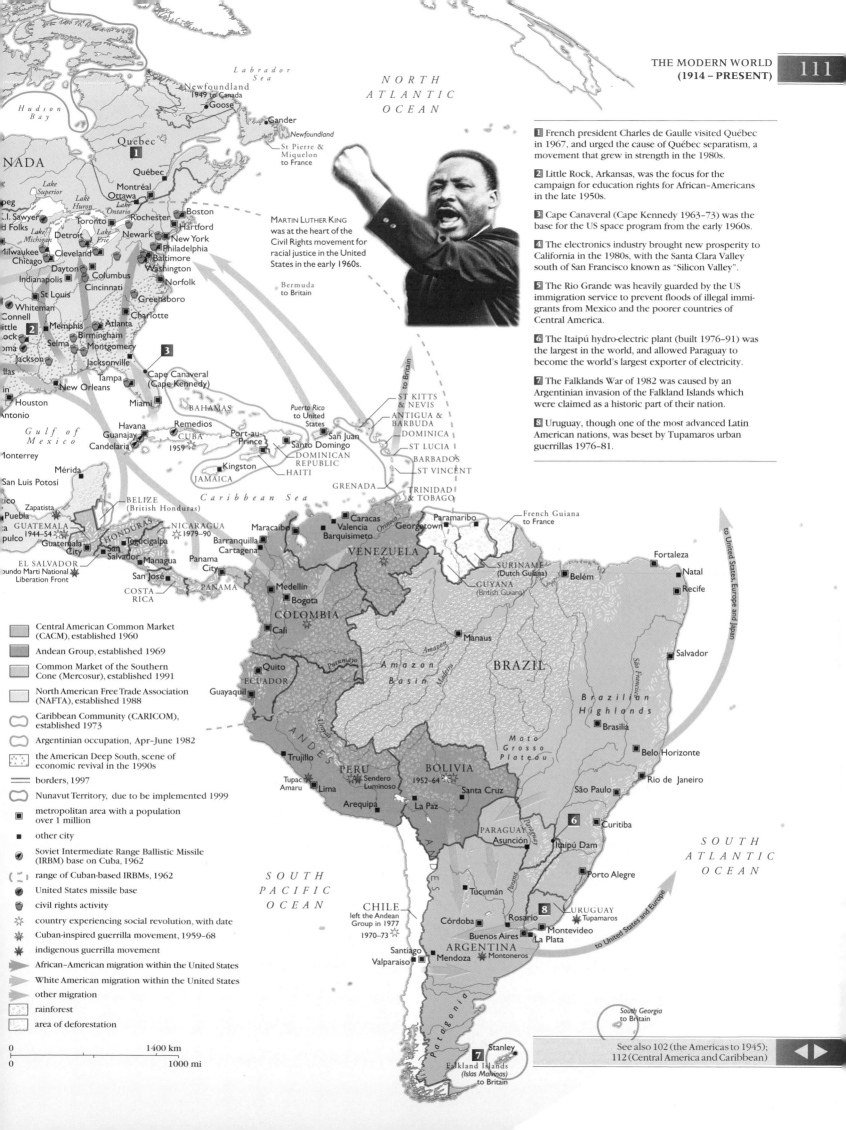

MARTIN LUTHER KING was at the heart of the Civil Rights movement for racial justice in the United States in the early 1960s.

1 French president Charles de Gaulle visited Québec in 1967, and urged the cause of Québec separatism, a movement that grew in strength in the 1980s.

2 Little Rock, Arkansas, was the focus for the campaign for education rights for African-Americans in the late 1950s.

3 Cape Canaveral (Cape Kennedy 1963-73) was the base for the US space program from the early 1960s.

4 The electronics industry brought new prosperity to California in the 1980s, with the Santa Clara Valley south of San Francisco known as "Silicon Valley".

5 The Rio Grande was heavily guarded by the US immigration service to prevent floods of illegal immigrants from Mexico and the poorer countries of Central America.

6 The Itaipú hydro-electric plant (built 1976-91) was the largest in the world, and allowed Paraguay to become the world's largest exporter of electricity.

7 The Falklands War of 1982 was caused by an Argentinian invasion of the Falkland Islands which were claimed as a historic part of their nation.

8 Uruguay, though one of the most advanced Latin American nations, was beset by Tupamaros urban guerrillas 1976-81.

Legend

- Central American Common Market (CACM), established 1960
- Andean Group, established 1969
- Common Market of the Southern Cone (Mercosur), established 1991
- North American Free Trade Association (NAFTA), established 1988
- Caribbean Community (CARICOM), established 1973
- Argentinian occupation, Apr-June 1982
- the American Deep South, scene of economic revival in the 1990s
- borders, 1997
- Nunavut Territory, due to be implemented 1999
- ▣ metropolitan area with a population over 1 million
- ▪ other city
- Soviet Intermediate Range Ballistic Missile (IRBM) base on Cuba, 1962
- range of Cuban-based IRBMs, 1962
- United States missile base
- civil rights activity
- ✻ country experiencing social revolution, with date
- ✺ Cuban-inspired guerrilla movement, 1959-68
- ✺ indigenous guerrilla movement
- African-American migration within the United States
- White American migration within the United States
- other migration
- rainforest
- area of deforestation

```
0        1400 km
0        1000 mi
```

See also 102 (the Americas to 1945);
112 (Central America and Caribbean)

All the eight states of Central America, together with several islands of the Caribbean, have suffered from similar problems in the later 20th century. All had subsistence agriculture, unfair land distribution and a deprived native peasant class. Tax evasion by the wealthy was endemic, and labor-intensive industries were lacking. The states were too poor to fund welfare sufficiently to prevent political revolt, so political violence and state repression were commonplace. Aid (overwhelmingly from the United States) tended to prop up military leaders committed to anti-Communist policies despite frequent corruption and human rights abuses.

Before its revolution, Cuba was dominated by United States interests, with US marines stationed at their Guantánamo Bay base. Cubans who demanded political independence were treated as rebels, and any government that supported US interests was guaranteed a supply of dollars. Fidel Castro's successful revolution led to hostility from the United States and the International Monetary Fund (IMF). The Soviet Union gave Castro support, especially after the American-supported but abortive counter-coup at the Bay of Pigs in 1961. The following year, United States air surveillance revealed that Soviet intermediate range ballistic missiles (IRBMs) had been stationed on the island, and all of eastern and most of the southern United States lay within their 3,200-kilometer (2,000-mile) range. The US president Kennedy imposed a naval blockade on the islands and even considered invasion, a step that seemed inevitably to lead to nuclear war. When Soviet leader Khrushchev removed the missiles, the threat of invasion was lifted, but Castro became an enduring Soviet ally. He grew into the first Caribbean leader to have a marked impact on world affairs, sending trained guerrillas to spread Marxism–Leninism in Africa (including Angola and Ethiopia). The Soviet Union supported Cuba's economy and funded its welfare state, but Cuba went into decline after 1990 and faced severe American sanctions.

The United States believed Cuba to have fostered guerrilla revolts in Nicaragua, El Salvador, Guatemala and Honduras, and feared that these countries would come under Soviet control. Cuban guerrillas were active in El Salvador, training rebels and organizing protests. By 1976 they were fomenting strikes on coffee and cotton plantations. The army responded by taking over the government and thousands of civilian suspects were killed. A similar cycle of events occurred in Guatemala. In Nicaragua, which was ruled by the wealthy Samoza family, Sandinista guerrillas occupied Managua and set up a Marxist–Leninist state in 1979. This was, however, subverted by rightwing Contra guerrillas trained by the United States. In 1990, with more than three-quarters of the population still below the poverty line, the Sandinista leader Daniel Ortega was voted out of office in a general election.

Mexico, the richest country in the region thanks to its reserves of oil, opposed foreign intervention and defended the Sandinistas as a "stabilizing factor" entitled to transform the people's way of life through

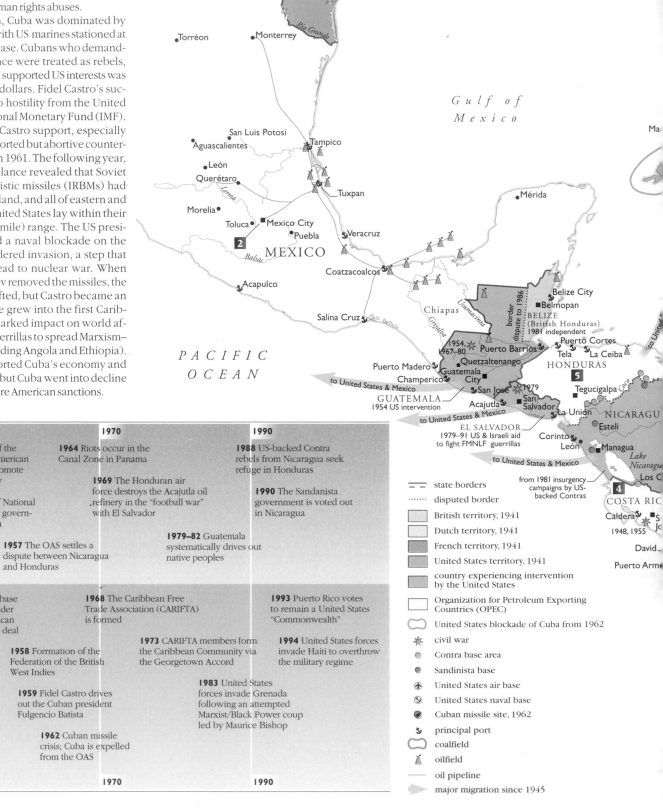

TIMELINE

Central America

1948 Formation of the Organization of American States (OAS) to promote peace and security

1948 The Army of National Liberation forms a government in Costa Rica

1957 The OAS settles a dispute between Nicaragua and Honduras

1964 Riots occur in the Canal Zone in Panama

1969 The Honduran air force destroys the Acajutla oil refinery in the "football war" with El Salvador

1979–82 Guatemala systematically drives out native peoples

1988 US-backed Contra rebels from Nicaragua seek refuge in Honduras

1990 The Sandanista government is voted out in Nicaragua

Caribbean

1941 A United States base is built on St Lucia under the 1940 Anglo-American "destroyers for bases" deal

1958 Formation of the Federation of the British West Indies

1959 Fidel Castro drives out the Cuban president Fulgencio Batista

1962 Cuban missile crisis; Cuba is expelled from the OAS

1968 The Caribbean Free Trade Association (CARIFTA) is formed

1973 CARIFTA members form the Caribbean Community via the Georgetown Accord

1983 United States forces invade Grenada following an attempted Marxist/Black Power coup led by Maurice Bishop

1993 Puerto Rico votes to remain a United States "Commonwealth"

1994 United States forces invade Haiti to overthrow the military regime

1950   1970   1990

Map legend

- ⹀ state borders
- ······· disputed border
- British territory, 1941
- Dutch territory, 1941
- French territory, 1941
- United States territory, 1941
- country experiencing intervention by the United States
- Organization for Petroleum Exporting Countries (OPEC)
- United States blockade of Cuba from 1962
- ✳ civil war
- ◉ Contra base area
- ◉ Sandinista base
- ✴ United States air base
- ⚓ United States naval base
- ◉ Cuban missile site, 1962
- ⚓ principal port
- coalfield
- ⛰ oilfield
- — oil pipeline
- ➤ major migration since 1945

1 In 1977 the United States agreed that the Canal Zone, under US control since the beginning of the century, would be handed over to Panama in 2000.

2 The population of Mexico City rose to more than 20 million in the mid-1990s. Many people lived on the streets or in squalid and dangerous conditions.

3 The last Soviet advisors left Cuba in 1993, when a renewed United States blockade of the island took effect. Many Cubans attempted to reach the United States illegally; Miami became a popular destination for Cuban exiles.

4 Costa Rica sought to avoid many of the political conflicts of Central America, and in 1987 its president Arias Sánchez won the Nobel Prize for his attempt to draw up a peace plan for the region.

5 In 1969 war between Honduras and El Salvador broke out following a World Cup soccer match between the two countries.

6 Barbados, which was a British colony until 1966, but which had enjoyed a degree of self-government since 1639, was used as a base for the United States invasion of Grenada in 1983.

CHE GUEVARA, from Argentina, helped Castro in Cuba. He was an icon of revolution through the Americas.

revolution. The country had few law and order problems, although the population quadrupled from 1940 and a recession hit in 1984. A Zapatista revolt in Chiapas province was crushed ten years later.

The United States intervened in the internal affairs of several Caribbean islands, again prompted by fear of Communism. The Dominican Republic was invaded by paratroopers in 1965, Grenada in 1983, and Haiti in 1994. Another United States intervention was the arrest of the president of Panama, Manuel Noriega, in 1989, on drugs smuggling charges.

In 1958-62 an unsuccessful federation of West Indian states was tried, after which most sought independence (achieved peacefully for the most part) or chose to remain as British dependencies. In the 1950s, Britain actively sought immigrants from the West Indies, but curtailed this in 1962. Jamaica faced overpopulation, unemployment and racial tension, but its educational programs and tourist attractions improved job opportunities. Trinidad and Tobago, richly endowed with oil, natural gas and asphalt, suffered from a high birth rate, strikes and sabotage due to Black Power groups and embittered Asians working on the sugar plantations. Belize, a former British colony, was the last Central American country to gain its independence; it remained a firm supporter of United States policies.

See also 102 (early 20th-century America); 111 (the Americas from 1945)

The end of World War II left the United States dominant but the Soviet Union was also moving strongly into east Asia. The Chinese civil wars were soon to be resolved, while the European colonies had been decisively altered by the experience of Japanese occupation and US liberation.

In September 1945 US forces landed at Inchon on the former Japanese colony of Korea, in response to the presence of Soviet troops in north Korea. No formula could be found for unifying the country and the UN approved an American plan to hold elections in the south. Syngman Rhee's Republic of Korea (South Korea) emerged in 1948, followed shortly by Kim Il Sung's Communist Democratic Republic of Korea (North Korea). The Soviet Union and United States withdrew in 1948 and 1949 respectively, leaving Korea divided.

Many US troops withdrew to Japan, where America was responsible for its military occupation and the repatriation of three million Japanese servicemen. The United States and its Commonwealth Allies met with unexpected cooperation from Japanese police and local officials. Emperor Hirohito remained, though only as titular ruler, and real power was in the hands of General MacArthur, Supreme Commander of Allied Powers. MacArthur introduced a democratic constitution, ensured that the United States shipped in adequate food supplies and generally charmed the Japanese with his dignity and benevolence. The Japanese came to admire Americans and their way of life. By 1949 Japan was willingly drawn inside America's defense perimeter.

By 1950 Mao Zedong had succeeded in unifying China, partly by demonstrating that the PLA was no warlord army. Soldiers, workers, the Party hierarchy (cadres) and the government were united. Mao assured the people that China was no longer isolated: the Sino–Soviet Treaty (1950) guaranteed their membership of a international socialist brotherhood. He promised land reform and development plans, and protection for China's frontiers. His first move was to invade Tibet in the winter of 1950–51 to recover what China considered a historic province.

North Korea invaded South Korea in 1950. This provoked a major United Nations response and an army from sixteen nations, spearheaded by the Americans, was sent to Korea to resist the invaders. UN forces attacked across the 38th Parallel dividing North from South, and a few reached the border with China on the Yalu River. At this point the PLA entered the war and forced a UN retreat. A static war ensued, with both sides digging in. An armistice was agreed at Panmunjom in 1953 and five years later the PLA left Korea, although a UN presence remained. After the war, North Korea remained a Stalinist state, while the South began to rebuild its shattered economy. Heavy industry and infrastructure, as well as electronics and consumer industries, were all constructed from scratch as Korea, like Japan, used the opportunity of war to build a new prosperity.

Chinese armed forces were also involved in 1954 when PLA gunners shelled the two small islands of Quemoy and Matsu that were claimed by the Nationalist government based in Taiwan. PLA forces landed on other Nationalist islands and in 1958 resumed the shelling of Quemoy. America mobilized a massive fleet in the Taiwan Straits in support of Jiang Jieshi, who still claimed to be the legitimate ruler of the whole of mainland China. In 1962 PLA forces attempted to push across the Indian border and were poised to enter Assam. After brief fighting against ill-prepared Indian troops, the Chinese withdrew. Along the Ussuri River Chinese patrols clashed with Soviet troops in 1969.

In the 1950s and 1960s, Mao Zedong attempted to forge a Chinese version of Marxism, based on a drive toward establishing economic modernization (especially in the chaotic "Great Leap Forward" of 1958–60) and the collectivization of agriculture. From the mid-1960s he fomented "permanent revolution" by encouraging the youthful Red Guards to challenge all forms of authority, especially in education, administration, industry and the Party itself, and to send many intellectuals to work on communes. China was almost totally cut off from the outside world until after Mao's death in 1976.

former colony, c.1939

	British
	Dutch
	French
	United States
	North Korea, 1948
	South Korea, 1948
	People's Republic of China (Communist), 1950
	Republic of China (Nationalist), 1950
	Tibet prior to the Chinese invasion, 1950
	North Vietnam, 1954
	South Vietnam, 1954
	Japan, 1972
	Indonesia, 1949
	United Nations Trust Territory
1946	date of independence as a nation-state
LAOS	Communist state by 1976
	insurgency, with date
	clash between Red Guards and the Army or workers, 1965–69
	disruption caused by Red Guards, 1965–69
	urban youth sent to Chinese provinces, 1974–76
	main center from where urban youth were removed
	Chinese troop movements, with date
	Nationalist Chinese attacks, 1954–55
	Nationalist Chinese evacuation to Taiwan, 1950
	borders, 1976
	disputed border, 1976

Korean War, 1950–53

	United Nations airbase
	Chinese and North Korean airbase
	North Korean advance, June–Sep 1950
	United Nations advance, July–Sep 1950
	Chinese and North Korean advance, Nov 1950–Jan 1951
	limit of North Korean advance, Aug–Sep 1950
	limit of United Nations advance, Nov 1950
	limit of Chinese and North Korean advance, Jan 1951

Islamaba

PAKISTAN
West Pakistan
until 1971,
1947

TIMELINE

China, Korea and Japan

1950

1945 The United States occupy Japan (to 1952)

1948 The states of North and South Korea are established

1949–50 Chinese Nationalists evacuate to Taiwan

1950 North Korea invades the South

1953 Korean armistice is signed in Panmunjom

1960

1958–60 Mao's "Great Leap Forward" establishes agrarian and industrial communes

1958 Agricultural collectivization in North Korea

1962 China challenges India in the Himalayas

1962 Start of policy of export-led growth in South Korea

1966–70 The Cultural Revolution to prevent revisionism causes internal disruption in China

1968 Japan is the world's second largest economy

1969 China confronts the Soviet Union in east Asia

1970

1971 People's Republic of China is admitted to the United Nations

1975 Death of Jiang Jieshi

1976 Death of Mao Zedong

Indo-China

1946 French forces return to Indo-China

1954 The French surrender at Dien Bien Phu

1954 Laos and Cambodia become independent states; Vietnam is divided

1964 The US assert that "all measures will be taken to resist aggression" in Vietnam

1965 US ground troops in action against the Viet Cong

1970 US troops enter Cambodia

1973 US troops leave South Vietnam

1976 Vietnam is reunited

Southeast Asia

1946 The Philippines become an independent republic

1948 Burma is independent

1956 Indonesia's last links with the Dutch crown are severed

1963 Federation of Malaysia set up, including Malaya, North Borneo, Sabah and Sarawak, Singapore (to 1965)

1971 The British military presence in Singapore is ended

1950   1960   1970

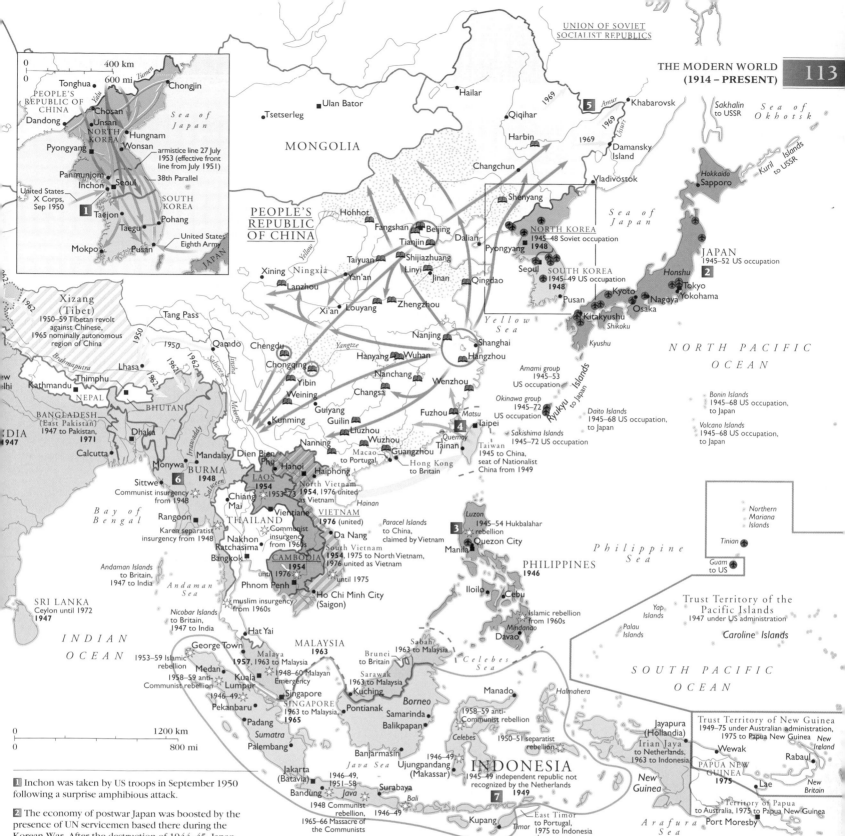

1 Inchon was taken by US troops in September 1950 following a surprise amphibious attack.

2 The economy of postwar Japan was boosted by the presence of UN servicemen based there during the Korean War. After the destruction of 1944–45, Japan became the driving force in east Asia's economy.

3 The Hukbalahar revolt from 1945 in Luzon, a peasant uprising over land ownership, was crushed by the government in 1953–54.

4 In 1958 US president Eisenhower sent "the most powerful fighting force in history" to confront the Communist Chinese in the Taiwan Straits.

5 Tension between the Soviet Union and Maoist China on the Amur River border from 1969 emphasized the rift between these former allies.

6 Burma, which pursued a neutral foreign policy after independence under U Nu, was under a socialist military regime led by Ne Win from 1962.

7 East Timor, a Portuguese colony until the Portuguese revolution of 1975, was invaded by Indonesia the same year, and annexed in 1976.

Independence and unity arrived slowly for many east Asian nations. The Philippines became an independent republic in 1946; Burma in 1948; after the partition of India in 1947, East Pakistan became Bangladesh in 1971. But the former French Indo-Chinese colonies of Laos, Cambodia and Vietnam became embroiled in the longest war of the century. During World War II the French had accepted Japanese domination of the area; only the Communist Vietminh forces led by Ho Chi Minh resisted, and declared independence in 1945. The return of the French led to a long guerrilla war in which the French initially drove the Vietminh from the major cities, but in 1953–54 the Vietminh general Giap won a remarkable and decisive victory over the French at Dien Bien Phu.

Maoist China was the chief supporter of the insurgents in Indo-China, and also of the Communists in Malaya who inspired a long guerrilla campaign against the British; eventually independence was achieved by the anti-Communist, Malay-led nationalists in 1957. Indonesia, which claimed its independence after the war and won Dutch acceptance of the fact in 1949 after a bitter struggle, also suffered Communist, regionalist and Islamist activity. To a lesser extent, the Philippines (where United States' influence was still paramount), Burma and Thailand also saw Communist movements.

See also 108 (World War II in Asia); 114 (Vietnam War); 120 (the Pacific Rim after 1976)

Following the victories of Ho Chi Minh's Viet-minh guerrilla forces in 1943–54, France withdrew from most of Indo-China. The subsequent Geneva Conference ruled that Vietnam would be divided between the North, ruled from Hanoi by the Vietminh, and the non-Communist South, with its capital in Saigon. Two neutral states, Laos and Cambodia, would also be formed and within two years the Vietnamese would hold free elections and be united under a government of their own choice.

The elections were never held. Vietnam stayed divided and weak: the North by being cut off from the rich rice-fields of the Mekong delta, and the South by the presence of the Vietminh. Land reform was a key issue in the Mekong delta where two million peasants were landless, with many more paying high rents to absentee landlords. Saigon was reluctant to redistribute the land, whereas the Vietminh soldiers gave land to the peasants and also handed over responsibility for food production and local government. The Communists thus began to win the hearts and minds of the people, who were alienated by the anti-Buddhist president Diem in Saigon. Coercion, too, was rife on the Communist side in intimidating or eliminating anti-Communists.

John Foster Dulles, US secretary of state from 1953, had never endorsed the Geneva agreements. He intended to save all of southeast Asia from Communism and to this end set up the South-East Asia Treaty Organization (SEATO) to prevent subversion within member states. When guerrilla uprisings began in Vietnam during 1955–56, the United States sent military advisers to train the ARVN (Army of the Republic of South Vietnam). Gradually the guerrillas, now termed the Viet Cong (Vietnamese Communists or VC), won control of half of Diem's provinces. Disillusioned ARVN officers killed him.

A succession of Saigon governments followed. For the United States, the war against North Vietnam (NVN) became "the great issue" of the 1960s. America's leaders accepted the "domino theory": if South Vietnam (SVN) succumbed to Communism, the same fate would in turn befall Laos, Cambodia, Thailand, Burma and Pakistan. After President

Kennedy's assassination in 1963, President Johnson left the conduct of the war in the hands of defense secretary Robert McNamara. More American troops arrived in the South as VCs and their supplies swarmed down the "Ho Chi Minh Trail". In an effort to halt the flow of war materiel from China and Russia via Hanoi, the US provoked the Tongking crisis in 1964: an attack on US destroyers became an excuse for bombing North Vietnam 1965–70.

Air attack failed to reduce VC activity. US soldiers (and others from Australasia and South Korea) were sent to fight an elusive enemy hiding in the hamlets, jungles and paddy fields. They had enormous firepower; but the fundamental issue – how to defeat well-armed, well-supplied nationalists operating in an agrarian economy – was never resolved. The Central Intelligence Agency (CIA) did not penetrate the VC high command; it did not warn of the Tet offensive of 1968 when Viet Cong battle-squads entered Saigon, Hue and other towns, and failed to reveal the buildup around the US base at Khe Sanh.

With antiwar sentiment growing in the United States, President Johnson authorized negotiations with North Vietnam in Paris. His successor Richard Nixon pledged to scale down US troop involvement and to "vietnamize" the war by boosting the ARVN military contribution. Even as US troops were quitting Vietnam, he backed the invasions of Cambodia and Laos plus Operation Linebacker II, a resumption of the air war designed to destroy the transportation systems of North Vietnam. US air power now proved irresistible, destroying bridges, truck factories and harbor installations. Linebacker II encouraged Le Duc Tho, the NVN delegation leader, to sign the Paris peace agreement with Henry Kissinger (US national security adviser). South Vietnam's President Thieu reluctantly agreed to the ceasefire, and the last American combat troops left Vietnam in 1973.

Nixon's subsequent resignation and the decline of US aid encouraged Le Duan (Ho Chi Minh's successor) to attempt the reunification of Vietnam. The Ho Chi Minh Trail now provided unhindered access to the south, and China and the Soviet Union had re-equipped the regular NVN Army so that it could put

infantry divisions, armored brigades and artillery regiments into the field. These advanced from the north and the west, fighting the kind of war that the Americans had always wanted them to fight. In 1975 SVN's president Thieu fled to Taiwan; American helicopters ferried their remaining personnel from the capital as NVN tanks entered Saigon. At the same time Laos and Cambodia, both destabilized by Viet Cong activity and by constant US air attack, also fell to the Communists: Pathet Lao guerrillas set up a People's Democratic Republic in Laos, while the Khmer Rouge captured Cambodia's capital, Phnom Penh. Vietnam was reunited as the Socialist Republic of Vietnam under the leadership of Le Duan.

Legend

— border, 1954
Communist control within Indo-China, 1954
under Vietnamese Communist control, 1970
Vietnamese Communist gains by Jan 1975
Vietnamese Communist gains by Apr 1975
Khmer Rouge control, 1975
Pathet Lao control, 1975
Communist guerrilla activity in Thailand, 1975
US carrier fleet on permanent station
US air base in South Vietnam and Thailand
North Vietnamese air base
Tet Offensive assault, Jan–Feb 1968
major combat area
interdiction by US Air Force
VI A zoned target area (Route Packages) of the US Air Force within North Vietnam
.... border of zoned target area
forbidden target for US air strikes until Operation Linebacker II, 1972
<u>Vinh</u> harbor mined by the US Navy
Viet Cong supply route
US and South Vietnamese offensive, 1970
Vietnamese Communist advance, Jan–Apr 1975
Vietnamese invasion of Cambodia, 1978–79
Chinese invasion of Vietnam, 1979
US evacuation, with date
— railroad

TIMELINE

Vietnam War

1960	1965	1970	1975
1954 Geneva agreements temporarily divide Vietnam	**1962** First Australian troops arrive in South Vietnam	**1966** US orders a bombfree zone around Hanoi	**1972** North Vietnamese troops cross the demilitarized zone (DMZ)	**1975** US Congress rejects president Ford's request for further aid to South Vietnam
1955 Ngo Dinh Diem, new president of South Vietnam rejects reunification	**1963** 15,000 US military advisers in South Vietnam	**1968** Tet offensive	**1972** The largest force of bombers takes part in Linebacker II	**1975** North Vietnamese troops capture Saigon
1959 Infiltration of South Vietnam begins via the Ho Chi Minh Trail	**1963** China promises more military aid to the North	**1968** VC besieges US marines at Khe Sanh, for 77 days		
	1964 The Tongking Gulf crisis: USS *Maddox* is attacked	**1968** US troops strength in Vietnam tops 540,000	**1973** The Paris Agreement is signed	
1960 Hanoi forms a National Liberation Front (NLF) to operate in South Vietnam	**1965** First US combat troops land at Da Nang	**1969** Death of Ho Chi Minh, succeeded by Le Duan	**1973** The last American troops leave Vietnam	

Other countries

1960	1965	1970	1975
1956 Prince Sihanouk of Cambodia adopts neutrality		**1968** Sihanouk permits US troops to pursue Viet Cong units within Cambodia	**1973** US Congress ends bombing of Cambodia
1958 Laos adopts anti-Communism with US support			**1973** Anti-government demonstrations in Thailand
1959 Hanoi sends weapons to guerrilla groups in Laos		**1970** South Vietnamese troops enter Cambodia, later supported by US troops	
1960 Khmer Rouge guerrillas active in Cambodia		**1971** South Vietnam troops enter Laos, but fail to cut Ho Chi Minh Trail	**1975** Pathet Lao form government in Laos; Khmer Rouge in Cambodia

| 1960 | 1965 | 1970 | 1975 |

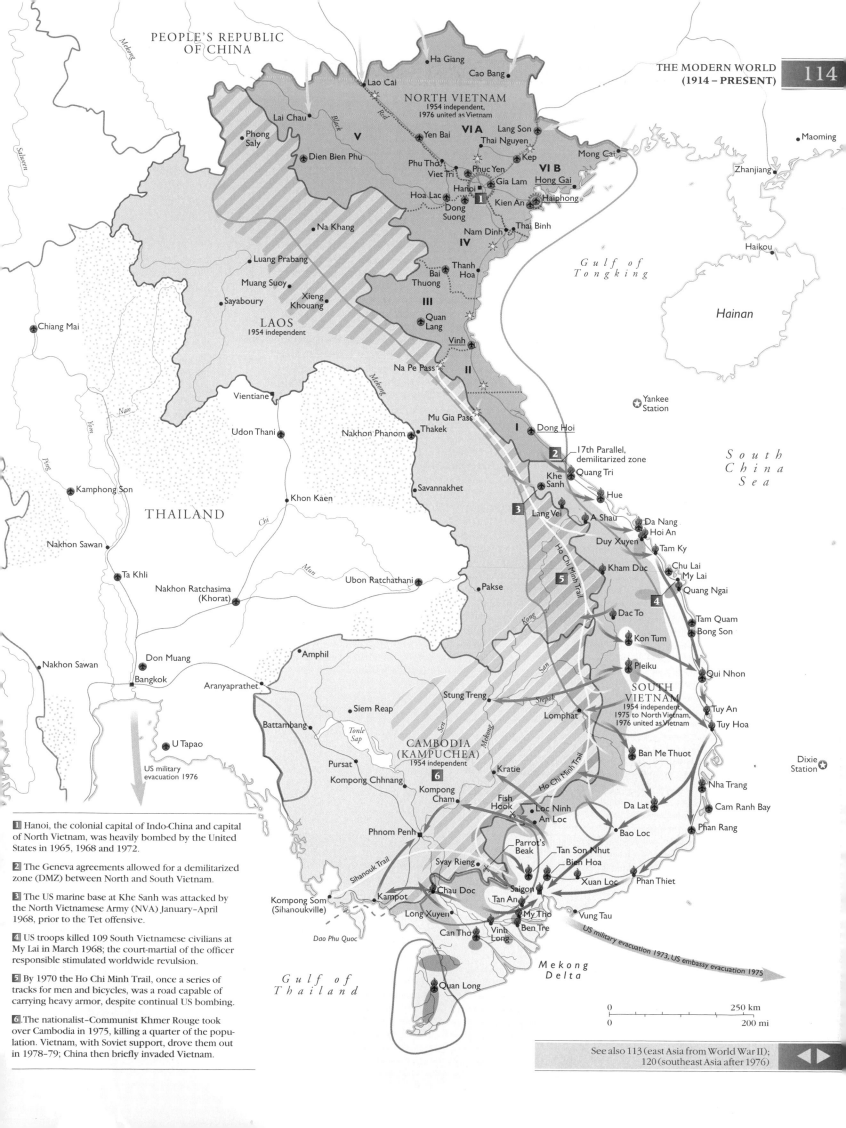

PEOPLE'S REPUBLIC
OF CHINA

Ha Giang
Cao Bang
Lao Cai
NORTH VIETNAM
1954 independent,
1976 united as Vietnam
Lai Chau
V
VI A
Lang Son
Maoming
Phong
Saly
Yen Bai
Thai Nguyen
Dien Bien Phu
Phu Tho
Viet Tri
Kep
Mong Cai
Zhanjiang
Phuc Yen
VI B
Hoa Lac
Hanoi
Gia Lam
Kien An
Hong Gai
Haiphong
Dong
Suong
Na Khang
Nam Dinh
Thai Binh
IV
Haikou
Luang Prabang
Bai
Thuong
Thanh
Hoa
Gulf of
Tongking
Muang Suoy
Xieng
Khouang
III
Sayaboury
Quan
Lang
Hainan
Chiang Mai
LAOS
1954 independent
Vinh
Na Pe Pass
II
Vientiane
Mu Gia Pass
Thakek
I
Dong Hoi
Yankee
Station
Udon Thani
Nakhon Phanom
Savannakhet
2
17th Parallel,
demilitarized zone
Khe
Sanh
Quang Tri
South
China
Sea
Khon Kaen
3
Hue
Lang Vei
A Shau
Da Nang
Hoi An
Nakhon Sawan
Duy Xuyen
Tam Ky
Ta Khli
Kham Duc
Chu Lai
My Lai
THAILAND
Nakhon Ratchasima
(Khorat)
Ubon Ratchathani
Pakse
5
Quang Ngai
Dac To
4
Tam Quam
Bong Son
Kon Tum
Nakhon Sawan
Amphil
Pleiku
Qui Nhon
SOUTH
VIETNAM
1954 independent,
1975 to North Vietnam,
1976 united as Vietnam
Don Muang
Stung Treng
Lomphat
Tuy An
Bangkok
Aranyaprathet
Siem Reap
Tuy Hoa
Battambang
Tonle
Sap
Ban Me Thuot
U Tapao
CAMBODIA
(KAMPUCHEA)
1954 independent
Kratie
Nha Trang
US military
evacuation 1976
Pursat
6
Cam Ranh Bay
Kompong Chhnang
Kompong
Cham
Fish
Hook
Loc Ninh
An Loc
Da Lat
Bao Loc
Phan Rang
Phnom Penh
Parrot's
Beak
Tan Son Nhut
Bien Hoa
Dixie
Station
Sihanouk Trail
Svay Rieng
Xuan Loc
Phan Thiet
Kompong Som
(Sihanoukville)
Kampot
Chau Doc
Saigon
Tan An
Vung Tau
Long Xuyen
My Tho
Ben Tre
Dao Phu Quoc
Can Tho
Vinh
Long
US military evacuation 1973, US embassy evacuation 1975
Gulf of
Thailand
Mekong
Delta
Quan Long

Mekong

Salween

Black

Red

Nan

Yom

Ping

Chi

Mun

San

Srepok

Sen

Mekong

Kong

Ho Chi Minh Trail

1 Hanoi, the colonial capital of Indo-China and capital
of North Vietnam, was heavily bombed by the United
States in 1965, 1968 and 1972.

2 The Geneva agreements allowed for a demilitarized
zone (DMZ) between North and South Vietnam.

3 The US marine base at Khe Sanh was attacked by
the North Vietnamese Army (NVA) January–April
1968, prior to the Tet offensive.

4 US troops killed 109 South Vietnamese civilians at
My Lai in March 1968; the court-martial of the officer
responsible stimulated worldwide revulsion.

5 By 1970 the Ho Chi Minh Trail, once a series of
tracks for men and bicycles, was a road capable of
carrying heavy armor, despite continual US bombing.

6 The nationalist–Communist Khmer Rouge took
over Cambodia in 1975, killing a quarter of the population. Vietnam, with Soviet support, drove them out
in 1978–79; China then briefly invaded Vietnam.

0   250 km
0   200 mi

See also 113 (east Asia from World War II);
120 (southeast Asia after 1976)

Only a few hours after the proclamation of the independent state of Israel on 14 May 1948, the armies of Syria, Jordan, Egypt and Iraq invaded, expecting to crush the Jewish state and establish an Arab Palestine. The Jews drew on reserves of experienced soldiers from around the world, defeated the Arabs and conquered territory as far as West Jerusalem. When East Jerusalem and the West Bank of the Jordan became part of the territory of Jordan the following year, Palestine ceased to exist. No Arab state would recognize the permanence of the new frontiers, though they received *de facto* acceptance at armistice talks in 1949. Israel's victory meant that the new state attracted thousands of Jewish immigrants to a new homeland, while more than a million Palestinians became refugees in their own land – a potentially explosive force in the politics of the region and of Jordan in particular.

Defeat led to a nationalist revolt in Egypt in 1952, when the British-sponsored ruling family was expelled and a republic instituted by a group of army officers. Colonel Nasser, president from 1954, relied on American dollars to subsidize the massive Aswan Dam project, regarded as essential for Egypt's economic and industrial development. When the United States withdrew in response to Nasser's increasingly anti-western foreign policy, he nationalized the Suez Canal, long seen as a strategic key to the east by Britain and France. These two old colonial powers decided to invade. Israel's support was secretly secured and Israeli forces invaded Sinai in October 1956, with Anglo-French troops arriving a week later. American pressure brought about a withdrawal and a United Nations force was sent in, while Nasser blocked the canal with sunken ships.

Widespread condemnation of Britain and France was followed by increased superpower involvement in the region: Arab states turned to the Soviet Union for weaponry while the United States became Israel's arsenal. Nasser was convinced that Egypt, allied with Syria (the two were united as the United Arab Republic in 1958–61), would defeat Israel. He assembled an alliance of Arab states and provoked a crisis by closing the Gulf of Aqaba. Israel, however, launched the most effective pre-emptive strike in history, attacking all of Egypt's air bases in June 1967. Most Egyptian combat aircraft were destroyed; Syria and Jordan suffered similar devastation.

When a ceasefire was agreed six days later, Israeli forces had occupied Gaza and the entire Sinai east of Suez, Jordan surrendered East Jerusalem, Bethlehem and Hebron, and Syria lost the Golan Heights, an area dominating the north of Israel.

The United Nations, however, passed resolutions requiring Israel to evacuate the occupied territories, deploring the loss of Palestinian civil rights, and confirming the Palestinian right to selfdetermination. These pointed to the deep divisions within Israel, where the Palestinians were treated as second-class citizens, many of them – particularly in the areas recently occupied by Israel – condemned to a life in refugee camps. The Palestinian Liberation Organization (PLO) was founded in 1964, and by the early 1970s had won, through a combination of terrorist tactics and moral pressure, a powerful and independent voice in the politics of the region. Seeming to endanger the fragile stability of Jordan, the PLO was evicted from the kingdom in 1970 and settled in Lebanon. The growing numbers of refugees there, most with little to lose, proved destabilizing to that country as well and contributed to the outbreak of civil war in Beirut in 1975.

In October 1973 Egypt's new president Anwar Sadat broke through into Israeli-held territory without warning on the Jewish Day of Atonement (Yom Kippur). The Israelis concentrated on holding the Golan Heights against Syrian tanks, but three weeks later Israel had defeated both attacks comprehensively while the two superpowers refused to intervene actively to support the protagonists.

In response to the United States' supply of military materiel to the Israelis, Saudi Arabia (where oil

1 Jerusalem, a holy city to Jews, Muslims and Christians, was divided after the failure of the Arab attack of 1948; the Israelis took the whole city in 1967, but disputes continued into the 1990s.

2 In 1953 the CIA (US intelligence agency) backed a coup against Iranian prime minister Mohammed Moussadeq, who had tried to nationalize the oil industry in 1951. The exiled shah returned to power.

3 Sharm el-Sheikh, a cove on the Sinai peninsula controlling entry to the Straits of Tiran, was captured by the Israelis in 1956 and controlled by the United Nations Emergency Force 1957-67.

4 This neutral zone between Kuwait and Saudi Arabia was partitioned between the two countries in 1966.

5 Israel bombed Palestinian bases in Jordan in 1968 and its troops defeated the Al Fatah (PLO military wing) guerrillas at the Battle of Karama.

6 Jordan expelled the Al Fatah guerrillas in 1970; many established new bases in southern Lebanon.

7 After ethnic conflict in Cyprus through the 1950s and UN intervention from 1964, a Turkish invasion in 1974 divided the island into Greek and Turkish zones.

revenues had grown dramatically since 1945 and which was the leading member of the Organization of Petroleum Exporting Countries, OPEC) imposed oil sanctions on the west, restricting OPEC exports and causing a sharp price rise. Despite this, the governments of Saudi Arabia and the Gulf states, including Iran (where the Allied occupation in World War II had left a legacy of popular bitterness toward "imperialists"), remained close to the United States and rejected the growing influence of the Soviet Union in the region. The main oil-producing states were reluctant to give military support to the anti-Israeli effort, and tensions developed between Saudi Arabia and Egypt over Egyptian policy in the southern Arabian peninsula. Syria and Iraq, however, were both under the control of the "anti-imperialist" and Arab nationalist Ba'ath Party, from 1963 and 1968 respectively. Libya too, another important oil producer, was in the control of a strongly anti-American regime inspired by the success of Nasser and led by Muammar Qadhafi from 1969.

Following the Yom Kippur War, Menachem Begin became prime minister of Israel, and realized that, like himself, Sadat was now interested in reducing Arab–Israeli tensions. Begin invited Sadat to Jerusalem, and a peace process was initiated which was formalized in the United States in 1979.

TIMELINE

Arab–Israeli Wars

1955	1965	1975
1948 Israel's foundation is followed by an Arab attack	**1964** Palestinian Liberation Organization (PLO) is founded in Jerusalem	**1973** Sadat launches the fourth war against Israel
1949 One million Palestinians flee Israel		**1977** Egypt's president Sadat offers Israel peace in return for a Palestinian state
	1967 Six-Day War ends with Israeli control over Sinai	
1956 Nasser's nationalization of the Suez Canal leads to British, French and Israeli invasions of Egypt	**1969** Yassir Arafat becomes PLO chairman	
1958 Nationalist revolution in Iraq overthrows the monarchy	**1970** The PLO are driven out of Jordan and settle in Lebanon; terrorist hijacking of civilian aircraft begins	

Other developments

1951 Moussadeq becomes Iranian prime minister and nationalizes the oil industry	**1965** Iran exiles Islamic leader Ayatollah Khomeini	**1975** Civil war breaks out in Beirut
1952 The Egyptian monarchy is overthrown	**1968** Ba'ath leader Saddam Hussein takes power in Iraq	
1953 The CIA sponsor a coup in Iran and reinstate Reza Khan Pahlavi as shah	**1970** General Asad seizes power in Syria	
		1973 OPEC countries raise the price of oil to exert political influence on the west
1961 Kuwait gains its independence, though it is claimed by Iraq		

1955	1965	1975

Mediterranean Sea

Derna

Tobruk

LIBYA
1951 independent
✳ 1969

Matrûh

0   300 km
0   200 mi

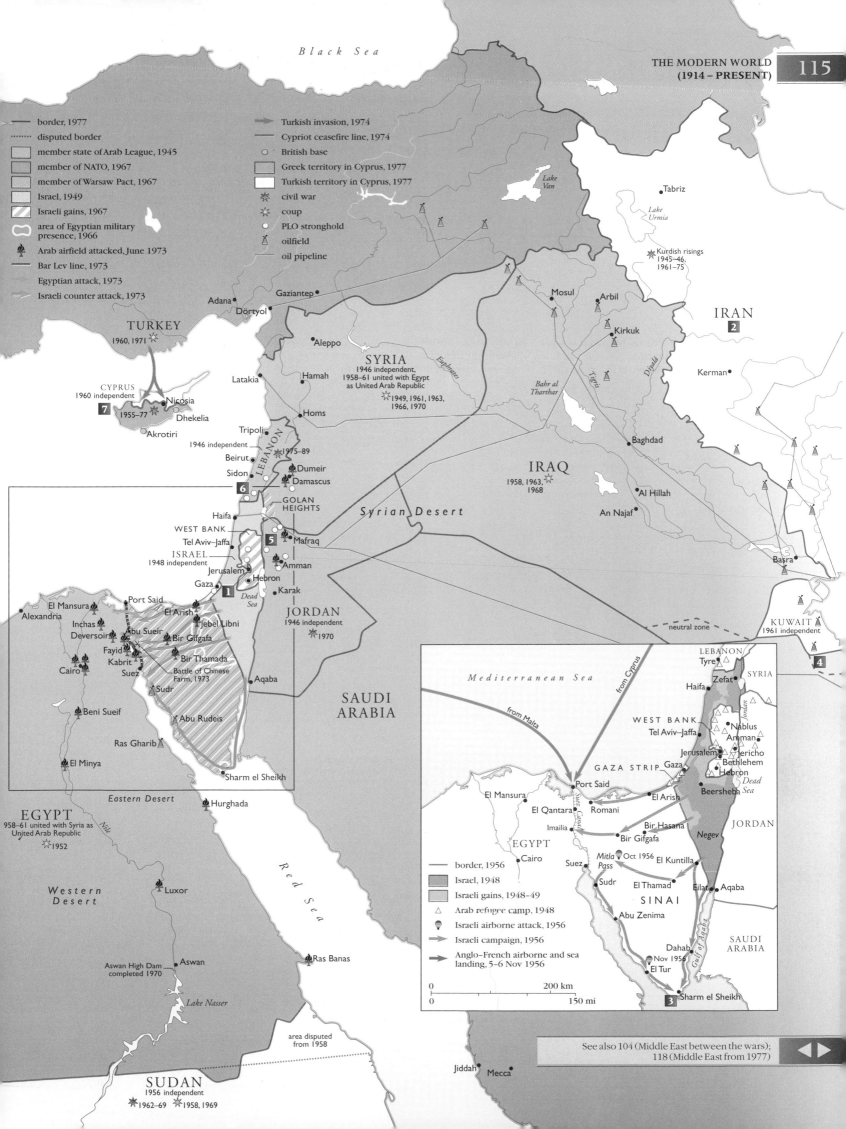

border, 1977
disputed border
member state of Arab League, 1945
member of NATO, 1967
member of Warsaw Pact, 1967
Israel, 1949
Israeli gains, 1967
area of Egyptian military presence, 1966
Arab airfield attacked, June 1973
Bar Lev line, 1973
Egyptian attack, 1973
Israeli counter attack, 1973

Turkish invasion, 1974
Cypriot ceasefire line, 1974
British base
Greek territory in Cyprus, 1977
Turkish territory in Cyprus, 1977
civil war
coup
PLO stronghold
oilfield
oil pipeline

Black Sea

TURKEY
1960, 1971

CYPRUS
1960 independent
1955–77
Nicosia
Dhekelia
Akrotiri

Adana
Dörtyol
Gaziantep

Aleppo

SYRIA
1946 independent,
1958–61 united with Egypt
as United Arab Republic
1949, 1961, 1963,
1966, 1970

Latakia
Hamah
Homs

Lake Van

Mosul
Arbil
Kirkuk

Tabriz

Lake Urmia

Kerman

Kurdish risings
1945–46,
1961–75

IRAN
2

Tripoli
1946 independent
Beirut
Sidon
LEBANON
1975–89
6

Dumeir
Damascus

Euphrates

Bahr al Tharthar

Tigris

Diyala

Baghdad

IRAQ
1958, 1963,
1968

Al Hillah

An Najaf

Haifa
WEST BANK
Tel Aviv–Jaffa
ISRAEL
1948 independent
Jerusalem
Gaza
1

GOLAN HEIGHTS
5
Mafraq
Amman
Hebron
Karak

Syrian Desert

Basra

El Mansura
Alexandria
Inchas
Deversoir
Fayid
Kabrit
Cairo
Suez
Beni Sueif
El Minya

Port Said
El Arish
Jebel Libni
Abu Sueir
Bir Gifgafa
Bir Thamada
Battle of Chinese Farm, 1973
Sudr
Abu Rudeis
Ras Gharib

Dead Sea

JORDAN
1946 independent
1970

Aqaba

SAUDI ARABIA

neutral zone

KUWAIT
1961 independent
4

Hurghada

Eastern Desert

EGYPT
1958–61 united with Syria as United Arab Republic
1952

Western Desert

Luxor

Nile

Aswan High Dam completed 1970

Aswan

Lake Nasser

Red Sea

Ras Banas

area disputed from 1958

SUDAN
1956 independent
1962–69   1958, 1969

Jiddah
Mecca

Inset map

Mediterranean Sea

from Cyprus
from Malta

LEBANON
Tyre
Haifa
Zefat

SYRIA

WEST BANK
Tel Aviv–Jaffa
Nablus
Amman

Jerusalem
Jericho
Bethlehem
Hebron

GAZA STRIP
Gaza

Dead Sea

Port Said
El Qantara
Romani
El Arish
Beersheba
Imailia
Bir Hasana
EGYPT
Cairo
Bir Gifgafa
Negev

JORDAN

Suez
Mitla Pass   Oct 1956
El Kuntilla
Sudr
El Thamad
Eilat
Aqaba
Abu Zenima
SINAI

SAUDI ARABIA

Dahab   Nov 1956
El Tur

Gulf of Aqaba

border, 1956
Israel, 1948
Israeli gains, 1948–49
Arab refugee camp, 1948
Israeli airborne attack, 1956
Israeli campaign, 1956
Anglo-French airborne and sea landing, 5–6 Nov 1956

0   200 km
0   150 mi

3   Sharm el Sheikh

Sharm el Sheikh

See also 104 (Middle East between the wars);
118 (Middle East from 1977)

By 1974 rivalry between the Soviet Union and the United States still dominated international affairs. The USSR guarded its European satellite states jealously. When, in 1956, Hungary tried to break free from the Soviet-dominated Warsaw Pact, the Red Army crushed the revolution. In 1961 the Berlin Wall was erected to enforce Soviet control over East Germany. And in 1968, Warsaw Pact forces ended the Czech attempt to introduce a more liberal form of socialist government (▷ 110). Yet Yugoslavia, Albania and Romania all won some independence from Soviet control.

In western Europe, institutions were set up to integrate the economies of the main industrial nations. The European Economic Community (EEC) was seen as a step to political union and the creation of a European superstate, but most countries (France was the main exception) still relied on the United States membership of NATO for security from possible Soviet aggression.

It was in America's "backyard" that superpower rivalry was most apparent. The Cuban missile crisis of 1962 brought a real threat of nuclear war until the Soviet Union withdrew its missiles from within range of the American mainland (▷ 112). Anxiety for the spread of Communism also lay behind the United States involvement in southeast Asia. Fearing that neighboring countries would fall to Communism (the "domino effect"), the United States sent troops and dollars to prop up an unpopular regime in South Vietnam. It was another war by proxy but, unlike Korea, American withdrawal from Vietnam led to the collapse of South Vietnam and the descent of Cambodia into civil war (▷ 114).

Conflict between China and the Soviet Union, underlain by centuries of mutual suspicion, showed that America's opponents were not a unified bloc, however. The Chinese version of Communism was different from the Soviet, as China tried to develop a locally-based economy centered on communes, in contrast to the centralized bureaucracies of the Soviet Union. Chinese Communism was more applicable to non-industrial societies. Communist insurgents worldwide, especially in southeast Asia, where rapid decolonization was followed by political upheaval, turned to it for inspiration and support. Eventual American recognition of the Sino-Soviet split led in the early 1970s to an attempt to exploit the dispute and brought a new era of détente (▷ 113).

In Africa, opposition to imperial rule was the driving force. The Suez crisis of 1956 showed the weakness of the old imperial powers, and a wave of

A.   Albania
AU.   Austria
B.   Belgium
CAR. Central African Republic
C.   Czechoslovakia
D.   Denmark
DR.   Dominican Republic
DY.   People's Democratic Republic of Yemen
EG.   East Germany
H.   Hungary
LE.   Lebanon
L.   Luxembourg
N.   Netherlands
NV.   North Vietnam
S.   Switzerland
U.   United Arab Emirates
WG.   West Germany
YA.   Yemen Arab Republic
YU.   Yugoslavia

1956 Hungarian revolt is crushed by the Warsaw Pact

1956 Egypt nationalizes the Suez Canal; Britain's invasion attempt fails

1955 The Warsaw Pact is created as a Soviet-bloc opponent of NATO

1962 Cuban missile crisis, as US president Kennedy insists on withdrawal of Soviet nuclear missiles

1961 The Nonaligned Conference is founded; OPEC is founded

1961 The Berlin Wall is built

1965 US troops are sent to Vietnam, and open bombing of the North begins

1965 India–Pakistan war

The Americas
Europe
Middle East
Africa
Asia and Australasia

1955

1960

1965

1951 USA, Australia and New Zealand, sign a defense treaty

1954 Algerian uprising begins against French rule

1954 Laos, Cambodia, South and North Vietnam gain independence

1957 The European Economic Community (EEC) is created

1957 The Soviet Sputnik II, the first artificial satellite, is launched

1958 Mao initiates the "Great Leap Forward" in China

1960 Fifteen African countries gain their independence

1962 US military advisors are sent to assist the South Vietnam regime

1963 Sino–Soviet split as Mao and Khrushchev determine different paths

1966-70 Mao Zedong leads the Cultural Revolution in China

1967 Israel defeats Egypt and the other Arab nations in the Six Day War

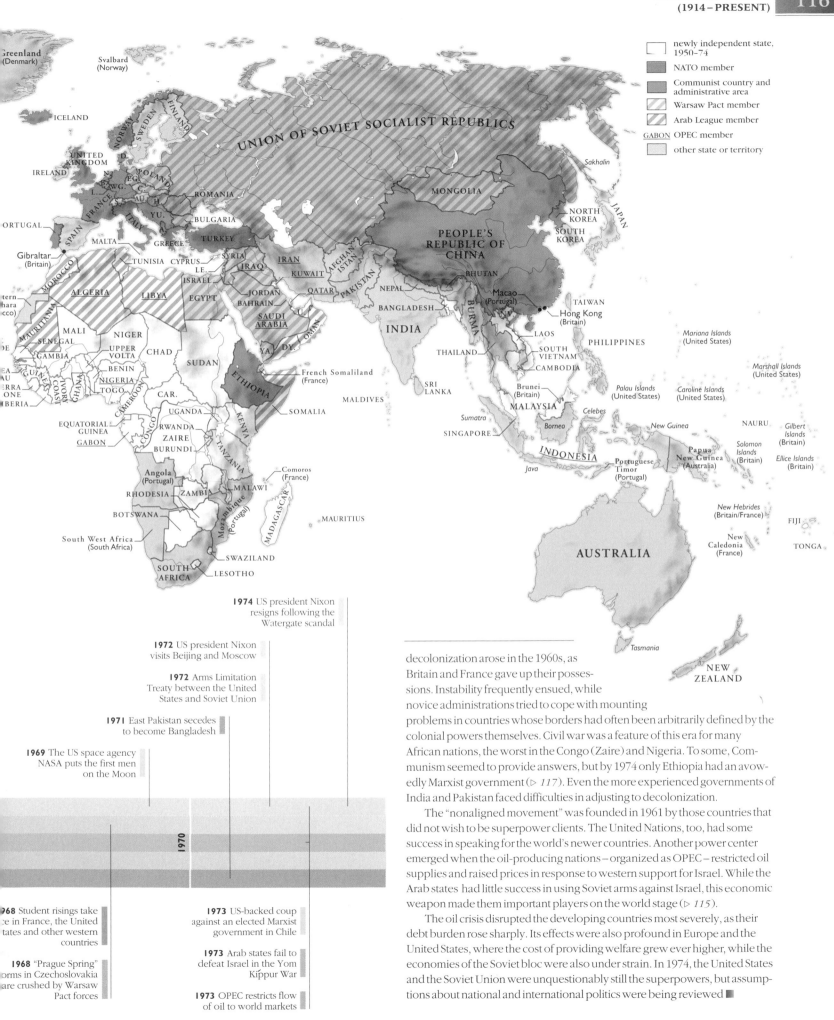

Legend:
- newly independent state, 1950–74
- NATO member
- Communist country and administrative area
- Warsaw Pact member
- Arab League member
- GABON OPEC member
- other state or territory

Map labels:

Greenland (Denmark) · Svalbard (Norway) · ICELAND · NORWAY · SWEDEN · FINLAND · UNITED KINGDOM · IRELAND · POLAND · ROMANIA · UNION OF SOVIET SOCIALIST REPUBLICS · MONGOLIA · NORTH KOREA · SOUTH KOREA · JAPAN · Sakhalin · PORTUGAL · FRANCE · ITALY · YU. · BULGARIA · GREECE · TURKEY · SPAIN · MALTA · Gibraltar (Britain) · MOROCCO · TUNISIA · CYPRUS · SYRIA · IRAN · AFGHANISTAN · PAKISTAN · NEPAL · BHUTAN · PEOPLE'S REPUBLIC OF CHINA · ALGERIA · LIBYA · EGYPT · IRAQ · KUWAIT · ISRAEL · JORDAN · QATAR · BAHRAIN · SAUDI ARABIA · OMAN · BANGLADESH · INDIA · BURMA · Macao (Portugal) · TAIWAN · Hong Kong (Britain) · Western Sahara (Morocco) · MAURITANIA · MALI · NIGER · CHAD · SUDAN · ETHIOPIA · French Somaliland (France) · SOMALIA · LAOS · SOUTH VIETNAM · CAMBODIA · THAILAND · PHILIPPINES · Mariana Islands (United States) · SENEGAL · GAMBIA · UPPER VOLTA · BENIN · NIGERIA · TOGO · GHANA · IVORY COAST · CAR. · UGANDA · KENYA · SRI LANKA · MALDIVES · Brunei (Britain) · Palau Islands (United States) · Caroline Islands (United States) · Marshall Islands (United States) · GUINEA · GUINEA BISSAU · SIERRA LEONE · LIBERIA · EQUATORIAL GUINEA · GABON · CONGO · RWANDA · ZAIRE · BURUNDI · TANZANIA · Sumatra · MALAYSIA · SINGAPORE · Borneo · Celebes · New Guinea · NAURU · Gilbert Islands (Britain) · Angola (Portugal) · ZAMBIA · MALAWI · Comoros (France) · INDONESIA · Java · Portuguese Timor (Portugal) · Papua New Guinea (Australia) · Solomon Islands (Britain) · Ellice Islands (Britain) · RHODESIA · Mozambique (Portugal) · MADAGASCAR · MAURITIUS · BOTSWANA · South West Africa (South Africa) · SWAZILAND · SOUTH AFRICA · LESOTHO · AUSTRALIA · New Hebrides (Britain/France) · New Caledonia (France) · FIJI · TONGA · Tasmania · NEW ZEALAND

Timeline:

1974 US president Nixon resigns following the Watergate scandal

1972 US president Nixon visits Beijing and Moscow

1972 Arms Limitation Treaty between the United States and Soviet Union

1971 East Pakistan secedes to become Bangladesh

1969 The US space agency NASA puts the first men on the Moon

1970

1968 Student risings take place in France, the United States and other western countries

1968 "Prague Spring" reforms in Czechoslovakia are crushed by Warsaw Pact forces

1973 US-backed coup against an elected Marxist government in Chile

1973 Arab states fail to defeat Israel in the Yom Kippur War

1973 OPEC restricts flow of oil to world markets

---

decolonization arose in the 1960s, as Britain and France gave up their possessions. Instability frequently ensued, while novice administrations tried to cope with mounting problems in countries whose borders had often been arbitrarily defined by the colonial powers themselves. Civil war was a feature of this era for many African nations, the worst in the Congo (Zaire) and Nigeria. To some, Communism seemed to provide answers, but by 1974 only Ethiopia had an avowedly Marxist government (▷ 117). Even the more experienced governments of India and Pakistan faced difficulties in adjusting to decolonization.

The "nonaligned movement" was founded in 1961 by those countries that did not wish to be superpower clients. The United Nations, too, had some success in speaking for the world's newer countries. Another power center emerged when the oil-producing nations – organized as OPEC – restricted oil supplies and raised prices in response to western support for Israel. While the Arab states had little success in using Soviet arms against Israel, this economic weapon made them important players on the world stage (▷ 115).

The oil crisis disrupted the developing countries most severely, as their debt burden rose sharply. Its effects were also profound in Europe and the United States, where the cost of providing welfare grew ever higher, while the economies of the Soviet bloc were also under strain. In 1974, the United States and the Soviet Union were unquestionably still the superpowers, but assumptions about national and international politics were being reviewed ■

fricans played an active part in World War II, fighting on behalf of the Allies, and building roads, railroads, naval yards and fuel depots. They met whites of a type quite different from the traditional colonial administrators, discovered that imperial powers were not invincible, and identified with democratic freedom for which the Allies were fighting. The war meant that African independence could not long be denied.

No entrenched white community gave up without a fight. In British west Africa, though, where the white population was minimal, the transfer of power was relatively swift and peaceful. In the Gold Coast, the Convention People's Party leader Kwame Nkrumah worked closely with the British governor, and the idea of a unitary independent state was tested in an election in 1956. The Gold Coast became independent as Ghana, with Nkrumah as prime minister. Britain gave independence equally readily to Nigeria, Sierra Leone and the Gambia by 1965.

France had recruited a large number of Africans to its armies in both World Wars, and in French West Africa "colonies" were replaced by "overseas territories" with all Africans made citizens of the French republic itself. While many Africans accepted French control provided that they could keep economic links with France, Algeria began its fight for independence on the day that World War II ended in Europe. In 1958 the nationalist freedom fighters were confronted by settlers, causing a crisis that brought Charles de Gaulle back to the French presidency. He abandoned the policy of direct rule from Paris, and by 1960 most French colonies had been given their independence. In Algeria, though, de Gaulle committed half the army to maintain French rule, but this too was abandoned in 1962 after the loss of more than 10,000 French troops.

In Kenya, where white settlers controlled all the best farming regions, the Mau Mau movement terrorized and murdered 20,000 people, mostly Kikuyu sympathetic to their white masters. The British army and air force were sent in before independence was granted with Mau Mau leader Jomo Kenyatta as prime minister. In contrast, the independence movements in Uganda, Tanganyika, Nyasaland and Northern Rhodesia were relatively peaceful.

The ends of both the Belgian and Portuguese

empires were violent. Belgium made no attempt to prepare the Congo for changes in government, and on independence the Congolese army mutinied and thousands of Belgian citizens became refugees. Belgian paratroopers went to their aid, and the copper-rich province of Katanga declared its own independence. Eventually, the Congolese general Mobutu crushed the Katangans and their mercenary supporters, creating a unified state which he renamed Zaire. Portugal was the last colonial power to leave Africa, and bitterly opposed the nationalists in Guinea, Angola and Mozambique. By 1975, though, when Portugal underwent its own political convulsions, the colonies became sovereign states.

Few African states found that independence brought stability or prosperity. Many faced ethnic conflict, a legacy of colonial borders that had little relevance to physical, social or economic realities. Most had impoverished, poorly educated and rapidly growing populations, and their economies proved vulnerable to multinational companies offering desperately needed investment to exploit the region's natural resources. Institutions of government were fragile, and arms manufacturers proved willing to supply weapons profligately. As a result, much of the continent experienced civil war, dictatorship and corruption, interrupted by humanitarian crises for which the world's aid agencies offered relief though they could never tackle the underlying problems.

The experience of Nigeria was typical: a civil war in the late 1960s brought on by a secessionist Igbo revolt led to widespread famine, and resulted in a cycle of weak civilian governments replaced by military strong men. Marxist forces, some with the support of the Soviet Union or Cuba, fought tenaciously in many countries including Mozambique and Angola, and won control of Ethiopia in 1974. Elsewhere, dictators such as Jean-Bédel Bokassa in the Central African Republic and Idi Amin in Uganda ruled by terror with few aims beyond personal aggrandizement. Environmental degradation, as the Sahara moved southward and the continent faced shortages of wood and fresh water, was matched in the 1980s by a demographic crisis as the AIDS virus swept through central and east Africa. Attempts to address such issues were made via the Organization of African Unity (OAU) and other regional groups,

but these often foundered through lack of leadership and political will, and in the face of the overwhelming economic problems. The problems of Rwanda in the 1990s, where old ethnic rivalries overflowed into genocide in 1994, creating a flood of refugees (including many responsible for mass murder) into Zaire – itself suffering from civil war as insurgents attempted to throw off the long-standing Mobutu regime that finally fell in 1997 – seemed to sum up the intractable problems of the continent.

1 Western Sahara was claimed by Morocco but was contested by Polisario guerrillas seeking to establish a Sahara Arab democratic republic.

2 Eritrea was annexed by Ethiopia in 1952, but won its independence in 1993 following a bitter civil war.

3 Zambia was ruled by Kenneth Kaunda from independence in 1964 until 1991; he became a leading figure in the Organization of African Unity.

4 A 20,000-strong United Nations force intervened in the Congo in 1960 to assist in expelling the Belgians.

5 Liberia was the only African country never to experience colonialism; but civil war broke out in 1985.

6 Italian and British Somaliland were united as Somalia in 1960, but civil war broke out in the 1980s over the disputed Ogaden region.

TIMELINE

North & east Africa

1944 French leader de Gaulle promises representative government to French colonies

1954 Algerian National Liberation Front (FLN) declares war on French

1974 Marxists oust emperor Haile Selassie in Ethiopia

1984–85 Civil war in Eritrea leads to widespread famine in Ethiopia

1946 Houphouet-Boigny of Liberia founds African Democratic Federation

1962 End of war in Algeria against French rule

1977–88 Somali forces clash with Ethiopia in a claim over the Ogaden area

1992 Civil war in Algeria between Islamic fundamentalists and government

1949 Mau Mau movement founded in Kenya

1963 State of emergency ends in Kenya with independence

West & central Africa

1954 Gold Coast's National Liberation Movement begins

1965 Southern Rhodesia's whites declare unilateral independence (UDI)

1975 Civil war breaks out in Angola immediately after independence

1994 Ethnic conflict in Rwanda results in mass slaughter and a refugee crisis

1956 Representative government promised to Nigeria

1967–70 Biafran war brings famine to eastern Nigeria

1958 French colonies hold referenda on independence

1961 Wars of liberation begin in Portuguese colonies

SPAIN

Tangier
Ceuta
to Spain
Oran
at
Fez
Melilla
to Spain
MOROCCO
1956 independent
arrakech
1960

Algiers
Annaba
(Bone)
Tunis
Sétif
Sousse
1958

ITALY

Malta

ITALY

TURKEY

GREECE

CYPRUS

SYRIA
IRAQ

LEBANON
ISRAEL
JORDAN

Crete

Mediterranean Sea

Gades
TUNISIA
1956 independent
Tripoli
Misurata
Benghazi
Derna
Tobruk

Alexandria
Port Said
1956
Cairo
Suez

EGYPT
1974

Nile

OMAN

ALGERIA
1962 independent
1954–62
1992
1962

LIBYA
1947–51 under Anglo–French administration,
1951 independent

HOGGAR
MASSIF
SAHARA DESERT

TIBESTI
MASSIF

Administrative border

Political border

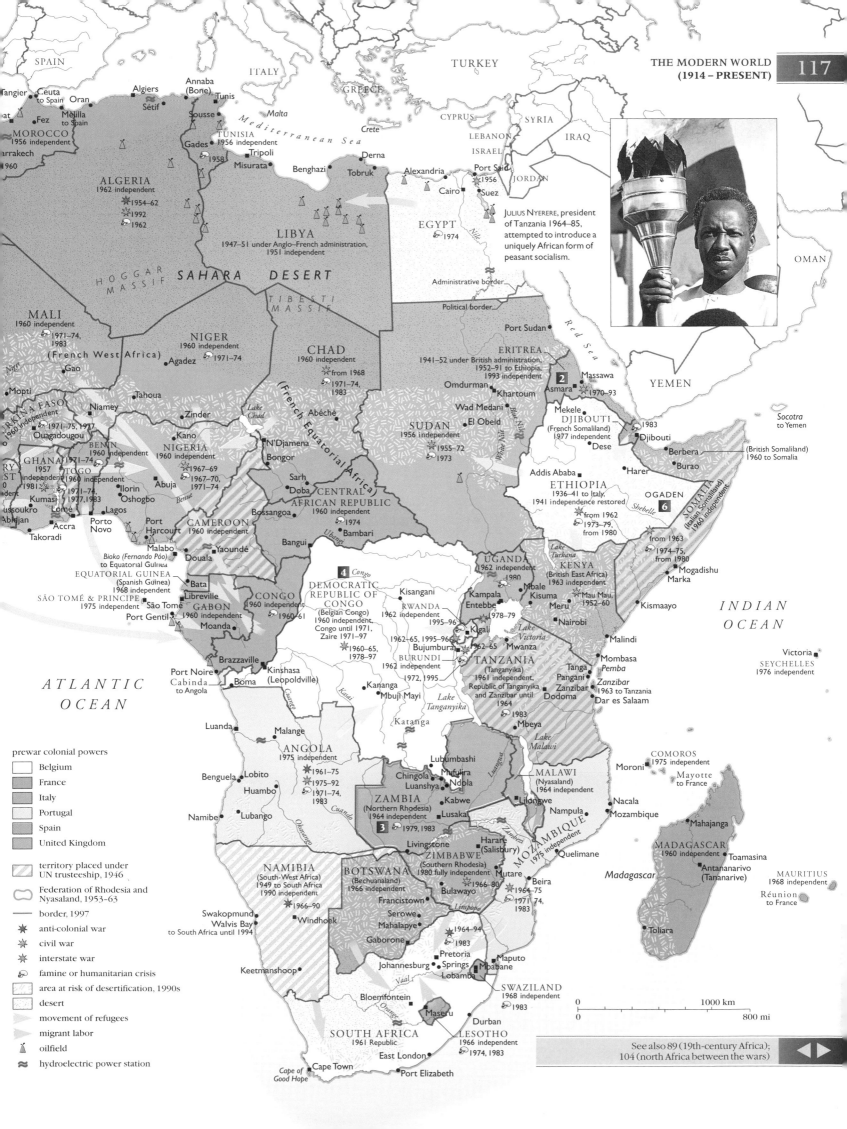

JULIUS NYERERE, president
of Tanzania 1964–85,
attempted to introduce a
uniquely African form of
peasant socialism.

MALI
1960 independent
1971–74,
1983
(French West Africa)

NIGER
1960 independent
1971–74

CHAD
1960 independent
from 1968
1971–74,
1983

Port Sudan

Omdurman
Khartoum

ERITREA
1941–52 under British administration,
1952–91 to Ethiopia,
1993 independent

2
Massawa
Asmara
1970–93

Red Sea

YEMEN

Socotra
to Yemen

Niger
Gao
Mopti

Tahoua

Zinder

Lake Chad

Abéché

Wad Medani
El Obeid

SUDAN
1956 independent
1955–72
1973

Mekele
Dese

DJIBOUTI
(French Somaliland)
1977 independent
1983
Djibouti

(British Somaliland)
1960 to Somalia
Berbera
Burao

RKINA FASO
independent
1971–75, 1977
Ouagadougou

BENIN
1960 independent
Niamey

Kano

NIGERIA
1960 independent
1967–69
1967–70,
1971–74

N'Djamena
Bongor

Sarh
Doba

CENTRAL
AFRICAN REPUBLIC
1960 independent
1974

Addis Ababa

Harer

ETHIOPIA
1936–41 to Italy,
1941 independence restored
from 1962
1973–79,
from 1980

OGADEN
6
Shebelle

SOMALIA
(Italian Somaliland)
1960 independent
from 1963
1974–75,
from 1980

GHANA
1957
independent
1971–74
TOGO
1960 independent
1981
nt
Kumasi
1971–74,
1977,1983

Ilorin
Oshogbo
Abuja

Bossangoa

Bambari

Mogadishu
Marka

ST
0

ussoukro
Lomé
Abidjan

Accra
Takoradi

Lagos
Porto
Novo

Port
Harcourt

CAMEROON
1960 independent

Bangui

Ubangi

*Lake
Turkana*

UGANDA
1962 independent
1980

KENYA
(British East Africa)
1963 independent
Mau Mau,
1952–60

Kismaayo

*INDIAN
OCEAN*

Malabo
Bioko (Fernando Póo)
to Equatorial Guinea
Douala
Yaoundé

EQUATORIAL GUINEA
(Spanish Guinea)
1968 independent
Bata

SÃO TOMÉ & PRINCIPE
1975 independent
São Tomé

Libreville
GABON
1960 independent
Moanda
Port Gentil

CONGO
1960 independent
1960–61

DEMOCRATIC
REPUBLIC OF
CONGO
(Belgian Congo)
1960 independent,
Congo until 1971,
Zaire 1971–97
1960–65,
1978–97

Congo

Kisangani

RWANDA
1962 independent
1995–96
Kigali
1962–65, 1995–96
Bujumbura
1962–65

BURUNDI
1962 independent
1972, 1995

Mbale
Kampala
Entebbe
1978–79

Kisuma
Meru

*Lake
Victoria*
Mwanza

TANZANIA
(Tanganyika)
1961 independent,
Republic of Tanganyika
and Zanzibar until
1964

Nairobi

Malindi

Mombasa
Pemba
Tanga
Pangani
Zanzibar
1963 to Tanzania
Dar es Salaam

Victoria
SEYCHELLES
1976 independent

*ATLANTIC
OCEAN*

Brazzaville
Port Noire
Cabinda
to Angola
Kinshasa
(Leopoldville)
Boma

Cuango
Kasai

Kananga
Mbuji Mayi

*Lake
Tanganyika*

Katanga

Dodoma
Zanzibar
1983

Mbeya

*Lake
Malawi*

Luanda
Malange

Cuanza

ANGOLA
1975 independent
1961–75
1975–92
1971–74,
1983

Lubumbashi
Mufulira
Chingola
Luanshya
Ndola
Kabwe

Lilongwe

MALAWI
(Nyasaland)
1964 independent

COMOROS
1975 independent
Moroni

Mayotte
to France

prewar colonial powers

	Belgium
	France
	Italy
	Portugal
	Spain
	United Kingdom

Benguela
Lobito
Huambo

Namibe
Lubango

Cuando
Okavango

ZAMBIA
(Northern Rhodesia)
1964 independent
3
1979, 1983

Lusaka

Nacala
Mozambique
Nampula

MADAGASCAR
1960 independent
Mahajanga

territory placed under
UN trusteeship, 1946

Federation of Rhodesia and
Nyasaland, 1953–63

border, 1997

anti-colonial war

civil war

interstate war

famine or humanitarian crisis

area at risk of desertification, 1990s

desert

movement of refugees

migrant labor

oilfield

hydroelectric power station

Livingstone

Harare
(Salisbury)

ZIMBABWE
(Southern Rhodesia)
1980 fully independent
1966–80
Mutare
Bulawayo
1964–75
1971–74,
1983

MOZAMBIQUE
1975 independent

Beira

Quelimane

Zambezi

NAMIBIA
(South-West Africa)
1949 to South Africa
1990 independent
1966–90

BOTSWANA
(Bechuanaland)
1966 independent

Francistown
Serowe
Mahalapye

Limpopo

Antananarivo
(Tananarive)

MAURITIUS
1968 independent

Réunion
to France

Toamasina

Madagascar

Swakopmund
Walvis Bay
to South Africa until 1994
Windhoek

Keetmanshoop

Gaborone

1964–94
1983

Pretoria
Springs
Johannesburg

Maputo
Mbabane
Lobamba

SWAZILAND
1968 independent
1983

Toliara

Bloemfontein

Vaal
Orange

Maseru

SOUTH AFRICA
1961 Republic

LESOTHO
1966 independent
1974, 1983

Durban

*Cape of
Good Hope*
Cape Town

East London

Port Elizabeth

0		1000 km
0		800 mi

See also 89 (19th-century Africa);
104 (north Africa between the wars)

After Egypt's President Sadat visited Jerusalem in 1977, US President Carter arranged meetings between Sadat and Israeli Prime Minister Begin at Camp David which led to a treaty in 1979 between Israel and Egypt (the first Arab state to take such a step). This recognized the state of Israel, promised autonomy to the Palestinians in Gaza and the West Bank, and returned the Sinai to Egypt.

The Palestine Liberation Organization (PLO) now took on the main task of fighting Israel, through terrorist activities in Europe and from its Al Fatah bases in Lebanon, where civil war was raging between Christian Phalangist and Islamic forces and where, since 1976, Syria had provided the main authority. In 1978 Israel invaded and UN forces struggled to keep apart the armies of Israel, Syria and the Christian militia. Sadat was assassinated by Islamic activists in 1981 but his successor Hosni Mubarak continued his policies. Trying to restore stability to the region, the United States brokered an agreement that the PLO leave Beirut for Tunis, but Lebanon's civil war continued until Syria restored peace in the early 1990s; but Hizbollah fighters, funded by Iran, still used Lebanese bases for raids on Israel.

The political force of Islam had been dramatically seen in Iran, where the pro-western shah was overthrown in 1979 by street demonstrations in support of the Ayatollah Khomeini. As president of the new theocratic republic, Khomeini severed diplomatic relations with Israel, welcomed PLO leader Yassir Arafat to Tehran and defined the United States as the "main enemy of mankind". US embassy staff were taken hostage; 52 stayed in captivity for more than a year, despite a trade embargo and an abortive rescue mission that summed up the US failure to deal with this new force in regional politics.

Khomeini's resurgent Shiite Islam and apparent intentions of dominating the Middle East, led Saddam Hussein, Ba'athist leader of predominantly Sunni Iraq, to invade Iran in 1980. War between the two states continued for eight years, mainly in the oil-producing region around Abadan. Neither won a clear victory despite almost a million casualties and great damage to oil installations on both sides. After the ceasefire in 1988, Saddam revived an old Iraqi claim on the rich, pro-western emirate of Kuwait, and invaded in 1990. To his surprise, the United Nations condemned the move and imposed sanctions on Iraq. Saudi Arabia, fearing further Iraqi expansion, permitted its territory to be used as a base for an attack on Iraq. Despite Soviet support for Iraq, the United Nations agreed to the use of force, and war broke out in January 1991. Iraq tried to draw the entire region into the conflict by goading Israel with missile attacks, but the American-led UN coalition (including Egypt and Syria) managed to limit the scope of the conflict and won a quick victory by bombing followed by a devastating ground attack.

The postwar settlement proved less than straightforward. The coalition had no mandate to topple Saddam and did not wish to take power in Baghdad.

Legend:

- border of Soviet Union to 1991
- member of OPEC
- member of NATO
- Egypt, 1983
- Israel, 1983
- territory restored to Egypt, May 1979–Apr 1982
- area occupied by Israel
- territory captured by Iraq, Sep–Dec 1980
- territory captured by Iran, Oct 1984
- Qom center of Islamic revolution in Iran, 1970s
- PLO diaspora, 1982
- Iran–Iraq war air strike, 1980–88
- area of Shiite population, 1983
- area claimed by Kurds as national homeland
- Anti-Iraq coalition state, 1990–91
- Coalition air base, 1990–91
- Coalition offensive, 1991
- UN-imposed Iraqi "no-fly" zone
- UN peace-keeping force
- movement of refugees
- migrant labor
- border, 1997
- oilfield
- oil pipeline
- desert

The attack ceased once Kuwait was liberated. Civil war broke out in Iraq as Shiites in the south and the Kurds in the north both sought to secede. Saddam remained in power, destroying the Shiite powerbase and forcing two million Kurds to seek asylum in Iran and Turkey, before the UN stepped in to enforce no-fly zones and safe havens from Iraqi attack. Devastating sanctions were imposed, but Saddam rebuilt his military base, including chemical weapons (forbidden by the postwar agreement); he also gradually restored his authority over the Kurdish areas.

Meanwhile, the Camp David agreements on Palestinian rights failed to materialize: Jewish settlers moved into the West Bank and built virtual fortresses there. In 1987 the Gaza and West Bank Palestinians began the *intifada* (uprising) against Israeli intransigence. Eventually a peace process was agreed, with phased Israeli withdrawals and recognition of a Palestinian National Authority under Arafat, initially only in Jericho but later intended to include Gaza and other areas. However, Israel faced a rightwing backlash and prime minister Rabin was murdered in 1995. Thereafter moves toward Palestinian self rule advanced slowly amid mutual suspicion.

TIMELINE

Arab–Israeli conflict

1978 First Israeli invasion of Lebanon

1978 The Camp David agreements are signed

1981 Assassination of president Sadat of Egypt

1982 Second Israeli invasion of Lebanon; PLO withdraws from Beirut; Christians massacre Palestinian refugees

1983 A suicide bombing in Beirut kills over 300 US and French troops

1985 Israel agrees to withdraw from Lebanon

1987 *Intifada* by Palestinians in occupied territories begins

1989 Israeli premier Yitzhak Shamir opposes the creation of a Palestinian state

1992 Lebanese elections mark the end of the civil war

1993 In the Oslo Declaration, Israel and PLO agree on the formation of a Palestinian state

1995 Israel agrees to begin withdrawal from West Bank towns; premier Yitzhak Rabin is assassinated

1996 Israel attacks Hizbollah strongholds in south Lebanon

The Gulf

1979 Islamic forces in Iran oust the shah; Khomeini comes to power

1980 Iraq invades Iran; Iraqi oil terminals are damaged by Iranian attacks

1981 Israel bombs an Iraqi nuclear installation

1983 Iranian forces invade northern Iraq

1988 Iraq uses chemical weapons on the Kurds of northern Iraq

1988 The UN arranges a cease-fire between Iran and Iraq

1990 Iraq invades and annexes Kuwait

1991 An American-led UN coalition defeats Iraq and liberates Kuwait

1996 The United States launches missile attacks on Iraq to enforce the no-fly zones

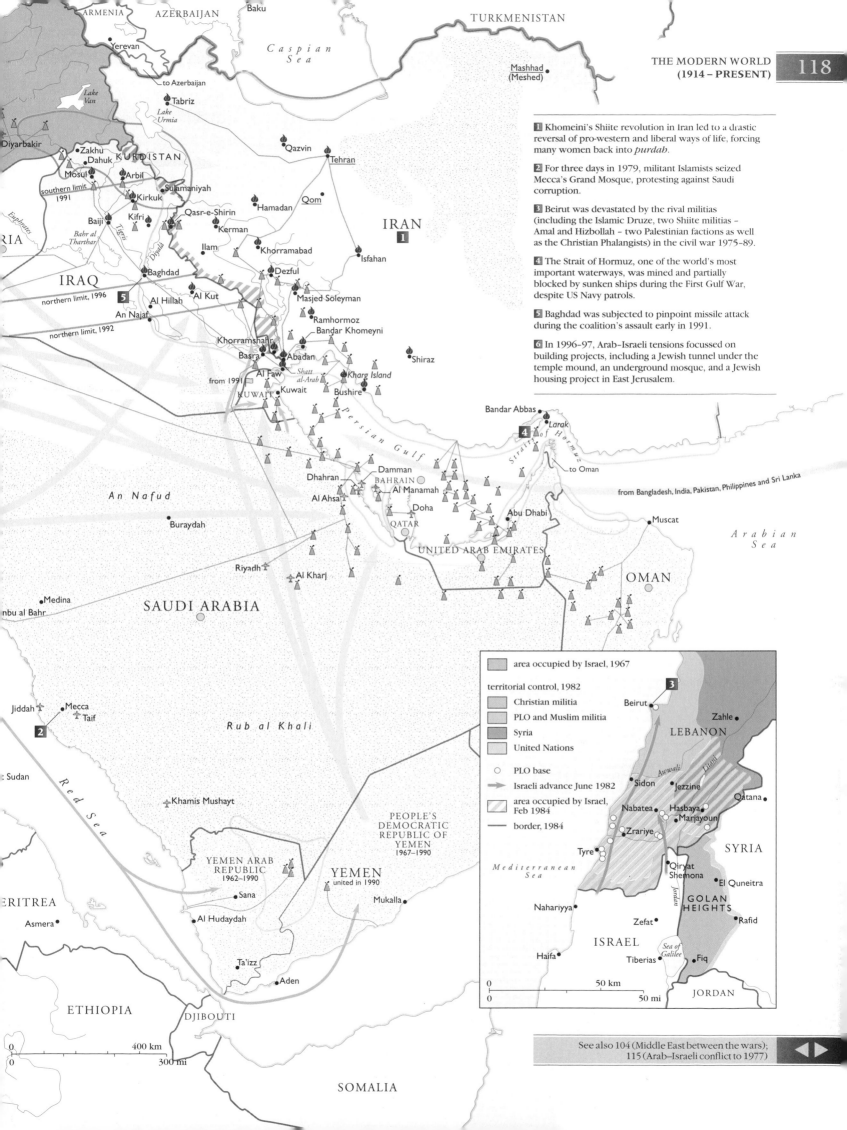

1 Khomeini's Shiite revolution in Iran led to a drastic reversal of pro-western and liberal ways of life, forcing many women back into *purdah*.

2 For three days in 1979, militant Islamists seized Mecca's Grand Mosque, protesting against Saudi corruption.

3 Beirut was devastated by the rival militias (including the Islamic Druze, two Shiite militias – Amal and Hizbollah – two Palestinian factions as well as the Christian Phalangists) in the civil war 1975–89.

4 The Strait of Hormuz, one of the world's most important waterways, was mined and partially blocked by sunken ships during the First Gulf War, despite US Navy patrols.

5 Baghdad was subjected to pinpoint missile attack during the coalition's assault early in 1991.

6 In 1996–97, Arab–Israeli tensions focussed on building projects, including a Jewish tunnel under the temple mound, an underground mosque, and a Jewish housing project in East Jerusalem.

- area occupied by Israel, 1967

territorial control, 1982
- Christian militia
- PLO and Muslim militia
- Syria
- United Nations
○ PLO base
→ Israeli advance June 1982
▨ area occupied by Israel, Feb 1984
— border, 1984

See also 104 (Middle East between the wars);
115 (Arab–Israeli conflict to 1977)

When Communist control over eastern Europe collapsed in 1989, tension between the North Atlantic Treaty Organization (NATO) and the Warsaw Pact dissolved. However, many former Soviet satellite countries and, from 1991, the old Soviet republics, suffered problems of social restructuring, while the western countries faced disagreements over how to cooperate politically and economically.

The rapid reunification of Germany signaled the end of the bi-polar Europe and demonstrated many of the problems inherent in the creation of a new one. There were fears that a resurgent Germany at the geographical center of the continent would dominate Europe and create an instability similar to that which existed before 1914. In the short term, however, the price of German reunification was high. To achieve its political aims, the former West Germany was faced with a huge bill for taking over East Germany's backward economy. Germany's dominance in European finance meant that the costs of reunion were felt beyond its own borders. Interest rates rose across Europe, and in 1992 Britain and others were forced to leave the Exchange Rate Mechanism (ERM), which had been introduced to guarantee economic stability in the European Union (EU) and lead to eventual monetary union.

The failure to maintain the integrity of the ERM called into question the creation of more unified financial structures within the European Union (EU; formerly EC). This failure caused doubts to resurface in several member-states about the need for, and price of, a single European currency, planned for introduction in the late 1990s. Parallel with the debate about "deepening" the union was the question of "widening" it to include countries that had formerly chosen or been forced to stay outside. While many of the formerly Soviet-dominated countries were clamoring to join the Union, some countries (including Britain and Denmark) saw vociferous anti-EU campaigns, and a referendum on joining led to a "no" vote in Norway. As fears rose of migration, international terrorism and drug smuggling, doubts arose of the wisdom of the agreement to allow free movement of goods, people and services across the EU from 1992. In 1995 several countries abolished border controls between them, though others viewed this decision with disquiet.

Western Europe's division over such questions was heightened by instability in the east. The euphoria surrounding the demise of communism was soon replaced by uncertainty. The new governments of eastern Europe and the states of the former Soviet Union faced unprecedented difficulties in turning state-run "command economies" into market-driven ones. The nascent democracies often appeared fragile, not least in Russia itself where Boris Yeltsin, a president of authoritarian instincts but failing health, was faced with powerful forces both of reaction and radical reform, and problems of high unemployment and inflation, potent organized crime, alarming ethnic conflict and resurgent Russian nationalism.

Meanwhile, war was seen within Europe for the first time since 1945. Resurgent nationalism led to ethnic conflicts in Armenia and Azerbaijan, then engulfed Europe's heart as Yugoslavia tore itself apart. Here as elsewhere, different nationalities had been held together by the shackles of authoritarian

Key / Legend:

- .... borders, 1997
- member state of EU, 1997
- associated state of EU
- member state of EFTA
- state with EU cooperation agreement
- SPAIN   member state of NATO
- **1989**   year of application for EU membership
- ——   former boundary of Warsaw Pact
- ——   implementation of "open frontier" Schengen agreement, 1995
- ✧   area of ethnic/nationalist tension

ethnic composition of Bosnia–Herzegovina, pre-1991

- more than 60 percent Croat
- more than 60 percent Muslim
- more than 60 percent Serb
- ethnically mixed area
- Bosnian–Croat Federation, 1995
- Bosnian Serb Republic, 1995
- Croatian territory under Serbian control, 1995
- ◉   UN-designated "safe havens"

0 ———————— 800 km
0 ———————— 600 mi

TIMELINE

Eastern Europe

1989 Fall of the Communist regimes in Poland, Hungary, Czechoslovakia, Bulgaria, East Germany, and Romania

1989 Ethnic conflicts begin in Azerbaijan and Armenia

1990 Slovenia breaks away from Yugoslavia

1990 Croat-held Dubrovnik is shelled by Serb forces

1991 A failed Communist coup leads to the breakup of the Soviet Union

1992 Bosnia-Herzegovina breaks away from Yugoslavia

1992 Siege of Sarajevo by the Bosnian Serbs begins

1993 Czechoslovakia splits into the Czech Republic and Slovakia

1993 Russia adopts a new constitution, giving the president increased powers

1994 Chechen nationalists are crushed by the Russian army at Grozny, southern Russia

1995 Croatia launches offensive against Serbs in Krajina and eastern Slavonia

1995 US president Clinton achieves agreement between the warring parties in Bosnia in Dayton Accord

1996 Elections in Russia confirm Yeltsin's position

Western Europe

1990 The European Bank for Reconstruction and Development is founded

1991 EU heads of government define a strategy for closer political and financial union at Maastricht

1992 The EU single market comes into force

1992 France and Germany found a joint army (Eurocorps) to strengthen the Western European Union

1994 Norway rejects membership of the EU

1995 Austria, Sweden and Finland join the EU

1995 Schengen agreement allows some open frontiers

1996 Intergovernmental Conference (IGC) is held to explore the future of Europe

1997 NATO offers membership to Hungary, Poland and Czech Republic (from 1999)

communism. The country split into its constituent republics but – unlike in Czechoslovakia where a similar divorce occurred – this took no account of the ethnic complexity on the ground.

With the Serbs in the grip of a militant nationalist spirit, and with Bosnia's population divided culturally and religiously between Bosnians, Croats and Serbs, the conflict focused on Bosnia–Herzogovina and its capital Sarajevo, which had provided the stage for the outbreak of European war in 1914. The states of the former Yugoslavia – especially Bosnia and Croatia – experienced four years of bloody civil war, where atrocities and policies of "ethnic cleansing" forced hundreds of thousands of civilians to flee their homes. The war revealed the political and military impotence of the rest of Europe, which was unable to agree a common policy on the problem, preferring to leave the task of peace-keeping to the United Nations. Behind this failure lay a fear of the war spreading. For this reason, western Europe's economic and military ties with the east, particularly Russia, continued to grow in importance: foreign

policy cooperation agreements were signed while the EU assisted with trade and communication links.

The relationship between Europe and the United States was uncertain. The Western European Union (WEU), an alliance excluding the United States, was promoted as a alternative to the US-dominated NATO. In 1995, however, the United States succeeded where Europe had failed, and brokered a settlement in Bosnia. And in 1997 NATO and Russia signed an agreement that allowed for NATO's expansion and ended what remained of the Cold War.

1 Berlin, symbol of the divided Europe from 1945, was quickly reunited and became capital of the new Germany in 1991.

2 In 1991 at Maastricht the EU agreed to move to common economic and social conditions. Britain rejected Europe-wide provisions on social issues.

3 In 1996, Venice was the focus of a movement, promoted by the separatist Northern League, for an independent "Padania", based on the Po valley.

4 Prague, like many cities of eastern Europe, saw a boom in the early 1990s, with tourists and industrialists attracted by new opportunities and low costs.

5 The mainly Muslim inhabitants of Sarajevo, capital of Bosnia, were besieged by Bosnian Serb forces from 1992 to 1995.

6 Grozny, capital of the Chechens in their attempt to break away from the Russian Federation, was destroyed by the Russians in December 1994; elections in 1997 confirmed the desire for independence.

7 A ceasefire from October 1994 to February 1996 interrupted 25 years of "troubles" in Northern Ireland, involving conflict between the Protestant majority, Catholic nationalists and the British government.

8 Moscow and much of Russia suffered inflation, shortages, gangsterism and unemployment in the early 1990s in the rush to build a market economy.

See also 110 (Cold War Europe); 118 (Middle East)

The balance of world power was dramatically altered by the rise of the Asian economies in the last quarter of the 20th century; these were expected to be responsible for no less than half the world's growth by the year 2000. The region had plentiful supplies of cheap labor able to take on work of a highly technical nature. Infrastructural projects, heavy industry, textiles and high technology were developed in parallel to allow these countries – many of them, such as South Korea and China, devastated by political turmoil in mid-century – to emerge from poverty to compete on the world stage within a few decades.

The economic power driving this development was that of Japan, which trebled its investments in many of the east and southeast Asian countries after 1985 when a revaluation of the Yen made home-produced goods uncompetitive. By the late 1990s, the east and southeast Asian countries had overtaken the United States as Japan's main trading partner, with Malaysia, Hong Kong, Taiwan and, increasingly, China, as the main beneficiaries.

As the region developed, new countries opened up for development. Japan and Korea competed for a position in the Vietnam economy, especially after relations between Vietnam and the United States were normalized in 1995. Vietnam's transport and energy infrastructure was particularly weak following the destruction from the war that ended in 1975.

The tiger, or dragon, economies of Asia – South Korea, Hong Kong, Taiwan and Singapore – grew up alongside Japan. These newly industrializing economies (NIEs) had a number of characteristics in common. None had significant raw materials, so all had to export in order to grow. From the 1950s all

nurtured their industries by government protection, and turned to export-oriented small light industries in the 1960s and 1970s. Like Japan, they had lost the advantage of low labor costs by the mid 1990s, and moved to invest in their neighbors with reserves of cheap labor, notably China.

By the 1980s South Korea had shifted its manufacturing base toward high technology, transport and heavy industry, and growth continued at a high rate. South Korean firms slowly opened trading links with the Communist regime in North Korea, but relationships between the two countries remained tense even after the death in 1994 of Kim Il Sung, ruler of North Korea since its foundation.

The foundations for Taiwan's economy were laid by Jiang Ching-kuo, the son of Chinese Nationalist leader Jiang Jieshi, from the late 1970s. He developed shipbuilding, petrochemicals and electronic industries, especially computers. By the mid-1990s this small island, remarkably, had the eighth largest trading power in the world. Mainland China, however, regarded Taiwan as a part of the People's Republic. Taiwan's democratic elections in 1987, and the election in 1996 of a leader more committed to an independent Taiwanese future, exacerbated tensions between the two. Hong Kong, China's small offshore island leased to Britain until 1997, moved toward trade and banking but retained its textile and other labor-intensive industries. Singapore, by contrast, pursued high-technology manufacture in conjunction with finance and business services.

In 1975, China had little or no foreign investment, no foreign loans and little direct trade with non-Communist states other than Japan. In 1978, vice-premier Deng Xiaoping embarked on economic

and educational reforms, aiming to replace Mao Zedong's class struggle with the goal of economic modernization. Political reform, however, was not pursued and a prodemocracy movement that arose in the wake of economic reform was crushed in 1989. Despite worldwide condemnation of China's human rights record, China actively sought investment, trade and technology from overseas. South Korea located plant and machinery in China's special economic zones; but the tiger economies that did most in China were those with the strongest political or ethnic ties with the country – notably Singapore and Taiwan (even though trade between Taiwan and mainland China was officially illegal). From 1984 Hong Kong, many of whose inhabitants came from Guangdong province, increasingly shifted its production to nearby Chinese provinces to take advantage of lower labor costs. The return of Hong Kong to China in 1997 was a step toward further integration of the two economies.

Japan retained its status as economic superpower thanks to its technological superiority, even though its growth was slowing in the 1990s, and other Asian countries beside China were industrializing fast. Thailand, Malaysia and Indonesia – which has large reserves of oil and gas to finance the growth of heavy industries such as petrochemicals, shipbuilding and steel – were growing. The Philippines, too, opted in the mid-1990s for policies modeled on the successes of other economies of the region.

A few countries did not form part of the "Asian miracle": notably Cambodia and Myanmar (formerly Burma), where oppressive regimes deterred foreign

Map legend

—— border, 1997

original newly industrializing economies

emergent newly industrializing economies

Chinese special economic zone

little industrialization

Organization for Economic Cooperation and Development

ASEAN member state (Association of Southeast Asian Nations), 1967

Japanese investment flow

population over 1,000,000

port

Manila industrial center

Chinese prodemocracy demonstration

separatist movement

------- fiber-optic cable, 1996

source of major resource

◇ gold

◆ copper

◆ nickel

◆ tin

◇ other metal

⚑ oilfield

| 0 | | 1200 km |
| 0 | | 800 mi |

BHUTAN
NEPAL
BANGLADESH
INDIA

TIMELINE

East Asia

1975 In Taiwan, Jiang Ching-kuo plans for rapid growth

1978 In China, Deng Xiaoping advocates economic reforms; China and Japan sign a trade agreement

1979 China and the United States normalize relations

1984 The NIEs begin to invest in China

1984 Revaluation of the Yen leads Japanese countries to invest in southeast Asia

1987 Democratic elections are held in Taiwan, and martial law is lifted for the first time since 1949

1989 Japan becomes the world's largest foreign aid donor and supplier of capital

1989 In China, the prodemocracy movement led by students is crushed at Tiananmen Square, Beijing

1993 Japan's Liberal Democratic Party loses power for the first time since 1955

1994 Kim Il Sung, Stalinist president of North Korea, dies

1997 Death of Deng Xiaoping; Hong Kong returns to Chinese rule

Southeast Asia

1975 The Khmer Rouge take over Cambodia, leading to mass killings

1975 Collapse of South Vietnam and creation of a single Vietnamese state

1976 Indonesia annexes Portuguese East Timor

1977 The Communist regime in Laos signs a friendship treaty with Vietnam

1978–79 Vietnam invades Cambodia to crush Khmer Rouge regime; China invades northern Vietnam

1986 Prodemocracy candidate Corazon Aquino takes over from Ferdinand Marcos after the Philippines presidential elections

1986 Laos signs an economic development agreement with Thailand

1987 Democratic elections are held in South Korea

1988 A military junta seizes power in Burma

1989 Australia initiates the Asia Pacific Economic Cooperation Forum

1991 Burmese prodemocracy leader Aung San Suu Kyi is imprisoned by the military government

1992 Vietnam opens a free-trade zone, funded by Taiwan

1980 1990

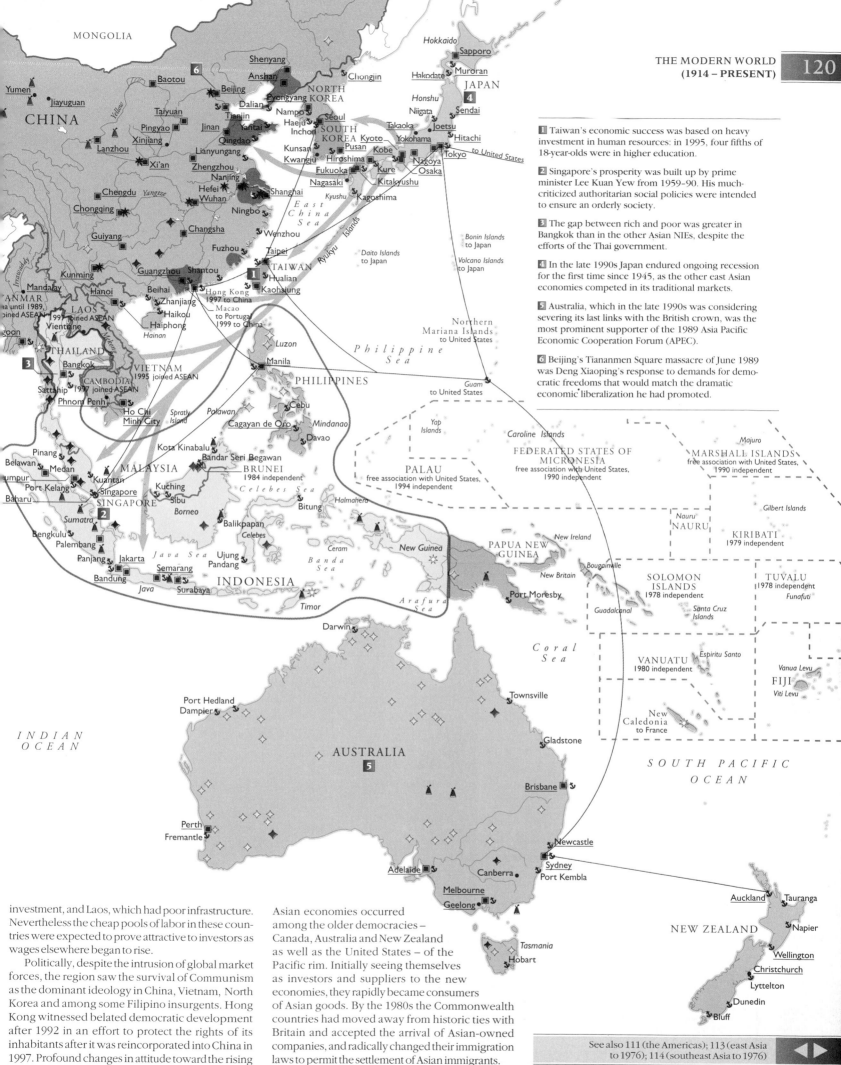

1 Taiwan's economic success was based on heavy investment in human resources: in 1995, four fifths of 18-year-olds were in higher education.

2 Singapore's prosperity was built up by prime minister Lee Kuan Yew from 1959–90. His much-criticized authoritarian social policies were intended to ensure an orderly society.

3 The gap between rich and poor was greater in Bangkok than in the other Asian NIEs, despite the efforts of the Thai government.

4 In the late 1990s Japan endured ongoing recession for the first time since 1945, as the other east Asian economies competed in its traditional markets.

5 Australia, which in the late 1990s was considering severing its last links with the British crown, was the most prominent supporter of the 1989 Asia Pacific Economic Cooperation Forum (APEC).

6 Beijing's Tiananmen Square massacre of June 1989 was Deng Xiaoping's response to demands for democratic freedoms that would match the dramatic economic liberalization he had promoted.

investment, and Laos, which had poor infrastructure. Nevertheless the cheap pools of labor in these countries were expected to prove attractive to investors as wages elsewhere began to rise.

Politically, despite the intrusion of global market forces, the region saw the survival of Communism as the dominant ideology in China, Vietnam, North Korea and among some Filipino insurgents. Hong Kong witnessed belated democratic development after 1992 in an effort to protect the rights of its inhabitants after it was reincorporated into China in 1997. Profound changes in attitude toward the rising Asian economies occurred among the older democracies – Canada, Australia and New Zealand as well as the United States – of the Pacific rim. Initially seeing themselves as investors and suppliers to the new economies, they rapidly became consumers of Asian goods. By the 1980s the Commonwealth countries had moved away from historic ties with Britain and accepted the arrival of Asian-owned companies, and radically changed their immigration laws to permit the settlement of Asian immigrants.

See also 111 (the Americas); 113 (east Asia to 1976); 114 (southeast Asia to 1976)

The years from 1975 saw seismic shifts in world politics. The end of the Cold War permitted longstanding problems in Europe, the Middle East and Africa to be addressed. Fears of imminent nuclear, environmental or demographic disaster, widely predicted in the preceding decades, calmed by the late 1990s, though the world's future political shape was still uncertain.

Central to these changes was the collapse of the Soviet Union. Under Leonid Brezhnev the country stagnated, and the *détente*, or cooling of the international tension, of the 1970s came to an end with a Soviet invasion of Afghanistan. The United States emerged from its post-Vietnam crisis of confidence under tough-talking president Ronald Reagan who changed the mood in the early 1980s. The soaring costs of arms production, combined with the Soviet Union's technological deficit, led the new leader Mikhail Gorbachev to try to improve superpower relations and liberalize the Soviet system. In doing so he unleashed disintegrative forces he could not control.

Gorbachev did not resist the demands for increased independence from many of the USSR's eastern European satellites. In 1989–90 the peoples of eastern Europe took the opportunity to overthrow their Communist governments. In the Soviet Union itself, the separate republics seceded from the Union and formed the Commonwealth of Independent States. The old order was not so easily replaced in Yugoslavia, which was ripped apart by ethnic conflict (▷ 119).

Meanwhile, greater centralization was occurring in western Europe, where the European Community (later the European Union) expanded in size, abolished many border restrictions and initiated moves toward political and economic union.

The collapse of the Soviet Union led to change in Africa, where problems of decolonization and debt had been exacerbated by superpower conflict. South Africa's role in opposing the spread of Communism vanished, and as American support for the regime was withdrawn, the burden of upholding *apartheid* grew. South Africa ceased interfering in the politics of other countries of the region, and in 1994 achieved majority rule under the charismatic president Nelson Mandela (▷ 117).

In the Middle East, both the west and the Soviet Union felt vulnerable to the threat posed by Islamist movements to oil supplies and the loyalty of the Muslim areas of the USSR. The Islamist takeover of Iran in 1979 complicated the politics of the Middle East: Iraq was supported in a long war

A.	Albania		
AR.	Armenia		
AU.	Austria		
AZ.	Azerbaijan		
B.	Belgium		
BO.	Bosnia-Herzegovina		
CAR.	Central African Republic		
CR.	Croatia		
C.	Czech Republic		
D.	Denmark		
DR.	Dominican Republic	RO.	Romania
GE.	Georgia	S.	Switzerland
GER.	Germany	SK.	Saint Kitts–Nevis
H.	Hungary	SV.	Saint Vincent & the Grenadines
LE.	Lebanon		
L.	Luxembourg	SL.	Slovakia
M.	Macedonia (Former Yugoslav Republic of)	SLV.	Slovenia
		U.	United Arab Emira
N.	Netherlands	YU.	Yugoslavia

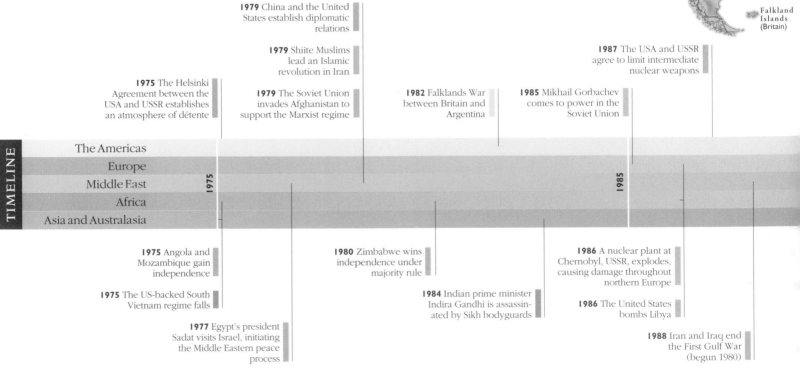

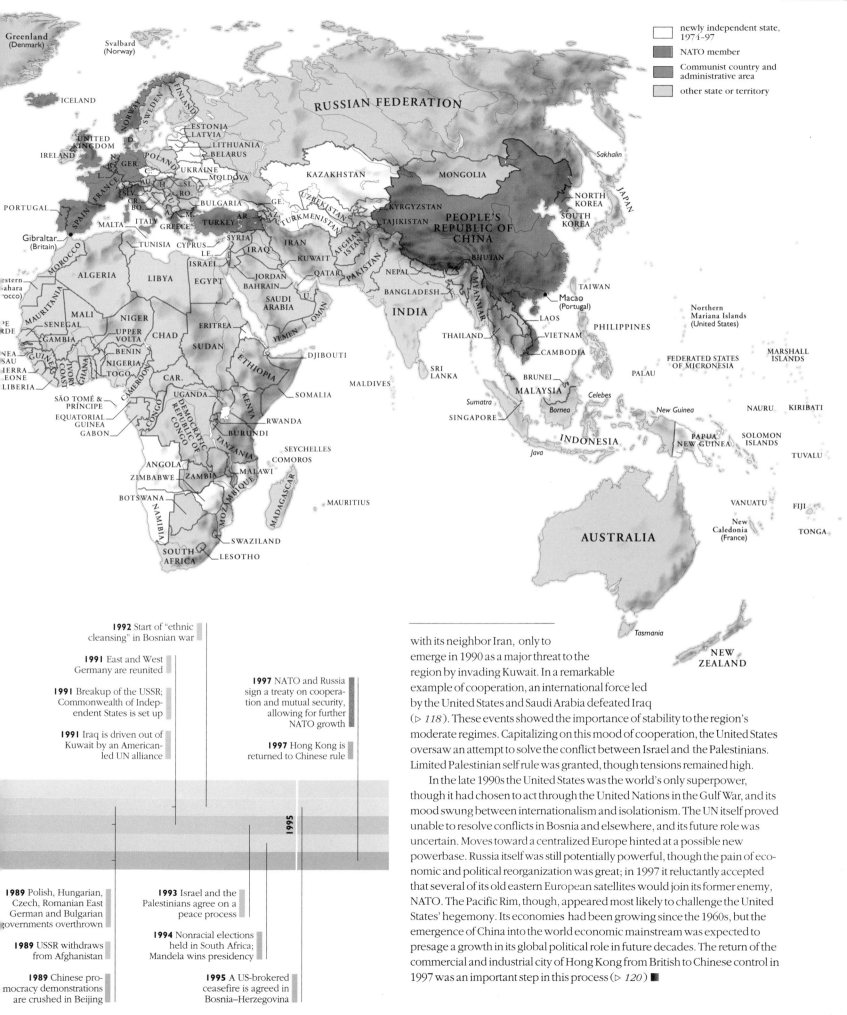

newly independent state, 1974–97

NATO member

Communist country and administrative area

other state or territory

Greenland (Denmark)

Svalbard (Norway)

ICELAND

RUSSIAN FEDERATION

Sakhalin

NORWAY SWEDEN FINLAND

UNITED KINGDOM

IRELAND

ESTONIA
LATVIA
D. LITHUANIA
POLAND BELARUS
GER. UKRAINE
B. MOLDOVA

KAZAKHSTAN

MONGOLIA

NORTH KOREA
SOUTH KOREA

JAPAN

PORTUGAL

FRANCE
SPAIN
CR. SLV.
BO. AU. H. RO.
IT. BULGARIA
GREECE TURKEY
GE. AZ.
ARMENIA
UZBEKISTAN
TURKMENISTAN
KYRGYZSTAN
TAJIKISTAN

PEOPLE'S REPUBLIC OF CHINA

TAIWAN

Gibraltar (Britain)

MALTA
ITALY

TUNISIA
CYPRUS
SYRIA
LE.
IRAQ
IRAN
AFGHAN-ISTAN

KUWAIT

PAKISTAN

NEPAL
BHUTAN

Macao (Portugal)

Northern Mariana Islands (United States)

MOROCCO

Western Sahara (Morocco)

ALGERIA

LIBYA

EGYPT

ISRAEL
JORDAN
QATAR
BAHRAIN
SAUDI ARABIA
U.
OMAN
YEMEN

BANGLADESH

INDIA

MYANMAR

LAOS

THAILAND
VIETNAM
CAMBODIA

PHILIPPINES

PALAU

FEDERATED STATES OF MICRONESIA

MARSHALL ISLANDS

MAURITANIA
MALI
SENEGAL
GAMBIA
NIGER
UPPER VOLTA
CHAD
SUDAN
ERITREA
DJIBOUTI
ETHIOPIA

SOMALIA

MALDIVES

SRI LANKA

BRUNEI
MALAYSIA

SINGAPORE

Sumatra
Borneo
Celebes

New Guinea

NAURU

KIRIBATI

GUINEA
GUINEA BISSAU
SIERRA LEONE
LIBERIA
IVORY COAST
GHANA
TOGO
BENIN
NIGERIA
CAMEROON
CAR.
UGANDA
KENYA
RWANDA
BURUNDI
TANZANIA

SÃO TOMÉ & PRÍNCIPE
EQUATORIAL GUINEA
GABON
CONGO
DEMOCRATIC REPUBLIC OF CONGO

SEYCHELLES
COMOROS

INDONESIA

Java

PAPUA NEW GUINEA

SOLOMON ISLANDS

TUVALU

ANGOLA
ZAMBIA
ZIMBABWE
MALAWI
MOZAMBIQUE
BOTSWANA
NAMIBIA

MADAGASCAR

MAURITIUS

AUSTRALIA

VANUATU

New Caledonia (France)

FIJI

TONGA

SOUTH AFRICA
SWAZILAND
LESOTHO

Tasmania

NEW ZEALAND

1992 Start of "ethnic cleansing" in Bosnian war

1991 East and West Germany are reunited

1991 Breakup of the USSR; Commonwealth of Independent States is set up

1991 Iraq is driven out of Kuwait by an American-led UN alliance

1997 NATO and Russia sign a treaty on cooperation and mutual security, allowing for further NATO growth

1997 Hong Kong is returned to Chinese rule

1995

1989 Polish, Hungarian, Czech, Romanian East German and Bulgarian governments overthrown

1989 USSR withdraws from Afghanistan

1989 Chinese pro-mocracy demonstrations are crushed in Beijing

1993 Israel and the Palestinians agree on a peace process

1994 Nonracial elections held in South Africa; Mandela wins presidency

1995 A US-brokered ceasefire is agreed in Bosnia–Herzegovina

with its neighbor Iran, only to emerge in 1990 as a major threat to the region by invading Kuwait. In a remarkable example of cooperation, an international force led by the United States and Saudi Arabia defeated Iraq (▷ *118*). These events showed the importance of stability to the region's moderate regimes. Capitalizing on this mood of cooperation, the United States oversaw an attempt to solve the conflict between Israel and the Palestinians. Limited Palestinian self rule was granted, though tensions remained high.

In the late 1990s the United States was the world's only superpower, though it had chosen to act through the United Nations in the Gulf War, and its mood swung between internationalism and isolationism. The UN itself proved unable to resolve conflicts in Bosnia and elsewhere, and its future role was uncertain. Moves toward a centralized Europe hinted at a possible new powerbase. Russia itself was still potentially powerful, though the pain of economic and political reorganization was great; in 1997 it reluctantly accepted that several of its old eastern European satellites would join its former enemy, NATO. The Pacific Rim, though, appeared most likely to challenge the United States' hegemony. Its economies had been growing since the 1960s, but the emergence of China into the world economic mainstream was expected to presage a growth in its global political role in future decades. The return of the commercial and industrial city of Hong Kong from British to Chinese control in 1997 was an important step in this process (▷ *120*) ∎

Acknowledgments

Text, timelines and maps

The authors and publishers readily acknowledge the work of a large number of scholars and published works, on which they have drawn in the preparation of this atlas. Many of these works remain in print, and can be used as reliable secondary reading on the many topics covered in this atlas. Among them are the following:

Adams, A.E., Matley, I.M. and McCagg, W.O. *An Atlas of Russian and East European History* (London 1967)

Ajayi, J.F.A. and Crowder, Michael (eds) *Historical Atlas of Africa* (Cambridge and New York 1985)

Allchin, B. and R. *The Birth of Indian Civilization: India and Pakistan before 500 BC* (2nd ed., London 1994)

Almond, M., Black, J. McKitterick, R., and Scarre, C. *The Times Atlas of European History* (London and New York 1994)

Ardagh, John with Jones, Colin *Cultural Atlas of France* (London and New York 1991)

Ashdown, P. *Caribbean History in Maps* (London and New York 1979)

Bagot Glubb, J. *The Great Arab Conquests* (London 1963)

Bahn, Paul G. (ed) *Cambridge Illustrated History of Archaeology* (Cambridge and New York 1996)

Baines, John and Malek, Jaromir *Atlas of Ancient Egypt* (Oxford and New York 1980)

Barraclough, G. (ed) *The Times Atlas of World History* (4th ed., London 1993 and New York 1994)

Bartlett, R. *The Making of Europe: Conquest, Colonisation and Cultural Change 950–1300* (London 1993)

Bayley, Christopher (ed) *Atlas of the British Empire* (London and New York 1989)

Black, C. and others *Cultural Atlas of the Renaissance* (London and New York 1993)

Black, Jeremy *The Cambridge Illustrated Atlas of Warfare: Renaissance to Revolution 1492–1792* (Cambridge and New York 1996)

Blunden, Caroline and Elvin, Mark *Cultural Atlas of China* (London and New York 1986)

Bolton, Geoffrey (ed) *The Oxford History of Australia* (Oxford and Melbourne 1994)

Braudel, Fernand *Civilization and Capitalism* (3 vols, revised ed., Princeton 1992)

Brown, Dee *The American West* (New York 1994)

Campbell, John (ed) *The Experience of World War II* (London and New York 1989)

Chadwick, Henry and Evans, Gillian R. (eds) *Atlas of the Christian Church* (London and New York 1987)

Champion, T., Gamble, C., Shennan, S. and Whittle, A. *Prehistoric Europe* (London 1984)

Chang, K.C. *The Archaeology of Ancient China* (Yale 1977)

Chard, C.S. *Northeast Asia in Prehistory* (Madison, USA 1974)

Coe, Michael, Snow, Dean and Benson, Elizabeth *Atlas of Ancient America* (London and New York 1986)

Coe, Michael *Mexico: from the Olmecs to the Aztecs* (4th ed., London and New York 1994)

Cohn-Sherbok, D. *Atlas of Jewish History* (London and New York 1994)

Collcutt, Martin, Jansen, Marius and Kumakura, Isao *Cultural Atlas of Japan* (London and New York 1988)

Connah, G. *African Civilizations: Precolonial cities and states in tropical Africa* (Cambridge and New York 1987)

Cook, J.M. *The Persian Empire* (London 1983)

Cornell, Tim and Matthews, John *Atlas of the Roman World* (London and New York 1982)

Cotterell, A. *East Asia* (London 1993, New York 1995)

Crawford, M. *The Roman Republic* (London 1978, Cambridge, Mass 1993)

Cunliffe, Barry (ed) *The Oxford Illustrated Prehistory of Europe* (Oxford and New York 1994)

Darby, H.C. and Fullard, Harold *The New Cambridge Modern History Atlas* (Cambrdge 1970)

Davies, R.H.C. *A History of Medieval Europe* (2nd ed., London and New York 1988)

Davis, Norman *Europe: a History* (Oxford and New York 1996)

Dear, I.C.B. and Foot, M.R.D. (eds) *The Oxford Companion to the Second World War* (Oxford and New York 1995)

de Lange, Nicholas *Atlas of the Jewish World* (London and New York 1984)

Elliott, J.H. (ed) *The Hispanic World* (London and New York 1991)

Fagan, Brian M. *The Journey from Eden: the Peopling of our World* (London and New York 1990)

Fagan, Brian M. *Ancient North America* (London and New York 1995)

Fage, J.D. and Oliver, R. (eds) *The Cambridge History of Africa* (Cambridge and New York 1975–)

Fernández-Armesto, Felipe (ed) *The Times Atlas of World Exploration* (London and New York 1991)

Fiedel, S.J. *Prehistory of the Americas* (2nd ed., Cambridge and New York 1992)

Freedman, Lawrence *Atlas of Global Strategy* (London and New York 1985)

Freeman-Grenville, G.S.P. *Historical Atlas of the Middle East* (New York 1993)

Frye, R.N. *The Heritage of Persia* (2nd ed., London 1976)

Gamble, C. *The Palaeolithic Settlement of Europe* (Cambridge 1986)

Gamble, C. *Timewalkers: the Prehistory of Global Colonization* (Stroud 1993, Cambridge, Mass. 1994)

Gaur, A. *A History of Writing* (London 1984, New York 1994)

Gilbert, Martin *The Atlas of Jewish History* (5th ed., London and New York 1996)

Graham Campbell, James (ed) *Cultural Atlas of the Viking World* (London and New York 1994)

Green, M.J. *The Celtic World* (London and New York 1995)

Griffiths, Ieuan L. *The Atlas of African Affairs* (London 1984) *Grosser Historischer Weltatlas* (3 vols, Munich 1981)

Hall, D.G.E. *A History of South-east Asia* (4th ed., London 1981)

Handlin, O. *The History of the United States* (New York 1967)

Hartman, Tom *A World Atlas of Military History 1945–1984* (New York 1985)

Haywood, John *Historical Atlas of the Vikings* (London and New York 1995)

Haywood, John *Dark Age Naval Power* (London and New York 1991)

Holt, P.M., Lambeth, A.K.S. and Lewis, B. (eds) *The Cambridge History of Islam* (Cambridge 1970–)

Homberger, E. *Historical Atlas of North America* (London and New York 1995)

Hooper, Nicholas and Bennett, Matthew *The Cambridge Illustrated Atlas of Warfare: The Middle Ages 768–1487* (Cambridge and New York 1996)

Hosking, G. *A History of the Soviet Union* (London 1985)

Johnson, Gordon, Bayly, C. and Richards J.F. *The New Cambridge History of India* (Cambridge 1987–)

Johnson, Gordon *Cultural Atlas of India* (London 1995, New York 1996)

Kemp, B.J. *Ancient Egypt* (London 1989, New York 1992)

Kinder, H. and Hilgemann, W. *Atlas of World History* (2 vols, Munich, London and New York 1974)

King, P.D. *Charlemagne* (London 1986)

Kuhrt, A. *The Ancient Near East* (London and New York 1995)

Kulke, H. and Rothermund, D. *A History of India* (London 1990)

Langer, William L. *An Encyclopedia of World History* (5th ed., London and New York 1973)

Lee, K. *A New History of Korea* (Cambridge, Mass 1988)

Levi, Peter *Cultural Atlas of the Greek World* (London and New York 1984)

Lynch, J.H. *The Medieval Church* (Harlow 1992)

Mallory, J.P. *In Search of the Indo-Europeans* (London 1989, New York 1995)

Matthew, Donald *Atlas of Medieval Europe* (London and New York 1989)

McEvedy, Colin and Jones, Richard *Atlas of World Population History* (London 1978)

Milner, C.A., O'Connor, C.A. and Sandweiss, M. *The Oxford History of the American West* (Oxford and New York 1994)

Milner-Gulland, Robin with Dejevsky, Nikolai *Cultural Atlas of Russia and the Soviet Union* (London and New York 1989)

Moore, R.I. (ed) *The Hamlyn Historical Atlas* (London 1981)

Morgan, D. *The Mongols* (Oxford 1986, Cambridge, Mass 1990)

Moseley, M.E. *The Incas and their Ancestors* (London and New York 1993)

Murray, Oswyn *Early Greece* (2nd ed., London 1993)

Nile, R. and Clerk, C. *Cultural Atlas of Australia, New Zealand and the South Pacific* (London and New York 1995)

Ostrogorsky, G. *History of the Byzantine State* (revised ed., New Brunswick 1986)

Parker, W.H. *An Historical Geography of Russia* (London 1968)

Paxton, John *The Statesman's Yearbook Historical Companion* (London 1988)

Phillipson, D.W. *African Archaeology* (Cambridge 1993)

Pitcher, D.E. *An Historical Geography of the Ottoman Empire* (Leiden 1972)

Porter, A.N. (ed) *Atlas of British Overseas Expansion* (London 1991)

Pounds, Norman J.G. *An Historical Geography of Europe* (Cambridge 1990)

Reid, Anthony (ed) *Southeast Asia in the Early Modern Era: Trade, Power and Belief* (New York 1993)

Riasanovsky, N.V. *A History of Russia* (5th ed., Oxford and New York 1993)

Riley-Smith, Jonathon *The Atlas of the Crusades* (London and New York 1991)

Roaf, Michael and Postgate, Nicholas *Cultural Atlas of Mesopotamia* (London and New York 1990)

Roberts, J.M. *The Hutchinson History of the World* (London 1976)

Robinson, Francis *Atlas of the Islamic World since 1500* (London and New York, 1982)

Rogerson, John *Atlas of the Bible* (London and New York 1985)

Scammell, G.V. *The World Encompassed: the First European Maritime Empires c.800–1650* (London 1981)

Scarre, Dr Chris *Past Worlds: The Times Atlas of Archaeology* (London and New York 1988)

Schmidt, K.J. *An Atlas and Survey of South Asian History* (New York and London 1995)

Schwartzberg, Joseph E. (ed) *A Historical Atlas of South Asia* (revised ed., Chicago and London 1992)

Segal, Aaron *An Atlas of International Migration* (London and New Jersey 1993)

Sharer, R.J. *The Ancient Maya* (5th ed., Stanford Ca. 1994)

Shepherd, William R. *Shepherd's Historical Atlas* (9th ed., New York and London 1974)

Sinclair, Keith (ed) *The Oxford Illustrated History of New Zealand* (Oxford and Auckland 1990)

Sinor, D. (ed) *The Cambridge History of Early Inner Asia* (Cambridge 1990)

Smith, B.D. *The Emergence of Agriculture* (New York 1995)

Spence, J. *The Search for Modern China* (London and New York 1990)

Spence J.E. (ed) *The World Today* (London 1994)

Taylour, W. *The Mycenaeans* (2nd ed., London and New York 1990)

The Times Atlas of the World (8th ed., London and New York 1990)

Thornton, John K. *Africa and Africans in the Formation of the Atlantic World 1400-1680* (Cambridge and New York 1992)

Tindall, G. and Shi, D.E. *America, a Narrative History* (New York 1996)

Todd, M. *The Early Germans* (Oxford and Cambridge, Mass. 1992)

Twitchett, D. and Fairbank, J. (eds) *The Cambridge History of China* (15 vols, Cambridge and New York 1978–91)

Vincent Mary and Stradling, R.A. *Cultural Atlas of Spain and Portugal* (London 1994, New York 1995)

Walbank F.W. *The Hellenistic World* (3rd ed., London 1992, Cambridge, Mass. 1993)

Wallace-Hadrill, J.M. *The Barbarian West 400–1000* (5th ed., Oxford and Cambridge, Mass. 1996)

Waller, Philip (ed) *Chronology of the 20th Century* (Oxford 1995)

Webster's New Geographical Dictionary (Springfield, Mass. 1984)

Whittle, A. *Neolithic Europe: a Survey* (Cambridge and New York 1985)

Winter, J.M. *The Experience of World War I* (London and New York 1988)

Wintle, J. *The Vietnam Years* (London 1991)

Photographs

Introductions: *Part 1:* Hutchison Library; *Part 2:* Images Colour Library; *Part 3:* Hutchison Library; *Part 4:* Images Colour Library; *Part 5:* Robert Harding Picture Library; *Part 6:* R. Ian Lloyd/Hutchison Library;

Maps: *104:* Saudi Aramco; *107:* ZEC/Dalkeith Poster Cards; *108:* Corbis-Bettmann/UPI; *111:* Popperfoto; *112:* Andromeda Oxford Limited; *117:* Hulton Getty.

Artwork references have been assembled from a wide variety of sources. Any individual or institution who can demonstrate that copyright may have been infringed is invited to contact Andromeda Oxford Ltd.

Figures refer to map numbers; **bold** type indicates major references.